STUDIES IN PERCEPTION

Edited by Peter K. Machamer and Robert G. Turnbull

STUDIES IN
PERCEPTION

Interrelations in the History of Philosophy and Science

OHIO STATE UNIVERSITY PRESS : COLUMBUS

Library of Congress Cataloguing in Publication Data

Main entry under title:
Studies in perception.
   Includes index.
1. Perception. 2. Philosophy—History. 3. Science—
History. I. Machamer,   Peter   K. II. Turnbull,
Robert G.
BF311.S733   153.7   77-10857
ISBN 0-8142-0244-6

CONTENTS

CONTENTS

PREFACE

This volume is the second and final product of a course development grant awarded to the editors by the National Endowment for the Humanities. The first volume, *Motion and Time, Space and Matter*, was composed of essays dealing with some of the issues at the interface of philosophy and the physical sciences. The essays of the present volume deal with many and varied topics in perceptual theory as they arose in their philosophical and scientific contexts. Our aim here, as in the first volume, is to stress the interrelated and encompassing character of these topics.

The essays printed herein have gone through at least three stages before reaching their present form. First, in conjunction with a year-long course taught by Ohio State University faculty members from various departments, outside consultants were brought in, in pairs, to speak to the class concerning aspects of the texts that were being studied. Second, in June 1974, a conference that brought back all of the consultants and the teachers of the course to read second drafts or re-writes of papers was held on the Ohio State campus. Those drafts or re-writes were discussed by all the consultants and teachers and by some thirty invited participants. Finally, the essays were again revised for the present publication. The major focus of the course, the conference, and the final essays was the study of the interconnections between scientific and philosophical approaches to issues in perception and of the similarities and differences that exist in the treatment of perceptual problems in different historical periods.

The editors were convinced at the outset of the project that studies in and of perception suffered from "compartmentalization" into academic disciplines and that greater understanding of the nature of perception and of the history of its study was to be gained by breaking down these artificial barriers. The course and conference were living evidence that the philosophical and scientific issues with which most theorists deal have overlapped or been identical. Historically, until very recent times, no rigid division into kinds of problems for distinct methods of inquiry has been insisted upon by most writers on perception. Historians of science, historians of philosophy, philosophers, psychologists, opticians, and physiologists all seem to have been dealing with similar issues, sharing similar assumptions, and accepting similar solutions.

In the essays that follow, it is striking how problems concerning the immediate objects of perception, the relations of perception to sensation, and the relations of perception to cognition and past experience appear and reappear in different historical periods. Berkeley's concerns, for example, were often those of Aristotle and Helmholtz, and issues treated by Gibson's theory find ready historical antecedents. The essays, dealing with materials from widely separate historical points, exhibit a striking regularity with which similar problems in similar terms have arisen again and again. Certainly different times and their concomitant prejudices and theories show differences among themselves, but this was far less the case than the editors had anticipated. We both wished for the time and the ability to lay out the coherent pattern exhibited by the essays presented here and thus to provide the reader with a general overview of the development of perceptual theories from Greek times until the present. Whether we have the ability must remain in doubt; the fact is that we have not had the time. The essays, however, speak for themselves, and some of the coherent pattern shows in the multiple references under various topics in the index. It may be worth noting that no work describing the history of doctrines of perception exists and that the present volume, with its broad scope and interdisciplinary approach, is an effort to fill this void.

It is the hope of the editors and of most of the participants that the kind of studies presented in this volume in their multi-disciplinary character will be continued. We hope that other universities will begin to offer the kinds of courses offered at the Ohio State University during the two program years (and which continue to be offered). Finally, we hope that the coopera-tion and mutual exchange of points of view and information that characterized this conference, and the one previously, will be continued. Philosophers, historians, and psychologists have much to learn from one another and much to lose by continued isolation.

The editors wish to give thanks to those persons who made the course, the conference, and the present volume successful. Thanks to the consultants for their enthusiastic and learned participation, to those who attended the conference and who enlivened its many discussions (formal and informal), to the National Endowment for the grant, to the Ohio State Uni-versity for its support, and to the students in the courses who provided the impetus for the whole project. Grateful apprecia-tion is owed to the staff of the Ohio State Philosophy Department for its work during the conference and in the preparation of this volume, in particular, to Virginia Foster and Mary Lee Raines, but especially to Elizabeth Hellinger. For our colleagues and their wives who hosted some of the parties we have many kind, if not sober, thoughts. To Marge and "Marty" who put up with much for many years, we can at least make public our debt. Our thanks to Stephen Lunsford for his help in editing many of the essays for this volume. Finally, we are much indebted to Roy Edelstein for his preparation of the index.

Peter K. Machamer

Robert G. Turnbull

STUDIES IN PERCEPTION

Robert G. Turnbull

Chapter One

THE ROLE OF THE "SPECIAL SENSIBLES" IN THE PERCEPTION THEORIES OF PLATO AND ARISTOTLE

For many years I was bewildered and more than a little fascinated by the fact that both Plato and Aristotle, when formally addressing themselves to problems of perception, concentrate upon color, sound, odor, and so on, and give little attention to shape, size, number, and the like. The much-discussed "secret doctrine" of the *Theaetetus* (155E-157C) purports to explain how the same wind may appear or seem and also "be" both cold and warm to different persons at the same time and to the same person at different times. It purports as well to explain similar facts concerning colors, tastes, sounds, odors, and such. But it nowhere attempts explanation of how, for example, the same coin may appear or seem and also "be" both elliptical and circular or large and small to anyone at all. Aristotle's major discussion of perception in books II and III of *On the Soul*, despite its differences from Plato's account(s) and its attention to "common sensibles", is vexing in an exactly similar way.

I think that an important clue in seeking an explanation of this apparently differential treatment of the sensibles is found in Aristotle's insistence in *On the Soul* that the several senses cannot be mistaken concerning their proper or special sensibles (color, sound, and so on) but can be mistaken concerning common sensibles (motion, rest, number, shape, and size). It should be noted, as well, that Plato's "secret doctrine" is stated in a context purporting to show how it is that perceptions cannot be mistaken and thus how it is that Protagoras' claim that "man is the measure" may be defended. And it is worth adding that, at the conclusion of the *Theaetetus* arguments against the claim of perception (*aisthesis*) to be knowledge (*episteme*), Plato denies that the secret doctrine can account for the "commons" (*ta koina*, 185E 1) by means of which the soul thinks colors, sounds, and such *to be*, to be *different* from one another, to be the *same* as themselves, to be *two* or some other *number*, or to be *like* or *unlike* one another. No doubt there is some connection to be made here with Platonic forms (and I shall say more of this later) but the point is that such "thinkings" about colors and sounds cannot allow for man's being the measure of *their* correctness.

Both Plato and Aristotle find the perceivings of special sensibles to be "infallible" because sensibles are themselves joint functions of the sense organs and certain causal characteristics of physical things in the environment. Thus no physical thing is in this "to-a-percipient" sense colored except *to* or *as perceived by* a sentient animal that has eyes. Of special importance in this connection it is to be noted that no attempt is made by Plato or Aristotle—nor could it be made—to distinguish the "real" color of a thing from the color it "appears" or "looks" to have. Perception of special sensibles is infallible because, given the to-a-sentient-animal condition, it could not (*logically* could not) be corrected.

Even so, colors as perceived are, for both Plato and Aristotle, the colors of physical things—to percipients. They are not ideas in the mind, sense-data, sensibilia, *sentiments*, or any other members of this general family of modern philosophical inventions. They are located in physical space and are, one might say, the perceived or perceptible surfaces of physical bodies (though, for Aristotle, as we shall see, one might better say that colors are at the surfaces of physical bodies).

As for the physical bodies *qua* unperceived, the Plato of *Timaeus* thinks of them as ultimately made up of elementary triangles that, in turn, make up the grosser physical bodies. Leaving aside the random "powers" that are allegedly given some degree of tidiness by the demiurge's geometric shapes, the physical bodies of *Timaeus qua* unperceived have shape,

4

size, number, position, and motion or rest (Aristotle's "common sensibles"). And bundles of the elementary solid figures also have the same properties. And they have those properties in themselves and not *to* or *as perceived by* a sentient animal. If, therefore, those properties can be perceived at all, it is possible for them to be *misperceived*. Something that is large *could* look or appear small. Something that is moving rapidly *could* look or appear to be moving slowly. And so on. But, as we have noted, something that is red or white *to* someone *could not* look or appear green or yellow to that percipient at the same time.

Though Aristotle's account of physical bodies *qua* unperceived is quite different from the *Timaeus* account, his "chunks" of earth, air, fire, or water also have, *in themselves* and *unperceived*, motion, rest, number, position, shape, and size. And as in Plato's account, *qua* having these properties, they *could* be misperceived in precisely the way in which, *qua* having special sensibles to percipients, they *could not* be misperceived.

But how are we to understand the perception of the common sensibles if they are not *to* or *as perceived by* a percipient being? If the paradigm of perception is seeing a color or hearing a sound, how does seeing a shape or seeing three X's (no matter what the X's are) fall under the paradigm? How is either of the latter a case of seeing at all? And, if we can make out how it is that common sensibles can be said to be perceived, how can they be misperceived? I think that this whole matter can best be approached by, first, giving a relatively unguarded and un-qualified statement of how I take Plato and Aristotle to under-stand the perceptual situation. Since the aim at this point is to expose the general nature of what those philosophers took to be the problem or problems of perception, I shall present the un-guarded account with little or no attention to the actual texts of either Plato or Aristotle. Second, in the light of the unguarded account, I shall attempt explanation of some crucial texts. For Plato these will be taken from *Theaetetus*, *Timaeus*, and *Republic*. Quite careful attention will be given to the celebrated analogies of the Line and the Cave from *Republic*. For Aristotle these will be taken from *On Sense and Sensible Objects* and *On the Soul* with special attention given to *On The Soul*, III.

5

THE UNGUARDED ACCOUNT

For both Plato and Aristotle there is a material world surrounding us and including us (*qua* bodies) that is made up of earth, air, fire, and water (however different their accounts of these "elements" may be) and that exists quite indifferently to its being perceived or sensed by any sentient being whatsoever. And it would or could exist even though it were never perceived or sensed. That world is, of course, spatial, and its parts have shape, size, number, position, and motion or rest. It is finite in extent and is entirely filled by its parts.

The motion (including other varieties of motion than local motion) of the material world and its parts is at least ultimately due to soul for Plato or due to activating of natural capacities or powers for Aristotle, though many derivative motions are due to contact. This requires, of course, that the ultimate parts of the material world be impenetrable and elastic and thus capable of transmitting local motion on contact. Both Plato and Aristotle think of there being a large number of bodies that are made up of smaller bodies in an immense variety of combinations. All of these larger bodies are capable of motion not only in the sense of movement in space but also in the sense of increase and diminution. They are also capable of changing from some number to another, i.e., they are capable of division and unification. Many of them are capable of growth, as plants and animals grow (and also decay). Even the ultimate bodies are capable of change that is other than local motion, i.e., change into one another (except for Plato's ultimate pieces of earth, which can only change from larger to smaller or smaller to larger pieces of earth).

Since all of the spatial material bodies are capable of motion and at least some of them are in regular local motion constantly, all of the motions can be thought of as temporal changes and all bodies as being in time. The clock for both Plato and Aristotle is, of course, the interrelated regularity of local motions of the heavenly bodies.

We may note, finally, that both philosophers think of there being a certain finite quantity of "matter" that fills the finite material world and to which there is no addition and from which there is no subtraction. How this is possible and how several other things in the account are possible are not, fortunately, important to this unguarded and relatively unqualified statement.

What are important are the following. First, the material world of Plato and Aristotle admits of characterization without reference to colors, sounds, odors, and such and exists quite independently of being perceived. Second, molar bodies of various kinds, all having shape, size, number, position, and motion or rest, are at various places in the world at various times. Third, bodies are larger and smaller in the degree to which they are made up of greater and smaller quantities of the elementary bodies, i.e., earth, air, fire, and water. Fourth, every body at a given time has a definite shape, size, number, and position. And it is either at rest or moving (in one or more of the several modes of movement) at a definite rate of change.

We must now turn to thinking of there being in this material world a number of relatively large and complex bodies that are characterizable in the above manner but that are also capable of perception, i.e., of *perceiving*. Without them there are no colors, no sounds, no odors, no tastes, no hards or softs, no hots or colds. (Whether there are moists and dries in the unperceived universe is, for Aristotle, an arguable issue, so I shall leave them out of the account.) As noted earlier, all of these exist in that peculiar way in which things that are *to* or *as perceived by* sentient beings exist.

I think it helpful to suppose that both Plato and Aristotle put to themselves the following question: Granted the existence of the unperceived material world, how is it possible for sentient beings, *qua* sentient, to become aware of it? Or, if you please, how is it possible for them to perceive it, or rather, parts of it? And I think that the answer that both gave to this question is: Only by way of perceiving colors, sounds, odors, hards and softs, and the like. By means of colors, the shapes, sizes, numbers, positions, and motions or rests of material things are *visible*. By means of sounds, *audible*. By hards and softs, hots and colds, *tangible*. Less usefully, by odors and tastes, one might say that material things (or their real properties) are *smell-*

7

able and *tasteable*. Taking 'perceptible' as a genus term for which the appropriate species terms are 'visible', 'audible', 'tangible', 'smellable', and 'tasteable', this would require that it is by means of colors, sounds, hards and softs, odors, and tastes that material things (having, in themselves, only shape, size, number, position and motion or rest) are *perceptible*. In and of themselves, they are *imperceptible*.

In order to make the shape, size, number, and such of a material thing visible, the color must be at, or immediately contiguous with, the surface of that material thing. Thus the seen color must be, as both Plato and Aristotle insist, external and must have the shape of (at least one side of) some molar physical thing. If we speak of a visual field of a given percipient at a given time, then the array of colors in that field is an array of colors having the shapes of (at least one side of) molar physical things—including, of course, among those things clouds, the sky (or so much of it as lies within the visual field), and the like. Lest one think of a primitive, Grandma Moses perspectiveless scene, however, I hasten to qualify the reference to shapes of molar physical things. They are, of course, shapes "from here" where "here" is a systematically ambiguous reference to the location of eyes and "from" is intelligible by means of the visual cones or pyramids of Euclid's optics (and, I believe, the relatively unstated optics of Plato and Aristotle). Thus eyes, roughly, are or provide the apices of visual pyramids. At any given moment in visual perception, within the pyramid of the entire visual field, smaller or narrower pyramids with variously angled bases delineate a perspectival array of colored shapes. With local movement of the pyramid of the entire visual field (or, if you please, with the generation of a continuous set of pyramids starting from "here"), continuous shifts of the two-dimensional bases of contained pyramids afford continuously different perspectives or size changes or both (assuming rest on the part of all or most of the physical things in the large field of vision). As one moves from, toward, above, below, and around a physical thing, the shifting perspectives allow for correction of single-location point-of-viewishness, especially when supplemented by another sense modality (say, touch) or by the

8

placing of a measuring rod on the several surfaces of the physical thing in question.

It is thus obvious from the visual cone or pyramid account that the shape made visible by color at a certain time may well be a misleading clue or index to the shape of a given physical thing. But one who is thus misled *can*—in principle at least—find out the shape by varying his perspective, measuring, and perhaps, making use of another sense modality. But he *cannot* —in principle—correct his color apprehension, for the colors are irremediably *to* or *as perceived by* him.

If what I have been saying in this unguarded account is correct in its general features at least, we have an explanation for the fact that both Plato and Aristotle, when formally addressing themselves to problems of perception, concentrate upon color, sound, odor, hard and soft, and so on. They are what need to be accounted for in perception, and they are what makes perception possible. I am tempted to say that their very subjectivity is necessary for our securing any perceptual purchase on the objective world of material things.

But—reaching this point—it is time to see how this general account may help in explaining some texts of both Plato and Aristotle.

THE TEXTS OF PLATO

In *Timaeus* Plato attempts a fairly detailed statement of the various physical or material conditions for the several sense modalities (i.e., vision, hearing, touch, and the like). Following time-honored custom in attending to vision to the neglect of the other sense modalities, partially because of its intrinsic interest and partially because of the attention Plato gives to vision in *Theaetetus* and *Republic*, I shall confine myself almost entirely to the texts concerning the material conditions of vision.

From 45C through 46C Plato states very succinctly his extramission theory of vision, though he does not until later (67C-68E) explain the physical conditions of color perception. Fire— the kind that does not burn but is "akin to daylight"—is emitted from the eye, presumably in straight-line pattern and spreading out in the form of the Euclidian cone or pyramid.

> For they [the gods] made within us the unmixed fire which is just like that of day [literally, brother of daylight] stream out through the eyes as a smooth and dense whole, compressing especially the material of the middle of the eyes so as to keep out all other fire which is coarser and allowing only this pure sort of fire to filter through. And so, when the light of day surrounds the stream of vision [opsis], then, like flowing out to like and coming to be compacted, a single kindred body is formed conforming to the linear pattern determined by the eyes [literally, according to the straight path of the eyes]. (44C)

Plato goes on to say that this "kindred body," in "touching" or being touched by various physical things in the near or remote environment, transmits "the motions" or whatever it touches or is touched by "right up to the soul." And this touching and transmission "produces that perception [sensation, *aisthesis*] that we call 'seeing' " (44D).

At night, when there is no "kindred" day-fire, the fire streaming from the eyes is "cut off" (*apotetmetai*), so no rigid body is formed to touch or be touched by objects in the environment. (Aristotle, in *On Sense and Sensible Objects*, notes another *Timaeus* passage which maintains that there is a "quenching" (*aposbesis*) of light in the dark and ridicules the idea as implying that we could not see in the daytime when it rains [473b 15-19].) And he notes that, when the eyelids are closed, the fire cannot stream out. More interestingly, he claims that his theory accounts for the "image-making" of mirrors. I say "more interestingly" for two reasons. First, his account of a man's seeing his own reflection in a flat mirror assumes the "coalescence" of fire from the face and fire from the eye on the smooth surface of the mirror. He speaks of reflections occurring "when the fire of the face comes to be coalescent (compacted) with the fire of vision [*opsis*] on the smooth and bright [surface]" (46B). Second, he uses this meeting of the fire from the face and the fire from the eye to account for the right-left, left-right image reversal in a mirror. It is difficult to see what he could possibly have in mind unless he is thinking of fire from the left side of the face traveling in a straight line (but at an angle- so as to meet fire traveling from the eye in a straight line (but at an opposite angle) so as to meet at the surface of the mirror and the reverse holding for fire traveling from the right side of the face. Indeed, in the course of the brief account of mirror-images, Plato shifts to use of the term "ray" (*auge*, 46C). This need for opposite angles of the ray from the eye and that from the side of the face seems clearly to require some such geometrizing of the "stream of vision" as that found in Euclid's visual cone or pyramid. The point is of considerable importance, for nowhere in any Platonic text is the visual cone as such described. Aside from the fact that some means must be assumed in the *Timaeus* account for narrowing the transmission medium for motions from (relatively) large objects in the environment in order to transmit those motions to the eye (and he does speak of the "straight path of the eyes"!), this brief section on mirror images seems to justify the assumption that Plato makes use of the Euclidean cone or pyramid, whether or not he has a completely worked out geometric optics.

At 64D-E, Plato speaks of the visual stream as, in daylight, being a body "connatural with" or "joined with" (*symphues*) our own body. And he is at pains to explain how cuttings and burnings of that body cause no pain and how a return to its form after disruption produces no pleasure. The explanation is that the visual stream is a body made up of subtle parts that are rather easily scattered and return to original form with comparative ease. "For violent force is in no way in its [the visual stream's] dissolution [*diakrisis*—commonly translated as 'dilation'] and its compounding [*synkrisis*—commonly translated as 'contraction']" (64E). I have called attention to the words *diakrisis* and *synkrisis*, for they play a key role, as we shortly shall see, in the understanding of Plato's theory of the physical conditions of color perception. I think that the most natural reading of the present passage is that the pleasure or pain would be felt in the eye as a result of transmission of motions along the visual stream to the eye, but some commentators have taken it that the visual cone is itself a sensitive body.

11

At 67C-68E, Plato explains the physical conditions of color perception. It is, perhaps, of some interest to note, with the general contention of this paper in mind, that the two standard Greek words for "color," *chroma* and *chros*, both used in the present passage, have as their primary meaning "the surface of the body" or "skin." Though there is no doubt that in the present passage they mean *color*, the association with surfaces adds a slight help to my claim that Plato thinks of colors as making surfaces visible.

The general contention of the passage is relatively clear. Plato speaks of flame (*phloga*) "streaming off" bodies. These are, of course, tetrahedra (i.e., fire particles), which are said to "break into" (*empipto*) the visual stream (*opsis*). Some are equal in size to those making up the stream. When they are encountered nothing happens except, perhaps, prolongation of the body going out from the eye, for they presumably join with the eye fire. They are therefore said to be "transparent." (Cf. Aristotle's remark in *On the Soul* that "light is, as it were, the color of the transparent" [418b 11-12].) When the stream encounters larger particles than its own, those larger tetrahedra are said to "compound" or "contract" (*synkrino*) the stream. I suppose this to be a relatively uniform pushing back of the stream over a given portion of it, thus transmitting a uniform motion back in that portion of the stream-body to the eye, in the pattern, of course, of a contained (within the whole stream) visual pyramid. The flame made up of these larger tetrahedra is said to be *black* (or, perhaps, *dark*). When the stream encounters smaller particles than its own, those smaller tetrahedra are said to "dissolve" or "separate out" (*diakrino*) the stream. The motion of the flame composed of such smaller particles is said to be "more rapid," and the flame made up of such particles is said to be *white*. He thinks of the several other colors being produced by the interaction of the quick-dissolving particles that get "quenched" by the moisture of the eye and the flashing out of the original eye fire. I omit any attempt to explain his account of mixtures of various kinds.

It is tempting to think that Plato takes the "flames" coming off the surfaces of material things as some sort of differential reflection of light, larger fire particles being reflected from molar Platonic bodies that we call *black*, smaller ones from molar bodies that we call *white*. But whether they are reflected fire particles or whether they "stream off" molar physical things in some other way, the point I am concerned about in discussing these passages is clear. The color transmission, whatever the detailed explanation of the color differences, *reveals* or, if you please, *outlines* the shapes of molar material things.

In *Theaetetus*, Plato expressly argues that colors, sounds, tastes, and the like are *to* or *as perceived by* sentient beings (156 ff.). Though the stated doctrine occurs in a context in which Socrates is made to refute the doctrine that perception (*aisthesis*) is knowledge (*episteme*), and he presents the doctrine as rendering intelligible a claim of Protagoras, most scholars take the doctrine—as an account of the nature of perception or sensation—as Plato's own. And I agree. A crucial and much-discussed part of that doctrine—concerning vision—occurs at 156C-E.

> All these are, as we say, in motion, and there is quickness or slowness in their motion. Now the slow [one] has its motion in the same place but is directed toward whatever [ones] approach, and in this way it begets. But the two that are begotten are quicker. For they are carried along and their motion is naturally in a rush. Thus when an eye and some approaching thing that is proportioned [*symmetron*] to it beget whiteness and perception [*aisthesis*], its twin (things that would not have come to be with either going to anything else), then, as the visual stream [*opsis*, the same term translated as 'visual stream' in the *Timaeus* passages, usually translated as 'sight'] from the eyes and the whiteness from that which joins in begetting the color are moving between [the eyes and the thing], the eye comes to be filled with the visual stream [*opsis*, usually translated 'sight'] and sees, coming to be not a mere visual stream but a seeing eye, and the joint parent of the color is filled with whiteness and comes to be not whiteness but white—whether a white stick, or a white stone, or a white whatever happens to be so colored.

I think it is obvious that there is a connection between this passage and the doctrine delineated in the three passages from *Timaeus*. My translation of *opsis* as 'visual stream' rather than 'sight' may be regarded as a bit suspect, but how else is one to

13

understand '*opsis* from the eyes'? *Whiteness* I understand to be the small fire particles streaming off the molar physical things, as in the *Timaeus* doctrine. Even as, in the above *Theaetetus* passage Plato speaks of the eye's *seeing*, so also, at *Timaeus* 45D, he speaks of *seeing's* occurring when the motion has been transmitted by the visual stream body "right up to the soul."

It is interesting to note, in connection with the main contention of this paper, that Plato, in the *Theaetetus* passage, speaks of the "joint parent" as coming to be not whiteness but *a white thing*. What a person is presented with in vision is not, of course, small particles of fire (which, on Plato's account, are at any rate not visible), but an expanse of white that is at the surface of a thing, i.e., the thing seen. And Plato insists that the color as seen is such as to warrant our characterizing it as the color of a thing.

There is a great deal of emphasis on the use of 'coming to be' [various forms of *gignomai*] in the context of, and in the passage quoted from, *Theaetetus*. The usage is, of course, connected with the blending of the doctrine of Heraclitus with the "man is the measure" dictum of Protagoras in the dialogue. The usage is, I think, connected with the "to a percipient" feature of perception, though arguing this with appropriate textual and contextual detail is impossible here. Just before the quoted passage, Socrates confronts Theaetetus with a puzzle concerning number. The puzzle is found in the fact that six dice are both more than four and less than twelve. If the six are compared with four, the six are large. If compared with the twelve, the six are smaller. Question: How can the six change from larger to smaller without going through a process of change? The point of the so-called puzzle is, I think, that *seeing* and *color* or *sensing* and *sensed* are irremediably relative. Each is necessarily "with respect to" the other. And thus, like the wind which, in the earlier example of the dialogue, is both warm and cold *to* different percipients at the same time, nothing simply is F, where F is a "special sensible"; it is also G or whatever, but always *to* a percipient. Hence its "becoming" is, paradoxical as that may sound, without benefit of going through a temporal process of change. Special sensibles, so considered, *radically* are and are not, and thus *radically* come to be.

Commencing at 184B, the matter of the "commons," mentioned in the introduction to this paper, comes up. It does so in connection with Socrates' insistence that *strictly speaking* it is not eyes that see or ears that hear but *souls* that see and hear colors and sounds by means of eyes and ears. Furthermore, if one has some awareness or thought of what is perceived through hearing and what is perceived through the visual stream *together* or *at once*, that thought cannot be a perceiving through, or by means of, a bodily sense organ. He goes on to assert that it is not through a bodily sense organ that one (185A-C) "thinks this same thing concerning both [a sound and a color] that both *are*," or "that each is *different* from the other but the *same* as itself," or "that both are *two*, but each is *one*," or that they are *like* or *unlike* one another. *Being, Same, Different*—a familiar list to readers of *Sophist* and *Timaeus*—as well as the others listed above are said to be "among those which the soul itself and by itself stretches itself towards [*eporegetai*]" (186A), i.e., making use of no bodily organ. And these are said to be "commons" (*koina*). Finally, Socrates says, at 186C, that human beings and animals from birth are capable of perception, but that it is only through education [*paideia*] with much difficulty that one becomes capable of "lines of reasoning [*analogismata*] concerning [what is perceived by the soul through the body] with regard to their nature [*ousia*] and utility." This, of course, sounds like a reference to the education of the guardians in *Republic*, and we shall be turning shortly to that dialogue.

It is worth noting here, however, that some of the functions assigned here to the soul working through no bodily organ, in particular, simultaneous awareness (or, if you please, thought) of the deliverances of different senses, are assigned by Aristotle, in *On The Soul*, III, to the "common sense" (*aisthesis koine*). I may also note that the Aristotelian "common sense" is especially the faculty for perceiving the common sensibles, and the list given at 425a and 16-17 includes "motion, rest, shape, size, number, and one [or unity]." Number and unity are, of course, in Plato's list of "commons." Elsewhere (in *Parmenides* 146A) Plato defines motion as *always in a* DIFFERENT and rest as *always in a* SAME. With a bit more ingenuity and reference to other dialogues (especially *Parmenides*), one could probably find

15

ways to think of Platonic "commons" that would encompass shape and size. However that may be, Plato thinks of his "commons" as forms that are gotten at by the soul by itself and thought of by the soul as (somehow) common to, or holding for, the sensibles that are perceived by the soul through bodily organs. It is hard to see, nevertheless, how such "commons" could be common unless there were a basis for their application or commonality in the deliverances of sense perception themselves. Aristotle, largely, I think, because of his rejection of the Platonic "separated" forms, assigns the "non-accidental" [*ou kata symbebekos*] apprehension of the common sensibles to the faculty of common sense.

In the celebrated and much-worked-over analogies of the Line and the Cave in *Republic* VI and VII, Plato is obviously drawing upon a doctrine or theory of perception that he does not in text or context explain. I assume that the general features of both analogies are known in what follows. My interest, of course, is not in full and detailed exposition but rather in how they relate to the general thesis of this paper concerning the role of the "special sensibles."

Commencing at 509D and continuing to the end of Book VI, Socrates describes four stages in the acquisition of complete knowledge by the analogy of a doubly-divided line. The left segment of the line after the first division is to represent "the visible kind" (*to horomenon genos*) and the right segment "the intelligible (or thinkable) kind" (*to noumenon*) (509D). Visibles are further divided into "images"—that is, "shadows" (*skiai*), and then "appearances" (*phantasmata*) in water and in smooth and shiny surfaces—and those of which the images are images— that is, animals, plants, and all the things (literally, "the inanimate kind") about us. The intelligibles are further divided into objects of geometry and other parts of mathematics and objects of "dialectical science" (*tes tou dialegesthai epistemes*). Corresponding to these four sorts of objects are, respectively, "imaging" or "likenessing" (*eikasia*), "belief" or "trust" (*pistis*), "understanding" (*dianoia*), and "reason" (*noesis*).

Earlier, especially at 508A-509C, Plato speaks of the sun as the cause of "the power of visibility" (*ten tou horasthai dyna-*

min) of the visibles and also of their "coming to be" (*genesis*) and growth and nurture (509B). Even earlier, at 507D, he says

> Don't you understand that both vision [or the visual stream—*opsis*] and the visible are in want of something?
>
> How is that?
>
> Even though vision [*opsis*] may be in the eyes and one having it may try to make use of it and even though color may be present in things, if a third kind that is peculiarly adapted to this special purpose is not also present, I'm sure you know both that vision will see nothing and also that the colors will not be seen.
>
> What is it?
>
> I speak of what you call *light*. (507D4-E4)

It is quite clear from the context that light is just the daylight, the connate fire of the *Timaeus* that mingles with eye fire to produce the rigid body that touches, and is touched by, various things in the material world. And it is for this reason, of course, that the sun is said to be the cause of the "power of visibility" of visibles.

Now what I should like to say about "imaging" or "likeness-ing" (*eikasia*) is that it is perception wherein no correction has been made for what I earlier called "point-of-viewishness" and that, despite Plato's talk of shadows and appearances in water and in smooth surfaces, he has in mind the uncorrected seeings and seens made possible by the visual cone when it has, as it were, not been moved around objects. Supporting this desire of mine are the following considerations. First, it is just possible that his intention in talking of shadows and appearances in water and smooth surfaces is to call attention to the two-dimensional character of surfaces made visible by the colors falling within the perspective array in the visual cone. Second, both in the explanation of the analogy of the Line provided by the analogy of the Cave in book VII and in the discussion of the painter's bed (i.e., the one of the painting) in book X, Plato makes a great deal of the immobility of the prisoners who can see only shadows on the wall and of the fact that one can walk around the bed make by the bed-maker but not around the bed

17

in the painting. Speaking of the bed made by the bed-maker, he says,

> A bed—if you look at it from an angle or straight down at it or some other way—does it differ from itself or not, though it appears in many different ways? And doesn't it go that way with other things?
>
> It does indeed. They appear in different ways but they don't differ.
>
> Then, consider this point. To what end is the painting made in each case? Is it made with a view to copying something just as it is or to copying an appearance [of it] as it appears? Is it an imitation of a reality [*aletheias*] or of an appearance [*phantasmatos*]?
>
> Of an appearance. (598A7-B4)

The contrast between appearances of a bed as one walks around it and the bed as it remains the same seems to me like the contrast between the objects of "likenessing" (*eikasia*) and the objects of belief (*pistis*) in the analogy of the Line. The painter imitates an object of "likenessing", not an object of believing. (If he were to imitate the latter, in the bed case, he would have to make another bed.) The immobility of the prisoners looking at the shadows of real objects being carried back and forth behind them must be supplemented by the fact that, had Plato made them immobile while looking at the real things, the movement of those things would have provided them with correcting perspectives. And they could have caught on rather quickly to the fact that there is a difference between two-dimensional appearances of an object and the object, i.e., in the terms of book X that the object remained the same while appearances of it varied. Third, it may be of some importance to note that the standard term for scene-painting is *skiagraphia*. It is defined in Liddell and Scott as "painting with shadows so as to produce an illusion of solidity at a distance." Plato uses the term earlier in the *Republic* (365C) in connection with cultivating or producing the appearance of virtue while all the while devoting oneself to the pursuit of one's own profit at whatever cost. He uses it in *Critias* (107D) in connection with the point that we are tolerant of inexactness of paintings of outdoor scenes but very

18

critical of paintings of our own bodies. He uses it in *Phaedo* in connection again with creating the illusion of virtue (69B). My point is, of course, that *skiagraphia* literally is 'shadow painting' and that the talk of shadows both in the Line and the Cave may well evoke in his listeners the use of shadows to create the illusion of reality. Fourth, it is noteworthy that reflections in water and other smooth surfaces would, of course, not be shadows but would be, as it were, in full color. With this in mind, there seems no reason to be overly attached to taking the shadows of either the Line or the Cave literally as shadows.

It therefore seems to me completely plausible that the Plato who wrote *Republic* knew at least in general outline the sort of thing he was to write about perception in *Timaeus* and *Theaetetus* and that he had it in mind in the analogies of the Line and the Cave. I might add to that plausibility by noting that Glaucon is very puzzled concerning the sun's being the cause of the visibility of the objects of perception and asks for clarification.

> Please don't hold back, but at least go through in detail the similitude [i.e., to the Good] of the sun, if you are leaving anything out.
>
> I am leaving out a great deal.
>
> Well, then, don't leave out the least bit.
>
> I believe that much will be left out. Even so, so far as the present occasion makes it possible, I shall not willingly omit anything. (509C)

And then Socrates proceeds to give the analogy of the Line. My point is, of course, that what is omitted is not merely the detail of the relation of the objects of *reason* to those of *understanding* and their dependence on the Good but also the detail of the technical accounts of perception in *Timaeus* and *Theaetetus*. And we are warned at the outset that much will be omitted.

I forgo any attempt to explain (and *a fortiori* to defend an explanation) of the remaining features of the analogies. It might be worth noticing, however, that, if my explanation of the relation between "likenessing" and belief and their objects plus the relation of both to the sun is accepted, the movement in the *paideia* from belief to understanding is readily intelligible. If, in correcting for the point-of-viewishness of "likenessing", one should measure and compare sizes, what more natural than that he would be led to numbers and to equality? Indeed, Plato suggests as much in later parts of book VII. And he suggests, as well, what was suggested in *Theaetetus* in the section concerning the soul's perceiving or recognizing a simultaneously perceived color and sound as two (523B-524D).

The Platonic evidence, taken as a whole, I submit, has the effect of confirming the thesis of this paper, namely, that the so-called "special sensibles" make visible the shape, size, number, and so on, of material things whose existence is by no means dependent upon our perception. We cannot be wrong in apprehending the special sensibles, but we can be wrong—and can correct ourselves—about the so-called "common sensibles".

THE TEXTS OF ARISTOTLE

Fortunately my case is easier to make out for Aristotle than it was for Plato. After all, tbe very terms of the distinction by which the thesis was originally stated, namely, "special sensibles" and "common sensibles", are Aristotle's. And he insists that "it is not possible to be deceived [*apatethenai*] concerning" special sensibles and goes on to claim that "each [sense, *aisthesis*] judges concerning these [i.e., its proper objects] and is not deceived that [something is] a color or a sound, but rather what it is which is colored or where it is, or what it is which makes a sound or where it is" (*On the Soul*, 418a 13-17). Aristotle, of course, makes a great deal of the distinction between *potential* and *actual*. To stay with the modality of sight, eyes that have passive potentiality or power and physical things (or their surfaces) that have active potentiality or power, are *qua*, having such potentialities, in the right conditions simultaneously actualized. But "the motions—both the acting [*poiesis*] and the suffering [*pathos*]—are in the acted upon" (*On the Soul*, 426a 2-3), i.e., in vision, they are in the eyes. In this way both "the actualizing [*energeia*] of the sensible and the sensing are one and the same" (425b 27-8), that is, the physical thing that is perceived is not changed in the perceiving, though the sense organ is changed. With respect to the status of colors, sounds, and such, when no perception is taking place, he says

> The earlier philosophers of nature [physiologoi] expressed themselves rather unhappily on this matter, thinking, as they did, that nothing is black or white without vision [opsis] nor flavored without taste. In one sense they were right, in another, wrong. For 'sensing' [aisthesis] and 'sensible' [aistheton] having double meanings, corresponding to potentiality and actuality. What they say holds for the one [i.e., actuality] but it does not hold for the other [potentiality]. (On the Soul, 425a 22-27.)

So we have Aristotle holding that in his world of physical things the molar ones have potentialities corresponding to the several colors and could have them even though there were no percipient beings in the world. In this sense the colors exist without "vision". But, with percipients around, i.e., beings with passive potentialities of the right sort, when the right conditions obtain, there come to be actual (rather than merely potential) colors.

Staying away from bothersome texts in Aristotle which suggest that he is undecided concerning extramission or intromission theories of vision, it is obvious that Plato's account of vision or seeing makes Aristotle uncomfortable, though he retains certain general features of it. He does not approve the idea that light travels and takes time in doing so, and he castigates Empedocles on this score (418b 21 ff.). As we saw earlier, he thinks that the Plato of Timaeus with his explanation of our failure to see at night (as Aristotle understands it, because of "quenching" of eye fire) cannot explain our ability to see when it is raining. Aristotle's own view is that there can be no perception without a medium of some sort: in the case of vision, commonly air or water. The introduction of fire into the medium transforms the medium from opaque to transparent. Of transparency I shall say something shortly. At this moment, however, I should like to attend to the claim of Aristotle that the action of the perceived thing on the medium (when it is transparent) is instantaneously transmitted to the eye. How it is transmitted is a bit unclear, but Aristotle makes it quite clear that the change produced in air, water, glass, or whatever when fire is introduced is an immediate actualizing of the potentially transparent that renders transparent a larger or smaller "piece" (my term) of the medium all at once. The presumption is that the transfer of motion from the perceived object to the eye is likewise immediate, or rather "mediate" in the sense that it requires a medium, but is nonetheless instantaneous. In chapter 12 of *On the Soul*, II we are told that the sense organ—in vision, the eyes, of course—must be extended, but "neither the being sensitive or the sensing [*aisthesis*] are extended." They are, rather, "a kind of ratio or power [*dynamis*] of it [i.e., the sense organ or the sensitive subject]" (424a 26-28). I think that this ratio, when the sense organ is not stimulated, is to be thought of as a "mean" (*mesotis*). Indeed, Aristotle says that "sensation [perception, *aisthesis*] is some sort of mean between opposed sensibles" (424a 4-6). The idea is that we do not actually perceive anything when the sense organ is in its "mean" condition, but departures of the organ from that condition produce actual perceptions. If the departures are extreme, the sense organ may be destroyed (as the power of vision may be destroyed by staring at the sun). In this same connection Aristotle speaks of "the sense [*aisthesis*] as receptive of the sensible forms [*ton aistheton eidon*] without the matter" (424a 18-19). What I understand this to mean is that an eye, for example, is made of certain materials (*which* materials being unimportant for the present purpose) that are naturally and normally in a certain ratio to one another. The eye is capable of departing from that mean condition so and so many "degrees" in either direction from the mean. If that amount is exceeded, the eye, as a functioning complex, is destroyed. When suitably stimulated by the medium's transmission of motions from a molar physical thing that has active "color power" (my expression), the eye takes on a ratio that is formally akin to, or, if you please, identical to, a certain ratio in the thing (which is or produces its "color power"). Thus the eye takes on the form of the sensitive object without its matter. (Aristotle compares this to the wax receiving an impression of the signet without the material of which the signet is made.) When this occurs, the eyes sees a color.

The whole account of book II of *On the Soul* is directed to explaining our perception of colors, sounds, hards and softs, and so on, and none of it is devoted to the perception of common sensibles as such. The account is also, of course, like Plato's, one in which the active powers of the thing and the passive powers of the sensitive organ are both needed for the perception to occur. If, for any reason, the sensitive organ is changed or not "normal", the special sensible perceived is changed. Thus Aristotle clearly thinks of the perception of the special sensibles as *to* or *as perceived by* a sentient being. But what is to be said of the common sensibles?

In *On Sense and Sensible Objects*, a document intended as a supplement to *On the Soul*, Aristotle says that color "is at the limit [*peras*] of the body, but it is not the limit of the body, but we must suppose that it is the same nature [*physis*] which is colored outside which is also inside" (439a 33-b 1). He goes on to speak of color as the "limit" of the transparent.

> Therefore in the degree to which the transparent holds for bodies (and it holds in greater or lesser degree for all of them), it [the transparent] makes them have a share of color. Since the color is in the limit, it must be in the limit of it [i.e., the transparent]. So that color would then be the limit of the transparent in a body that is defined [i.e., that has a definite shape]. (439b 8-12.)

He is concerned in this passage both to claim that the surface of water (or glass, or other transparent medium) is colored and to claim that the actually seen color in perception is at the surface of a material object. Thus one can think of a present visual perception, phenomenologically considered, as a set of colored planes lying at the limits or surfaces of various bodies in a visual field. Between "here" (the location of the eyes) and any one of them is, of course, the "transparent". I noted earlier that Aristotle, in *On the Soul*, comments that "light is as it were the color of the transparent". I did so in connection with Plato's treatment of the transparent as due to the eye fire's meeting fire-particles of exactly similar size. It is difficult to see what

23

Aristotle's "as it were" comment can mean unless he is thinking of air or water *qua* rendered transparent by fire as producing in itself approximately the same ratio as the natural ratio or mean of the eyes when opened as well as being the transmitter of whatever motions from colored objects at its limits.

Aristotle does not discuss perspective as such, and thus there is no account of how it is that we see physical bodies as having different sizes and shapes from varying distances and angles. It is quite clear that he does not do so in his general and in his detailed accounts of perception. Here, except for some hints in the early part of book III of *On the Soul* in the discussion of "common sense", we really hear only about the special sensibles and that the common sensibles are "essentially" (naturally, properly, *kath auta*) objects of the several senses (as contrasted with "incidentally", *kata symbebekos*, as a certain man is perceived "incidentally"). He does, however, at *Physics*, II, 193b 32-194a 11, talk about *optics*. He does so in a context where he is attempting to distinguish physics from mathematics. The mathematician, he says, treats of the surfaces, volumes, lines, and points of physical bodies, but he does not treat them as actual "accidents" [*symbebekota*] of bodies. "Therefore he separates them" (193b 34), i.e., considers them in separation from the physical bodies. He then writes,

> For geometry investigates physical lines, but not *qua* physical, but optics [*optike*] investigates [*skopei*] mathematical lines, but not *qua* mathematical, but rather *qua* physical. (194a 10-13)

It is very hard to resist the temptation to think that Aristotle, the long-term colleague of Eudoxus in Plato's Academy, is thinking of optics very much as Euclid did and to think of his neglect of the use of the Euclidean visual cone or pyramid in his writings as a simple indication that he thought that to be a mathematician's work and probably that he thought of it as being done or having been done by others. At any rate it is difficult to think what he could be talking about in treating optics as giving a mathematical treatment to physical "lines" if he is not thinking of a treatment of vision like that of Euclid's *Optics*.

I wish to conclude with a few remarks concerning Aristotle's treatment of the "common sense" in *On the Soul*, III.

But there cannot be some special [*idion*] sense organ for the commons [i.e., common sensibles], those that we sense accidentally [*kata symbebekos*] by each sense, for example, motion, rest, shape, size, number, one. For we sense all of these by motion, for example, size by motion. So also shape. For shape is a sort of size. Rest [is sensed] by the not-moved. Number by the denial of the continuous and by the special [sensibles]. For each sense senses *one*. So that it is clearly impossible for there to be a special sense for any whatsoever of these [i.e., common sensibles], for example, motion. For, if so, it would be as we now sense the sweet by sight. But this would be because we happen to have a sense for both by which we also recognize when they occur together. If not, we would in no way sense them except accidentally [*kata symbebekos*], for example, as we sense Kleon's son—not because he is Kleon's son, but because he is white. And it is accidental for this to be Kleon's son. But for the non-accidental [apprehending] of the commons [common sensibles] we already have a common sense. Thus they are not special [sensibles]. Otherwise we would sense them in no other way than as we said we see Kleon's son. The senses sense the special [sensibles] of one another accidentally—not *qua* themselves [or *qua* in the plural, as it were] but *qua* one, when there comes to be the sensing [of different sensibles] in the same thing, for example, bile because it is bitter and yellow. For it is not for different [senses] to say that both are one. Thus sense may even be deceived; if an object is yellow, it may believe it to be bile. It might be asked what is the reason we have many senses and not one only. It may perhaps be in order that the accompanying and common sensibles can elude us less easily, for example, motion, size, and number. For if there were only vision and it were of white [only], the [common sensibles] would rather elude us and all would seem to be the same because of the simultaneous coincidence with one another of color and size. As things are, since the common [sensibles] hold in different sensibles [i.e., special sensibles], it is clear that they [the common sensibles] are different from each and every one of them [i.e., the special sensibles]. (425a 14-425b 12).

According to the passage it is not accidental that we sense the common sensibles, as it is accidental that we sense, say, Kleon's son. But it is accidental for a given sense, say sight, to sense a common sensible, because that common sensible is available in more than one sense modality and not merely in sight. Aristotle thus argues that there must be a common sense by means of which we quite properly (and not accidentally) sense, e.g., that a shape as colored and a shape as hard are one. Otherwise we are in the situation of sensing the sweet by sight. The last part of the passage, that about the reason for our having many senses, is interesting for the main thesis of this paper. The obvious point of having the common sensibles "elude us less" is that, by having them be visible, tangible, and so on, we can hope to get them right—not merely to separate them from the special sensibles in each sense modality. But that point is, after all, the major thesis of this paper.

Edward N. Lee

Chapter Two

THE SENSE OF AN OBJECT:
EPICURUS ON SEEING AND HEARING

I. PRELIMINARIES

This paper is mainly devoted to an exegesis (and only a partial one, at that) of sections 46-53 in Epicurus' "Letter to Herodotus," the sections containing his account of seeing and hearing.[1] Familiar, even shopworn, as those sections are, the interpretation of them to be given here will be rather different from the usual. Before beginning our argument, it may be helpful if I mention certain details in Epicurus' text that strike me as inadequately dealt with in the usual interpretations of his view. One of my main aims has been to "do justice" to these features, and introducing them here may help to set the exegetic project of the paper in perspective.

A. The first is the term *phantasia*, which plays a focal role (at §50.1) in Epicurus' account of seeing. Aristotle had analyzed *phantasia* (in *De Anima* III.3) in such a way as to distinguish it from all perceiving. Epicurus' flaunting of the term within his own analysis of perception seems a deliberately anti-Aristotelian move. Just what the force of *phantasia* actually *is* for Epicurus is, however, most unclear, as is the detail of the relation between his view and Aristotle's. Both issues will be dealt with here.[2]

B. The term *sympatheia* appears no less than four times in Epicurus' fairly brief account of perception, both in the case of seeing and in that of hearing. The term would be quite at home in the Stoics' pan-vitalist physics, where all parts of the cosmos bear internal and organic bonds of "sympathy" to all the others. But Epicurus' atomistic form of materialism takes as its basic units independent atoms bearing nothing but mechanical and external relations to one another: just what the sense of *sympatheia* can be, in such a context, and with what right Epicurus can employ it, clearly calls for some explaining.[3]

C. Epicurus' theory of seeing is an exclusively "intromissionist" one.[4] He explicitly rejects (§49) Plato's notion that any visual ray extends from the seeing eye out to the object seen, and holds instead to a one-way flow of atoms from the object into the eye. Nonetheless, in his account of hearing—although it follows much the same lines as that for seeing—he makes explicit mention (§52.8–9) of some sort of feature that "extends out to the [sound-] emitting object."[5] Once again, the role of this notion seems to demand elucidation.

My present argument (to state it very roughly) will be that we can use the role of *sympatheia* (B) in Epicurus' two accounts so that they illuminate one another, and that we can then see how the "outward-extending" feature in the hearing account (C) helps to clarify the sense in which vision's *phantasia* also represents or "reaches out toward" its object (A). We shall thus see that both accounts treat perceptual awareness (in these importantly differing modalities) as the "sense of an object"—the direct and uninterpreted, purely perceptual apprehension of an external physical object. Sections II-V of the paper will be spent in working out details of these occasionally tangled matters. In sections VI and VII I shall take up (what may by then seem long overdue) some assessment of the wider philosophical, psychological, and historical import of Epicurus' position as I analyze it here.

28

II. EPICURUS ON SEEING (PART I)

Epicurus' account of visual perception, of course, begins with the infamous *eidola* unceasingly pumped out by objects. There is no end of problems with that theory of idol-propagation,[6] but what matters most to us for the present is that these *eidola* are *only* the beginning terms in his account.

The very term *eidolon* (most often translated "image" or "idol"; cf. Lucretius' *simulacrum*) naturally tends to suggest something representing or depicting something else: one thinks of it as something like a picture. Yet it is essential to remember that an *eidolon* is but a single fleeting film of flying atoms, a diaphanous sheet or screen or convoy of atoms, thinner than any gossamer (only one atom thick) and traveling all on its own through space at some amazingly high speed. Any such single spurt or pulse of atoms is in fact very little like any traveling picture (it is not something that one might, say, intercept *en route* and *view*) but is instead the merest, most fleeting physical episode. It is only (1) when and if all of the members (or most of them, at least) of a *stream* of such idols bear certain relations to one another (and to their source) and (2) when and if they strike successively upon an appropriate sense organ, that they will generate a *phantasia* of the object (§49.6–50.4). The conditions required for the generation of such *phantasiai* are in fact both more complex and more subtle than they may first appear, and a close look at Epicurus' unfortunately highly obscure remarks about them will be required. These remarks occur first in his discussion of vision and are then supplemented by his account of hearing. We shall make use of each of these accounts to illuminate the other.[7]

The key points about the idols' propagation are these:

A. *Each film* moves away from its source-object very rapidly, and all the parts of each move out in the same speed and manner, so that these parts retain, as the idol travels, the over-all form and interrelation that they had in (or on the surface of) the object.[8]

B. *Successive films* are generated in extremely rapid succession, one after the other (though they do form a discrete, discontinuous series, of course). (§48.1–4, etc. They are all presumably emitted at the very same, very fast rate, somehow, lest some should overtake their predecessors, or some of them lag and so cause interferences between the films; cf. §50.2–3.)

C. Because all the films come from the same object, and because each retains that object's basic features (as it was upon each film's departure), a certain affinity or similarity will obtain between the films within a series. This is not to say, of course, that they must all be the *same*. The source object may itself be changing as the films are being produced, so the films may vary widely among themselves. Films very widely separated in time may show precious little similarity at all, but at least rather closely successive ones—even though they may be *somewhat* different—must "preserve their *sympatheia* from the underlying object" (§50.2–3).

We must go into more detail about this crucial *sympatheia* in a moment, but, just to sketch in the main conclusion of all this for now: given that these conditions (A)-(C) are satisfied, then (D) when the film-stream strikes an appropriate sense organ, it "produces a *phantasia* of a single and continuous [object]" (§50.1–2).[9] In order to understand the way *phantasia* does present a "single and continuous object," we must better understand the *sympatheia* mentioned in (C), and the needed clarification comes from the subsequent account of hearing. Several elements appear in that account of hearing that seem at first to have no exact parallel in the case of vision: there is mention of an *akoustikon pathos* (§52.6) and of something called *epaisthesis* (§52.9, 53.2); there is no mention at all of any *phantasia*, although more is said—indeed, some quite remarkable things are said—about *sympatheia*. The entire discussion of hearing raises several obscure and complex points, and some wrestling with those will be unavoidable; but in that way a clarification of *sympatheia*, and of the various ties and asymmetries between the accounts of hearing and of vision, may in the end emerge.

III. EPICURUS ON HEARING

Epicurus begins his account by remarking that hearing must, like seeing, come about through some sort of outflow from the object, an outflow whose impact upon us produces in us auditory stimulation (the *akoustikon pathos* of §52.6 and §53.7).[10] He then adds, obscurely enough, that this flow subdivides into "homoiomerous segments" (*onkoi*: literally, "bulks" or "masses"). Some commentators have assumed that he means by this phrase the atoms (of breath or voice or whatever), but the idea that any physical phenomenon is ultimately reducible to atoms is so trivially true within Epicurus' physics that *that* point seems scarcely worth making here; nor does that reading help make sense of his calling these particular *onkoi* "homoiomerous" nor of his noting that the audible stream can be segmented into them.[11] What *does* Epicurus mean, then?

I would suggest that he has in mind simply the succession of distinct or distinguishable stretches of uniform sounding that together make up the auditory stream. One sort of case Epicurus had in mind (cf. §53.4–7) is that of a person's speaking. There the vocal output would obviously be segmentable into the various phonic subsections of "articulated" speech, these distinct segments each being identifiable and recordable in, say, the International Phonetic Alphabet. Each distinct stretch of sounding out one of these phonetic units would, I suggest, be one of the "homoiomerous segments" that he here refers to.[12] The point about segmentability is not, of course, confined to the case of speaking. Music also offers excellent and easy examples: one might think of the perforations in a player-piano roll as a kind of visual display of the "homoiomerous stretches"— i.e., the segments of the sustained sounding of some uniform tone—whose ensemble will constitute a playing-through of the piece of music. (In a less graphic, more symbolic way, *any* musical score must represent thus the disposition, duration, and succession of the sound-stream's "homoiomerous segments," especially as the piece gets realized on some instrument that produces continuously sustained tones—like an organ or a violin.) The point about the segmentability of a sound-stream is clearly fully general in application. Think, for instance, of the way that

31

sound effects on a radio program might convey this sequence of events: a car drives up, it stops, the door opens, someone gets out and walks along a sidewalk, up some wooden steps, and then rings a doorbell. The ten seconds that such a sequence might take up would fall into several obvious distinct parts: within each part, the requisite sound effect would have to be produced by some one distinctive means or other, and the sound thus produced would have its own distinctive character, the same throughout that part.[13]

In any event, the "homoiomerous segments" that an auditory stream may be divided into would be not *atoms* but rather patterned sequences or clusters of atoms, each producing some (more or less) uniform noise for some period of time. We need not settle upon any very exact candidates for these homoiomerous clusters now, but we do need to have some idea of what Epicurus meant by them, because it is *between* these "segments" that, in the case of hearing, two very interesting relations are next said to hold: (A) though these segments clearly must be different in sound from one another (since each one is one of the internally homogeneous segments into which some longer stretch of sounding can be broken down), these segments "maintain a certain *sympatheia* toward one another" (§52.6–8), and (B) maintain a "distinctive unity extending out to the object that emitted them" (§52.8–9).

A. What Epicurus here has in mind by *sympatheia* might, I think, best be illustrated by way of some examples of some opposite cases. Think of a bad job of tape-splicing —one where, although the same voice is heard speaking throughout, the voice levels, background noises, and ambient resonances all vary rather abruptly here and there, so that the "falsified" or "patched-up" character of the product is very evident to the ear. Here, one might say, there is segmentability of the auditory stream, but no *sympatheia* bonding and interrelating its parts: lacking is the complex of features that cooperate somehow to convey or sustain the confident sense that some single, genuinely continuous process of sound-producing (speaking or whatever) is being heard going on (or: *was* thus going on at the time the recording was made). The *sympatheia pros allelous* of the many *varying* parts of the sound is that coherence, continuity, or subtle affinity among them all that attests to their production in some continuous single session of sound-emission. It would no doubt not be easy to say very specifically what this feature *is* in any given case, yet it seems to be a genuine and an important feature of hearing. To put it negatively once more: it is that whose absence from a stretch of sounding makes it evident that we are not hearing one single continuous case of sound-production by some single thing, but rather some sort of falsification or fabrication bringing several distinct sound productions together.[14]

B. Scarcely separable from this feature is the second one that Epicurus mentions: "the distinctive unity extending out to the source" (§52.8–9). What he has in mind, I think, is simply the familiar role of features of timbre in identifying any sound. When we hear someone speak, then despite the fact that we hear many distinct sounds articulated (and even if we do not understand the language being spoken), it may be recognizably, even obviously, the same voice speaking throughout. In hearing music, it is clearly the same instrument playing throughout, despite the fact that it plays many different tones and may not even repeat a single one of them. (If I hear a chromatic scale played, only once, on a piano, then I do not hear any one tone more than once, and yet hear a-scale-played-*on-a-piano*.) This sort of timbre-"unity" pervades the entire stretch of sound-production, and, *if* we happen to have the requisite information, it may enable us to identify the object or person making the sound just by means of this "distinctive unity." But these two points need to be kept distinct.

1. On the one hand, we can simply *hear* that the sound being made throughout some stretch is being made

33

by the same instrument; that the voice that is speaking is the same voice throughout. This much we can simply hear,[15] even if we do not know *what* it is that makes that noise, or *who* it is that is speaking. Thus a person might discern or (on a later occasion) recognize the characteristic sound of an oboe, a bassoon, or a French horn—without knowing what the instrument in question is called, or even what it looks like; just as one may hear that some one person is speaking, and even recognize his voice (as one you have heard before), but not know whose voice it is. This sort of "distinctive unity" is genuinely a feature *of* the auditory display—i.e., is a genuinely intrinsic, aesthetic, or "phenomenological" attribute: we *hear* it, and do not need to bring special information to bear in order *to* hear it.

2. On the other hand, to be sure, some modicum of extra information may enable us to identify the source of such "heard distinctiveness." Once we have such information, we may even tend to think of the distinctive unity of sound as "belonging *to*" its source: as something *so* connected with the object that we can regard it as that object's "own": "That is Nixon's voice," or (generically, rather than individually), "That is the sound of an oboe."[16] What Epicurus is saying, however, does not at all require that we should thus be able to *identify* the source of the sound we near: merely that we hear it as a sound being made by some one something. It is in this sense that the presence of (A) the *sympatheia* between segments of the sound, and (B) of this "distinctive unity" throughout the sound, enables us to *hear* the sound as "extending to the source of the sound": i.e., to hear it as the sound *of* some one thing's sounding in its characteristic way—and this whether or not we happen to be able to identify the sounding thing.

C. Having said all this about the structure and interrelatedness of the auditory stream, Epicurus then goes on to say that this "distinctive unity extending to the source of the sound" also produces—much of the time, at any rate— something that he calls *ten epaisthesin ten ep' ekeinou* (§52.9). This obscure phrase has been the target of a good many learned guesses. In the light of what we have said before, two main possibilities suggest themselves as readings of this phrase—but only one of those, I think, will really work.

1. *Epaisthesis* may here mean—in much the way that we discussed a little while ago (B.2)—the recognition or identification of the source of the sound. Epicurus' point could be that the very distinctiveness of the "distinctive unities" we hear often enables us to go on and identify their source, no doubt by associating with it some one of the conceptions that we have, already, ready-to-hand (i.e., our *prolepseis*): "I know that voice; that is so-and-so."[17] The contrasting case that Epicurus goes on to describe in §52.10– 53.1 would then be our earlier example of knowing merely that there is *something* (or someone) out there making that noise (cf. *to eksothen monon*), but not knowing what (or who) it was. However, though this may be a possible reading, three considerations seem to me to weigh against it: *a*) it would not, on this account, be strictly true that such identification is "produced" *by* the "distinctive unity" we hear;[18] *b*) it is not at all clear, on this account, why the intensive appositive specifying phrase *ten epaisthesin TEN EP' EKEINOU* should have been added, or what it conveys; and *c*) it is not clear why, on this account, the ensuing explanatory (*gar*) clause in §53.1–2 should have seemed necessary or even useful in explaining the entire *epaisthesis* business. If some other reading can take care of these unclarities, it would seem a preferable view.

2. My second (and preferred) suggestion is that *epaisthesis* here means, quite specifically, a spatially oriented directional auditory awareness, one pointed right at or toward the location—the *heard* location—of the sounding object.[19] On this reading, the contrasted case that Epicurus describes in §52.10–53.1 would be one where, in the dark of night, say, we hear intermittently some indistinct sort of sound—e.g., the rustling of something moving through the bushes surrounding our campsite—but we are not able to tell what it is, nor to locate just exactly where it is. All we know is that there is "something out there *somewhere*" (*to eksothen monon endelon paraskeuazousan* [§52.10]). Such occasions are (mercifully) fairly rare—just as §52.9 *hos ta polla* says they are—but they *could* happen if all we heard were snatches of some "distinctive unity of sound." Such isolated snatches just do not suffice for localization, since, as Epicurus himself goes on to say (and very aptly, on this reading), "we cannot achieve that [localization] without some sustained coherence (*sympatheia*) in the signal emanating from the object" (§52.1–2). Under normal circumstances, such a sustained signal will be present; and it was by taking its presence for granted that Epicurus could earlier say (in §52.9–10) that the "distinctive unity of sound extending out toward the object" would, in most cases, be sufficient to produce a clear sense of the object's location: i.e., an auditory awareness directed at the place of the sound-producing source. But our auditory awareness might also sometimes be more vaguely focussed "somewhere out there"—in which case we would not have any *clear* sense of hearing something making its characteristic noise.

Epicurus' use of the term *epaisthesis* is not sufficiently clear to settle this issue (not in the surviving material, at any rate), I shall discuss some of the evidence and the alternatives briefly in the next section, but for the present I shall anticipate my conclusion

there and opt for the second reading (C.2 above) that I have offered here. Given this choice, the four essential constituents
of any clear case of hearing will be these:
1. the occurrence (stimulated by the emissions from some
    external sound-producing source) of some auditory im-
    pression or stimulation in us (the *akoustikon pathos* of
    §52.6 and §53.7);
2. a *sympatheia* obtaining among the sundry segments of
    the auditory stream that is produced by that source (this
    sympatheia manifesting, or attesting to, the continuity of
    their generation from that single source);
3. a "distinctive unity" within that auditory stream, "ex-
    tending out toward that source" (this unity manifesting,
    or attesting to, the singleness of the source and perhaps
    enabling us to identify it); and
4. our directional awareness, pointed out from ourselves into
    space at the specific location out there *of* that source.
When all four of these are satisfied, something out there is making a noise, and our auditory awareness is focused toward it,
through those very noises that it is making—focused upon it as
the maker *of* those noises we are hearing. It is this constellation
of components that explains what happens when we simply
"hear" (§52.5, *to akouein*).

IV.   ABOUT THE TERM "EPAISTHESIS"

Among the many terms that Epicurus coined in developing
his philosophical views, an important number were constructed
with the prefix *epi-*. Their interpretation remains highly controversial.[20] For the term *epaisthesis*, which most concerns us
now, three main interpretations vie with one another, each one
turning on a different nuance in the prefixed *epi-*. I shall review
these alternatives under the headings of (A) the additive, (B)
the directional, and (C) the intensive reading.

A.   *Additive*. This reading takes *epaisthesis* as a supplemen-
     tation to "mere" *aisthesis*, one produced through the
     introduction of some factor (a learned or conceptual one)

37

over and above (*epi*) the basic *aisthesis*. Cyril Bailey and A. A. Long have both espoused this view of the term. Bailey gives it a rather special twist in suggesting that *epaisthesis* is relevant specifically to the case of listening with understanding to spoken human language. He cites "the special case of speech, in which there is added to the sensation (*aisthesis*) a perception (*epaisthesis*) of significant words";[21] and elsewhere he holds that Epicurus "distinguishes between mere noises and the articulate words of a speaker, which involve perception (*epaisthesis*) and a subsequent mental understanding of the meaning."[22] This view of the term would as readily apply, however, to recognizing a birdcall or hearing the doorbell ring; it belongs to a fully general view of perception as the psychic sum of sensation and interpretation.

B. *Directional.* In their recent (and highly controversial) book, the Bollacks have suggested yet another reading for our term as perception spatially oriented toward its external object: "L'afflux des corpuscles d'air qui, en un faisceau, convergent vers l'objet, suscite la perception orientée (*ten epaisthesin ten ep' ekeinou*)."[23] They explain their view of the force of the prefixed *epi-* in these terms: "Le préfixe *ep-* souligne ce que, dans le cas de l'ouïe, la sensation a d'appréhensif. . . . Cet aspect est encore mis en lumière par la reprise de la préposition dans *ep' ekeinou*. La perception remonte jusqu'à l'objet."[24] This interpretation has some marked affinities with the view that I myself adopt here, but the Bollacks' way of grounding the view seems unacceptable because the directional or orientational use of *epi* calls for an object in the accusative or possibly dative case and not in the genitive, as here.[25] Alluring as their reading is, it seems that there is no "reprise" of the preposition in the *ep' ekeinou* phrase of §52.9, a phrase that must have its common sense of "in this (particular sort of) instance."[26]

C. *Intensive.* Arrighetti has argued that the prefixed *epi-* implies no non-perceptual or inferential addition to immediate data, but rather an intensification within the field of the immediate itself, a heightened attentiveness to the very content presented in perceptual awareness. Although the counterarguments by De Lacy, and now by Sedley, concerning *epiLOGISMOS* are powerful indeed, Arrighetti's view still carries conviction as regards *epaisthesis* and seems to me much the most defensible and promising reading. We might most effectively consider this sort of *epaisthesis* as a rudimentary Gestalt configuration of perceptual "data." This falls very far short of a conceptual "interpretation" or elaboration of such data. It amounts to an apprehension of their immanent organization, a structuring of the perceptual given as the sense of some presented perceptual object. The point is not that one knows or can identify what one is perceiving (as in the "additive" reading above) but simply that one has a "good Gestalt." Ambiguous figure-ground examples offer a useful case in point. We can describe one well-known instance of these figures alternatively as a white vase on a black ground, or as two black faces confronting one another across a white ground. The specification of the shapes in question as those of "vase" or of "faces" must of course involve conceptualization (the application of *prolepseis*, in Epicurus' terms); but the two fundamental organizations of the perceptual field do not depend on that: whether or not we know *what* to call what it is we perceive in the two cases, we may still see the configuration in two distinct ways—either as one object on a ground partly masked by that object and extending laterally to both its sides, or as two objects with an intervening ground. Each way of seeing the picture, I would suggest, is an *epaisthema*: a configuration of the perceptual field itself as the sense of some object (or objects) being presented to us. Thus, even though I follow Arrighetti in an "intensive" reading of the etymological force of the compound term, *epaisthesis*, the Gestalt-configuration sense that I associate with it rather closely resembles the "directional" reading

39

that the Bollacks advocate. As indicated in section III above, I take Epicurus' use of the term at §52.9 to refer to auditory localization—a "Gestalt-configuration" of the auditory field in terms of a directedness of hearing upon the heard location of an object being heard: the auditory "sense of an object." I do not pretend that I can demonstrate this reading. My present aim has mainly been to delineate the main alternatives. Resolving the issue with finality may well be precluded by a simple lack of evidence,[27] but the present reading, building both upon the detailed content of Epicurus' exposition in the *Letter* and on the etymology of the term he coined, seems to me much the most plausible alternative.

V. EPICURUS ON SEEING (PART II)

With all that was earlier said about the case of hearing, it can, I think, begin to be clear that the tactics of Epicurus' account of hearing very closely match those of his account of vision and may help to shed some important light back upon that earlier account.[28] I shall be quick about coming to these similarities, having so long lingered with the case of hearing.

A.   Though he does not mention *phantasia* in his account of hearing, the *epaisthesis* mentioned in §52.9–53.2 plays a fully analogous role: each is, within its own modality, "the sense of an object"—an orientation of perceptual awareness toward or upon the relevant object of perception for that modality (the object-as-seen, or the object-as-heard).

B.   Just as the continuity (the "authenticity," we might even say) of sound's emanation from its source is attested by the *sympatheia pros allelous* (§52.7–8) of the various segments of that sound, different though they are from one another, so the continuity (and "authenticity") of the visual stream is attested by the way that various films within it (and especially, of course, the closely successive ones) "maintain their *sympatheia* from the underlying object" (§50.2–3)—i.e. maintain that *sympatheia with one another* (cf. the §52.7–8 phrase) which derives from their common mode of generation from a common source (50.3–4, *kata ton ekeithen symmetron epereismon* etc.), and do this even though they may also differ widely from one another (e.g., as the object changes or moves). That objective *sympatheia* among the inflowing films is thereby the ground for vision's *phantasia* being "of" one *continuous* object.[29]

C. Nothing in Epicurus' account of vision seems exactly to match his remarkable mention (in the hearing account) of a "distinctive unity extending toward the source" (§52.8–9; again, as in the previous case of *sympatheia,* notice that the phrase describes a character of the *objective relations* between the "homoiomerous segments" of the auditory stream that emanates from the source). However, I think we can readily see its correlate in the repeatedly emphasized idea that all of the idols come from the same source and that each of them has the same shape and color as its source.[30] That doctrine—coupled with that of a *sympatheia* between idols that is sustained even as the object changes in various ways—serves as the objective ground for vision's being a viewing of the *one* thing that it is a viewing of (*tou henos phantasia,* §50.1): i.e., for the fact that visual awareness, just like auditory awareness, is the apprehension *of an object,* and "extends out to its source" (§52.8–9: *diateinousan pros to aposteilan*).

D. Although no mention is made in the account of vision of any immanent alteration in the sense organ to correspond to the *akoustikon pathos* of §52.6, it is surely easy enough to supply one (in the form of whatever immanent stimulation of, or impression on, the eyes or retina or whatever must correspond to the impinging sound waves' stimulation of the ears or auditory canals or whatever).[31]

With the enumeration of these affinities[32] between Epicurus' accounts of vision and of hearing, I have taken my exegesis of the text as far as I would want to on the present occasion.

At the risk of some redundancy, it may perhaps be useful to suggest an analogy that departs from Epicurus' account (but is, I would submit, firmly based on our comparison between his two analyses), an analogy that may help to bring out the structure of Epicurus' analysis of vision and also help to make some of the philosophical points that I want to stress more clear. Let us compare the case of analyzing visual awareness (along Epicurean lines) to that of analyzing the production of a picture on a television screen.

1. To Epicurus' *eidolon* there would correspond each separate "scanning" of the surface of the tube by the electron beam gun at its base. Alternatively, we might think of each *eidolon* as the coded content of any one such "scanning," transmitted from the television camera in the studio to the receiver. Note that this "content" exists, while in transmission, in nonpictorial form (and can be exhibited thus, as it is, e.g., on the video analyzer or wave-form monitor screen on any television control console), and that it must be converted in the receiver so as to generate a "picture." But it is not itself to be thought of as a picture; even if we think of the *eidolon* as "any one complete scanning of the surface of the tube," the individual *eidolon* is not properly a "picture," but just a physical event, a conveying of information from the object to the eye; it is something that *happens* (and happens very fast indeed, in one sixtieth of a second) along all the 525 scan-lines on the television picture tube. No one such individual "exciting" of the surface of the tube is itself a "picture."

2. When a *series* of such scannings strike successively across the surface of the television tube, each one's instantaneous excitations of the phosphors on that surface will blend visually with the next to produce an impression of

42

the continuous presence of illumination (perhaps patterned, perhaps not: that depends on the form of the input). This excitation of the surface of the tube, thought of just *as such*—i.e., as the purely immanent physical disturbance or alteration of the phosphors lying right there *on* the surface of the tube—corresponds to the "visual stimulation" or *horatikon pathos* (that which I posited, in section D above, in this section, to correspond to the *akoustikon pathos* of Epicurus §52.6). But again, this excitation is not *per se* a "picture."

3.   When the content of a series of such scannings is related, one to another, with the sort of consistency or *sympatheia* that we have tried to characterize above, *then*—and just by virtue *of* the fact that those objective relations hold—we will get the generation of a picture: the presentation of some scene. Then, when we look at the surface of the tube, we will be seeing—not just the surface of the tube, and not just "a picture" either—but rather "what is going on" (sc., what is going on with whatever object the camera is scanning at that time—or *was* scanning, when this content was recorded for presentation at this time).

I believe these points hold fairly enough for my electronic analogue, and also hold for Epicurus' analysis of vision. Were we to convert the example to the "scanning" of retinal images— the retina's transducing photic energy into photo-chemical events, and the transfer of that excitation in the form of neural signals to the optical projection areas of the brain—we might perhaps bring the example even closer to home!

VI.   IMPLICATIONS OF THE PRESENT READING

The gist of my argument is that, for Epicurus, the object of perceptual awareness is the physical object itself. The *eidola* are not at all the objects (not even "proper" or "immediate" objects) of perception, but just the physical means by which information about the object is conveyed to the senses and by which perception is sustained. (Neither, of course, is the appearance *of* the physical thing such a "proper object" of perception: Epicurus' "*phantasia* of a single and continuous object" [§50.1] *is* itself perceptual awareness of an object, and is not the immanent object *of* such awareness.) Two late Epicurean texts offer strikingly clear expressions of this realist thesis that it has been my main concern to establish, and it may be useful to cite these before continuing. The first is from Lucretius:

> You must by no means think the fact peculiar that, even though the idols which impinge on the eye cannot themselves be seen individually, nonetheless the external objects themselves are perceived (*res ipsae perspiciantur*).[33]

The second occurs in a very recently discovered (1970) fragment from the massive inscription erected by Diogenes of Oenoanda:

> The images that flow away from objects impinge upon our eyes and are the cause of our seeing the external realities (*ta hypokeimena*). . . .[34]

Both texts affirm particularly clearly the "realist" strain in Epicurean theory of perception that I have sought to disclose in the master's own *Letter to Herodotus*. Returning now to Epicurus himself, some further aspects and implications of this reading need to be examined.

A. *The Relation to Aristotle's Theory.* As analyzed here, Epicurus' theory shows a close but complex relation to Aristotle's views. For Aristotle, seeing results from an actualization (by the special or "proper" object of vision, i.e., color) of the medium between the object and the eyes, an actualization thus transmitted to the eye where (assuming the animal is awake and percipient) "the form of the object is received without its matter." In Epicurus, the steady succession of form-preserving, form-communicating *eidola* replaces Aristotle's con-

tinuum of actualization across the intervening medium.
The stream of idols thus serves (in part) as a functional
equivalent of Aristotle's mechanism of "actualization of
the transparent." (Rather *unlike* the Aristotelian notion,
it may be added, the idol-stream—for all that theory's
serious limitations—does give some concrete physical
sense, a specific and comprehensible model, for a process that, on Aristotle's account, intractably resists
explication via *any* specific physical process.) For Epicurus, as for Aristotle, external objects are not the unseen causes of our perceivings, nor are they the unperceived targets of proleptic inferences from, through, or
beyond our "immediate" data, nor are they proleptic interpretations *of* such data.[35] On both theories, perception is *au fond* the awareness of an external physical
object, and an awareness produced in percipient beings
precisely by the perceptible features of that object.
Yet, despite that much similarity with Aristotle, Epicurus' treatment of the object-directed character of seeing (or of hearing) is distinctively his own. For even
though Aristotle does assume that perception is the apprehension of a present external object, the "special
sensible" for vision is just the *color* of that object (that
is what "actualizes the transparent") and it remains
rather unclear, in his view, how the relevant common
sensibles get to be associated with or perceived with
that color so as to produce the integrated, object-oriented
character of seeing. Epicurus' theory provides an account for precisely that point: the properly *visual* information conveyed by the *eidola*-stream includes not only
color but shape, texture, form ("slant of surface") and
object-unity or object-character: items categorized by
Aristotle as "common sensibles" rather than as proper
sensibles of sight are all of them presented to the eye as
information given in the optical array—i.e., as represented
in *eidolon*-configurations or in the relations of *sympatheia* that obtain among various *eidola* or both. (The
items classified by Aristotle as "incidental sensibles"—

e.g., Corsicus' being who the seen object is—would be handled by Epicurus, in a way analogous to Aristotle's, as proleptic interpretations of our primary perceptions.)

What is more, Epicurus' account even more substantially differs from Aristotle's in holding that objects are not "really" colored:[36] although color, as a secondary quality of things, is grounded securely enough in their objective atomic structure (*contra* Democritus), we do not see things "as they are" (*contra* Aristotle) but only as they necessarily appear to us in virtue of our sensory apparatus. That is the reason that Epicurus' account takes its fundamentally anti-Aristotelian turn in employing the term *phantasia* within the analysis of perception. For Aristotle, *phantasia* was a faculty entirely *distinct* from perception (*de Anima* III.3). That position of Aristotle's had been an integral part of his opposition to Plato, for whom *phantasia* had been nothing less than the master-concept for our entire perceptual relation with the physical world.[37] That view had of course marched hand in hand with Plato's metaphysical derogation of phenomenal reality as the imaging in space of separate Forms, but Aristotle totally rejected that metaphysical assessment. He sought accordingly to displace *phantasia* from its position of Platonic preeminence, taking *aisthesis* instead as the normal and fundamental form of our relation to nature, and segregating *phantasia* from *aisthesis* in such a way as to establish a version of direct realism. Epicurus' atomism led him to reject any such direct realism and so to reinstate *phantasia* within his analysis of perception.[38] Nonetheless, his account does share with Aristotle's view (if the present account is correct) a focal commitment to an anti-representationalist realism for which the proper object of perceptual awareness is the external physical object itself.[39] His theory thus steers between (and borrows from both) the Aristotelian and Platonic views—a self-conscious strategy, I believe, and one whose further implications we must next examine.

B. *Epicurus' "Empiricism."* Our present interpretation helps show how Epicurus could evade some systematic difficulties forced upon him by the usual view. On that representationalist reading, Epicurus' empiricist claims must all seem a kind of whistling in the dark, his attempt to depart from Democritus' agnostic strain an empty manifesto. Despite himself, he can at best hold (on that reading) that we have our subjective sense impressions as our basic data, and he would thus be a kind of Cyrenaic in a self-deluding disguise.[40] One might alternatively emphasize, instead of the subjective status of the basic data, the fact that all object-perception must (on this reading) be effected by proleptic interpretations *of* these data—a view which thus forces Epicurus into the mentalistic or intellectualistic camp of Plato or of Strato of Lampsacus, a view perhaps best expressed in the famous verse of Epicharmus that "Mind (*nous*) does the seeing and Mind does the hearing; the others [i.e., the senses] are deaf and blind."[41] The standard reading of Epicurus on perception in fact proves doubly disastrous for his empiricist program, steering it either into the Scylla of Cyrenaic subjectivism or the Charybdis of Strato's pan-noeticism. Either extreme proves "unfair to the senses" and would undermine the very empiricism it is supposed to underlie. Since Epicurus was quite alive to the views of the various schools with which he was in competition, it seems incredible to me that his theory should collapse thus into the very alternatives he wanted to avoid.

As I have tried to show, Epicurus' solution was to adapt certain aspects of Aristotle's epistemological direct realism within his own atomistic theory, and so to undergird his empiricist project. Perhaps the crucial test for this (or any) interpretation is the sense that it can make of Epicurus' infamous dictum that "all perceptions are true." The best sense most commentators have been able to find for that thesis is the numbingly unsatisfactory one that perception involves a "real event" in the stimulation of the organs of sense: during perception, our sense organs are in fact moved or stimulated as they are actually impinging stimuli.[42] On the present analysis, however, these interpreters have erred in taking perception (for Epicurus) as an instantaneous and purely immanent process (i.e., in terms of our earlier distinctions, by conflating it with the *pathos*) and so making it something whose "truth" must be either wholly self-contained or wholly problematic. If perception is rather the object-stimulated, object-sustained awareness *of* that external object itself, then a clearer significance at once attaches to Epicurus' dictum as a claim for this very "objectivity" of perception.

What goes wrong with the usual reading of Epicurus, I believe, is that it construes him in the mold of later forms of empiricist theory, like them in conceiving the "data" of sense in the shallow terms dictated by assumptions about the receptive capacities (very limited) of our external sense-organs. In his case, this takes the form of concentrating on the content of individual *eidola* receivable there (e.g., color patches and such). On the present reading, however, the data of perception are by no means thus limited; they also include the complex relationships of *sympatheia* that obtain between the members of an *eidola*-stream and so provide an enormously densely textured base in sense experience on which his empiricism could rely. Very much in Epicurus' spirit, I believe, are some of Maurice Mandelbaum's observations opposing an oversimplified "empiricism" by insisting upon "object character" or "reality character" as a phenomenological feature of perception.[43] Following this lead, even effects like the bent oar can be comfortably accommodated: perhaps because the underwater portion does not really have the same sort of appearance as the out-of-water portion (its contours and color features are seen to tremble *with* the water's surface, and are not simply seen through it, as if under glass), or perhaps because the *sympatheia*-relations can obtain between temporally disparate views of the oar (both before, during, and after its immersion), in either case perception does not present "a bent oar," but rather an oar in water. Looking really closely at what we do see in such cases, we should not be led to say that the oar is bent (error thus arising, in Epicurus' terms, through the added opinion [*to prosdoxazomenon*]). Very subtle and complex forms of coherence or continuity (*sympatheia*) within the *eidola*-stream may thus secure those features crucial to the "truth" of our perceptions. The dictum that all perceptions are true may indeed, in this view, be just another way of saying that perceptions *are* object-presentations stimulated and sustained by a stream of *eidola* from those objects that are presented *in* them: it is our presentations of objects (*phantasiai*) that are true, and true precisely *to* the very objects that they present, as they present them. But to appreciate the point and force of the dictum, we must keep in view the full complexity of what is perceptually presented and not misrepresent (by oversimple assumptions) *what* it is that is "true."

C. *Epicurus and J. J. Gibson.* Quite apart from Epicurus' historical relation to the various alternatives in Greek philosophical theory, it may be useful to consider his view in the light of modern controversies in the psychology of visual perception. Broadly speaking, Epicurus' view (as interpreted here) lines up with the theory of "direct visual perception" lately developed by Professor James J. Gibson, as against the "empiricist" view according to which optical stimuli receive interpretation, or spark an "unconscious inference" process, that only then issues in perception (such a modern version of the two-stage theory deriving via Helmholtz from the British Empiricists).[44] On our reading, Epicurus' *eidola* are not the objects of perceptual awareness but merely his means of conveying optical information to the observer so that perception of the object itself can occur. Epicurus insists on the complex structure of the *eidola*-stream and thus, in a manner directly analogous to Gibson's, on the availability "*in* ambient light" of information fully specifying the perceptible world. To be sure, this basic point of similarity between the Epicurean and Gibsonian strategies is accompanied by a fundamental difference between them: Epicurus never dreamed of the complex operations needed for perceivers to *extract* the information presented in the optical array; he no more dreamed of the role of eye motions or of cortical receptive fields and feature detection systems than of rods and cones or the lateral geniculate nucleus. He just assumed that one registers the given information by attentive openness *to* it—by a careful "application" (*epibole*) of the mind to the influx of somehow objectively coherent *eidola*. And yet the basic similarity remains. Epicurus' very conception of the *eidola*—for all the physical implausibilities or sheer absurdities in his theory of their propagation—resembles Gibson's emphasis on surfaces and their textures (rather than the abstract points-and-lines of "empiricist" theory) as the elements of our visual world. Though the details of Epicurus' *eidola* view may all be sheerest fantasy, yet he seems to be trying to maintain by means of it that the eye (or "the visual system") itself registers spatial form (bulge) and slant-of-surface (i.e., that it does so in the "first stage," rather than "supplying" these through "unconscious inferences" based on optically given "cues"); and in this respect his view resembles Gibson's.[45] Again, Epicurus' basic distinction between the individual *eidolon* and the continuous *phantasia* that a stream of *eidola* sustain has fundamental affinities with Gibson's stress upon the temporal succession of stimuli (as opposed to the tendency, epitomized in the Ames demonstrations, to seek all "real" optical data in a single fixation from a fixed point of view). I am not suggesting, obviously, that Epicurus was a "Gibsonian" *avant la lettre*. He did, however, adopt an approach to perception that has strong affinities with certain parts of Gibson's approach, and noting these may at least help us to see where the philosophical thrust of Epicurean realism lies.

VII. EPILOGUE

In concluding, I would like to emphasize some major themes of this analysis. Although the *mechanics* of perception all depend, for Epicurus, upon emanations from external objects and influx to the perceiver (his is, to *that* extent, at least, a thoroughly "intromissionist" theory) his analysis also includes some essential and remarkably strong accounts of perceptual awareness as directed upon, and even "reaching out toward," the external object. His theory is not quite so strictly "intromissionist" as it may seem. Perhaps some confusion on this point has resulted simply from the fact that he called the atomic films from objects *"eidola"*—"images" or "pictures." Those films do, to be sure, have a wholly intromissive direction of movement. But they are also lacking entirely in any intentional character, and though they are, so to say, the only concrete items in his account of perception, they are not really the *operative* elements in that account at all: that is, they do not contribute to it through any capacity of theirs *as "eidola"* (i.e., intentional entities, pictures). It is rather the objective relations of *sympatheia among* these idols, and of a kind of pervading unity among them "that extends out to their source," that provide the ground of the outward-directed, and, more strongly still, the *object*-directed, intentional core of perception on Epicurus' view. To be sure, all such language of outward-directedness is now purely "phenomenological," and is not reimporting any emissionist physical theories. Nonetheless, the emissionist language is quite essential to Epicurus' philosophical approach to perception.

Having said this much concerning Epicurus' epistemology, I would like to venture some few remarks about his physics, or that part of it dealing with the propagation of the *eidola*. It is certainly true that Epicurus' views in physical optics are a weirdly peculiar, almost ludicrous affair. Yet the philosophical analysis that rises upon those unlikely foundations proves, I think, to have a real conceptual power. What happened, I would suggest, is simply that Epicurus fitted his physics to his phenomenology and his epistemology. He knew that he did not want real visual rays that emanate from the eyes, and yet that he did want to keep the phenomenological or metaphorical equivalent of those. (Parallel in philosophical strategy: he knew he did not want direct realism, but he did not want subjectivistic representationalism either; he retains emissionist language at the core of his realism—though it is now a "critical realism.") In order to ground that "emissionist" language—without backsliding into any genuinely emissionist theory—he made use of several fairly subtle phenomenological features of perceptual experience. He made *peculiar* use of these, to be sure: e.g., he noticed the phenomenon of auditory localization and certain instances of what would nowadays be called perceptual constancy, and then projected these phenomenological features into his physics as the (purportedly) objective relations of *sympatheia* among the idols that were the best he had to work with in the physics that he had at hand.

Epicurus knew in his heart that somehow images of things do get conveyed from the things to our eyes. Seeing no better way by which to show how this could be, he simply posited a physical theory that—however bizarre it might seem in and of itself—would enable him to end up with the philosophical theory of vision that he wanted. One cannot help wishing that he could have had some help from Alhazen![46] Epicurus' curious and even preposterous theory of the emanation of coherent *eidola* that somehow get whittled down to an appropriately pupillary size in the course of their transit to the eye—that bizarre theory was, in its bizarre way, the functional equivalent of Alhazen's idea that, out of the infinite array of light rays streaming out from every point on an object, only the single *one* that chances to be perpendicularly incident upon the surface of the eye can penetrate into its inner sanctum and so cooperate in producing there an image that corresponds, in the end, exactly to the form of the object seen. It is very much the same "image" that Epicurus wanted to get in there somehow, too—but Epicurus simply did not know how to do so, apart from the fanciful theory he devised. What he *did* know, however, were the philosophical strategies and perspectives, and the phenomenological insights that he wanted to preserve and ground within his theory. So—he brazenly fabricated a physical theory that (once you swallowed, somehow, or could disregard its many and massive implausibilities) would carry him where he really wanted to go. For the historian of science, I suppose, that must seem the story of a rather dismal episode—one enormous step sideward, if not backward, for the history of physical optics. For the historian of philosophy, I think, it stands in a somewhat different light. Epicurus well knew what he *did not* want philosophically: he did not want the idealist metaphysical reductionism of Plato, *or* the phenomenalist subjectivism of the Cyrenaics, *or* skepticism, *or* the direct realism of Aristotle. What he wanted was to skirt *all* of those alternatives, and he knew in his bones that one can. What he wanted, simply, was to be a critical realist. In modern times, philosophers have traveled that road with the help of, or even under pressure from, the various physical and psychological sciences. Epicurus could not look to any such established scientific theories to help him along. Instead, he made one up. If some rather arbitrary physical theories were the *only* price he had to pay for securing the philosophical approach to perception that he knew in his heart was right, he can hardly have hesitated for a minute in constructing that theory. Plato had done much the same thing in the *Timaeus*, after all. To the historian of philosophy, the story is not only familiar—it is almost endearing![47]

1. References to the *Letter* will be made by citing section and line number of the text as given in Graziano Arrighetti's *Epicuro, Opere* (Turin: Einaudi, 1960), pp. 43–49. (A second, revised edition of this work was published in 1973 but was unavailable to me at this writing.) Epicurus' fragments will also be cited from this edition, using Arrighetti's numbering for the passage and also giving the page of his book; for example, "Arr. 27.23, 6–13 (p. 262)" will mean lines 6–13 of fragment 23 in section 27, a passage found on p. 262.

2. See especially section VI.A below. The term *phantasia* is fairly common in Hellenistic epistemology, but, as I shall argue below, Epicurus' use of it here has a specifically anti-Aristotelian force. His use of the term must also be assessed within the complex detail of these sections of the *Letter*, and should not be assumed without

question to have the same force it might have in other writers (e.g., the Preface to Theon's Recension of Euclid's *Optics, Euclidis Opera Omnia*, ed. J. L. Heiberg [Leipzig: Teubner, 1883–1916], 7:153.15 and 25).

3. Interpreters often enough endow Epicurus with some alleged technical meaning for this term. Thus Bailey asserted that it "means the corresponding affections in the images to the atomic positions and movements in the original, to which are due the qualities of colour, &c., and any incidents of change" (*Epicurus: The Extant Remains* [Oxford: Clarendon, 1926], p. 194). And Bignone renders it as "la costante continuità delle proprietà sensibili degli oggetti esterni sino a noi" (*Epicuro, Opere* [Bari: G. Laterza, 1930], pp. 83 and 84). But these quite lack foundation. In fact, as Arrighetti countered (p. 456), "La *sympatheia* è una proprietà degli *eidola*." We shall shortly see that the term's occurrence at §52.7–8 compels quite another reading of the term from those of Bailey and Bignone. (See also note 8 below.)

4. For the emission vs. intromission controversy in optical theory, see David Lindberg's contribution to this volume, as well as his "Alkindi's Critique of Euclid's Theory of Vision," *Isis* 62 (1971): 469–89, and his "Alhazen's Theory of Vision and Its Reception in the West," *Isis* 58 (1967): 321–41.

5. His words are *diateinousan pros to aposteilan*. The exact term for Plato's extramissionist theory would appear to be rather *APOteino* (cf. Ar., *De Sensu*, 438a25–27 and *De Mem.*, 452b9–11), but Epicurus' language here is still remarkable for a militant "intromissionist."

6. Epicurus did deal with some details of the theory in the books of his treatise "On Nature" that are summarized in the *Letter*. Most of that is lost, but enough remains from book II to show at least that much was attempted. For discussion of these fragments (marred, however, by some idiosyncratic interpretation) see A. Barigazzi, "Cinetica degli *eidola* nel *peri physeos* di Epicuro," *Parola del Passato* 13 (1958): 249–76, and the persuasive counterarguments by Arrighetti, pp. 526–35.

7. The two accounts naturally differ somewhat, since seeing and hearing are importantly different modes of perception, and Epicurus' account renders (rather acutely, as we shall see) some of the differences between them. But the two treatments also exhibit deep affinities, and these will help us to see how, in both cases, Epicurus analyzes perceptual awareness as "the sense of an object." I believe an important philosophical moral lies behind the fact that Epicurus' discussion of hearing helps bring out some crucial issues more clearly than does the case of vision. On the disparity between vision and hearing, and that disparity's relevance to philosophical strategies and arguments in the analysis of perception, see Maurice Mandelbaum's remarks in his *Philosophy, Science, and Sense Perception*, (Baltimore: Johns Hopkins, 1964), pp. 179–82 (as well as his own use of the hearing case there to press his argument for critical realism). Epicurus' two accounts do not serve to "illuminate" one another merely because *he* was (woodenly, as it were) "locked on" to the same rigid and simplistic gimmicks for solving all his problems. There are important affinities as well as disparities between the two cases, and Epicurus, as we shall see, suggests a remarkably subtle account of both of these—one embracing both the similarities and the differences.

8. This point is stressed in §46.1 and 5–6, §48.4–6 and §49.6–9. Much of my present argument rests on the claim that §50.2–3 (about *sympatheia*) is making an importantly different point. When Epicurus speaks of the fidelity of *eidola* to the object, he speaks of their having constituents the same as the object (Arr. 23.33, 2–4 [p. 197] and 27.26, 6–9 [p. 268]), or of their bearing a certain relation toward (*pros*) the object (cf. Arr. 23.48, 10–12 [p. 211] and esp. 127.13–15 [p. 443]). In distinction from all these remarks, his terminology at §50.2 of the *Letter* is that the *eidola* "preserve a certain *sympatheia* from the object (*apo tou hypokeimenou*)." As I shall argue shortly, the reason for this difference of terminology (matched only in the problematic lines §48.10–11) is that this *sympatheia* is not of the *eidola* toward the object, but toward each other (as at §52.7–8).

54

9. In Epicurus' text, point (D) in fact precedes the clause I have given here as item (C). I understand item (C) as a kind of appositive clause or restating of the present point (D) and therefore list it as I do, but I believe that nothing appreciable turns on this expository device: items (A) and (B) are presupposed for *both* (C) and (D), if one prefers, but the present ordering will better serve to bring out the analogy with hearing (where the counterparts of [C] and [D] are not so closely interconnected).

10. My reasons for not identifying that *pathos* with the actual hearing (*to akouein* in §52.4) will emerge more clearly as we proceed.

11. Note that, properly speaking, an audible stretch of sound does not, as such, "segment" into atoms at all—no more than does the stream involved in vision. The smallest proper parts or segments of the visible stream are individual *eidola*, not the atoms that compose them. Several commentators note that the *primordia vocum* of Lucretius IV.531 are not properly *atoms* (cf. Bailey *ad* 530-32, Robin *ad* 524); I agree, but my present suggestion about Epicurus differs from Lucretius' point, and from theirs (see next note).

12. This suggestion finds little if any support in Lucretius' account of sound and hearing in book IV, and since he knew the portions of Epicurus' "On Nature" now lost to us, that may well seem a strong mark against my reading. We cannot presume, however, that Lucretius has transmitted everything he found in Epicurus. We know he sometimes changed the order of what he found, and can be sure that he both added and omitted some images and some ideas (whether on his own, or influenced by other Epicurean sources). At any rate, I do not suggest that Lucretius missed or misunderstood the point I find in Epicurus' text here: merely that he omitted it. My view rather *roughly* resembles Lucretius' account of the dividing and shaping of a speech-stream (IV.549-56; cf. 551 *articulat*, 552 *figurat*, and 555 *articulatim*), but I do not restrict this segmenting to the case of speech. Many commentators link Epicurus' remark about the "Splitting up of sound" to Lucretius IV.563-67 (explaining why a crier can be heard in all directions), but that seems to me quite without foundation.

13. No doubt such "homoiomerous segments" might be more technically defined in terms of clusters of fairly constant frequency patterns, but I am anxious to keep my suggested readings as simple-minded and as phenomenologically accessible as possible. Much as in the player-piano-roll example above, one might simply *see* the "homoiomerous segments" of any sound displayed as visually similar patterns in a sound spectrograph.

14. Any readers who think this suggestion overly inventive might consider what might be meant by other views: "a current . . . is split up into particles, each like the whole, which preserve a correspondence of qualities with one another. . . . A number of separate particles each preserving exact correspondence with the others and with the original emission" (Bailey, *Lucretius, de rerum natura*, vol. III, [Oxford: Clarendon Press, 1947] p. 1243), "particules . . . qui gardent une conformité réciproque" (Robin *ad* Lucr. IV.54-69), "un certo reciproco accordo di qualità sensibili" (Bignone).

15. We can very often "simply hear it," at any rate, though there are of course exceptions: the sound of a violin played *pizzicato* is not so obviously "from the same instrument" as sounds produced by full bowing, and many people are surprised to learn that it is even possible to produce harmonics on a violin or a guitar. So, too, one can be amazed by the way an impressionist can "do" so many other people's voices. Nonetheless, in standard and simple cases there is an audible consistency of timbre to the sounds produced by some one instrument or some one person.

16. Here I am trying to bring out various features suggested by Epicurus' term *idiotropon* (§52.8)—those of uniqueness (being distinctive of some one object and no other) and thus of exclusiveness to that one object, and thus of a proprietary relation

to the object as the sound's "owner", as that "whose" sound the sound *is*. (Cf. voice-prints and our earlier example of an impressionist who does "other people's voices.")

17. This interpretation of *epaisthesis* as the "fitting" of percept to concept was advanced by Bailey (*The Greek Atomists and Epicurus*, [Oxford: Clarendon, 1928], pp. 420, 440, and 240 n.6) and has lately been defended by A. A. Long in his "Aisthesis, Prolepsis and Linguistic Theory in Epicurus," *BICL* 18 (1971): p. 130 n. 11. As Long notes, this view of the term strongly resembles the "wax tablet" model in Plato's *Theaetetus* (191C ff.).

18. Rather, the identification is "produced" by *us*, by our retrieving the appropriate prolepsis and applying it to the percept. But according to §52.8–10, it is the "distinctive unity" (*henoteta idiotropon*) that "produces" the *epaisthesis*, and thus that "wax tablet" reading does not seem appropriate.

19. The phenomenon of auditory localization plays an important role in modern treatments of hearing but, of course, is not itself any modern discovery. For sample modern accounts, see J. J. Gibson, *The Senses Considered as Perceptual Systems* (Boston: Houghton Mifflin, 1966), pp. 81 ff., or the experiments reported by D. N. Elliott and C. Trahiotis, "Cortical Lesions and Auditory Discrimination," *Psych. Bull.* 77 (1972): 211 ff. For an interesting non-scientific discussion of the topic, see R. M. P. Malpas, "The Location of Sound," in R. J. Butler, ed., *Analytical Philosophy* (Oxford: Oxford University Press, 1965), 2:131–44.

20. See Arrighetti, "Sul valore de *epilogizomai, epilogismos, epilogisis* nel sistema epicureo," *Parola del Passato* 7 (1952): 119–44 (hereafter cited as "Valore"), along with counterarguments by Phillip de Lacy, "Epicurean *epilogismos*," *American Journal of Philology* 79 (1958): 179–83, and now by David Sedley, "Epicurus, On Nature, Book XXVIII," *Cronache Ercolanesi* 3 (1973): 5–83 (see especially pp. 27–34).

21. *Lucretius, de Rerum Natura*, III.1247. See similar remarks in his *Greek Atomists and Epicurus*, p. 420.

22. *Lucr.* III.1243. Taken strictly, these words of Bailey suggest that *epaisthesis* does not include the "subsequent mental understanding" of the words one hears. If so, he may have had in mind a sort of preliminary phonological organization perhaps akin to the kind of Gestalt configuration that I argue for below; however, such an interpretation is difficult to reconcile with his express remarks in *Greek Atomists*, pp. 418–21.

23. Jean Bollack, Mayotte Bollack, and Heinz Wismann, *La Lettre d'Epicure* (Paris: Editions de Minuit, 1971), p. 201.

24. Ibid., p. 202. (For the parenthetical remark omitted here, see note 25).

25. (a) When signifying actual physical motion in some direction, *epi* clearly needs the accusative (cf. §62.2,4, 23.37, 9–10 [p. 200], etc.). So does the metaphorical "motion" of referring (§36.1–2, §38.3, §63.1, §72.3). In the words omitted from my quotation from the Bollacks' page 202, they claim "la même valeur" for *epi-* in *epibole*. But when that term is elsewhere "reprised," it takes the accusative (§36.3). (b) For the more elusive cases of lasting intentional orientation, cf. Plato's use of *epi* with the dative. The clearest cases are at *Rep.* 477–80, where *episteme* is taken—as in the Bollacks' etymology for *epaisthesis*—as "standing over against its object." (Cf. Ernst Hoffman's reminder about Plato's forms: "Der 'Gegenstand' des Denkens 'steht' bei Platon tatsächlich dem menschlichen Denken 'gegen-über' (entsprechend der antiken Etymologie von *epistasthai*) . . . " ("Anhang" to E. Zeller, *Philos. der Griechen* [Leipzig: O. R. Reisland, 1922], II.1, p. 1089). See also H. Cherniss' discussion "*Timaeus* 52C2–5" in *Mélanges de philosophie grecque, offerts à Mgr. Diès*·(Paris: J. Vrin, 1956), pp. 49–60. But I have noted no clear Epicurean cases of this use.

26. Although the *ten* . . . *ten* . . . construction at §52.9 does make the notion of a "reprise" attractive, the genitive seriously undermines it.

27. *Epaisthesis* and *epaisthema* occur in some fragments of "On Nature" (which

book is uncertain) in ethical contexts where any contrast with "mere *aisthesis*" seems irrelevant—though, to be sure, the actual force there is unclear (Arr. 31.16, 10 [p. 328] and 31.31, 13 [p. 350]). Although Arrighetti says (p. 572), that 31.16 shows the use of *epaisthesis* "in maniera assai chiara," he has also retreated there from the restoration of lines 8-9, which he advanced with some confidence in "Valora," pp. 126-27 (and there used as part of his basis for his view about *epaisthesis* [p. 127]); now he suggests that the lacuna makes the force of several terms insoluble and makes the entire "contenuto di questa colonna . . . tutt' altro che perspicuo" (p. 572). David Sedley's recent examination of the papyrus has shown now that *neither* of Arrighetti's readings of it is tenable, though Sedley's own reading also yields no coherent sense (Sedley, *Epicurus*, p. 34). Aëtius' brief remark about Epicurus' usage of the term (*Epicurea*, ed. H. Usener [Leipzig: Teubner, 1887], fr. 249) only dimly reflects the present problems and cannot be referred to to resolve the issue.

28. As I have stressed in note 7 above, the present attempt to associate the two accounts is in no sense meant to collapse the real distinction between seeing and hearing. Though there are, if I am right, significant affinities between the two accounts, Epicurus is by no means forcing them into the same straitjacket, but retains careful respect for the differences between the two phenomena. (See also note 32.)

29. Notice here that the point is not merely the non-intermittency of visual experience (that our visual "picture" is not seen going on and off, as in a slow-changing slide projector with black spaces "seen" between the showings of the slides). That feature is explained merely by the rapid succession of the idols. What needs explanation is not merely the non-intermittency of our view of unchanging scenes but the continuity of our view of changing scenes (not just the continuous appearance-of-a-picture, but the appearance of a picture-of-continuous-process). This is the feature, I believe, that the *sympatheia* between idols (idols that do, of course, succeed one another very rapidly) is supposed to ground or explain.

30. See items (A) and (B) in section II above, and the references in note 8.

31. No mention of any *horatikon pathos* happens to occur in Epicurus' surviving texts, but his account can scarcely do without this item. It may well have appeared in one of the lost Books of "On Nature" and does appear, for instance, in Theon's statement of a view (apparently an Epicurean view) that he is attacking (cf. *Euclidis Opera Omnia*, 7:148.25 and 152.2-3).

32. As emphasized in notes 7 and 28 above, I am making no claim that the two modalities can be analyzed in exactly the same way: the fact that there is no "auditory *phantasia of* an object" as there is a visual one, is an important and irreducible difference between the two. Whereas we see the object itself, we only hear the object making its characteristic sounds; we do not, analogously, see it emitting its characteristic look—but simply see *it*. (Cf. again the discussion by Mandelbaum cited in note 7 above.) In place of an "auditory *phantasia* of the object," therefore, there is a complex of heard features of the auditory stream that "stretch back out to its source" and a directional awareness of the location of that source. Though Epicurus had no inkling of the way that differential binaural reception contributes to such localization, he did notice the phenomenon of aural localization and quite properly and neatly incorporates it in his account of hearing. Throughout his treatment of perception, I believe, he exhibits a great deal more phenomenological subtlety and sensitivity to features of perceptual experience than he has begun to get credit for.

33. *Lucr.* IV. 256-58. Bailey's note *ad loc.* seeks to replace this realist assertion with the orthodoxies of a banal representationalism, but his effort goes squarely against the text and is quite misguided, as is shown by our second text cited here.

34. New Fragment 5, col. II, lines 9-14; text from Martin Ferguson Smith, "New Fragments of Diogenes of Oenoanda," *American Journal of Archaeology* 75 (1971): p. 359 (for his translation and comments, see p. 362). This fascinating fragment seems

to have continued (though the crucial lines of col. III are unfortunately effaced) by saying that what the eye apprehends is then taken up by the *psyche*—no doubt for further proleptic processing. Smith (pp. 362–63) thinks that the two-stage process thus suggested is the same as that which Bailey surmised (in *Greek Atomists*, p. 417), but he has quite missed the crucial difference that for Bailey the object of the first stage is *not* the external object itself (*to hypokeimenon*) but an immanent representation *of* that object (see notes 17, 21, and 22 above for Bailey's views). That the Epicurean theory should allow for or involve a second, elaborative or interpretative stage is, of course, quite consistent with our present reading: it is the nature of the *first* stage that most concerns us here.

35. Aristotle's own theory has also been interpreted as a two-stage representationalism, akin to the Bailey and Long view of *epaisthesis* (cf. I. Block, "Aristotle and the Physical Object," *Philos. and Phenom. Res.* 21 [1960]: 93–101, esp. 99–100). I believe that view to be mistaken, obviously, but I cannot argue the issue here.

36. For useful discussion of the evidence on this matter, see J. M. Rist, *Epicurus: An Introduction* (Cambridge: At the University Press, 1972), pp. 61–65.

37. *Sophist* 264A–B (with all of 259E ff.) is the basic text for his express views of *phantasia*, but the same doctrines (though without the term) also permeate the *Timaeus*: see *Tim.* 28A2–3, 28C1, and 52A7, and note that Aristotle quotes the *Sophist's* definition along with these passages from the *Timaeus* when attacking Plato's view (*De An.* III.3, 428b25–26).

38. The terminology of Stoic epistemology may perhaps have had an influence as well, but the main influence seems to me to be the contest with Aristotelianism. Aristotle's sharp separation of *phantasia* from *aisthesis* is the very hallmark of his direct realism (very much as in Ryle or Austin): the banishing of all "appearance"-talk from the philosophical analysis of perception (*De An.* III.3, 428a12–15—a very Austinian point—is highly revealing in this regard).

39. Thus where Plato likes to emphasize that *aisthesis* all by itself is blind (*alogos* in *Tim.* 28A2–3, and cf. the argument at *Tht.* 181B–186E), Aristotle emphasizes that *aisthesis* is an innately "discriminative" faculty, one that apprehends external objects and, even in animals that "want discourse of reason," provides a basis for appropriately responsive behavior toward them (cf. *De An.* III.7). In Epicurus, the mechanics of the *eidolon*-stream effect a similar intrinsic object-orientation for perception as such, and do this prior to, and independently of, mentalistic (or "proleptic") adumbration.

40. As a symptom of the enfeebled anti-skepticism of the two-stage interpretation, notice Long's revealingly disowning remark in the midst of his account of Epicurus' view: "the function [of *phantasia* and *aisthesis*] is to provide the data on the basis of which we perceive, or think we perceive, train whistles . . . etc." (Long, "Aisthesis," p. 118).

41. Cf. Strato, fr. 112, in F. R. Wehrli, *Die Schule des Aristoteles*, 5 (Basel: B. Schwabe, 1950): 34, and discussion, pp. 71–75. See also the comments by H. B. Gottschalk, *Strato of Lampsacus: Some Texts* (Leeds: Leeds University Press, 1965), pp. 163–64. Epicurus surely knew Strato's views. It may be, as Usener suggests (*Epicurea*, p. 377) that §53.2–4 of the *Letter* is referring specifically to him.

42. See N. W. DeWitt, "Epicurus: All Sensations Are True," *TAPA* 74 (1943): 19–32, and Elizabeth Asmis' brief but useful remarks on problems with this doctrine in her review of J. M. Rist's *Epicurus: An Introduction* in *Philos. Rev.* 83 (1974):413–14. Ms. Asmis' own distinction there between "the act of sensing" and "the object of sensation" has some analogies with our present reading, but we have drawn that distinction here, in the relevant Epicurean idiom, between the immanent *pathos* generated in the sense organs and the *phantasia* (or *epaisthesis*) with its intentional object.

43. See Mandelbaum (note 7 above), pp. 152–54, as well as pp. 225–32 and 238, on phenomenological "steadiness" as a visible feature. Epicurus' obscure remark at §48.9–11 (where a textual corruption has often been suspected) might be read almost straightforwardly along these lines, as an affirmation of this sort of "object character": to attend to what is presented clearly to us (*tas enargeias*) from objects without, precisely *is* to attend to the *sympatheiai* that enable the *eidola* from them to produce the coherent and cohering presentation of a single and continuous object. Cyril Bailey adduces some analogous ideas about the validating role of coherence among *eidola*, but in a different connection (*Greek Atomists*, pp. 240–41, n. 6, in explaining Diogenes Laertius' remark at X.32—*before* the quote from Epicurus' *Letter* starts); however, Bailey never brings these ideas into his account of Epicurus' own views on perception (except in connection with our ideas of the gods, cf. p. 440).

44. For bibliography, see the contributions by Gibson and by Machamer in the present volume. For a helpful account of the two approaches to seeing (one given in the context of an extended defense of the Gibsonian alternative), see R. N. Haber and M. Hershenson, *The Psychology of Visual Perception*, (New York: Holt, Rinehart & Winston, 1973), chapter 12. It should be noted that Gibson's views have important links with the Gestalt tradition that also influences Mandelbaum's book (referred to several times above) so that the present comparison between Gibson and Epicurus "lines up" closely with our earlier remarks. (It may also be noted that this comparison helps underline the error involved in reading Epicurus on the model of the opposite, "empiricist" view.)

45. See ibid., chapter 13. This instance is, in some ways, embarrassing for Epicurus. If the *eidola* retain the surface contour of their source, they must travel as molded three-dimensional films and must be received thus at the eye. Quite apart from the problems of their transit, that reception raises problems, since the foremost portion of any one film might "make contact" before the hindmost portion of the previous film had done so—and how could the eye differentiate them? Awkward as such questions are for Epicurus, they arise from his interesting attempt to *save* "bulge" and "slant-of-surface" as directly given features of visual experience and to resist explanation of them through conceptual (proleptic) interpretations, "inferences," or additions. To that extent, at least, his odd view has true analogies with Gibson's approach. Similar remarks might apply to the odd expedients reported by Lucretius (IV.244–55) as an Epicurean way of explaining our perception of objects' distance; crude and peculiar as the explanations are, they should be seen as pursuing the extremely interesting goal of staying faithful to the phenomenological point that apparent distance is an intrinsic feature of the optical "given" (cf. ibid., chap. 14).

46. For Alhazen's optical theory, see A. I. Sabra's contribution to this volume, as well as his article ("Ibn Al-Haytham") in the *Dictionary of Scientific Biography*, 6 (New York: Scribner's, 1972): 190–94. See also the papers by David Lindberg referred to in note 4 above.

47. I am indebted to several participants in the Ohio State University Conference for their helpful discussions and to Professor David Glidden for showing me several of his unpublished papers on issues in the theory of perception from Protagoras to Lucretius. For better or for worse, however, I alone am responsible for the views advanced in the present paper.

David E. Hahm

Chapter Three

EARLY HELLENISTIC THEORIES OF VISION
AND THE PERCEPTION OF COLOR

The complete history of the Greek science of vision or optics has not yet been written.[1] Time has dealt so harshly with the Greek treatises on the subject that we do not even have the culmination of that science, Ptolemy's *Optics*. Ptolemy's final synthesis of the science of vision is known only from a Latin translation of an Arabic translation of the original; what is worse, the crucial first book, containing Ptolemy's discussion of the principles of vision and visual perception, is totally lost. Modern scholarship has been able to reconstruct the main ideas of the first book on the basis of later references and so has taken an important step in understanding the history of Greek optics.[2] However, the developments leading up to Ptolemy are still largely unknown. The works of Plato, Aristotle, and Euclid allow us to glimpse the state of the science in the fourth century B.C., but from the fourth century B.C. to the second century A.D. virtually nothing survives. This is particularly disappointing since we know that the century after the death of Aristotle was one of the most creative periods in the history of Greek science and philosophy. In fact, we know that there was hardly a philosopher or scientist during that time who did not write one or more treatises on vision, the senses, mirrors, or some other aspect of the science of vision.[3] Yet we cannot claim to possess a single one of these creative efforts in the field in its entirety.[4] The situation is not hopeless, however. Enough references survive here and there to reconstruct at least pieces of the picture of the science of vision in the late fourth and early third centuries B.C.; hopefully, patient effort will one day compensate somewhat for the unfortunate disappearance of all the original treatises. As a contribution to this reconstruction, I would like to sketch out what appear to be the predominant theories of vision in this period and the application of these theories to one of the chief problems of perception—the perception of color.

From the Hellenistic period down through late antiquity three distinct theories of vision competed for attention—namely, those of the mathematicians, the Epicureans, and the Stoics. By the first century B.C. these three theories had eliminated all earlier competitors. A fragment of an optical treatise attributed to Geminus (first century B.C.) states that optics is not concerned with the physics of vision, but only demands that the rectilinear propagation of light or vision be preserved. Hence optics does not decide whether (1) "rays are poured out from the organs of sight and effluences travel to the surfaces of objects, or (2) images (εἴδωλα) streaming off from perceptible bodies in rectilinear motion penetrate the eyes, or (3) the intervening air [between the object and the eye] is extended together with, or carried along with (συνεκτείνεται ἢ συμφέρεται), the raylike *pneuma* of the eye."[5] Apparently, these three theories were the only options a student of optics had to consider. Moreover, no substantially different theory arose to compete with these three down to the end of antiquity. For in the second century A.D. a work that has come down to us under the name of Alexander of Aphrodisias includes refutations of essentially the same three theories: (1) "that vision occurs through rays," which are poured out and fall upon the object, (2) "that vision occurs through the stretching (συνέντασις) of the air," and (3) "that vision occurs through the impact of images" (εἴδωλα), which stream off from objects.[6] Two centuries later Calcidius summarizes the same three theories in a survey of "current opinions" on the subject ("opiniones . . . quae sunt in honore; de visu probatae sententiae veterum," *In Tim.* 236, 243) and claims that they are all ultimately derived from Plato, each incorporating but one aspect of Plato's view.[7] The fact that these three theories, which were developed in their basic form in the late fourth and early third centuries B.C., were still the only theories that had to be refuted or absorbed by the proponents of the revived Aristotelian and Platonic philosophies at the end of antiquity demonstrates the vitality and longevity of the Hellenistic theories of vision and earns for them a secure place in the history of optics.

Difficulties arise, however, when we try to reconstruct these theories in detail and to identify the problems to which the proponents of these theories addressed themselves. The theory that vision occurs by the movement of some kind of image or film (εἴδωλον) from the object directly to the observer's eye is clearly the theory of Epicurus. And even though Epicurus' more specialized works on physics and vision are lost,[8] his *Letter to Herodotus* and the surviving fragments of his *Physics* make his basic theory amply clear. Every object consists of a multitude of tiny particles called atoms. From the surface of these objects the outer layer of atoms is continually flowing off. Each of these layers or films of atoms (called *eidola*)[9] maintains its shape and atomic arrangement as it races in a straight line through space. If it should happen to strike an eye (specifically, the pupil) facing in the direction of the object, the *eidolon*, or rather the series of successive *eidola*, will affect the eye in such a way that perception will occur.[10] Since this theory of vision became characteristic of the Epicureans and of no one else, there can be little doubt that throughout later antiquity descriptions and refutations of the theory of images referred to the Epicurean theory.

The theory that rays are poured out from the eye and fall upon the object is attributed by Calcidius to "the geometers, who agree with the Peripatetics" (*In Tim.* 238), and it is true that the mathematicians who wrote optical treatises, from Euclid through Ptolemy and beyond, assumed that rays (ἀκτῖνες, ὄψεις) are emitted from the eye to the object. The earliest representative of this group, Euclid, whose optical treatise is dated about 300 B.C., but who probably drew on material from a somewhat earlier date,[11] clearly presupposed the theory in his third definition, although he does not elaborate on the physics behind it: "Those things are seen upon which the visual rays fall; the things upon which the visual rays do not fall are not seen."[12] These rays were assumed to extend from the eye in straight lines in the shape of an ever widening cone (Defs. 1–2).

In addition to the mathematicians, who were the primary proponents of this theory, Calcidius mentions that the Peripatetics share this view (*In Tim.* 238). At first glance this may seem to be an error, since Aristotle explicitly rejected the theory that something is sent out of the eye in vision (*De Sensu* 2.438a16–b16).[13] But a closer look at Aristotle suggests that in some texts he himself did hold a theory like that of the mathematicians. In *On the Heavens* he attributes the apparent twinkling of the stars to a jiggling of the sight as it extends too far into the distance. The planets do not twinkle, he maintains, because they are closer and the sight reaches them with full strength (*Cael.* 2.8.290a 17–24). Furthermore, the third book of the *Meteorology* presupposes and even explicitly states that the sight reaches out from the eyes, penetrates into the sky, and in the case of certain meteorological phenomena like rainbows is reflected to the sun.[14] This book, which includes proofs for the shape of halos and rainbows, seems to be dependent on contemporary geometrical optics, a science that Aristotle elsewhere characterized as the science that provides the explanation for the rainbow (*Post. Anal.* 1.13.78b32–79a13). From this we may infer not only that mathematical optics was older than Euclid, but that it actually influenced Aristotle's thought at some time.[15]

Furthermore, even after Aristotle had rejected the theory of visual rays, it does not seem to have died out in his school. Only a few pages after rejecting the theory, he himself slips back into its phraseology by saying that a fraction of a visible grain of millet may escape notice "even though the sight comes to it" (*Sens.* 6.445b31–446a1). Moreover, when he comes to account for variations in keenness of sight in *On the Generation of Animals*, he points out that it makes no difference whether one assumes that sight issues from the eye to the object or a motion passes from the object to the eye (*Gen. An.* 5.1.781a3–13). This suggests that the issue was still very much alive in the circles for which Aristotle was writing.

The works of Aristotle's successor, Theophrastus, show a comparable ambivalence. Though Theophrastus seems to have followed Aristotle's analysis of perception, he also seems to have made use of a theory of visual rays.[16] According to Simplicius, Theophrastus maintained that flame is emitted from the eye.[17]

63

He also explained the superior nocturnal vision of certain animals by the theory that the fire in their eyes is exceptionally strong (*De Sensu* 18). Furthermore, the reason we cannot look at the sun, he believed, is that a strong fire extinguishes a weaker (*De Sensu* 18). Finally, his explanation of dizziness depends on a theory of visual rays, and he says explicitly that people become dizzy upon heights because "their vision, stretching out far in the distance, is shaken and jiggled, and being shaken and moved in this way disturbs and moves the things within."[18] Finally, the treatises of the Peripatetic school are divided on the theory of vision. Some of the Pseudo-Aristotelian *Problems* speak of sight issuing from the eyes (e.g., *Prob.* 11.58; 15.6, 7, 12; 25.9; 31.8, 15, 16, 19, 20, 21, 25), whereas others (*Prob.* 31.7, 11) and *On Colors* speak of sight, motion, or light entering the eye. Since the theory of visual rays occurs in Aristotle, Theophrastus, and the works of the Peripatetic school, Calcidius cannot be accused of error in seeing some measure of agreement between the mathematicians and the Peripatetics.[19]

With this wealth of material based on the theory of visual rays in the fourth and third centuries B.C. we might expect to know the physics of the theory in some detail. Yet, in fact, we know less about the physical basis of the theory of visual rays in the Hellenistic period than of either of the other theories. About the elemental composition of the rays Euclid tells us nothing, not even whether a ray is continuous or corpuscular. Nor does he give us any hint how a mathematician imagines that this ray may perceive or transmit sensations. All we can conclude is that the visual rays are discrete linear entities, which diverge from each other as they advance from the eye, so that the regions of a visible object that lie between the rays are not perceived (cf. Prop. 1, 2, 3). Aristotle adds nothing to our knowledge of the physical nature of the rays, and Simplicius' remark that Theophrastus believed flame emerges from the eye hardly clarifies either the elemental nature of the visual ray or its relation to the light of the sun and of fire. Thus it may be significant that the refutation by Alexander and the summary by Calcidius do not attribute any specific characterization of the rays to the proponents of the theory. Therefore, though the importance of this theory in the early Hellenistic period is firmly attested, the physics of the theory is far from clear and, in fact, may not have been developed at this time.

Having reviewed two of the three Hellenistic theories of vision, we may turn to the third. Calcidius attributes this theory to Heraclitus and the Stoics. We need not take his brief summary of Heraclitus' view very seriously, since his statement about this traditional ancestor of Stoicism has a Stoic coloring.[20] But his summary of the Stoic view is more detailed and significant. He says, "The Stoics attribute sight to the tension [or "stretching," *intentione*] of the innate *pneuma*, whose shape they liken to a cone. When this has proceeded from the interior (*penetrali*) of the eye, which is called the pupil, and when from this fine beginning its beginning has been enriched to solidity the further it extends, then when illumination has been placed near the visible thing, sight is poured out and extended in every direction."[21] This description of the Stoic view makes their theory sound very similar to the theory of visual rays; that it is not the same is clear from the other descriptions of the same theory. The fragment attributed to Geminus describes this theory as one which attributes sight to the co-extension or the concomitant movement of the intermediate air with the ray-like visual *pneuma* (συνεκτείνεται ἤ συμφέρεται ὁ μεταξὺ ἀὴρ τῷ τῆς ὄψεως αὐγοειδεῖ πνεύματι). Alexander describes the theory as one that attributes sight to the "tension" (συνένταστς) of the air and explains that on this theory "the air touching the pupil [of the eye] is pricked by the sight and shaped into a cone; and when this [conically-shaped air] is struck at the base by the visible objects, sensation occurs, as also in touch through a rod."[22] These descriptions refer just as obviously to the Stoic theory, but they do not make the theory sound like the theory of visual rays. One big difference is that the medium, air, is directly involved in vision in some way.

To understand the Stoic theory and the discrepancy in the descriptions, we must turn to other evidence for the Stoic view.[23] Unfortunately, for the Stoic theory we do not have any original account, but must depend on later handbooks. Two of these handbooks summarize for us the theory of Chrysippus, who was the head of the Stoic school in the late third century B.C. According to Aëtius, "Chrysippus says we see by virtue of the stretching (συνέντασις) of the intervening air. This air is pricked (νυγέντος) by the visual *pneuma*, which advances (διήκει) from the principal part [of the soul] to the pupil. Upon its impact (ἐπιβολή) against the surrounding air the visual *pneuma* stretches (ἐντείνοντος) the air conically, whenever the air is homogeneous [of the same kind]. Fiery rays (ἀκτῖνες), not black misty ones, are poured forth from the sight. Hence darkness is visible."[24] According to Diogenes Laertius, "vision occurs when the light between the sight and the object is stretched (ἐντεινομένου) conically, as Chrysippus says in the second book of his *Physics* and Apollodorus too. The conical form of the air arises at the sight, with the base at the visible object. Thus the visible object is reported back through a rod, as it were, of stretched air."[25] These two accounts not only agree with each other but with the summary in Alexander, and so can offer some grounds on which to reconstruct the theory of Chrysippus.[26]

According to these accounts (Aëtius, Diogenes Laertius, and Alexander) the visual *pneuma* in the eye performs some action on the air outside. This action is called "pricking" ("stabbing," νύσσω) or "impact" (literally, "hurling against," ἐπιβολή). As a result of this action the air outside becomes stretched taut in some way in the form of a cone, provided that the air is "homogeneous." The latter condition seems to refer to the presence of daylight, which is in some manner similar to, or homogeneous with, the optic *pneuma*. If we may trust the hostile allusion in Alexander, the proponents of this same theory believed that "illuminated air because it is dilated (διακεκρίσθαι) has more strength and is able to move the sense by pressure, whereas unilluminated air, because it is slack, is unable to be stretched by the sight."[27] Thus the sun with its light apparently performs a similar action on the air (viz., stretching) to that performed by the optic *pneuma*, though this stretching is presumably to a lower degree or in some way different from the additional tensioning that occurs in vision. Once this tensioning occurs, the cone of illuminated, optically tensed air is able to transmit back to the *pneuma* in the eye any motion it encounters at its base. Drawing on an analogy, Chrysippus compares the cone to a rod that may be used (even by a blind man) to feel objects at a distance, and so suggests that the eye may use the tensed cone of air to sense visually objects at a distance.

Though the evidence for Chrysippus' view strongly suggests that the optic *pneuma* does not itself proceed to the object, but instead enlists the illuminated intervening air to transmit the sense-producing motions back to it, nevertheless this evidence does not make clear the precise relationship between the optic *pneuma* and the external air. The action of the optic *pneuma* on the air is called "stabbing" ($\nu\acute{\upsilon}\sigma\sigma\omega$). This is an old Greek word that is used not only for the action of swords and spears penetrating the flesh, but of a horse's hoof on the ground, and an elbow in the ribs.[28] Thus it may suggest either that the *pneuma* emerges from the pupil into the tip of the cone, or that the *pneuma* merely exerts a physical impact on the air outside. "Impact" ($\dot{\epsilon}\pi\iota\beta o\lambda\acute{\eta}$) suggests that the *pneuma* strikes a blow on the air outside at the point of the pupil, but the word does not clarify the precise effect of the *pneuma* on the air.[29] One conceivable model for this action of the *pneuma*, which is literally wind and was defined by Chrysippus as "moved air,"[30] might be an "inflation" of some kind; one could imagine the visual cone of air outside being "blown up" like a conical balloon. But if this notion is present, it is probably not conceived literally, for there is no suggestion that a substantial quantity of *pneuma* leaves the eye. Alternatively, we also know that Chrysippus conceived of *pneuma* as a mixture of air and fire, a special kind of warm air.[31] Thus in its elementary composition it is similar to the illuminated air outside, which our text calls "homogeneous." Perhaps we may imagine the transmission of a special state or quality to the similar air outside, a quality that, in accord with the picture of inflation, may be described as "dilation" or "stretching," but which is not accomplished by the transfer of any material substance. This would be in harmony with Chrysippus' general view of psychic states as qualitative states of the psychic *pneuma* and the movements transmitted in sensation as qualitative changes of state ($\dot{\epsilon}\tau\epsilon\rho o\iota\acute{\omega}\sigma\epsilon\iota\varsigma$) in the *pneuma*.[32]

But how, then, are we to explain the statements in the same

handbook summaries that a fiery ray or rays (αὐγή, ἀκτῖνες πύριναι) are poured forth from the sight?[32] Do these terms refer only to the transmission of a state of tension? Or does this summary really refer to a different Stoic philosopher, an earlier or later Stoic who accepted a theory similar to that of visual rays and then imagined these rays to be streams of fire? Or is it yet another aspect of Chrysippus' theory, (say) an oversimplified reflection of a theory in which the optic *pneuma* (the air-fire mixture) *per se* is not emitted, but some of the heat in it is sent out to aid and strengthen the fire already illuminating and tensing the air around us? If so, Chrysippus' theory comes close to that of Plato, who claimed that vision is a form of fire that flows out of the eye, coalesces with the fire of daylight in the air, and so forms a coherent body in a straight line from the eyes.[34] As such, Chrysippus' theory could represent an attempt to adapt Plato's theory to the Stoic physical assumptions.[35] But this, of course, must remain in the realm of speculation as long as our evidence for Chrysippus is so meager.

The evidence presented here suggests that Chrysippus near the end of the third century B.C. held a theory of vision that is compatible with the summary presented by Alexander, but not with the descriptions of the (presumably) Stoic theory in Geminus (1st century B.C.) and Calcidius (5th century A.D.). For Calcidius claims, "The Stoics attribute sight to the stretching of the innate *pneuma*, whose shape they liken to a cone," whereas Chrysippus actually seems to have said that sight is due to the stretching of the *intervening air*, when it is pricked by the *pneuma* and thereby stretched into the shape of a cone. And Geminus says, "The intervening air is coextended (συνεκτείνεται) or moved along with the ray-like visual *pneuma*," whereas Chrysippus actually claimed that the intervening air is stretched (συνεντείνεται) by the visual *pneuma*.[35] One possible explanation for these discrepancies might be that the summary of Chrysippus' view had become distorted by transmission through many generations of handbooks, and so Geminus and Calcidius were misled. Another possible explanation is that the Stoics themselves modified their theory of vision after the third century B.C., and Geminus and Calcidius were actually referring to

Stoic theories of a later time.[37] But to settle this question is beyond the scope of this paper.

So far we have surveyed only the outlines of the physical principles underlying the three clearly discernible theories of vision in the Hellenistic Age. For a deeper understanding of these theories we must examine the issues that these theories addressed. One of the oldest problems of perception among the Greeks, going back at least to the beginning of the fifth century, was the perception of color. According to Theophrastus, Empedocles believed that there are pores of fire and of water in the eye. By the pores of fire we see white, by the pores of water, black. An effluence from visible objects brings along the color, and the color is perceived in accord with whichever pores the effluence fits.[38]

Theophrastus gives us slightly more detail on the color theory of Democritus, the fifth century atomist, who like the Epicureans seems to have attributed vision to a stream of effluences from the object.[39] Theophrastus tells us that, according to Democritus, what is smooth and hard and what has straight, open passages is white, though loose friable substances are white when their particles are round and arranged close to each other. Black comes from things that are rough, irregular, and dissimilar. For these cast shadows, and the passages are not straight or easy to pass through. Also, their effluences are sluggish and confused.[40] From this we may gather that color is due to the arrangement of atoms in an object and in the effluences from the object, but the mechanism of color perception is puzzling. For he speaks of shadows on the rough surface as an explanation of a black color, yet he gives no evidence of postulating a "light" that might cast such shadows.[41] We might assume that, in groping for an analogy to explain color, he hit upon the light and shade of illuminated scenes.

The question then arises how he could explain "light" and "shade" in terms of effluences from the object without introducing an external source of light. Perhaps the answer is found in his use of pores or passages to explain color. In this Democritus makes use of a concept that Empedocles had already tried. In the theory of Democritus straight, easy passages are

69

associated with transparency and a white color; passages that are not straight or easy to pass and effluences moving with a sluggish, disordered motion are associated with the color black. From these associations we might conjecture that Democritus makes the perception of white and black analogous to transparency and opacity in substances. As a transparent object allows light to pass through easily, and an opaque object blocks the passage of light, so a white object has passages so arranged among its atoms as to allow the effluence to pass out readily to the eye, whereas a black object has its atoms arranged in such a way as to slow down and impede the exit of the effluence. Now the shadowy surface of a dark object becomes intelligible in terms of effluences. For a rough, shadowy surface is one from which effluences cannot flow with ease to the observer, and hence the observer, deprived of most or all of the vision-producing effluences, will see shade or the color black.

If the ease of passage is what differentiates white from black, Democritus' explanation of other colors becomes more intelligible. Red, he said, consists of configurations of atoms similar to those that produce heat, but larger (Theophrastus, *De Sensu* 75). Now the atoms of heat and fire Democritus regarded as spherical and therefore the most mobile of atoms.[42] And he maintained that the spherical shape is a kind of angle that cuts because of its mobility (Arist. *Cael.* 3.8.307a17–18). Moreover, another kind of angular, piercing atom, that of sour things, Democritus claims has the tendency to penetrate everywhere and gather atoms together so that voids are formed. When this happens the object is heated, "for that which has the most void becomes the hottest" (Theophrastus, *De Sensu* 62). Putting these bits of information together, we may infer that the mobile fire atoms move rapidly through the void spaces that are found in warm objects. Red objects are constituted similarly. But since their atoms or aggregations of atoms are larger, the movement of their effluences is presumably somewhat slower.[43] If white objects are such that their effluences pass on toward the eyes very quickly and easily, and red objects transmit their effluences less easily and freely, these slower effluences from red objects could be expected to produce the sensation of a color falling somewhere between white and black.[44] On this interpretation Democritus' theory of colors proves to be more coherent than it first appeared. It would also seem to be in harmony with the widespread Greek idea (which we will meet again) that the color scale consists of a series of colors varying, not in spectral hue, but in intensity from white to black.[45] Finally, Democritus now appears to be a significant predecessor of Plato in his theory of color perception.

Turning directly to Plato's theory of vision, we find that the eye sends out a stream of fire that coalesces with the daylight to form a single homogeneous body in a straight line in the direction in which the stream issues forth. This body has the capacity of experiencing and transmitting back to the observer the motions of objects that it encounters (Tim. 45b-d). Now visible objects also emit a stream of fire, and at some point the two streams meet (*Tim.* 67c). Since for Plato all elements consist of geometrically shaped particles, these two streams of fire will be two streams of particles impinging on each other. The color perceived, Plato maintains, will depend on the relative size of the two sets of particles. "Of the parts moving from the other things and falling on the sight some are smaller, some larger and some equal to the parts of the sight itself. The ones that are equal are imperceptible, which, in fact, we call transparent; the greater compress [or congeal] it [i.e., the sight], the less separate it" (*Tim.* 67d). Plato then compares the action of white and black on the vision to the action of hot and cold on the flesh and astringent and pungent on the tongue, which likewise depend on separation and combination (*Tim.* 61d-62b, 65c-66a). But then he continues "What separates the sight is white, and the opposite black," adding that if the particles from the object are very sharp, they may cleave the visual stream and travel all the way up into the eye and produce the sensation of brightness (*Tim.* 67e-68a).

What Plato seems to be saying is that the effluences from colored bodies have an effect on the stream of visual particles such that the particles are either crowded together or driven apart, and that the color perceived will depend on the alteration of the visual stream. So much seems clear, but beyond that

71

problems arise. The first is how the alteration of the arrangement of particles in the visual stream is communicated back to the eye, for Plato had explicitly stated that the motions encountered by the visual stream when it comes into contact with objects outside are transmitted back to the body and the soul (*Tim.* 45c-d). In the case of the more piercing (ὀξύτεραν) motion of "a different kind of fire," the particles divide the visual stream and open a channel all the way to the eye allowing these particles actually to enter the very texture of the eye and affect it directly. This produces the sensation of "dazzling," and the object that produces it is called "bright" or "flashing" (λαμπρόν, στίλβον, *Tim.* 67e-68a). Similarly, in the sensation of red, fire enters the eye (*Tim.* 68b). Here the motion seems to be communicated back directly by the effluences. But this happens presumably only in the case of certain strong colors and lights. In the perception of other colored objects the effluences apparently never reach the eye. This is certainly true in the case of black.

Plato does not explain how the alteration of the arrangement of visual particles outside the eye is transmitted to the eye, but we might make a guess on the basis of his contention that the visual stream, when it meets the similar illuminated air without, is "compacted with it" (συμπαγές) and becomes a "unified, homogeneous body" (ἓν σῶμα οἰκειωθέν), which seems capable of exerting pressure in the direction of the object until it meets an opposing pressure.[46] Whatever it experiences by making contact with an external object or its effluent fire, it experiences throughout the totality of its substance (ὁμοιοπαθὲς δὴ δι᾽ ὁμοιότητα πᾶν γενόμενον, *Tim.* 45c-d). Since this entire substance is "compacted" (συμπαγέν) and "grown together" (συμφυές) with the fire within us (*Tim.* 45c, 64d), the entire complex of fire in the eye and out in the visual stream will experience the same alteration simultaneously. Thus Plato may say, with justice, that the motions encountered upon impact with the fire from the object are "transmitted (διαδιδόν) to the body as a whole right up to the soul" (*Tim.* 45d).

The next question is what the nature of this movement is. Plato's words are *synkrisis* and *diakrisis*, words usually used of the mixing together and separation of aggregates.[47] How Plato imagined this affecting the currents of visual fire is not at all clear. Any attempt to reconstruct the mechanics of the process in detail for the differently sized particles leads to problems and inconsistencies, a fact that suggests that Plato never worked out the details. But it does seem clear that underlying the processes of color perception is a characteristic that we might call accessibility. If the particles of the object's effluence are large, the stream of fine particles of the visual fire will be mixed together and confounded upon impact. This is the motion of *synkrisis*. In this condition no particles of fire will ever penetrate the visual stream; their access to the sensory apparatus of the eye is thus prevented and the observer will see black (*Tim.* 67d-e). Similarly, at night, when the stream of fire from the eyes meets the dark, fireless air outside, the fire from the eyes is "cut off" (ἀποτέτμηται) and cannot make contact with any effluences from the object (*Tim.* 45d). With access between the object and the eye blocked, the observer will presumably experience the sensation of blackness, just as he does when looking at a black object. On the other hand, when in normal daytime vision the particles of the object's effluence are smaller than those of the visual stream, they will penetrate easily between the particles of the stream and will divide them, thereby producing the sensation of whiteness (*Tim.* 67d-e).

But then Plato gives the motion of separation a new twist, an elaboration that allows him to account not only for whiteness but for the remaining colors as well. He adds that the most powerful of the dividing particles, the ones with "sharper motion," will continue penetrating the stream until they enter the eyeball where two events will occur: (1) the passages of the eye will be pushed apart violently and dissolved, causing pain and releasing some of the water of the eye in the form of a tear;[48] and (2) the entering fire will then meet (presumably near its source) the visual fire tending to leave the eye, and in the encounter the exiting fire will flash out like lightning, the entering fire will be quenched, and all kinds of colors will be seen (*Tim.* 68a). This experience accounts for the color called "bright" or "flashing." There is also an intermediate variety of fire (τὸ δὲ τούτων αὖ μεταξὺ πυρὸς γένος), which likewise travels up the

73

visual stream and enters the eye. This kind of fire, however, does not penetrate so far as to encounter the fire of the eye at its source, but reaches only the moisture of the eye ($\pi\rho\grave{o}\varsigma$ $\tau\grave{o}$ $\tau\hat{\omega}\nu$ $\grave{o}\mu\mu\acute{a}\tau\omega\nu$ $\grave{v}\gamma\rho\grave{o}\nu$ $\grave{a}\phi\iota\kappa\nuο\acute{v}\mu\epsilon\nu ov$), where it is mixed with the moisture. In this case the fire from the object must be sensed through the moisture, which presumably has an inhibiting and darkening effect and yields a sensation of red.[49] Thus the specific color sensation turns out to be dependent on the degree of access that the fire from the object has to the source of the visual fire. The farther it penetrates, the brighter the color sensation produced. Colors will, therefore, range from "bright/flashing," in which the effluence penetrates deep into the eye, down to "black," in which the effluence does not enter the stream at all. Intermediate colors, like red, penetrate to an intermediate degree.

In this way Plato attempts to bring together into one theory of color vision the notion of penetrability and the notion of the relative size of particles.[50] The attempt is not completely satisfactory for we are left with two incompatible color scales. The one in which the relative size of the effluent particles determines the color produces a scale ostensibly ranging from *synkrisis* to *diakrisis*, but which, strictly speaking, can have only one intermediary—the neutral state that is transparency, not a color at all. The other scale produces the various colors presumably in proportion to the depth of penetration of the effluent particles that "separate" the stream. But on this scale not every *diakrisis* will produce white, but only *diakrisis* in the highest degree. Other degrees of *diakrisis* will produce the other colors. Thus the definition of white as "whatever divides the stream" is contradicted by the claim that red also divides the stream.

Nevertheless, in spite of its deficiencies, Plato's theory of color is extremely important for bringing to a culmination the early Greek theory of color vision, a theory based on the mechanical effect of particles from the object. In this theory the size, shape, arrangement, and motion of the material particles coming from the object, and of the particles of the eye and an emission from the eye, are used to account for the various colors we see. The primary colors, from which the others are derived by mixture, are themselves explained as quantitative variations of certain mechanical effects. The mechanical effects may be called "ease of approach," "speed," or "depth of penetration"; but the underlying assumption is that the higher degree of access there is between the object and the eye, the lighter or brighter will be its color. One might say that this theory reduces vision to a tactile sensation, and the mechanical physics of the theory as well as its vocabulary supports this judgment.[51] Yet the proponents of the theory reduce tactile sensation as well to the same mechanical interaction of particles.[52] Hence the theory might more usefully be described as one that reduces vision, and all the senses, to the local movement of solid particles and quantitative variations of this movement.

This theory of color vision has been discussed at some length because it provides the background against which the Hellenistic theories of vision had to work, and it is not too surprising that each of the Hellenistic theories shows an influence of its basic assumptions. Let us begin by examining the theory of color perception among the Hellenistic atomists. When Epicurus entered the philosophical scene at Athens, atomism was hardly a respectable philosophy. Not only had Plato spent a lifetime pulling down the materialist assumptions of the atomists, but Aristotle had attacked virtually all the physical assumptions and so had rooted atomism out from even the small place Plato had left it. Epicurus, therefore, had to devote a great deal of his energy to defending the physical assumptions of atomism against Aristotelian criticisms. This shows up in the extant evidence for the Epicurean theory of the perception of color. For to a large degree what we have preserved is simply a defense of the basic presupposition of the theory of Democritus and Plato, namely that the elementary particles are not themselves colored, but color arises from an interaction of these particles with the sensory apparatus. Epicurus contends that color is not even tied to a specific shape of atom, although in some sense modalities a specific shape does produce a specific sensation; rather, color is due to the arrangement ($\theta\acute{\epsilon}\sigma\iota\varsigma$) of the atoms in the object and in the emerging films.[53]

The great emphasis on position and the total absence of any

reference to the size of the atoms suggests that the Epicureans have made at least a minor modification in the traditional theory. What the change really consisted in, however, remains a mystery. It could be part of an attempt to eliminate the visual stream and all that went with it in Plato, like proportional particles. But in the absence of evidence it is idle to speculate, especially since we cannot even be sure that Epicurus did eliminate size from consideration. A better-attested Epicurean modification is giving light an explicit role in the emission and character of the color-producing effluences. If Democritus introduced light into his theory of color in some way, we hear nothing about it in our sources. Plato's talk of fire from visible objects, including objects made of earth, presupposes that the sun's fire is reflected in some way by objects, but he never brings the subject up for discussion. Epicurus, however, seems to have made the active role of light explicit. For Lucretius maintains there can be no color without light, and the way light falls on an object affects the color. This we can see in the changing hues of the tail of a peacock and the way things under a colored awning take on the color of the awning (Lucr. 2.795–809, 4.72–86). But this modification is a minor one; the basic mechanics of the theory are accepted by the Epicureans without change.

Unfortunately, there is little evidence to show how the Epicureans used the mechanical theory for explaining the discrimination of colors. Direct evidence is completely lacking, and the only clue we have that the concepts of *synkrisis* and *diakrisis* were used comes in Lucretius' explanation for the fact that a person in a dark room can look out and see things in the light, whereas a person in the light cannot see into a dark room. His explanation is that when a person looks out of the darkness at something in the light, the illuminated object sends off films that drive the air ahead of them into the eyes of the viewer. First the dark air enters, but then the light air follows and cleans out and scatters (*purgat, discutit*) the dark air, and opens (*patefecit*) the passages that had been "besieged" (*obsederat*) by dark air. Filled with light once again, the eyes can receive the films when they arrive. On the other hand, if a person looks from the light into darkness, the light comes first and is followed by the dark air, which is denser (*crassior*) and which fills and "besieges"/(*obsidit*) the passages so that the films cannot enter and arouse vision (Lucr. 4.337-352). Obviously the Epicureans have preserved the basic premise of the mechanical theory that free access is a necessary condition for vision, and that dark air blocks the movement of effluent films.

Having accepted this premise, it should have been possible for the Epicureans to construct an explanation for variations in color. In fact, Calcidius gives one in his summary of the Epicurean theory of vision: "When the bulk of the film is more delicate (*delicatior*), the vision will be separated and opened (*separatur panditurque*), I believe, and the things sensed then will seem white; if it is more dense (*corpulentior*), they will mix together (*confundunt*) the sight and seem black" (*In Tim.* 236). If Calcidius is reporting the Epicurean view accurately, we can, indeed, conclude that the Epicureans have adopted the accessibility theory of color vision in its purely mechanical, but more refined, Platonic form, fitting it to an atomic physics such as the one for which it was originally designed. Of course, they had to rid it of any remnants of the theory of visual rays that it may have acquired in the Platonic version, but this was a relatively simple task; and in addition, or as part of this cleansing, they substituted the density of the films for the size of the particles as the differentiating characteristic of color sensation.

Now the only reservation we need have arises from the fact that Calcidius adds the qualification, "I believe" (*opinor*), as though he did not find the theory spelled out in his sources. This must give us pause and make us at least consider the possibility that Calcidius himself has elaborated upon the Epicurean theory or has even invented it on the basis of the Platonic theory and his knowledge of basic Epicurean physics. Thus there can really be no certainty as long as the detailed physical treatises of Epicurus are lost. Yet it seems probable that Epicurus did hold something like this theory.

Though the evidence for the Epicurean theory of color discrimination is slim, the evidence for the theory of visual rays, the earliest of our three Hellenistic theories, is relatively abundant. Euclid's *Optics* gives us no information whatsoever because color is beyond the scope of that work. But Aristotle in the third book of his *Meteorology* does give us a theory of color adapted to the theory of visual rays. In explaining the colors of the rainbow, Aristotle says that our sight is reflected by droplets of water to the sun. In being reflected, it is bent and thereby weakened. The degree of weakening determines the color: "Just as sight, being reflected (literally, "broken," κλωμένη) makes black appear blacker on account of weakness (ἀσθενία), so also it makes white appear less white and approach black. For the relatively strong sight changes the color to red, the next to green, the still weaker sight to purple" (*Meteor.* 3. 4.374b28–33). It is not only the bending of the sight in reflection that may weaken it, but also mixture with the medium; for if one looks at the sun through the dark mist or smoke, it appears red (*Meteor.* 3.4.374a4–8, b9–11; 3.6.377b11–13).

To understand this theory we must first elucidate the term "weakening." Its meaning comes out most clearly in the three postulates with which Aristotle prefaces his explanation of the rainbow:
1. "Bright in or through black makes red."
2. "Sight extended becomes weaker and less."
3. "Black is a kind of negation (ἀπόφασις), for the appearance of black consists in the failure (ἐκλείπειν) of sight. Therefore further things appear blacker because the sight does not penetrate (διικνεῖσθαι)" (*Meteor.* 3.4.374b9–15).

Since black is a negation and failure of sight, occurring when the sight does not reach something, and since less than total failure to reach may be called "weakening" and will result in colors intermediate between white and black, "weakening" may reasonably be taken to mean "a diminishing of the power of penetration or access." This interpretation may be confirmed by Aristotle's account of the weak-sighted man who allegedly saw a reflected image of himself before his eyes as he walked. The reason give for this by Aristotle is that his sight was so weak and thin (λεπτή) that it was unable to push aside (ἀπωθεῖν) the nearby air, but was instead reflected backward off the air (*Meteor.* 3.4.373b2–10). Strength of sight here apparently consists in an ability to penetrate and weakness in an inability to penetrate. If this interpretation of the concept of "weakening" is correct, it is understandable why reflection and a dark medium would cause weakening and a corresponding change of color. The sight could perhaps be compared to a stream flowing through a tube. If the tube is bent backward on itself, the flow will obviously be impeded. Also if an opposite, a negation of its contents, intervenes, the flow can likewise be expected to be impeded.

This theory of vision looks like a relative of the older mechanical theory. Even though the Platonic concepts of combination and separation have been abandoned, the underlying principle of penetrability or degree of access still survives to determine the color. Only now the visual ray reaches out, and resisting factors impede its penetration to produce the various colors. In part, at least, this difference is due to the fact that Plato's theory dealt with colored objects, and the color theory of Aristotle's *Meteorology* deals only with rainbows and atmospheric phenomena. We have no evidence how it would deal with colored objects. But two things are clear. The visual ray theory has totally eliminated effluences from the object, whose physical structure could affect the condition of the ray. Secondly, the visual ray theory has eliminated the atomistic physical assumptions. The effect of this is to preclude the reduction of color vision to the perception of moving particles by the agency of other moving particles. Obviously, a new model of color perception has been introduced. What it is we cannot even guess, but "strength" and "weakness" or "failure" are considered appropriate descriptions of the qualities the ray possesses. The terms would most appropriately be applied to an animate object, and it may be significant that two centuries later Hipparchus, the mathematician and astronomer, will compare the visual rays to hands reaching out to the object and returning the apprehension of it to the visual perceptor (τὸ ὁρατικόν, Aët. 4.13.9). But whatever model of perception the theory of visual rays has adopted, it has in some way incorporated the principle of the degree of accessibility between observer and object and so perpetuates this basic premise of the classical theory of color vision.

Before turning to the third theory of color perception, we might pause to consider the one extant Hellenistic work on color, namely, the Peripatetic treatise *On Colors*. This work has come down to us in the Aristotelian corpus, though it is clearly not by the hand of Aristotle.[54] It seems to be a research proposal, laying out the principles that should govern a scientific investigation of coloration and color change in plants and animals. As such it does not deal directly with the perception of color, but rather with the physical basis of color in plants and animals. Nevertheless, a few traces of the author's assumptions about vision and color perception may be gleaned from the treatise.

The assumption with which the treatise begins seems to be that colors are fundamental properties of substances. Each element by nature possesses a simple color; the colors we see are mixtures of the simple colors, arising ultimately from mixtures of the elements (*Col.* 1.791a1–12). The seeing of objects cannot occur except by the impression (φαντασία) of color (*Col.* 1.791b15–17), and vision apparently is completed only when the color reaches the eyes (*Col.* 3.793b23–30). If this were all there were, we could regard the treatise as a development of the orthodox doctrine of Aristotle's *On the Soul* and *On Sense and Sensible Objects*, with color the proper sensible for vision and differences in color due to various mixtures of certain primary colors.[55] But the treatise goes on to develop these basic ideas in a direction that deviates considerably from the theory of *On the Soul* and *On Sense and Sensible Objects*. For the author of *On Colors* makes no mention of the medium, of the transmission of movement from the object to the eye through the medium, or of any of the other major ideas that occupy Aristotle in *On the Soul* 2.7. Instead, it is light that moves from the object to the eye and serves as the vehicle whereby the color is transmitted to the eye. Light, the author of *On Colors* contends, is the color of fire (*Col.* 1.791b6–14) and so apparently also of the sun (cf., e.g., *Col.* 2.792a10–11, b22–23). It is by virtue of the light that fire is visible, as it is by virtue of their own colors that all other bodies are visible (*Col.* 1.791b15–17). Darkness is simply the failure or absence of light (*Col.* 1.791a12–13, b2–3).

Now the color of the light reaching the eye depends on a number of factors. First of all, it may vary in hue depending on its source, e.g., the sun, the moon, fire, or a lamp. Moreover, before it reaches the eye, it may undergo one or more processes of mixture that will alter its color. For example, it must penetrate a medium and so will be additionally colored by mixture with the color of the intervening substance. Then, too, it may strike an object and be reflected. In this process it will be mixed with a third color, the natural color of the object. Moreover, it may be affected even by the strength with which it strikes the object or the angle of impact. Eventually a mixture of at least three, and possibly many more, colors will reach the eye to produce a sensation corresponding to the predominant color of the light (*Col.* 3.793b12–794a2; cf. 2.792a4–29, b16–25).

Precisely what light is and how it changes color through mixture is never fully explained, but there are a few clues to the general direction of the author's thought. The author claims that black can appear in three ways. A naturally black object will appear black. An object that reflects no light, when the surrounding region does, will also appear black. Finally, whatever reflects very little light appears black, like a rough sea or a very thick, rough cloud.[56] This indicates that in falling on an object and being reflected from it, light may be scattered and thereby lost, and the loss will affect the color seen. If the loss is total or nearly total, so that little or no light is reflected, the color black will be seen.

In a later passage dealing with the mixture of colors the author gives an example of how the medium affects the color seen. He points out that air near the eye seems to have no color because the "denser" rays "conquer" ($\kappa\rho\alpha\tau\epsilon\hat{\iota}\tau\alpha\iota$) the rare air and shine through it. However, air seen through a depth looks deep blue, because where the light fails ($\lambda\epsilon\acute{\iota}\pi\epsilon\iota$), there the air, being rare, is interspersed or grasped by ($\delta\iota\epsilon\iota\lambda\acute{\eta}\mu\mu\epsilon\nu\sigma$) darkness.[57] This suggests that light in passing through a medium encounters resistance, even though the medium is rare. In the case of the air in the sky the author seems to imagine the rays of light proceeding out of the air toward the eye.[58] If this light has to travel through a relatively short distance, the rays of light can overcome ($\kappa\rho\alpha\tau\epsilon\hat{\iota}\nu$) the resistance of the air and emerge unaffected. Thus air near an observer seems to have no color. But if

81

the distance is great, the light will "fail" or "be wanting" (λείπειν). Wherever this happens, the air will be interspersed with, or grasped by (διειλήμμενος), darkness and appear blue. Thus the color of rare, transparent air depends on the distance the light must travel before reaching the observer: the greater the distance, the more darkness and hence the darker the color.[59] Thus the writer's underlying assumption is that the color of light passing through a medium depends on the relative strength of the light in comparison to the resistance offered by the medium; the lower the degree of penetration, the darker the color will be.[60]

Still further light is shed on the theory of color by the discussions of colored substances in nature. Each element is said to have its own natural color. Air, water, and earth are naturally white; fire is naturally yellow. If earthy things sometimes seem to possess other colors, it is because they are dyed. Now the "dye" (βαφή) that colors things presumably has water as its base. But the water, which is by nature white, is colored by the admixture of other elements. For example, the treatise claims that sand becomes yellow "when flame-colored (φλογοειδής) and black color the water" (Col. 1.791a8–9). We may assume that the flame-colored shade comes from fire. But black is not the color of any element, and so the writer explains that black accompanies elements as they undergo transformation into another element (Col. 1.791a9–10). By this device the writer is apparently hoping to bring in black as a component not only for the color of sand but for all the colors in nature beside white and yellow. Precisely how he conceives the physics of his theory is not clear, but he repeatedly calls upon the processes of ripening (πέψις, which is literally "cooking") and of drying to account for a "darkening" of color (e.g., Col. 1.791b17–792a3; 2.792b5–11; 5.794b19–795a27, 795b22–796a9, 21–31). From all this we may conclude that processes involving elemental change bring black into mixture with the white and yellow of the elements and so can be called upon to account for the whole spectrum of colors in nature.

If these inferences about the color theory of the treatise *On Colors* are correct, we may begin to assess the place of the treatise among the early Hellenistic theories of color vision. The theory underlying the treatise obviously has connections with the theory of Aristotle's *On Sense and Sensible Objects* that various colors are mixtures of the primary colors, which, in turn, are intermediates between white and black. But it just as obviously goes beyond that treatise and shows, in addition, the clear influence of the theory of Aristotle's *Meteorology*. For it shares with the *Meteorology* the idea that black is due to a "failure" or "eclipse," and that there is a correlation between the "strength" of the light and the color, so that the weaker the light, the darker its color will be.[61] Now this is not surprising in a treatise emerging from Aristotle's school. What is surprising is that there is a crucial difference between *On Colors* and Aristotle's *Meteorology*. Whereas the *Meteorology* presupposes that a visual ray travels from the eye to the object, *On Colors* assumes that a ray of light moves from the source of light to the object and then to the eye. This makes it impossible to regard *On Colors* as a mere extension of the theory of the *Meteorology*. It is even doubtful that *On Colors* should be regarded merely as a "correction" of the theory of the *Meteorology* on the basis of Aristotle's later theory of vision expressed in *On the Soul* and *On Sense and Sensible Objects*. For the key Aristotelian concepts, such as light being the color of the transparent and the transparent being the medium of vision, do not appear at all in *On Colors*. Of course, we cannot here enter into a discussion of all the historical connections of *On Colors*, but we can notice that it bears some relation to the Epicurean theory. The strong intromissionist point of view, the notion of light as a material substance capable of mixing with, or affecting and being affected by, other substances (*Col.* 1.791a1–12; 2.792a29–3.794a2), the ideas that color varies with the angle of light and that there is no color without light (*Col.* 2.792a20–24; 1.791b15–17, cf. a12–b6), and finally, the concern with the changing color of the sea and of the feathers of birds (*Col.* 1.791a20–24; 2.792a20–29; 3.793a14–16; cf. 3.793b8–12), can all be paralleled in Epicurean texts.[62] This creates the strong presumption that the writer of *On Colors* had more to work with than the texts of Aristotle and that among these were discussions (perhaps Peripatetic) with which the Epicureans also were familiar, or pos-

83

sibly the Epicurean texts themselves. Thus the Peripatetic treatise *On Colors* is a useful indication of the complexity that is likely to have characterized the science of vision in the Hellenistic age. Each of the three theories that came out of the Hellenistic age may seem to have its own formal identity, but the boundaries between them may well have been fluid; mutual interaction and the demands of particular problems very likely produced numerous variations, of which this is the only one to survive.

Yet despite the mixed heritage of the treatise and its apparent attempts to harmonize principles derived from different theories of vision, its underlying principle of color perception appears to be the same as that of all the theories we have been examining. Of course, its initial assertion that the simple colors are natural concomitants of the elements sounds like the orthodox Aristotelian theory that makes color an irreducible property of the surface of an object, but this assertion is overshadowed by a strong tendency to make the color seen by an observer depend on the amount and strength of the light that reaches the eye from the object. Thus once again the degree of access between the object and the observer is the determining factor in the perception of color.

The third distinct theory of color perception at which we must look is the Stoic theory. The evidence for it is slim but suggestive. We know, in general, how the Stoics conceived of sensation. They thought of it as a presentation (φαντασία) apprehensible through a sense organ.[63] The object makes an impact (literally, "falls against," προσπεσόντος) from without and creates a motion that is transmitted to the principal part of the soul.[64] The presentation that is offered to the soul was defined by Zeno as "an imprint (τύπωσις) on the soul," a term that in time caused the Stoics interpretive problems. Cleanthes, Zeno's successor, interpreted it as a relief impression in three dimensions, like the imprint of a seal in wax.[65] Chrysippus, Cleanthes' successor and the one whose theory of vision we have been reconstructing, ridiculed the naïveté of Cleanthes' view and insisted that the imprint must be understood as a qualitative change of state (ἑτεροίωσις).[66]

Within this general scheme of perception the Stoics developed their theory of color perception. The presentation that an object imprints on the soul includes the color of the object. Zeno defined colors as "the primary shapes" (πρῶτοι σχηματισμοί) of matter or as "the surface coloration" of matter (ἐπίχρωσις).[67] Thus the color will also be part of the "shape" of the imprint produced by the object. Chrysippus apparently agreed that color, like temperature, was a quality residing in the object and having the power to move the soul so as to produce a presentation. However, since Chrysippus understood the presentation to be a qualitative state, isomorphic with the state of the qualified object of perception, he called the presentation produced by a white object a *pathos*, a passive state, produced by a white object.[68] Furthermore, the white object, he contended, was white by virtue of the state of the *pneuma* or air in it. Matter is given form and shape by a *pneuma* or "airy tension" permeating it. The states of matter that constitute its forms and qualities are nothing but "airs," Chrysippus said. This tensed air or *pneuma* is what makes an object hard or dense or white.[69]

The physical explanation of the transmission of this color state from the object to the soul is described briefly by Calcidius: "The Stoics believe that the mind perceives in the way in which it is driven by the *pneuma*, which transmits to the depths of the mind that which it itself has experienced from uniting with the visible forms [i.e., objects] (*ex visibilium specierum concretione*). If it is extended and as it were opened (*porrectus et veluti patefactus*), it announces that the things seen are white; but if it is further mixed together and clogged (*confusus porro et confoecatior*), it signals that the thing is black and shady." Then Calcidius compares the process of perception to what happens when the shock from an electric eel is passed through the net, rod, and hands to the fisherman.[70] If we combine this information with what we know from elsewhere about Chrysippus' theory of visual perception, we may conclude that in seeing colors the tensed cone of air standing between the eye and the object experiences a change of state induced by the state of the object; this state is communicated back to the eye and the soul. The change of state is not left undefined, but is described by

85

the terms "separating" and "mixing together" or by the terms "opening" and "closing"—the very same terms we have found so often in Greek color theory.

The suspicion may arise that since our witness is a Platonist, writing summaries of theories he claims have descended from Plato, he might have distorted the evidence. Alternatively, since we have already found that his statement of the basic principles of the Stoic theory are, if not misrepresented, then derived from a later Stoic remodeling of the theory, we might reasonably wonder how reliable his statement about the perception of color is. But in this case Calcidius' testimony is backed up by a second century A.D. witness who alludes to the same theory and expressly attributes it to Chrysippus, although he is not at the moment interested in theories of vision at all. Plutarch in an essay *On the Principle of Cold* discusses Chrysippus' theory that air is basically cold and paraphrases Chrysippus as follows: "Since fire is both hot and bright, the nature opposite fire must be cold and dark. For as dark is opposite bright, so cold is opposite hot. For as the dark tends to fuse together (συγχυτικόν) sight, so the cold does to touch. And heat dissolves (or "diffuses," διαχεῖ) the sensation of the thing touched, as brightness does for the thing seen."[71] This proves that Chrysippus, like Democritus and Plato, tried to explain sight and touch in parallel fashion, reducing both to the same physical process. Moreover, the process is similar, but not identical, to the one we have met in Plato. Where Plato spoke of combination and separation (σύγκρισις and διάκρισις), Chrysippus speaks of fusing and diffusing (συγχυτικόν, *confusus*, διαχεῖ). But this difference in terminology is understandable, if we remember that Plato's process involved groups of discrete particles and was named accordingly, whereas Chrysippus' process involves a continuous substance whose change in physical state must be called fusion or diffusion. Perhaps we may think of it as a change in density.[72] There is confirmation for this if Alexander is expressing a genuine Stoic claim when he suggests that the Stoics would agree that slack, unilluminated air is denser (πυκνότερον) than expanded, illuminated air.[73] Even so, the underlying assumption is that the open access that accompanies a diffused state produces white, whereas the "clogged" condition of a fused state produces darkness and black.

What we have in Stoicism is still another transformation of the original Greek theory of color perception, in which color depends on the accessibility of the sense organ. But it is remodeled to bring it into line with the Stoic theories of matter and of perception. The Stoic theory of matter required that the visual cone be made of a continuous substance, tensed air. The only way to conceive of it being "separated" or "dilated" was to think of it as being rarefied. On the other hand, the Stoic theory of visual perception was developed after Aristotle had rejected the theory of visual rays and had argued for vision taking place by the transmission of a qualitative state through a medium. Hence the Stoic theory postulates a state of density or of tension being impressed on the base of the cone of tensed, visual air. This state is communicated back to the *pneuma* of the eyes and through it to the principal part of the soul where a presentation arises.

The Stoic theory of color, therefore, provides for a continuum of states within which the color scale may be located. We have no information on how Chrysippus explained colors other than white and black. We might guess he would have said that they are all intermediate degrees of density or tension.

We have now examined the three main theories of color perception in the early Hellenistic age. All three show evidence of attempting to maintain the basic assumptions of the classical theory as it was developed by Democritus and Plato. All three seem firm in the belief that color is not a primary quality of objects, but is reducible to physical principles.[74] All three appear to reduce the multiplicity of colors to a linear scale in which the various hues are conceived of as intermediates between black and white. Finally, all three attempt to reduce this scale to one of degrees of accessibility between the object and the observer. The basic conflict among the three theories is really over the physical basis of the theory, and it is at this level that all the battles seem to be fought. There is an obvious dispute whether matter is atomic or continuous, and whether in vision the eye sends something out to the object, co-opts the medium to transmit information back, or simply waits for something to come from the object. The basic task confronting the Hellenistic theorists was to adjust the orthodox theory to fit their individual physical theories. There is no evidence I have been able to find that any facts or observations appeared after Plato's day to undermine the basic approach of the classical Hellenic theory of color perception. Accordingly, when viewed in historical perspective, the investigation of visual perception in the Hellenistic age seems to have given color relatively little emphasis. One gets the impression that color was simply not a critical issue. Now this impression may be due to our lack of primary sources, but on the basis of our present information, we would have to conclude that Hellenistic investigators had turned their attention to other things. Color, which occupied the attention of fourth-century thinkers, had been satisfactorily "solved," at least for the time being. Attention was now turning toward the perception of shape and size and the enigmas posed by viewing things from a distance. It was these problems that gave the Hellenistic theories their real test.

1. Some aspects and periods of it have been surveyed by J. I. Beare, *Greek Theories of Elementary Cognition from Alcmaeon to Aristotle* (Oxford: Clarendon Press, 1906); E. Haas, "Antike Lichttheorien," *Archiv für Geschichte der Philosophie* 20 (1907): 345–86; J. Hirschberg, "Die Optik der alten Griechen," *Zeitschift für Psychologie und Physiologie der Sinnesorgane* 16 (1898):321–51, and "Die Seh-Theorien der griechishen Philosophen in ihren Beziehungen zur Augenheilkunde," *Zeitschrift für Augenheilkunde* 43 (1920):1–22; and W. Jablonski, "Die Theorien des Sehens im griechischen altertume bis auf Aristoteles," *Sudhoffs Archiv für Geschichte der Medizin* 23 (1930): 306–61.

2. See A. Lejeune, *Euclide et Ptolémée: Deux stades de l'optique géométrique grecque* (Louvain: Bibliothèque de l'Université, 1948). Lejeune has also edited the Latin translation of Ptolemy's treatise, *L'Optique de Claude Ptolémée dans la version latine d'après l'arabe de l'émir Eugène de Sicile* (Louvain: Bibliothèque de l'Université, 1956).

3. For example, in the Peripatos, Theophrastus wrote *On Sensation, On Visual Films (Idols), On Vision* (four books), and *On Things That Change Color*; Strato, *On Vision, On Sensation,* and *On Colors.* The Stoic Zeno wrote *On Vision* and Cleanthes *On Sensation.* Epicurus wrote *On Seeing* and *On Visual Films (Idols).* Archimedes wrote *Catoptrics* (the properties of mirrors). And, of course, most philosophers dealt with the subject in their general works on physics.

4. Only one treatise relating to the subject survives intact, the Pseudo-Aristotelian work *On Colors.* Though attempts have been made to attribute this work both to

Theophrastus and to Strato, conclusive evidence has not yet been discovered and its authorship remains in doubt; cf. W. Capelle, "Straton von Lampsakos," *Real-Encyclopädie der classischen Altertumswissenschaft* (Stuttgart: J. B. Metzler/A. Druckenmüller, 1894–1973) Series 2, Vol. 4a (1932), pp. 283–84; O. Regenbogen, "Theophrastos von Eresos," *Real-Encyclopädie*, Suppl. 7 (1940), pp. 1543–44; and H. B. Gottschalk, "The De Coloribus and its Author," *Hermes* 92 (1964): 59–85. Hence we cannot say with certainty that we possess a treatise on vision by either of these philosophers. Nevertheless, Gottschalk has shown that *On Colors* most likely emanates from close to Theophrastus. Theophrastus' critical survey of his predecessors' opinions on sensation (the *De Sensu*) comes close to being an extant treatise in this field, but it is not a statement of his own ideas. His own writings on the subject are all lost.

5. The most recent edition of this fragment is R. Schoene, ed., *Damianos: Schrift über Optik, mit Auszügen aus Geminus* (Berlin: Reichsdruckerei, 1897), pp. 22–31. The passage quoted is on page 24.

6. *De Anima Libri Mantissa*, ed. I. Bruns, Supplementum Aristotelicum 2.1 (Berlin: G. Reimer, 1887), pp. 127–38. This work has come to us under the name of Alexander of Aphrodisias, but its authenticity is questionable (cf. P. Moraux, *Alexandre d'Aphrodise: Exégète de la Noétique d'Aristote* [Paris: Les Belles Lettres, 1942], pp. 24–28). Nevertheless, since the question of authorship is irrelevant for my purposes, I will, for the sake of convenience, continue to refer to this text under the name of Alexander. The text also adds a fourth theory that seems to combine the essential elements of the first and third theories. This seems to be a schematized version of the Platonic theory that Theophrastus, *De Sensu* 5, also characterized as midway between an extramission and an intromission theory.

An interesting application of the three theories at about the same date occurs in Plutarch, *Quaest. Conviv.* 1.8 (= *Mor.* 625e–626e). Here Plutarch records three explanations of why old men hold their books farther from their eyes. He uses the theory of visual rays, of images from the object, and of a theory that he calls Platonic, but that shows an admixture of ideas from the theory of the optic *pneuma*. A fourth explanation for the phenomenon is mentioned briefly, but its underlying theory of vision (if any) remains obscure. Cf. also Aulus Gellius' brief reference to three theories of vision: Stoic, Epicurean, and Platonic (*Noct. Att.* 5.16).

7. *In Tim.* 236–46. On the much-disputed date of Calcidius, see J. H. Waszink, ed., *Timaeus a Calcidio Translatus Commentarioque Instructus*, Corpus Platonicum, Medii Aevi, Plato Latinus, Vol. 4 (London: Warburg Institute; Leiden: Brill, 1962), pp. ix–xv.

8. He is known to have discussed the subject in detail in books II and III of his thirty-seven-volume treatise on physics, of which a few fragments survive (see G. Arrighetti, ed., *Epicuro: Opere* [Torino: Einaudi, 1960], pp. 186–215). He must also have treated the subject in his *Great Epitome*, *On Seeing*, and *On Visual Films* [*Idols*]. Fragments of his treatises *Against Theophrastus* and *Twelve Elements* deal with vision and suggest he at least touched on the subject in these books (see H. Usener, *Epicurea* [Leipzig: Teubner, 1887], pp. 101–2 [frs. 29–30], 114 [fr. 56]).

9. Epicurus also described them as "outline images" ($\tau\acute{\upsilon}\pi\omega$) and "effluences" ($\dot{\alpha}\pi\acute{o}\rho\rho\omega\iota$); cf., e.g., *Ep. ad Herod.* 46, and *Physics* fr. 32, section 10, line 2 (Arrighetti, page 359).

10. Epicurus, *Ep. ad Herod.* 46–50, and *Physics* II, supplemented by Lucretius 3.359–69, 407–15, 4.29–268. For a convenient summary of Epicurus' theory with fuller documentation, see K. Kleve, *Gnosis Theon: Die Lehre von der natürlich Gotteserkenntnis in der epikureischen Theologie*, Symbolae Osloenses, Suppl. 19 (Oslo: University of Oslo, 1963), pp. 13–22, supplemented by D. Lemke, *Die Theologie Epikurs: Versuch einer Rekonstruktion*, Zetemata 57 (Munich: C. H. Beck, 1973), pp. 5–22. Recently, R. E. Siegel, "Did the Greek Atomists consider Non-Corpuscular Visual Transmission? Reconsideration of Some Ancient Visual Doctrines," *Archives Inter-*

nationales d'histoire des sciences 22 (1969):3–16; *Galen On Sense Perception* (Basel: S. Karger, 1970), pp. 19–23, has attempted to refute the traditional interpretation and construe Epicurus' theory as a non-corpuscular theory. Siegel's interpretation, however, is forced and, what is more, is contradicted by the fragments of Epicurus' *Physics*, of which Siegel seems to be unaware.

11. Euclid's *Optics* is extant in two versions, the original and a modified version by Theon of Alexandria (fourth cent. A.D.). Cf. J. L. Heiberg, *Litterargeschichtliche Studien über Euklid* (Leipzig, 1882), chap. 4.

12. Euclid, *Optica*, ed. J. L. Heiberg (Leipzig: Teubner, 1895) p. 3, Definition 3. A complete English translation can be found in H. E. Burton, "The Optics of Euclid," *Journal of the Optical Society of America* 35 (1945):357–72, and an abridged translation in M. R. Cohen and I. E. Drabkin, *A Source Book in Greek Science* (Cambridge, Mass: Harvard University Press, 1958), pp. 257–61.

13. This is the view of B. W. Switalski, *Des Chalcidius Kommentar zu Plato's Timaeus*, Beiträge zur Geschichte der Philosophie des Mittelalters, Texte und Untersuchungen, vol. 3, no. 6 (Münster: Aschendorff, 1902), p. 40, note 4, who believes that Calcidius confused the Peripatetics with the Pythagoreans.

14. Cf. esp. *Meteor.* 3.2.372a19–21; 3.372b34–373a19; 4.373a35–b13; b32–33; 374b11 12; 6.377a30–378a12.

15. Aristotle's *On the Soul* and *On Sensation* are generally regarded as being written later than the *Meteorology*: see, e.g., W. Jaeger, *Aristotle: Fundamentals of the History of his Development*,[2] trans. R. Robinson (Oxford: Oxford University Press, 1948), chaps. 11–12. I. Düring, *Aristoteles: Darstellung und Interpretation seines Denkens* (Heidelberg: Carl Winter Verlag, 1966), pp. 51–52, 558–62, is more cautious, particularly on dating the psychological treatises. He suspects that the optical aspects of the *Meteorology* are influenced by the work of Eudoxus and his school (p. 393).

16. For Theophrastus' theory of perception and vision, see G. M. Stratton, *Theophrastus and the Greek Physiological Psychology before Aristotle* (London: Allen & Unwin; New York: Macmillan, 1918), pp. 18–32.

17. Simplicius, *In Aristotelis De Caelo Commentaria*, ed. J. L. Heiberg, Commentaria in Aristotelem Graeca, no. 7 (Berlin: G. Reimer, 1894) p. 602, lines 5–6.

18. *De Vertigine* 8 and *passim*; cf. Stratton (above, n. 16), pp. 30–32.

19. How extensive this agreement was and how long some measure of agreement persisted we cannot say. We do know that the theory of visual rays was vigorously rejected in the third century A.D. by the author of the text attributed to Alexander of Aphrodisias, *De Anima Libri Mant.* 127.27–130.12 Bruns.

20. Cf. Waszink (above, n. 7), p. 249, note on line 11.

21. *In Tim.* 237. I have translated the most recent text by Waszink (above, n. 7). H. von Arnim, *Stoicorum Veterum Fragmenta*, vol. 2 (Leipzig: Teubner, 1903) (hereafter *SVF*), no. 863, offers a slightly different reading of this text. His reading does not alter the sense, however.

22. *De Anima Libri Mant.* 130.14–17 Bruns. The text can also be found in von Arnim, *SVF*, no. 864.

23. For a brief survey of the Stoic theory of vision see S. Sambursky, *Physics of the Stoics* (New York: Macmillan, 1959), pp. 23–29.

24. Aëtius 4.15.1 = von Arnim, *SVF*, no. 866; Aëtius 4.15.2 = *SVF*, no. 869.

25. *Diog. Laert.* 7.157 = von Arnim, *SVF*, no. 867.

26. Galen, *De Hipp. et Plat. Plac.* 7.7 (vol. 5, p. 643 Kuhn) = von Arnim, *SVF*, no. 865, refers briefly to the Stoic theory. I am here deliberately avoiding discussion of Galen's own theory of vision, which manifests many similarities to the Stoic view. Galen's theory has been variously interpreted as: (1) essentially Stoic (Chrysippean),

but incorporating some old Platonic ideas and the new anatomical discoveries (cf. R. E. Siegel, *Galen on Sense Perception* [Basel: S. Karger, 1970] pp. 37–40, 46); (2) as virtually identical to Posidonius' (first century B.C.) version of the Stoic theory, but not to the old theory of Chrysippus (cf. K. Reinhardt, *Kosmos und Sympathie: Neue Untersuchungen über Poseidonios* [Munich: C. H. Beck, 1926], pp. 188–92; cf. Sambursky [above, n. 23], p. 28); and (3) as Galen's own personal theory, synthesized from the theories of Plato, Aristotle, and the Stoics (cf. H. Cherniss, "Galen and Posidonius' Theory of Vision," *American Journal of Philology* 54 [1933]:154–61.) But the interpretation of Galen's theory and any other possible permutations of the old Stoic theory after the third century B.C. is beyond the scope of this paper.

27.　Alex. Aphr., *De Anima Libri Mantissa*, p. 131.31–34 (Bruns) = von Arnim, *SVF*, no. 868. Cf. page 132.37 (= *SVF*, no. 432) where Alexander in his refutation of the Stoic view used a definition of light as "dilated air."

28.　H. G. Liddell and R. Scott, *A Greek-English Lexicon* (Oxford: Clarendon Press, 1940), s. v. νύσσω.

29.　A little further light is shed on the process by a quotation from Chrysippus' predecessor Cleanthes. In a different context Cleanthes said, "Tension is a blow (πληγή) of fire; if it becomes sufficient in the soul to accomplish the impacts (ἐπιβάλλοντα) it is called strength and force," von Arnim, *SVF*, vol. 1, no. 563. Though here it is fire, and not *pneuma*, which is acting, the process is described as a "blow," and "impacts," and the effect as "strength" and "tension."

30.　See von Arnim, *SVF*, vol. 2, no. 471; cf. also no. 697.

31.　Cf. von Arnim, *SVF*, vol. 2, no. 841; cf. nos. 310, 442.

32.　See von Arnim, *SVF*, vol. 2, no. 56. For further discussion M. Pohlenz, "Zenon und Chrysipp," *Nachrichten der Göttingen Gesellschaft der Wissenschaften*, Phil.-hist. Kl., Fachgruppe I, n.s. 2, 9 (1938):174–77, 181–82; and Sambursky (above, n. 23), pp. 25–27.

33.　Aët. 4.15.2–3 = von Arnim, *SVF*, vol. 2, nos. 866, 869. Cf. also Aulus Gellius, *Noct. Att.* 5.16.2 = *SVF*, vol. 2, no. 871.

34.　*Tim.* 45b–d; cf. R. Turnbull, "The Role of the 'Special Sensibles' in the Perception Theories of Plato and Aristotle," this volume.

35.　Their particular adaptation could be intended to avoid Aristotle's strictures against the emission of physical substances through the membrane of the eyes (*Sens.* 2.438a27–b2) and to replace Plato's fire with the more subtle *pneuma*, which in contemporary biology and psychology had been emerging as the proper vehicle of sensation and movement (cf. F. Solmsen, "Greek Philosophy and the Discovery of the Nerves," *Museum Helveticum* 18 [1961]:159–84).

36.　Aulus Gellius (second century A.D.), *Noct. Att.* 5.16.2 (= von Arnim, *SVF*, vol. 2, no. 871) assigns a similar theory to the Stoics: "The Stoics say the causes of seeing are the emission of rays from the eyes to the things which they are able to see and the concurrent stretching (*intentionem*) of the air."

37.　It would be tempting to conclude that Geminus and Calcidius are summarizing Posidonius, the Stoic polymath of the first century B.C., who was both a teacher of Geminus and (some have thought) a commentator on Plato. G. Pfligersdorffer, *Studien zu Poseidonios*, Österreiche Akademie der Wissenschaften, phil.-hist. Kl. Sitzungsberichte, vol. 232, no. 5 (1959), pp. 54–55, draws this conclusion for the statement of Calcidius. However, with the "Posidonian question" in a state of flux and most of the earlier reconstructions of Posidonius' thought now under suspicion (see the introduction to the new edition of fragments by L. Edelstein and I. Kidd, ed., *Posidonius: I. The Fragments* [Cambridge: At the University Press, 1972], pp. xiii–xix), it might be better to await further evidence.

38.　Theophrastus, *De Sensu* 7 (= H. Diels and W. Kranz, *Die Fragmente der*

Vorsokratiker[6] [Zürich-Berlin: Weidmann, 1952], 31A86 (vol. 1, p. 301, lines 26–35); cf. W. Kranz, "Die älteste Farbenlehren der Griechen," *Hermes* 77 (1912):126–28; and W. K. C. Guthrie, *History of Greek Philosophy*, (Cambridge: At the University Press, 1965), 2.148 n. 1; 231–38.

39. Cf. Diels-Kranz (above, n. 38) 67A29 (vol. 2, p. 78, line 30–page 79, line 5). Theophrastus, *De Sensu* 50 = Diels-Kranz 68A135.50 (vol. 2, pp. 114.28–115.3) describes a more complex theory of vision, which includes effluences from the object and the observer and an imprint in the intervening air. This theory is difficult to understand and to harmonize with the simpler theory mentioned by Alexander. But the subtleties of Democritus' theory are beyond the scope of this paper and, in any event, do not affect his theory of color, which makes color depend only on the effluences from the object. For full discussion of Democritus' theory see Beare (above, n. 1), pp. 23–37; C. Bailey, *The Greek Atomists and Epicurus* (Oxford: Clarendon Press, 1928), pp. 103–5, 165–70; K. von Fritz, "Democritus' Theory of Vision," in E. A. Underwood, ed., *Science, Medicine, and History: Essays on the Evolution of Scientific Thought and Medical Practice, Written in Honour of Charles Singer* (Oxford: Oxford University Press, 1953), pp. 83–99; R. E. Siegel, "Theories of Vision and Color Perception of Empedocles and Democritus: Some Similarities to the Modern Approach," *Bulletin of the History of Medicine* 33 (1959):145–59; and Guthrie (above, n. 38), 2.442–45.

40. Theophrastus, *De Sensu* 73–74. Cf. Kranz (above, n. 38) and Guthrie (above, n. 38), 2.445.

41. Guthrie (above, n. 38), 2.445–46, assumes that he does, and he might have cited Theophrastus' vague remark that "it is likely that he derives the white from light or something else (*Sens.* 80). Von Fritz (above, n. 39), p. 99 n. 68, suspends judgment and explains shade very plausibly in terms of the passages in the structure of the object. I have followed his interpretation.

42. Cf., e.g., Aristotle, *De An.* I.2.403b31–404a9, 405a8–13.

43. The extant text of Theophrastus is not clear whether Democritus claimed the atoms or their aggregates are larger than those of heat (cf. Stratton [above, n. 16], p. 197 n. 177). Von Fritz (above, n. 39), pp. 96–99, argues persuasively that Democritus was associating the colors with configurations of atoms, not with individual shapes of atoms. There are two questions here, what Democritus believed and what Theophrastus claimed for him, but they cannot be settled here.

44. He also considered yellow-green ($\chi\lambda\omega\rho\acute{o}\nu$) to be a primary color, but Theophrastus, *De Sensu* 75, 82, complains that all he said about it was that it consists of solid and void, with the shade varying by the position and order of the solid and void. Theophrastus thinks he should have assigned it a distinct shape, but if my interpretation is correct, he need not have done so. He may have imagined it as having a structure and porosity corresponding to its position in the color scale.

45. This is the theory of Aristotle, *Meteor.* III; see below, pages 78–79.

46. *Tim.* 45c. Plato says that that which "falls against from within *presses reciprocally* ($\grave{\alpha}\nu\tau\epsilon\rho\epsilon\acute{\iota}\delta\eta$) against what falls together with it from the things outside". "Falling" is used to describe the activity of both the visual stream and the effluence, and "mutual pressure" to describe the effect of the impact (*Tim.* 45c). At 64e Plato says that the sight "hurls against" ($\pi\rho\sigma\beta\alpha\lambda o\hat{v}\sigma\alpha$) and "touches" ($\grave{\epsilon}\phi\acute{\alpha}\pi\tau\eta\tau\alpha\iota$) its object.

47. Cf. Liddell and Scott (above, n. 28), s.v. $\sigma\upsilon\gamma\kappa\rho\acute{\iota}\nu\omega$, $\sigma\acute{\upsilon}\gamma\kappa\rho\iota\sigma\iota\varsigma$, $\delta\iota\alpha\kappa\rho\acute{\iota}\nu\omega$, $\delta\iota\acute{\alpha}\kappa\rho\iota\sigma\iota\varsigma$.

48. *Tim.* 67e–68a. In this passage Plato does not mention pain, but at 64d–e Plato points out that in normal perception the penetration of the fire from without in *synkrisis* and *diakrisis*, though it might appear to be a cutting or burning, does not cause pain because it occurs without violence($\beta\acute{\iota}\alpha$)This is because the particles of the visual stream are so small. Only bodies made of larger particles that do not yield so readily suffer violence with the resulting sensation of pain. Thus the violent entry of particles

92

from "bright," "flashing" objects could be expected to cause pain. The speculation of F. M. Cornford, *Plato's Cosmology* (London: Routledge & Kegan Paul, 1935), p. 268, n. 1, that *Tim.* 64d–e refers to the effect of cuts, burns, and so on, on the visual stream outside the body finds no support in the text.

49. Aristotle and Theophrastus shed some additional light on the process involved. Both assume that white seen through a dark intervening substance will give the sensation of red. So the sun seen through smoke or mist appears red, and fire burning in black coals appears red (Arist. *Meteor.* 3.4.374a3–8; Theophr. *De Igne* 75).

50. Relative size enters into the theory, not only in the distinction between black and white, but in the depth of penetration. The most deeply penetrating particles are "sharper," a quality that increases as the size decreases (*Tim.* 78a; cf. 55e–56b). The slightly less penetrating particles that produce red are impeded by mixture with the much larger water particles.

51. Cf., e.g., the words for "touching" in *Tim.* 45d1, 64e3.

52. Cf., e.g., Democritus according to Theophr. *Sens.* 61–63 and Plato in *Timaeus* 61d–64d.

53. Epicurus states that the *eidola* convey the shape and the color of the object (*Ep. ad Herod.* 49). According to a scholiast he maintained in his book *Twelve Elements* that color changes according to the position |($\theta\acute{\epsilon}\sigma\iota\varsigma$) of the atoms (Usener [above, n. 8] p. 9; cf. his treatise *Against Theophrastus* fr. 30 [Usener, p. 102] and Lucretius 2.757–794, 810–825).

54. See above, note 4.

55. *De Anima* 2.6–7; *De Sensu* 3.439a6–440b25; 4.442a19–25; cf. R. Turnbull (above, n. 34), pp. 21–25.

56. *Col.* 1.791a13–b2 (For the reading of this corrupt text I have followed Gottschalk [above, n. 4], pp. 61–62). The examples are difficult to understand. I take it that the author is in all examples attributing the dark color to rough surfaces that reflect little light, even in the case of the cloud, although it may at first appear that the writer is attributing the cloud's dark color to its thickness and consequent non-transparency (cf. *Col.* 7.791a24–26). I believe there are three arguments in favor of such an interpretation: (1) $\delta\iota\grave{\alpha}$ $\tau o\hat{\upsilon}\tau o$ (line 24) and $\kappa\alpha\tau\grave{\alpha}$ $\tau\grave{\alpha}$ $\alpha\grave{\upsilon}\tau\grave{\alpha}$ $\delta\grave{\epsilon}$ $\tau o\acute{\upsilon}\tau o\iota\varsigma$ (line 25) suggest that the explanation for darkness in clouds, air, and water ought to be exactly the same as the darkness of the rough sea; (2) the succeeding lines (791a26–b1) state that the reason for the black color is the small quantity of reflected rays; and (3) at *Col.* 3.794a14–15 it is stated that dense air like dense water is white, not black. There is no inconsistency in the author's view if we understand 971a25–26 to be a qualification limiting the discussion to air and water when they are sufficiently dense that not all the light will pass right through, but some will be reflected, or, in other words, when air and water are regarded not as a medium of vision but as visible objects. In such cases the conditions of the surface may determine the color. A rough, thick cloud will be dark; a smoother one, white.

57. *Col.* 3.794a8–14. The text goes on to add that when the air or water is dense, rather than rare, it will be white instead of blue. This must be understood in the light of the statement immediately preceding the text under discussion. There the author states that white, translucent ($\delta\iota\alpha\phi\alpha\nu\acute{\epsilon}\varsigma$) substances, like air, water, and glass, appear airy when rare, but a mist ($\dot{\alpha}\chi\lambda\acute{\upsilon}\varsigma$) when dense, because the rays fail ($\alpha\grave{\upsilon}\gamma\hat{\omega}\nu$ $\dot{\epsilon}\kappa\lambda\epsilon\iota\pi o\upsilon\sigma\hat{\omega}\nu$) on account of the density and so we cannot see the interior clearly (*Col.* 3. 794a6–8). What he means is that air, water, and glass may be either transparent or opaque depending on their density. When air is rare and transparent one can see through it; but when it is dense and non-transparent, it will reflect light and be what we call a cloud ($\dot{\alpha}\chi\lambda\acute{\upsilon}\varsigma$). This is in agreement with Aristotle's view in *Meteor.* 3.3.372b34–373a2; 4.373a35–b10; 6.377b14–22. As a dense cloud it reflects light and is white

against the blue sky (though it may also be black as we learned earlier [cf. n. 56]).

58. The alternative is to imagine the rays of the sun proceeding from the sun into the air, but leaving the regions at a great distance from the sun unilluminated. But then the color becomes a function of the distance from the sun, whereas the text clearly makes the color depend on the distance of the observer (ὁ ἀήρ ἐγγύθεν μὲν θεωρούμενος, . . . ἐν βάθει δὲ θεωρουμένου).

59. There are some difficulties in this theory, notably the source of the light passing through the air. If it is from the sun, not only will the distance of the sun also affect the color (which the author could well have admitted), but a process of reflection will have to be incorporated, and this will then have to be harmonized with the author's notion that dense air reflects and rare air transmits light. But the treatise does not enter into these problems, and they do not, in any case, affect the underlying principle.

60. In addition to the text discussed above (*Col.* 3.794a8–14), the role of "strength" in determining color is stated at *Col.* 3.793a2–6, where the author claims light and shade differ quantitatively, so that mixtures of them with each other or with other colors will produce differences in color, either "because the ingredients differ in quantity and strength (δυνάμεσι) or because they do not have the same proportions." It is also implied in the discussion of compound colors, whose differences are due to the hue and quantity of the component colors (*Col.* 2.792a4–6). Weak (ἀσθενεῖς) rays of the sun, such as those in the sky at dawn and dusk or those that strike water at an angle, produce darker colors like purple (*Col.* 2.792a15–24). Again, wheras much (πολύ) light makes feathers appear bright red, less (ἐλάττονος) light makes them look grey-brown (*Col.* 2.792a24–28). The vocabulary of *Col.* 3.793b29–30 (ἐπικρατούντων) sheds further light on the author's presuppositions.

61. For black as deprivation or failure cf. *Col.* 1.791a12–13, b2–6 with *Meteor.* 3.4.374b12–14; cf. also *Phys.* 3.1.201a3–6; *Metaph.* 10.2.1053b30–32; 11.9.1065b10–11; *Sens.* 3.439b14–18; 4.442a25–26. For the correlation between the strength of light and the color cf. the texts discussed above (pp. 81–82 and n. 60) with *Meteor.* 3.4.374b11–15. 28–33, where the "weaker" or "less" the sight is, the darker the color will be (see above, pp. 78–79). For a full discussion of the relation of *On Colors* to Aristotle and Theophrastus see Gottschalk (above, n. 4).

62. For the concept of light mixing with and affecting substances see Epicurus, *Ep. ad Pyth.* 109; Lucretius 2.795–809; 4.72–83. Both the author of *On Colors* and Lucretius use the vocabulary of dyeing when talking of colored light and objects (cf. *Col.* 1.791a4–8; 2.793a19–33; *Lucr.* 2.734–36, 776–77. For the idea that there is no color without light see Epicurus, *Against Theophrastus,* according to Plutarch, *Adv. Colot.* 1110c (= Usener [above, n. 8] p. 102, fragment 29); and also Lucr. 2.795–98; for color varying with the angle of light cf. Lucr. 2.799–800; and for the discussion of the color of the sea and of feathers of birds cf. Lucr. 2.764–94, 801–7.

63. Von Arnim, *SVF,* vol. 2, no. 850.

64. Ibid., vol. 1, no. 151.

65. Ibid., vol. 1, nos. 58, 484.

66. Ibid., vol. 2, no. 56; see above, n. 32.

67. Von Arnim, *SVF,* vol. 1, no. 91.

68. Ibid., vol. 2, no. 54.

69. Ibid., no. 449.

70. Calcid. *In Tim.* 237 = von Arnim, *SVF,* vol. 2, no. 863.

71. Plutarch, *De Primo Frigido* 9.948d = von Arnim, *SVF,* vol. 2, no. 430. Plutarch here assigns the theory only to the Stoics in general; but when he returns to the theory later, he explicitly attributes it to Chrysippus (*Prim. Frig.* 952c–d = *SVF,* vol. 2, no. 429; cf. Plut. *Stoic. Repugnant.* 1053f = *SVF,* vol. 2, no. 429).

72. The Stoic theory will then be parallel to the Epicurean theory described by Calcidius in which the specific color sensation depends (at least in part) on the density of the films (*In Tim.* 236).

73. *De Anima Libri Mantissa,* 131.31–35 (Bruns) = von Arnim, *SVF,* vol. 2, no. 868.

74. It might seem that Zeno makes colors irreducible qualities of matter when he calls them "primary shapings" (cf. von Arnim, *SVF,* vol. 1, no. 91); but we would probably find that even he reduces them to a species of some other genus, since colors will have to be among the effects of the form-giving active principle upon matter (cf. von Arnim, *SVF,* vol. 1, nos. 85–88). The Peripatetic treatise *On Colors,* on the other hand, almost certainly makes the colors of objects irreducible qualities of the elements, at least in some passages; but this text presents special problems and must be considered separately (see above, pp. 80–84).

Heinrich von Staden

Chapter Four

THE STOIC THEORY OF PERCEPTION AND
ITS "PLATONIC" CRITICS

There has been a tendency in the history of philosophy to line up
the Stoics on the "Platonic-Aristotelian" side of most issues
(infinity, divisibility, continuum, number of worlds), while putting the Atomists on the opposite side.[1] There certainly is justification for this, and the selective integration of Stoic and Platonic
thought from Antiochus of Ascalon[2] to Plotinus[3] also points to a
significant kinship between Platonism and Stoicism. This affinity
makes it particularly intriguing that one of the major philosophical confrontations of the third and second centuries B.C. occurred between Stoics and leaders of the Platonic Academy. At
issue were not only ethical[4] and theological questions but especially the Stoic theory of perception. In this paper I shall argue
that this protracted epistemological battle illuminates fundamental respects in which Stoicism and Platonism are in fact
philosophically incompatible. (It might be objected at once that
the Platonists of this period, notably Arcesilaus and Carneades,
were not authentic representatives of the Platonic tradition but
skeptical revisionists who more than deserve the pejorative label
"New Academy"[5] and therefore should not be allowed to stand
as "Platonic" opponents of Stoicism. This is indeed a serious
objection, and it will be taken up below.) The paper is divided
into two main sections: (I) a brief exposition of the Stoic theory
of perception; and (II) an examination of the "Platonic" (New
Academic) criticism of this theory. (In neither section will
numerous related issues that do not bear directly on the main
argument be addressed.)[6]

I

In the dynamic materialism of the Stoics a human being is viewed as a continuum of constantly moving and changing pneuma, a mixture of air and fire that is capable of varying degrees of tension or tautness in its parts.[7] Central to this view is the Stoic conception of the psyche: it is a particularly taut, warm, dry part of the pneuma (i.e., corporeal, unlike the Platonic psyche). It is also innate, composed of fine particles, extended continuously through the entire body, and blended with the rest of one's pneuma. This elastic psyche is the principle of life and as such is responsible not only for one's procreative capacity, motions, drives, and speech, but also for all sensory and other cognitive functions.[8] It has a command center, *to hēgemonikon* or 'the part capable of leading/commanding', located in the heart. (The brain is explicitly denied any cognitive—or, for that matter, motor and affective—functions by most Stoics,[9] who in this respect, too, deviate from Plato.)

From this cardiac command center, which is at times identified with the dianoetic or thinking part of the psyche, the five 'senses' extend to the sense organs. Each of these 'senses' is a continuum of pneuma, capable of transmitting information about external objects back to the command center, performing best when more taut, but yielding murky data when slack.[10] An example of such transmission is analyzed in Professor Hahm's contribution, and I shall therefore pick up the cognitive process after relay of a datum back to the command center has been completed.

What is received through the senses in the command center is described by the Stoics as a *phantasia*, i.e., an 'appearing', 'becoming apparent,' or 'presentation'[11] of an external entity in the ruling part of the psyche. This presentation is an experience of being affected (*pathos*) that occurs in the command center and 'indicates' or reveals both itself and its external cause.[12] Sometimes it is also described as 'the making of an imprint' or 'impression' (*typōsis*) in the center.[13] Although not all Stoics interpret this making of an imprint the same way,[14] it is clear that all of them understood it to be an involuntary physiological event within a cosmic chain of determined processes, i.e., as an experience that does not lie within the percipient's power.

Not all sensory presentations have equal cognitive value or potential: some lead to a 'grasp' or 'apprehension' (*katalēpsis*) of what is presented,[15] whereas others do not. Presentations that render a grasp possible[16] are called *phantasiai kataleptikai*, those that fail to do so are *phantasiai akatalēptoi*. The notion of 'a presentation that makes apprehension possible'—'cognitive presentation' is Professor Sandbach's felicitous rendering[17] used in the remainder of this paper—is at the center of the epistemological controversy between the Stoa and the Platonic Academy and therefore merits closer scrutiny.

A well attested[18] Stoic definition of the cognitive presentation is: "A cognitive presentation is a presentation from an existing object and in accordance with the existing object itself, moulded and stamped in (sc. upon the command center of the psyche), of such a kind that it could not occur from an object that does not exist." Each part of this crucial definition requires some explication, especially since the translation offered here is unlikely to excite universal enthusiasm.

1.1. *Cognitive presentation.* Much depends upon the validity of this rendering of *phantasia kataleptikē*, and I therefore beg the reader's patience during a brief philological interval. It has been interpreted very differently: thus Eduard Zeller calls it *begriffliche Vorstellung*; Max Pohlenz, *Anschauungsbild*; J. M. Rist, 'recognizable presentation'.[19] If, however, *katalēpsis* is perceptual grasp or apprehension, as will be argued below, then *kataleptikos* would seem to mean 'making grasp possible',[20] 'apprehensive,'[21] or 'cognitive', i.e., to have primarily an 'enabling', active, not a passive sense (as in 'recognizable'). By contrast *kataleptos* means 'capable of *being* grasped' or 'apprehensible'. Verbal adjectives in -*tos* were increasingly reserved for passive use after the active, 'enabling' verbal adjectives in -*tikos* had been popularized by Aristotle;[22] an illuminating parallel is provided by the difference between *aisthēton*, 'capable of being perceived/sensed', and *aisthētikon*, 'capable of perceiving/sensing' or 'making perception/sensation possible'.

Taking a middle road, Sandbach and others have maintained

that *katalēptikos* is in fact ambiguous, having now an active, now a passive, sense.[23] Although 'deliberate ambiguity' is always a seductive explanation, it is also perhaps more insidious in philosophical than in literary contexts. The main evidence for a passive sense is said to be Cicero's renderings of *phantasia katalēptikē* as 'visum quod percipi posset' (a presentation that can be perceived) and 'visum comprehendibile' (an apprehensible presentation).[24] But (a) the extensive Greek sources do not provide conclusive support for this passive interpretation of *katalēptikos*, and (b) Cicero himself perhaps unwittingly reveals what I take to be his confusion about *katalēptikos* and *katalēptos* (would this be so surprising in a complex epistemological dialogue, *Academica*, written in perhaps no more than two or three months?).[25] Having called a cognitive presentation "comprehendibile", Cicero's strawman Varro asks: "Will you bear with these Latin coinages?", to which Atticus responds: "Indeed we will, for how else could you express *katalēpton?*"[26] In other words, the passive renderings in Cicero are inconclusive, because he is apparently not even trying to translate *katalēptikos* but rather *katalēptos*—which I too concede to be passive, but which has no legitimate place in the Stoic definition of cognitive presentation. *Katalēptos* is all the more glaring because Cicero often mentions Stoic concepts in Greek in the *Academica* (including *phantasia*, *akatalēptos*, *katalēpsis*, *kritērion*, *epochē*, *ennoiai*, *prolēpsis*, and *synkatathesis*, all of which belong in the same context as *katalēptikos*),[27] but never once *katalēptikos*.

Furthermore, as I shall argue below, while the cognitive presentation is something *of* which the percipient is also aware and *to* which he assents in the act of grasping, in the Stoic view it is the external object which is 'grasped.' If I am right on this controversial point, it would make little sense to call a presentation rather than an external entity 'graspable', 'apprehensible' or 'recognizable', and more sense to say that it 'enables a grasp' of a presented object to take place.

I.2. *From an existing object.* It has been pointed out that the Greek word translated as 'existing' here, *hyparchein*, has several interrelated meanings in Stoic usage, including 'to be the case' (i.e., 'to be true'), 'to exist', 'to be predicated' of a subject. That it means 'to exist' in this definition seems likely in the light of the Stoic statement that *to hyparchon* is "that which causes (sets in motion) a cognitive presentation" (Sextus Empiricus, *Adversus Mathematicos* VIII.85–86). Now whatever causes such a presentation must be a material body, because according to the Stoics only bodies can act or be acted upon; but since existence can be predicated of all bodies—and of them only— while 'being the case' or 'being true' can be said only of a proposition (which numbers among the incorporeals), therefore whatever causes a presentation must be something that exists.

Pierre Hadot has suggested, however, that *to hyparchon* here must be used in the sense 'is the case', which is normally predicated of a true proposition. According to Hadot it cannot designate the external ('existing') object presented in the control center, because "wenn es sich so verhielte, vermöchte man nicht recht einzusehen, woran es manche Vorstellungen (sc. *phantasiai*) mangeln könnte, um 'erfassende Vorstellungen' (sc. *phantasiai katalēptikai*) abzugeben," and because this would mean that Sextus was confusing the homonyms *hyparchein*, 'exist', and *hyparchein*, 'be the case'.[28] The second objection seems weak, especially inasmuch as one topos of skeptical refutation is the demonstration of internal contradiction or circular reasoning by juxtaposing propositions containing homonyms. (See I.5 infra for a fuller discussion of *hyparchein*.)

Let us test Hadot's first objection by asking, What indeed is it that characterizes a *non*cognitive presentation? It can be a presentation that is (a) not from an existing object (*tēn mē apo hyparchontos*); or (b) from an existing object but not corresponding to the existing object itself; or (c) not clear and not distinctly imprinted (Diogenes Laertius VII.46). Sextus seems to suggest that a presentation (d) from a nonexistent (*apo mē hyparchontos*) is another candidate for 'noncognitive' (*M.* VII. 249). If there is a distinction between (a) and (d), as the difference in word order suggests,[29] it might be that (a) refers to what Professor Rist (*Stoic Philosophy*, p. 137) has called a presentation derived "from what is not the existing object" (with the Stoics [Sextus, *M.* VII.244] I would add 'at the present moment',

t_1), whereas (d) refers to a presentation of, for example, a unicorn, which does not correspond to any external entity and, as I shall suggest in I.3, at t_1 is not triggered by one. Thus in case (a) a presentation x at t_1 *from* (*apo*) the existing (i.e., also present) object Emma might be mistaken for a presentation y *of* her (absent) 'identical' twin Ella.[30] Although Ella at t_1 is not the existing object *from* whom presentation x is transmitted to the percipient's command center, she is not a 'nonexistent' in the same sense as a unicorn, since she happens to be a trim and taut extension of animated pneuma, a real external entity, which the unicorn as a mere phantom or *phantasma*[31] of the mind is not. An existing object, Secretariat, might however have triggered a presentation of a nonexistent unicorn in an insane person, as I.3 infra suggests. The Stoic insistence on '*from*' (*apo*) is not fortuitous: a presentation must be *from* an existent (at t_1), not just *of* it, to be cognitive.

Furthermore, unlike many modern philosophers the Stoics seem to view the 'existence' of an external object as independent of its cognition. That its cognition conversely is dependent on its existence and presence and, moreover, cannot be disassociated from linguistic expression about it, is a different matter. (More on this problematic distinction between 'nonexistent' and 'not an existing object' in I.3 and I.5 infra.).

As (a), (b), and (c) indicate, that a presentation is from an existing object, though a necessary condition of a cognitive presentation, does not in itself render a presentation cognitive. This is also recognized in the next two segments of the definition, which provide a further response to the objection raised by Hadot.

I.3.   *In accordance with the existing object itself.* The Stoics' rationale for including this phrase in the definition is explained as follows (Sextus, *M.* VII.249):[32] "Some presentations do not resemble the existing object itself even though they are *from* an existing object." An example is provided by the mad Orestes: "While he did derive a presentation from an existing object, Electra, it did not correspond to the existing object itself, for he supposed that she was one of the Furies. . . . " This seems to

101

imply that if Orestes had experienced a presentation of a Fury not triggered by the presence of the existing Electra, it would have been called 'from a nonexisting object' and not 'from an existing object.' This further illuminates the significance of 'from' (*apo*) in I.2: although all Furies are nonexistents, presentation x_1 *of* Fury X can be '*from* an existing object' (Electra) whereas an 'identical' presentation x_2 *of* Fury X could be '*from* a nonexistent' (not even Electra is there). The Stoics sometimes call x_2 a *phantastikon*[33] or *phantasma*[34] arising from no 'presented' object or *phantaston*, but this kind of 'being affected' is often included among the presentations and becomes a standard part of the Stoic-Academic debate (cf. II.1 infra).

I.4. *Molded and stamped in upon* . . . This addition suggests that being from an existing object and corresponding to it are necessary but not sufficient conditions of a cognitive presentation. It must also reproduce "all the specific properties (*idiōmata*) of the presented objects with technical precision" (*technikōs*; Sextus, *M.* VII.250). Just as signet-rings always mould all their characteristics or *charaktēres* onto wax, so those who procure a grasp of substances[35] should apprehend them with all their specific properties (ibid., p. 251). If a presentation is to be cognitive, the correspondence between presentation and presented object must therefore be exact and comprehensive.

I.5. *Of such a kind that it could not occur from an object that does not exist.* This part of the definition seems to have been a relatively early[36] Stoic response to some of the Academic criticisms to be examined in part II. A fundamental tenet of Stoic philosophy is that every existing object is unique, that no two objects, whether 'identical' twins, two apparently identical eggs, two kernels of grain, or two strands of hair, are identical: "Omnia sui generis esse, nihil esse idem quod sit aliud" (Cicero, *Academica priora* II [*Lucullus*] 85). In order to be cognitive a presentation must therefore also be capable of communicating to the command center of the psyche the differences between the 'identical' twins Emma and Ella, and to do so with the technical precision referred to in I.4. If a presentation of Emma were indistinguishable from a presentation of Ella, it could not be a cognitive presentation, because it would not be transmitting the distinctive uniqueness of the presented object. But, say the Stoics, there are many presentations that do communicate the distinctive uniqueness of objects and that are accordingly distinguishable from all other presentations; and it is from such cognitive presentations that knowledge is derived.

This part of the definition does not let one off the hook quite that easily, however. It is commonly translated 'such as could not be derived from a nonexistent object', but, as I mentioned in I.2, Rist (p. 137) argues for 'of such a kind as could not come from what is not *that* existing object' (italics mine). Andreas Graeser[37] has objected to Rist's interpretation on the grounds that neither Sextus (*M.* VII.248–51) nor Cicero (*Ac.pr.*II.77) supports it. And indeed, (a) Sextus seems to say "of such a kind as could not be from a non-existing (object)," *apo mē hyparchontos*, not only in the passage to which Graeser refers but also in VII.402–3, VII.426, and in his *Outlines of Pyrrhonism*, II.4. (b) Cicero too seems to lend support to Graeser's objection, saying that "Zeno had the acute insight that no presentation could be perceived [i.e., could be cognitive; see I.1 supra] if a presentation from what is (*quod est*) could be of such a kind that one from *what-is-not* (*quod non est*) could be of the same kind." (c) Diogenes Laertius (VII.50) also seems to understand the clause this way, reading *apo mē hyparchontos*, 'from a non-existing (object).'

There does, however, also seem to be some evidence in support of Rist's interpretation, and my own interpretation of I.2 and I.3 is based on the—admittedly tentative and hesitant—conclusion that the Stoics found use for both of these interpretations.[38] The evidence for 'a nonexistent object' has been mentioned; that for 'not that existing object' must now be taken up.

First, our earliest source, Cicero, does not always use *ab eo quod non est*,[39] "from that-which-is-not," in this part of the definition of cognitive presentation, but more often uses the phrase *ex eo unde non esset*,[40] "from an object from which it does not come." This suggests that some ambivalence about 'nonexistent' (*quod non est*) and '(at t_1) not the existing object' (*ex eo unde non esset*) entered into I.5 of this definition at least as early as Cicero. Second, the difference between *tēn mē apo hyparchontos* (*phantasian*) and (*hē*) *apo mē hyparchontos* (*phantasia*) in Diogenes Laertius (VII.46 vs. VII.50) must not be overlooked. Even in the hands of Diogenes, Greek retains its capacity for nuance and precision, and the switch from *mē apo* to *apo mē* does not need to be frivolous or fortuitous. In the first passage we seem to have: "the presentation which [at t_1] is *not from* (the) existing object";[41] in the second: "the presentation which is *from* (the) *non*existing object"—in short, again perhaps the difference between Ella and unicorn. Third, the discussion of 'acataleptic' presentations (see I.2 *supra*) and madmen (I.3) suggested that there must be a distinction between acataleptic presentations that at t_1 are not from the existing object and those which are from nonexistents.[42]

Although one cannot be dogmatic about such problems, Cicero's vacillation between *quod non est* and *unde non esset* might ultimately be due to such a distinction between 'nonexistent' and 'not the existing object' at t_1. The confusion may have been compounded by the fact that the Stoics did not consistently and explicitly refer to time-at-which and percipient-for-whom in their discussions of 'existing' and 'not existing'. But the percipient is of course implied by the very concepts of presentation and imprint, and the t-factor is entailed by their use of 'exist' (*hyparchein*), since *hyparchein* can only be predicated of the present, not of past or future (for which *hyphestanai* is reserved).[43]

There is a further significant instance of vacillation in Cicero's rendering of I.5. Instead of a presentation 'such as could not be of the same kind (if) it came from an object from which it did not (actually) come' (Ella? *Ac. pr.* II.18) or 'such as could not be of the same kind (if) it came from a nonexistent' (unicorn? II.77), Cicero sometimes calls it a presentation 'from a true object (*a vero*), such that one from a false object (*a falso*) could not also be of the same kind' (ibid.). The switch within a single passage from 'existing' and 'not existing' object to 'true' and 'false' object, suggesting that 'true' and 'existing' could be used interchangeably (almost as though they provide an opportunity for rhetorical *variatio*), is puzzling because of the illuminating Stoic insistence elsewhere that 'true'[44] and 'false' can be said only of statements or propositions (*axiōmata*) which, although they somehow 'are', *qua* incorporeals are not existents. If true and false can be predicated of propositions but not of external entities, then 'existing' and 'true' are, strictly speaking, not interchangeable; what is worse, it would make no sense to talk of 'true *objects*' and 'false *objects*'.

I suspect that Cicero's application of 'true' and 'false' to external entities may be traced[45] to the Greek participle *hyparchon*. The problems that arise from its homonymy ('being the case': *verum*, and 'existing': *id quod est*; see I.2 above) are formidable, and as hasty a writer as Cicero may not always have been alert to the correct distinction. Furthermore, Seneca's famous complaint about the lack of a Latin word for the Greek *an-hyparxia* ('nonexistence')[46] suggests that the same Latin poverty extends to *hyparchon* and that this exercised additional pressures on its translator.

It is important to recognize, however, that *hyparchein* provides more than a homonymic link between significant discourse and material objects, inasmuch as a proposition that 'is the case' (*hyparchei*), though not 'existing' as a material object, does accurately describe a material object (or objects) that 'exists' (*hyparchei*) at a given time in a certain state. As the Kneales suggest, "the true proposition has a structure corresponding to a similar structure in the object described."[47] Only a presentation of an existing material object (*hyparchon*) can be expressed in a true proposition, i.e., in a statement of what is the case (*hyparchei*).[48]

This brings me to what appears to be an authentic Stoic use of 'true' and 'false':[49] the application of 'true' and 'false' not to propositions (legitimate) or to external objects (Ciceronian and questionable) but to presentations. Since presentations are part of a corporeal process—they are pneumatic alterations in the cardiac command center—a similar question arises, as members of the Platonic Academy were quick to point out: How can a corporeal affectation be 'true' or 'false' if 'true' and 'false' can be said only of an incorporeal proposition? Furthermore, what is the relation of a *true* presentation to a *cognitive* presentation, and conversely of a *false* to an *acataleptic* presentation?

First, the evidence. (a) Instead of rendering I.5 of the definition as 'of such a kind that it could not occur from what does not exist', several sources also attribute a different version, '*true* and of such a kind that it could not be *false*', to the Stoics.[50] Its authenticity has apparently been accepted by most, though not all, critics; as eminent a scholar as Professor Sandbach recently wrote: "At issue . . . was whether there were any cognitive presentations; *that is* whether there was any *true* presentation of such a nature that an identical one could not arise which was *false* . . . " (*The Stoics* [1975], p. 91; italics mine). Also outside the strict framework of the definition of a cognitive presentation, sources frequently report that the Stoics called presentations 'true' or 'false.' (b) According to Cicero, "Zeno claimed that some, but not all, presentations are false" (*De natura deorum* I.70; *SVF* I.63). (c) Aëtius confirms that this is Stoic: "Perceptions are true, but of the presentations some are true, others false" (*Placita* IV.9.4 = *Doxographi Graeci*, p. 396 = *SVF* II.78). (d) Plutarch twice attributes the use of 'false presentations' to Chrysippus.[51] Indirect, and perhaps less important, confirmation is provided by (e) the Stoicizing Antiochus, who says that he can agree to the Academic premise[52] that there are false presentations (*visa falsa*; Cicero, *Ac. pr.* II.41 and 83; *SVF* I.59); and (f) Saint Augustine who, probably relying on Cicero (*Ac. pr.* II.34), says that Zeno defined a cognitive presentation[53] as "tale (sc. visum) . . . quale cum falso (sc. viso) non haberet signa communia" (*Contra Academicos* III.ix.18).[54]

'True' and 'false' presentation therefore seems to have been an entrenched part of Stoic terminology, and the Stoics themselves justified this apparently anomalous use of 'true' and 'false' as follows: "True then are those (presentations) about which one can[55] make a true (affirmative) predication, such as, at the present moment 'it is day' or 'it is light'; false are those about which one can make a false predication, as 'the oar in the deep water is bent' or 'the porch tapers off to a thin point'. . . ." (Sextus, *M.* VII.244 = *SVF* II.65). This explanation reconciles the location of true and false in the *lekta* with the notion of veridical and nonveridical presentations, by making clear that the true, as that which is the case, is applicable to a presentation only when the presentation can be accompanied by a true proposition, i.e., by a statement in which the predicate asserted corresponds in sense and time ("at the present moment") to the state of the presented object being described—and such a correspondence is only possible if the presented object is in fact an existent in that state at t_1. The relationship of true statement to 'true' presentation is therefore similar to that of 'existing' (*hyparchon*) object and 'true' (*hyparchon*) proposition discussed above.

A question still not answered by this Stoic response to Academic criticism of their use of 'true' and 'false' is, however, that of the relation of a *true* presentation to a *cognitive* presentation.

That true presentation and cognitive presentation are not identical is clear from another part of the same account in Sextus (*M.* VII.242–48), which reports a Stoic[56] classification of presentations that can be schematized as in figure 1. In other

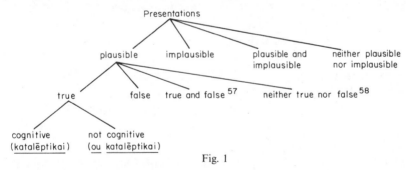

Fig. 1

words, although all cognitive presentations are true, not all true presentations are cognitive. (Cf. c. 247: "Of the true presentations some are cognitive, some not.") When a presentation is from an existing object and one can make a true predication about it, it is true; but in order to be cognitive as well, say the Stoics, it must induce a strong, assertive assent. If a subjective psychological or pathological condition such as melancholia causes a percipient not to make a positive affirmation and not to assent to a presentation, then even if it happens to be true

107

("occurs externally and fortuitously" as true, ibid.), it cannot be called cognitive.[59] It was perhaps the possibility of such deviant conditions, which sometimes render true presentations non-cognitive, that later gave rise to an addition to the definition of a cognitive presentation.

I.6. Later Stoics, perhaps again in response to Academic criticism,[60] argued that a cognitive presentation could serve as the criterion of truth only if one added the clause '*provided that it has no obstacle*' (Sextus, *M.* VII.253–7). There are cases, say these Stoics, in which a presentation fulfills all the conditions enumerated in I.1–I.5 above but remains disbelieved (*apistos*). Because of prior expectation and belief, a percipient might be disposed to distrust a presentation or fail to 'yield' to it and to accept it as valid. In such cases the presentation—even if it, strictly speaking, makes grasp *possible*, even if it is from an existing object, in accordance with the existing object itself, moulded and sealed in upon the command center, and is distinguishable from presentations that are either not from this existing object or from a nonexistent—will not be the criterion of truth (though it is technically 'cognitive'), because there is no assent to it and hence no apprehension of the presented object[61] and no corresponding action.

Although the obstacles (*enstēmata*) are described by Sextus as being due to external circumstances (*dia tēn exōthen peristasin*, ibid., c. 254), this is so only in a qualified sense, for the two examples he cites both refer to inhibiting or obstructing dispositions developed by the percipient him- or herself. (Perhaps 'external' is used in contradistinction to those 'internal' deviant conditions of a percipient that are pathological, e.g., delirium, melancholy, insanity; but then even 'reason' in a state contrary to nature is considered an 'external' obstacle.)[62]

This brief analysis of a cognitive presentation provides most of the necessary background to the Academic criticisms, and remaining elements of the Stoic theory of perception will therefore be presented in barest outline.[63]

First, although not all presentations are caused directly by existing external objects—some also occur in dreams, hallucinations,[64] and so on, others arise through mental activity[65]—it should be emphasized that Stoic psychology always retains a strong empirical bent. The mind at birth is like a 'sheet of paper well serviceable for writing',[66] with dispositional potentialities (see below) but no cognitive content, and the first presentations must be received through the senses. All mental activity is hence at least to some degree dependent upon sensory experience, and sensory presentations of the kind discussed in I.1–I.6 therefore always remained a cornerstone of the Stoic theory of cognition. In concentrating on presentations from sensibles in the preceding analysis rather than on 'rational' presentations, I accordingly followed the Stoic lead.

Second, the relation of cognitive presentation to 'higher' stages of cognition deserves brief mention. A presentation is followed by an assent to it (*synkatathesis*) or by a refusal to assent to it (this refusal could occur as *epochē*, suspension of judgment, or *hēsychia*, silence). Just when, how, and why an involuntary, physiological affectation (presentation) induces a voluntary mental act (assent) is a vexing question not answered satisfactorily by the extant sources.[67] One source suggests that a cognitive presentation without an obstacle, being evident (*enargēs*)[68] and striking (*plēktikē*), "virtually seizes us by the hair, dragging us off into assent, *requiring nothing else* to impress us as a presentation of this kind or to suggest its distinctiveness vis-à-vis other presentations" (Sextus, *M.* VII.257).[69] This sounds pretty involuntary from beginning to end,[70] but another source offers this view: "To these presentations which are, as it were, received by the senses, (Zeno) joins our minds' act of assent which he wants to be located in us and to be voluntary" (Cicero, *Ac. post.* I.40 = *SVF* I.60).[71] Intermediate between these extremes are milder but also vaguer formulations of the relation of presentation to assent, for example, " . . . Some presentations are cognitive in so far as they *induce* (*epagontai*) us to give assent" (Sextus, *M.* VII.405 = *SVF* II.67).

Though the sources provide frustratingly sparse information, they suggest that Chrysippus was acutely aware of problems concerning voluntary and involuntary inherent in this part of Stoic doctrine. He tried to solve them by resorting to two closely related distinctions: (1) between proximate (or antecedent or auxiliary) cause and ultimate (or principal or perfect) cause, and (2) between 'fated' and 'necessary' (cf. Cicero, *De fato* 39–45 = *SVF* II.974).[72] Assent, Chrysippus says, cannot take place unless it has been prompted by a presentation; but since this presentation has only a proximate, not a principal, cause, the assent too will have the presentation only as its proximate cause. In a characteristic Stoic simile Chrysippus tries to illustrate this point as follows: "Just as someone who pushes a cylinder forward gives it its beginning of motion (*principium motionis*) but not its ability to roll rapidly (*volubilitas*), so a presentation (*visum*) that has impinged (*obiectum*) will indeed impress and, as it were, stamp its appearance on one's mind, but assent will be in our power and, as was said in the case of the cylinder, though it has been given an impulse from without, for the rest it will move itself by its own power and nature" (ibid., c. 43).[73] Chrysippus accordingly concedes that a presentation is a proximate cause of assent (and hence that assent is part of the chain of fate), but not that this kind of cause has an assent as its necessary effect. Hence assent, though 'fated', remains in our power, inasmuch as it is not 'necessitated' (ibid., c. 44). To put it differently: although a presentation is a *conditio sine qua non*[74] and in that sense a 'necessary' condition of assent, it is not also a sufficient condition thereof. The Stoic principle of causality is hence maintained, but it is stripped of what they called 'necessity', and thereby a claim to voluntariness is reserved for assent. It is clear then that assent follows *upon*, and is usually *to*,[75] a presentation, and that it has a voluntary dimension—even though, like presentation, it is a corporeal, dispositional alteration in the heart (command center of the psyche).[76]

Not all assent is, however, assent to a cognitive presentation, for percipients also 'yield' or assent to unclear, false, and, generally, acataleptic presentations.[77] In such cases the assent is called precipitate, false, or weak;[78] and the act of assenting (*synkatatithesthai*) is an act of being precipitate, being deceived, opining, being in error, "missing the mark"[79] due to the percipient's lack of virtue.[80] Belief and error, in other words, are weak or false assent, usually to acataleptic presentations.

If an assent is to a cognitive presentation, it constitutes an apprehension or 'grasp' (katalēpsis, comprehensio) of the external object that is 'indicated' by the presentation.[81] Like presentation and assent, grasp occurs as a physical change of the command center; it is a disposition of the mind or ruling part.[82]

That the object of this grasp is an external object is not an undisputed view, and I adopted it only after some hesitation. Professor Sandbach rightly observes that there are "surprisingly few passages that explicitly state katalēpsis to have external reality as its object" (Problems, p. 21 n. 14), and argues that "grasp, apprehension, cognition, whatever we call it, is primarily of the presentation" and only "secondarily of the external object" (ibid., pp. 13–14). As I indicated above (in I.1), the passages on which this view relies are, however, first, a Ciceronian passage that reveals a fundamental misunderstanding on the part of Cicero, who seems to have confused katalēptos and katalēptikos, and, second, a passage from Augustine (n. 24) the value of which is compromised by the fact that he relied on Cicero.[83] Elsewhere (a) Cicero himself (Ac. post. I.42) makes unmistakably clear that it is in fact the external object that is 'grasped'. (b) In his section on Zeno, Diogenes Laertius likewise says without qualification that grasp, when it comes about directly through sense experience, according to the Stoics is "of white, black, rough, and smooth objects" (VII.52), i.e., of traditional Greek sense objects.[84] (c) Furthermore, in a discussion of the Stoic cognitive presentation, Sextus reports that "those who obtain a grasp of real objects (hypokeimena) should apprehend[85] all their distinctive characteristics" (M. VII.251). Finally, (d) in Ac. pr. II.23 we also find the phrase comprehensionem . . . rerum.[86] These four texts strongly suggest that the Stoics thought of external objects as primary, if not the only, objects of grasp or apprehension. This is not to deny that one is also aware of the cognitive presentation, which, after all, reveals both itself and the external object; but when assenting to such a presentation, one grasps the presented external object. The Stoics were, after all, as Bréhier suggested and Sandbach grants, interested in knowledge of external reality, not just in passing judgment on presentations.

It is significant that this grasp or apprehension is also called 'perception' (*aisthēsis*)[87] by the Stoics. That they used *aisthēsis*, a word traditionally reserved for elementary, sensory cognition, to designate veridical cognition is not only a reflection of their view that cognition is always rooted in sensory experience (despite our innate capacity to form general concepts, *prolēpseis*), but also a measure of their revalorization of the sensible world after its devaluation by Plato. This perceptual grasp, *aisthēsis* or *katalēpsis*, is after all valid and 'true',[88] even though (a) it is not of Ideas or Forms but of sensible bodies (*sōmata*);[89] (b) its instrument is a sense organ (*aisthēterion*);[90] (c) its assent is usually to a sensory presentation (*aisthētikē phantasia*);[91] and (d) it is itself a *physical* state of the command center. Because *aisthēsis* (*qua* perception) is always veridical, reason, thought, and knowledge can and do depend upon it. If one considers, in addition, the ontological concomitant of this epistemological revaluation of *aisthēsis*—viz., that all reality including even the *psychē* and its ruling part, mind, is corporeal (incorporeals like *lekta*, void, place, and time admittedly also somehow 'are,' but they are not 'real')—then it becomes even clearer that the Stoics' identification of *aisthēsis* with *katalēpsis* and their ascription of cognitive reliability and validity to this common perceptual act that is accessible not only to the divine Wise Man but to Jack and Jill too, constitutes a radical departure from Platonism.[92] It is against this fundamental Stoic deviation from the Platonic course that members of the Platonic Academy seem to have directed some of their criticism.

II

Much of the "Platonic" criticism focuses on the Stoic claim that cognitive presentations are reliable because (*per definitionem*, I.5 *supra*) they are 'of such a kind that they could not be from an object that does not exist' or 'true and of such a kind that they could not be false'. The Skeptics of the Platonic Academy, of whom Arcesilaus (ca. 316–241 B.C.) and Carneades (ca. 190–129 B.C.) are best known,[93] argue just the contrary: that no presentation is found of such a kind that it could not be false, and hence that there are no cognitive presentations.

If a criterion of truth does exist, says Carneades, it must lie in being affected by, or having a *pathos* of, evidentness (*enargeia*).[94] This affection must furthermore display or 'indicate' both itself and the thing that caused it (Sextus, *M.* VII.160–61). Carneades agrees with the Stoics that only presentation (*phantasia*) could meet these requirements and must therefore be the foundation of any viable epistemology (ibid., 161–63). He also agrees that although there are some true presentations,[95] not *every* presentation could be a criterion since a presentation at times, "like a bad messenger," is misleading or at a discrepancy "with those things which despatched it" (ibid., c. 163). And such a presentation, being false, cannot, of course, be a source of perceptual grasp.

Up to this point Carneades' argument makes use, in characteristic Socratic-Platonic fashion, of premises that are also acceptable to his opponents, and indeed he is willing to concede all but one (I.5 supra) of the premises implicit in the Stoic definition of cognitive presentation.[96] Whereas the Stoics claimed not only that each external entity has its own distinctiveness—it is *sui generis* and *nihil est idem quod sit aliud*—but also that this distinctiveness is transmitted to a percipient with technical precision (see I.4 supra) by a cognitive presentation, Carneades argues as follows (Sextus, *M.* VII. 402–3; 164):

> Presentations arise also from objects that do not exist just as from existing ones. And proof of the *indistinguishability* (*sc.* of these two kinds of presentations) is that they are found evident and striking to an equal degree; and proof, in turn, that they are striking and evident to an equal degree is that corresponding consequent actions are joined to them. . . . There is no true presentation of such a kind that it could not be false but, for every presentation that seems true, a false presentation is found to exist which is *indistinguishable* from it.[97]

It is therefore *not* the Stoic assertion that there are presentations that report objects or facts correctly that is challenged,

as Brochard suggests, but the Stoic claim that such presentations can be recognized as reliable and 'cognitive' by a percipient.
Omnis pugna, Cicero says, is about the immediate identifiability
versus indistinguishability of true and false presentations, and
it is on this aspect of the Stoic-'Platonic' controversy that my
analysis will accordingly concentrate.

Arcesilaus and Carneades had recourse to several sets of
'false' but nonetheless apparently and evidently 'true' presentations to illustrate their point about indistinguishability (*aparallaxia*). I have singled out four for closer scrutiny.

II.1. In a first group of examples the Academics discuss
presentations experienced by a percipient in a psychological or
physiological state that deviates from normal perceptual conditions, e.g., in dreams, ecstasies, deliria, insanity, and hallucination.[98] In these states a percipient (a) experiences presentations
from nonexistent objects (e.g., unicorn); or (b) presentations
without any *immediate* external cause (i.e., from what at t_1 is
not an existing object for the percipient, as, in a dream, a presentation of quenching my thirst at the Arethusa spring); or (c) he
involuntarily distorts whatever presentations he has from existing present objects (e.g., the mad Heracles receiving a presentation from his own children, who are present at t_1, as though
they were those of Eurystheus, who are not present).[99] In the
Stoic view these presentations must be acataleptic (see I.2 and
I.3 supra). Yet, says Carneades, to the percipient they often seem
as evident and striking as any cognitive presentation, and the
percipient accordingly assents to them and, what is worse, acts
upon them (e.g., Heracles actually kills what *manifestly appear*
to be his enemy's children but *are* in fact his own). To claim
that the intrinsically evident distinctiveness of cognitive presentations induces assent does not help the percipient's effort to
distinguish between reliable and unreliable presentations if,
for the percipient, noncognitive presentations are indistinguishable from cognitive ones in 'appearance', evidential impact, and
immediate effect (i.e., assent and action).

The Stoics could presumably have replied that they were
aware of cases of false assent and had accounted for these in

their explanations of belief, error, and ignorance.[100] They could furthermore claim that they covered such instances by including in their classification of presentations (see fig. 1) plausible or persuasive presentations, some of which are explicitly said to be false (i.e., those about which one could make a false predication), and others to be 'both true and false' (see note 57 for examples). The Stoics did, in other words, acknowledge that only *some* plausible presentations are also true, and even that only *some* true presentations are in turn also cognitive. Later Stoics could, moreover, emphasize (a) their acceptance of the obstacle clause (I.6 supra) in their treatment of the cognitive presentation as criterion, and (b) their insistence that no link may be missing or impaired in the cluster of five things that must concur for cognitive presentation to occur (sense organ, sense object, space, disposition, and mind; Sextus, *M.* VII.424; *SVF* II.68).[101] They had said (I.6) that if even only one of these elements is missing or not functioning normally (e.g., Heracles' mad mind), perceptual grasp would not be preserved—and all of this, the Stoics might claim, more than takes care of the 'Platonic' examples of mad Heracles or a dream vision of quenching my thirst.

Such responses are, however, unlikely to be considered adequate by the Academic Skeptics. Although the Academics do not quarrel with the need for concurrence, coherence, and verification—on the contrary, Carneades' three stages of probabilism incorporate these notions[102]—or with the Stoic distinctions between plausible/implausible and true/false presentations *per se*, they do insist on asking, How could the perceiving subject, at the very moment of having presentation *x*, recognize it with certainty as 'true'? Hence the critical emphasis on equal intensity or evidentness, and on the Stoic claims about the *intrinsic* distinctiveness of a cognitive presentation.

II.2. In a second argument for indistinguishability the Academic Skeptics turn from the subjective experience of presentations to examples that, in their view, also illustrate more 'objective' obstacles to a true perceptual grasp of external entities. In these instances the presentations are from existing objects that are different in substance (*hypokeimenon*)[103] but

115

similar in form (*morphē*). A favorite example is that of some eggs, say, A, B, and C, that seem to be exactly alike (i.e., their presentations *a*, *b*, and *c* are indistinguishable). They are offered to the Stoic Wise Man for inspection—if then shown just egg A, "will he be able to say with infallibility whether it is this one or that one?", i.e., to tell apart A, B, and C 'cataleptically', solely on the basis of *a*, *b*, and *c* (Sextus, *M.* VII.409)? Will *a*, which happens to be 'true' because its cause A is visible and present at this moment, have a distinctive, intrinsic peculiarity (*idiōma ti*, ibid., c. 411) so evident that the Wise Man could recognize that it differs from *b* (which is noncognitive because B at present is not being shown)? The Academic answer is, of course, no. Similar arguments are derived from 'identical' twins, Castor and Polydeuces, a hundred 'identical' seals imprinted in wax by the same signet-ring, a hundred 'identical' copies of Lysippus' bronze bust of Alexander the Great (Cicero, *Ac.pr.* II.85–86), and from the notorious Megarian 'Veiled Argument' (i.e., many different snakes of similar appearance in turn poke their heads out of a snake hole; who could tell them apart? Sextus, *M.* VII.410).

At issue here are, significantly, not deviant *subjective* conditions as in II.1. Instead of a madman or a dreamer, we have that paragon of cognitive ability, the Stoic Wise Man. But even he is said to face considerable problems whose roots lie in the very nature of experienced reality: different particular substances can cause not only similar but indistinguishable presentations also in the most discriminating percipients.

It is important to remember that, in the empirical psychology of the Stoics, presentation and grasp are in the first place of objects as particulars, not of objects as kinds. Thus a cognitive presentation of Emma would in the first instance entail that she be apprehended infallibly as a particular substance, distinct from her 'identical' twin Ella (cf. I.4 supra). Cognition of objects as kinds[104] must be preceded by, and is dependent upon, cognition of sense objects as particulars, despite our innate dispositional capacity to form general or 'natural' concepts that operate discriminatingly upon perceptual data and test them for coherence and for generalizable elements. "The first manner of inscrib-

ing (sc. upon the so-called *tabula rasa*) is through the senses"
(Aëtius, *Placita* IV.11.2 = *Dox. Gr.* p. 400; *SVF* II.83); "all
thinking proceeds from perception or not without perception,
. . . and as a universal rule it is impossible to find anything in
conception which one does not possess as known by direct
experience" (Sextus, *M.* VIII.56, 58; *SVF* II.88; cf. p. 87). Given
this dependence of other stages and forms of cognition upon the
sensory perception of particulars, the Stoic theory stands or falls
with its assertion of the individual perceptibility of external
entities *qua* distinctive particulars.[105]

It is perhaps significant that the Academics do not argue that
the identical appearance or 'form' (*morphē*) of eggs A, B, and C
or of the Peel twins Emma and Ella or of the snakes cannot be
grasped, nor that one *infima species* of snake cannot be distinguished from another. The form of these plural substances is
in each set identical and distinctive, and hence also distinguishable; it is the individual particulars of a subspecies or species
that are different yet often indistinguishable. This distinction
between one 'specific' form, which does not cause epistemological problems, and 'indeterminate' plural particulars,
which do, is intriguing in the light of Plato's view that only the
eidos qua unity is knowable, whereas the plurality subsumed
under the *eidos* cannot be truly known, not even individually.[106]
I am far from suggesting that Plato's theory of Forms is being
retained here or that the New Academic distinction between
unity of form and plurality of corporeal substances is, in this
form, authentically Platonic. But it does not seem farfetched
to suggest that a strong epistemological residue of Plato's view
of the epistemic relation of corporeal particulars to generic or
universal form might be operative in this Academic criticism
of the Stoic theory.[107]

II.3.   The nature not only of percipients but also of the sensible world is again at issue in a further set of Academic examples aimed at illustrating the indistinguishability of cognitive
and noncognitive presentations. The nature of the *qualities* of
sense objects, it is argued here, precludes sensory presentations
from being cognitive.

117

According to the Academic Skeptics the qualities of sensible objects are not apprehensible, because they are subject to constant change. Not even color, the proper object of the sense traditionally said to enjoy primacy among the senses (i.e., sight),[108] can be grasped, "for *it changes* according to seasons, activities, natures, ages, circumstances, diseases, health, sleeping, and waking, so that though we recognize that it is variable in this way, we are ignorant of what in truth it is" (Sextus, *M.* VII.413; this also involves changes in the percipient, to which I return below). These sensible qualities are central to the Stoics' theory of perception—they say, for example, that perception (*aisthēsis*) is of *white* and *black* objects[109]—and the Stoics therefore insist on their apprehensibility. If the Academics are right in claiming that the flux character of these qualities renders them noncognible, the Stoic position would be seriously undermined.

About the Platonic provenance of this New Academic view of sensible qualities being in flux and 'confused' or 'indistinguishable' there cannot be much doubt. Although Plato, especially in his later dialogues, seems to have recognized that extreme 'fluxism' is undesirable and might even entail aphasia and apraxia,[110] the Academic Skeptics could in good conscience claim that their argument is based on authentic Platonic ontology, i.e., on the view that the phenomenal world is characterized by motion and change, and hence is not truly knowable.[111] (It might be objected that the New Academics, having abandoned the theory of Forms, as it seems,[112] were left to defend the worst part of Plato's heritage—a submathematical sensible world that permits only very elementary and provisional forms of cognition—but this does not affect the Platonic legitimacy of their characterization of sensible qualities.)

It is, however, not primarily the Academic reassertion of flux that presents a challenge to the Stoic theory of perception. The material continuum of the Stoics is, after all, itself not static but in flux: *hylē* and *sōmata* are in flux (*reustos*), subject to alteration (*alloiōtos*), and liable to change (*treptos, metablētos*) throughout their extension.[113] Furthermore, this change or alteration is specifically said by the Stoics to occur by transformation of qualities.[114] The disagreement then is instead about the epistemological consequences that follow from this flux theory.

Under what might be more than vestigial Platonic pressures the Academic Skeptics still operate with an ideal of knowledge— now no longer regarded as realizable—that requires stability, immutability, and permanence of knowledge *and* of the objects of knowledge. Since they find no such objects in the absence of Forms,[115] they resolve the relation of cognition to the phenomenal world—and of ethics to *aisthēsis*—by resorting to probabilism, which, given Plato's affection for 'likely' (*eikōs* and *eikotōs*) in the *Timaeus* and elsewhere,[116] is perhaps not the worst heresy a Platonist could have committed in the wake of the aporetic ending of the *Theaetetus*.

The Stoics too retain central aspects of the Platonic ideal: knowledge is secure, firm, not subject to change or falsification (see note 92); yet they make perception (which *per definitionem* is veridical) of individual material objects in constant flux a cornerstone of their epistemology. How could they answer the Platonic objection that change precludes true cognition? Are all of the problems raised by Plato, for example, in the course of refuting the first major hypothesis of the *Theaetetus* (knowledge is sense perception) by means of Heraclitean flux and Protagorean *mensura*, now resolved definitively by Stoic empiricism?

The Stoics could point, first, to their distinction[117] between the very rare *knowledge* of the Wise Man, which is secure, immutable, and incontrovertible, and Everyman's perceptual *grasp*, which, although veridical at the moment, is subject both to further testing for coherence and to further mental processing into cohesive clusters of percepts, which in turn are a basis for generalization. (The omnipresence of an immanent Logos is what ultimately makes flux and knowledge compatible—but this would lead us astray.)

Second, they introduced the time factor, which the New Academics (like Plato) could not reconcile with true cognition because of their insistence on the supratemporal or atemporal quality of knowledge and its objects. The Stoics by contrast emphasize that one can predicate 'true' of a cognitive presentation or of a perceptual grasp—or make a true statement about an existing object—only at the present moment and in the present tense.[118] This does not reduce the cognitive value of perceptual grasp, because under the circumstances prevailing at t_1, it remains a valid, veridical grasp of an existing object, expressible in a statement that 'is the case'. That Martha is presented cataleptically as beautiful at t_1 and cataleptically as ugly at t_2 does not bother the Stoic, because he can produce a true proposition 'Martha is beautiful' at t_1, and then again at t_2 a true proposition 'Martha is ugly'; but the Platonist wants to know 'what is (*ti esti*) Martha really and truly?', and different answers at different times will not satisfy him. (That is why, in the early Academy, he resorts to unchanging Forms, of which Martha partakes; cf. Plato, *Republic* 523–24.)

A third component of the Stoic position tries to meet a different aspect of the challenge posed by flux: the flux to which the qualities of the percipient himself are subject (and the relativity associated with changes in the percipient due to age, climate, health, disease, and so on). Later Stoics try to resolve this problem through the obstacle clause (I.6 supra) and the associated notions of 'normality' or 'naturalness';[119] also, the *subjective* conditions of perception (sense organs, disposition, reason) must be in unimpaired natural order for a cognitive presentation to serve as criterion of truth (II.1 and I.6 supra). In an argument possibly derived from the Academics and again strongly reminiscent of arguments used by Plato,[120] Sextus suggests that this is an impossibility, generally because of many internal and external circumstances that generate incessant change in a percipient, and specifically because of constant change in a percipient's 'sensory passages'. If constant change in the perceiver is conceded—as it is by both parties—then at what moment in time and under what circumstances should the organs of perception be considered *normal*?[121] Correspondingly, if there is a direct correlation between 'normal' and 'reliable', is it at t_1 or t_2 or t_3—at each of which the sensory channels are 'different'—that they transmit information reliably? And, to return to II.1, how does a changing percipient distinguish presentations transmitted by organs in a 'natural' state from other presentations? The upshot of these *aporiai* is that "although one could say that such a thing is appearing by this particular sense in this particular circumstance, we cannot ever have an authoritative guarantee that it is in truth such as it also appears, or is of one sort but appears to be of another" (Sextus, *M.* VII.424-25).

Plato's requirement that whatever is known must be knowable and predicable in and of itself, *kath' hauto*, and not relative to other things, *pros ti*, cannot be met easily by a theory which, like the Stoics', makes a *Platonic* ideal of knowledge dependent upon, and in part identical with,[122] veridical perception of sensible particulars which, like their percipients, are in constant flux.

II.4. Classic examples of sensory illusion, confusion, and limitation provide the Academic Skeptics with a further challenge to Stoic claims about the identifiable distinctiveness of a cognitive presentation. Thus the smooth surface of a painting can also be made to have an apparently rough texture by an artist; a tower in a distance appears now round, now square; when partially in water, an oar appears bent, when out of it, straight;[123] trees seem stationary when viewed from a stationary position but in motion when viewed from a moving vehicle;[124] conversely, the sun is conceptually 'presented' as traveling with inconceivable velocity (in a geocentric cosmology) but nevertheless at t_1 appears to us to be standing still.[125] Although these examples do not, strictly speaking, all fall in the same category,[126] for the Academics they illustrate a further type of indistinguishability, which has its roots in the general cognitive inadequacy of the senses even of a sound and alert percipient. (Note that this is different from the preceding types of indistinguishability that are rooted in exceptional subjective states [II.1 supra], in the phenomenal indistinguishability of individual substances as opposed to form [II.2], and in the flux and corporeality that encompass all subjective and objective reality [II.3]; but that it has in common with II.1-3 a problem faced by the percipient: how to *distinguish*[127] between equally evident presentations that are not all cognitive.)

That the fundamental perceptual inadequacy of the senses is

121

at issue is also suggested by Cicero's discussion, in the context of some of these examples, of the inaccuracy and limited range of human vision. The telescopic vision of a legendary figure, Strabo, provides a measure of just how weak our vision usually is: Strabo could see an object 1,800 stades (slightly more than 205 miles) away, which, says Cicero (*Ac.pr.* II.81), is not even a record since certain birds can see farther. From a promontory on the southern coast of Sicily, Capo Boeo (then Lilybaeum), Strabo could see the Punic fleet sailing from Carthage (Libya) —and he even reported the exact number of ships correctly![128] This reveals how rotten the visual capacity of the average person is.

How then can a faculty that, because of its intrinsic inaccuracy and weakness, often transmits vague, misleading, or contrary (but equally 'evident') presentations to the command center, function as a cornerstone not only of cognitive presentation but also of all other stages and forms of cognition?

The Stoics, of course, agree that absolute certainty is not always possible in each particular case and argue that *hēsychia* or *epochē*, silence or suspension of judgment, not assent, would be the appropriate response when faced with genuine phenomenal indistinguishability, whatever its cause.[129] Some Stoics also seem to have stressed the need for repeated 'attentiveness' and for verification in the case of a dim (*amydra*) presentation of a real object (Sextus, *M.* VII.258). Gerard Watson has furthermore argued persuasively that the very act of assent involves some form of comparison and that the ordering operation of *prolēpseis*, or universal concepts, upon percepts entails the principle of coherence, as do the resulting articulations.[130] This is perhaps why some Stoics also called *prolēpsis* a criterion.[131] But the Academics zero in on the Stoic claim that the cognitive presentation itself has *intrinsic* qualities that permit it to function as a criterion of truth, and not on the Stoic view of the *relation*[132] of a cognitive presentation to other 'criteria', such as general concepts, knowledge, and right reason. It is not the integration of a new presentation into an already established body of information that is at issue, but the identifiability of a cognitive presentation per se.

The New Academic emphasis in II.4 supra on the inadequacy
and unreliability of our senses is again authentically Platonic.
Thus in the *Republic* Socrates and Glaucon, warming up for a
discussion of mathematics and dialectic, agree on the insuffi-
ciency of the senses (and also touch significantly upon the
contrary qualities of sensibles [II.1] and their equal evidentness
[II.1–4]):

> Some things urgently demand that thinking do the examining
> because sense perception produces no sound result.
> Obviously, he said, you mean things appearing at a distance and
> perspective paintings.
> You didn't quite get my meaning, I said.
> What kind of thing do you mean then? he asked.
> Those things . . . which at the same time pass (from one percep-
> tion into the opposite perception) I call 'summoning help', because
> sense perception fails to make *clear* 'this' more than its opposite,
> regardless of whether it comes upon the subject from a distance or
> nearby. But from this you'll see more clearly what I mean—here,
> we agree, are three fingers, the little, the second, the middle.
> Right, he said.
> . . . But now, does sight *adequately* see their largeness and
> smallness, and does it make no difference to it whether a finger
> lies in the middle or on the outside? And similarly touch, with re-
> gard to thickness and thinness or softness and hardness? Don't
> the other senses also make such things clear *deficiently*? In fact,
> each of them produces these results. . . . Won't the sense assigned
> to 'hard' perforce also be assigned to 'soft', and doesn't it report to
> the psyche that one and the same thing it perceives as both hard
> and soft?
> Yes, that is so, he said.
> Then, said I, won't the psyche necessarily be at a loss (*aporein*)
> about just what this perception signifies as the hard, since it says
> the same thing is also soft . . . ?[133]

In several other passages Plato also scores the inadequacy of
the senses as a source of insight,[134] while not denying them
a 'triggering' role in *anamnēsis*[135]—as little as the New Academics denied that whatever limited cognition one does gain is
dependent upon the reception of plausible sensory presentations.
More often than not Plato also links this inadequacy to the
nature of sensible objects (as did the New Academics in II.2–3

supra). But this does not prevent Plato from giving an account of the genesis and structure of the phenomenal world and of our sensory apparatus by resorting to a 'likely story' (*eikōs logos, eikōs mythos*) in his *Timaeus*—as little as Arcesilaus' aporetic skepticism seems to have prevented him from resorting to the 'reasonable' (*eulogon*)[136] as a criterion for dealing with the phenomenal world, and as little as Carneades' rejection of the Stoic brand of empiricism inhibited him from resorting for his criterion to a 'plausible' (*pithanē*) presentation that, in optimal cases, is also tested for contradiction, concurrence, and genetic context.[137]

Aparallaxia, the evidential or phenomenal indistinguishability on which the New Academy harps, is not a word used by Plato; but, as suggested in II.1–4, key elements of the Academic argument are derived from Plato's view of perception. In addition to Platonic texts already mentioned, other famous passages exemplify the extent to which some New Academic arguments were in essential respects preformed by Plato. I mention only a few to buttress this point: (a) *Phaedo* 78d10–79c8: the many beautiful things that are perceptible by the senses are always in a state of change, are "never and in no way (*oudepote oudamōs*; emphatic) identical with themselves or one another" and hence not distinctively or indistinguishably discernible. What is visible is in change, and hence cannot be the object of true cognition. When the psyche perceives through senses, it is "dragged by the body into the region of the things that are never the same and . . . wanders and is confused; and her head spins as though she were drunk, when she touches change." A pretty pessimistic picture compared with the Stoics' sanguine assessments! (b) *Symposium* 210e2–d1: in Diotima's description of the passage of the true initiate to a sudden vision of an amazing beauty marked by eternal being, by self-identity, by simplicity, and by incorporeality, the phenomenal world the initiate leaves behind is characterized *inter alia* as "in one way beautiful, in another ugly; at one time beautiful, at another not; in one relation beautiful, in another ugly; at one place beautiful, at another ugly; as if to some people beautiful but to others ugly" (211a2–5). Again, it is the change of sensible qualities into their opposites that precludes them from having that stable distinctiveness demanded by Platonists of knowable objects. (New Academic arguments based on this aspect of Plato's philosophy are, of course, elaborations growing out of a Hellenistic context, e.g.: because characteristically at t_1 Joe will have a presentation x_1 from an existing person X that 'X is beautiful' but at t_2 a presentation x_2 from X that 'X is ugly' and, moreover, because x_1 and x_2 are *indistinguishable* both in terms of evidence and in terms of inducing assent and action, therefore presentations from X cannot serve Joe as a criterion of truth.) (c) In the *Republic* (V.478e7–480a12) Socrates, arguing for the absoluteness and knowability of the one, induces Glaucon to concede the relativeness of the many, which allow only belief, not knowledge. The opponent of the theory that there is only one idea of beauty, says Socrates, will be asked:

> Of these many beautiful things, kindly tell, noble sir, if there is any one which will not appear (*phanēsetai*) ugly? And of the just, which will not appear unjust? Or of the holy, not unholy?
> No, he said, they inevitably appear (*phanēnai*) both beautiful in some way and ugly, and so on in all the other cases you ask about.
> But how about the many things 'twice the size'? Do they appear (*phainetai*)[138] any less to be half than twice the size?
> Not at all.
> . . . Then in the case of each of these many things 'is' it more than it 'is not' whatever one says it is?
> They are like those ambiguous riddles (asked) at dinner parties or like the children's riddle about the eunuch. . . . (479a5–b12).

This conclusion is similar to that reached in *Republic* VII.523c1–2: "*aisthēsis* in no respect reveals this more than its opposite"; and it is this ambiguity and indeterminacy associated with sensibles that, also in the New Academic view, disqualify them from being objects of true, secure cognition. (d) In the 'secret doctrine' introduced by Socrates at *Theaetetus* 155d9 ff., it is said that everything becomes and becomes relatively to something else: "Hard and hot and so on . . . are not anything in themselves . . . but all of them of whatever kind come to be by means of change in their meetings with one another . . . " (156e7–157a2). From all this follows that one may not legitimately use the terms 'something', 'somebody's', 'mine', 'this',

125

'that', nor any other word that implies stability, of the perceptible world (157b2-5). And for the Platonist stability is essential
to true cognition. (Again, that what seems to be 'this' perceptible
object at t_1 becomes 'that' one at t_2 can be accommodated by
Stoic epistemology but not by the Platonic model in which the
Academic criticism is rooted.) (e) Even the *Timaeus*, for all its
emphasis on the ways and senses in which changing things can
be apprehended and talked about, still reasserts (28a1-4): "That
which is apprehensible (*perilēpton*) through thought accompanied by reason (*logos*) is being (*on*) that is always the same,
whereas that which is opinable (*doxaston*) through belief accompanied by unreasoning *aisthēsis* becomes and passes away
but never is really being (*on*)." So too 49c7-d3: "Since these
things indeed in this way never singly become apparent (*phanta-
zomenōn*) as the same things, which of them can one firmly and
confidently affirm to be 'this'—whatever it is—and not something
else, without embarrassing oneself? It is impossible . . . " (cf.
49e2-4). The first hypothesis of the *Parmenides* suggests
that some of these arguments go back to the Eleatics, but it is
from their Platonic father that the New Academics seek sanction.

The skepticism of Arcesilaus and Carneades is then neither
aphasic nor as radically and consistently self-referential as that
of Sextus.[139] Their arguments are, as their critic Antiochus apparently said, the weapons "of persons who are confident that
what they are defending is in fact true and firm and certain."[140]
Although the suggestion that their aim was more aporetic than
skeptical[141] is not without merit, one should not overlook the
fact that these Academics not only (true to the parasitical tradition of Skepticism) accepted many tenets of the Stoic theory[142]
—even a central term of skepticism, *epochē*, is expropriated from
the Stoics[143]—but also have a distinct view of the nature of the
material world and of its knowability.

If the New Academy's view of the phenomenal world is
Platonic in key respects, so are its methods: the use of Stoic
endoxa for an immanent critique that reveals internal inconsistency or contradiction; *in utrumque partem disserere*; *ou
mallon*[144] and *isostheneia*; *epagogē*; *reductio ad impossibile*,

and so on. Gilbert Ryle, Paul Moraux, and others have argued that these and similar methods were formalized in the dialectical theory of the early Academy as reflected especially in Aristotle's *Topics*,[145] and H. J. Krämer has offered detailed, subtle analyses of their use in the New Academy (*Hellenistische Philosophie*, esp. pp. 14–58).

By using these "old" methods, and by using arguments that reveal a fundamental incompatibility between the Platonic[146] view of the material world and a theory that, like the Stoics', makes material entities its epistemological and ontological cornerstone, the New Academy restored to philosophy a critical function that, as one recent critic observed, "it was in danger of losing."[147]

I am indebted to Professors Paul Eisenberg, David Glidden, David Hahm, Edward Lee, Margaret Reesor, Wilfrid Sellars, and Robert Turnbull for comments on an earlier draft of Part II.

1. More recently, e.g., David J. Furley, *Two Studies in the Greek Atomists* (Princeton, N.J.: Princeton University Press, 1967), p. v.

2. See G. Luck, *Der Akademiker Antiochus von Askalon* (Bern: P. Haupt, 1953), especially pp. 21–51.

3. Cf. Andreas Graeser, *Plotinus and the Stoics* (Leiden: Brill, 1972).

4. Cf. A. A. Long, *Phronesis* 12 (1967): 59–90.

5. Antiochus seems to have been the first to apply the label "New Academy" (disparagingly) to the skeptical phase of the Platonic Academy.

6. Such significant issues include the putative differences between Zeno and Chrysippus about a criterion, and those between Cleanthes and Chrysippus concerning the making of an imprint in the psyche.

7. *Stoicorum Veterum Fragmenta*, ed. Hans von Arnim (Leipzig: Teubner, 1903–24), vol. III, nos. 160, 84; vol. II, nos. 742–71, 439–61 (henceforth cited as *SVF*, along with volume and number).

8. *SVF* II.773–911. Cf. II.458.

9. Diogenes of Babylonia (a Stoic) said that "some Stoics" located the command center in the head (*SVF* III. Diogenes 33), but the extant evidence suggests that the heart was overwhelmingly favored: *SVF* III.Diog. 29–30; II.837–39, 879–81, 894, 896, 901, 910. Cf. I.148; II.885.

10. Cf. *SVF* II.863 (Waszink reads *confaecatior* with the MSS, which is preferable to von Arnim's *confoecatior*; C. J. Herington has made the plausible suggestion *concaecatior*). Cf. *SVF* II.879.

11. *Phantasia*, from *phainomai* ('appear', 'become apparent', 'be shown'), is a translator's nightmare. A few samples: (1) 'presentation' (A. A. Long, ed., *Problems in Stoicism* [London: Athlone, 1971], p. 91; F. H. Sandbach, "Phantasia Kataleptike," in ibid., p. 9; J. M. Rist, *Stoic Philosophy* [Cambridge: At the University Press, 1969],

pp. 133 ff.; G. Watson, *The Stoic Theory of Knowledge* [Belfast: Queen's University, 1966], p. 35 and passim; Johnny Christensen, *An Essay on the Unity of Stoic Philosophy* [Copenhagen: Munksgaard, 1962], pp. 56 ff.); (2) 'impression' (A. A. Long, *Hellenistic Philosophy* [London: Duckworth, 1974], pp. 123 ff.); (3) 'Erscheinung' (O. Rieth, *Grundbegriffe der stoischen Ethik* [Berlin: Weidmann, 1933], p. 114); (4) 'Anschauungsbild' (M. Pohlenz, *Die Stoa*, 2d ed. [Göttingen: Vandenhoeck and Ruprecht, 1959], 1:55); (5) 'Wahrnehmungsbild' (Pohlenz, op. cit.); (6) 'Vorstellung' (Pohlenz, op. cit., p. 56; P. Hadot, *Archiv für Begriffsgeschichte* 13 [1969]: 123; E. Zeller, *Geschichte der griechischen Philosophie*, 3d ed. [Leipzig: O. R. Reisland, 1880], vol. 3, pt. 1, pp. 71–85; Pohlenz, op. cit., 1:56).

12. *SVF* II.54, 63.

13. Ibid., II.53, 55, 56, 59.

14. Ibid., 56. Cf. A. Bonhöffer, *Epictet und die Stoa* (Stuttgart: F. Enke, 1890), pp. 148–51; Watson, op. cit., pp. 34–35 (and p. 34 n. 1); F. H. Sandbach, *The Stoics* (New York: Norton, 1975), pp. 85–86; G. Verbeke, *Kleanthes van Assos* (Brussels: Paleis der Academiën, 1948), pp. 96–99; J. B. Gould, *The Philosophy of Chrysippus* (Leiden: Brill, 1970), pp. 53–55.

15. Whether it is the 'presented' external object or the presentation itself that is grasped is a controversial issue taken up below.

16. This 'active' interpretation of *kataleptikos* is not accepted by all critics; see I.1 infra.

17. In Long, *Problems*, pp. 9–21, and *The Stoics*, pp. 85–89, 120–21. Long uses 'apprehensive presentation' in *Problems*, p. 91, but switches to 'cognitive impression' in *Hellenistic Philosophy*, pp. 90 ff., 123 ff.

18. *SVF* I.59: Cicero, *Academica priora* (hereafter, *Ac. pr.*) II.18 and 77; Sextus, *Adversus Mathematicos* (hereafter, *M.*) VII.248 and 426; idem, *Outlines of Pyrrhonism* II.4; Diogenes Laertius VII.50. Cf. *SVF* II.60, 65.

19. Zeller, op. cit., vol. 3, pt. 1, pp. 83–84; Pohlenz, op. cit., 1:55 (but p. 50: a *phantasia* that "die Erfassung des Objektes selbst *ermöglicht*"); Rist, loc. cit.

20. I emphasize the potential, since a cognitive presentation, although making apprehension *possible*, does not *ensure* it according to some later Stoics (Sextus, *M.* VII.253–57). More on this under I.6 infra.

21. 'Apprehensive' is perhaps a more accurate rendering than 'cognitive', but its epistemological use seems to have been usurped by the sense of 'uneasy or fearful about a possible future event'.

22. A significant distinction, because on it hinges to some degree the question of whether external objects or presentations are perceived and grasped. Sandbach, in "Phantasia Kataleptike," p. 21 n. 15, refers to two instances of adjectives in *-tikos* with a passive sense, but they are both early (Plato); examples from the Hellenistic period would be more conclusive. (But that *-tikos* sometimes simply signifies 'associated with' I grant.) The active interpretation is supported by Zeller, op. cit., III.i.83; E. Bréhier, *Chrysippe et l'ancien stoïcisme* (Paris: Presses universitaires de France, 1951), p. 97; Pohlenz, op. cit., 1:60, 62; Watson, op. cit., p. 35; the passive by Rudolf Hirzel, *Untersuchungen zu Ciceros philosophischen Schriften* (Leipzig: S. Hirzel, 1883), 2:185, and Rist, loc. cit. It is important to recognize that my 'active' or 'enabling' interpretation of *kataleptikos* attributes no 'activity' to the essentially passive presentation beyond its inherent capacity to 'show both itself and its cause'; it is the mere *passive* existence of a certain kind of presentation that renders grasp *possible*.

23. Sandbach, *The Stoics*, p. 89; idem, "Phantasia Kataleptike," pp. 14–15, 21 n. 15; L. Stein, *Die Psychologie der Stoa* (Berlin: S. Calvary, 1888), 2:170; Ernst Grumach, *Physis und Agathon in der alten Stoa* (Berlin: Weidmann, 1932), pp. 74–75.

24. *SVF* I.59: Cicero, *Ac. pr.* II.77; *SVF* I.60: *Academica posteriora* (hereafter

Ac. post.) I.41; and so on. So too Augustine, *Contra Academicos* XIII.ix.18 (but probably dependent on Cicero).

25. Cf. Cicero, *Letters to Atticus* XII.45.1; XIII.6.1; XIII.12.3; XIII.13.1; XIII.32.3; all written in May–June 45 B.C.

26. *Ac. post.* I.41. Sandbach, "Phantasia Kataleptike," pp. 20–21 n. 13, finds support for *kataleptos* in Papyrus Herculanensis 1020 (*SVF* II.131), which, however, seems to be a single, inconclusive occurrence that goes counter to the evidence in Diogenes, Sextus, Aëtius, Philo, and so on. It also does not occur in a definition of 'cognitive presentation'. No solution is without its difficulties: I leave for consideration elsewhere whether *ou kataleptikos* and *akataleptos* are synonyms, and whether *phantastikon* (*SVF* II.54) also has the 'active' sense proposed for *kataleptikos*.

27. Long, *Problems*, pp. 89–95; Andreas Graeser, "A propos *hyparchein* bei den Stoikern," *Archiv für Begriffsgeschichte* 15 (1970–71): 303 f.

28. P. Hadot, op. cit., pp. 122 ff.

29. Diogenes: *mē apo hyparchontos* vs. Sextus: *apo mē hyparchontos* (cf. I.5).

30. This is possible because of memory, which is "a treasure house of presentations" (*SVF* I.64; II.56) and constitutes an enduring modification of the mind. Cf. Christensen, op. cit., p. 57.

31. Such an apparition or phantom is sometimes called not a *phantasia* but a *phantasma* (*SVF* II.55) or *phantastikon* (*SVF* II.54, where *phantasma* is reserved for the 'object' presented) or *emphasis* (*SVF* II.61); but see I.3 infra.

32. This is still a Stoic argument: *phasin* and indirect discourse.

33. Aëtius, *Placita* IV.12.1 (*Doxographi Graeci*, p. 401) = *SVF* II.54.

34. Diog. Laert. VII.50 = *SVF* II.55.

35. Substances: *hypokeimena*. I adopted 'substances' only after some hesitation; used of the Stoic first category, it means 'subject referred to' according to A. C. Lloyd, *Problems*, p. 73 n. 34; but Rist, op. cit., chap. 9: 'substance' and 'substrate' (so too Zeller, op. cit., III.i.93, 102–3); Margaret Reesor, "The Stoic Categories," *American Journal of Philology* 78 (1957): 63–82: 'substratum'; Phillip De Lacy, "The Stoic Categories as Methodological Principles," *Transactions, American Philological Association* 76 (1945): 246–63: 'substance'.

36. Cf. Sextus, *M.* VII.253 ("the older Stoics"), referring back to 248–52, and Cicero's ascription of it to Zeno in *Ac. pr.* II.77.

37. Review of J. M. Rist's *Stoic Philosophy*, *Gnomon* 44 (1972): 17.

38. This distinction might signal a development within later Stoicism.

39. In the light of my conclusions about Cicero's use of *katalepton*, these observations must remain tentative.

40. *Ac. pr.* II.18.

41. 'The' is troubling (as is Rist's 'that') in the absence of an article. (A presentation that is 'not from the existing object' could, of course, be strictly either from an 'existent' not presented at t_1 [Ella] or from a nonexistent [unicorn]).

42. Cf. Sextus, *M.* VII.249. (Ibid., VIII.57: Sextus implies that even 'false presentations' from nonexistents ultimately depend upon direct, sensory experience of external entities.)

43. Cf. A. A. Long, "Language and Thought in Stoicism," in Long, *Problems*, p. 89.

44. The use of 'true' rather than 'truth' is important: the true is a statement and hence incorporeal, whereas truth is corporeal since it is "knowledge assertive of all that is true, and all knowledge is the command center in a certain condition" (Sextus, *M.* VII.38–39), discussed in Long, "Language and Thought in Stoicism," pp. 98–104.

45. There are, however, also 'rational presentations' that have *lekta* (i.e., also propositions) as their objects, and the mind rather than the senses as their instrumental medium. See *SVF.* II.61, 181, 187; Long, "Language and Thought in Stoicism," pp. 82–84, 108 n. 25; Sandbach, "Phantasia Kataleptike," pp. 11–12; and n. 49 infra.

46. *Epistulae morales* 87.40.

47. William and Martha Kneale, *The Development of Logic* (Oxford: Oxford University Press, 1962), p. 153.

48. Much of this is given pregnant expression in Diog. Laert. VII.49 (*SVF* II.52): " . . . Presentation is the antecedent (sc. of assent, grasp, and thought), and then reason, being capable of expression, 'ex-presses' (*ek-pherei*, carries outside) in speech (*logos*) that which it experiences at the hands of the presentation."

49. To Cicero this use may also have seemed to sanction his substitution of 'the true' for 'the existing'.

50. Sextus, *M.* VII.152 (*SVF* II.90), explicitly attributes this version to the Stoics. *Ac. pr.* II.18, II.33, and II.113 also suggest that Cicero allowed "tale (visum) verum quale falsum esse non possit" to stand as I.5 of the definition (here it is significantly not *visum a vero* but *visum verum*). Carneades' objection at Sextus, *M.* VII.164, and Alexander of Aphrodisias' identification (*De anima* p. 71 Bruns.; *SVF* II.70) of cognitive presentations with 'true and strong presentations' and of an 'acataleptic presentation' with 'a false presentation', provide further confirmation. Cf. also Cic., *Ac. pr.* II.47 (*SVF* II.66); Sextus, *M.* VII.405 (*SVF* II.67).

51. *Moralia* 1055F–1056A (*SVF* II.994); 1057A–B.

52. Among others, H. J. Krämer, *Platonismus und hellenistische Philosophie* (Berlin: De Gruyter, 1972), pp. 37–47, has shown in convincing detail that the Academics tend to use the Stoics' own premises when they attempt to refute the Stoics; see nn. 142–43 infra.

53. See n. 24 supra.

54. In *Ac. post.* I.42 Cicero claims that Zeno called not only some presentations but also 'grasp' (which is an assent to cognitive presentation) true. Since perceptual grasp is also a corporeal process, similar questions about the use of 'true' arise here.

55. It is not specified whether only the *possibility* of a true statement must accompany a presentation for it to be true.

56. Sextus, *M.* VII.242–60. Long, *Problems,* p. 109 n. 31, calls it "a late Stoic catalogue" but p. 111 n. 79 seems to use it as orthodox Stoic doctrine. Sextus himself does not seem to regard it as late: this section is launched (227) as an account of orthodox Stoic epistemology; Zeno, Chrysippus, and Cleanthes are quoted; 'older Stoics' are referred to in 253 re 242–48; in 260 it is concluded simply with "such then is the doctrine of the Stoics." Certainty about its date remains elusive, but cf. also Cicero's allusion, *Ac. pr.* II.40, to Academic and Stoic classifications of presentations and Diog. Laert. VII.51 ff.

57. E.g., the mad Orestes' experience of a presentation from an existing object (Electra)—hence true—which, however, he mistakes—hence false—for a Fury (Sextus, *M.* VII.245). It is not clear why 'bent oar' (which is also from an existing object, oar *X*) should be classified as a 'false presentation' whereas Orestes' presentation of Electra is 'both true and false'. The only difference seems to lie in the source of perceptual error: Orestes' is more 'subjective' (insanity), the case of the oar more 'objective' (refraction).

58. Generic presentations (*genikai phantasiai*), e.g., 'Man', ibid., 246.

59. Numerous problems remain; some of them are discussed in my monograph *Aisthesis* (Göttingen: Vandenhoeck und Ruprecht, forthcoming).

60. No later than Carneades, this 'obstacle' (*enstēma*) issue seems to have been raised; cf. Cic., *Ac. pr.* II.33. It was perhaps this problem that gave rise to Carneades'

introduction of *aperispastos* into his own probabilistic theory of cognition (n. 102 infra).

61. This seems to lend support to my emphasis in I.1 on the 'enabling' and 'potential' dimension of *kataleptikos*. Cf. n. 20 supra.

62. Reference to perceptual obstacles is also found in the Stoics' statement that five things should concur for a sensory presentation to occur: a sense organ, a sensible object, place, disposition or condition, reason. A malfunction or absence of only one is enough to render apprehension (*antilēpsis*) impossible; Sextus, *M.* VII.424 (*SVF* II.68).

63. Details in Pohlenz, op. cit., 1:54–63 and 2:32–36; Watson, op. cit.; Sandbach, "Phantasia Kataleptikē" and "Ennoia and Prolēpsis" (and my review, *American Journal of Philology* 96 [1975]); idem, *The Stoics*, pp. 82–91; Long, *Hellenistic Philosophy*, pp. 123–31; Bonhöffer, op. cit., pp. 113–232; Christensen, op. cit., pp. 54–61; Bréhier, op. cit., pp. 80–107.

64. Strictly speaking, not 'presentations' (*phantasiai*) but *phantastika, phantasmata* or *emphaseis* (see nn. 31, 33–34 supra).

65. These are presentations apparently required for discursive reasoning and for meaningful linguistic communication. Cf. n. 45 supra.

66. Aëtius, *Placita* IV.11.1 ff. (= *Dox. Gr.* p. 400; *SVF* II.83): *chartēs euergos eis apographēn* (not 'tabula rasa'!).

67. Cf. Sextus' account of its dual (voluntary/involuntary) aspects (*M.* VIII.397). How authentically Stoic all details are, is not clear.

68. Not a prominent concept in Stoicism, its earliest use by a Stoic seems to be *SVF* III.Antipater 33. Carneades may have prompted the Stoics to pay more attention to the problem of 'evidence' (see Part II). Cicero's use of *declaratio* (*Ac. post.* 1.41 = *SVF* I.60) is taken by J. S. Reid (*Academica* [London, 1884]) to translate *enargeia*, but *Ac. pr.* II.17 and 105 establish *evidentia* and *perspicuitas* as the Latin equivalents; like *enargeia* they refer to 'being clear' while *declaratio* is 'a making clear'. I am therefore inclined to interpret 'quae . . . haberent declarationem' as Cicero's translation of *endeiktikos* or *parastatikos* (*SVF* II.63, 221, 266; cf. also *endeiknymi, epideiknymi,* and *deiknysi,* ibid., II.54–57).

69. *Phasi*: Sextus is still talking about Stoics.

70. A different aspect, not to be confused with this apparent involuntariness, is that the capacity to assent, like that of appetition, is given to human beings in accordance with fate (*SVF* II.991).

71. Cf. also *SVF* II.974, 979–81, 991–94.

72. For details see Rieth, op. cit., pp. 134–68; Pohlenz, *Abhandlungen der Gesellschaft der Wissenschaften, Göttingen,* phil.-hist. Kl. 3, 26 (1940): 104–12; Long, *Problems,* chap. 8; Margaret Reesor, "Fate and Possibility in Early Stoic Philosophy," *Phoenix* 19 (1965): 285–97.

73. According to Chrysippus 'Fate' then implies only that no event is produced without an antecedent cause. Cf. Long, "Freedom and Determinism in the Stoic Theory of Human Action," in *Problems*, pp. 180–85, and "The Stoic Concept of Evil," *Philosophical Quarterly* 18 (1965): 329–43.

74. Cf. Cicero, *De fato* 36.

75. Assent is also given to impulses and, in such cases, leads to action: Seneca, *Epist. Mor.* 113.18 (*SVF* III.169); cf. *SVF* III.177. More interesting, but less well documented, is the case of assent to propositions. Arcesilaus had already criticized the Stoics for saying assent is to presentations rather than to propositions, since only propositions can be true or false (Sextus, *M.* VII.154). At least some Stoics seem to have conceded the point or to have tried to answer it: Stobaeus, *Eclogae* II.vii.9, p.

88.3 ff. Wachsmuth (*SVF* III.171). These propositions will, if the context is cognitive, usually be *about* external objects, e.g., that "Emma is beautiful." Cf. S. G. Pembroke, "Oikeiosis," in Long, *Problems*, pp. 130, 145–46 n. 77; Sandbach, "Phantasia Kataleptikē," pp. 12–13.

76. Plutarch, *Against the Stoics on Common Concepts* 45 (*Moralia* 1084 A–B = *SVF* II.848): assent is a *sōma*.

77. Plutarch, *On Stoic Discrepancies* 47 (*Moralia* 1056F–57C; cf. *SVF* II.993 and III.177).

78. Galen, *On the Errors of the Soul* 1 (V p. 58 Kühn = *SVF* III.172). Cf. also the descriptions (a) of belief (*doxa*) as 'weak and false assent' (*SVF* I.67; II.90), as 'assent to the acataleptic' (Sextus, *M.* VII.156; *SVF* III.548), and as 'a weak supposition' (ibid.); (b) of committing error (*hamartanein*) as 'assenting to acataleptic presentations' which are false but nevertheless plausible (Plutarch, loc. cit.); (c) of ignorance (*agnoia*) as 'a weak assent subject to change' (*SVF* I.68, III.548).

79. Plutarch, loc. cit.

80. Ibid., 1057B (*phaulous*); Cic., *Ac. post.* I.42 = *SVF* I.60.

81. Cf. Cic., *Ac. post.* I.41 = *SVF* I.60 (a very confusing formulation!); Sextus, *M.* VIII.397 = *SVF* II.91, etc. The most famous illustration of the relation between presentation, assent, grasp or apprehension, and knowledge is Zeno's hand simile: "Showing one his hand with fingers outstretched, he would say 'a presentation is like this'. Next he contracted his fingers a little: 'assent is like this.' Then he pressed his fingers together completely, making a fist of it, and said that this was grasp (apprehension) . . . But when he had moved up his left hand and pressed his fist with it tightly and hard, he would say that knowledge was a thing of that kind, of which none except the wise partake" (Cic., *Ac. pr.* II.145). Cf. *Ac. post.* I.41; and Sandbach, "Phantasia Kataleptike," pp. 11 ff.; id., *The Stoics*, 87 f.; Bonhöffer, op. cit., pp. 178 f.; Rist, op. cit., pp. 139 f.

82. Sextus, *Pyrrh.* III.188 = *SVF* III.96; Clement, *Strom.* VIII.5, vol. III, p. 90 Früchtel = *SVF* II.121.

83. Herculanean papyrus 1020 (*SVF* II.131; see n. 26 supra) gave me considerable pause, as did Sandbach's comments, but my conclusions seem to have stronger support. Cf. nn. 19–24 supra.

84. Just as there are presentations not directly derived from sense objects (*logikai phantasiai*), so too the Stoics distinguish between 'grasp through sense' and 'grasp through *logos*'. The objects of the latter are propositions 'presented' in non-sensual presentations: they are arrived at through reasoning or argumentation, including analogy, inference, 'resemblance', 'transposition', 'composition', 'contrariety'. Cf. Diog. Laert. VII.52 and n. 45.

85. *Epiballein*: 'throw (one's mind) upon', 'attend to'.

86. This is a weaker piece of evidence, because it is attributed to the (Stoicizing) Antiochus by Lucullus (but expropriated for Chrysippus in *SVF* II.117).

87. *Aisthēsis* is a polysemic term in Stoicism. Cf. Diog. Laert. VII.52 (*SVF* II.71): "*Aisthēsis* is said by the Stoics to be (1) the pneuma extending from the command center to the senses (organs?): (2) the grasp (*katalēpsis*) that occurs through them; (3) the equipment of the sensory organs (impaired in some people); (4) also its actual exercise (*energeia*)." Aëtius, *Plac.* IV.8.1 (*SVF* II.850) likewise emphasizes its homonymic aspect. Cf. *SVF* II.108.

88. While *aisthēsis* qua perception must be veridical, since it is an assent to a cognitive presentation, *aisthēsis* qua sensation can deliver a *phantasia* that will be a source of error and is not necessarily 'cataleptic'. But perception, though veridical, is not co-extensive with knowledge: only in the Wise Man will it be knowledge (*SVF* I.60; II.90; 108).

89. E.g. Aëtius, *Placita* IV.8.8 (*Dox. Gr.* p. 395 = *SVF* II.851).

90. Cf. *SVF* I.62; II.850.

91. *SVF* II.74.

92. Other elements of Stoic epistemology need not detain us here. They also discussed memory, experience, natural or general concepts (*prolēpseis*; cf. Sandbach, "Ennoia and Prolepsis," in *Problems* pp. 22–37), reason, science or art, and knowledge.

93. I shall distinguish between Arcesilaus and Carneades only when the sources do. Since Arcesilaus and Carneades followed the Socratic tradition of not writing anything (cf. Diog. Laert. IV.32; Plutarch, *Moralia* 328A), we have to rely exclusively on reports in later authors for their views. I have profited from using the following: von Arnim, "Arkesilaos" (no. 19), in *Pauly-Wissowas Realencyclopädie* (Stuttgart: J. B. Metzler, 1896), 2:1, cols. 1164–68, and "Karneades," ibid., 10:2 (1919), cols. 1964–85; Victor Brochard, *Les Sceptiques grecs*, 2d ed. (Paris: Imprimerie nationale, 1887), pp. 93–208; Charlotte Stough, *Greek Skepticism* (Berkeley: University of California Press, 1969), pp. 6–8, 40–66; Roderick Chisholm, *Theory of Knowledge* (Englewood Cliffs, N.J.: Prentice-Hall, 1966), pp. 41–45, 52–54; Hirzel, op. cit., 3 (1883): 22–39, 251–341; Albert Goedeckemeyer, *Die Geschichte des Skeptizismus* (Leipzig: Dieterich, 1905), pp. 30–130; Krämer. op. cit., passim.

94. Sextus identifies Carneades as the author of these and the following arguments in *M.* VII.159 and 166. On *enargeia* in Stoicism see n. 68 supra.

95. Brochard (128) erroneously regards 'there are no true presentations' as the core of Carneades' position (as n. 96 shows).

96. This is also clear from Cicero's summaries of Carneades' argument (*Ac. pr.* II.40–43, 47–50, 83–90):
1. Some presentations are true, others false.
2. A false presentation is not cognitive.
3. If two presentations are indistinguishable, it is impossible that one is cognitive and the other not.
4. For every true presentation it is possible for a false presentation to be indistinguishable from it.
5. Therefore no true presentation is cognitive.
6. Therefore there is no cognitive presentation.
Omnis pugna de quarto est, Cicero rightly observes (ibid. II.83). See also Sextus, *M.* VII.163–66, 403 ff.; Stough, op. cit., pp. 42 ff.

97. This argument, in slightly different formulations, is also attributed to the Academic Skeptics in other passages: Cic., *Ac. pr.* II.40; 77; 83; Sextus, *M.* VII.154.

98. Sextus, *M.* VII.403–8; VIII.67–68; Cic., *Ac. pr.* II.88–90.

99. Sextus, *M.* VII.406; Cic., *Ac. pr.* II.89.

100. See p. 000 and n. 78 supra.

101. The absence of time in this enumeration is puzzling. That time is a *lekton* and hence not 'really real' would not be an adequate explanation, since space too is an incorporeal (Sextus, *M.* X.218; *SVF* II.331), conceived of by inference (Diog. Laert. VII.53; *SVF* II.87).

102. Carneades' own criteria for the conduct of life and the attainment of *eudaimonia* were (a) vivid, plausible presentation (*pithanē phantasia*) that has intrinsic power to produce conviction but no absolute truth claim; (b) if the presentation is both plausible and consistent, *aperispastos* ('incapable of being dragged hither and thither'), a higher degree of probability is attained—there now must also be concurrence, a consistency of presentational experience, no easy reversal (reminiscent of the Platonic *ametablētos*, but not as strong); (c) still more 'probable' is a presentation which is not only plausible and consistent, but also tested: *diexōdeumenē*, it has been scrutinized from every angle (the probabilist's version of Plato's rotational model of

133

nous pantachothen, as Lee suggested?). Cf. Sextus, *M.* VII.166–89; *Pyrrh.* I.226–31; Cic., *Ac. pr.* II.99.

103. On *hypokeimenon* see n. 35 supra.

104. The Stoics did recognize the existence of generic presentations (*genikai phantasiai*), e.g., of generic Man. It is, however, a significant measure of the Stoics' departure from Plato that these presentations are not classified as 'true'—and hence do not include cognitive presentations—but as 'neither true nor false' (see p. 000 and Sextus, *M.* VII.246; only a presentation of a particular object or fact could accordingly be cognitive).

105. The Stoics could respond that the Academic examples are exceptional cases which may not be generalized, and that they had made provision for the Wise Man to suspend judgment (exercise *epochē* or *hēsychia*, *SVF* II.276–77) by refusing assent in such cases. The Academics would, however, find this rejoinder inadequate, and could (a) apply a Megarian *sorites*—one of their favorite forms of argumentation—to the concept 'exceptional' (as they did to the question of the boundary between cataleptic and acataleptic); and (b) use the Epicurean argument that while exceptions may not be generalized, one case of perceptual error or confusion is sufficient to invalidate the Stoic generalizations about perception.

106. E.g., *Republic* 476a4–480d13; *Phaedo* 72e3–77a5. Cf. *Theaetetus* 148d4–7; *Symposium* 205b4–212a7; *Timaeus* 30c2–31b3, 38a8–b5, etc.

107. Krämer, op. cit., pp. 68–75, maintains that the Academic Skeptics used Platonic arguments that they based not on the Platonic dialogues but on the proofs of the Forms as these had been systematized and transmitted in oral instruction in the Academy, and as reflected in the extracts from Aristotle's *Peri ideōn*. He marshals very impressive but, in my view, not entirely conclusive evidence.

108. Cf. Plato, *Phaedrus* 250d3–4. But cf. Aristotle's vacillation between sight and touch: *Metaphysics* 980a23–4 and *De anima* 429a2–3 *vs. De an.* 413b4–5, 434b22–25, 435a12–13, b2–3, 414a2–3, etc.

109. Diog. Laert. VII.52; cf. *SVF* II.860.

110. In the *Parmenides* 134e8–135c4 it is suggested that all thought and discourse (*dialegesthai*) is impossible without the Forms, and a similar conclusion is stated at the end of the *Cratylus*. Cf. also the criticism of extreme Heracliteanism in *Theaetetus* 181b8–183c7, and the emphasis on 'things of such a kind that they always recur as similar things' (*Timaeus* 49e5). On related issues see E. Lee, "On Plato's *Timaeus*," *American Journal of Philology*, 88 (1967): 1–28; idem, *Essays in Ancient Greek Philosophy*, ed. John P. Anton and George L. Kustas (Albany, N.Y.: State University of New York, 1971), 219–235.

111. While extreme, comprehensive Heracliteanism is rejected and the need for unchanging Forms is stressed implicitly or explicitly, the applicability of the flux doctrine to the phenomenal world is not denied. Cf. *Theaetetus* 182c1–183c7; *Cratylus* 439b4–440e2; *Timaeus* 49c7–50a4.

112. Ever since antiquity there have been those who maintained that a 'dogmatic' strand of Platonism which included the theory of Forms and, in particular, Plato's lecture *On the Good*, continued to be transmitted esoterically within the Academy, even during its sceptical phase. I find the evidence inconclusive. Cf. Sextus, *Pyrrh.* I.234; Eusebius, *Praeparatio evangel.* XIV.6.6, XIV.8, 12, and 14 (Numenius); Cic., *Ac. pr.* II.60; Augustine, op. cit., III.xvii.37 ff.; A. Weische, *Cicero und die Neue Akademie* (Münster: Aschendorff, 1961), pp. 20–26; Krämer, op. cit., pp. 54–56.

113. Cf., for example, *SVF* II.305, 318, 324, 594, and 989.

114. E.g., *SVF* II.409, 494.

115. Just why the Forms were jettisoned remains an intriguing puzzle. The revival of Socratic *aporia* in the face of a pervasive empirical tendency in philosophy, science,

and rhetoric might have been at least as significant as Pyrrhonism. On empiricism cf. P. and E. De Lacy, *Philodemus on Methods of Inference* (Philadelphia: American Philosophical Society, 1941), pp. 120–37; id., "Ancient Rhetoric and Empirical Method," *Sophia* 6 (1938): 523–30; K. Deichgräber, *Die griechische Empirikerschule* (Berlin: Weidmann, 1930); and von Staden, "Experiment and Experience in Hellenistic Medicine," *Bulletin of the Institute of Classical Studies* 22 (1975): 178–99.

116. *Timaeus* 30b7, 44d1, 48d2, 57d6, 68b7, 68d2. Cf. *Theaetetus* 162e5, 8 (also *pithanologia*); *Sophist* 231b9–c5, etc. See also Lee's comments (*Essays*, p. 234 n. 32, etc.) on a connection between *eikos* (likely) and *peithō* (persuasion) in Plato. Already Augustine linked the New Academic 'plausible' (*pithanon*) to the Platonic 'likely' (*eikos*): *Contra Academicos* III.xx.43.

117. *SVF* II.90. Cf. I.60, 68–69; II.130, 117 (with the qualification that this is Antiochus), 93, 95, etc.

118. See pp. 99–102 (with nn. 27–28, 43) and *SVF* II.509.

119. Sextus, *M.* VII.424, suggests that "reason in a state contrary to nature" (*dianoia para physin echousa*) would be an example of an obstacle (*enstēma*).

120. Ibid. (*SVF* II.68). This occurs in the context of frequent reference to arguments that Academic Skeptics used against the Stoics: VII.401, 402 ff., 408–11, 412 ff. 416 ff., 422, 424 ff., 433–35, etc. For a Platonic precedent cf. *Theaetetus* 157e1–160a3.

121. A Stoic answer might be that they are 'natural' and efficacious when their psychic pneuma is taut, but abnormal and unreliable when it is slack (n. 10 supra). This still would not clarify how a *percipient* could recognize normality.

122. In a Wise Man, perceptual grasp, being secure, firm, and incontrovertible even by reason, *is* knowledge according to *SVF* II.90 (Sextus, *M.* VII.151–52), I.60 (Cic., *Ac. post.* I.41). See n. 88 supra.

123. For these and similar examples see, inter alia, Cicero, *Ac. pr.* II.79.

124. Similar examples in Cicero, ibid., 81–82.

125. Ibid.

126. Thus distance perception is in part texture dependent (cf. Bela Julesz, "Cooperative Phenomena in Binocular Depth Perception," *American Scientist* 62 [1974]: 32–43), whereas 'bent oar' depends on refraction (which is 'correctly' perceived). These examples are lumped together by Sextus (*M.* VII.414) as illustrations of a single point: our deficient ability to distinguish *schēma*. *Schēma* might refer to 'shape' or 'form', but it could also allude to 'appearance' as in the Platonic opposition of *schēma* and reality: Plato, *Rep., 365c* (cf. Ps.-Plat. *Epinomis* 989c).

127. Cf. Cic., *Ac. pr.* II.80.

128. Varro according to Pliny (who puts Strabo's visual range at 135,000 Roman paces or almost 125 miles), *Natural History* VII.xxi.85. Cf. also Solinus, *Collectanea Rerum Memorabilium* I.99 (p. 27 Mommsen); Strabo, *Geography* VI.2.1 (C.267); Aelian, *Variae Historiae* XI.13; Valerius Maximus, *Facta et Dicta Memorabilia* I.cap.8 (De Miraculis), ext. 14; Isidorus, *Etymologiae* II.xii.4.

129. See nn. 105, 143.

130. Watson, op. cit., pp. 35, 37, 44–5, 51, 53, etc.

131. *SVF* II.105; Suda, *s.v. prolēpsis.* Cf. Sandbach, "Ennoia and Prolēpsis," pp. 22–37.

132. As defined by the Stoics this relation implies comparison, coherence, testing, verification—in short, the very principles given systematic application in Carneades' three-stage probabilism. See also *SVF* II.135, 223, 87–88, for the Stoic interest in inference, transition, analogy, synthesis, etc.

133. *Rep.* VII.523b2–524a8.

134. E.g., *Theaetetus* 157e1–159e5; *Phaedo* 65e6–66a6.

135. Cf. *Phaedo* 72e–76e.

136. The concept *eulogon* again reveals the parasitical nature of much of Academic skepticism: it is taken from the Stoic definitions of *kathēkon* (moral duty?) and *katorthōma* (right act): *SVF* III.284, 493–94.

137. See nn. 102 and 116 supra, and Sextus, *M.* VII.166–89; id. *Pyrrh.* I.226–31.

138. This and the foregoing are forms of *phainomai* (n. 11 supra). Cf. also Plato's frequent use of *phantazomai* in contexts similar to those of the New Academy: *Tim.* 43e8, 49d1; *Repub.* 380d2, 476a7.

139. On Sextus: Arne Naess, *Scepticism* (London: Routledge & Kegan Paul, 1968), pp. 1–35. There are, however, indications that the Academics at times conceded that skepticism has to be self-referential in order to be viable. Cf. Cicero, *Ac. post.* I.45; Goedeckemeyer, op. cit., pp. 37 ff.; Krämer, op. cit., p. 54.

140. Antiochus, as 'reported' by Lucullus, in Cic., *Ac. pr.* II.43.

141. Léon Robin, *Pyrrhon et le scepticisme grec* (Paris: Presses universitaires de France, 1944), pp. 46 f.; Rieth, op. cit., p. 165 n. 3; Krämer, op. cit., passim (especially pp. 48, 50–58, 103–6); so too Hegel, *Lectures on the History of Philosophy*, trans. Haldane and Simson (London: Kegan Paul, Trench, & Trübner, 1894), 2:312.

142. See Pierre Couissin, "Le Stoïcisme de la Nouvelle Académie," *Revue d'histoire de la philosophie* 3 (1929): 241–76; Krämer, op. cit., pp. 14–58.

143. Pierre Couissin, "L'Origine et l'évolution de l'Epochē," *Revue des études grecques* 54 (1929): 373–97.

144. On *ou mallon* both in Plato and in skepticism, see Phillip De Lacy, *"Ou mallon* and the Antecedents of Ancient Scepticism," *Phronesis* 3 (1958): 59–71.

145. See *Aristotle on Dialectic: The Topics*, ed. G. E. L. Owen (Oxford: Oxford University Press, 1968), pp. 69–79 (Ryle), 277–311 (Moraux), and Owen's caveats, pp. 103–25.

146. The genealogy of the "Skeptical" Academy remains a controversial topic, and my analysis of Platonic elements is not meant to be an exhaustive statement about their heritage. In both modern and ancient times, Pyrrho, Socrates, Plato, the Megarians, and the Peripatetics have had their turns as fathers of the New Academy. (A useful summary with extensive references to secondary literature can be found in Krämer, op. cit., pp. 5–13).

147. *Hellenistic Philosophy*, p. 93.

David C. Lindberg

Chapter Five

THE INTROMISSION-EXTRAMISSION CONTROVERSY IN
ISLAMIC VISUAL THEORY: ALKINDI VERSUS AVICENNA

I. INTRODUCTION

Despite three-quarters of a century of serious scholarship, the
history of early visual theory still suffers from an underestima-
tion of the issues involved.[1] Ancient and medieval visual theory
continues on occasion to be portrayed as a simple struggle between extramissionists, who naïvely believed that rays emerge
from the observer's eye, and intromissionists, who recognized
that in any sensible visual theory radiation must pass from the
observed object to the observer. The impression is thus given
that the central and overriding issue of visual theory was the
direction of radiation—an innocent question that elementary observation (and perhaps even armchair reflection) should quickly
have settled. And from this it follows that philosophers who puzzled over the matter for well over a thousand years must have
lacked either good will or good sense—or, at any rate, good arguments.

   The truth, of course, is that the issues were far more difficult
and complex than this stereotyped account admits. The direction of radiation was by no means the only issue at stake (or
even the most important one), for it was thoroughly intertwined
with basic questions about the aims and criteria of visual theory.
Moreover, there was no simple test, either experimental or logical, by which the direction of radiation could be determined.
Finally, philosophers in fact discoursed on the subject of vision
with skill and subtlety. In order to defend these claims, to dispel any suggestion that the issues or arguments were simple-minded

and to give a clearer picture of the controversy and the shape of the battle lines, I propose to examine the arguments of two of the most important protagonists, Alkindi and Avicenna.

II. ALKINDI AGAINST THE INTROMISSION THEORY OF VISION

Ya'qūb ibn Ishāq al-Kindī (d. ca. 873) was the first Islamic philosopher to take a serious interest in the science of optics.[2] He was of Arab descent, born into a powerful and cultured family, and educated in Basra and Baghdad. He was patronized by the caliph al-Ma'mūn and his two immediate successors, but fell out of favor during the caliphate of al-Mutawakkil, who reacted against the Mu'tazilite theology of Alkindi and his early patrons. Some 260 works have been attributed to Alkindi, and in his chief optical work, *De aspectibus*, he undertook to defend and supplement Euclid's theory of vision.

One of the points at which Euclid was most in need of supplementation, in Alkindi's view, was the claim that the rays by which an object is perceived issue from the observer's eye; for whereas Euclid had made this a postulate, Alkindi was convinced that it could be demonstrated. Alkindi began his demonstration with a brief summary of the alternatives:

> Therefore I say that it is impossible that the eye should perceive its sensibles except [1] by their forms travelling to the eye, as many of the ancients have judged, and being impressed in it, or [2] by power proceeding from the eye to sensible things, by which it perceives them, or [3] by these two things occurring simultaneously, or [4] by their forms being stamped and impressed in the air and the air stamping and impressing them in the eye, which [forms] the eye comprehends by its power of perceiving that which air, when light mediates, impresses in it.[3]

The first of these alternatives is clearly the intromission theory of the atomists, according to which a thin film of atoms (likened by Lucretius to the skin of a cicada) is stripped off a visible object and propagated intact to the observer's eye; the second is the extramission or visual ray theory of Euclid and Ptolemy; the third is the combined intromission-extramission theory of

138

Plato;[4] and the fourth is the mediumistic theory of Aristotle, according to which colored bodies produce qualitative changes in a transparent medium, and these changes are transmitted by the medium to the transparent humors of the eye.[5] Now it will be Alkindi's strategy to disprove the first, third, and fourth theories and to show that only the Euclidean theory is consistent with the known facts of visual perception.

Alkindi has a variety of arguments. He repeats Aristotle's argument about weak-sighted people who see their own image before them because "the power proceeding from sight, when it cannot penetrate the air because of weakness, is made to return by the air to the body of the observer."[6] He also argues, following Theon of Alexandria, that the structure of a sense organ implies the mode of its functioning. The ears, for example, are hollow in order to collect the air that produces sound. But God made the eye spherical and mobile. It does not, therefore, collect impressions; rather, through its mobility it shifts itself about and selects the object to which it will send its ray.[7]

Another argument for the extramission theory is that it alone, of all theories of vision, can explain the selectivity of sight and the dependency of acuity on position within the visual field. When we read a book, sight must strain to locate a particular letter and perceives it only after an interval of time; it is thus evident that we perceive objects in the visual field in temporal sequence rather than all at once. Moreover, objects situated at the side of the visual field or far from the observer are poorly perceived. Now if sight were to occur through an impression made in the eye by the form of the visible object (i.e., by any theory but the Euclidean, since all the others include at least a component of intromissionism), everything within the visual field would be seen simultaneously and with equal acuity; for once forms have entered the eye, it does not matter how far they have traveled or from what direction they have come. Furthermore, if objects as far off as celestial bodies are visible, surely objects at the distance of a palm or cubit (such as the letters of a book) must impress their forms on the eye all the more clearly and should not have to be sought by the eye. One must conclude, therefore, that the intromission theory is false; rather, a visual power issues from the eye, weakening as it diverges from direct opposition to the center of the eye, and selects its objects successively.[8]

Alkindi's claim that the strength of the visual power varies with its position in the visual cone introduces the geometry of the visual process—the *raison d'être* of the extramission theory.[9] Another argument, Alkindi's key argument in my judgment, continues along mathematical lines. If sight were to occur through intromission of the forms of sensible things, Alkindi argues, a circle situated edgewise before the eye would impress its form in the eye and consequently would be perceived in its full circularity. But this does not occur. "On the contrary, when circles and observer are in the same plane, the circles are by no means seen. Therefore it remains that a power proceeds from the observer to the visible objects, by which they are perceived."[10] This power proceeds from the eye in straight lines and falls only on the edges of the circles, perceiving them merely as straight lines.

Now this is an obscure and difficult argument, but it will pay us well to pause and consider its meaning and import. If we are to grasp the argument at all, we must first understand what Alkindi means by "form." What he does *not* mean is a composite impression produced by a large number of individual rays, as in the modern conception of an optical image. Rather, it seems that forms are coherent images or likenesses, not susceptible of analysis into individual rays, which (according to any of the intromission theories, Alkindi believes) would be impressed in the observer's eye. They bear a resemblance to the *simulacra* or thin films of the Epicurean theory of vision, except for the fact that they represent the entire object rather than merely the surface opposite the observer.[11] There is no justification, of course, for Alkindi's application of the same conception of forms to Plato and Aristotle, who made no attempt to treat the perception of shape.[12] But whether fair to his predecessors or not, Alkindi's conception of vision by intromission (i.e., of all theories except the Euclidean) is clear: if a circle placed edgewise before the eye should be seen by the entrance of its form into the eye, this would not be the result of radiation from each

140

point on the near edge of the circle entering the eye to produce an image (as in the modern view); rather, the form of the circle would enter the eye as a unit, and there its spatial orientation would have nothing to do with its perception, for within the eye the laws of perspective no longer apply.[13] Indeed, this appears to be the essential point of Alkindi's argument: if the perception of an object is to depend on its spatial orientation, if visual theory is to be submitted to mathematical analysis, one must hold to the theory of visual rays. In short, Alkindi sees no means by which the intromission theory, which for him is the theory of coherent forms, can be made compatible with the laws of perspective.

This may seem to be a fatuous argument. After all, is it not self-evident that light radiates independently from each point on the surface of a visible object, and that on this conception of radiation we can build an intromission theory in which perception depends on the spatial orientation of the perceived object? But this self-evidence is purely the result of hindsight, for we have learned from Alhazen and Kepler (both of whom lived long after Alkindi) how to construct an intromission theory on the punctiform analysis of the visible object. What would surely have been self-evident to Alkindi and his ancient predecessors is that a coherent visual impression can result only from a coherent process of radiation and therefore that the image must depart from the visible object as a unit.[14] Alkindi has thus taken the intromission theory as he conceived it (or, more specifically, the only intromissionist account of the perception of shape yet presented)—the theory of coherent forms—and demonstrated that it is not mathematically viable.

III. AVICENNA AGAINST THE EXTRAMISSION
       THEORY OF VISION

One of the most influential medieval defenders of the Aristotelian theory of vision was the Persian natural philosopher Abū 'Alī al-Husain ibn 'Abdallāh ibn Sīnā, known in the West as Avicenna (980-1037).[15] Avicenna dealt with visual theory in a variety of presently extant works, including the *Kitāb al-Shifā* (*The Book of Healing*, known in the West as *Sufficientia*), *Kitāb al-Najāt* (*The Book of Deliverance*), *Maqāla fī 'l-Nafs* (*Epistle* or *Compendium on the Soul*), *Dānishnāmā* (*Book of Knowledge*), and *Kitāb al-Qanun fī 'l-Tibb* (*Liber canonis* or *Canon of Medicine*).[16] But before considering the content of these works, it is necessary to say a word about their composition, and hence their interrelationships. It appears to have been established that the *Compendium on the Soul* was Avicenna's first work.[17] The *Shifā* and *Canon* were works of Avicenna's maturity and clearly represent his most complete thought on medical and natural subjects.[18] Finally, the *Najāt* and *Dānishnāmā* were abridgements of longer works (the *Najāt* an abridgement of the *Shifā*) prepared toward the end of Avicenna's scholarly career; their importance is that they represent Avicenna's own view of what was essential to the longer works.

Although the short compendia offer a bare sketch of Avicenna's theory of vision, all of them reveal his Aristotelian sympathies. One of Avicenna's more succinct (if somewhat confused) summaries of the various alternatives appears in the *Compendium on the Soul*, where he writes:

> As to the seeing power, philosophers have differed on the question of how they perceive. Thus one set among them asserts that they perceive wholly and solely through a ray that shoots out beyond the eye, and so encounters the sensible objects that are seen. This is Plato's way.[19] Others assert that the perceiving power itself encounters the sensible objects that are seen, and so perceives them.[20] Still others say that visual perception consists in this:—When an intervening transparent body becomes effectively transparent by light shining upon it, then an impression of the outspread [flattened] individual of such sensible objects as are seen is effected in the cristalline lens of the eye, just such a pictorial impression as is effected in looking-glasses [mirrors]; indeed the two effects are so similar that were mirrors possessed of a seeing power they would perceive the form imprinted in them. This is Aristotle's way; and it is the sound reliable opinion.[21]

In the *Najāt*, at the other end of Avicenna's philosophical career, basically the same conclusion is expressed. After describing the emission theory of Euclid and Alkindi, Avicenna adds:

"But true philosophers hold the view that when an actually transparent body, i.e., a body which has no colour, intervenes between the eye and the object of sight, the exterior form of the coloured body on which light is falling is transmitted to the pupil of the eye and so the eye perceives it."[22] This is Aristotle's theory, only a little elaborated.

But to understand Avicenna's theory of vision, it is not enough to recognize that he boldly proclaimed himself an Aristotelian. We must see how he defended the Aristotelian theory and refuted the alternatives. His emphasis was on disproving all forms of the extramission theory; to the positive defense of the Aristotelian theory of vision he devoted relatively little effort. The most general statement of the theory to be disproved is simply that sight occurs through the emission of a power or ray from the eye. The theory might be defended in this general form by noting that an object in direct contact with the eye cannot be observed and therefore that separation between the eye and its object is an indispensable condition of sight. The same can be said of any substantial emanation from the object (because it too is an object), and the accidents of the object (e.g., its color and shape) cannot be transported without matter.[23] Therefore only one alternative remains: "the sensitive power must extend to the place of the perceived object to encounter it."[24]

But how can the sensitive power be extended to the visible object? Here we must qualify the general statement that sight occurs through the emission of a ray by defining the nature of the ray; we thereby elaborate the extramission theory into its particular versions—the Euclidean, Galenic, and so forth. Avicenna attempts this process of elaboration in each of the works where he treats vision, but unfortunately with little consistency, and no two works contain identical schemata; even the *Najāt* and the *Shifā*, the one conceived as an abridgement of the other, are not organized along identical lines.[25] However, if we look beyond the organization of Avicenna's arguments to their content, it becomes apparent that all the theories to which Avicenna addresses himself fall loosely into two main classes, covered by the rubrics "Euclidean" and "Galenic."[26] I propose, then, to recount Avicenna's refutation of these two versions of the theory.

The term "Euclidean," by which I have denominated the first

version of the extramission theory, is to be broadly construed to mean that "something issues from the eye, meets the object of sight, takes its form from without—and that this constitutes the act of seeing."[27] Moreover, it is essential to this theory, in Avicenna's view, that the ray issuing from the eye be a material substance, because "the sensitive power cannot be transported except by the mediation of body."[28] Avicenna recounts several of the arguments by which this theory had been defended, including the observation that a man sees rays emanating from his eyes under certain circumstances as when he has just awakened, and the claim of Galen and others that when one eye is closed the pupil of the other is dilated, proving that there is a material substance emanating from the eye.[29] There is another defense of the Euclidean theory, from the nature of images formed by reflection, to which Avicenna devotes an entire chapter; but this takes us into the finer points of the theory of reflection and is much too intricate to go into here.[30] Suffice it to say that Avicenna finds internal contradictions within it, which demonstrate its untenability. But to discredit one defense of the Euclidean theory is not, of course, to discredit the theory itself. To achieve the latter end, Avicenna finds that he must further divide the Euclidean theory into four subcategories, which are separately refutable: (1) The radial corporeal substance emanating from the eye constitutes a single homogeneous conical body, which is in contact with the entire visible object and also with the observer's eye. In this case, "there will have emerged from the eye, despite its smallness, a conical body of immense size, which will have compressed the air and repulsed all the heavenly bodies, or [else] it will have traversed an empty space."[31] (2) That which issues from the eye is a continuous substance, which makes contact with the entire visible object but loses contact with the observer's eye. Apparently Avicenna is here attempting to overcome the obvious objection to the first version of the Euclidean theory, namely, that a continuous body could not emerge from the eye and fill all the space between the eye and the fixed stars; by breaking contact with the eye, this substance need only spread itself over the visible object to whatever depth its quantity permits. (3) The substance issuing from the eye consists of separate rays or parts, not in mutual contact. These rays thus touch only certain portions of the visible object. (4) The radial corporeal substance does not make contact with the visible object at all.[32]

Avicenna rejects the first version of the Euclidean theory as absurd, because it suggests that from something as small as the eye can emerge a continuous substance large enough to fill a hemisphere of the world.[33] Moreover, this process must be repeated each time the eyes are opened: that is, either the radial substance must repeatedly issue forth and return, or else a new ray must be sent forth each time eyes are opened.[34] A further difficulty of this version of the Euclidean theory is that the extension of a continuous radial body as far as the fixed stars would require that the intervening air (and even the celestial spheres) be swept out of the way, unless, of course, this entire space were void; but to Avicenna neither possibility is conceivable.[35]

Avicenna concludes his assault on the first version of the Euclidean theory by arguing that if the visible object were perceived by a conical body issuing from the eye, then the remoteness of a visible object should not affect its apparent size and shape, and the size of the angle intercepted by a visible object at the eye would be irrelevant.[36] In his opinion, the extramission theory of Euclid entails that the power of perception is located in the base of the visual cone and therefore perceives the magnitude of the visible object by contact;[37] consequently, if the extramission theory were true, the true magnitude of a remote object should be directly perceived, and the laws of perspective would not apply. This argument, which strikes at the very foundations of the mathematical theory of vision, would surely have perplexed Euclid, Alkindi, Alhazen, and other practitioners of the mathematical approach; for their position was precisely the opposite, namely, that only an extramission theory (through its visual cone) makes the perception of magnitude intelligible.[38] This radical difference in interpretation can be understood only by recognizing that the real issue between Avicenna and the mathematicians was over the criteria by which to evaluate a theory of vision. Their position was that only the extramission theory (with its visual cone) can make sense of visual perception *mathematically*. His position was that the mathematics of the visual cone is made irrelevant and inapplicable by the fact that the visual power is not, according to the version of the extramission theory under consideration, fixed in the eye, where it can perceive the angle between rays touching the extremes of the object, but in the base of the visual cone, where it is able to acquire immediate knowledge of the object's true size; thus a *physical* or *psychological* understanding of the extramission theory reveals its inability to explain such facts of perception as the diminution of objects with distance from the observer.

The second version of the Euclidean theory is more obviously absurd than the first and can be dismissed with greater ease. If that which issues from the observer's eye should lose contact with the eye, what purpose could it serve, for the whole point of the extramission theory is to establish contact between the observer and the visible object? To maintain that one can perceive objects through rays that are no longer in contact with the eye is as foolish as to maintain that one can perceive things with his hand (by touch) after the hand has been severed from his body.[39] The only salvation for this theory is the supposition that contact is established through a medium that returns impressions from the disconnected ray to the eye; this, however, leads either to absurdity or to the Aristotelian theory, as will become apparent below.

The third version of the Euclidean theory, which maintains that the substance issuing from the eye consists of discrete rays in contact with both the eye and the visible object, is the closest of Avicenna's four versions to Euclid's own teaching. This version of the theory escapes the troublesome problem of a continuous body half as large as the universe emanating from the eye, since the rays can be regarded as diffused to whatever extent is required to explain their increased volume. However, there is also a most serious difficulty: rays perceive only what they encounter (for encounter between the visual power and the object is the essence of perception), which means that the observer "will perceive spots where the ray falls to the exclusion of the spots where it does not fall, so that he will only partially perceive the body, sensing some points here and there but missing the major part."[40] The difficulty can be escaped only by supposing that the rays use the medium that occupies the spaces between, rays, endowing it with the power of perception by changing it into their own nature and "becoming [with it] as one thing."[41] However, this maneuver has serious difficulties of its own:

> What would we say concerning the heaven when we observe it? Can we say that the heaven is changed into the nature of the issuing ray so as to be sentient with it, as though they are one thing, so that it encounters Saturn and sees the whole of it, and also Jupiter and the other great stars? The falsity of this is obvious.[42]

If it should be argued that the medium is not united with the ray (to become sentient) but only endowed with the power to return forms to the ray, then of what use are visual rays in the first place? Why not suppose that the medium is transformed directly from the surface of the eye and returns forms to the eye without the mediation of visual rays? Moreover, the air intermediate between two rays would necessarily return the same form to each of them, with the result that the same object would be perceived twice.[43]

A second argument against the theory of discrete visual rays (this third version of the Euclidean theory) is derived from the nature of matter, both celestial and terrestrial. It is known that void is nonexistent and therefore that the celestial spheres are without vacuities or pores. It is therefore impossible for them to be penetrated by rays, and if vision were to occur through the passage of material rays from the observer to the object, there would be no way of seeing the celestial bodies beyond them. A similar problem arises in vision through a body of water. On the theory that discrete rays are emitted from the eye, how it is possible to see the earth in a continuous fashion beneath a body of water, there being no void?[44] If it is that rays force their way into the water, creating passages where previously there were none, why does not the bulk of water increase because of the superaddition of the radial corporeal substance? Moreover, if there were void there [in the water], how great would the magnitude of its vacuities have to be in view of the fact that water is a heavy body, which [naturally] descends into vacuities and fills them? It is evident that the whole water would have to be vacuous, or its greater part, or [at least] half, so that this issuing substance could penetrate to the whole of that which is beneath it. . . .[45]

The fourth and last version of the Euclidean theory, namely, that the substance issuing from the eye does not reach the visible object, can be dismissed for reasons already discussed in connection with the second and third versions of the theory. If the visual ray does not reach the object, then the form of the object must be communicated to the ray by the air between the object and the terminus of the radiation. But if air has this property, "why does it not return [the form] to the pupil and avoid the labor of spirit issuing into the air?"[46] Whether the air acquires this property simply by virtue of its transparency or as the result of a permutation, the issuance of the ray is redundant and this theory untenable. Avicenna thus concludes the first and most extensive phase of his refutation of the extramission theory. By demonstrating the absurdity of each of the four possible versions of the Euclidean theory, he claims to demonstrate that vision cannot occur through the emission of a substance that proceeds from the observer's eye to the object of sight.

In the second phase of his refutation, Avicenna disputes the other major form of the extramission theory of vision—the Galenic theory, according to which the ray issuing from the eye does not itself perceive the visible object, but employs the intervening air (and any other transparent media present) as its instrument.[47] Avicenna's fullest refutation of this theory appears in the *Shifā*, where he points out that the air may become the instrument of the eye in either of two senses: it can either be rendered a true optical medium, capable of transmitting visual impressions to the eye, or be converted into a visual organ, percipient in itself.[48] Before pursuing these alternatives, however, Avicenna presents what he calls his general judgment or universal proposition, namely, that in either case the air cannot acquire a new disposition or state whereby it comes to possess a certain quality or property in itself. This is impossible because

148

a state (even a temporary one, which exists only so long as its efficient cause[49] continues to act) would exist in relation to all observers, whereas vision is clearly an individual phenomenon. For example, if the effect of the visual power should be a new state of the medium, it would follow

> that weak-sighted people would see better when they congregate . . . and that a man of weak sight would see better when he is near another man whose vision is stronger. . . . However, we observe that a weak-sighted man is not aided at all in his sight by congregating with those who see better or by joining many people of weak sight. Therefore it is evident that this [opinion] is false.[50]

To return to our two alternatives, then, the effect of the visual power must be to convert the air into a medium for the transmission of visual impressions (though only in relation to one observer) or else to convert the air into a sentient organ of sight.[51] The latter alternative is impossible, Avicenna points out in the *Najāt*, because if the air itself were sentient, then any disturbance of the air would necessarily distort vision;[52] furthermore, the laws of perspective would not hold because the sentient power would be in direct contact with the visible object.[53] In the *Shifā* he argues that it would be absurd to maintain

> that air is altered so as to possess sensibility, so that it would perceive the fixed stars and return to sight what it has perceived. Besides, air does not touch everything that is seen, for we see the fixed stars, which air does not touch; and it would be absurd to say that the heavens, which are between [us and the fixed stars] are affected by our sight and become its instrument. . . .[54]

Nor can it be reasonably maintained, as an alternative version of the theory, that light is a body dispersed throughout the air and the heavens, which is united to our eyes and becomes their instrument; for this would entail that the heavens contain pores through which the light passes,[55] which in turn would entail that only parts of the stars are visible. Finally, air and light are not conjoined to one observer to the exclusion of others; why then would they return their perceptions to one observer and not another?[56]

The other alternative, that the visual power perfects the air as a medium, cannot stand either. What kind of affection could air receive from sight so as to become capable of transmitting impressions (and, what is more, transmitting them only to the single observer whose visual power produced the transformation in the air)? Surely air cannot receive "the power of life," since it remains a simple element.[57] Nor is it reasonable to suppose that sight renders the air transparent in actuality, since the sun is much more efficacious in that regard. Sight cannot result from the heating or cooling of the air, for if it did, the contrary effect (as a result of the presence of other hot or cold bodies) would lead to a cessation of vision.[58] Perhaps, then, sight produces some quality that lacks a name; but "how, then, could proponents of this view know of it, and how did they apprehend it?"[59] Moreover, as Avicenna points out, he has already refuted (in his "general judgment") the possibility of changes that constitute a state or disposition of the medium. The conclusion then seems inescapable: if the air is actually transparent, if colors exist in actuality, and if the eye is healthy, nothing more is required for the occurrence of sight. As Avicenna expresses this conclusion in the *Dānishnāmā*, "since the air itself is in contact with the eye, it goes without saying that it transmits [the image] to the eye, and there is no need for a ray to issue [from the eye]."[60] In the final analysis, the Galenic theory must be rejected because it is redundant.

The true theory of vision, in Avicenna's opinion, is the Aristotelian. In the *Shifā* he outlines its essential elements:

> Just as other sensibles [than color and light] are not perceived because something extends from the senses to them and encounters them or is joined to them or sends a messenger to them, so vision does not occur because a ray issues forth in some way to encounter the visible object, but because the form of the thing seen comes to sight, transmitted by a transparent medium.[61]

The theory outlined in this passage is identical in its principal features to that of Aristotle, who wrote in his *De anima*: "Colour moves the transparent medium, e.g., the air, and this, being continuous, acts upon the sense organ. . . . For vision occurs when the sensitive faculty is acted upon; as it cannot be acted upon by the actual colour which is seen, there remains only the medium to act on it. . . ."[62] If Avicenna's account of his own theory seems unduly economical, the reason is that Aristotle had been equally terse.

There is more to Avicenna's theory of vision than I have here presented. In the *Najāt* and the *Dānishnāma* we find a comparison of sight to image-formation in a mirror, in the course of which Avicenna explains how remoteness of the visible object affects the perception of magnitude. And in the *Canon of Medicine*, he introduces certain elements of the Galenic theory of vision, including a description of ocular anatomy, the claim that the crystalline humor is the principal organ of sight, and an account of the transmission of the visual power to the crystalline humor through the visual spirit that fills the optic nerves.[63] But rather than pursue any of these efforts to develop his own theory, I wish to inquire how successfully Avicenna has combatted the extramission theory of his opponents.

The "Euclidean theory," in Euclid's hands, had been largely a mathematical theory of vision, effective so long as physical issues were set aside.[64] Although Ptolemy and Alkindi invested the theory with additional physical content, it remained primarily a mathematical theory, the success of which was to be judged by mathematical criteria.[65] By contrast, Avicenna ignores the mathematics of the Euclidean theory and makes a series of devastating physical points. He argues that if the rays remain in contact with the observer's eye, they must either form a continuous body and fill all of the space up to the fixed stars (an obvious physical impossibility) or separate and thus achieve a spotted impression of the visible object (an apparent observational falsehood); if they do not remain in contact with the observer's eye, they are useless in explaining perception. The theory of a material substance emanating from the eye is thus inconsistent either with the medieval (as well as modern) conception of material substance or with the universally accepted facts of visual perception. To this argument there is no reply.[66] Although he has not discredited the mathematical utility of the Euclidean theory of visual rays, Avicenna has adequately established that it does not represent the physical nature of the visual process.

Avicenna presents an equally convincing refutation of the Galenic theory. The claim that air becomes a sentient instrument of vision is untenable because it cannot explain how one manages to perceive clearly when the wind is blowing, or how it is that the same air can serve simultaneously as the visual instrument for a whole crowd of observers (to which one will the air return its perceptions?), or what kind of change occurs to make the air an instrument of vision. Nor is there escape in claiming that the air is not percipient, but only a medium for the transmission of visual impressions. This maneuver not only leaves unanswered the question about what kind of change could occur in the medium to give it the power of transmitting impressions to the observer (and only to the one observer whose visual power provoked the transformation of the medium), but makes the whole Galenic theory redundant, for it is perfectly obvious (to an Aristotelian, at any rate) that the medium is capable of returning impressions to sight without the issuance of visual rays. With a few strokes, Avicenna has deftly destroyed both the Euclidean and Galenic versions of the extramission theory as viable physical explanations of the process of sight. The Aristotelian theory seemed to be the only remaining alternative.

IV. CONCLUSION

What can we conclude from this analysis of arguments for and against the intromission and extramission theories of vision? First, I hope to have dispelled any impression that the intromission-extramission controversy was trivial or silly—unworthy of the attention lavished on it by natural philosophers from Aristotle to Alhazen. The issues were exceedingly complicated and by no means easily resolved; indeed, I would suggest that within the conceptual framework of the protagonists the issues were unresolvable.

Secondly, the arguments of Alkindi and Avicenna reveal that the controversy touched deeper issues than merely the direction

152

of radiation. It is true, of course, that the direction of radiation was much discussed; but at a more fundamental level the controversy reveals a basic disagreement between intromissionists and extramissionists about the aims and criteria of visual theory. Alkindi argued effectively against the intromission theory on *mathematical* grounds, revealing its inability to account for the laws of perspective; only the extramission theory with its visual cone, he claimed, could give a geometrical explanation of the perception of space. Avicenna, on the other hand, devastated the extramission theory on *physical* and *psychological* grounds, showing that the extramissionists' cone of visual rays is not a viable physical explanation of sight. Alkindi and Avicenna were thus arguing past one another: Alkindi ignoring the physical advantages of the intromission theory in order to expose its mathematical disadvantages, Avicenna ignoring the mathematical capabilities of the extramission theory in order to call attention to its physical deficiencies.

This failure to meet one another head-on was not simply the outcome of a strategy of attacking the opposition at its weakest point; nor was it due to lack of courage or intellect or honor; rather, it was an expression of the aims and fundamental assumptions of the several optical traditions. The extramission theory had always been essentially mathematical in character; Euclid's purpose had been to formulate a mathematical theory of perspective, and he had managed to hold physical content to a bare minimum. The extramission theories of Ptolemy and Alkindi, although endowed with more physical content, remained principally mathematical; and they were therefore to be judged by mathematical, rather than physical, criteria. The intromission theory, by contrast, was chiefly physical in purpose, designed to explain how the visible qualities of the perceived object are communicated to the organ of sight; it had no mathematical pretensions and was not to be judged by mathematical criteria. Thus the optical enterprise was deeply split into separate traditions having radically different aims, and the potential practitioner found himself compelled to choose between the mathematics and the physics of the visual process.[67] This is the same profound dilemma faced by the medieval astronomer, who

153

discovered that no single theory could successfully treat both the physics and the mathematics of the heavens and that he must choose between Aristotle's physics and Ptolemy's mathematics.[68] It should be clear then that when a Euclidean attacked the Aristotelian theory of vision on mathematical grounds, he was merely expressing his basic conception of the optical enterprise; since the purpose of visual theory was to provide a mathematical account of the perception of space, if it failed at this it was untenable, and any advantages it might possess from a physical standpoint were strictly irrelevant. Similarly, an Aristotelian could justifiably reject the Euclidean theory of vision for failing as a physical account, since (in his view) physics was what visual theory was all about.

Could this gulf between differing opinions of the aims of visual theory be bridged? Avicenna's contemporary, Alhazen (d. ca. 1039), showed that it could. Alhazen devised a new intromission theory, which incorporated the Euclidean and Ptolemaic visual cone and thus combined the mathematical advantages of the extramission theory with the physical advantages of the intromission theory.[69] Indeed, Alhazen also incorporated the achievements of the Galenists, thereby creating a theory that simultaneously satisfied mathematical, physical, and medical criteria. He thus obliterated the old battle lines and initiated a new optical tradition, the fundamental aims and assumptions of which have prevailed until the present.

1. I do not wish to quibble about the date at which serious scholarship on the history of early visual theory began. For convenience one might date the origins from J. L. Heiberg's edition of Euclid's optical works (*Euclidis opera omnia*, ed. J. L. Heiberg and H. Menge, vol. 7 [Leipzig, 1895]); or Julius Hirschberg's "Die Optik der alten Griechen," *Zeitschrift für Psychologie und Physiologie der Sinnesorgane* 16 (1898): 321–51; or J. I. Beare's *Greek Theories of Elementary Cognition from Alcmaeon to Aristotle* (Oxford: Clarendon Press, 1906).

2. Portions of the following account are taken from my "Alkindi's Critique of Euclid's Theory of Vision," *Isis* 62 (1971): 469–89, which the reader should see for a fuller discussion of Alkindi's theory of vision. The most convenient sources on Alkindi's life and works are George N. Atiyeh, *Al-Kindi: The Philosopher of the Arabs* (Rawalpindi: Islamic Research Institute, 1966); Majid Fakhry, *A History of Islamic Philosophy* (New York: Columbia University Press, 1970), pp. 82–112; Nicholas

Rescher, *Al-Kindi: An Annotated Bibliography* (Pittsburgh: University of Pittsburgh Press, 1964). For other sources see my "Alkindi's Critique," p. 469 n. 1.

3. Alkindi, *De aspectibus*, in Axel Anthon Björnbo and Sebastian Vogl, "Alkindi, Tideus und Pseudo-Euklid. Drei optische Werke," *Abhandlungen zur Geschichte der mathematischen Wissenschaften*, vol. 26, pt. 3 (1912), p. 9.

4. This third alternative might also be taken as a description of the Stoic or Galenic theory of vision. In this paper I will not be concerned to correct Alkindi and Avicenna when they oversimplify, distort, or misunderstand ancient visual theories.

5. For a fuller account of ancient theories of vision, see the articles in this volume by Robert Turnbull, Edward Lee, and David Hahm; also chap. 1 of my *Theories of Vision from Alkindi to Kepler* (Chicago: University of Chicago Press, 1976).

6. *De aspectibus*, p. 10. Cf. Aristotle *Meteorologica* III.4.373ᵇ3–10. Aristotle employs an extramission theory of vision in the *Meteorologica*; in his later psychological works he defends the intromission theory usually associated with his name.

7. *De aspectibus*, p. 12. Cf. Theon's preface to his recension of Euclid's *Optica*, in Euclide, *L'Optique et la Catoptrique*, trans. Paul Ver Eecke (Paris: Albert Blanchard, 1959), pp. 55–56.

8. *De aspectibus*, pp. 11–12.

9. The principal defense of the extramission theory had always been that it alone could explain the geometrical features of the perception of space. That is, it could explain the localization of a given point in the visual field by the location (within the visual cone) of the ray intercepted by that point; and it could explain the apparent size of objects in the visual field by the size of the angles formed (at the eye) by rays proceeding to their extreme points.

10. Ibid., p. 9.

11. And, of course, Alkindi says nothing about the corporeality of the forms. In suggesting that Epicurean *simulacra*, like Alkindi's forms, are coherent images, I do not wish to imply that the atoms comprising a *simulacrum* were thought to be physically hooked; following Edward Lee (above, p. 29) I admit that *simulacra* were regarded merely as "convoys of atoms" maintaining a fixed configuration as they leave the body. This might be called mathematical, as opposed to physical, coherence. On the Atomistic theory of vision, see Epicurus, "Letter to Herodotus," in Diogenes Laertius, *Lives of Eminent Philosophers*, trans. R. D. Hicks (London: Heinemann, 1925), 2:577–79; Cyril Bailey, *The Greek Atomists and Epicurus* (Oxford: Clarendon Press, 1928), pp. 406–9. Alexander of Aphrodisias, not himself an atomist, rejected any attempt to consider atomistic forms as incoherent entities; see Bernard Saint-Pierre, "La Physique de la vision dans l'antiquité: contribution à l'établissement des sources anciennes de l'optique médiévale" (Ph.D. diss., University of Montreal, 1972), pp. 224–28, 290–91.

12. Except the negative justification that Plato and Aristotle issued no denial of the theory of coherent forms that Alkindi wishes to attribute to them; indeed, since they presented no alternative theory to explain how shapes are perceived, Alkindi might well suppose that he has captured their view. On the perception of shape in the Platonic and Aristotelian theories, see Robert Turnbull's discussion, above.

13. Alkindi gives no detail regarding the process of radiation, but I think one may surmise that the form, as it is propagated toward the eye, would maintain the same "edgewise" orientation with respect to the eye possessed by the circle of which it is the form. Once inside the eye the form is not perceived according to the laws of perspective because the visual power entirely surrounds it.

14. Alkindi himself (in a different context) stated the principle of punctiform analysis on which Alhazen would build a successful intromission theory; see Lindberg, "Alkindi's Critique," pp. 485–86.

15. The following discussion is taken largely from chapter 3 of my forthcoming *Theories of Vision*. Avicenna's autobiography (with additions made after his death by his friend al-Juzjani) is most readily available in a translation with commentary by A. J. Arberry, "Avicenna: His Life and Times," in *Avicenna: Scientist and Philosopher*, ed. G. M. Wickens (London: Luzac & Co., 1952), pp. 9–28. The secondary literature on Avicenna is immense, but particularly useful summaries (in addition to the articles assembled by Wickens) are Carra De Vaux, *Avicenne* (Paris: Félix Alcan, 1900); Soheil M. Afnan, *Avicenna: His Life and Works* (London: Allen & Unwin, 1958); F. Rahman, "Ibn Sina," in *A History of Muslim Philosophy*, ed. M. M. Sharif, vol.1 (Wiesbaden, 1963), pp. 480–506; A. M. Goichon, "Ibn Sī nā," *The Encyclopaedia of Islam*, new ed., vol. III, fascs. 55–56 (Leiden/London, 1969), pp. 941–47; and Fakhry, *History of Islamic Philosophy*, pp. 147–83.

16. The best bibliography (in a Western language) of Avicenna's extant works is that of M. M. Anawati, O.P., "La Tradition manuscrite orientale de l'oeuvre d'Avicenne," *Revue thomiste* 51 (1951): 407–40. On the translation and Western dissemination of Avicenna's works, see M. T. d'Alverny, "Les Traductions d'Avicenne (Moyen Age et Renaissance)," in *Avicenna nella storia della cultura medioevale* (Accademia Nazionale dei Lincei, Problemi attuali di scienza e di cultura, Quaderno 40 [Rome: Accademia Nazionale dei Lincei, 1957]), pp. 71–87; "Notes sur les traductions médiévales des oeuvres philosophiques d'Avicenne," *Archives d'histoire doctrinale et littéraire du moyen âge* 19 (1952): 337–58; and "Avendauth?" in *Homenaje a Millás-Vallicrosa* (Barcelona: Consejo superior de investigaciones científicas, 1954), 1: 19–43.

Avicenna's fullest treatment of vision is in pt. IV, bk. 6 (the psychological section) of the *Kitāb al-Shifā*. This section was translated into Latin in the second half of the twelfth century by Avendauth (who rendered it orally into Castilian) and Domenicus Gundissalinus (who put it into Latin) and circulated as *De anima* or *Liber sextus naturalium*; the Latin text is available in a modern critical edition by Simone Van Riet, *Avicenna Latinus: Liber de anima seu sextus de naturalibus, I-III* (Louvain: E. Peeters; Leiden: E. J. Brill, 1972). I have employed this (hereafter cited as *De Anima*) and the critical edition and French translation of the Arabic text by Ján Bakoš, *Psychologie d'Ibn Sīnā (Avicenne) d'après son oeuvre aš-Šifa*, 2 vols. (Prague: Académie Tchécoslovaque des Sciences, 1956) (hereafter cited as "Bakoš"). For editions and translations of the other works in which Avicenna treats vision, see below.

Avicenna's theory of vision has been almost entirely neglected by historians of optics. The principal exceptions are Eilhard Wiedemann, "Ibn Sînâ's Anschauung vom Sehvorgang," *Archiv für die Geschichte der Naturwissenschaften und der Technik* 4 (1913): 239–41; and Vescovini, *Studi sulla prospettiva* (Turin: G. Giappichelli, 1965) chap. 5; however, neither makes full use of the available sources.

17. S. Landauer, "Die Psychologie des Ibn Sînâ," *Zeitschrift der deutschen morgenländischen Gesellschaft* 29 (1875): 336–39.

18. Arberry, "Avicenna," pp. 20–23; Afnan, *Avicenna*, pp. 65–68.

19. Actually it is Euclid's, Ptolemy's, and Alkindi's way, but not Plato's.

20. This description is applicable to the Galenic or Stoic theory, though (as will be seen below) Avicenna probably intends it to apply to the Euclidean theory as well.

21. Avicenna, *A Compendium on the Soul by Abû-'Aly al-Husayn Ibn 'Abdallah Ibn Sînâ*, trans., Edward A. van Dyck (Verona: Nicola Paderno, 1906), pp. 51–52; I have altered van Dyck's parentheses to brackets, since they clearly represent the editor's explanatory additions. The Arabic text and a German translation of the *Compendium* are contained in Landauer, "Psychologie des Ibn Sînâ." In fact, Aristotle had explicitly denied the comparison between vision and the formation of mirror images; see *De sensu* II.438a5-7.

22. F. Rahman, *Avicenna's Psychology: English Translation of the Kitāb al Najāt* (London: Oxford University Press, 1952), p. 27.

23. Both the Latin translation of Avendauth and Gundissalinus and the French translation of Bakoš are obscure at this point, but Avicenna's intent is clear.

24. I quote here from the medieval Latin translation of *De anima* (pt. IV, chap. 6 of the *Shifā*), ed. Van Riet, p. 214. Cf. Bakoš' French translations, p. 82. I would like to express my gratitude to Mlle Van Riet for permitting me to see her text while it was still in typescript.

25. One example will suffice to illustrate the kind of schema devised by Avicenna. In the *Najāt*, he argues that what emanates from the eye is either (A) material or (B) immaterial. If it is material, than either (A1) it remains a coherent body, in contact with the eye and reaching to the fixed stars, or (A2) it is dispersed into discrete rays, or (A3) it is united with the air and the heavens to form a coherent and sentient instrument of vision. If it is immaterial, it must be a quality that transforms the air and renders it either (B1) a medium of transmission or (B2) sentient in itself. In the discussion below, I have largely followed the arrangement employed by Avicenna in the *Shifā*.

26. Avicenna does not refer to either Euclid or Galen by name, but it is clearly to their theories (broadly defined) that he was directing his refutation. For example, theories A1 and A2 (n. 25) are fundamentally Euclidean, and A3, B1, and B2 are Galenic. The extramission theory of vision would have been available to Avicenna not only in the words of Euclid and Galen but also of Alkindi and Ḥunain and perhaps of Ptolemy and Tideus.

27. Rahman, *Avicenna's Psychology*, p. 27.

28. *De anima*, p. 214; cf. Bakoš, p. 82.

27. Rahman, *Avicenna's Psychology*, p. 27.

28. *De Anima*, p. 214; cf. Bakoš, p. 82. Avicenna also notes that the radiating substance assumes a conical shape and that vision occurs best through its central axis (Van Riet, pp. 212 13; Bakoš, p. 81); he thus reveals that he has in mind not simply the theory of Euclid in its original form, but the later elaborations of Ptolemy, Damianus, and Alkindi.

29. *De anima*, pp. 214-15; Bakoš, p. 82. See Aristotle, *De sensu*, II.437^{a}24; Galen, *On The Usefulness of The Parts of the Body*, trans. Margaret T. May (Ithaca: Cornell University Press, 1968), 2:476.

30. Avicenna first presents this defense in chap. 5 of *De anima* (pp. 216–19, Bakoš, pp. 83-84); he then devotes all of chap. 6 to its refutation.

31. Rahman, *Avicenna's Psychology*, p. 28. Cf. *De anima*, pp. 226–27; Bakoš, p. 87.

32. At one point Avicenna maintains, of this fourth alternative, that the substance also loses contact with the eye (*De anima*, ed. Van Riet, p. 226; Bakoš, p. 87), but later he appears to admit that in fact contact is maintained (*De anima*, p. 234; Bakoš, p. 91). Avicenna's refutation will prove to be equally effective in either case.

33. *De anima*, p. 226; Bakoš, p. 87. Cf. Rahman, *Avicenna's Psychology*, p. 28; Avicenna, *Le livre de science* [the *Dānishnāmā*], trans. Mohammad Achena and Henri Massé (Paris: Société d'Édition "Les Belles Lettres," 1958), 2:58. Avicenna apparently accepts a visual angle of 180 degrees, perhaps having binocular vision in mind. This objection of Avicenna to the extramission theory had been anticipated by Aristotle and Alexander of Aphrodisias; on the former, see *De sensu* II.438^{a}26-27; on the latter, see Saint-Pierre, "La Physique de la vision," p. 215.

34. *De anima*, p. 226; Bakoš, p. 87.

35. Rahman, *Avicenna's Psychology*, p. 28.

36. *De anima*, pp. 226–27; Bakoš, pp. 87–88. *Livre de science*, 2:59, 61.

37. There is no evidence that Euclid, Alkindi, and other Euclideans ever in fact dealt with this question.

38. The position of the mathematicians was that one judges the size of an object by

the angle between the visual rays that proceed from the eye to the extremities of the object. The apex of the visual cone thus serves as a center of perspective. Though not of the mathematical school, Galen agreed that only on an extramission theory can magnitude be discerned; see his *De placitis Hippocratis et Platonis*, in *Claudii Galeni opera omnia*, ed. C. G. Kühn, (Leipzig: Cnobloch, 1823), 5:618. A similar view was expressed by Tideus and Ḥunain ibn Isḥāq; see Tideus, *De speculis*, in Björnbo and Vogl, "Drei optische Werke," p. 75; *The Book of the Ten Treatises on the Eye Ascribed to Hunain ibn Is-hâq (809–877 A.D.)*, trans. Max Meyerhof (Cairo: Government Press, 1928), p. 32. Even Alhazen, who completely rejected the extramission theory, admitted grudgingly that it is useful for a mathematical understanding of vision; see David C. Lindberg, "Alhazen's Theory of Vision and Its Reception in the West," *Isis* 58 (1967): 326–37. And finally, Averroes acknowledged that the mathematical achievements of the Euclideans were evidence for the extramission theory of vision; see Averroes, *Epitome of Parva naturalia*, trans. Harry Blumberg (Cambridge, Mass.: Mediaeval Academy of America, 1961), p. 15.

39. *De anima*, p. 227–28; Bakoš, p. 88.

40. Rahman, *Avicenna's Psychology*, p. 28. See also *De anima*, p. 228; Bakoš, p. 88; *Livre de science*, 2:59.

41. *De anima*, p. 228; cf. Bakoš, p. 88. With this supposition the third version of the Euclidean theory becomes very like the Galenic theory of vision.

42. *De anima*, p. 228; cf. Bakoš, p. 88.

43. *De anima*, p. 229; Bakoš, pp. 88–89.

44. The more appropriate question would seem to be: How is it possible to see the earth at all in the absence of void, or to see it continuously even if vacuous pores should exist?

45. *De anima*, p. 230; cf. Bakoš, p. 89.

46. *De anima*, p. 234; cf. Bakoš, p. 91.

47. When he first describes the Galenic theory in the *Shifā*, Avicenna makes a statement that could be construed to mean that the ray itself meets the visible object (along with the air to which it is conjoined): "Another opinion is that of him who holds that a ray issues from the pupil; but out of the pupil comes that which touches a hemisphere of the heaven only by a dispersion [of the ray], from which comes the enlarging of vision [in the form of a cone]." However, not only is this remark highly ambiguous, but it is followed immediately by another that seems to assert the traditional Galenic view that the ray is not itself conveyed to the visible object: "But when it [the ray] issues forth and is conjoined to illuminated air, the air becomes its instrument, and it apprehends through the air" (*De anima*, p. 213; cf. Bakoš, p. 81). Moreover, a little later in the argument, Avicenna points out that the Galenists attack the Euclideans on the grounds that if a body actually traversed the space between the eye and the fixed stars, a perceptible time would be required; the obvious implication is that since no time is perceived, the substance issuing from the eye cannot be conveyed to the fixed stars (see *De anima*, pp. 215–16; Bakoš, p. 82).

When Avicenna gets down to a systematic refutation of the Galenic theory, he describes two principal versions of it. The visual ray, which transforms the transparent medium into an instrument of vision can be either a material substance or an immaterial quality. However, he refutes both views with the same argument, and I see no point in making any more of the distinction than he made. What is essential to the Galenic theory is that the air is transformed into an instrument of vision, and it is to this point alone that Avicenna directs his argument (see *De anima*, pp. 219–20; Bakoš, p 84; cf. Rahman, *Avicenna's Psychology*, pp. 28–29).

48. To be quite precise, Avicenna mentions yet a third possibility: the air can be converted into a visual organ capable of returning impressions to the eye (rather than percipient in itself). However, the distinction between this view and the claim that the air may become a *medium* capable of transmitting visual impressions to the eye is a

very fine one indeed, and Avicenna makes little of it in *De anima* and overlooks it altogether in the *Najāt*. In either case, the air returns visual impressions to the eye, and it is not relevant to a refutation of the theory whether one calls the transformed air a transmitting medium or a visual organ. See *De anima*, p. 222; Bakoš, p. 85; cf. Rahman, *Avicenna's Psychology*, p. 29.

49. In this case the visual power.

50. *De anima*, p. 222; cf. Bakoš, p. 85. See also Rahman, *Avicenna's Psychology*, pp. 28 29; *Livre de science*, 2:58.

51. This recalls a similar distinction made by Tideus, *De speculis*, in Björnbo and Vogl, "Drei optische Werke," pp. 74-75.

52. On the similar argument of Alexander of Aphrodisias, see Saint-Pierre, "La Physique de la vision," p. 216.

53. Rahman, *Avicenna's Psychology*, p. 29. On the latter argument, see above.

54. *De anima*, pp. 222-23; cf. Bakoš, pp. 85-86.

55. In his own theory of vision, Avicenna can argue that light is a form or quality, rather than a body, and thus escape this difficulty.

56. *De anima*, p. 223; Bakoš, p. 86.

57. *De anima*, p. 224; Bakoš, p. 86.

58. Cf. Aristotle *De sensu* II.437^{b}17-24.

59. *De anima*, p. 225; cf. Bakoš, p. 87.

60. I have translated this from the French version of Achena and Massé, *Livre de science*, 2:59.

61. *De anima*, pp. 213-14; cf. Bakoš, p. 81.

62. Aristotle *De anima* II.7.419^{a}13-19, trans. W. S. Hett, rev. ed. (London, 1957), p. 107.

63. For a full account of these aspects of Avicenna's theory, see chap. 3 of my *Theories of Vision*.

64. See Lindberg, "Alkindi's Critique, pp. 471-74.

65. On Ptolemy, see Albert Lejeune, *Euclide et Ptolémée. Deux stades de l'optique géométrique grecque* (Louvain: Bibliothèque de l'Université, 1948), pp. 15-84. On Alkindi, see Lindberg, "Alkindi's Critique," pp. 478-87.

66. If somebody should argue that the ray is not a material substance, Avicenna would reply that a medium is then required, which brings us to the equally untenable Galenic theory.

67. To be precise, there was also a third alternative—the Galenic or medical tradition— to complicate the decision. I have been able only to touch upon the Galenic theory in this paper; for a fuller discussion, see my *Theories of Vision*, chaps. 1, 3, and 8. For a picture of a fourteenth-century natural philosopher struggling with this same choice, see A. G. Molland, "John Dumbleton and the Status of Geometrical Optics," *Actes du XIIIe Congrès international d'histoire des sciences, Moscou, 18-24 août 1971* (Moscow, 1974), 3-4:125-30.

68. Neither in astronomy nor in visual theory was the dichotomy complete. Ptolemaic astronomy possessed a certain amount of physical content (e.g., the centrality and fixity of the earth), while Aristotle's system of homocentric spheres was not devoid of mathematical capability. In visual theory, we have seen that Alkindi and other extramissionists made certain physical claims, while Avicenna (in a section of the *Dānishnāmā* that I have not touched upon) added a brief geometrical discussion to his intromission theory.

69. See A. I. Sabra "Ibn al-Haytham, Abū 'Alī al-Ḥasan ibn al-Ḥasan," *Dictionary of Scientific Biography*, 6:191-94; also my "Alhazen's Theory of Vision," pp. 328-29; and my *Theories of Vision*, chap. 4.

Chapter Six

SENSATION AND INFERENCE
IN ALHAZEN'S THEORY OF VISUAL PERCEPTION

I

Alhazen's theory of visual perception occupies a considerable part of his *Optics*, itself a large work in seven books averaging about forty-three thousand words each.[1] Of the eight chapters that constitute the Arabic text of the first book, five are taken up by a theory of vision that includes a discussion of the effect of light upon sight, a description of the structure of the eye, an explanation of the manner of vision, a statement of the uses of the various parts of the eye, and finally an account of the conditions of vision.[2] Book II, on the objects of vision and the manner of their apprehension, contains the core of the theory of perception. Book III is on the errors of direct vision and deals, among other things, with errors of "pure sensation," of recognition, and of perceptual inferences. The errors of vision through reflection from mirrors of various types are the subject of Book VI, and the last chapter of Book VII is concerned with errors due to refraction. Some of these considerations already figure, sometimes prominently, in Ptolemy's *Optics*, from which Alhazen's own investigations clearly started. But no such detailed, elaborate, and systematic treatment of the subject of perception has come down to us from any writer in antiquity or in the Middle Ages prior to the eleventh century.[3]

Nevertheless, Alhazen's views, and, to a slightly lesser extent, those of Ptolemy, have been almost totally neglected by historians,[4] and, it seems, for the same reason. Historians of philosophy who are concerned with the history of perception have usually regarded works on optics as scientific or mathematical and therefore falling outside their domain, whereas historians of science and mathematics have tended to ignore the psychological sections in such works as properly belonging to philosophy. Even historians of optics who have given attention to Alhazen's doctrine of vision appear for the most part to have assumed that it was feasible to elucidate the account presented in book I of the *Optics* without exploring the subsequent account on perception, as if the two could meaningfully be divorced from one another.

The questions that can be asked about Alhazen's theory of perception are many and of different kinds. Some are historical and concern its relation to preceding theories (for example, those of Ptolemy and Aristotle), or the extent and consequences of its influence on later thinkers in the Islamic world and in Europe. Others concern the nature of Alhazen's approach to the problem of perception, the character of his treatment, or the details of his explanations. In the following pages an attempt will be made to clarify certain key concepts in Alhazen's treatment of perception, with emphasis on the connection between the accounts of the first and second books of the *Optics*, and on the distinction between sensation and inference that is basic to the second book.

II

The account of vision (*ibsār*: *visio*)[5] in book I is an account of how a faithful representation (the word is not Alhazen's) of the distribution of light and color on the surface of a visible object is conducted through the medium to the eye and thence to the brain. Strictly speaking, however, there is no vision *of the object* without the concurrence of certain mental operations that it is the aim of book II to expound. And though Alhazen speaks of the occurrence of the representation in the brain as a sensation (*ihsās*: *sensus*), this sensation, according to him, never takes place without being accompanied by some of those operations. His first account may therefore properly be described as a theory of the physical and physiological conditions of vision.[6]

This theory combines two concepts that it had become traditional to oppose to one another: the concept of form (*sūra*,

161

eidos, forma) associated with Aristotle and his followers, and the concept of ray on which mathematicians like Euclid and Ptolemy had based their geometrical explanations of vision.[7] Alhazen regarded this combination as a synthesis between a physical and a mathematical approach to the study of light and vision. He characterized the physical approach as one concerned with *what* things are—*what* light and transparency, for example, are—and the mathematical approach as one aiming to determine *how* things behave; for example, *how* light extends in transparent media or *how* it is reflected from polished surfaces or refracted when passing from one medium into another.[8] From the physicists or natural philosophers he obtained such statements as: light is an "essential form" of self-luminous bodies, and an "accidental form" in bodies that are illuminated from outside; transparency is an "essential form" in virtue of which light is transmitted from one point to another; and a ray is an "essential form" that extends rectilinearly in transparent bodies.[9] From the mathematicians, and from Ptolemy in particular, he inherited the experimental and mathematical character of his entire book.

The Arabic version of Ptolemy's *Optics* that was known to Alhazen, like the extant Latin translation made from it in the twelfth century, lacked the first part in which Ptolemy proposed a theory of luminous and visual radiations.[10] This accident had important consequences for the subsequent history of optics. It signaled the absence of a theoretical basis that students of the subject were invited to make up for as best they could. Alhazen's achievement can be viewed as an attempt to fulfill this task by subjecting the "physical" or peripatetic doctrine of vision to a geometrical treatment in terms of rays. In the *Optics* he identified the physicists' position as that according to which "vision is brought about by a form (*ṣūra*) that comes from the visible object to the eye and through which sight perceives the form (*ṣūra*) of the object"; whereas mathematicians agreed that "vision is brought about by a ray that goes from the eye to the visible object and by means of which sight perceives the object; that this ray extends on straight lines whose extremities meet at the center of the eye; and that each ray through which a visible object is perceived has as a whole the shape of a cone whose vertex is the center of the eye and whose base is the surface of the object."[11] Obviously, these two doctrines could not simply be juxtaposed without modification. The resulting synthesis retained the mathematicians' rays, for example, but only as imaginary lines on which the forms extended.[12] And, for the first time, it provided an answer to the question of how a form representing the object passed without distortion through the eye considered as a dioptric structure. It is this question and the answer given to it by Alhazen that should now concern us.

The Greek atomists had explained vision as the impinging on the eye jelly of a stream of skins or idols that are continually being separated from the surfaces of visible objects. Now Alhazen's "forms" are not corporeal, but they are supposed by him to radiate in a manner that would have well suited an atomistic theory. For just as it would have been natural in such a theory to assume that atoms went off from all points of the object-surface in all directions (for why should they behave otherwise?), so Alhazen's forms radiated not from the object as a whole but from every point on it rectilinearly in every direction. And the fact that these forms were immaterial would make them less vulnerable to objections which the earlier atomists might perhaps have found more difficult to answer.

The forms that radiate in this manner are forms of the light and the color in the object, whether essential or accidental. Accidental or acquired light and color are *not reflected* from an opaque object, but, rather, having been "received" and "fixed" in the object, they behave like essentially inherent light and color, i.e., radiate from all points in all directions. Reflection proper is a case of sending back the impinging light and color, and it takes place in a given plane at a given angle. Colors, it must be emphasized, are no less real that light. They may even be capable of sending out their forms independently of light, but they are never visible without it. The forms of color are always found mingled with those of light.[13]

Alhazen's explanation of the manner of vision, in the limited sense indicated above, as an application of this principle of the radiation of forms to a certain view of the construction and functioning of the eye. Starting from current anatomical knowledge originally derived from Galen, he conceived of a geometrical arrangement of the principal coats of the eye that served his own purpose. The uvea is a sphere that contains the albugineous, crystalline, and vitreous humors, in this order. It is placed close to the cornea and therefore eccentrically to the eyeball. The front surface of the crystalline is, however, concentric with the cornea, or rather with that part of the cornea which directly faces the pupil. The middle of the pupil, the center of the uvea, and the center of the eyeball all lie on one straight line that extends to the middle of the optic nerve. The center of the eye lies behind the interface that separates the crystalline and vitreous humors. This interface is either plane or spherical so that the line of centers is perpendicular to it. It follows that lines drawn from the eyecenter to the surface of the cornea (the so-called lines of the ray, or radial lines) are all perpendicular to that surface and to the crystalline-surface.[14]

Now, in accordance with the stated principle, the light and color (or their forms) that extend along divergent lines from a given point on an object placed opposite the eye, will spread over the eye-surface. As this is true for every point on the object, the light and color from all these points will concur at every point of the eye-surface. And since refraction will take place at all points of that surface, still more confusion of forms will occur on the crystalline-surface. To make sure that a form preserving the order of the parts of the object as a whole is laid out on the crystalline-surface, Alhazen assumes that only forms going through the eye along lines perpendicular to its surface are effective in the process of vision. Those lines are, of course, the radial lines drawn outward from the eye-center. The points where these lines intersect the crystalline-surface will have a one-to-one correspondence with all points on the object.[15] The sensation that, according to Alhazen's repeated statements, takes place first at the crystalline is a sensation of the ordered form as it penetrates the body of the crystalline along the radial lines.

III

The doctrine that the crystalline is the sensitive organ in the eye had been urged by Galen and his many followers;[16] and, as Alhazen stated, "That sight perceives the visible objects through the straight lines whose extremities meet at the center of the eye is accepted by all mathematicians, there being no disagreement among them about it. And these lines are what mathematicians call lines of the ray."[17] These ideas, however, now receive certain refinements as a result of their being taken into a new theoretical scheme. First, the reception of light and color through lines of the visual cone is attributed simply to the "nature" of sight.[18] Gradually, however, a distinction between two modes of reception emerges:

> . . . The crystalline is disposed both to receive and perceive [the forms]. Thus the forms traverse it on account of the receptive and also perceptive power in it and through which it is disposed to have perception. And since it is disposed to receive these forms through the radial lines, the forms traverse its body along those lines.[19]

Again—the distinction becoming clearer:

> As for the sensitive organ, i.e., the crystalline humor, it does not receive the forms of colors and lights in the way they are received by the air and the non-sensitive transparent bodies, but in a different manner from that in which the transparent bodies receive them. For this organ being disposed to sense those forms, it receives them *qua* sensitive in addition to its receiving them *qua* transparent.[20]

And, finally, in book II:

> The sensitive organ [i.e., crystalline] does not receive the forms in the same way as they are received by transparent bodies. For the sensitive organ receives these forms and senses them, and the forms go through it on account of its transparency and on account of the sensitive power that is in it. Therefore it receives these forms in the manner proper to sensation (*qabūla iḥsāsin*), whereas transparent bodies receive them only in the manner proper to transmission

165

(*qabūla ta'diyatin*) without sensing them. And if the sensitive body's reception of these forms is not like their reception by non-sensitive transparent bodies, then the forms do not extend through the sensitive body along the lines required by transparent bodies, but rather along the extension of the parts of the sensitive body. Sight is thus characterized by receiving the forms along the radial lines alone, because it is a property of forms to extend in transparent bodies along all straight lines and therefore they come to the eye along all straight lines. But if sight received them along all lines on which they arrive, the forms would not [appear] to it ordered. And therefore sight has come to be characterized by receiving the forms through those [radial] lines alone, so that it would perceive the forms with the order they have on the surfaces of visible objects.[21]

That sensation takes place by means of lines perpendicular to the crystalline-surface is not, therefore, simply or primarily due to the superior strength of action along those lines,[22] but rather to a property of the crystalline itself, namely, its selective sensitivity. It is a function of the crystalline, as a sensitive body, to sort out the forms coming to it from different sides, pick up those forms that extend on the perpendiculars, and hand them down along the same privileged directions to the vitreous humor. The latter thus receives a total form whose elements correspond one-to-one with their origins in the visual field. The vitreous humor, in addition to its transparency and sensitivity, has the further property of conveying the total form as an integral whole to the optic nerve,[23] where different points of the form will sensitize different parts of the visual spirit. Since these parts are separately confined to different filaments along which they travel, a total form, undisturbed by the bending of the nerve, will eventually arrive at the brain. Already, at the common nerve, the form coming from one eye will have coincided with the form from the other symmetrically disposed eye, and it is this united form that the *ultimum sentiens* perceives.[24]

IV

Two questions may now be briefly considered: what, in the light of what we have seen, could be the meaning of Alhazen's statement that sensation first takes place in the crystalline, and what should we make of his concept of form? Both questions are clearly important for an understanding of his theory of perception.

Alhazen speaks generally of the effect of light in the eye as something "of the nature of pain"; and it is the pain felt in the eyes when gazing at intense light that he cites as an empirical evidence in support of the intromission hypothesis.[25] At one place he appears to be saying further that the visual sensation *in* the crystalline does not itself differ generically from the sensation of pain, even if no pain is felt:

> The effect that light produces in the crystalline is of the nature of pain. But while some pains are such that they disturb the organ suffering them and upset the soul, others, being slight, are found to be bearable. . . . Pains of this description are not felt, and the subject suffering them does not judge them to be pains on account of their slightness. . . . Now the effects of lights in the eye are all of the same kind and only vary by more or less. That being so and the effect of strong lights being of the nature of pain, all luminous effects in the eye are of the nature of pain and only vary by more or less. But due to the slight effect in the eye of weak and moderate lights they are not perceived as pain. The crystalline's sensation of the effects of lights is therefore of the same nature as the sensation of pain.[26]

A few pages later, however, Alhazen makes his position clearer:

> It may be said [objected] that the forms occurring in the eye do not reach the common nerve, but rather it is the sensation taking place in the eye that extends to the common nerve in the same way that the sensation of pain and of tangible objects extend; and when this sensation reaches the common nerve the last sentient perceives the sensible object. . . .
> We reply that the sensation produced in the eye no doubt reaches the common nerve. But the sensation produced in the eye is not only a sensation of pain, but a sensation of an effect of the nature of pain, and a sensation of luminosity, and of color, and of the order of the parts of the object.[27] Now the sensation of colors and of the order of the object's parts is not of the nature of pain. We shall show later on [in bk. II] how the eye's sensation of each one of these things is produced. But the sensation of the form of the visible object as it is can only be produced by the sensation of

167

everything in this form. Further, if the sensation that takes place in the eye reaches the common nerve and it is from the sensation produced in the common nerve that the sensitive faculty perceives the form of the visible object, then the sensation occurring in the common nerve is a sensation of the light and the color and the order. Thus, in any case, the thing that comes from the eye to the common nerve and from which the last sentient perceives the form of the object is a thing from which the last sentient perceives the light and color in the visible object and the configuration of its parts. But the thing from which the last sentient perceives the light and color and order is a certain form. Thus from the form produced in the eye there comes, in any case, to the common nerve a certain ordered form. And from the ordered form occurring in this nerve the last sentient perceives the form of the object as it is in itself. Therefore, the sensation of the effect produced in the surface of the crystalline reaches the common nerve, and so does also the form of the light and color that occurs in the surface of the crystalline, and it gets there with the order it has on the crystalline-surface.[28]

No sensation, whether of pain or of form, is "accomplished" until it arrives at the last sentient, which resides in the front of the brain.[29] When the effect produced in the eyes by a bright light reaches the brain, it is perceived as pain that, indeed, is felt in both eyes. But the sensitive faculty does not become aware of the forms coming to it as located in the crystalline. In what sense, then, is the crystalline said to be the place where *sensation* of forms *first* occurs? There can, I think, be only one simple answer to this question: by selecting the forms that extend in certain special directions, the crystalline performs in fact the *first* necessary operation in the process of vision. Alhazen asserts: "It is only at the crystalline that the forms of visible objects are set in order by means of the radial lines, for it is at that organ that sensation begins."[30] This, of course, can be put the other way round: sensation begins at the crystalline *because* it is there, and only there, that the forms are properly arranged in respect to veridical perception; visual sensation is therefore said to begin at the crystalline because it depends, in the first place, on a property that exclusively belongs to the crystalline humor.

V

"Form" is an undefined term in the *Optics*. Two expressions in the long passage just quoted perhaps come nearest to a definition: form is that "thing that comes from the eye to the common nerve and from which the last sentient perceives the form of the object," "a thing," that is, "from which the last sentient perceives the light and color in the visible object and the configuration of its parts." Though it may be described as an optical array, a form in Alhazen's sense is not a picture depicted anywhere in the eye, and should not therefore be mistaken for the image produced in a pin-hole (or lens) camera, or the impression made by a material *eidōlon*.[31] As a representation of the object, it is perceptible only after it has been singled out from a multitude of confused rays on the crystalline-surface and transmitted to the brain; and it is perceptible only to the faculty of sense. From a historical point of view one may say that the crystalline's selective power performs a function corresponding to, but only corresponding to, that which Kepler later ascribed to the crystalline by regarding it as a lens that casts a distinct picture on the retina. It organizes the visual matter before this matter is presented to the sense faculty.

More insight can be gained into Alhazen's concept of form by considering what he has to say about "ascertained forms." It may be profitable to look now at his account of this special category, though it occurs in the last chapter of book II, after the general theory of perception has been given.[32] Sight, it has been said, perceives a visible object by receiving its form. This form is composed of the particular properties that make up the visible appearance of the object, such as its shape, size, color, and so on. A particular property, say color, thus comes to the sensitive faculty as part of a composite form that combines a multitude of properties. Now some properties, such as shape or color, may appear to the sense of sight as soon as the eye looks at the object. That is, they are visible at a glance. Others, however, such as the letters of small script, only become apparent after the object has been contemplated and scrutinized.

There are thus two modes of perception, the one immediate (*idrāk bi 'l-badīha, comprehensio superficialis*),[33] the other contemplative (*idrāk bi 'l-ta'ammul, comprehensio per intuitionem*). Alhazen then introduces the concept of "ascertained form" (*ṣūra muḥaqqaqa, forma certificata*). A true form (*forma vera*) of an object, he says, is one that manifests all visible properties of the object. How can we ascertain that such a form has been received? Only by contemplation, he answers. For it is only by contemplation that we may apprehend the fine features of objects. And even if such subtle features were totally absent from an object, so that a quick glance at it would give us *all* its visible properties, we could not be certain of this without scrutinizing the object. A true form may, therefore, be present to the sensitive faculty by virtue of an immediate perception; but contemplative perception, an operation involving the inspection of all parts of the object, is a condition for obtaining an ascertained form.

Contemplation is an operation effected both by the eye and the faculty of judgment (*virtus distinctiva*),[34] which, as we shall see, is involved in all normal acts of perception. The eye, by successively orienting itself to various parts of the object, causes the forms of those parts to be received along the axis of the visual cone or along lines close to it; and vision along such lines is clearer than vision along other lines. The faculty of judgment then discerns (*tumayyiz, distinguet*) the colors of various parts, their similarity or difference, their relations to one another, and so on, until, in the end, the disposition of the whole object composed of all those parts becomes clear to it.[35]

Alhazen explains the manner in which the form of a visible object is ascertained as follows. When the eye looks at an object, the sense perceives the total form of the object as a whole in some vague way, while clearly perceiving that part of the object where it is intersected by the visual axis. By moving the eye over the whole surface of the object, the sense gains a succession of perceptions of the object's total form, each focusing on a different part of it. The ascertained form of the whole object is the outcome of this succession of perceptions. As a result of the faculty of judgment's comparing and discerning of the various details contained in each one of these perceptions, there is finally formed "in the imagination" (*al-takhayyul, imaginatio*) a total configuration truly representative of the visible object.[36] Alhazen finally remarks, however, that to "ascertain fully" the form of an object is to ascertain it to the limit (*ghāya*) possible for sense perception. Ascertainment is a relative concept—relative, that is, to the faculty of sense.[37]

All this means that to obtain a form approximating the visible features of an object is a highly complex affair that involves other operations besides those explained in book I of the *Optics*. The forms sent out to the visual faculty every time the eye glances at the object, though unconfused and organized, are but the raw material from which the "true form" will be built up, insofar as it is attainable, by the faculty of judgment. Even as layers in the process of building up the increasingly truer form, the successively grasped total forms do not remain unchanged in the final product; some of their features (e.g., their peripheral fuzziness) must be thrown out in order to be replaced by others more truly representative of the object.

But let us now go back to the beginning of book II where these complicated ideas are introduced.

VI

All objects of vision (*al-maʿānī al-mubṣara, intentiones visibiles*), says Alhazen, are properties of physical bodies.[38] Not all properties are perceived in the same manner. Two of these, color and luminosity, are perceived by "pure sensation." Perception of all others involves acts of comparison, discernment, and inference, all of which are performed by the faculty of judgment. Consider the similarity (or difference) of two objects, taken by Alhazen as a paradigm case and presented by him in a rather striking manner. This can only be perceived through perception of the similarity (or difference) between their forms. But the similarity (or difference) of two forms is not identical with either or both of them. And nothing is received from the objects other than their respective forms. In particular, they do not send out a third form from which their similarity (or difference) can be perceived. Perception of similarity (or difference) can therefore be achieved only by comparing (*qiyās, comparatio*)[39] the forms and grasping that property which they have in common (or in respect of which they differ). "That being the case, the sense of sight's perception of the similarity and difference of forms is not by pure sensation, but rather through comparison of the forms that it perceives by pure sensation."[40]

The case of perceiving two similar colors, say two greens of which one is brighter than the other, is particularly instructive, involving as it does an object of pure sensation. The sense (*al-ḥāss, visus*) will perceive their similarity in being green and also their difference in respect of brightness. "Now to distinguish between the two greens is not the same as the sensation of green, for the latter is due to the eye's becoming green through the agency of the green; and the eye has become green through the agency of two greens; and as a result of becoming green through the agency of both greens the sense perceives them to be of the same kind. Thus its perception that one green is brighter than the other, and that they are of the same kind, is a judgment (*tamyīz, distinctio*) of the coloring that takes place in the eye, and not the sensation of the coloring itself."[41] By analogy we may say that the eye's sensation of light is due to the eye's being illuminated through the agency of light and, again, that the sense of sight perceives the similarity and difference of lights through comparison and discernment.

The preceding account, couched in terms very close to those of Alhazen, is misleading in two respects. It gives the impression, or rather states, that forms, as well as light and color as such, are perceived by pure sensation; and it ascribes the acts of comparison and discrimination to "the sense of sight." That neither of these conceptions is intended quite as it stands is made clear by later statements. First, we read:

> Not everything perceived by the sense of sight is perceived by pure sensation, but rather many visible properties are perceived by discernment and inference in addition to the sensation of the visible object's form, and not by pure sensation alone. *Now sight does not possess the power of discernment* (*quwwat al-tamyīz*), but rather it is the *faculty of judgment* (*al-quwwa al-mumayyiza*) *that discrimi-*

nates those properties. But the discrimination performed by the faculty of judgment cannot take place without the mediation of the sense of sight.[42]

This clears up one point: the sense of sight is said to be capable of certain acts beyond pure sensation because it is the medium through which these acts are performed by the faculty of judgment. But we still have the assertion in which it is seemingly implied that the object's form is perceived by pure sensation. The following passage should dispel any doubt regarding this point too. In it Alhazen is primarily concerned to distinguish the role of recognition, an act involving memory and comparison, from that of pure sensation, but in the course of making this distinction he specifically states that perception of forms as forms is a function of the faculty of judgment.

> Now recognition is not pure sensation. For the sense of sight perceives the forms of visible objects from the forms that come to it from the colors and lights of those objects. And its perception of lights *qua* lights and colors *qua* colors *is* by pure sensation. But those features in the form which, or the like of which, it previously perceived, and which, or the like of which, it remembers having perceived, are at once perceived by recognition from significant traits (*amārāt*) in that form. *The faculty of judgment then discerns (tumayyiz) that form, thus perceiving from it all of its properties, such as order,* outline (*takhṭīṭ*), *similarity, difference and all properties of the form whose perception is not effected by mere sensation or recognition.* Therefore, among the things that are perceptible by the sense of sight, some are perceived by pure sensation, others by recognition, and others still by a discerning and an inference that exceeds the inference of recognition.[43]

The presence of form in the eye is a coloring and illumination produced by the colors and lights coming from points on the object. A form, however, is not just light and color (light *qua* light and color *qua* color), but a pattern whose outline and order of parts are discerned only by the faculty of judgment. If, as Alhazen says, pure sensation is only of light as such and of color as such, then it follows that there exists no state of consciousness that can be described as pure sensation. We are aware of the sense of coloring and illumination only as part of the discerned form whose perception *qua* form must involve judgment by the discerning faculty. Thus the concept of form, first introduced in book I of the *Optics* as a necessary condition for veracious vision, is seen to be ultimately absorbed into a psychological concept elaborated by the theory of perception given in book II.

VII

To recapitulate. A form is an optical array disengaged by the crystalline humor and presented through the optic nerve to the faculty of sense. The visual material of which this form is composed, the light and color in it, are registered as light and color sensations. But the perception of the received configuration as an ordered disposition of light and color is the work of a mental faculty over and above mere sensation. There is a process that turns the disentangled visual material into a perception of form and, ultimately, into a perception of an object lying out there with all its visible properties—shape, size, position, and so on. Seeing an object is not the result of a mere imprinting on the mind (brain) of a form emanating from the object. It is an inference from the material received from the object as sensation.

A special category of inferential perception is what Alhazen calls perception by recognition (*idrāk bi 'l-ma'rifa*, *comprehensio per cognitionem*). Through it sight, or rather the cognitive faculty, recognizes an individual to be a member of a certain species or as the same individual it previously had acquaintance with. Memory (*dhikr*, *rememoratio*) is an essential element of recognition—a proof that the latter is not a result of merely registering the form given in sense perception. In the case of recognizing an individual as such, the conclusion "this is my friend *x*" is arrived at by means of comparing the presently received form of *x* with the previously received but presently memorized form or forms of *x*. In the case of recognition of a species ("this is a horse"), the conclusion is derived from a comparison of the form present in sense-perception with the previously received and presently memorized forms of individuals

174

belonging to the same species.[44] Together with this account in terms of separate individual forms, Alhazen introduces a concept of "universal form" (*ṣūra kulliyya, forma universalis*) that is remarkable for its thoroughly empirical character, no matter what one might think of its degree of philosophical sophistication.

A universal form is established "in the imagination" as a result of repeated perceptions of individuals that belong to the same species. Such individuals have visible properties of which some, e.g., color or shape, are the same for all of them. A universal form consists of the totality of *particular* properties that individuals of the same species have in common. Every time an individual is presented in sense perception, the sensitive faculty, *qua sensitive*, perceives the universal form which exists in that individual. To recognize what a thing is (*māʾiyya, quidditas*), therefore, is nothing more than to recognize the coincidence of the presently perceived universal form in the individual with the universal form already present "in the imagination." Perception of such a coincidence or similarity is something that the faculty of judgment automatically seeks to achieve. When an object is seen, the faculty of judgment immediately undertakes to search for a similar form among those stored in the imagination. No recognition will take place if no such form is found.[45] What is remarkable about this explanation is that, unlike those of all major Islamic philosophers of the peripatetic school, such as al-Kindī, al-Fārābī and Avicenna, it nowhere appeals to an *intellectus agens* as a source of *sui generis* universal forms. It should be emphasized that, according to Alhazen, the universal form in an individual object is merely a collection of some of the particular properties making up the concrete form of the object, and it is conveyed to the cognitive faculty along with the object's total sensible form. No sensible object, whatever the sense faculty, is perceived to be what it is (*māʾiyya*) except by recognition.[46]

Recognition is distinguished from other inferential perceptions by the fact that it does not require inspection (*istiqrāʾ, inductio*) of all features of the recognized form or object, and this explains why it takes place in an exceptionally short time.[47] A familiar

175

word on a piece of paper, for example, is recognized, not by scrutinizing the order and shape of every letter, but, perhaps, by simultaneously noticing the first and the last letter in it, or by "perceiving the configuration (*tashakkul*) of the totality of the form" representing the written word.[48] Such features, which, as a result of being grasped and compared with a memorized form of a whole object give rise to recognition of the object, are called by Alhazen "significant traits" or "signs" (*amārāt, signa*), and he accordingly calls "perception by sign" (*comprehensio per signum*) such a mode of apprehension. It is an example of how inferences may take place within us without our being aware of them. His aim is to argue that if we are not conscious of inferential perceptions as inferences, that is only because repetition and habit have turned them into perceptions by recognition or sign, which take place in an extremely short time:

> . . . The perception of many of the objects of vision that are perceived by discernment and inference (*bi 'l-tamyīz wa 'l-qiyās, per rationem et distinctionem*) takes place in an extremely short interval of time, and in many cases it is not manifest that their perception occurs through discernment and inference because of the speed of the inference through which those objects are perceived. . . . For the shape or size of a body, or the transparency of a transparent body, and such like properties of visible objects, are in most cases perceived extremely quickly, and not immediately, since they are perceived by inference and discernment. . . . The quickness of the perception of these properties by inference is only due to the manifestness of their premises and to the fact that the faculty of judgment has been accustomed to discern those properties.[49]

Again:

> And similarly with all objects of vision that are perceived by inference: when the faculty of sight repeatedly perceives them, its perception of them turns into [perception] by recognition without resuming the inference by which it [formerly] perceived their identity.[50]

Still using the term *idrāk* (here consistently rendered as "perception"), Alhazen extends his account to include "perception" of syllogistic conclusions and uses this example to make a distinction between performing an inference and being aware of how it is done. Upon hearing the statement "this thing can write," a man of "sound judgment" will "without an appreciable interval of time" conclude that "this thing is a man." His inference will be effected by means of a universal premise that is "established in the soul" (undoubtedly as a result of previous experience), "manifest" to the faculty of judgment, and "present to the memory." But "the faculty of judgment does not syllogize by ordering and combining and repeating the premises as in the verbal ordering of syllogism." " . . . For that faculty perceives the conclusion without the need for words or for repeating and ordering of premises, or the need for repeating and ordering words."[51] Alhazen continues: "The order of words that make up the syllogism is but a description (*ṣifa*) of the manner in which the faculty of judgment perceives the conclusion, but the faculty of judgment's perception of the conclusion needs neither a description (*naʿt*) of that manner nor the order of the manner of perception."[52] That is to say, the faculty of judgment need not be aware of the forms of inferences as these forms are displayed in *our* descriptions of them, nor does it need the means (words) *we* employ to perform those inferences. It need not be a "little man" within. "Perception" of a visible property, or of a conclusion in an inference about objects, should therefore be distinguished from "perception" of the manner in which it is achieved. A higher-level inference is required to identify those inferences that the faculty of judgment performs without discerning their manner of production.[53]

The visible properties are "many," but they generally fall under twenty-two categories:[54] light (*ḍawʾ, lux*), color (*lawn, color*), distance (*buʿd, remotio*), position (*waḍʿ, situs*), solidity (*tajassum, corporeitas*), shape (*shakl, figura*), magnitude (*ʿiẓam, magnitudo*), discreteness (*tafarruq, discretio & separatio*), continuity (*ittiṣāl, continuum*), number (*ʿadad, numerus*), motion (*ḥaraka, motus*), rest (*sukūn, quies*), roughness (*khushūna, asperitas*), smoothness (*malāsa, levitas*), transparency (*shafīf, diaphanitas*), opacity (*kathāfa, spissitudo*), shadow (*ẓill, umbra*), darkness (*ẓulma, obscuritas*), beauty (*ḥasan, pulchritudo*), ugli-

177

ness (*qabīḥ, turpitudo*), and the similarity (*tashābuh, consimilitudo*) and dissimilarity (*ikhtilāf, diversitas*) between any of these properties or any of the forms composed from them. Alhazen calls these "particular" objects of vision to distinguish them from the more complex properties that fall under them: such as order, which comes under position; curvature, which comes under shape; equality and inequality, which come under similarity and dissimilarity; laughter and weeping, which come under shape and movement; and so on. He is convinced that there exist no visible properties that cannot be reduced to the "particular properties" (*intentiones particulares*) either individually or in combination. Alhazen's major contribution to the history of perception lies in the impressively detailed and often original explanations of how each of these particular properties is apprehended. To discuss his explanations here without being able to give them their due share of attention would be a sign of failure to appreciate his achievement and a disservice to the history of our subject. He devoted to them two thirds of the entire second book of the *Optics*. One thing, however, that can and should be pointed out here is that these explanations are all guided by one logical conclusion of the distinction outlined above. If "light as such" and "color as such" are the only objects of pure sensation; further, if the apprehension of all the other properties is an act of a discerning faculty, which accompanies the optical stimulation reaching the brain from the eye; and, further, if this act is in the first place an inference that may not appear as such because it is performed automatically and often very quickly; then to explain the manner of perception of all those inferential properties will be to formulate descriptions of the inferences involved in apprehending each of them. Alhazen was quite clear and indeed persistent about this. He saw his task as one of providing models of inference whose conclusions are judgments about the nature of a color, the distance, size, or shape of a visible object, or the beauty of a human face.[55] This was an ambitious program that cannot fail to impress readers of the *Optics* by its consistent application. While describing inferences at the basis of our perception of objects as distant from us (disappearance of the object when the eyes are closed or turned away from it, and so on), Alhazen finds occasion to answer an objection raised by the visual ray theorists against the intromission hypothesis. The answer is worth quoting here because it reveals the extent to which his general view of vision was involved in his psychological theory:

> Because the visible object is perceived in its own place, the up-holders of the doctrine of the ray came to believe that vision occurs by means of a ray issuing from the eye and ending at the object, and that vision is achieved by the end points of the ray. They argued against natural scientists, saying: if vision takes place by a form that comes from the object to the eye, and if the form exists inside the eye, then why is the object perceived in its own place outside the eye while its form exists in the eye? But these people forgot that vision is not accomplished by pure sensation alone, but is rather accomplished by means of discernment and prior recognition, and that without these no vision can be effected by sight, nor would sight perceive what the visible object is at the moment of seeing it.[56]

1. The Arabic text of Alhazen's *Optics* (*Kitāb al-Manāẓir*) has not been published. The Latin translation made by an unknown person in the late twelfth or early thirteenth century, and known in the Middle Ages as *Perspectiva* or *De aspectibus*, was published by F. Risner in the volume bearing the collective title *Opticae thesaurus. Alhazeni Arabis libri septem, nunc primum editi, eiusdem liber de crepusculis et nubium ascensionibus, item Vitellonis Thuringo-Poloni Libri X, omnes instaurati, figuris illustrati et aucti, adjectis etiam in Alhazenum commentariis a Federico Risnero* (Basel, 1572; repr., New York, 1974). Reference will be made to the Arabic MSS and to Risner's edition. In all instances my English translation will be from the Arabic, but Risner's text will sometimes be quoted for comparison.

2. These are chapters 4-8, which, alone, make up the entire bk. I in the medieval Latin version. Chapters 1-3 (preface; properties of sight; properties of light and manner of its radiation) have not been found in any of the Latin manuscripts of the *Optics*.

3. Alhazen died ca. 1040 in Cairo, where he spent the latter part of his life. For biographical and bibliographical information, see the article "Ibn al-Haytham" in *Dictionary of Scientific Biography*, ed. C. C. Gillispie (New York, 1972), 6:189-210.

4. The most detailed study of Alhazen's psychology of vision is in Arabic: M. Naẓīf, *al-Ḥasan ibn al-Haytham, His Researches and Discoveries in Optics*, 2 vols., (Cairo, 1942-43); see vol. 1, chaps. 2-3, pp. 240-338. There is an account in German: H. Bauer, *Die Psychologie Alhazens auf Grund von Alhazens Optik dargestellt*, in the series *Beiträge zur Geschichte der Philosophie des Mittelalters*, vol. X, no. 5 (Münster in Westfalen, 1911). G. F. Vescovini studies Alhazen's influence on fourteenth-century empiricist theories of cognition in *Studi sulla prospettiva medievale* (Turin, 1965). The best account of Ptolemy's theory of perception is in A. Lejeune, *Euclide et Ptolémée, deux stades de l'optique géométrique grecque* (Louvain, 1948).

5. Alhazen's *baṣar*, like the Greek *opsis* and the Latin *visus*, means both eye and sight or sense or faculty of sight. He has a special word for the activity of seeing or vision, namely *ibṣār*, corresponding to the Greek *horasis* and the Latin *visio*.

6. The limited scope of the explanation of vision in bk. I is indicated by Alhazen toward the end of that book as follows: "This is the manner of vision generally. For that which sight perceives of the visible object by mere sensation is only the light and color in that object. As for the other things that sight perceives of the visible object, such as shape, position, magnitude, movement, and the like, these sight does not perceive by mere sensation, but through inference and signs (*bi-qiyās wa-amārāt: per rationem et signa*). We will later explain this thoroughly in the second Book when we enumerate the things perceived by sight" (*Optics*, I.6; Fatih MS 3212, fol. 105ª). See Risner, p. 15, lines 11-15.

7. Thus al-Kindī in the ninth century argued against any explanation of vision in terms of "form," and in favor of a theory exclusively formulated in terms of rays; while Avicenna in Alhazen's own time took precisely the opposite view (see Lindberg's chapter, this volume). In medieval Islam not only the mathematicians but practically all the early *mutakallimūn* or dialectical theologians adopted the visual-ray theory. It is more than likely that the writings on *kalām*, of which large sections were devoted to discussion of "physical" questions, constituted the immediate source of Avicenna's detailed knowledge of the arguments in support of that theory.

8. In the *Discourse on Light* (*Maqāla fī 'l-ḍaw'*), a short work composed after the *Optics*, Alhazen wrote: "Discussion of the nature (*māhiyya*) of light belongs to (*min*) the natural sciences (*al-'ulūm al-ṭabī'iyya*), and the discussion of the manner (*kay-fiyya*) of the radiation (*ishrāq*) of light depends on (*muḥtāj*) the mathematical sciences (*al-'ulūm al-ta'līmiyya*) on account of the lines on which the lights extend. Again, discussion of the nature of the ray belongs to the natural sciences, and the discussion of its shape (*shakl* and *hay'a*) belongs to the mathematical sciences. And similarly with regard to the transparent bodies through which the lights pass: the discussion of the nature of their transparency belongs to the natural sciences, and the discussion of how (*kayfiyya*) light extends through them belongs to the mathematical sciences. Therefore, the discussion of light and of the ray and of transparency must be composed of (*yajibu an yakūna murakkaban*) the natural and the mathematical sciences" (*Majmū' Rasā'il Ibn al-Haytham*, Hyderabad, 1357 A.H., no. 2, p. 2). There is a French translation of the *Discourse*: R. Rashed, "Le 'Discours de la lumière d'Ibn al-Haytham," *Revue d'histoire des sciences et de leurs applications* 21 (1968):198-224. In the *Optics* Alhazen speaks of the synthesis in terms that directly refer to the question of vision: "Our inquiry combines the natural and the mathematical sciences. It is dependent on the natural sciences because vision is one of the senses and these belong to the natural things. It is dependent on the mathematical sciences because sight perceives shape, position, magnitude, movement and rest, in addition to its being especially concerned with straight lines. Since it is the mathematical sciences that investigate these things, the inquiry into our subject truly combines the natural and the mathematical sciences" (bk. I, ch. 1, Istanbul MS Fatih 3212, fols. 2ª⁻ᵇ).

9. These statements occur in the *Discourse*, cited in the preceding note.

10. One of Alhazen's earlier works on optics was a summary of Euclid and Ptolemy in which he reconstructed the contents of the first part, which, he said, was missing from Ptolemy's *Optics*; see the article in *Dictionary of Scientific Biography* referred to in note 3 above, p. 190, col. B. That work is now lost. A modern attempt at reconstruction is in A. Lejeune's *Euclide et Ptolémée*. Ptolemy's Greek text has not survived. A critical edition of the Latin version is A. Lejeune, *L'Optique de Claude Ptolémée dans la version latine d'après l'arabe de l'émir Eugène de Sicile* (Louvain, 1956).

11. MS Fatih 3212, fols. 2ª-3ᵇ.

12. *Optics*, 1.6; MS Fatih 3212, fol. 104ª: "Moreover, all that mathematicians who

hold the doctrine of the ray use in their reasonings and demonstrations are imaginary lines, which they call lines of the ray. And we have shown that the eye does not perceive any of the visible objects except through these lines. Thus the opinion of those who take the radial lines to be imaginary is correct, and we have shown that vision is not effected without them. But the opinion of those who think that something issues from the eye other than the imaginary lines is impossible, and we have shown its impossibility by the fact that it is not warranted by anything that exists, nor is there a reason for it nor an argument that supports it." See Risner, p. 15, lines 1-5, where these statements are somewhat compressed. See also D. C. Lindberg, "Alhazen's Theory of Vision and Its Reception in the West," *Isis* 58 (1968):325-27.

13. *Optics*, I.6; MS Fatih 3212, fol. 82[a]: "Moreover, the form of the color is always mixed with the form of the light and not distinct from it, for sight perceives light always mingled with color. It is therefore most appropriate that the eye's sensation of the color of the visible object and of the light that is in it should only occur through the form that is mixed of that light and color, and that comes to the eye from the surface of the object." See Risner, p. 7, sec. 14, lines 11-13.

14. The structure of the eye is the subject of *Optics*, bk. I, chap. 5; MS Fatih 3212, fols. 72[a]-81[b]; Risner, bk. I, chap. 4, pp. 3-7. The following chapter expounds the manner of vision.

15. The picture is complicated in book VII where Alhazen tries to explain how objects lying outside the visual cone are seen. This explanation in terms of refraction has been left out of the above account because the questions that concern us here are independent of it.

16. See Galen, *On the Usefulness of the Parts of the Body*, trans. M. T. May (Ithaca, N.Y., 1968), vol. 10, chap. 3, pp. 469-74.

17. *Optics*, I.6; MS Fatih 3212, fol. 98[a]; Risner, p. 13, lines 16-18.

18. *Optics*, I.6; MS Fatih 3212, fol. 97[b]: " . . . The nature of sight is to receive what comes to it of the light of visible objects, and . . . its nature is further characterized by receiving only those forms that come to it through certain lines . . . , namely, the straight lines whose extremities meet only at the center of the eye, these lines being alone characterized as diameters of the eye and perpendicular to the surface of the sensitive body [i.e., the crystalline humor]. Thus perception occurs through the forms coming from the visible objects, and these lines are, as it were, an instrument of sight by means of which the visible objects appear to it distinct and the parts of each visible object ordered." See Risner, p 12, sec. 20, line 28-p. 13, line 5. For "surface of the sensitive body" (*saṭḥ al-jism al-ḥāss*), the Latin has "*superficiem visus sentientis.*"

19. *Optics*, I.6: MS Fatih 3212, fols. 106[b]-107[a]; Risner, p. 15, sec. 25, lines 7-9; "Et etiam glacialis est praeparatus ad recipiendum istas formas, et ad sentiendum ipsas. Formae ergo pertranseunt in eo propter virtutem sensibilem recipientem."

20. *Optics*, I.6: MS Fatih 3212, fol. 117[a]; Risner, p. 17, sec. 30, lines 1-4: "Membrum vero sentiens, scilicet glacialis, non recipit formam lucis et coloris, sicut recipit aer, et alia diaphana non sentientia, sed secundum modum diversum ab illo modo. Quoniam istud membrum est praeparatum ad recipiendum istam formam; recipit ergo istam, quatenus est sentiens, et quatenus est diaphanum."

21. *Optics*, II.2: MS Fatih 3213, fol. 7[a-b]; Risner, p. 26, sec. 4, lines 1-9: "Et receptio formarum in membro sentiente non est, sicut receptio formarum in corporibus diaphanis; quoniam membrum sentiens recipit istas formas, et sentit eas, et pertranseunt in eo propter suam diaphanitatem et virtutem sensibilem, quae est in eo. Recipit ergo istas formas secundum receptionem sensus. Corpora autem diaphana non recipiunt istas formas, nisi receptione, quae recipiunt ad reddendum, et non sentiunt ipsas. Et cum receptio corporis sentientis ab istis formis non sit sicut receptio cor-

porum diaphanorum, non sentientium; extensio formarum in corpore sentiente non debet esse secundum verticationes, quas corpora diaphana exigunt. Visus ergo non est appropriatus receptioni formarum ex verticationibus linearum radialium tantum, nisi quia proprietas formarum est, ut extendantur in corporibus diaphanis super omnes verticationes rectas." The remainder of the quoted passage is lacking in Risner's text.

22. *Optics*, I.6: MS Fatih 3212, fol. 90^b; Risner, p. 10, lines 27–30: "But the effect of the lights that come along the perpendicular is stronger than the effect of those that come along inclined lines. Therefore, it is most appropriate that the crystalline should perceive, through each point on it, the form that comes to this point along the perpendicular alone, without perceiving through the same point that which comes to it along refracted lines."

23. *Optics*, II.2; MS Fatih 3213, fol. 8^a: "In addition to sensing these forms, the posterior part [of the crystalline], namely, the vitreous, and the receptive power that is in it, has the property of only preserving their arrangement." Risner, p. 26, sec. 4, lines 12-13: "Posterior autem pars quae est humor vitreus, et virtus recipiens, quae est in illo corpore, non est appropriata cum suo sensu istarum formarum, nisi ad custodiendum eorum [*sic*] ordinationem tantum."

24. See Risner, pp. 26–27, secs. 5–6.

25. See *Optics*, bk. I, chap. 1, sec. 1, in Risner's edition.

26. *Optics*, I.6; MS Fatih 3212, fols. 107^a–108^a. See Risner, p. 15, sec. 26, line 1–p. 16, line 4.

27. Strictly, as the theory of bk. II makes clear—see below, perception of the order of the parts of the object is not perception "by pure sensation," which can only be of "light as such" and of "color as such." The question that concerns Alhazen here, however, is not "what is sensation?", but "what are the conditions for veridical perception?" He is concerned to argue that a "form" must in any case be presented to the last sentient. Some features of the form, including order, are only discerned by the faculty of judgment.

28. *Optics*, I.6; MS Fatih 3212, fols 112^b–113^b. This whole passage, including a part not quoted here, is reduced to nine lines in Risner's text: see p. 16, sec. 27, line 45 p. 17, line 3.

29. Risner, p. 16, sec. 27, lines 31–32: "sensus non completur, nisi per illud [ultimum] sentiens tantum, non per oculum tantum."

30. *Optics*, II.2; MS Fatih 3213, fol. 6^b; Risner, pp. 25–26: "Lineae ergo radiales non iuvant ad ordinationem formarum rerum visibilium, nisi apud glacialem tantum, quoniam apud membrum istud principium est sensus."

31. Kepler, in *Ad Vitellionem paralipomena* (Frankfurt, 1604), p. 193, makes the distinction, which should be borne in mind here, between image as a theoretical entity and as a picture: "Definitio. Cum hactenus Imago fuerit Ens rationale, iam figurae rerum vere in papyro existentes, seu alio pariete, picturae dicantur."

32. See Risner, pp. 67 ff.

33. *Optics*, II.4; MS Fatih 3213, fol. 132^a; Risner, p. 67, sec. 64, esp. lines 20–22. In the Latin version the more commonly used expression for *idrāk bi 'l-hadītha* is *comprehensio per aspectum*.

34. Alhazen's *al-quwwa al-mumayyiza* (faculty of judgment), which he often calls simply *al-tamyīz* (discernment), corresponds to some extent to Aristotle's *dynamis kritikē*. The cognate verb *mayyaza*, also frequently used in the *Optics*, means to differentiate, distinguish, discriminate, discern. The Latin version employs *virtus distinctiva, distinctio*, and *distinguere*. For these terms in Ptolemy see A. Lejeune, *L'Optique de Claude Ptolémée*, Index.

35. *Optics*, II.4; MS Fatih 3213, fol. 133^b: "The faculty of judgment discerns all

the forms that come to it: thus it discerns the colors of [their] parts, and their difference if they are different, and the order of the parts in relation to one another, and their details, and the structure (*hay'a*) of each of them, and all [other] features (*ma'ānī*) that appear as a result of contemplating the object, and the structure of the whole object as composed of those parts and features." Risner, p. 67, lines 14–17: "Et virtus distinctiva distinguet omnes formas venientes ad ipsam, et distinguet colores partium, et divarsitatem colorum, et ordinationem partium inter se. Et generaliter distinguet omnes intentiones rei visae, quae apparent per intuitum et formam totius rei visae compositam ex illis intentionibus."

36. *Optics*, II.4; MS Fatih 321, fol. 136^a; Risner, p. 69, sec. 66, lines 1–3: "Et etiam dicamus, quod quando visus comprehenderit aliquam rem visam, et fuerit certificata forma eius apud sentientem, forma illius rei visae remanet in anima, et figuratur in imaginatione. . . . "

37. *Optics*, II.4; MS Fatih 3213, fol. 152^{a-b}: "This ascertainment is relative to the sense. For 'ascertained' and 'perfectly ascertained' (*ghāyat al-taḥqīq*) here mean the limit (*ghāya*) of what the sense (can) perceive. In addition to all that, the sight's perception of visible objects takes place in accordance with the sight's strength, for sights vary in respect of strength and weakness." Risner, p. 75, lines 8–12: "Et ista certificatio, quae est respectu sensu, est intentio certificata, et est dicere finem certificationis in istis locis, finem illius, quod potest comprehendi a sensu. Et cum omnibus istis comprehensio visibilium a visu est secundum fortitudinem visus; quoniam sensus visus oculorum diversatur secundum vigorem et debilitatem." As in several other places the Latin is clearly inadequate.

38. The Arabic *ma'nā* (pl. *ma'ānī*) means sense, notion, concept, and so on. In medieval and particularly philosophical literature, it was frequently used in the general sense of "thing," "matter," "affair," and so on, and referred to objects that lacked a special name. As employed by Alhazen, the word has nothing to do with *intentio* as a directing of the mind.

39. In Alhazen's *Optics*, the word *qiyās* is used to mean comparison, analogy, analogical argument, inference, syllogism. All of these were established usages in his time. The Latin version renders *qiyās* variously as *comparatio, ratio, syllogismus*. It has *ratiocinatio* for *istidlāl* (inference), which is sometimes used by Alhazen.

40. *Optics*, II.3; MS Fatih 3213, fol. 20^{a-b}; Risner, p. 30, sec. 10, lines 20–21: "Et cum ita sit, comprehensio ergo sensus visus a consimilitudine formarum, et diversitate illarum, non est per solum sensum, sed per comparationem formarum inter se." The Latin omits the clause "which it perceives by pure sensation."

41. *Optics*, II.3; MS Fatih 3213, fol. 21^a; Risner, p. 30, sec. 10, lines 25–30: "Sed distinctio inter duas viriditates non est ipse sensus viriditatis, quoniam sensus viriditatis est ex veridificatione visus ab utraque viriditate, et comprehendet, quod sunt unius generis [sic]. Comprehensio ergo visus, quod altera viriditas est fortior altera, et quod duae sunt unius generis, est distinctio colorationis, quae est in visu, non ipse sensus coloris."

42. *Optics*, II.3; MS Fatih 3213, fol. 22^{a-b} (italics added); Risner, p. 31, lines 2–4: "Non ergo omne, quod comprehenditur a visu, comprehenditur solo sensu, sed multae intentiones visibiles comprehenduntur per rationem et distinctionem cum sensu formae visae. Visus autem non habet virtutem distinguendi, sed virtus distinctiva distinguit istas res; attamen distinctio virtutis distinctivae in istis rebus visibilibus non est, nisi mediante visu."

43. *Optics*, II.3; MS Fatih 3213, fols 24^b–25^a (italics added). The whole passage is rendered in Risner's text by two sentences: "Cognitio autem non est solo sensu. Intentiones ergo quae comprehenduntur a sensu visu quaedam comprehenduntur solo sensu, quaedam per cognitionem, quaedam per rationem et distinctionem" (p. 31, sec.

183

11, lines 31-33).

Another explicit statement occurs later, on fol. 37^b: "The faculty of judgment perceives most of the particular properties in the visible object by discerning the properties in that form [of the object], namely, the order of its parts, the shape of its periphery, the configuration of those parts, the difference between them in respect of color, position and order . . . [and so on]." Risner, p. 35, lines 6-10: "Et virtus distinctiva comprehendit plures intentiones particulares, quae sunt in re visa, ex distinctione intentionum, quae sunt in illa forma ab ea, scilicet ex ordinatione partium formae, et ex figuratione illius, quod continet formam, et ex figuratione partium eius, et diversitate colorum, et situum et ordinationum, quae sunt in partibus illius formae, et ex consimilitudine et diversitate earum."

44. *Optics*, II.3; MS Fatih 3213, fols 22^b-23^a; Risner, p. 31, line 5-sec. 11, line 16.

45. *Optics*, II.4; MS Fatih 3213, fols. 138^b-140^a; Risner, p. 69, sec. 67-p. 70, sec. 68.

46. *Optics*, II.3; MS Fatih 3213, fol. 24^b; Risner, p. 31, sec. 11, lines 29-30: "Et non comprehendetur quidditas alicuis rei visae, neque alicuis rei sensibilis alio sensu, nisi per cognitionem."

47. *Optics*, II.3; MS Fatih 3213, fol. 23^b; Risner, p. 31, sec. 11, lines 11-16.

48. *Optics*, II.3; MS Fatih 3213, fol. 24^a; Risner, p. 31, lines 16-18. The clause in quotation marks is missing from Risner's text. The Arabic is "*aw min idrākihi li-tashakkul jumlat al-sūra.*"

49. *Optics*, II.3; MS Fatih 3213, fol 25^{a-b}; Risner, p. 31, sec. 12, lines 1-8.

50. *Optics*, II.3; MS Fatih 3213, fol. 27^b. Risner's text starts "Et similiter sunt omnes intentiones, quae comprehenduntur per rationem, . . . " but omits the rest of the passage; see p. 32, lines 18-19.

51. *Optics*, II.3; MS Fatih 3213, fol. 26^{a-b}; Risner, p. 32, lines 4-8; "Quod virtus distinctiva non arguit per compositionem et ordinationem propositionis, sicut componitur argumentatio per vocabula. . . . Quoniam virtus distinctiva comprehendit conclusionem sine indigentia in verbis, et sine indigentia ordinationis propositionum, et ordinationis verborum."

52. *Optics*, II.3; MS Fatih 3213, fol. 26^b; Risner, p. 32, lines 8-11: "Quoniam ordinatio verborum argumenti non est, nisi modus qualitatis comprehensionis virtutis distinctivae a conclusione. Sed comprehensio virtutis distinctivae ad conclusionem non indiget modo qualitatis, nec ordine qualitatis comprehensionis."

53. *Optics*, II.3; MS Fatih 3213, fols. 30^a-31^a; Risner, p. 32, sec. 13, line 1 p. 33, line 13: "Et etiam multoties non apparet qualitas comprehensionis intententionum visibilium, quae comprehenduntur ratione (i.e., *qivās*, inference) et cognitione (i.e., *ma'rifa*, recognition), quoniam comprehensio earum non fit valde velocior, et quia comprehensio qualitatis comprehensionis non est nisi per secundum argumentum post primum argumentum, per quod fuit visio. Virtus autem distinctiva non utitur isto secundo argumento, in tempore, in quo comprehendit aliquam intententionem visibilem, neque distinguit qualiter comprehendit illam intentionem. . . . Comprehensio ergo qualitatis comprehensionis, et quae comprehensio eiusmodi comprehensionis est, non est, nisi per argumentum et distinctionem non velocem. Et propter hoc non apparet multoties qualitas comprehensionis rerum visibilium, quae comprehenduntur ratione apud comprehensionem."

54. *Optics*, II.3; MS Fatih 3213, fol. 34^{a-b}; Risner, p. 34, sec. 15. As Alhazen mentioned elsewhere, Ptolemy had counted seven, see A. I. Sabra, "Ibn al-Haytham's criticisms of Ptolemy's *Optics*," *Journal of the History of Philosophy* 4 (1966): 46. Ptolemy wrote: "Dicimus ergo quod uisus cognoscit corpus, magnitudinem, colorem, figuram, situm, motum, et quietem" (Lejeune, *L'Optique de Claude Ptolémée*, p. 12). But since his list does not include light, it is doubtful that he meant it as a complete enumeration.

184

55. *Optics*, II.3; MS Fatih 3213, fol. 34^{a-b}; Risner, p. 34, sec. 15, lines 1-3: "Et cum declarata sint omnia ista, incipiemus modo ad declarandum qualitates comprehensionis cuiuslibet intentionum particularium, quae comprehenduntur per visum, et qualitates argumentorum (*kayfiyyat al-maqāyīs*, manner of inferences), per quae acquirit virtus distinctiva intentiones comprehensas sensu visus."

56. *Optics*, II.3; MS Fatih 3213, fol. 49^{a-b}; Risner, p. 38, line 1-p. 39, line 4: "Et ex comprehensione rei visae in suo loco, opinati sunt ponentes radios, quod visio esset per radios exeuntes a visu, et pervenientes ad rem visam, et quod visio esset per extremitatem radii, et ratiocinati sunt contra physicos, dicentes. Cum visio fuerit per formam venientem a re visa ad visum, et illa forma pervenit ad interius visus, quare comprehenditur res visa in suo loco, qui est extra visum, et forma eius iam parvenit ad interius visus. Et non sciverunt isti, quod visio non completur solo sensu tantum, et quod visio non completur, nisi per cognitionem et distinctionem antecedentem, et si cognitio et distinctio antecedens non esset, non compleretur in visu visio."

185

Chapter Seven

A MEDIEVAL THEORY OF VISION

The medieval period produced its own theory of vision, the dates of which are roughly 1000–1600. Although this theory has antecedents in earlier accounts of vision, there is quite enough new about it to mark it off cleanly from its predecessors. And although Kepler's theory (published in 1604) advertised itself as mere "supplements to" or "omissions from" this medieval account ("Omissions from Witelo"; *Paralipomena ad Vitellionem*), the omissions turned out to displace what they were omitted from. Thus the theory is medieval from beginning to end.

I have spoken of *a* medieval theory. Someone might want to quarrel with me about whether what I have in mind is one theory, or several. I suspect we have no very good criterion for individuating theories, and there are special problems in this case about whether certain differences in those several medieval accounts of vision that I have in mind are merely terminological, or are also substantive. But I think a plausible case could be developed for saying that the various writers I shall name are expositors of a single theory. The originator of this theory is the Arabic philosopher Alhazen (ca. 965–1039). The other chief expositors are Roger Bacon (ca. 1214–94), John Pecham (ca. 1240–92) and Witelo (ca. 1220–70).[1]

From among these four writers I choose for discussion Roger Bacon. In what follows I shall assume that, with relatively minor qualifications and reservations, the theory of vision that emerges in part V of Bacon's *Opus majus* is a standard account of this theory.

I

Perhaps a good way to understand what is most distinctive about this medieval theory of vision is to begin with the following comment from chapter 5 ("*De modo visionis*") of Kepler's *Omissions from Witelo*:

> I say that vision occurs when the image (*idolum*) of the whole hemisphere of the world which is in front of the eye, and a little more, is formed on the reddish white concave surface of the retina (*retina*).[2]

Kepler's comment is arresting. One thing that makes it arresting is the fact that it comes after centuries of ignorance as to the role of the retina in vision, ignorance even of the existence of the retinal image. But it is arresting for an even more interesting reason. Suppose we grant that in vision an image is formed on the inside surface of the eye, more or less according to principles of optics known to Kepler—an image that pictures "the whole hemisphere of the world which is in front of the eye, and a little more." That in itself is an intriguing fact about an organ of the human body. But why should the upshot of this formation be that someone *sees* something?

Consider this passage from Leibniz:

> It must be confessed, however, that Perception, and that which depends upon it, are inexplicable by mechanical causes, that is to say, by figures and motions. Supposing that there were a machine whose structure produced thought, sensation, and perception, we could conceive of it as increased in size with the same proportions until one was able to enter into its interior, as he would into a mill. Now, on going into it he would find only pieces working upon one another, but never would he find anything to explain Perception.[3]

I can imagine your eye enlarged until I am able to go into it as into a mill—or better, as into a modernistic, spherical cinema. There I would find a huge inverted image "of the whole hemisphere of the world which is in front of the eye," but nothing, one feels like saying with Leibniz, to explain Perception. (In itself the phenomenon of the retinal image is like a moving picture playing to an empty house.)

Two different ways of responding to Leibniz's disdain come to mind. One way would be to add to Kepler's comment something like this:

Addendum to Kepler's Comment:
Of course, receiving an image on the surface of the retina is not really enough for there to be vision. The "information" the retina receives on its light-sensitive surface needs to be processed before there is vision.

There are, in turn, two ways of taking this addendum. First, one might think of it as requiring a mind or soul as a processor of information—in the way Descartes does in his *Dioptrics*. (" . . . It is the soul that sees, not the eye" [*Discourse* VI].)

In a way Kepler himself invites a Cartesian addendum by following up his comment with this incredible sentence:

I leave it to natural philosophers [*Physicis*] to discuss the way in which this image or picture [*idolum seu pictura*] is put together by the spiritual principles of vision residing in the retina and in the nerves, and whether it is made to appear before the soul or tribunal of the faculty of vision by a spirit within the cerebral cavities, or [whether] the faculty of vision, like a magistrate sent by the soul, goes out from the council chamber of the brain to meet this image in the optic nerves and retina, as it were descending to a lower court.[4]

And when, after the long digression that this follow-up sentence leads him into, Kepler finally returns to his first point, he states it somewhat more guardedly, this way:

Thus vision is brought about by [*fit per*] a picture of the thing seen being formed on the concave surface of the retina.[5]

But the tone of Kepler's remarks in this section and elsewhere suggests that he does not expect enlightenment from any addendum the "natural philosophers" will be able to flesh out; their disputes, he seems to suggest, are idle. So although Kepler does allow for a Cartesian addendum to his comment that vision takes place when an image is formed on the surface of the retina, the allowance is minimal and perfunctory.

There is a second way of taking the addendum to Kepler's comment that I provided above. One might think of it as requiring at least, and perhaps at most, a neurophysiological account of how the "information" on the retina gets processed. Such an addendum finds favor among many of our contemporaries.

An entirely different way of responding to Leibniz's disdain is possible. Instead of adding the addendum given above, one might just dig in one's heels and insist that no addendum is required; to see something just *is* to receive a visual impression of it and the image on the retina is the impression one receives.

Many difficulties stand in the way of making this last-mentioned response attractive. For one thing, a man in a stupor, or even a dead man, might have just the same images on his retina as a live and sober man—yet see nothing. Then, too, there is the fact that the image on the retina is inverted. How can it be that to see something just is to receive a retinal image of it when one sees the object upright and receives on the retina an inverted image?

But there is another difficulty even more basic than the two I have mentioned so far; it is so basic that it is easily overlooked. In normal vision I receive but a single visual impression of the table in front of me. I receive one impression, but I have two retinal images—one on each retina. Of course I might be blind in one eye or have closed one of my eyes; but in the standard, binocular, case there are two images and only one visual impression.

Enter the medieval theory of vision. It does not, like Descartes, attempt to account for vision as a partly noncorporeal process. Quite the reverse, it is an openly physicalistic account. Nor does it postulate a neurophysiological processor of information behind the eyes in the brain. It wants to account for vision as the receiving of an impression—a "*species*" in Bacon's terminology. But it does not know about images on retinas. Instead of conceiving our two eyes as two cameras that produce two images containing "information" that gets processed by some physiological, or nonphysiological, processor, it conceives the eyes as the collars of two funnels that direct species or impressions (in the normal case, one from each eye) to the optic chiasma, where they merge and where, as Bacon puts it, vision is completed. The funnel model is explicit in Bacon where he says this:

> . . . Since the bone of the eye [i.e., the skull socket into which the eye fits] is concave with an opening toward the head, the nerve enters the opening of the eye and spreads out into the hollow of of the bone like the utensil with which wine is put into jars. (5.1.2.1; Burke, 432)[6]

II

Bacon lists ten conditions that are, he says, necessary for vision. They are, first,

1. that there be an impression of a visible object (5.1.5.1; Burke, 449);

and then

2. that there be light (5.1.8.1; Burke, 473);
3. that there be sufficient distance between the eye and the visible object (for in general, he says, a sensible object placed *on* the organ of sense is not perceived) (5.1.8.1; Burke, 474);
4. that the visible object confront the eye (5.1.8.2; Burke, 475);
5. that the object be of a magnitude perceptible by the sense (5.1.8.3; Burke, 477);
6. that theevisible object must exceed the density of the air and the heavens (5.1.9.1; Burke, 481);
7. that the medium be sufficiently rare (5.1.9.2; Burke, 484);
8. that there be sufficient time for perception (for a thing brought suddenly before our eyes is not, he says, seen distinctly and perfectly) (5.1.9.2; Burke, 485);

190

9. that the eye be healthy (5.1.9.4; Burke, 492); and
10. that the *species* or impression be positioned or oriented properly (5.1.9.4, 5.2.2.1; Burke, 492, 510).

Bacon treats the first condition separately from the rest. As I read him, he makes the first condition both a necessary and a sufficient condition for vision.[7] The other nine conditions are therefore as much requisites for the fulfillment of the first condition as they are requisites for vision.[8]

The first condition is, moreover, not just necessary and sufficient for vision. It tells us what, according to Bacon, vision is.[9] It is, so to speak, Bacon's gross analysis of vision. I therefore begin with it.

a) x sees y at t if and only if x receives a visual impression of y at t (5.1.5.1; Burke, 449)

I should here call attention to the fact that I am rendering '*species*' in Bacon as 'impression'. I am doing this in a deliberate effort to capture as much as possible of the immediate plausibility of Bacon's theory. To use a more technical-sounding English word, or to preserve the original Latin term, would make it more difficult to grasp the attractiveness of Bacon's theory.

Talk of vision as the receipt of an impression suggests that vision is a passive, rather than an active, affair; and Bacon indeed says that vision is passive ("*visus est virtus passiva*" [5.1.5.1; Burke, 449]). But it is well to note, as will come out later on, that, according to Bacon, some minimal perceptual judgment is an ineluctable part or aspect of every receipt of a visual impression. So the receipt of an impression has an active aspect as well. And so a Baconian impression is not to be thought of as an immediate or uninterpreted "given".

It is also very important to be clear that impressions (*species*) are not themselves perceptible, according to Bacon. They are therefore not the proper objects of vision, or what is directly seen, since they are not normally perceived or seen at all.[10]

The other principles of the theory that I shall highlight are not highlighted by Bacon himself, but they are, I think, implicit in his discussion in a rather important and unmistakable way. Here is a second principle, and an argument for it:

b)   x receives a visual impression of y if and only if there is some place at which x receives a visual impression of y.

Argument for (b)

(1)   Visual impressions are like corporeal things. (Obvious fact)

(2)   Nothing is like a corporeal thing except another corporeal thing. (*A priori*)

(3)   Visual impressions are corporeal things. (1,2)

(4)   If x receives z and z is a corporeal thing, then there is a place where x receives z. (*A priori*)

(5)   If x receives a visual impression of y, then there is some place at which x receives a visual impression of y. (3,4)

(6)   If there is some place at which x receives a visual impression of y, then x receives a visual impression of y. (*A priori*)

b)   x receives a visual impression of y if and only if there is some place at which x receives a visual impression of y. (5,6)

To call visual impressions "corporeal things", as in (3) above, may be misleading. Bacon denies that an impression (*species*) is a body (*corpus*) (5.1.9.4; Burke, 489). Instead, he says, it has corporeal being (*esse corporeale* [5.1.6.4; Burke, 462]). And it has, he says, corporeal form (*forma corporalis* [5.1.9.4; Burke, 490]). It is perhaps well to think of it as a state of a transparent, physical medium that gets passed on from the object perceived to the perceiver by what Bacon calls "the multiplication of species."[11]

Bacon tries to establish (3) in more than one way. His use of (2) seems to me the most interesting. (*Et hoc iterum patet, quoniam species est similitudo rei corporalis et non spiritualis; ergo habebit esse corporale* [5.1.6.4; Burke, 462].)

The reasoning to (5) and to (*b*) itself is meant to make explicit what seem to me to be assumptions of Bacon's discussion.

Here is a third principle:

c) x sees y single at t if and only if x receives a visual impression of y at t and any two visual impressions of y that x receives at t merge completely.

The argument for (c) in Bacon is a mixture of *a priori* and *a posteriori* considerations. It is an *a posteriori* affair that when you close the left eye and leave the right open, under normal conditions you get a visual impression; when you close the right eye and leave the left open, then again under normal conditions you get a visual impression. Finally, when you leave both eyes open, again, under normal conditions you get an impression— one impression mind you, not two. When you push one eye aside in a certain way, however, you get not one impression but two. All this so far is more or less *a posteriori* (see 5.1.5.2, 5.2.2.2; Burke, 451, 512).

But it is, I take it, an *a priori* consideration, or mostly an *a priori* consideration, that leads Bacon to consider the double vision case a case of unmerged impressions. Thus Bacon says case a case of completely merged impressions. Thus Bacon says that in perception "the two species coming from the eyes must become one, so that the object seen may appear as one and not as two" (5.1.6.4; Burke, 464). But it isn't as though he supposes we can determine in a given case whether the two species merge independently of determining whether the object seen appears "as one and not as two."

Here is another principle:

d) Visual impressions merge if and only if there is some place at which visual impressions merge.

The argument for (d) rests on considerations adduced for (b). Impressions are corporeal things (or anyway have corporeal being). If two corporeal things merge, they merge somewhere. Therefore, if two visual impressions merge, they merge somewhere.

By putting (c) and (d) together we get this:

e) x sees y single at t if and only if x receives a visual impression of y at t and there is some place at which any two visual impressions of y that x receives merge completely.

The place of merging in normal, "non-double" vision is what we shall call the center of visual perception, the *ultimum sentiens* in the case of vision.[12] It is natural to think of this as the place where seeing really goes on.[13]

Clearly, the center of visual perception is not in the right eye or in the left eye; anatomy, including especially the anatomy of the so-called concave or visual nerves, suggests that the nerves are conduits of visual impressions and that the visual center is in the front of the brain. Thus:

f) The center of vision is not in the right eye or in the left eye but somewhere else, presumably more or less between them.

Bacon seems to support the idea that the center of vision is more or less between the eyes by *a posteriori* considerations of anatomy. (Consider, for example, this: "But naturally eyes that are well formed and healthy have a position similar with respect to the common nerve, and therefore the two species come to the same place in it and become one, so that thus through one species and one perception one judgment is formed regarding a single object" [5.1.5.2; Burke, 451]). But (*f*) might be given some support from mostly *a priori* considerations as well. One might argue that, since the two eyes are similar, there could be no sufficient reason for the center of vision to be in one rather than in the other. Since it cannot be in both, it is in neither.

I first thought that several facts, or apparent facts, about the "focus of attention" in vision might have played some role in Bacon's conclusion that there is a single center of vision. What I had in mind was this.

It is natural for us, I think, to suppose that a chicken, say, or some other creature with eyes in the side of its head, could not "look through"—that is, focus its attention on something through —more than one eye at a time. The other eye would doubtless remain light-sensitive in the way one's peripheral vision is light-sensitive. But (this thinking goes) there could be at most only a single focus of the chicken's attention at any one moment. To put the point very crudely, the "inner chicken" has to decide which window to look out.

Insofar as it is natural for one to think this, one is drawing on what one takes to be a limitation in the human case. A human being can, to be sure, shift her or his attention from one point to another in the visual field. Perhaps a human being can do this very, very quickly—perhaps in 1/5 of a second. But no one (so this thinking goes) can concentrate on two disparate points in the visual field at once.

There is, in fact, some experimental evidence in support of this "natural supposition." M. D. Vernon summarizes it this way:

> It appears that a time interval of the order of one fifth of a second is necessary to transfer the direction of attention from one event to another, in the sense of perceiving them as different. This time appears to be about the same whether attention is being transferred from one part of the visual field to another, or from a visual to an auditory stimulus.[14]

I say I first thought that this "natural supposition" might have played some role in Bacon's confidence that there is a single center of vision. His reasoning would presumably go this way. If you grant that *attention stems from some point in space* (the "point of view," thought to be behind the eyes somewhere), then the fact that we can have no more than one focus of attention at a time suggests that there is only one point from which vision is directed (namely, the center of vision). If there were, say, two points (perhaps one in the left side of the brain, the other in the right; or one in the left eye, the other in the right) then, it seems, one would be able to focus one's attention simultaneously or two different locations in one's visual field.

In fact I find no such reasoning in Bacon, and no evidence that what I have called a "natural supposition" plays any role whatsoever in the way Bacon conceives vision. And it now seems to me instructively appropriate that there should be none. Such reasoning would be appropriate to a philosopher like Augustine, who distinguishes between having a visual impression

and attending to something within it—or perhaps better, to something within the visual field it portrays. (See *De trinitate* 11.2.2.)
But I find no such distinction in Bacon. To see x is simply to
receive a visual impression of x—and that ends the matter.

III

What, especially, should one criticize in this medieval theory of
vision?

One might begin with the point mentioned earlier that a person
in a stupor, or just distracted (or, of course, dead), sees nothing
—even though that person's eyes, if they are open, could be
thought to receive impressions as before.

I do not know for sure what Bacon's answer to this kind of
objection would be, but I am inclined to think he might appeal
to his doctrine of optic emissions. The doctrine of optic emissions seems to be a vestige of the earlier emission theories of
vision retained either out of an incurable eclecticism or else from
a genuine respect for his predecessors. For whatever reason,
Bacon has the doctrine, and here is the way he tries to keep it
from being obviously otiose:

> . . . The species of the things of the world are not fitted by nature
> to effect the complete act of vision at once because of its nobleness.
> Hence these must be aided and excited by the species of the eye,
> which travels in the locality of the visual pyramid, and changes the
> medium and ennobles it, and renders it analogous to vision, and
> so prepares the passage of the species itself of the visible object,
> and, moreover, ennobles it, so that it is quite similar and analogous
> to the nobility of the animate body, which is the eye. (5.1.7.4;
> Burke, 471)

It would be easy enough for Bacon to say that in the case
of a dead person, and also, perhaps, in the case of one stupified
or distracted, neither the medium nor the species of the object
has been properly "ennobled" for passage to the eye. Of course,
if this were to be Bacon's response, he should have included
something about the necessity of preparing the object and the

medium in his list of necessary conditions of vision. And he does not do that.

In the case of a dead person Bacon can add in the point that, to get to the center of vision, a species must pass through twisting nerves with, persumably, no internal mirrors to facilitate passage. In the case of a normal, alert viewer impressions manage this treacherous passage, Bacon thinks, because they are in an animated medium (*in medio animato* [5.1.7.1; Burke, 467-68]). The animation, he thinks, draws them through the twisting routes. Upon the death of the viewer, however, the medium would no longer be animated and the impressions would never reach the optic chiasma.

One promising line of criticism would reverse a common objection to representative theories of perception. The representationalist who claims that sense data are both (1) the only direct objects of vision and (2) similar to the physical objects they represent may be asked how, since physical objects are not direct objects of vision, we can know that sense data are like them. With Bacon we may reverse the query. Since impressions (*species*) are not direct objects of vision—are normally not even perceived at all—we may ask what basis there can be for thinking of them as likenesses (*similitudines*) of what they are impressions of. (The claim that "visual impressions are like corporeal things" figures in the argument for principle (*b*) above.)

To answer this criticism Bacon would need to argue that there are ways of determining that *a* is like *b* without having to take a look (or otherwise perceive) both *a* and *b*. In particular, he would need to argue that there are legitimate ways of determining that one's visual impression of, say, an apple resembles the apple itself without one's having to take a look at both the apple and the impression.

Another good thing to worry about is the account of perceptual judgment and error implicit in Bacon's treatment of vision.

Bacon discusses a number of kinds of error in vision. In some cases he seems to attribute error to reasoning consequent upon

197

the basic perception. In other cases he says that error is the result of excess or deficiency in the fulfillment of one or more of the nine conditions mentioned above. In other cases he appeals to refraction as an explanation of error. (Refraction does not seem to fit under any of the nine conditions.)

But Bacon also talks as though a basic perceptual judgment is an ineluctable part of the very process of receiving an impression. Just as one cannot have a pain without taking it to be painful, so, perhaps Bacon thought, one cannot receive the impression of light or color without taking it to be an impression of light or color. Further discrimination may call upon a more explicit reasoning process, but a minimal judgment, on this view, is an unelimable part of the process of receiving a visual impression.

Anyway Bacon certainly does not try to get down to an ultimate "given" that is bereft of judgment. In particular (as I have already tried to emphasize), the notion of an impression (*species*) in Bacon is not the notion of a visual "given."

Historically it was, no doubt, the fact that its optics are faulty that did the medieval theory in. And that brings me to make a final comment. Although huge chunks of the medieval theory are purely *a priori* (as I have tried to emphasize in my reconstruction), the theory ended up being refuted decisively by experimental evidence. This evidence shows the theory wrong, not just in detail, but in conception. The experiments conducted by Christophorus Scheiner in 1625, inspired by Kepler, show that what the crystalline lens does is not to stuff a *species* down the optic nerve for transmission to the optic chiasma but rather to project an image on the full globular expanse of the retina. That evidence demolishes Bacon's account of the optics of the crystalline lens and the vitreous humor (5.1.7.1; Burke, 466–67) and, with it, the conception of vision that underlies the medieval theory. The eye is not really the collar of a funnel; it is a camera. The medieval funnel theory of vision is wrong.

1. For a defense of the view that, "aside from citations and format, the theories of vision presented by Bacon, Pecham and Witelo are essentially the same as Alhazen's," see David Lindberg's "Alhazen's Theory of Vision and Its Reception in the West." *Isis* 58 (1967): 321–41. See also Alistair C. Crombie, "Kepler: *De Modo Visionis*," in *Mélanges Alexandre Koyré*, I: L'Aventure de la science (Paris: Hermann, 1964), pp. 136–72.

2. Johannes Kepler, *Gesammelte Werke* (Munich: C. H. Beck'sche, 1939), 2:151. The English translation is from Crombie, op. cit., p. 147.

3. *The Monadology*, no. 17, trans. George Montgomery, *The Rationalists* (Garden City, N.Y.: Doubleday, 1960), p. 457.

4. Kepler, op. cit., p. 151; Crombie, op. cit., pp. 147–48 (translation).

5. Kepler, op. cit., p. 153; Crombie, op. cit., p. 150 (translation).

6. Roger Bacon, *Opus majus*, ed. J. H. Bridges (Frankfurt: Minerva, 1964), vol. 2. The citation "5.1.2.1." means "Part Five, Part One (i.e., Part One of Part Five), Second Distinction, Chapter One." Part five of the *Opus majus* is devoted to the science of optics ("De scientia perspectiva"). The translation is from Robert Belle Burke, *The Opus Majus of Roger Bacon* (New York: Russell & Russell, 1962), vol. 2. The citation "Burke, 432" refers to page 432 of Burke's translation. Later citations from Bacon will be abbreviated in this same way.

7. "The first requisite here considered is, that vision needs the impression of a visible object, for without this there can be no vision [i.e., the condition is necessary] . . . when every impediment is removed, so that the impression comes to the eye, the object is seen [i.e., the condition is sufficient]" (5.1.5.1; Burke, 449).

8. Later on Bacon says that the eight or nine remaining conditions (either [2]–[9], or else [2] [10]) are such that if they are fulfilled by either excess or defect, error or defect in vision occurs (5.2.3.1; Burke, 517).

10. The surrounding discussion suggests that this is the point in Bacon's saying that "vision arises through an impression" (*visio fiat per speciem*) (*ibid.*).

10. *Species sunt insensibiles* (5.1.6.4; Burke, 464). Bacon allows in the surrounding discussion that impressions may be seen, in some circumstances, *per accidens*. He seems to have in mind, for example, the phenomenon of seeing (what we should describe as) rays of light. *In* seeing the rays, we do not, of course, see their source, though we may see the source as well.

11. See Bacon's treatise, *De multiplicatione specierum*, appended to Bridges's edition of the *Opus majus* (407–552). Bacon's insistence on corporeality is reflected in his claim that impressions (*species*) "must obey the laws of material and corporeal things" (5.1.6.4; Burke, 462).

12. In 5.1.5.3. (Burke, 452) Bacon explains that '*ultimum sentiens*' may be taken in two ways. Taken in one way, it stands for the common sense. Taken in the other way, it is the center of perception for a specific sense (e.g., vision). It is the *ultimum sentiens* for vision that is, he supposes, located at the optic chiasma.

13. I mean to be highlighting those passages (e.g., 5.1.5.2; Burke, 450–51) in which Bacon insists that vision is incomplete until the two impressions merge at the *ultimum sentiens*. In other passages Bacon seems to balance that point with an insistence that the "double-barreled" reception of the impression, from the two eyes to the optic chiasma, be counted as a "single and undivided visual act" (5.1.5.3; Burke, 453).

14. *The Psychology of Perception* (Harmondsworth: Penguin, 1962), p. 171.

Chapter Eight

INNATE IDEAS

I want to suggest that the doctrine of innate ideas, particularly the versions held by Descartes and Leibniz, is a natural extension of the doctrine of natures and dispositions held by Aristotelian metaphysicians. To be more specific, I shall suggest that innate ideas stand to minds in the way that Aristotelian natures stand to bodies; that just as a leaf that changes from green to red in the fall must have it in its nature so to change, a mind that is first ignorant of and then knows some truth must have it in its nature to know that truth. It is well known that Leibniz and Descartes hold that, for example, mathematical ideas are innate; but many historians have either ignored or just noted in passing that both claim, when pressed, that all ideas, even those we may term perceptual, are innate. The extension of the innateness doctrine to all ideas is indeed what Locke criticizes and takes to be a *reductio* of the theory. I hope to make clear why the extension of the theory to ideas of perception is natural and necessary. The key ideas are rather simple: the new science, with its new ideas about causation, plus the distinction between mind and body emphasized by Descartes, creates a crisis in the explanation of how we come to have ideas. I believe, and hope to make plausible, that this problem is strikingly analogous to the problem of change of quality that Aristotelians had wrestled with for centuries. Though I think this striking analogy more than accidental, I shall not, for reasons given below, try to take the discussion beyond the analogy. Before proceeding to the main sections of this paper, then, I want to make a string of preliminary remarks.

The doctrine of innate ideas constitutes a theory, and theories are supposed to explain something. I think it safe to say that both historians of philosophy and those, like myself, who take history as a tool for analysis of contemporary problems, have been baffled by the theory of innate ideas for two reasons. First, it is and, I think, always has been unclear what phenomena the theory was meant to explain. Second, even when relatively clear proposals were made about the phenomena, it was completely unclear how the theory explained them. Indeed, the central criticism of the theory, propounded by Locke and recently echoed by Goodman against Chomsky, is that we know no more when we believe there are innate ideas than we know when we believed there were no innate ideas. The theory simply has no explanatory value whatever. Less pejoratively, the critics hope that—given that we can isolate the phenomena to be explained—anything that can be explained by using the theory of innate ideas i.e., any insight the theory provides, can be given without it. Thus, for example, one hopes that Chomsky's allegedly scientific theory of language learning can be stated without the metaphysical baggage of the theory of innate ideas.[1] For the classical theory of innate ideas is metaphysical if it is anything. This claim is something else I hope to make plausible in this paper. I shall not try to make plausible the claim that science and metaphysics should not mix as Chomsky seems to mix them; nor will I try to show that he mixes them.

Many philosophers who are not professional historians know of the theory of innate ideas through a welter of somewhat obscure doctrines, plus some intuitive hunches. Does not the theory have something to do with the *Meno* problem? Is it not a theory that is intended to explain our acquisition of mathematical knowledge and, perhaps, our knowledge of the principles of logic? Is it not a theory of what the mind brings to experience? The latter question conjures up names and images: Kantian idealism, perhaps, or seeing the world through a certain kind of glasses. These names and images evoke stock responses: how could we know what the mind contributes to experience? How can we step outside our own 'conceptual framework' to take a neutral look at what is given in experience? What does "bring to experience" mean? How can we ascertain the kind of glasses by means of which we see the world, if we cannot take the glasses off?

I hope, in this paper, to shed a little light on a few of these issues. I believe that it can be made clear what phenomena Descartes and Leibniz, at least, were trying to explain by the theory of innate ideas. Once one sees this, it will also become clear how the theory relates to problems of perception with which, as a contributor to this volume, I have been enjoined to deal. The theory, in brief, was not intended to explain sense perceptions in any straightforward way. But if my own view is correct, then a problem arises for any innate idea theorist (Locke sees the problem in his usual, confused way): the logic that drives one to claim that some ideas are innate seems to lead inevitably to the claim that all ideas are innate. This logic, to repeat my earlier claim, is at least analogous to the logic that leads to Aristotelian dispositions in material bodies.

Finally, I wish to issue some caveats. Earlier versions of this paper have undergone the following severe criticisms. First, the view I allude to of Aristotelian natures and dispositions, which I claim is analogous to the theory of innate ideas, is terribly wrongheaded. Aristotle, it has been alleged against me, simply did not hold such a view. Second, the view I present of Descartes as an Aristotelian is, at least with respect to his account of bodies, ridiculous. I held that Descartes is committed to natured bodies or, more accurately, to the view that material substances have a nature. It is alleged against this that, for Descartes, material substance 'is' its nature.[2] Since I do not pretend to be a historical scholar, my initial embarrassment, especially on the second score, was severe. It was considerably lessened with respect to the Cartesian point, however, when I came to realize, in rethinking the paper, that my point about Descartes and his view of innate ideas does not depend on whether or not material bodies 'are' their natures. Furthermore, some recent work has taken my side in this matter.[3] As to the Aristotelian controversy, it comes to the old problem of Aristotle's exact view of prime matter and the problem of individuation. I think I have, in the present version of this paper, skirted this difficult issue. At least, I do not see that any of my points entail a stand on the question of prime matter.

In sections I and II I shall lay out, in a very general way, some of the issues about dispositions in bodies and about innate ideas. In section III I shall explore how Descartes and Leibniz fit the patterns developed in the earlier sections.

I

When one billiard ball strikes another and causes it to move, we must, in order to explain the effect, take into account some of the properties of the moved ball, e.g., its shape and mass. No one doubts that such properties must be mentioned in any adequate account of the motion of the ball. Nor have most philosophers and scientists doubted that, in order to explain causally how a sentient being comes to perceive and to know, the structure of the sentient being must be taken into account. What complicates matters is that a change in a perceiver, e.g., from not perceiving to perceiving the color of a leaf, *prima facie* has at least three aspects that are missing in the case of the billiard balls. (1) The leaf, we want to say, causes the perceiver to perceive *it*, and the knower has knowledge *of* what causes him or her to have that knowledge. To put the point in more modern terms, what we get as a result of the causal process is information about something. (2) The causal process is more complex, for the leaf exists at a distance from the perceiver's body. This fact enormously complicates the problem of explaining how we get information about physical objects.[4] (3) In billiard ball interaction, both the striking and the struck object may significantly change some of their properties. But in perceived-perceiver interaction, only the perceiver seems to change. This further adds to the difficulty of trying to understand how the object 'transfers' information about itself to a perceiver. To put the point slightly differently, the striking ball changes by 'transferring' something to the struck ball; but the leaf does not change by 'transferring' information to the perceiver.

I think it could be plausibly argued, though I shall not argue it here, that (1), (2), and (3) are facts that every philosopher of perception, including, of course, Plato and Aristotle, have taken into account. However, (1), (2), and (3) neither separately nor jointly entail any philosophical theory; specifically, they do not entail either a theory of representative perception or a theory of innate ideas. Many philosophers, though, embracing certain other philosophical and/or scientific views, have arrived at the latter two theories. Later I shall deal with such a set of assumptions. Before proceeding, I wish to make some comments about the *present* standing of the old doctrine of innate ideas.

The puzzlement generated by the theory of innate ideas has made it one of the curios of the history of philosophy; until quite recently, the theory was mentioned only in passing in discussions of Locke, Leibniz, and Descartes. Indeed, though idealism, representationalism, phenomenalism, the mind-body problem, and the argument from illusion are still very much alive, the theory of innate ideas had, it seemed, long ago died a merciful death. Small wonder, then, that many philosophers were dismayed by the return of this phoenix within the context of linguistics, most notably in the work of Chomsky. Close attention to trends in both psychology and neurophysiology are as dismaying. The doctrine of innate ideas seems to be alive and well, thriving especially in accounts of perception.

It is not my purpose to assess these modern views, though I shall presently draw a lesson from Chomsky's. Nor do I mean to assert that what linguists and psychologists call a theory of innate ideas cannot be made scientifically respectable. But there are clear dangers. The seventeenth-century doctrine is patently metaphysical. It would thus be unfortunate if the revival bore the metaphysical freight of the old doctrine. To see the dangers just alluded to, I want to turn briefly to Chomsky's work in *Cartesian Linguistics.*[5]

Chomsky is a scientist. He tries, as he should, to be very careful about crossing the metaphysical line. This care is evident in *Cartesian Linguistics.* Yet much uneasiness remains. Chomsky sees a definite structural similarity between seventeenth-century metaphysical and twentieth-century linguistic problems. Even this need not be fatal, if one is careful not to be misled. Chomsky is too often misled, as the following passage shows:

It is important to realize that seventeenth-century rationalism approaches the problem of learning—in particular, language learning—in a fundamentally non-dogmatic fashion. It notes that knowledge arises on the basis of very scattered and inadequate data and that there are uniformities in what is learned that are in no way uniquely determined by the data itself. Consequently, these properties are attributed to the mind, as preconditions for experience. This is essentially the line of reasoning that would be taken, today, by a scientist interested in the structure of some device for which he has only input-output data. In contrast, empiricist speculation, particularly in its modern versions, has characteristically adopted certain a priori assumptions regarding the nature of learning (that it must be based on association or reinforcement, or on inductive procedures of an elementary sort—e.g., the taxonomic procedures of modern linguistics, etc.) and has not considered the necessity of checking these assumptions against the observed uniformities of "output"—against what is known or believed after learning has taken place. Hence the charge of a priorism or dogmatism often levelled against rationalistic psychology and philosophy of mind seems clearly to be misdirected.[6]

The empiricists referred to are Locke in the seventeenth century and the behavioristic psychologists of the twentieth. The passage makes it clear that Chomsky sees more than a mere structural similarity between the problem of accounting for language learning and the problem of knowledge acquisition. At best, he is simply mistaken in believing that Descartes, Leibniz, and other innate idea theorists are in some sense doing science in postulating the existence of innate ideas. The case against Chomsky can, I think, best be put as follows: Consider the problem of accounting for change in material bodies. Both Descartes and Leibniz accept the impact theories of the new science to account for such changes. But both also postulate the existence of natures—in Leibniz's account, active natures—to solve the metaphysical problem of change.[7] The same, as I shall argue presently, is true of their theories of knowledge acquisition.[8] Chomsky, on the other hand, rejects behaviorism for another scientific theory. Neither Descartes nor Leibniz doubt that one can formulate laws correlating physical stimuli with mental states (of at least some kinds). Yet they also hold to a theory of innate ideas. Chomsky's discussion, then, is dangerously misleading. It not only misconstrues what the rationalists were

205

doing but places him in their footsteps. Thus there is a clear danger that he holds an ostensibly scientific theory for metaphysical reasons.

It is not too difficult, however, to generate some sympathy for Chomsky's view. There is a formal similarity between the problem that the linguist faces in explaining verbal behavior and the problems of perception and knowledge that worry Descartes and Leibniz. When, to use Chomsky's terms, output 'differs' from input or when the effect is 'different' from the cause—in both cases, in 'significant' ways—it is natural to look for an intervening variable to explain the discrepancy. Let me illustrate this with an example. Chomsky claims against Skinner's and other behaviorists' theories of language acquisition that no such theory can account for the fact that speakers of a language can recognize and understand sentences they have never heard or seen before.[9] Suppose that we could, contrary to what Chomsky believes is the case, at least find a functional relationship between the sentences that speakers do learn, and the sentences that they come later to recognize and understand and have never, in this sense, learned. Even if such a relationship could be found, most linguists I think, would be unsatisfied; they would still look for an intervening variable to explain the 'discrepancy'. There is a philosophical puzzle that arises here and that very quickly leads us to Hume and the heart of problems concerning causation. What precisely is this 'discrepancy'? Why do we assume there is an intervening variable? And what do we assume about the nature of this variable? As we shall see, the doctrine of innate ideas is intimately tied to these questions. My point here, however, is that the scientist, in positing the existence of the intervening variable and its structure, neither asks a philosophical question nor poses a philosophical answer. Rather, it is the scientist's procedure and the structure of scientific laws that generate philosophical puzzles and philosophical answers.

II

When I come to know something that I have not known previously, there is a change in me. What accounts for such

206

changes? This is the key question behind the innate ideas controversy. For Locke, the question is a causal one, in the sense of 'cause' that accompanied the new science with which he was so impressed. For Leibniz, the question is not merely causal in the new sense but also in the old sense of the Aristotelians. Locke's answer is in terms of learning from experience: the cause is external to the substance that changes. Leibniz's answer is additionally in terms of innate ideas.

Leibniz's answer is at least analogous to the Aristotelian account of change in physical objects. The former, I believe, is structured by the latter. Conclusively showing the historical inference is beyond the scope of this paper; such a demonstration calls for an extended discussion of the history of the Aristotelian notion of change. What I hope to do, instead, is to draw on salient and relatively uncontroversial features of the Aristotelian theory of change in order to make the claim a plausible *suggestion*.

Consider the green leaf that changes to red in autumn. What accounts for the change? This is the problem of change in physical objects; a physical body changes one of its characteristics, in an unproblematic sense of 'characteristic' that we all commonsensically understand. Suppose that one is told that the reason X, a physical object, is now red—though it was not red a moment ago—is that (a) it was square a minute ago, and (b) it was dipped into water at that moment. Neither (a) nor (b) in any way mentions the present color of the object. Hence, so far the new color seems to have 'come from nothing.' Put another way, there seems to be no more reason, looking at (a) and (b) alone, to expect that X will be red the next moment than to expect that it will be green, or brown, or circular, or that it will exist at all.

In effect, we have returned to the problem, Hume's problem, mentioned at the end of section I. Certainly one classical response to Hume's puzzlement over the fact that the present state of an object gives us no clues to its future states (or the future states of other objects), or, perhaps more suggestively, that the effect is not 'contained' in the cause, is to posit some intervening variable. In the situation above we want to know why, if the relationship between the earlier and the later states is a functional one, a physical object's shape and its being dipped into water produce a color change. We could, for example, appeal to the microstructure of the object. Scientific tradition would support this move; but for the philosopher it merely raises the same problems with respect to the entities of the microstructure.[10] The properties of an atom do not seem to necessitate that any change take place, let alone what sort of change. One way round this difficulty—if one sees it as a difficulty—is to claim that the properties of objects are not what they seem, i.e., the properties that objects or events have are not limited to those one can perceive. This response involves the notions of disposition and potentiality, which, of course, has nothing to do with the microscopic-macroscopic distinction that the scientist invokes.

Why do philosophers turn to dispositions and potentialities? In classical solutions to the problem of change, the principle that something cannot come from nothing is pervasive.[11] Indeed, the whole philosophical tradition before Hume is controlled by it and the concomitant (if not equivalent) principle that effects must be like their causes. For if the effect has a property that the cause does not have, the effect would seem to have come from nothing. This is precisely the problem with the invocation of (a) and (b) above as an explanation for the fact that the physical object is now red. The positing of dispositions allegedly bridges the gap between the effect and (a) and (b); for if the object has the potential to change its color to red under conditions (a) and (b), it is not sbrprising that when (a) and (b) are realized, there is a change in the object. Stace, in his discussion of the Aristotelian theory of causation, puts the matter thus:

> Aristotle claims, by means of the antithesis of potentiality and actuality, to have solved the ancient problem of becoming, a riddle, propounded by the Eleatics, which had never ceased to trouble Greek thinkers. How is becoming possible? For being to pass into being is not becoming, for it involves no change, and for not-being to pass into being is impossible, since something cannot come out of nothing. For Aristotle, the sharp line drawn between not-being and being does not exist. For these absolute terms he substitutes the relative terms potentiality and actuality, which shade off into

each other. Potentiality in his philosophy takes the place of not-being in previous systems. It solves the riddle because it is not an absolute not-being. It is not-being inasmuch as it is actually nothing, but it is being because it is potential being. Becoming, therefore, does not involve the impossible leap from nothing to something. It involves the transition from potential to actual being. All change, all motion, is thus the passage of potentiality into actuality, of matter into form.[12]

Stace also exhibits the logic of these ideas with more precision. He claims that matter and form are relative notions in that an acorn, for example, can be considered a substance—formed matter—as well as just matter that can grow into something, an oak. Insofar, however, as the acorn is considered as matter for change, it is not without some qualities, i.e., it is not pure (prime) matter. That is, there is a sense in which the changes that can be wrought in the acorn are limited.

For when we say that matter is the potentiality of what it is to become, this implies that what it is to become is already present in it ideally and potentially, though not actually.[13]

It should be clear that what is potentially and ideally in the acorn is not just its structural properties but in some rather mysterious way the properties it can, as matter, take on under certain conditions.[14]

Let me try to illustrate these ideas a bit more fully. Suppose that X, the physical object mentioned above that changes from some other color to red, has the disposition to change to red under conditions (a) and (b). It is of course not the case that one can know, prior to perceiving the change, that X has the disposition in question (assuming that this fact cannot be inferred from the other knowledge), but this is merely an epistemological problem. The world runs on whether or not we know that X has the disposition. The point is that X 'must' have this disposition. Hume claimed that he did not *perceive* any necessary connection between an effect and its cause, and for him, this was enough to dismiss necessary connections and, what classically goes with them, powers and dispositions.[15] Hume thus translates his epistemological point into an ontological criterion: we cannot justifiably claim that any property or relation exists that cannot be perceived. Descartes and Leibniz held no such criterion. Neither, I think, did Aristotelians, who believed in the existence of natures, powers, and dispositions. The Aristotelian point about the disposition of the leaf is not put in terms of expectations. The point, rather, is this: change is lawful; different sorts of entities change in different ways. Why is it, for example, that birds fly and cows do not? The Aristotelian answer is of course complex: the matter of a particular cow differs significantly from that of a particular horse, limiting the sort of changes each can manifest; and, just as significantly, the form of a particular cow differs from that of a particular horse. This form, or nature, is perhaps best understood in terms of a set of properties expressible in terms of dispositional predicates. All existents are substances, combinations of form and matter; and it is form, nature,[16] that provides a major part of the explanation of change. Take, again, our object X that has the disposition to turn red under conditions (a) and (b). Does the fact that X has this disposition allay the worry that, without it, we are faced with the problem that something has come from nothing? *Prima facie*, the answer is *no*. The object X is, after all, only potentially red before (a) and (b) are realized; we seem, in other words to have traded the problem of the change from not being to being red for the more general problem of the change from potentially to actuality. Let us see what the possibilities are here.

1. One could claim that, prior to its actualization, redness is 'in' X in such a way that, under conditions (a) and (b) it 'emerges' or 'shows itself.' Change would thus be an 'uncovering' of 'hidden' properties.

2. One could define dispositional predicates in the familiar positivistic way, using the material conditional.

3. One could claim that, prior to its actually being red, X has a property best expressed in terms of a subjunctive conditional: If (a) and (b) were to occur, X would be red.

(3) seems to leave us where we began, in that the relationship between the peculiar property expressed by the subjunctive conditional and the fact that X is (now) red is just the relationship

between potentiality and actuality. (1) is more suggestive, in that it seems to imply that there is a sense in which X is always red; like a red wall that has an overlay of some other color of paint. Whether such a metaphor can be satisfactorily explicated is another matter. My purpose, fortunately, is not to try to explicate fully the Aristotelian notion of potentiality and actuality, but to show that, in the case of innate ideas, a problem similar to that of change in material bodies arises for minds, and is solved in similar ways. Nor do I suggest that Descartes invests bodies with natures in the classical way; I take it that one meaning of his claim that bodies are passive is that they have no hidden powers, either in the sense of dispositions waiting to be actualized or in the sense of entelechies that actualize them. Indeed, Liebniz takes Descartes to task for this failure to metaphysically ground the possibility of change in bodies[17] But because Descartes does not have such powers in bodies does not imply that he forgoes them in his analysis of minds.

I will not rehearse here all the standard criticisms of (2). One such criticism, however, is important in understanding the analogy between the theory of innate ideas and the Aristotelian explanation of change in material bodies. It is not merely that the material conditional as used in (2) is in no way equivalent to the subjunctive conditional in (3). Even the subjunctive conditional does not express the notion of final causality that enters into the full Aristotelian explanation for change.[18] One way to fill the gap between potentiality and actuality mentioned in criticizing (3) is to posit the existence of wills in material bodies. That Aristotle actually did take this step is very controversial, and I certainly do not wish to argue the point here. I merely wish to observe that if any entity has the desire to become red, then, given the opportunity—conditions (a) and (b)— it will carry out its intention. Carrying this suggestion to its conclusion, X contains red, before it is actually red, in *idea*. In the case of Leibniz, I believe, this suggestion is not so far-fetched, at least on the monadic level.

In summary, I view the Aristotelian solution to the problem of change in material bodies as a solution to the problem of how something can come from nothing. This solution is in terms of dispositional properties. Exactly how this solves the problem is unclear, though one tolerably clear model can be given in terms of willing changes to occur. I want to turn now to the problem of change in mental substances. I have stated that the acquisition of knowledge, whether perceptual or mathematical, is for Descartes and Leibniz problematic in a way analogous to the problem of change in material bodies. Whether or not ancient and medieval philosophers had considered that such acquisition called for a causal theory is a moot point here (certainly, in the case of perception, they seem very concerned with its 'mechanics' as well as with its metaphysical ground). Descartes gives the problem a new impetus. Not only does he face the difficulty of accounting for the acquisition of mathematical knowledge, but the new science drastically complicates the account of perceptual knowledge. Consider first the case of mathematical knowledge. A long tradition stemming from Plato, and including Saint Augustine, had established that (a) we cannot learn mathematical facts from sense experience, even though such experience may be a necessary condition for learning such facts, and (b) the 'location' of these facts cannot be the physical world. The argument for (a) usually goes something like this. We know, for example, that $2 + 2 = 4$; we do not know it either directly from sense experience (as we, for example, know that this piece of wood is brown) or indirectly, i.e., we cannot justify our knowledge claim on the basis of inferring it from what we know directly from sense experience. Then there seem to be two alternatives. Either, by a special act of mind, e.g., conception, we conceive this fact as located in some other world than the physical—the mind of God or a Platonic heaven—or we find it in ourselves. Of these possibilities, Malebranche chooses the former, Descartes and Leibniz, the latter.

But this point about mathematical knowledge, that we cannot learn mathematical facts from sense experience, was made long before the mechanical theories of Descartes, and long before the metaphysical theories of dualism and representationalism had any currency. The claim that we cannot learn mathematical facts from perception seems, before Descartes, to be independent of any particular theory of perception. Whether or not this independence is maintained by Descartes is not so clear. Leibniz does seem to maintain it; he argues for innate ideas of mathematical truths in rather classical fashion. One point I wish to elaborate in the remainder of this paper is that Descartes' theory of perception, and Leibniz's, would be enough to establish (a) above. Descartes, as we shall see, claims that we cannot even learn the characteristics of physical bodies directly from perception; the whole mechanism of mind-body interaction precludes it. Thus, for Descartes at least, sense experience is not a sufficient condition for even perceptual knowledge, let alone mathematical knowledge. Leibniz, for not altogether the same reasons, concurs; his theory of perception also, as we shall see, would be enough to establish that we cannot learn mathematical facts from sense experience. I thus want to maintain that, whatever the relation of theories of perception before Descartes to (a) and (b) above, after Descartes perception theories play a major role in establishing (a) and (b).

Leibniz invokes innate ideas to explain both the acquisition and location of mathematical knowledge. Although he claims such ideas are dispositions, he uses language reminiscent of Plato: he speaks of uncovering the covered, of remembering the forgotten.[19] Innate ideas are like the unconscious ideas or drives of the Freudians; they exist in the mind, waiting for their hour. This is not how we normally think of dispositions. We say that a piece of sugar is soluble, and in so doing we attribute to it a property different from the one that it manifests when it dissolves. We do not think of its dissolving as in it, lying in wait, before it dissolves.[20] We have, of course, discussed one way of understanding such talk about physical objects. A willing being contains the qualities it will later manifest, by way of idea. Though this is certainly controversial as a plausible doctrine in itself, let alone as an interpretation of Aristotle or the medievals, it is hardly implausible as a theory of change within a mental substance. It may be implausible to attribute intentions to rocks and leaves, but it is not so unreasonable to suppose that an intelligent being has ideas that go unrecognized unless certain conditions obtain. And, for philosophers coming

213

out of an Aristotelian tradition, it might be quite natural to think of the progression from ignorance to mathematical knowledge as a passing from the potential to the actual, analogous to the way in which a leaf that turns red passes from the potential state of being red to the actual state of being red.

III

I am trying to suggest that the theory of innate ideas would rather naturally stem from certain metaphysical views about causation. It is not just an accident that Locke, Berkeley, and Hume will have no official truck with innate ideas, or that all three speak of learning mathematics, for example, in a radically different way than do Leibniz and Descartes.[21]

Locke claims that the mind is a blank tablet. Experience writes upon it. The cause of perceiving and of knowing is external to the perceiver and the knower. Leibniz, too, understands Locke this way, as the following passages from the *New Essays* show (the context is a discussion of Locke's critique of innate ideas and Locke's own view of perception and knowledge):

> I have made use also of the comparison of a block of marble which has veins, rather than a block of marble wholly even or of blank tablets. . . . For if the soul resembled these blank tablets, truths would be in us as the figure of Hercules is in the marble, when the marble is wholly indifferent to the reception of this figure or some other. But if there were veins in the block which should indicate the figure of Hercules rather than other figures, this block would be more determined thereto, and Hercules would be in it as in some sense innate, although it would be needful to labor to discover these veins, to clear them by polishing, and to cut away what prevents them from appearing. Thus it is that ideas and truths are for us innate, as inclinations, dispositions, habits, or natural potentialities, and not as actions. . . .[22]
>
> Is our soul then by itself such a blank that besides the images borrowed from without, it is nothing? This is not the opinion (I am sure) that our judicious author [Locke] could approve. And where do we find tablets that have no variety in themselves?[23]

And a bit later, he adds:

. . . Two individual things cannot be perfectly alike, and . . . they must always differ more than *numero*; a fact which destroys the blank tablets of the soul, a soul without thought, a substance without action, a vacuum in space . . . and a thousand other fictions of philosophers.[24]

On Locke's view, according to Leibniz, the marble is receptive to any form whatever. As he describes Locke's view, "besides the images borrowed from without, it (the mind) is nothing." Of course, on one level the image of the block of marble is merely suggestive and metaphorical. For a block of marble is a physical object and, on the Aristotelian view, a combination of form and matter. There is not a long and established tradition before Descartes of taking the mind as a substance, itself a combination of form and matter; the tradition is rather that a *person* is a substance wherein the soul is the form of the body. Leibniz's image of the block of marble is dangerously misleading, in that it seems to invite us to think of the soul as matter (the marble) that is preformed (written on from its beginning) rather than informed by external forces (experience writing on it). On the other hand, we should perhaps be prepared to take the image seriously. That Locke thought of the soul in 'material' terms is beyond doubt. That Descartes at least claimed that mind was a different sort of substance from body is also beyond doubt. Whether or not Descartes and, for that matter, Leibniz, took this substantival notion and, explicitly or implicitly, gave it an Aristotelian underpinning, is just the question at issue.[25]

Let me, then, for the sake of argument, take Leibniz's image seriously. If Locke is right, according to Leibniz, then the mind is a sort of unformed, qualityless stuff, i.e., a bare substratum. This is made quite clear by the contrast, in the quotations above, between Leibniz's view of the difference between substances (the invocation of the identity of indiscernibles) and Locke's (alleged) view that one mind, like a chunk of 'pure' matter, is merely numerically different from another mind, like another chunk of 'pure' matter. The mind, in other words, could not be, at birth, just an unqualitied substratum waiting for ideas. There

are no substrata without any qualities. The mind must, therefore, be born with some qualities, and those qualities that are
proper to mind are, of course, ideas. Thus minds have ideas
like marble has veins. Leibniz's problem is to explain how a mind
can have ideas without knowing it does; his answer is that
it has ideas before it knows them (in my view in a way analogous to how a leaf contains a color it does not yet actually show),
i.e., dispositionally. I want to explore this latter notion now in
some detail.

That Leibniz believes in the 'preexistence' in the mind of
unknown ideas is absolutely clear:

> I have already replied to the objection which claimed that when it
> is said that innate notions are implicitly in the mind, the state-
> ment must mean simply that it has the faculty of knowing them;
> for I have pointed out that besides this it has the faculty of find-
> ing them in itself.[26]

> The mind is not only capable of knowing them [necessary truths]
> but further of finding them in itself; and, if it had only the simple
> capacity of receiving knowledge, or the passive power therefore, as
> indeterminate as that which the wax has for receiving figures and
> the blank tablet for receiving letters, it would not be the source of
> necessary truths.[27]

> It [the mind] is not, then, a naked faculty which consists in the
> mere possibility of understanding them [the truths]; it is a dis-
> position, an aptitude, a preformation, which determines our soul
> and which makes it possible for them to be derived from it. Just as
> there is a difference between the figures which are given to the
> stone or the marble indifferently, and between those which its
> veins already indicate, or are disposed to indicate, if the workman
> profits by them.[28]

> . . . The *idea* being taken for the immediate internal object of a
> notion, or what the logicians call an incomplex term, there is
> nothing to prevent its always being in us, for these objects can
> persist when they are not perceived.[29]

What shall we make of this 'preexistence'? It is clear that
Leibniz at least *prima facie* claims that innate ideas exist as
dispositions or, as he sometimes puts it, preformations. What
this comes to is an attempt to explain how an idea is related

to the mind prior to its being known. As far as I can make out, Leibniz tries three ways of explicating the dispositional idea: two of these he seems to accept (they are distinct although he does not clearly distinguish them) and one he rejects. The three ways correspond closely to the ways, already discussed, of explicating the notion of dispositions in physical objects.

(1′) To say that a subject S has an idea P dispositionally, is to say that S 'knows' P, where the term *knows* is not used in the sense of actual knowing, but in some other sense, e.g., unconscious knowing. Another way of making the distinction between two senses of 'know' is to claim that under certain conditions (sense perceptions), P is 'revealed' to S; P is 'known' all along, but S does not know that.

(2′) To say that a subject S has the idea P dispositionally, is to say that if certain conditions obtain, S knows P.

(3′) To say that a subject S has an idea dispositionally, is to say: (a) P is in the mind prior to being consciously apprehended, and (b) if certain conditions were to obtain, P would be consciously apprehended. Condition (a) does not imply that P is in any way cognized before (b) obtains.

Beginning with (1′), it is, I believe, most clearly indicated by the example of the block of marble. Descartes, in a revealing metaphor, once spoke in a similar vein. He described the process of doubt as a method of clearing away the mental rubbish that accumulates in order to reveal the diamonds of truth there all along. What we know is thus originally 'covered' and must be 'revealed', just as the sculptor, according to Leibniz, reveals the figure of Hercules. The implication is that when P is recognized, it does not stand in some new relation to the mind, but is rather revealed to stand in a relation in which it has always stood. Do we thus always 'know' what we later come to know that we 'know'?

There are, of course, contemporary theories of knowledge that have as a consequence that one can know something without knowing that one knows it. One can, for example, behave as if one knows P without ever formulating P to oneself. Indeed, it is rather difficult to maintain such a view without defining some nonepisodic sense of 'know', unless, perhaps, one takes a Freudian view. Now surely Leibniz did not have in mind such a behavioral sense of 'know' when he spoke of innate knowledge of mathematical ideas: for a savage innately knows, for example, that a triangle has three sides even if he never behaves as if he knows it.[30] Nor does it seem that Freudian theory can help us understand Leibniz's view, even if there are some structural similarities. It is doubtful that Freud wanted to speak of unconscious ideas being known. Furthermore, in classic Freudian cases, the existence of unconscious ideas is posited to explain how conscious acts have the import they do, e.g., a slip of the tongue reveals an unconscious goal, and it is because this slip seems to be intentional that Freud posits the existence of some underlying unconscious intention that is a partial cause of the slip. But Leibniz is not concerned with the symbolic import of ideas. There is no parallel reason for taking the fact that one knows some proposition P as symptomatic for some previously existing, though consciously unknown, idea. Freud's theory cannot help us understand how one arrives at a theory of innate (unconscious) ideas, and insofar as Freud has trouble explicating the notion of the unconscious, he is of no help in understanding Leibniz.

The problematic explication of the dispositional notion of innateness, then, comes with the metaphor of the block of marble. It also comes with Leibniz's discussions of the use of innate principles without the user being conscious of their use, the implication being that in some sense S 'knows' them. For how else can we make sense of our use, say, of the principle of contradiction, in affirming what according to Leibniz is not an innate truth, namely, that the sweet is not the bitter?[31] The problem with (1') is that it invokes what seems to be an unexplicated notion of unconscious intentionality. The advantage of (3') over (1') is that it contains no such notion.

Leibniz explicitly rejects (2'); (2') merely expresses Locke's view of the unnatured mind that is capable of receiving ideas from the outside. It is clear from the quotations given above that Leibniz considers such a notion too weak. P must be 'in' the mind prior to being known, and (2′) does not express this adequately.

This brings us to (3′). Leibniz's most persistent explication of the dispositional character of innate ideas takes the form of a comparison to the way remembered knowledge is in the mind prior to remembrance.[32] It is tempting to dismiss such comparisons out of hand, since after all in the case of an innate idea P, it does not follow the normal sequence of being learned, forgotten, then remembered; this is a quite different sequence than if P is forgotten before it is ever learned. However, I think one can counter such an objection in favor of Leibniz by simply pointing out that the origin of an idea does not necessarily dictate its relation to the mind. Whatever the way innate ideas get into the mind, why cannot they have the same relation to the mind when not being attended to as any idea not being attended to? We need not, to put the point another way, assume that an innate idea is one that is in some sense being *thought of*, though not consciously thought of, before it is actually known. Thus instead of thinking of some special sense of 'know', in which the mind 'knows' its innate ideas before it consciously knows them, innate ideas are simply in the mind, in the same sense any ideas are in the mind prior to being consciously thought.

Let us then grant Leibniz the point that innate ideas are in the mind prior to being known, in the same sense in which any idea is in the mind when not being consciously apprehended. Under certain conditions the idea will be consciously apprehended; these conditions, Leibniz maintains, are most likely sensory.[33] It seems, though, that this way of looking at Leibniz makes the comparison I am stressing, between innate ideas and dispositions of physical bodies, rather strained. One way to describe the strain is this: the explication (3) for the notion of a disposition in physical bodies is not really analogous to (3′) for innate ideas. (3) offers us the standard subjunctive conditional as an explication for dispositional notions, and any further attempt to explicate this, say, in terms of 'ideas' that physical objects 'entertain' as goals, and then actualize under certain conditions, is at best highly controversial, i.e., it is controversial that any Aristotelian would hold such a view. Thus (3) leaves us with a problem that (3′) seems not to have. For it may be that the notion of memory, and the question of the location of ideas and their relation to the mind prior to memory, is philosophically problematic; but these difficulties are not necessarily a function of the inherent difficulty of explicating the notion of a disposition. The move from an idea's being in the mind and not known, to its being in the mind and being known, appears different from the actualization of potential we describe when we say a leaf changes from green to red. I do not minimize the limits of my comparison. Nonetheless, what I wish to maintain is that the positing of dispositionals in the form of innate ideas is a response to the same problem that motivates the positing of dispositionals in bodies. The logic of the two sorts of dispositional notions might turn out to be different (even if closely allied), but the motivation, I shall try to show, is quite the same.

I have suggested earlier that the doctrine of dispositions in physical bodies constitutes an attempt, as Stace puts it, to solve the problem of becoming. Without the potentiality-actuality distinction, one is faced with the problem of how something, e.g., the color of the leaf in the fall, comes from nothing. I have also suggested, without in any way arguing the case, that the *ex nihilo* principle seems closely allied to the doctrine that effects must somehow be like or 'contained in' their cause; since otherwise the effect will seem to have come *ex nihilo*. It has been objected to me that any philosopher who has a doctrine of efficient causation embraces the *ex nihilo* principle still, since, after all, such a philosopher maintains that an effect does have a cause of *some* sort. My intuition here, which again I shall not try in any way to justify fully, is that this objection is mistaken. Plato, we know, clearly distinguished the condition from the cause when he had Socrates claim that the cause of his sitting in prison was not that his bones and muscles were in a certain state, but that he wanted to sit in prison. Aristotle was certainly aware of the necessary external conditions for change— he called this 'efficient causality'—but he distinguished this sort of cause from others. If

Aristotle had been content with such conditions as a sufficient explanation for (natural) change, why did he posit the potentiality-actuality distinction as a solution to the problem of becoming? The case of the leaf changing from green to red in the fall brings home the point: in citing the changes in weather, and so on, as the cause of change of color, there seems to be a puzzle. We cannot see clearly how such conditions could bring about such a change; dispositions fill the gap.

Surprisingly, perhaps—since he is so fuzzy about so much—Locke appears to be the first major historical figure who challenges the *ex nihilo* doctrine. The following passage, I think, is remarkable, not only because it poses this challenge, but because it clearly brings together the problem of change in material bodies and the problem of change in perceiving things:

> . . . Nor can reason show how bodies, *by their bulk, figure, and motion*, should produce in the mind the ideas of blue or yellow, &c. But, in the other case, in the operations of bodies changing the qualities one of another, we plainly discover that the quality produced hath commonly no resemblance with anything in the thing producing it; wherefore we look on it as a bare effect of power. For, through receiving the idea of heat or light from the sun, we are apt to think *it* is a perception and resemblance of such a quality in the sun; yet when we see wax, or a fair face, receive change of color from the sun, we cannot imagine *that* to be the reception of resemblance of anything in the sun, because we find not those different colors in the sun itself. . . . Our senses, not being able to discover any unlikeness between the idea produced in us, and the quality of the object producing it, we are apt to imagine that our ideas are resemblances of something in the objects, and not the effects of certain powers placed in the modification of their primary qualities, with which primary qualities the ideas produced in us have no resemblance.[34]

One must tread carefully here, of course. In discussing the powers of bodies Locke divides them into active and passive. The sun has the active power to melt wax. Wax has the passive power to be melted by the sun. It is clear that Locke thinks of perception as just another causal interaction, in the same boat as interaction between inanimate bodies. He does not think of

221

bodies as in some sense producing change in themselves; his is certainly a doctrine of efficient causality. True, he speaks of passive powers; thus a perceiver must possess the passive power to have, for example, color ideas under certain conditions. But he stops short of claiming that the color idea must in any sense preexist, in the perceiver, prior to its production by an external body. Locke, I submit, means by this notion of passive power exactly what we have seen Leibniz attribute to him: to say that the perceiver S has the capacity to apprehend some idea P is merely to say that, under certain conditions, S apprehends P, i.e., (2′) above. Locke insists on the causes of changes in bodies *being external to them; and, in laying heavy stress on the psychology of learning, he shows that he considers the genesis of ideas to be a species of the general explanation of change.

The view of Descartes on the production of ideas from sense perception is both strikingly similar and strikingly different from that of Locke. In short, Descartes sees the same difficulties about the causes of ideas as does Locke; but whereas Locke is content to let matters rest with efficient causality, Descartes invokes the notion of innate ideas. Consider the following passage:

> . . . any man who rightly observes the limitation of the senses, and what precisely it is that can penetrate through this medium to our faculty of thinking must needs admit that no idea of things, in the shape in which we envisage them by thought, are presented to us by the senses. So much so that in our ideas there is nothing which was not innate in the mind, or faculty of thinking. . . . For nothing reaches our mind from external objects through the organs of sense beyond certain corporeal movements . . . but even these movements, and the figures which arise from them, are not conceived by us in the shape they assume in the organs of sense, as I have explained at great length in my *Dioptrics*. Hence it follows that the ideas of the movements and figures are themselves innate in us. So much the more must the ideas of pain, colour, sound and the like be innate, that our mind may, on occasion of certain corporeal movements, envisage these ideas, for they have no likeness to the corporeal movements.[35]

Consider the red square patch that I now see. Why cannot what Descartes so revealingly calls the occasion of certain corporeal movements, i.e., the interaction of physical bodies with my body, which interaction finally produces certain motions in the brain, cause, in some Humean sense, the patch? Why need one claim that color and shape ideas are innate? Descartes quite pointedly remarks that our ideas have no *likeness* in corporeal movements. So, he concludes, they must be innate. The conclusion only follows if one adds the suppressed premise that effects must be like their causes. More important is the implication as to what an innate idea *is*. It is not merely the disposition or passive power to have such ideas. Descartes says that the idea of, say, colors and shapes are innate so that when certain physical events occur, we envisage *these* ideas. So where Locke speaks of a passive power, and leaves the relationship between this power and the idea that springs from it to be explicated in terms of (2) or (2'), Descartes posits the existence of innate ideas to explain the origin of ideas of sense. Interestingly, Descartes does not have the sort of problem he outlines in the last quoted passage in his analysis of body-body interaction, since in that case, he thinks, there is no problem of effects being unlike their causes. Locke, on the other hand, gives the same sort of analysis to body-body interaction as he does to body-mind interaction. In both cases, the above quoted passage makes clear, effects can be unlike their causes. Even considering the most secret powers of bodies, he says, it is mysterious as to why certain actions have the effects they do.[36] As far as I can tell, what Locke means is that the sort of causal connection he discusses with respect to the sun and the wax repeats itself on the micro-level. To call the relation mysterious is not to give it analysis, of course, but rather to deny that any analysis can be given. Locke, in other words, refuses to take the step that others take; he refuses to countenance hidden essences, powers, or dispositions in the sense that the Aristotelians do. Had Descartes seen (as Hume did later) that even in the case of body-body interaction, effects are unlike their causes, he would have had to claim, as he did in the case of body-mind interaction, that there are dispositional qualities in bodies. Most likely this would have involved him in the very notion of bodily activity that he is famous for descrying.

Before turning, for the last time, to Leibniz, let me conclude this part of my speculations (and indeed, I know that the above is highly speculative) by claiming that the mind-body problem for Descartes is in a perfectly clear sense a species of the problem of how effects can be like their causes. That problem makes the contrast between Descartes, who believes in innate ideas, and Locke, who does not, very sharp. Both agree that ideas of perception are unlike those physical bodies that are the necessary conditions for their existence. Yet Locke is satisfied to call these bodies (or physical events) causes of the ideas. True, he implies the mind has the passive power to have such ideas caused in them. But he in no way implies that such ideas are innate. Descartes, on the other hand, refuses to grant that physical objects cause our perceptions, even though they are necessary conditions for their existence. Or, if one claims that for Descartes such conditions are causally necessary, it is clear that no set of such conditions is sufficient for the production of ideas of sense. Locke does think that such conditions are sufficient, in that his argument against powers and dispositions and essences in the classic sense implies that, for him, the statement of the conditional that describes the physical conditions in its antecedent and the effect in its consequent is all that we can hope for. The difference between the dispositions or passive powers of Locke and the innate ideas of Descartes is vast.

Descartes certainly would have found Locke's doctrine of the causation of ideas of sense ineffective. Leibniz found Descartes' wanting as well. Missing from both is the notion of *activity*.[37] How can Descartes explain the actualization of innate dispositions? Is it by will? Descartes does not say. Leibniz does say; he erects a philosophy around the issue.

What is the final upshot of Descartes' worry about the cause of sense ideas? In effect, he makes all ideas, those of mathematics as well as those of sense, innate. So strong is the doctrine that it appears from the quotation above that it it is not merely, say, my idea of a certain shade of color and my idea of a certain shape that are innate, but also the idea I am now perceiving, *this* red square, is innate.

It is precisely this form of the innate idea theory that is fatal to it. Read somewhat sympathetically, this is Locke's primary objection to innate ideas.[38] If only some ideas are innate, the distinction between innate ideas and, say, ideas we derive from sense experience might seem viable. But if all ideas are innate, perhaps Occam's razor can be used to rid us of these entities. Surprisingly, Leibniz himself raises the same objection through Philalethes in the *New Essays*:

> . . . If you can say of some particular proposition that it is innate, you could maintain by the same reasoning that all propositions which are reasonable, and which the mind could always regard as such, are already impressed upon the soul.[39]

Leibniz does not really answer this objection. He merely distinguishes what he calls "pure ideas" from "the phantoms of the senses," and holds out for a certain subset of reasonable propositions as innate. The problem here is that Leibniz is rather shortsighted about his own views, and it is this very shortsightedness, I think, that has kept his (and Descartes') readers from grasping the fact that the theory of innate ideas is a response to the problem of the causation of ideas, ideas of perception *and* mathematical ideas. After all, what does lead Descartes to claim that all ideas, even those of sense, are innate? The problem is one over causation, over the interaction of the physical world with the mind. When Leibniz argues that we cannot learn mathematical truths from perception, he also claims that we *can* learn certain other truths from perception.[40] But this claim, which is over the necessity of mathematical truths and the impossibility of ascertaining this necessity by induction, is a smoke screen. Leibniz's own view of perception precludes the learning of any truths from sense experience and the derivation of any ideas from sense experience, except insofar as events in the physical world are, on the phenomenal level, a necessary condition for the activation of innate ideas. Consider the following passage:

> I think, however, that I can say that our ideas, even those of sensible things, come from within our own soul, of which view you can the better judge by what I have published upon the nature and

225

connection of substances and what is called the union of the soul with the body. . . . I am nowise in favor of Aristotle's *tabula rasa*; and there is something substantial in what Plato called *reminiscence*. There is even something more; for we not only have a reminiscence of all our past thoughts, but also a presentiment of all our future thoughts. . . . Thus it is true in a certain sense, as I have explained, that not only our ideas, but also our sensations, spring from within our own soul, and that the soul is more independent than is thought.[41]

Leibniz alludes here to his doctrine of preestablished harmony, and his views both of the 'independence' of substances and the causal interaction between substances. These doctrines are well known, and I shall not discuss them here. I wish to point out, however, that there is certainly a strong suggestion, in the above passage, that Leibniz follows Descartes in his claim that all ideas, even those of sense, are innate, and that his reasons are quite similar insofar as he is worried, as is Descartes, about the effect of bodies on the mind. If I am correct in this speculation, then Leibniz's attempt to distinguish pure ideas from phantoms of the senses is indeed a smokescreen. At best, the distinction could only be made at the superficial phenomenal level. At the monadic level, alluded to in the quoted passage above, the distinction could only be made contextually, in terms of the different sorts of conditions necessary for different sorts of innate ideas to come to consciousness. On the phenomenal level and, so to speak, going with common sense, only some ideas are innate; on the monadic level, all are innate. Thus is Leibniz open to the objection of Philalethes, and Locke.

Summary

According to Stace, Aristotle solves the problem of becoming by going between the horns of a dilemma: either something comes from nothing, which is impossible, or the something already exists, in which case it does not become, i.e., there is no change. Aristotle's solution is that the something does already exist, but only potentially and not actually. If a leaf becomes red, the color must exist potentially in the leaf. In order to avoid the dilemma, the color must preexist in the leaf but not, if I may so put it, in the same relation to it as when the leaf is actually red.

I have tried to suggest that the theory of innate ideas is a response to the same problem of becoming, except that what becomes are ideas. Despite or, even more surprisingly, because of the new notion of mechanics and the passivity of matter, Descartes holds that all ideas are innate. This is because, when considering how ideas of sense are caused, he sees that no interaction theory can explain how such ideas come into being, since as effects they are unlike their causes. Leibniz, in his critique of Locke, wants to maintain the distinction between ideas of sense and innate ideas, say, of mathematical objects, but he can only do so on the phenomenal level. He himself admits that the soul is more independent of the body than is usually thought and there is a sense in which all ideas are innate, on the deepest (monadic) level of analysis. Though I do no more than sketch my case here, I have inferred from this step of making all ideas innate that Leibniz, too, is responding to the problem of becoming in the case of ideas in an Aristotelian way.

1. Throughout this paper I assume what once was a widely shared view of the difference between philosophy and science; nowadays, of course, due mainly to the work of Quine, the distinction has drowned in the Pragmatic Sea. That there is a difference, for example, between the claim that there are electrons and the claim that there are irreducible dispositional properties seems to me so fundamental that I scarcely know how to go about defending it. Yet I know the defense must be made, and made better than heretofore it has been, if the move toward the total naturalization of metaphysics and epistemology is to be forestalled. Very fortunately this is not a task I have set for myself in this paper. I shall content myself, if not the reader, with the simple claim that I invoke the distinction between metaphysics and science very much in the spirit of Carnap and positivism (though not completely: see Gustav Bergmann, "Logical Positivism, Language and the Reconstruction of Metaphysics," in *The Metaphysics of Logical Positivism* (New York: Longmans, Green, 1954, pp. 30-77), and the formula, which I know is inadequate, that whereas the scientist searches for the actual mechanism of change, the philosopher searches for that which makes change possible at all.

2. In discussion of an earlier version of the paper read before the meeting that inspired this volume, Professors Alan Donagan and Wilfrid Sellars adamantly raised this point. My use of single quotation marks around 'is' shows that I think their usage problematic. I shall continue to use single quotation marks throughout this paper for uses I consider problematic.

3. Stephen Schiffer, "Descartes on His Essence," *Philosophical Review* 85 (1976): 21–43. See especially p. 25. Schiffer argues that Descartes holds both that the essence of matter is extension and that the essence of material *bodies* is more than extension. For extension is a quantity of matter, and an individual body is made up of a quantity of matter; but whereas a particular body can perish, matter cannot. Schiffer concludes that "viewed thus, Descartes' matter would bear a striking resemblance to the prime matter of the Aristotelian-Thomistic tradition." However one views the place of Cartesian matter, Schiffer's argument that the essence of a particular body cannot be just extension, and hence the body is not identical with extension, is convincing. The interesting question to me, which unfortunately Schiffer does not clearly address, is whether matter itself is *identical with* extension.

4. To many philosophers it has seemed almost axiomatic that because (a) objects that we perceive are at a distance from our bodies, and (b) they cause us to perceive them by a complex chain of intermediary causes, that we do not 'directly' perceive such bodies.

5. Noam Chomsky, *Cartesian Linguistics* (New York: Harper & Row, 1966). See also his review of Skinner's *Verbal Behaviour* in *Language* 35 (1959): 26–58.

6. Chomsky, *Cartesian Linguistics*, p. 65.

7. See note 1 above. Again, as I understand them, traditional metaphysicians have been concerned with the question of what physical objects, and minds, must be like in order for change in them to be possible. For these metaphysicians, what science tells us about the mechanisms for change is at best a starting point for inquiry and not, as it is for many today, the end point of *all* inquiry.

8. I fear this is much oversimplified, for several reasons. First, Leibniz accepts the new impact theories on what might be called the phenomenal level. This is all the better for my own view of the matter; for the fact that there is another, deeper level of analysis (the monadic level) in which Leibniz goes beyond science shows his commitment to a difference between science and metaphysics (though it is not, of course, the one to which the positivists subscribe). Second, to speak of the nature of extension as postulated to solve the problem of change would, in Descartes' case, be criticized by at least Leibniz. Leibniz would argue, I think, that the notion of a nature is useless unless such natures are active. One could argue that for Descartes 'extension' refers neither to a disposition nor something active, but rather to a certain set of attributes that all bodies have necessarily. See Schiffer's aforementioned paper. On the other hand, I think that for Descartes the notion of an essence with respect to mind is radically different than the notion of essence with respect to body.

9. Chomsky, review of *Verbal Behaviour*, pp. 42–44, 56.

10. Some philosophers and scientists have claimed, perhaps in response to questions like those raised by the change in the leaf, that all is atoms in motion, e.g., that all change is a function of one entity taking on the 'same' properties that another entity, of the same kind, 'gives' or 'transfers' to it (for example, momentum or velocity). Hume's insights can of course easily be restructured to fit even this scientific news.

11. In the Christian tradition, the most important cases where this principle is violated is in the *ex nihilo* creation of the world. Such violation is a miracle, but miracles do not often occur; they do not occur at all in the regular course of nature.

12. W. T. Stace, *A Critical History of Greek Philosophy* (London: Macmillan, 1960), pp. 279–80.

13. Ibid., p. 280.

14. I think one could plausibly argue that this notion is the source of the claim, accepted by many philosophers, that Aristotle invests every material body with a soul, i.e., that every natured body has a soul. For one reasonable explication of how the

228

qualities can be in the acorn potentially is modeled on thought: I can think of becoming a physician, so that the quality I later take on is in me in the sense of my thinking about it, in the way a thought contains its intention. I shall return to this point later in the main body of the paper.

15. See my "Hume's Theory of Relations," *Nous* 1 (August 1967): pp. 264 ff.; also my "Some Counsel on Humean Relations," *Hume Studies* 1 (November 1975): 48–65.

16. For an excellent discussion see Ellen Stone Haring's, "Substantial Form in Aristotle's *Metaphysics Z*," *Review of Metaphysics* 10 (1956–57): 308–32, 482–513, 698–713.

17. Leibniz criticizes Descartes on two counts: (1) Descartes does not give a coherent mechanical explanation of change in material bodies, and (2) Descartes does not adequately ground, metaphysically, change in bodies.

18. Stace, op. cit., p. 280. My discussion that follows in the main body of the paper is derived from Stace's ideas.

19. Gottfried Wilhelm Leibniz, *New Essays Concerning Human Understanding* (La Salle, Ill.: Open Court, 1959), p. 78.

20. Leibniz speaks of innate ideas as potentialities, just as Descartes does. Descartes in fact compares an innate idea to innate generosity. See *Notes Directed against a Certain Programme*, in *Philosophical Works*, vol. 1, ed. E. Haldane and G. Ross (Cambridge: At the University Press, 1957), p. 442. Such a comparison could of course be taken to show the doctrine of innate ideas as harmless, one to which a positivistically interpreted Locke could agree. For to say that a person is innately generous could be taken to mean that, under many different sorts of conditions, the person is generous, whereas a person who is not generous innately merely does not show generosity under such a variety of conditions. I think and shall show that Leibniz would reject such an interpretation of his claim that there are innate ideas; such ideas exist in the mind before they are known. Descartes, despite the aforementioned comparison, more often leans towards Leibniz's view. For an interesting discussion see Anthony Kenny, "Descartes on Ideas," in *Descartes: A Collection of Critical Essays*, ed. Willis Doney (Garden City, N.Y.: Doubleday, 1967), pp. 230 ff. All future references to Descartes are to the Haldane and Ross translation.

21. Whether or not Locke is forced to some notion of innateness, e.g., innate faculties, whether he wants it or not, is another matter. And one could argue that for Berkeley, notions function in a way similar to innate ideas. In my view the issue comes down, at least in large part, to whether or not any philosopher trying metaphysically to account for change must turn to dispositions in the Aristotelian sense.

22. Leibniz, op. cit., pp. 45–46.

23. Ibid., pp. 46–47.

24. Ibid., p. 51.

25. To repeat the point made in note 3 above, I am not claiming that what Descartes calls matter is anything more, in his view, than its essence, though individual bodies are more than their matter. Minds (as opposed to mind? Is there such a notion in Descartes?), like individual physical bodies, are, by parallel reasoning, more than thought. Perhaps, to follow Schiffer's suggestion (see note 3) with respect to bodies, individual minds have as their 'matter' (their substratum) thought, while the 'form' imposed on this 'matter' combines with it to make up an individual mind. I do not think that the exact specification of the ingredients of a *particular* mental substance makes a difference to my point, however—since my idea is that innate ideas are somehow 'in' minds, where minds are viewed as substances. I suppose that one way to challenge this claim would be to maintain that, for Descartes, there are only two created substances, mind and body. Perhaps one can plausibly argue that there is

only one body, according to Descartes, namely extension, but is there really only one created mind?

26. Leibniz, op. cit., pp. 74–75.

27. Ibid., pp. 80–81.

28. Ibid., p. 81.

29. Ibid., p. 21. The entire discussion on page 21 and following is of interest here. There is an unmistakable connection with Platonic doctrines. Leibniz is claiming that ideas are not dependent on being known in the sense of being perceived in order for them to exist. They may subsist, 'in' a substance, by having a different relation to it than that of being perceived. Leibniz is not, of course, using 'perceived' in the sense of sense perception. A perceived idea is one that one is conscious of.

30. Ibid., p. 80.

31. Ibid., pp. 82–84.

32. In the *New Essays* there are, in fact, arguments about *both* the acquisition of mathematical ideas in the sense of acquiring the concepts of individual numbers, and the acquisition of truths such as $2 + 2 = 4$. In the latter case, Leibniz argues that we cannot explain our knowledge that such truths are necessary by appeal to sense perception (p. 82). These are separate arguments, even if Leibniz does not clearly separate them. For even if it were the case that, in order to explain our knowledge of the necessity of $2 + 2 = 4$, we must claim to find this truth in ourselves, it does not follow that we must hold that we acquire the concept of twoness, for example, from ourselves, from a storehouse of innate concepts or ideas. Leibniz holds both that such concepts *and* their relations are innate. See the *New Essays*, pp. 74–82, especially p. 82.

33. Ibid., p. 82.

34. John Locke, *An Essay Concerning Human Understanding*, ed. by A. C. Fraser (New York: Dover Publications, 1959), vol. 1, bk. 2, chap. 8, pp. 180–81.

35. Descartes, *Notes Directed against a Certain Programme*, pp. 442–43.

36. Locke, op. cit., vol. 1, bk. 2, chap. 23, p. 412.

37. Leibniz, op. cit., p. 112. Theophilus says, "Real powers are never simple possibilities. They have always tendency and action." Thus neither Locke's active nor passive powers would count as real powers in Leibniz's view, or, more accurately, neither those active and passive powers that Locke places in bodies, nor those powers of mind to receive ideas. Locke's whole discussion of such powers robs them of activity; the only reapply active entities are minds. See *Essay*, vol. 1, bk. 2, chap. 21, pp. 310–13.

38. Locke, op. cit., vol. 1, bk. 1, chap. 1, pp. 51 ff.

39. Leibniz, op. cit., p. 78.

40. Ibid., p. 84. The proposition "The sweet is not the bitter" is, he says, a mixed conclusion, and is not innate, since the ideas of bitter and sweet come from the senses.

41. Ibid., p. 15.

Chapter Nine

NEWTON'S ADVERTISED PRECISION AND HIS
REFUTATION OF THE RECEIVED LAWS OF REFRACTION

The principal aim of this paper is to achieve a satisfactory analysis of Newton's refutation of "the received laws of refraction." This refutation was based primarily on the results of Newton's well-known formation of the spectrum by refracting the sun's rays through a prism. At first glance, Newton's argument appears straightforward. The received laws are to be rejected because they predict a circular image, whereas what is observed is oblong. I will show, however, that Newton's actual argument was considerably more sophisticated than this. It had to be, given the difficulties of achieving an acceptable quantitative description of the experiment. In fact, as will be seen, Newton's advertised precision considerably exceeded what was actually available to him. Although Newton did not explicitly calculate the errors that would result from his exaggerated precision, he did perform a variation on his experiment that showed that even relatively gross inaccuracies in his quantitative descriptions would not affect the refutation of the received laws. It is this supporting argument that I wish to draw attention to, since it shows that Newton had some awareness of the importance of errors of measurement. My historical reference point for Newton's description of the prism experiment will be its first published version, the classic 1671/72 paper sent to the Royal Society. This version will, at the appropriate times, be compared with other manuscript and published versions.

Newton's 1671/72 optics paper begins with the claim that in 1666 Newton procured a "Triangular glass-Prisme, to try therewith the celebrated *Phenomena* of Colors."[1] The description that Newton gave of his first experiment does not, however, reflect this aim in any obvious way. Image size and shape are the descriptive parameters, not color and color location. In particular, it is the oblong shape of the sun's projected image that is of interest, not the continuous distribution of colors along that image.

> . . . Having darkened my chamber, and made a small hole in my window-shuts, to let in a convenient quantity of the Suns light, I placed my Prisme at its entrance, that it might be thereby refracted to the opposite wall. It was at first a very pleasing divertisement, to view the vivid and intense colours produced thereby; but after a while applying my self to consider them more circumspectly, I became surprised to see them in an *oblong* form; which according to the received laws of Refraction, I expected should have been *circular*.
>
> They were terminated at the sides with streight lines, but at the ends, the decay of light was so gradual, that it was difficult to determine justly, what was their figure; yet they seemed *semicircular*.
>
> Comparing the length of this coloured *Spectrum* with its breadth, I found it about five times greater; a disproportion so extravagant, that it excited me to a more then ordinary curiosity of examining, from whence it might proceed.[2]

Unfortunately, the manuscript evidence shows that Newton's engaging anecdotal style is most probably a historical fabrication. (Its very elegance should have by itself suggested this!) The claimed train of events in no way corresponds to Newton's earliest (1664–65) observations as recorded in the unpublished notebook, "Quaestiones quaedam Philosophicae."[3] There Newton set forth a series of experiments where variously colored objects were viewed *through* a prism. The descriptions of these experiments are primarily in terms of displaced colored images, and not in terms of image sizes and shapes. One of the most important of these experiments consisted in the observation through a prism of a thread divided into blue and red halves. On the basis of the visual separation of these halves, Newton concluded, "That ye rays which make blew are refracted more yn ye rays which make red appears from this experiment."[4]

There is however in "Quaestiones" no clear statement of what was later to become the cornerstone of Newton's optical

232

theory, namely, that white light consists of individual rays of different and unchangeable refrangibility and color. The rays of the above quotation do not have the immutable refrangibility and color that they will acquire in Newton's later work. In fact, at the time of the "Quaestiones," Newton saw the explanation of color phenomena as a choice between modification theories, and not in terms of a ray separation theory: "Colours arise either from shaddows intermixed wth light or stronger & weaker reflection or parts of ye body mixed with & carried away by light."[5]

Even if Newton did hold a modification theory at the time he first projected the sun's rays through a prism, his knowledge of the difference in refrangibility between the colors (however produced) would have been sufficient to suggest an oblong image (if only for a single refraction).[6] Therefore, if Newton was genuinely surprised by the shape of the spectrum, it was because he had not yet sufficiently worked out the geometry of the situation.

To further investigate this question of Newton's anticipations would take us wide of the aim of this paper, which is to analyze Newton's refutation of the then received laws of refraction. It will be relevant, though, to consider, why Newton thought the oblong shape would surprise his contemporaries who were unaware of Newton's so far unpublished optical theory. As Newton notes in the 1671/72 paper, the image ought on the basis of "the received laws of Refraction . . . to have been *circular*." And by "the received laws," Newton meant "the Hypothesis of the proportionality of the *sines* of Incidence, and Refraction," along with the relevant light ray axioms.[7] The received view of this "Hypothesis" had it that there is only one refractive index for each substance, or as Newton described it in his optical lectures, "Now from the commonly received Opinion, those Rays having the same Incidence ought also to have all the same Refraction."[8]

If what later became known as Snell's law is understood in this restricted way, and if it is combined with the assumption that the incident rays from the distant sun source are *parallel*, then it follows that the image ought to be circular and not oblong.[9] Therefore, what was perceived to stand in need of explanation was a deviation from a theoretically established norm. Newton considered four candidates for the explanation of this deviation. They were that the image is oblong because of (1) "the various *Thickness* of glass, or the termination with shadow or darkness"; (2) some "contingent irregularity" in the glass prism; (3) "the difference of the incidence of Rays coming from divers parts of the Sun"; (4) the possibility that "the Rays, after their trajection through the Prisme . . . move in curve lines."[10] Only the third candidate, the most developed by Newton, will be considered in this paper. This proposed explanation depends on the fact that because of the finite size of the sun, not all of the light coming from it can be considered as parallel rays. The observed deviation from the theoretically established norm is on this account to be explained in terms of a deviation from the (initial) conditions used to calculate that norm, and not in terms of a deviation from "the received laws."

In order to test this then received theory and associated explanation, Newton had to supplement his description of the prism experiment with the necessary quantitative data.

> I . . . measured the several lines and angles, belonging to the Image. Its distance from the hole or Prisme was 22 foot; its utmost length 13 1/4 inches; it breadth 2 5/8 inches; the diameter of the hole 1/4 of an inch; the angle, which the Rays, tending towards the middle of the image, made with those lines, in which they would have proceeded without refraction, 44 deg.56'. And the vertical Angle of the Prisme, 63 deg.12'. Also the Refractions on both sides the Prisme, that is, of the Incident, and Emergent Rays, were as near, as I could make them equal, and consequently about 54 deg.4'. And the Rays fell perpendicularly upon the wall.[11]

One feature of this supplementation that is of considerable importance is the equality of incident and refracted ray angles. This equality and its implicit precision stand in marked contrast to the ingenuousness expressed in the initial description. ("It was at first a very pleasing divertisement.") As Newton was later to clarify, it is the fact that the image is oblong for the case of equal incidence and refraction that is to be explained.[12] The reason for this restriction is that given the assumption of non-parallel incident sunrays, the received laws have as a consequent that the projected image ought to be oblong for all other inclinations. This reason, however, was not revealed in the 1671/72 optics paper. Nor was it revealed that Newton had at this time a general geometrical proof showing that even on the assumption of non-parallel incident rays, the received laws would yield a circular and not oblong image for the case of symmetrical incidence and refraction.[13] While the 1671/72 paper is clearly motivated by this proof, Newton's published procedure is more empirical. That is, measurements of the relevant proportions were substituted for much of the geometrical reasoning of the suppressed proof. The details and consequences of Newton's geometrically inspired procedure form most of the substance of this paper.

Given the importance, thought somewhat concealed, of the configuration of equal incidence and refraction, it is noteworthy that Newton did not in the 1671/72 paper describe how this equality was measured. This claimed equality is not, however, exceptional in this respect, since Newton did not in that paper reveal how any of the quantitative data was gotten. Instead of discussing his experimental technique, Newton went on to *re-describe* the experiment in a way that transforms the actual case into one that is mathematically more tractable. Specifically, Newton subtracted the aperture size from the vertical and horizontal dimensions of the projected image, and then used these reduced dimensions to calculate the angular divergence of the doubly refracted rays in both vertical and horizontal planes.

> Now subducting the diameter of the hole from the length and breadth of the Image, there remains 13 Inches the length, and 2 3/8 the breadth, comprehended by those Rays, which passed through the center of the saide hole, and consequently the angle at the hole, which the breadth subtended, was about 31' . . . the angle, which its length subtended, was more then five such diametors, namely 2 deg.49'.[14]

This subtraction and consequent calculation gives in effect what the case would be *if* the aperture were infinitesimal since it utilizes "those Rays, which passed through the center of the saide hole." Consequently, the terms of the sought-after expla-

235

nation are transformed from finite source and aperture into finite source but infinitesimal aperture.[15] Although Newton did not here or elsewhere explicitly justify this calculation (and resultant transformation), the geometry of the reduction in the horizontal plane is straightforward, but not exact (see fig. 1).

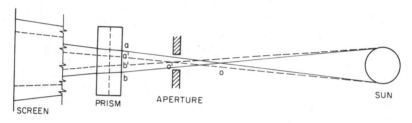

Figure 1

The simple subtraction of aperture size from image size will not yield the proper angular divergence of the sun's rays that pass through the center of the aperture, because *ao* and *bo* are not parallel to *a'o'* and *b'o'*. The resultant error is, of course, very small. Newton's procedure does yield an exact counterpart if the envisioned infinitesimal aperture is placed at *o* instead of in the middle of the finite aperture. (I will discuss below Pardies' objection to the reduction as applied in the vertical plane.)

After calculating the angular divergences of the refracted rays, Newton immediately noted that the 31' divergence in the horizontal plane is "answerable to the Suns Diameter."[16] Despite Newton's breezy manner, there are several problems posed by this apparently straightforward explanatory claim. Part of its justification depends on the fact that given the parallel sides of the prism (in the horizontal plane), it follows from Snell's Law (on *both* the received and Newton's interpretation) that the incoming and outgoing refractions are reciprocal. Hence, the angular divergences of the incident and doubly refracted rays are equal. In terms of the following figure, angle *x* can be identified as 31'. And presumably this angle *x*, equal to 31', is "answerable to the Suns Diameter" because on both the received view and Newton's, there could be no other explanation (see fig. 2).

236

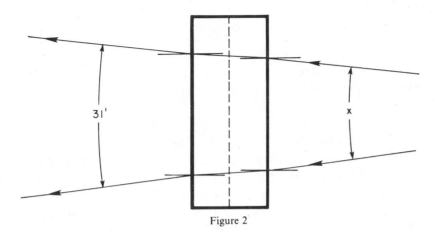

Figure 2

The importance of this identification of x as 31′ is obvious, since, given the (assumed) symmetry of the sun, it follows that the angular divergence of the incoming rays in the vertical plane is also 31′. And it is this 31′ that must be the basis of any successful calculation of the vertically refracted divergence of 2° 41′.

As can be seen, several assumptions including Snell's Law are needed in order to justify Newton's identification of the incoming divergence as 31′ in both vertical and horizontal planes. These assumptions, though, are all shared by both Newton's theory as well as "the received laws." Therefore, proponents of these two competing theories could at least agree on the determination of this crucial initial condition. For example, Pardies, though anxious to uphold the received view, readily accepted Newton's calculation of the incoming divergence of the sun's rays:

. . . The two surfaces of the prism may be considered as parallel, with respect to the inclination to the axis, since they are both parallel to it. But the refraction through two parallel plane surfaces is accounted none, because by how much a ray is refracted one way by the first surface, by just so much is it refracted the contrary way by the other surface. Therefore since the solar rays, transmitted by a hole through a prism, are not refracted sideways, *they proceed in that respect as if no prism at all stood in*

237

their way, that is with regard to the lateral divarication . . . (my italics).[17]

This agreement (with Newton's treatment in the horizontal plane) was essential because Newton's calculation provides greater accuracy than the nonrefractive and hence less theoretical procedure of directly measuring the divergence of the sun's rays in the absence of the prism. Such a direct measurement would have less accuracy because the unrefracted path length is only about seven feet long as opposed to the 22 feet of the theoretical calculation. This shorter path length is due to the sun's elevation, which, at the time of the experiment, would have to have been around 45°. Another nonrefractive alternative would be to measure the divergence when the sun was lower in the horizon. Using a lower elevation has the advantage of increasing the unrefracted path length, and thus restoring some of the lost accuracy. This procedure has the disadvantage of having to assume the non-existence of differing disturbing influences between high and low elevations. And, in fact, the effect of clouds as a disturbing influence was much discussed by Newton and his contemporaries.

Newton's next move was to compute "the refractive power of the Glass," so that the divergence of the outgoing doubly refracted rays (in the vertical plane) could be calculated on the basis of the 31′ divergence of incident rays. Although Newton does not give the details of his computation of the refractive power, his value of "20 to 31" indicates that the computation was based on the refraction angles of the incident ray (from the center of the sun) that was equally refracted by the prism. The incident angle of this ray has already been claimed to be 54°04′, while the refracted angle works out (on the basis of Newton's other claimed measurements) to be 31°36′. The ratio of their respective sines is, indeed, as Newton claims (nearly) "20 to 31." As will be noted, this measurement gives what might more properly be called the *mean* refractive power of the glass. And from the point of view of Newton's theory, this is indeed the case. From the point of view, however, of the to-be-tested "received laws," Newton's procedure gives *the* refractive power.[18]

Using this "20 to 31" measure of the refractive power, Newton then calculated, or claimed to calculate, that the angle of divergence of the refracted rays (in the vertical plane) should be "about 31" and hence about equal to that of the incident rays. But this calculated value of "about 31" corresponds, as Newton notes, to one "which in reality 2 deg.49'." Newton does *not*, however, at this stage of the 1671/72 paper use this large disparity to argue against the received laws. In order to show and adequately appraise Newton's argument against the received laws, it will be necessary to first critically examine the quantitative details of Newton's measurements and calculations. Unfortunately, as I have already noted, the details of these calculations and measurements were not given in the 1671/72 paper. Furthermore, except for the means used to determine equality of refraction, they do not appear in the later *Opticks*, nor do they appear in the *Lectiones Opticae*.[19] The revealed procedure for determining the equality of refraction is, however, an important clue. Another available related clue is the fact that Newton was before the publication of his first paper already in possession of a geometrical proof showing that (given the confirguration of symmetrical refraction for the mean incident ray) the angle of divergence of the doubly refracted beam is equal to that of the incident cone, that is, that the projected image is circular. This proof appears in a manuscript as well as the final version of the *Lectiones Opticae*, where it forms the basis for two arguments against the received laws.[20] The first is that, according to the received laws, there is a prism orientation such that the sun's rays will be projected into a circular image. The received laws are to be rejected because no actual prism orientation yields such an image. The second argument against the received laws is closer in form to that given in the 1671/72 paper. *Given* symmetrical refraction, the angular divergences of the doubly refracted cone in both the vertical and horizontal planes ought according to the received laws to be equal. Measurement, though, showed this not to be the case.

> . . . I so disposed the Prism, that the Refraction as well of the imerging as the emerging Rays, might be as it were equal, I measured . . . the Angles PFT, and YFZ, [the vertical and horizontal angles of the projected light cone] and found the Angle YFZ, in-

deed equal to half a Degree or the Diameter of the Sun; but the Angle PFT exceeded the same Diameter four times, and above, to which however it ought to be equal. . . .[21]

Note that only three quantitative determinations are required here: the equality of incident and finally refracted ray angles; and the vertical and horizontal angles of the doubly refracted light cone.[22] Newton's proof showed that the first equality would, assuming the received laws, guarantee the second equality. But as already noted, this proof does not appear in the 1671/72 paper. What Newton did in its absence was to substitute more extensive measurements of the experimental particulars so as to empirically derive the result of his proof for the special case of his experimental apparatus. The preexistence, however, of the general geometrical proof suggests that many of Newton's measurement and calculational claims are merely for show, to affect the appearance of a multitude of careful ruler and protractor measurements, when in fact a more *a priori* method was used. I will now begin a reconstruction of that method and, while doing that, show that the precision and accuracy of Newton's measurements is largely illusory. However, because of the distribution of experimental errors, no real harm is done. That is, since Newton's refutation of the received laws did not require the sort of precision he claims, Newton was not left in the position of claiming a result that requires an accuracy and precision that his data do not possess. Although Newton did not explicitly make the sorts of error calculation needed to show this, he did perform an experiment that vividly shows how the relevant experimental errors behave. There is, however, the danger that Newton's experiments, because of their purported precision and accuracy, will appear more authoritative than is warranted, especially with respect to the experimental work of his contemporaries. The point is that Newton's experiments are better, but not as much better as he would have us believe.

Finally, it is to be noted that though Newton used his measurements to refute the then received laws of refraction, he did *not* use those measurements as the basis for a calculation of image size using his own theory. This lack of a direct demonstration of the superiority of his own theory gives added force to the need to determine the exact nature and legitimacy of Newton's refutation.

I will first consider Newton's claim that the vertical (or refracting) angle of his prism is 63° 12′. Note that the measurement is given in minutes. Newton does not tell us how this precision was arrived at. For example, is the given value an average of measurements taken at different locations, or is it the angle measured between the places on the prism surface of the sun's incident and refracted rays?[23] Furthermore, is there any real need in this case for precision to within a minute of a degree? In the dispute with Lucas over the proper length of the projected spectrum, Newton attempted to explain away at least part of their disagreement as a mere appearance due to their differences of precision in reporting their data. And among the relevant data, Newton included the prism angle. He contrasted his precise value of 63° 12′ with Lucas' reported value of 60 degrees.

The angle indeed wch I used was but about 63 degr. 12 min. & his is set down 60 degr: the difference of wch from mine being but 3 degr. 12 min, is too little to reconcile us, but yet it will bring us considerably nearer together. And if his angle was not exactly measured, but ye round number might be two or three degrees less than 60, if not still less: & all this, if it should be, would take away the greatest part of ye difference between us.[24]

Newton then gives the following tables "that it might appear experimentally how ye increase of ye angle increases ye length of ye Image."[25] The first table was compiled on a "pretty clear" day, whereas the second was made on "a day as clear as I desired."

The angles of degr min		The lengths of ye image
54.	0	7 1/3
62.	12	10 1/8
63.	48	10 3/4
54.	0	7 2/3
62.	12	10 1/2
63.	48	11

Note that according to Newton's figures, an error of a whole degree with respect to the determination of the prism angle will result in an image length error of only about 2/5 of an inch. On a cloudy day, this error is less. But remember that Newton gives the value of his prism angle to within a minute, which correlates with a length variation of about 1/150 of an inch, a clearly imperceptible difference. Even an angle determination within ten minutes corresponds to what is still probably an imperceptible difference of 1/15 of an inch. These perceptibility claims are based on the following difficulties involved in determining the length of the projected image. First, Newton admitted on several occasions that the ends of the spectrum are quite faint and consequently difficult to measure. Furthermore, the spectrum length is, as already noted, a function of the weather, and hence, liable to change with passing clouds. Second, the spectrum length, it must be remembered, is to be that length when the incident and doubly refracted angles are the same for the mean incident angle of the sun. As Newton later revealed in the *Optics*, this equality was established by rotating the prism to that orientation where the image was at its lowest point.[26] This test is complicated, though, by the fact that the image size as well as location change as the prism is rotated. Errors in the location of the lowest point will therefore have corresponding errors in image size. And given that the image was 22 feet away from the prism, it seems impossible that Newton could have perceived image location and size changes to within 1/150 or even 1/15 of an inch. I will have more to say about this important test below.

Lucas responded to Newton's criticisms with the observation that since his prism angle was "between 59 and 60 deg.," Newton's angle suggestions would not account for their differences of claimed spectrum length. Lucas apparently had the good sense to realize the absurdity of measuring the prism angle closer than a degree. Newton, though, had the better sense to realize the argumentative or rhetorical value of claims to precision.[27] Unfortunately, by not taking Lucas's claims seriously, Newton and his contemporaries missed an opportunity to develop the concept of *dispersive* power. (Note that Lucas need not have been correct in his claims, only the mere possibility needed to have been taken seriously.)[28]

It is clear then that Newton's claimed precision even if correct, i.e., accurate, will be of little perceptible value with respect to (any proposed calculation of) the length of the projected image. Furthermore, the accuracy of Newton's claimed precision must be in doubt since, as Newton eventually admitted, his prism was *convex*.[29] This convexity means, of course, a varying angle across the face of the prism.

Accuracy to within a minute was also (implicitly) claimed in the other essential angle measurement that Newton gives. He reported that "the angle, which the Rays, tending toward the middle of the image, made with those lines, in which they would have proceeded without refraction, [is] 44 deg.56′."[30]

As usual, we are not told how this angle has been measured. It cannot have been directly measured from the location of the midpoint of the refracted image, since the unrefracted ray would at a distance of 22 feet be approximately the same distance underground. Given Newton's measurement of "44° 56′" and assuming a prism height of approximately five feet, the unrefracted rays of the sun would hit the floor about five feet away. An accuracy to within a degree of arc would require, therefore, linear accuracy of about 1/6 of an inch. Newton advertised to within a minute. Such precision would require linear measurements accurate to within 3/1,000 of an inch. This is clearly an imperceptible figure, especially when it is remembered that the incoming packet of sun rays has a thickness, so that a center must be visually estimated. Even accuracy to within 10′ requires linear accuracy of 3/100 of an inch, which certainly borders on the imperceptible. The unavailability of Newton's claimed precision becomes even more certain given the smaller than 5 foot protractor that Newton discusses in *Lectiones*, as well as in its earlier manuscript version.[31]

The two, just discussed, angular measurements of 63° 12′ and 44° 56′ were used to calculate the (symmetrical) angles of refraction: ". . . The Refractions on both sides of the Prisme, that is, of the Incident, and Emergent Rays, were as near, as I could make them, equal, and consequently about 54 deg.4′."[32]

243

The above calculation is clearly intended to be based on the assumption that the angles of refraction are equal. As noted above, Newton's procedure for determining this equality was to rotate the prism until the image is at its lowest point.

> About this prism Axis I turned the Prism slowly, and saw the refracted Light on the Wall, or coloured Image of the Sun, first to descend, and then to ascend. Between the Descent and the Ascent, when the Image seemed Stationary, I stopp'd the Prism, and fix'd it in that Posture, that it should be moved no more. For in that Posture the Refractions of the Light at the two Sides of the refracting Angle, that is, at the Entrance of the Rays into the Prism, and at their going out of it, were equal to one another.[33]

That such a procedure yields a prism symmetrically placed with respect to the incoming and outgoing rays clearly depends on a theory. In section III, of the first part of the *Lectiones Opticae*, Newton proved that the case of symmetrical refraction provided the minimum angular deviation for an incident ray.[34] While this proof is clearly to be the theoretical basis for the prism-locating procedure, Newton nowhere explicitly showed exactly how it was to yield that procedure in the case of a convergent incident cone of either single or varying refrangibility.[35] If a single refrangibility is assumed (as required by the received laws), then the test is ambiguous. Because the sun's rays are taken not to be parallel, it follows that not all of these rays can be symmetrically refracted by the prism. Newton's unpublished proof shows that a circular image will result (assuming the received laws) if the mid-ray along the axis of the incoming light cone is symmetrically refracted. Therefore, Newton's test must position the prism so that this ray is symmetrically refracted. Is it true, then, according to the received laws that the required sort of symmetrical refraction will result when the prism is fixed "between the Descent and Ascent, when the Image seemed Stationary." It is with respect to this fixing of the prism that ambiguity enters. Assume, for example, that the lowest point of the bottom edge of the spectrum is taken to be the *measure* of the lowest point of the spectrum as a whole; that is, that this bottom edge gives "the Place where the Image of the

244

Sun formed by the refracted Light stood still between its two contrary Motions, in the common Period of its Progress and Regress."[36] When this bottom edge is at its lowest point, the mid-ray will *not* be symmetrically refracted. This is because the ray or rays forming this bottom edge will have to be symmetrically refracted in order to obtain this minimum position. But if these bottom rays are symmetrically refracted, the mid-ray will not be so refracted because of its different incident angle. A similar result ensues if the lowest point of the upper edge of the spectrum is taken as the measure of the lowest point of the spectrum as a whole. The problem then is to find an unambiguous measure of the lowest point of the refracted image that will yield symmetrical refractions for the mid-ray. Stopping the prism midway in its rotation between the lowest points of the upper and lower edges of the image will do the trick, but only at the cost of an inconvenient and accuracy-robbing intermediate measurement. The angular positions of the prism would have to be noted, along a protractor, for example, and then divided.

Newton's prism test is in somewhat worse shape when conjoined with his own theory. The discrepancy between the desired symmetrical position and the lowest points of the upper and lower edges will be greater because of dispersion. Stopping the prism midway will work, as in the case of the received laws, but again at the cost of an intermediate measurement.[37]

The natural response to these complications is that they do not have observational significance. This response is not true, since very small errors in the determination of the relevant image location result in large errors in the sought-after symmetrical refraction. And, as I will show, Newton knew this correlation, yet persisted in using the lowest image point as a test for symmetrical refraction.

The discussion so far of available precision generates two questions. Does Newton's refutation of the received laws depend on the advertised precision? Did Newton show any awareness of the above sorts of interaction between error, claimed accuracy, and precision? Fortunately for Newton, the answer to the first question is no. Fortunately for me, the answer to the second is yes. Newton's awareness of the relevant error behavior and his subsequent demonstration that the refutation of the received laws did not depend on the accuracy of his data show that my analysis of his experimental methodology is not a mere carping anachronism.

Although Newton's claims of precision may be called to question, his refutation of the received laws will stand firm because of the way the experimental or measurement errors behave. The experimental errors are such that large errors in the measured initial conditions "cancel out" and result in small errors in the to-be-calculated effect, the image size. Therefore, the inaccuracies in Newton's claimed measurements will not have a significant calculational effect since accuracy to within perceptible limits does not require the sort of precision Newton advertises. Newton did not, unfortunately, make the calculations necessary to show that his measurement errors would behave in this fortuitous way. He did, however, describe an experiment that vividly shows the requisite error behavior, and thus also shows an awareness on Newton's part of the significance of error behavior. The description of this experiment follows immediately after Newton's calculation of a 31' divergence of the doubly refracted beam.

> But because this computation was founded on the Hypothesis of the proportionality of the *sines* of Incidence, and Refraction, which though by my own & others Experience I could not imagine to be so erroneous, as to make that Angle but 31', which in reality was 2 deg.49'; yet my curiosity caused me again to take my Prisme. And having placed it at my window, as before, I observed that by turning it a little about its *axis* to and fro, so as to vary its obliquity to the light, more then by an angle of 4 or 5 degrees, the Colours were not thereby sensibly translated from their place on the wall, and consequently by that variation of Incidence, the quantity of Refraction was not sensibly varied.[38]

The experiment clearly shows that large changes in prism orientation will have small effects with respect to changes in image length. This means that errors in the determination of the relevant initial conditions will have a small effect on the error of any image length calculated on the basis of a correct theory. Therefore, if the received view is correct, then improvements in the accuracy of the determination of the initial conditions will not help much in approaching more closely the observed divergence. If, on the other hand, improvements do help in the calculation, then the received view is not correct. I think that an argument of this sort was intended, however dimly, to be the essential point of the experiment.

If my interpretation of Newton's rotation experiment is correct, then Newton's refutation of the received laws is a two-step affair. First, the received laws do not fit the experimental facts. Second, improvements in the determination of the relevant initial conditions will not help, because even large improvements will have but imperceptible effects on the calculated size of the spectrum. Some support for this interpretation is supplied by the fact that Newton did not reject the received laws after showing that they yielded a 31' divergence instead of the observed 2°49'. That rejection occurs after the rotation experiment. In Newton's own words,

> By this Experiment therefore, as well as by the former computation, it was evident, that the difference of the Incidence of Rays, flowing from divers parts of the Sun, could not make them after decussation diverge at a sensibly greater angle, than that at which they before converged; which being, at most, but about 31 or 32 minutes, there still remained some other cause to be found out, from whence it could be 2 deg.49'.[39]

A nice bit of additional supporting evidence is Newton's use of the modal locution "could not make them," in referring to the possible causal efficacy of the divergence of the sun's rays. Newton's conclusion also forces a qualification on what has been said, for, as Newton was careful to note, what has been refuted is the sufficiency of the conjunction of the received laws and "the difference of the Incidence of Rays, flowing from divers parts of the Sun." Clearly, Newton's experiment and computation do not show that further or different supplementation will not salvage the received laws. In fact, Newton considered three additional supplementations in the 1671/72 paper and found them wanting. No argument was given, however, to show that the supplementations considered exhausted what was possible.

A powerful objection to my emphasis on the importance of Newton's rotation experiment is the fact that this experiment does not appear in either the *Opticks* or the *Lectiones*. The disappearance from the *Opticks*, at least, should not be surprising, since the principal opposition was always to Newton's own theory, and not to his rejection of the received laws. It was held by, for example, both Pardies and Hooke that "diffusion" theories could account for the oblong shape of the spectrum as well as Newton's ray separation theory.[40] Since there was no serious support for light having a single and immutable degree of refrangibility, an elaborate refutation of such a theory was not required. This response to the objection does not work nearly so well for the *Lectiones*, since the relevant section existed in manuscript form before the 1671/72 optics paper. The near identity of the rotation experiment and Newton's procedure for establishing symmetrical refraction will provide a strong reason for Newton not to have included the rotation experiment in either the *Lectiones* or the *Opticks*. This reason will also explain why Newton did not include his prism-locating procedure in the 1671/72 paper, for to have conjoined this procedure with the rotation experiment would have created difficulties for him. Although the combination of small image error and large prism orientation error is favorable (as shown) for the refutation of the received laws, this error combination must cast some doubt as to the general usefulness of Newton's procedure for prism location. The whole point of the rotation experiment is that to locate the prism this way will result in variations from symmetry that are as high as several degrees. But surely, such an error, if revealed, would weaken the forcefulness of Newton's other experiments that depended on a symmetrical prism orientation. Therefore, the conjunction of the rotation experiment and Newton's procedure for prism location would have had a debilitative effect on the latter. In the 1671/72 paper there is, unlike the *Lectiones* and *Opticks*, only one experiment that requires a symmetrical prism orientation: the projection of the spectrum. Newton apparently chose, therefore, not to reveal how this experiment was set up so that he could, without serious cost to himself, strengthen his refutation of the received laws with the rotation experiment. On the other hand, given the vast number of prism experiments in the *Opticks* and the *Lectiones*, Newton must have felt the need to explain how these experiments were performed. Finally, it is to be noted that though the rotation experiment does not appear in the *Lectiones*, its result does: "Moreover, although the Position of the Prism should be otherwise than I have described, supposing the Rays on each Side did not suffer a very unequal Refraction; yet the Figure of the Image would scarce on that Account be altered."[41]

No argument *per se* is given for this claim. The case of the *Opticks* is similar, although here Newton deliberately, I believe, confused the relevant issues by emphasizing the small error in image size, and by ignoring the correspondingly large error in prism orientation: "And because it is easy to commit a Mistake in placing the Prism in its due Posture, I repeated the Experiment four or five Times, and always found the Length of the Image that which is set down above."[42]

To summarize, Newton's first published refutation of "the received laws of refraction" consisted of the following steps. It was first calculated that the received laws would yield, given Newton's claimed experimental determinations, an angular divergence of 31', whereas the measured divergence was (after some calculation) shown to be 2°49'. Newton next showed by means of his rotation experiment that even if there were substantial errors in his measurements, better values would not significantly improve the correctness of any calculation based on these better values and the received laws. The received laws were to be rejected because of the large disparity between the calculated and observed values and, *more importantly*, because the calculated values could not be significantly improved by means of more accurate experimental determinations. Perhaps, surprisingly, Newton did *not* use his own theory and quantitative data to show that a closer "fit" of the observed data could be obtained. While this superiority of fit appears obvious, to have actually shown it would have involved Newton in calculational difficulties, so that the "appearance" is worth more than the "reality."[43] Newton's argument against the received view is not that his theory fits the facts better, but that the received view can do no better than it now does. This arguments suggests that experimental fit *per se*, or even superiority of (existing) experimental fit, is not as important for theory testing as is the demonstration that an existing fit can or cannot be improved. The availability of such demonstrations makes the comparison of alternative theories with the facts unnecessary as a mode of argument. This downgrading of comparative testing, suggested by Newton's procedure, is at apparent odds with one of the more popular slogans of recent philosophy of science, which has it that there is no theory testing without theory comparison. Kuhn, for example, is responsible for the following:

> In the sciences the testing situation never consists, as puzzle-solving does, simply in the comparison of a single paradigm with nature. Instead, testing occurs as part of the competition between two rival paradigms for the allegiance of the scientific community. . . . Verification is like natural selection: it picks out the most viable among the actual alternatives in a particular historical situation. . . . As has repeatedly been emphasized before, no theory ever solves all the puzzles with which it is confronted at a given time; nor are the solutions already achieved often perfect. . . . If any and every failure to fit were ground for theory rejection, all theories ought to be rejected at all times. . . . All historically significant theories have agreed with the facts, but only more or less. There is no more precise answer to the question whether and how well an individual theory fits the facts. But questions much like these can be asked when theories are taken collectively or even in pairs. It makes a great deal of sense to ask which of two actual and competing theories fits the facts *better*.[44]

Feyerabend has argued for the necessity of theory comparison for testing with an essentially similar argument: " . . . There does not exist a single interesting theory that is not in some kind of trouble. Singular statements, and even experimental laws that *prima facie* refute the theory, can always be found fairly easily. . . . Troublesome facts, taken by themselves, are almost never sufficient to eliminate the theory. What is needed is an alternative. . . ."[45]

It is an obvious corollary of this position that until Newton

250

demonstrates the superior experimental fit of his own theory, he cannot be said to have refuted the received view.[46] The position, however, that a more successful alternative is needed before a theory can be said to be refuted by the experimental facts is, as the Newton case indicates, false. This confrontation suggests a distinction between theories such that (known) non-zero limits exist on how close explanations utilizing those theories can approach the observed quantitative values of some to-be-explained phenomena and theories such that no such (known) limits exist. This distinction can be quadrupled by adding the epistemic operator 'known' at the places indicated.

Examples of the first type of theory and associated explanation include, in addition to the Newton case, the explanation of specific heats by kinetic theory and the Cartesian explanation of the lack of ether resistance. In the first example, the program was to postulate more and more complex molecular structures as a means of approaching the real specific heats of gases. The equi-partition theorem, however, put an absolute limit to the success of such a program. Kinetic theory was, therefore, said to be refuted by the specific heats of gases because all consistent resources for improvement were exhausted. Similarly, Newton showed in *Principia* II that no matter how small and smooth the etherial particles were made, the ether would still have a substantial resistance because of the essential *vis inertia* of its constituent particles.

One of Kuhn's favorite examples, Newtonian mechanics and increasingly more accurate treatments of the pendulum, is an example of a theory-explanation pair of the second sort. Another example is provided by the special theory of relativity and associated explanations of the Michelson-Morley experiment. That experiment did not give an actual null effect, i.e., it was not the case that there was no fringe displacement upon rotation. In fact, there was in both the original Michelson-Morley experiment as well as in Miller's extensive repeats a small positive effect of proper period through anomalous (for the ether theory) phase. Despite this positive effect, it was not claimed that special theory was refuted by the experiment. This was because no limit could be shown to exist to the degree of

251

successful fit of explanations consistent with, and utilizing, special theory.

I have so far spoken of an explanation based on, or associated with, a theory. The concept of explanation I have in mind is sometimes also denoted by 'model'; namely, an explanation, in the sense intended, consists of a particular treatment or description of the apparatus (or situation) in question, along with a theory that determines the behavior of the apparatus under the given description. (Clearly, such "explanations," though common in the physical sciences, e.g., micro-explanations, do not exhaust the concept.) Very often these descriptions are "idealized" in the following ways (among others). (1) The most accurate experimental values are not always used. (2) Properties not treatable, or not easily treatable by the theory, are either ignored or simplified. Pardies objected, for example, to Newton's simplification of the influence of the aperture size, where Newton's simplification consisted of reducing the image size and treating the aperture *as if* it had no width. (See above for discussion of Newton's reduction in the horizontal plane.) Pardies' objection is based on his geometrical treatment of the experiment (see fig. 3).

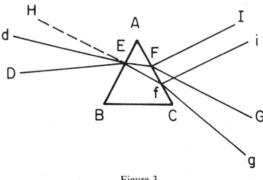

Figure 3

HE and *FI* are normal to the faces of prism *ABC*. *DE* and *dE* are incoming sun rays that define the maximum divergence of about one-half degree. Pardies has three rays meet at *E*, thus, in effect, providing an infinitesimal aperture. Because of their difference in incidence, the rays *DE* and *dE* will diverge after refraction to, respectively, *F* and *f*, and thence on to *G* and *g*. The infinitesimal aperture is thereby transformed by the prism into the finite aperture *Ff*.

> Therefore, in order to render the calculation just, it is not sufficient barely to subduct the diameter of the hole from the length of the image; for supposing the hole E to be invisible, or almost nothing, yet there would be formed a great hole as it were, in Ff, in the second surface of the prism.[47]

Newton's response was to first flatly assert "that the refractions of the rays . . . may be justly calculated from my principles."[48] Although no supporting argument was given for this claim, Newton did include in his response a diagram that reveals his geometrical thinking (see fig. 4).

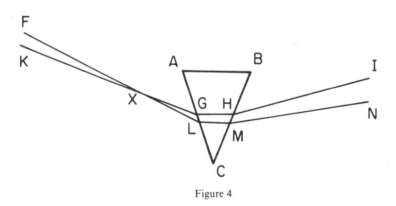

Figure 4

Newton, as will be remembered, claimed that his reduction technique gave the angular divergence of "those Rays, which passed through the center of the saide hole." Assuming that Pardies also wanted to calculate the angular divergence of these rays, it is clear from the differences between their diagrams that Pardies placed his finite aperture on the surface of the prism, whereas Newton placed his some distance away.

The second part of Newton's response was to note that even if Pardies' approach were correct, "the breadth of the hole in the posterior surface, if such there be, would hardly produce an error of two seconds, and in practice may well be neglected."[49]

Newton's parry here is very much like his rotation of the prism, which showed that even if Newton were in error with respect to the values of the necessary initial conditions, these errors would be inconsequential for the calculation of image size. The aperture reduction problem suggests, therefore, that just as there may be arguments or demonstrations that improvements in the determination of initial conditions will not help a theory, so too there may be arguments or demonstrations that show that improvements in the treatment or description of the (operation of the) experimental apparatus will not help. A more modern and clearer example of this latter sort of argument is Lorentz's variational proof that no wave account of the Michelson-Morley experiment, however detailed and realistic, would eliminate the periodicities obtained by simple ray accounts. Some theorists had sought to show that a detailed and more realistic application of Huygens's principle to the Michelson-Morley experiment would yield a null result.[50]

I have tried in this study to accomplish three goals. First, to provide an analysis of Newton's refutation of the then received laws of refraction that would reveal the full subtlety of Newton's thinking. Second, to show the existence and importance of scientific arguments that bear on the possibility of improving the experimental fit of given scientific theories. Finally, to show that attention to the concept of experimental error is necessary if scientific arguments are to be adequately analyzed. The particular merit of the Newton spectrum case is that it shows that even apparently simple cases have significant argumentative depth if error behavior is considered.

I would like to thank Professors A. I. Sabra, David C. Lindberg, Michael J. Crowe, Richard S. Westfall, and David Hahm for their many helpful comments on an earlier version of this paper.

1. Newton to Oldenburg, 6 February 1671/72, *The Correspondence of Isaac Newton*, vol. 1, ed. H. W. Turnbull (Cambridge: At the University Press, 1959), pp. 92–107 (hereafter cited as *Corr.*, with volume and page numbers). Newton's letter was originally published in the *Philosophical Transactions* 6 (1671/72): 3075–87. The double-

year notation is due to the use of Julian and Gregorian calendars. See "Preface," *Corr.* 1:xxvi.

2. *Corr.*, 1:92.

3. Cambridge University Library, Add. 3996, ff. 88–135. Actually, Newton's title contains "Questiones" and not "Quaestiones." Although I prefer to believe that Newton meant what he wrote (laments), grammar and Newton's personality indicate otherwise. Cf. "Newton to a Friend, c. 1661," *Corr.*, 1:1. For a brief description and some selections, see A. R. Hall, "Sir Isaac Newton's Note-Book, 1661–65," *Cambridge Historical Journal* 9 (1948): 239–50.

4. "Quaestiones," f. 123.

5. "Quaestiones," f. 106. But see ff. 122–23 for the beginnings of the separation theory.

6. Newton later devised the famous *experimentum crucis* to answer the question whether colors, and their associated refrangibilities, once produced, would change after additional refraction.

7. As given, for example, at the beginning of the *Opticks*, as well as in *Lectiones Opticae*, part I, section III. Henceforth, all page references to the *Opticks* will be from the fourth, 1730 edition (New York: Dover, 1952). Three versions of *Lectiones* will be referred to. First, the 1669 manuscript, Cambridge University Library Add. 4002 (henceforth, 4002). Second, the later posthumously published version (henceforth, *Lectiones*) as it appears in Horsley's *Newtoni Opera*, vol. III (Londini, 1782). Finally, the anonymous eighteenth-century translation *Optical Lectures Read in the Publick Schools of the University of Cambridge, Anno Domini 1669 . . .* (London, 1728) (henceforth, *Lectures*). For more complete bibliographic particulars, see *The Mathematical Papers of Isaac Newton*, ed. D. T. Whiteside (Cambridge: At the University Press, 1969), 3:435–43.

8. 4002, 2; *Lectiones*, 255; *Lectures*, 5.

9. My use of the premise of parallel incident rays as explaining how a circular image was to be gotten from the received laws is not the usual interpretation. Usually it is claimed that Newton had in mind his unpublished proof in the *Lectiones* that the spectrum ought (within, as Newton notes, a small error) to be circular, even assuming non-parallel incident rays. And in fact the two arguments (not usually distinguished) in the *Lectiones* explicitly depend on this proof. (These arguments along with Newton's proofs are discussed in the paper.) This proof is also repeated, though in very abbreviated form, in the *Opticks*. If Newton intended then that this proof also be the basis in the 1671/72 paper for the expectation that the image be circular, then as Sabra notes: "Newton's expectation that the image should be circular rather than oblong was based on calculations involving a great deal of information drawn from geometrical optics . . . Newton's was thus, to a certain extent, responsible for his paper being misunderstood by his contemporaries" (A. I. Sabra, *Theories of Light From Descartes to Newton*, [New York: American Elsevier, 1967] p. 235 and n.9). For a similar view see Richard S. Westfall. "The Development of Newton's Theory of Color," *Isis* 53 (1962): 352. Strictly speaking, the relevant issue is how Newton intended his readers to understand the initial anticipation that the image be circular, and not what Newton's own anticipations were based on. Combining the two does not square very well with the text of the 1671/72 paper. If Newton already had his proof in mind, and expected his readers also to have had it in mind, then why did he explicitly add the assumption of non-parallel incident rays as a possible way of *escaping* the already announced consequences that the image be circular? The sense of the text is, clearly, that the original premises leading to a circular image are to be modified or supplemented. In support of his interpretation Sabra notes Newton's several protestations that the 1671/72 paper was never really meant for publication, and that had he known its future, he would have modified it considerably (*Theories*, 235 n.9; 267 n.44). As against New-

ton's claims it is to be pointed out that the form of the argument used against the received laws differs in several very significant respects from those used in the *Lectiones* and the *Opticks*. As I will show, Newton in the 1671/2 paper empirically shows that his proof is correct for the specific experimental configuration in question. That is, the 1671/2 paper does *not* logically rely on the *Lectiones* proof; that result is derived in the body of the 1671/2 paper, but not in a purely geometrical way. That is, of course, not to say that Newton was not motivated by the proof of the *Lectiones*, but only that the logic of the 1671/2 paper does not require that proof. This difference, in the logical structure of the 1671/2 paper and the *Lectiones*, shows that Newton exercised considerable care in the composition of the 1671/72 paper. For additional supporting evidence see footnote 27.

10. *Corr.,* 1:92–94.

11. *Corr.,* 1:93.

12. "Newton to Oldenburg, 13 April 1672," *Corr.,* 1:140–41.

13. 4002, 4–7, *Lectiones,* 256–60; *Lectures,* 8–17.

14. *Corr.,* 1:93.

15. Actually, as will be seen, the image size drops out altogether as something to be explained. What remains to be explained are the angular divergences as here determined.

16. *Corr.,* 1:93.

17. "Pardies to Oldenburg, 30 March 1672," *Corr.,* 1:131. The translation is from *Philosophical Transactions*, Abridged, ed. by Hutton, Shaw, Pearson (London 1809), I, 728. This translation as well as the original are reprinted in *Isaac Newton's Papers and Letters on Natural Philosophy*, ed. I. Bernard Cohen (Cambridge: Harvard University Press, 1958), pp. 80, 88. Henceforth, this edition will be denoted *Papers.*

Pardies, perhaps deliberately, missed the fact that Newton made a mistake in favor of the received theory in his calculation of the angle of the incoming cone of the sun's light. The angle here identified as x, and calculated to be 31′, is the horizontal projection of the incoming divergence. Because the vertical incidence of the incoming cone is approximately 45° the actual angular spread of that cone is around 26′. For Newton's general awareness of the problem see the lemma to the proof referred to in footnote 13.

18. "To compare the Sines of Incidence with the Sines of Refraction, it will be proper to use the mean Sort, viz, that Sort of Rays, which exhibit a green Colour, or rather a Colour between Green and Blue: For I believe those, who hitherto have measur'd Refractions, (whether it was done in order to confirm the Hypothesis of *Cartes*, or for other Reasons) I believe, I say, they accommodated their Measure to the Middle of the refracted Light; that is, if we regard the Space occupied by the Colours, to the Confine of Green and Blue." 4002, 70–71; *Lectiones* 272; *Lectures* 50.

19. The manuscript Add. 3975 (Cambridge University Library) which contains the first known description by Newton of the projection of the spectrum, is also not very helpful.

20. See footnote 13. Newton's proof has the aperture on the wrong side of the prism, that is, between the prism and the spectrum instead of between the sun and the prism. Right after the proof Newton discusses several variations, none of which has consequences for the size of the image. Among these variations is the placement of the aperture. "Nor does it much signify, whether the opake Body . . . , in which is bored the Hole . . . to transmit the Rays, be placed on this Side of the Prism or beyond it . . ." While Newton's proof procedure could be empirically justified by this lack of significant effect, the rays on Newton's proof diagram can also be read backwards, so that the circular image is the sun, and the sun becomes the circular image. There is a slight complication here, since as Newton notes, the image (on the original

configuration) is not exactly circular. For the proof that the symmetrical configuration is the only one that yields a circular image see part I, section III, proposition 26. Cf. 4002, 126-27.

21. 4002, 8; *Lectiones*, 260; *Lectures*, 18.

22. It is implicit in this text that the angular divergence of the light cone from the sun has already been determined to be half a degree. This determiniation, then, should be added to the list. It is possible, though, that Newton is simply assuming (on the basis of his proof) that the divergence of the refracted light in the horizontal plane must be equal to the divergence of the sun's cone. In fact, as I have shown, this was Newton's procedure in the 1671/72 paper.

23. In an earlier section of the 1671/72 paper Newton reported that he varied the "circumstances" of the experiment, but found "none of those circumstances material." One of the variations was to transmit "light through parts of the glass of divers thicknesses," that is, to vary the positions on the prism of the incident and refracted beams.

Michael Crowe suggested, in conversation, that Newton's precision might be obtainable if light were *reflected* off the prism faces, and the resulting angles of reflection compared with the incident angles. Newton, though, makes no mention of having used such a method.

24. *Corr.*, 2:76.

25. *Corr.*, 2:77.

26. *Opticks*, pp. 27-28. This test also appears in 4002, ff. 8-9; *Lectiones*, pp. 260-61; *Lectures*, pp. 19-20.

27. As an example of Newton's success, Richard Westfall in commenting on the dispute asserts that " 'between 59 and 60 deg.' is not an impressive measurement besides Newton's . . . ," ("Newton Defends His First Publication: The Newton-Lucas Correspondence," *Isis* 57 [1966]: 309).

Interestingly enough, Newton gives the prism angle as "about 60 degrees" almost everywhere else: 3975, 2; 4002, 3; *Lectiones*, 256; *Lectures*, 8. In the *Opticks* experiments are described as having been conducted with prisms of refracting angles of 64, 62 1/2, and 63 1/2 degrees (29-30). This difference in reported precision should strengthen my claim that Newton's precision as advertised in the 1671/2 paper was unavailable to him. This difference also strengthens my claim that the logic of the 1671/72 refutation of the received laws of refraction is different from that of the *Lectiones* and the *Opticks*. This difference is also relevant for the interpretive issue discussed in note 9.

28. By the dispersive power of a substance I mean the measure of the variation in refraction between the ends of the spectrum. This measure (whatever it turns out to be) is to be contrasted with the measure of refraction (for a substance) of the mean refrangible color. Newton seems to have missed the possibility that the two could be independent. How close, or if Newton ever got to such a concept, will not be discussed here.

29. *Corr.*, 2:78.

30. *Corr.*, 1:93.

31. The accuracy requirements were calculated by using the variations in the tangents of $1°$, $10'$, and $01'$ deviations from a $45°$ incidence. Newton's instructions for the protractor are given in the *Lectiones Opticae*, part I, section II. My discussion here and elsewhere is, of course, rather simplified because it does not distinguish the initial calibration of measuring instruments from their accurate usage. This complication, would, I believe, only serve to reinforce my argument that Newton's advertised precision was not available to him.

32. *Corr.*, 1:93.

33. *Opticks*, p. 28. Cf. note 26 above.

34. 4002, f. 125; *Lectiones*, pp. 326–27; *Lectures*, pp. 164–66.

35. Newton did not even note the relevance of this proof. It was noted in footnotes by the anonymous editors of the fourth edition of the *Opticks*, and of the English and Latin versions of the *Lectiones*. Those editors did not note that the following proof (proposition 26), is also relevant, since it shows that image size is a minimum for the case of a symmetrically refracted central ray.

36. *Opticks*, p. 28.

37. Actually, the procedure of stopping the prism in the ways indicated will introduce a small error.

38. *Corr.*, 1:93-94.

39. Ibid., p. 94.

40. Ibid., pp. 110-14, 156-58.

41. 4002, ff. 7-8; *Lectiones*, p. 260; *Lectures*, p. 17.

42. *Opticks*, p. 30.

43. To demonstrate superiority of fit would require determining the relevant parameters (e.g., difference in refrangibility for the colors) from the case described, and then using these parameters to calculate the expected image size for different experimental situations (e.g., with different prism angles and different aperture sizes). To predict image size, however, in other appropriately varied cases would have involved Newton in the inevitable discrepancies between fact and theory. Newton used other experiments, most notably, the *experimentum crucis*, to argue for the truth of his own theory.

44. Thomas S. Kuhn, *The Structure of Scientific Revolutions*, 2d ed. (Chicago: University of Chicago Press, 1970), pp. 145–47.

45. Paul K. Feyerabend, "Problems of Empiricism," in *Beyond the Edge of Certainty*, ed. Robert G. Colodny (Englewood Cliffs, N.J.: Prentice-Hall, 1965), p. 250.

46. The wording here is deliberate, since I mean the condition to be necessary but not sufficient. My claim that the corollary is obvious is also deliberate, but unfair, since Kuhn and Feyerabend make many qualifications to their positions quoted here. My unfairness, though, is tempered by the fact that whether these qualifications leave Kuhn and Feyerabend with a coherent position is, as many have noted, open to serious doubt. Furthermore, my interest here is not primarily to criticize Kuhn and Feyerabend, but to draw attention to a form of argumentation neglected by most philosophers of science.

47. *Corr.*, 1:132. *Papers*, pp. 80–81, 88.

48. *Corr.*, 1:141. *Papers*, pp. 84, 730–31.

49. *Corr.*, 1:141.

50. Lorentz's proof, several references, as well as discussion, appear in "Conference on the Michelson-Morley Experiment," *Astrophysical Journal* 68 (1928): 341–73. A discussion of this proof along with an analysis of the significance of some of the measurement errors of the Michelson-Morley experiment are given in my "The Michelson-Morley Experiment: Descriptive Dependence on To-Be-Tested Theories," in *Motion and Time, Space and Matter: Interrelations in the History of Philosophy and Science*, ed. Peter Machamer and Robert Turnbull (Columbus: Ohio State University Press, 1976).

A *prima facie* difference between the Lorentz and Newton cases, and some earlier examples, needs to be noted. To motivate interest in scientific arguments that purport to draw limits to the possibility of experiment fit, I gave the examples of kinetic theory and specific heat, and Cartesian physics and resistance. These examples, though similar to the Lorentz and Newton cases, differ in that it was not the description of the experimental apparatus that was at issue but the description of matter and its configuration.

Chapter Ten

BERKELEY AND DESCARTES: REFLECTIONS ON
THE THEORY OF IDEAS

PART ONE

I

1. Descartes appends to his reply to the second set of objections a brief formulation, *more geometrico*, of his argument in the *Meditations* for the existence of God and the distinction between soul and body. Of particular relevance to my topic are certain of the definitions with which this appendix begins:

I. *Thought* is a word that covers anything that exists in us in such a way that we are immediately conscious of it. Thus all the operations of will, intellect, imagination and of the senses are thoughts. . . .

II. *Idea* is a word by which I understand the form of any thought, that form by the immediate awareness of which I am conscious of that said thought; in such a way that, when understanding what I say, I can express nothing in words, without that very fact making it certain that I possess the idea of what those words signify.

III. By the *objective reality of an idea* I mean that in respect of which the thing represented in the idea is an entity insofar as that exists in the idea; . . . whatever we perceive as being as it were in the object of our ideas, exists in the ideas themselves objectively.

IV. To exist *formally* is the term applied where the same thing exists in the object of an idea in such a manner that the way in which it exists in the object is exactly like what we know of it when aware of it. . . . [1]

2. Of these definitions the most interesting is the third, for to work out its implications is to find oneself at the very center of the Cartesian philosophy. The second is interesting, but also puzzling. It implies that all thoughts, i.e., everything that exists in us in such a way that we are immediately conscious of it, are ideas. But this conflicts with the classification of thoughts in the third *Meditation*, according to which only certain thoughts are properly called 'ideas,' namely those which "are, so to speak, images of the things . . . examples are my thought of a man, or of a chimera, of heaven, of an angel or [even] of God."[2]

3. As examples of thoughts that are not ideas, he gives "willing, fearing, approving, denying." He emphasizes, however, that although a "willing" or an "affection" or a "judging" is not an idea, it must be conjoined with an idea, for "I always perceive something as the subject of the action of my mind."[3] In other words, one can not will or fear or affirm without a willing or fearing or affirming *something*, and this something is in the mind by virtue of an idea.

4. I shall return in a moment to the problem posed by the definition of the term 'idea' in the appendix to the reply to *Objections* II, but the important thing to note is that it is the narrower account given in the *Meditations* themselves that has the most direct connection with the definition of the 'objective reality of an idea' which follows that definition.

5. The most general theme in Descartes' account of 'ideas' in the narrower sense is that *ideas* represent things—where 'thing' is used in that inclusive sense in which *anything* is a thing. He seems to have taken for granted that the term 'represents' as applied to thoughts is univocal. Thus in explaining what it is for a thought (or modification of the mind) to represent something (and hence to be an idea), he has no hesitation in appealing to one type of paradigm, namely, mental states in which we are *conceiving* of something, e.g., an angel.

6. Now it is obvious that when we are conceiving of an angel, the thought, which is a modification of our mind, is not itself an angel. It is angelic only in the sense that it represents an angel. Again, when we conceive a chimera, we represent something that does not exist. How are these facts to be under-

stood? Descartes offers just two metaphors, only one of which is sufficiently elaborated to be a proto-theory. The simple metaphor is that of an image. After all, the image of a chimera is not itself a chimera, although it is serving to represent it. But, unless the image is a physical image—in which case Descartes is not interested—it has none of the characteristics of what it represents; thus the mental image of a chimera has no shape at all, let alone one that, in some generic way, might resemble that which a chimera would have. For mental images, being modes of thought, simply do not have shape.

7. That is to say that they do not have shape *formally* as, according to the fourth definition, an actual chimera would. Thus, according to the extended system of metaphors that is Descartes' proto-theory of representation, there are two aspects of ideas, i.e., of thoughts that represent:

a. their character as modifications of the mind
b. their character as representing what they represent.

The latter is explained in terms of the metaphor of containment, and the concept of a mode of 'reality' ('objective reality') other than that of actual existence. It is a familiar fact that this concept has a scholastic origin and that the term 'objective reality' connotes 'being as an object of thought' rather than 'what is the case regardless of what we think' as it does today.

8. Anything, whether it actually exists or not, is the objective reality of a thought if it is what the thought is *about*. It, the 'anything' or entity in question, exists 'in' the idea. Thus 'ideas' are those thoughts that 'contain' entities which exist 'objectively' in them.

9. The contrasting term to 'objective reality' is 'formal reality.' Thus we could say that *a man* or, perhaps, the character of being a man has objective reality in our thought of President Nixon, but formal reality in that Nixon actually exists and is a man.

10. Thus when I conceive of a triangle, my thought is not triangular, but 'contains' a triangle objectively. The terminology is flexible. Thus the thought can even be said to *be* triangular, but only 'objectively', for the character of being a triangle is

only 'objectively' present in the thought, whereas it is 'formally' present in a triangular material surface.

11. Descartes has little to tell us about the first aspect of those thoughts that represent, i.e., their character as modifications of the mind. One is tempted to say that the only respect in which they differ (apart from occurring in different minds or at different times or in different contexts) is that they 'contain' different entities, i.e., that different entities exist 'in' them 'objectively'. Yet, although the metaphor of containment is to be taken seriously as an essential element in this proto-theory of representation, it should not be given exclusive rights, for metaphors always limp and need to be buttressed, in proto-theories, by other metaphors. Thus we have seen that instead of saying that a thought contains a triangle that has objective existence in it, we can say that the thought is objectively, though not formally, triangular. In this terminology the contrast is between two ways of being triangular, rather than between a material triangle and a triangle that is 'contained' in a thought 'in' which it exists objectively.

12. Thus ideas would differ as modifications of the mind with respect to different characters, even though they had them only 'objectively'. If, now, we return to the definition of 'idea' in the appendix to the reply to *Objections* II, we see that every thought, whether or not it represents (i.e., is an idea in the narrower sense), has a form, i.e., a character by virtue of which it is the sort of thought it is. Thus a volition has the form *volition*, and when we are conscious of a volition we are conscious of it as a volition, i.e., of its form.

13. Though the volition is not an idea in the narrower sense, in being conscious of it as a volition we do have an idea, in the narrower sense, *of* a volition. We have an idea of what the word 'volition' signifies.

14. On the other hand, when I am conscious of an idea in the narrower sense, e.g., an idea of an angel, I am conscious of it *as* an idea of an angel, and, hence, of its form, which is the character of being an angel. But whereas the volition has the character of being a volition *formally*, the idea of an angel has the character of being an angel only *objectively*. Of course, we

can also say that the form of the idea is *containing an angel as its objective reality*. But then my purpose has only been to show that Descartes' proto-theory enables him to make consistent (if highly metaphorical) sense of the wider definition of 'idea'.

II

15. In the definition of the wider sense of 'idea', Descartes speaks of our consciousness of our thoughts, but does not give an account of this consciousness. We do, however, find such an account in the treatise *The Passions of the Soul*, and it will be useful to consider it briefly, for it will enable some relevant distinctions to be made. In Article XIX ("Of the Perceptions") he distinguishes between two sorts of perceptions, those "which have the soul as a cause" and those which have "the body [as a cause]."[4]

> Those which have the soul as a cause are the perceptions of our desires, and of all the imaginations or other thoughts which depend on them. For it is certain that we cannot desire anything without perceiving by the same means that we desire it; and, although in regard to our soul it is an action to desire something, we may say that it is also one of its passions to perceive that it desires. Yet because this perception and this will are really one and the same thing, the more noble always supplies the denomination, and thus we are not in the habit of calling it a passion, but only an action.[5]

16. I have quoted this passage at length because it is easily misunderstood, and contains distinctions that are highly relevant to the understanding of other philosophers of this period. The first thing to note is that Descartes thinks it appropriate to limit the term 'action' as applied to mind to volitions and to items that are akin to volitions, thus to desires, which, like volitions, are ascribed to the 'will'. We find in Descartes no distinction between mental *act* and mental *action*, such that it would be appropriate to speak of any (occurrent) state of mind as a 'mental act', so that merely by virtue of being an *actualization* of a mental capacity it would be an *act* (as contrasted with a *po-*

tency). In the latter sense of 'act' a state could be one in which the mind was passive and still be an act. The concept of a 'passive act' would be a coherent one. Descartes would not *object* to such a distinction. He simply does not use the term 'act' in this purely Aristotelian sense in connection with the mental. And obviously he would not be happy with the concept of a 'passive *action*'.

17.   Yet the fundamental theme of the above passage is Aristotelian. For when he says that "this perception and this will are one and the same thing," we must bear in mind the opening paragraph of *The Passions of the Soul*, where he makes the general metaphysical point that

> all which occurs or that happens anew is by the philosophers, generally speaking, termed a passion, in so far as the subject to which it occurs is concerned, and an action in respect to him who causes it to occur. Thus, although the agent and the recipient [patient] are frequently very different, the action and the passion are always one and the same thing, although having different names, because of the two diverse subjects to which they may be related. (Pp. 331–32)

An example of this general metaphysical thesis would be that when fire heats a piece of metal, the actualization of the capacity of the fire to heat metal is 'the same thing' as the actualization of the capacity of the piece of metal to be heated by fire. Thus the fire's heating the metal is the same event as the metal's being heated by the fire. On the other hand, two *changes* involved in this event are *not* identical, namely, the fire becoming cooler and the metal becoming warmer, although these changes are aspects of that one identical event.

18.   Thus when Descartes tells us that "the perception and the will are one and the same thing," we must be careful not to conclude that the perception and the will are one and the same mental state *simpliciter*. What is one and the same state is the desire causing itself to be the object of a perception and a perception of the desire being caused by the desire. Being a perception caused by the mental state that is its object is the counterpart of being *heated* by something hot.

19.   Those who are inclined to say, and they are legion, with

an air of puzzlement that according to Descartes a mental act is identical with the awareness of that act are likely to be misinterpreting this passage.

III

20. It is high time that topics more closely related to perception were adumbrated. The best way to do so is to turn directly to Descartes' theory of sensation. The term *sensation*, as he uses it, includes visual sensation (e.g., a sensation of a certain shade of blue), sensations of the other senses, also bodily sensations (e.g., sensations of warmth) and sensations of pain or pleasure. Sensations are modifications of the mind of which we are immediately conscious, and hence are, according to Descartes' definition, 'thoughts'. But the definition is a bit puzzling, because to say that something is an immediate object of consciousness is to give it a relational or extrinsic characterization, whereas to classify it as a thought looks like an intrinsic characterization. What, we are inclined to ask, does a feeling of pain have intrinsically in common with a mental affirming, or a conceiving of an angel, and what is implied about its intrinsic character by classifying it as a modification of the *mind*? Of course, they share the negative character of not being definable in terms of the attribute of extension, but how much further does that get us?

21. Instead, however, of answering these questions directly, let us ask: Which are sensations more akin to, those thoughts that represent ('ideas') or those thoughts (e.g., volitions) that do not represent, though they are intimately related to those which do?

22. We are immediately pulled in different directions. Thus a sensation or feeling of pain does not *represent* a pain, it *is* a pain. In this respect it resembles an 'action of affirmation'. The latter does not *represent* an affirmation, it *is* an affirmation. The phrases 'of pain' and 'of affirmation' are, in grammatical terms, subjective genitives and serve to classify what is referred to by the terms they modify.

23. Shall we say, then, that sensations belong to that species

of thoughts which do not represent, and which therefore are not ideas in the narrower sense? Descartes does not press this question, and no coherent position is implied by the relevant texts. And there is good reason for this lacuna. To be sure, in the *Principles of Philosophy* he writes (part I, LXXI):

> . . . Such sensations were encountered as we called tastes, smells, sound, heat, cold, light, colors, etc., which in truth represent nothing to us outside of our mind, but which vary in accordance with the diversities of the parts and modes in which the body is affected.[6]

But the primary burden of this passage, in the context in which it occurs, is to emphasize the falsity of our childhood belief that material objects or processes resemble our sensations, e.g., that a material thing can resemble a sensation of blue.[7]

24. Yet if a feeling of pain does not *represent* but *is* a pain, this does not mean that it can not legitimately be said to represent *something*. And, indeed, the most plausible candidate is a bodily state, e.g., some aspect of the state of a hammered finger. This state need not be thought of as *resembling* the pain,[8] but nevertheless as being represented by it in accordance with a systematic manner of representation. And if, with Descartes, we construe a sensation of blue on the analogy of a feeling of pain, we might well be inclined to say that although a sensation of blue does not *represent* blue but *is* blue, it nevertheless does represent something, perhaps a certain state of the physical object that is its external cause.

25. And, indeed, Descartes stresses the functional role of pains and other modes of sensation in enabling men to find their way around safely in their environment. As a matter of fact, he stresses the kinship of men with animals in this respect —though the sensory states of animals, of course, as purely mechanical systems are limited to what, in the human case, are the physical correlates of feeling and sensation. The latter faculties were given us, not to illuminate the nature of the world, but to enable us to survive.[9] Pain keeps our hands off hot stoves.

26. But it is one thing to interpret sensations as having, in

a *generic* sense, a representative function, and quite another to interpret this function in terms of the categories that are appropriate to conceivings. Yet Descartes implicitly does this by taking the latter as his paradigm of the modifications of the mind that represent. And in the absence of an explicit, if only schematic, account of an alternative variety of representation in the generic sense, the temptation to do so must inevitably be present—and, as we shall see, was clearly present in Leibniz and Spinoza.

27. Descartes himself does refer to sensations on a number of occasions not only as thoughts, but as *confused* thoughts.[10] He connects this character of being confused with the intimate, indeed 'substantial', tie between the human mind and its body. Thus he writes:

> Nature also teaches me by these sensations of pain, hunger, thirst, etc., that I am not only lodged in my body as a pilot in a vessel, but that I am very closely united to it, and so to speak so intermingled with it that I seem to compose with it one whole. For if that were not the case, when my body is hurt, I, who am merely a thinking thing, should not feel pain, for I should receive this wound by the understanding only, just as the sailor perceives by sight when something is damaged in his vessel; and when my body has neither drink nor food, I should clearly understand the fact without being warned of it by confused feelings of hunger and thirst. For all these sensations of hunger, thirst, pain, etc., are in truth none other than certain confused modes of thought which are produced by the union and apparent intermingling of mind and body.[11]

This characterization of sensations, if taken at its face value, would require that sensations, although confused, belong to the same generic kind as clear and distinct thoughts, and would therefore require that they be analyzable in terms of the contrast between formal and objective reality. I shall return to this topic in a later section and shall limit myself for the moment to pointing out that *sometimes* when Descartes speaks of confusion in the context of sensation, he has in mind that as children, and, in the absence of sound philosophy, as adults, we tend to have confused beliefs about a similarity of sensations to their physical causes. Although, strictly speaking, it is the *beliefs* that are confused, the sensations may be said to be confused because of their role in this confusion.[12]

IV

28.   Now it is most important to note that when Descartes speaks of visual sensations, the examples he has in mind are not of the form 'sensation of a blue triangle' or 'sensation of a triangular expanse of blue', but simply 'sensation of blue.' In a perception of a shape we are conscious of or represent the shape, but we do not have a sensation of it. Thus, after the passage quoted in paragraph 23 above, he continues,

> The mind at the same time also perceived magnitudes, figures, movements and the like which were exhibited to it not as sensations, but as things or the modes of things existing, or at least capable of existing, outside thought, although it did not yet observe this distinction between the two.[13]

29.   This difference in status between the color and the shape involved in perceptual experiences generates puzzles which were endemic in seventeenth- and eighteenth-century philosophy, bound up as it is with the distinctions between primary and secondary qualities and between the mental and the physical. It is time we began to take a closer look at some of the conceptual pressures involved.

30.   Descartes is clearly committed to the view that when we have a perception of a shape, the shape has only 'objective' existence in the perceptual act or state. The perception has a shape 'objectively' but not 'formally'. One way of symbolizing this would be to introduce a new form of the copula, thus '[is]'. Accordingly we would say, where α is a perceptual act,

α [is] a triangle

whereas, x being a physical surface, we would say

x is a triangle.

268

If we now ask, "What can be predicted *formally* of α that pertains to its 'objective' triangularity?", we can, of course, be given a true but unilluminating answer, 'The character of being objectively a triangle', or, perhaps,

α is something that [is] a triangle.

The answer is unilluminating because what is desired is a 'formal' predication that is not derivative from an 'objective' predication. The answer

α is a triangle

would, of course, be ruled out by the principle that mental acts cannot be extended.

31. Notice, however, for future reference, that instead of introducing a new mode of predication, '[is]', we could have introduced a new predicate, '[a triangle]', and expressed the proposition that α is objectively a triangle by

α is [a triangle].

In the absence of a longer story, of course, there is no significant difference between these two modes of representation. They both indicate that α has a *special* connection with *ordinary* triangularity. Yet there is one difference worth noting. The second, unlike the first, is designed to give at least a nominal reply to the challenge: Granted that it is differentiated from other acts by occurring in *this* mind at *this* time, must not α actually (i.e., formally) have a character other than that of simply being a perception? And, in particular, must not a perception of a triangle differ in some character that it actually has from a perception of a circle? "Yes," the reply is, "it differs by having the character of being an [a triangle] perception."[14]

32. It is essential to remember that both the special copula and the special predicate of the above symbolic forms are, by virtue of Cartesian presuppositions, tied to the paradigm of conceptual thinking. Thus we would have

α [is] an angel

α is [an angel]

269

where α is the act in which Jones at a time, t, conceptually represents ('intends') an angel.

33.   But might there not be another way in which ordinary physical triangularity might be 'in' a mental state without that state being physically triangular? Is there no *via media* between being physically triangular and being a conceptual representation of a physical triangle? The answer, I shall argue, is, Yes, there is. But the failure of this period to consider, or if considered to elaborate, this alternative had serious consequences for philosophy.

34.   Now if Descartes is clearly committed to the view that when we have a perception of a shape, the shape has only 'objective' existence ('intentional inexistence') in the perception, he seems equally committed (though not perhaps as *distinctly*) to the view that when one has a sensation of blue, the sensation is a case of blue *formaliter*. I use this circumlocution rather than speaking of the sensation as blue *formaliter*, since Descartes does not attribute color to visual sensations.

35.   One might put this by saying that whereas Descartes might well have been uncomfortable about the statement, where α is a sensation,

   α is blue,

he would have been at least as uncomfortable about the claim that blue is in a sensation only as an angel is in a thought of an angel.

36.   At this point one might attempt to capture a possible Descartes by introducing either a new copula '{is}' or a new predicate '{blue}' to express this unique presence of blueness in a sensation of blue. But to do so would imply that the actual Descartes was in a position to ask, but simply failed to ask, the question: Why could not a perception be an {a triangle} perception or {be} a triangle? That is, why could it not involve physical triangularity in a way that does not require the perception to be *either* a physical triangle *or* a mere conception of a triangle? It is important to bear in mind that nothing which could reasonably be construed as a form of this question is explicitly raised by Descartes. Yet the question is a useful one to bear in mind when studying the Cartesian tradition.[15]

V

37.   Let us return to our main line of thought. We have found
Descartes to be committed to the view that blue and triangle
enter in different ways into perceptual experience. Yet as far as
the phenomena are concerned—and it was not left to phenome-
nologists to point this out—the shape we perceive is the shape
of a color expanse, and the color has a shape. Indeed, the shape
is there because color contrasts are there. Thus there is enormous pressure to say that the shape and the color have the
same 'mode of being.'[16]

38.   If we say that the color has formal reality, i.e., is a case
of color *formaliter* as a case of pain is a case of pain *formaliter*,
then the shape of the color is the shape of a case of color
formaliter, and must surely be a case of shape *formaliter*. Indeed, if a sensation *is* a case of color *formaliter*, the shape must
surely be the shape of a sensation—though perhaps not itself a
sensation. If the color is a modification of the mind, the shape
would be a modification of a modification of the mind.

39.   Could we expect Descartes to consider for a moment the
view that a shape could be even a modification of a modification
of the mind, let alone a modification of the mind?

40.   If, on the other hand, the shape of which we are conscious
is merely the objective reality of a *cogitatio*, i.e., characterizes
the latter only 'objectively,' then surely the same must be true of
the color expanse of which it is the shape!

41.   Thus either we pay one price and assimilate the status of
the experienced shape to that of the experienced color or we pay
another and assimilate the status of the experienced color to
that of the experienced shape. Descartes does not resolve this
dilemma; indeed, he does not face it. How can this be? did he
think that one and the same modification of the mind could be
both a case of blue *formally* and a triangle *objectively*, and,
by virtue of this hermaphroditic character, be an experience of
a triangular expense of blue? Yet he does, after all, think that
a modification of the mind can be both *formally* a case of desire
and *objectively* a case of a sloop, and by virtue of these facts be
a desiring of a sloop.

42.   Or, which is more likely, did he think that the case of

271

blue which has the shape is not the case of blue which is the sensation? He can be interpreted as holding that when we look at a blue and triangular object in standard conditions, the resultant state of the pineal gland causes us to have a *sensation*, α_1, of blue and, at the same time, a *perception*, α_2, of a triangle. We thereupon form an additional cogitatio, α_3, which is the idea of a blue triangle, i.e., an idea of which the objective reality is a blue triangle, thus

α_1 is a case of blue;

α_2 [is] a triangle;

α_3 [is] a blue triangle. —

43. But why should the mind connect the blue with the shape? Of course the modification of the pineal gland that, by virtue of its microstructure, causes the sensation of blue is also, in its gross character, triangular. And perhaps this is all that needs to be said.[17]

44. If Descartes had dwelt on this issue, it would have confronted him with the question: Why is it not *evident* that the experience of blue-*cum*-triangle is either constituted by, or derivative from, two radically different kinds of experience, one of which is of blue and the other of which is of a triangle? Descartes holds not only that we can be. immediately conscious of our sensations but that we can have a *clear* knowledge of them. To be sure, *clear* knowledge need not be *distinct*, and it is the latter which is presupposed by the above challenge. Yet Descartes does tell us that "we have a clear or distinct knowledge of pain, color, and other things of the sort when we consider them simply as sensations or thoughts."[18]

45. Descartes, however, is content to remind us that in ordinary perceptual experience we do not ask these questions. After all, the point of perception is to guide practice rather than to inspire ontology, and in this respect the philosopher's experience does not differ from the child's. Nevertheless, when, as philosophers, we *do* ask these questions, should not the answers be evident? A well-convinced philosophy must be able to account not only for the knowledge that it is true but for the fact that otherwise intelligent philosophers are convinced that it is false. If

Descartes had explored with sufficient care the above problems, he would surely have been forced to realize that the categories of his philosophy of mind were arrived at dialectically, rather than by philosophically inspired inspection.

46. There remains the possibility that Descartes simply took for granted that the relation of blue to the sensation of blue is the same as that of triangle to the perception of a triangle. This would mean that blue has merely *objective* existence, even in a sensation of blue. On this alternative the classification of blue as a sensation would amount to the thesis that objective reality is the only kind of reality of which blue is capable.[19] Shape, on the other hand, would also have reality as a modification of material things.

47. Again, on this alternative, the confused belief about blue shared by children and unsophisticated philosophers would be *not* the belief that 'blue' material things have a property that belongs formally only to sensations, but rather the belief that 'blue' material things have a property that belongs formally to *nothing*, not even sensations, for it is possessed only *objectively* by those *cogitationes* which are sensations of blue. Since the concept of a property that, though not self-contradictory, can be possessed formally by nothing is, to say the least, paradoxical, the point should be made in a way that involves no commitment to the idea that blue is a property or quality or even a modification (for the concept of a modification that cannot be *formally* the modification of anything is equally paradoxical). Fortunately there remains the catch-all categoory of *nature*. Blue, then, unlike shape, would be a nature that is capable only of objective being, though it can be confusedly believed to have formal being in the material world.

48. How could such a position be held, even 'implicitly,' by a subtle and perceptive mind? How could a philosopher of Descartes' caliber assimilate the status of blue in a sensation of blue (let alone the twinge in a feeling of pain) to the status, say, of the number Two in a mathematician's reasoning? The general clue to such a possibility lies in the absence from Descartes' philosophy of a clear and distinct theory (as opposed to a highly metaphorical proto-theory) of intentionality. This absence

made it possible to think that the difference between sensation of blue and conception of Two consists not in a difference between the relation of blue to the sensation and the relation of Two to the conception, but in a difference between the natures *blue* and *Two*.

49. What difference? There is an obvious candidate. A sensation of blue is always a sensation of a determinate shade of blue, thus $blue_{29}$. Two, on the other hand, is, in some sense of this slippery term, an 'abstraction'. Might not the striking phenomenological difference between a sensing of blue (or even a feeling of a specific kind of twinge!) and a conceiving of Two be the striking difference between the *determinate* nature $blue_{29}$ (or $twinge_{63}$!) and the abstract nature *Two*? Would not this step also illuminate the distinction between *sensing* $blue_{29}$ and *conceiving* generic blue or color as such? Generic blue and color as such are also 'abstractions', and our awareness of them falls on the side of conceiving rather than sensing or imaging.

50. It is a familiar fact that, as hinted above, the term 'abstraction' covers a number of distinctions. Is *Two* abstract in the same way in which *blue* as such is abstract? Is there not perhaps a sense in which $blue_{29}$ is abstract? These questions are lurking in the background and will play their role in the development of Cartesian themes, particularly across the channel. But let us continue to collect before we divide.

51. Notice that the alternative we have been exploring since paragraph 46 above would mitigate the problem of how $blue_{29}$ and triangularity get together in the experience of a $blue_{29}$ triangle. There would be no need to posit a transition from sensing $blue_{29}$, where the sensing is *formally* a case of $blue_{29}$, to conceiving $blue_{29}$, on the ground that this latter alone, as *objectively* a case of $blue_{29}$, would be suited to merge with the perception of a triangle. $Blue_{29}$ would *ab initio* have the same status as the triangular shape. Thus instead of the α_1, α_2, and α_3 of paragraph 43 above, we would need to postulate only one mental act, the perception of a triangular expanse of blue. We would add, of course, that just as the blue must be a determinate shade of blue, so the shape must be a determinate sort of triangularity.

52. But why, then, distinguish between a *sensation* of color and a *perception* of shape? This distinction would presumably

be justified by the fact that shape is a nature which *can* be realized by material things, whereas color is not. This categorial difference would find expression in the presumed fact that shape presents itself to us as a modification of an extended object,[20] whereas color does not so present itself to us, but is (confusedly) believed to be such a modification.

VI

53. I pointed out (above, paragraph 24) that even if a feeling of pain is interpreted as a case of pain *formaliter*, there is nevertherless a sense of 'represent' in which the feeling can be said to represent a bodily state, e.g., that of having a hammered finger. In such a case the feeling is not only a constituent of the seeming to feel one's finger to be hammered, it is also a feeling of a sort that is normally brought about by a hammering of one's finger, but that, in abnormal circumstances (e.g., in the case of a finger amputee), can be brought about by a state of one's animal spirits which is itself normally brought about by such a hammering.

54. As in the case of visual sensation one takes blue to be a feature of a material thing, so in the case of the hammered finger one takes a pain of that kind to be a feature of the finger. Pain-as-feature-of-finger would be the content of a confused belief. As in the case of color, the feeling itself could be said to be confused (in a derivative sense) by virtue of the fact that people have a natural tendency to be confused *about* it. But might there not be a deeper sense in which the feeling is *intrinsically* a confused idea? If, as in the case of color, one were to assimilate the 'in-ness' of pain in the feeling with the 'in-ness' of *Two* in a conceiving, and if we were to assimilate the sense in which pain 'represents' the bodily state with which it is correlated to the sense in which a conceiving 'represents' (i.e., 'intends') that which has objective being in it, we would have the tiglon (or liger) notion of a certain complex bodily state (the bodily correlate or pain) as having objective reality in the feeling. The objective reality of the feeling could be described both as *pain* and as *complex bodily state*.

55. There is, I suppose, a use for the form of words 'pain is

really a complex bodily state', in which it stands for a coherent idea. But the implications of the above conceptual tangle are paradoxical in the extreme. For it has built into it the notion that the *nature* pain$_{30}$, which is 'in' my feeling, is identical with the *nature* bodily-state$_{53}$ which is also 'in' this feeling. An *identity* of natures is, of course, no mere 'correlation'.

56.   Shall we say that *qua* pain$_{30}$ the nature is 'confused,' whereas *qua* bodily state$_{53}$ is not? How do *natures* become confused? One gropes for an answer. One comes up with something like this. Consider a conceiving which is 'of a bachelor', and a conceiving which is 'of an unmarried adult male human'. One is tempted to say there there is a legitimate sense in which the same nature is objectively present in the two conceivings. Yet is there not the following difference? Can we not suppose that in the second case the articulation of the conceiving as mental state, i.e., its form,[21] is (more) adequate to the articulation of the nature that is its objective reality than is true in the first case.

57.   Perhaps, in the first instance, a confused (*con-fusa*: fused together) idea is one that stands to a clear and distinct idea as a conceiving of a bachelor stands to a conceiving of an unmarried adult male human. Certainly clarity and distinctness is connected by Cartesians with definability.

58.   Now the touch of nutmeg. We elaborate this analogy by drawing the following distinction. An idea is *non-essentially confused*, if it could be replaced, in the mind that has it, by an idea that stands to it as an idea of an unmarried adult male human stands to an idea of a bachelor. If ideas were linquistic entities, we would speak of replacing *definienda* by *definientia*. Let us add this to our analogy.

59.   It now occurs to us that since, for humans at least, all definitions must involve a finite number of steps, the above suggestion has as a consequence that a human idea which contains a nature of *infinite* complexity would be *essentially* confused —though its counterpart in the mind of God would, of course, be ideally clear and distinct.

60. Since we must shortly move across the channel, there is no time to do more than throw out some hints as to how bridges might be built from the above analysis to the philosophies of Leibniz and Spinoza.

61. Thus if we add to the above the idea that the nature of an individual must be infinitely complex, since it must distinguish that individual from every other *possible* individual, we would have the Leibnizian thesis that an adequately individuating idea of a given individual must be infinitely complex, so that only God could have a clear and distinct *adequately* individuating idea of that individual. We humans could have *adequately* individuating ideas of individuals—but they would be *essentially* confused. Indeed, according to Leibniz, our *petites perceptions* are exactly such essentially confused ideas. On the other hand, humans can have clear and distinct ideas pertaining *to* individuals, but they would pick them out (successfully, *for practical purposes*) by means of generalities that hold of an infinite number of possible individuals, and hence are not *adequately* individuating ideas. Our *petites perceptions* of Adam are *adequately* individuating but *essentially* confused. Our clear and distinct idea of Adam is really the general idea of *an Adam*, and does not adequately individuate.[22]

62. Again, to point the discussion toward Spinoza, if the nature of any modification of any finite mode involves the nature of every other modification of every other finite mode—the whole face of the universe, then every human idea of that modification which does not pick it out in terms of common notions, but which contains all the content necessary to *understand* exactly *that* modification (why it exists, why it has the features it does) must be *essentially* confused. As in the case of Leibniz, these *essentially* confused ideas are the ideas of sense. The natures that are (objectively) in such confused ideas are the natures that are realized *formaliter* by states of the brain. But these natures essentially involve the natures of all other modifications of all other finite modes. If *every* such nature involves *every other* such nature, are they not all the same? One is

277

tempted to reply that each such nature involves every other such nature 'from a point of view'. But *this* profound kinship between Leibniz and Spinoza must be left unexplored.[23]

PART TWO

VII

63. The presence of traditional categories, as reshaped by Descartes, in British philosophy, and it is pervasive, has been less clearly discerned, particularly by British historians and commentators, than in the case of Continental philosophy. I shall have almost nothing to say about Locke, though many of the points I shall make in connection with Berkeley are of equal relevance to Locke's *Essay*. No one would be surprised to find traces of the most divergent frameworks in Locke's amiable syncretism. Berkeley and Hume, on the other hand, seem to be, as they conceived themselves to be, veritable paradigms of radical originality, illuminating the murky philosophical scene like flashes of lightning and capable of being understood apart from carefully articulated traditions (as even that kindred spirit Descartes was not) as though they had sprung from the Modern Spirit like Minerva (as yet un-owled) from the head of Zeus.

64. But before looking in detail at Berkeley's theory of 'ideas', it is important to take advantage of hindsight and draw some distinctions that are clearly required by an adequate phenomenology of perception, and that were seen as through a glass darkly in seventeenth- and eighteenth-century philosophy. The history of philosophy is appropriately rewritten by each generation, not because they have better historical methods, but because philosophy itself has made available not only finer distinctions but finer distinctions between distinctions. We can understand Plato better than Plato understood himself not primarily because we see things that Plato did not see but because we see more complicated patterns of sameness and difference in the things he saw.

65. Moving, as sooner or later must be done, to the proper

(and common)[24] sensibles, and constructing the concept of a 'basic' perceptual experience as an analytic tool, let us take as our paradigm an ostensible seeing of an object *over there* that is red and triangular on the facing surface. By an *ostensible* seeing of an object let us understand an experience that would be a seeing of such an object, if it were both true,[25] i.e., there is an object *over there* that is red and triangular on the facing surface, and if the experience had the right causal connections, i.e., the object is appropriately responsible for the occurrence of the experience.

66. As capable of truth, an ostensible seeing belongs to the conceptual order. Appropriately characterized in semantic terms, it is analogous to a linguistic episode. *Not*, however, to a *sentential* occurrence, thus

There is a cube of pink over there which faces me cornerwise

or

That, over there, is a cube of pink which faces me cornerwise

but, rather,

That cube of pink over there facing me cornerwise . . .

where the dots indicate the place for explicit predication, e.g., 'is made of ice'.

67. One might put this by saying that what is taken by a perceptual taking is an *object*, rather than a *state of affairs*. Yet the 'object' is not *simply* an object as contrasted with a state of affairs, for it implicitly *contains* a state of affairs much as

That cube of pink over there . . .

'implicitly contains'

That over there is a cube of pink.

68. This portmanteau ability of terms to encapsulate predications is no mere device of economy. For in perceptual contexts, the subject term (which refers to the perceptual object) is not only a subject of predication but also, *as term*, a perceptual

279

response. And to refer to an object, it must be not only a *response* but a response to a (correctly or incorrectly) identified object. And it is, of course, the predication contained *in* the subject term that carries the criteria of identification.

69. Failure to appreciate this fact has led to the incoherent notion of a purely demonstrative reference, a pure 'this', everything else falling into an explicitly predicative position, thus:

> *This* is a cube of pink and is over there and faces me cornerwise.

It has also generated the mistaken idea that a perceptual taking is a 'judgment', a believing *that* something is the case. Thus (relaxing, for the moment, our limitation to the proper sensibles), taking there to be a cat on the roof would have the form

> *That* is a cat and it is on the roof

whereas, according to the position sketched above, it actually has the form

> That cat on the roof . . .

70. Roughly, what is *taken* is what is packed into the *subject term*. If we regiment the concept of *belief* for perceptual contexts, we should say that perceptual taking is a form of 'occurrent' believing *in* rather than believing *that*. The distinction would be an important one, even if perceptual takings always occurred (as they do not) as *constituents* of believings *that*, e.g.,

> That cat on the roof is hunting for birds.

71. Perceptual beliefs have been characterized as examples of 'thinking without question' that something is the case, and as 'snap judgments'. But the psychological distinction between judgments that do or do not answer a prior question, or answer it without a pause for reflection, misses the point, which is that the distinction between what is 'taken for granted' and what is 'up for grabs' in a given statement is embodied in grammatical structure.

> That cat on the roof is ϕ

takes for granted, that is, in one sense of the term, presupposes, that there is a cat on a certain roof and asserts that it is ϕ Of course, the statement may have been preceded by the dialogue (or monologue)

What is that over there (in the trees)?
A roof.
What is that on the roof?
A cat.
What is that cat on that roof doing? . . .

But, of course, it *need* not—in which case it can be said to be an *original* as contrasted with a *derived* presupposition.

72.   Perceptual presuppositions or takings can be either original or derived. Observation, i.e., looking with questions in mind, as contrasted with merely happening to look in a certain direction, generates derived presuppositions. But looking with questions in mind itself requires a subject *term* that 'contains' a predication that is not itself in question, thus,

What is that over there *in the trees*?
A roof.

73.   Philosophers have searched for basic perceptual takings. One way of describing them has been to say that they are takings that do not presuppose anything that is vulnerable to certain kinds of challenge.

That over there in the trees is a roof.
But are those things over there trees?

The term 'tree' carries with it a rich cluster of implications. Trees are richly endowed with unperceived aspects, thus opposite sides, wooden insides, not to mention capacities, propensities, indeed, a wide variety of causal properties that specify the results of hypothetical transactions with other objects, including perceivers. We see trees, but *of* trees we do not see their opposite sides or their insides or their causal properties. Yet in perceptually taking a *tree*, we are *ipso facto* taking something having an opposite side with *some* kind of bark and branches, an inside of *some* kind of wood, and endowed with *some* form of the causal

281

properties characteristic of trees. Thus the sortal concept involved in the perceptual taking of an object carries with it generic or specific implications concerning *that of the object* which is not perceived.

74. In a limiting case, the sortal is simply *physical object*, and the implications are of the categorial character explored by Kant. In other words, the more we press the question 'But do we see *that* feature of the object?', (a) the more what we see *of* the object tends to be limited to occurrent proper sensibles, and (b) the more the sortal in terms of which the object is identified approximates the concept of an 'object in general'.

75. A 'basic' perceptual taking, then, is a taking that is minimal in two respects: (a) it is minimal in that it is restricted to features that are proper sensibles; (b) it has minimal implications concerning what is not seen *of* the object. It is the first respect that has tended to occupy the center of the stage. Thus the concept of pure occurrent sensible qualities and relations has been thought to define the 'content' of minimal perceptual takings.

76. But, as emphasized above, to eliminate *specific* implications concerning what is not perceived *of* an object need not (and, indeed, cannot) be to eliminate *generic* or *categorial* implications. This, of course, was Kant's brilliant insight. Thus, the perceptual taking

This now occurring yellow flash over there

where 'flash' does not carry with it the specific sortal 'of lightning', has no *specific* implications concerning future developments, and is minimal in both the above respects. Even so, it implies that *something* has happened *before now* and that *something* will happen *after now*, in places other than *there*. Indeed, if Kant is right, it implies that the flash belongs to a world of changing and interacting things, a spatial-temporal-causal system.

77. In the absence of Kant's insight, the categorial sortal (physical) object (or event), which remains after all the above pruning, is treated as though it were the mere notion of a *something* (I know not what?), or, as I shall put it, an *item*, that

has sensible 'qualities'.[26] Thus the idea that perceptual takings can be appropriately *minimal* and yet carry rich categorial commitments was lost to the empiricist tradition.

78. In other words, though it is obvious that a *quality* is always a quality of a thing, a *relation*, a relation between things, and a *manner*, a manner of what a thing does, the temptation to suppose that to minimize the *specific* implications of basic perceptual takings is to minimize their implications *simpliciter* proved well nigh irresistible. After all, *being a quality of a thing* is not itself a perceptible characteristic, nor is *having some causal property or other*, let alone *having the causal properties characteristic of some sort of thing.*

79. With these reflections in mind, let us contrive a minimal perceptual taking, the concept of which will help illuminate the internal structure of Berkeley's 'ideas'. We begin with a reasonably sound example of a minimal perceptual taking, thus

> This red and triangular on the facing side physical object over there . . .

We then, ostensibly continuing to minimalize in the same manner, cut it down to

> This red and triangular surface perpendicular to my line of sight . .

and continuing to cut, eliminating everything smacking of perspectives in three-dimensional physical space, and of surfaces as surfaces of physical objects,

> This triangular expanse of red . . .

which we finally telescope into

> This red and triangular item . . .

or

> This red triangle . . .

80. We are now *almost* in a position to take into account a radically different dimension of perceptual taking. Before doing so, however, we must pick up a thread that was laid aside at

the beginning of the above analysis. The perceptual taking expressed by

That cat over there . . .

was characterized as a perceptual taking *of a cat*. This classifies the taking by specifying one constituent of its conceptual content, i.e., as

(demonstrative) *cat*

rather than, for example,

(demonstrative) *dog*

The phrase 'of a cat' can be so used, of course, that a perceptual taking can be the taking of a cat, even though no cat is there to be taken. In this sense, 'of a cat' serves to classify a taking without commitment to its success in either its referential or (implicitly) predicative dimensions.

81. Again, the above perceptual taking is, in an obvious sense, a perceptual awareness of something *as a cat*. The 'as a cat' locution simply formulates in the material mode of speech the conceptual-grammatical point that the referring expression

That cat over there . . .

is a transformation, appropriate to perceptual contexts, of an expression in which 'a cat' occurs as an explicitly predicative expression, thus,

That over there is a cat.

82. The perceptual taking can be a *mis*taking, not only because there is no appropriately located cat, but, more radically (as in the case of hallucination), because there is no object *over there* that might be a cat. If the taking successfully picks out such an object, then, even if the object is not in fact a cat, the taking has a limited referential success. That it can succeed to this limited extent is, in our example, a function of the identifying criteria other than 'cat' that are contained in the referring expression. Thus 'that [object which could be a cat] over there' where 'over there' carries (by virtue of the context) information of the form 'in direction D'.[27]

284

83. The above is intended to explicate the idea that our contrived taking is an awareness *of something as a red triangle* and, in the case of fully successful reference, an awareness of a red triangle as a red triangle. But can the reference involved in such a minimal perceptual taking fail? Can there fail to be an object? Can the object fail to be a red triangle? These obviously relevant questions must be left at the margin. An attempt to answer them would take us too far into a systematic theory of perception proper, and away from our historical concerns.[28]

VIII

84. I have been constructing a frame of reference in terms of which to account for the idea that basic perceptual experiences are, for example, of something *as a red triangle*, and, indeed, *of a red triangle as a red triangle.* This frame of reference has taken as its point of departure the conceptual character of perceptual takings, i.e., that character by virtue of which a perceptual taking of a red triangle is analogous to a candid tokening, in perceptual contexts, of the referring expression

This red triangle.

It must now be noted that a perceptual taking is not an *exclusively* conceptual episode. The point is a crucial one for a full understanding of the problem that we were helping Descartes wrestle with in the first part of this paper.

85. In its conceptual aspect, a minimal perceptual taking is *of a red triangle as such*, in a sense analogous to that in which an appropriate tokening of the expression 'this red triangle' is a demonstrative reference to a red triangle as such.[29] To characterize it as an 'ostensible' reference is to classify it functionally as a demonstrative singular term. To characterize it as a reference *to a red triangle as such* is to classify it as including a sortal that plays the same inferential and non-inferential roles as does 'triangle' in our language, which sortal is modified by an adjective which plays the same inferential and non-inferential roles as does 'red' in our language. Thus an appropriate tokening by a Frenchman of

Ce triangle rouge-ci

would also be a demonstrative reference *to a red triangle as a red triangle*.

86.   The important point is that the semantic classification of linguistic items is not only functional classification but functional classification that, at its core,[30] is a matter of how the expression functions in inferences. Thus to say that an utterance by Jones of a certain term *refers to a red triangle as such* is to classify the utterance in a way that attributes to a knowledgeable user propensities to say such things as

So, it is not green
So, it has three sides
Etc.[31]

87.   Thus, by analogy, the core of the criteria in terms of which we classify by a minimal perceptual taking as one of the *of a red triangle as a red triangle* kind[32] is constituted by the inference patterns appropriate to the concepts *red, triangle,* and, last but not least, *this*.

88.   I have implied that minimal perceptual takings also have a non-conceptual aspect, the understanding of which is essential to the resolution of Descartes' problem. The modifying clause is the heart of the matter, for that perceptual takings have non-conceptual aspects is vague enough to be non-controversial. Thus it is reasonable to suppose that a taking which is of a red triangle as such has as proximate cause a bodily state that is brought about in standard conditions by the influence of an object that is red and triangular on the facing side, and in non-standard conditions by other influences that may or may not involve external objects.[33]

89.   The crucial step is that in which we think of the immediate cause[34] of the conceptual aspect of a perceptual taking as having an occurrent character that consists in its *somehow* exemplifying the perceptible qualities and relations of physical objects,[35] where the 'somehow' carries with it the rider 'other than by being a conceiving of an item exemplifying such qualities and relations'.

90. For, as I have argued on a number of occasions, the perceptual experience that we have been characterizing as a taking of a red triangle as such, and that, therefore, involves a conceiving of a red triangle (indeed, a conceptual reference to a red triangle), also involves the presence of redness and triangularity in a manner other than mere conception. If we say that a red triangle has being-for-sense in the experience as well as being-as-*conceptum*, we establish direct contact with Descartes' puzzle.

91. But the Cartesian, with his sharp dualism of mind and matter, is disposed to think of the being-for-sense of a case of red as equivalent to a modification of the *mind* being a case of red.[36]

92. If, now, we bear in mind that redness like triangularity is initially tied to the category of physical objects, we could say that for a case of red to have being-for-sense in a state of a perceiver (or of his sensorium) is neither for that state to be red as physical objects are red, nor for it to be red as *conceivings* that intend a case of red are red. The state in question (let us call it s) is properly characterized not by

s is a case of red

nor by

s is [a case of red]

but, as adumbrated above in paragraph 36,

s is {a case of red}, or s is {a red item}

where to be {a red item} is to be a state that has a character *analogous*[37] to the physical redness of a facing surface.

93. Thus s, which we can now call a sensation, can be {a blue item} without being either a case of blue or [a blue item]. If this seems like multiplying distinctions *praeter necessitatem*, the proper reply is that exactly these distinctions are necessary. For it enables us to see that s, which is {a blue item} without being blue, might also be {a triangular item} without being triangular, and yet without being merely [a triangular item], i.e., a triangular item that has being-as-*conceptum*.

287

94. If the minimal perceptual experience the conceptual aspect of which was characterized above as a perceptual taking *of a red triangle as a red triangle*, and, hence, as of the [this red triangle] kind, also has an aspect in which it is of the {a red triangle} kind, i.e., of the {a red and triangular item} kind, then color and shape each enter into the experience in the same two ways, and the problem of getting them together would disappear.

95. In other words, what I have so far referred to as *the* explication of the perceptual taking of a red triangle, namely its construal as a believing *in* a red triangle, is but one aspect of a more complex state that also includes a *sensing* of a red triangle, i.e., a state that is of the {a red triangle} kind. It is this more complex state, about the structure of which far more needs to be said than is possible on the present occasion, that is properly described as the state of ostensibly seeing (or seeming to see) a red triangle *as* a red triangle.

96. We are now in a position to comment on the fact that when, in the *Meditations*, Descartes attempts to specify exactly what he has in mind by 'sensation,' he writes,

> Finally, I am the same who feels, that is to say, who perceives certain things as by the organs of sense, since in truth I see light, I hear noise, I feel heat. But it will be said that these phenomena are false and that I am dreaming. Let it be so; still it is at least quite certain that it seems to me that I see light, that I hear noise and that I feel heat. That cannot be false; properly speaking it is what in me is called feeling [sentire]; and used in this precise sense that is no other thing than thinking.[38]

97. A number of things should be noted about this passage. (1) It begins the *equation* of sensing with *seeming to see* (*hear*, etc.) which has become endemic in Anglo-American theories of perception. Since *seeming to see* does, indeed, have a conceptual *aspect*, the interpretation of sensing, thus construed, as a mode of 'thinking' is not completely wrongheaded. (2) Descartes does not explicitly include shape in his examples of what is sensed, although it is surely the case that we can seem to see a shape as we can seem to see 'a light'. The pain model (which is lurking near warmth) is still exerting its influence.[39] (3) The

passage collapses into one supposedly homogeneous state, a sensation, items that, correctly understood, are distinguishable aspects (one conceptual, a believing *in*; one non-conceptual, the sensation proper) of a seeming to see.

98. Before advancing to Berkeley, we should remind ourselves that, like any other experience, the experience of seeming to see a red triangle as a red triangle does not wear its analysis on its sleeve. The analysis requires a painstaking philosophical dialectic that touches on most of the sensitive issues in ontology and the philosophy of mind. Solutions can be quick and obvious—arrived at almost by 'scrutiny'—only because one begins with so much inherited dialectic that there is room for only one alternative which is either not absurd, or the absurdity of which can be parsed as the paradoxical wisdom of the learned.[40]

99. Berkeley, as is well known, formulates the 'act-object' account of perceiving in the *Three Dialogues between Hylas and Philonous*, only to reject it. His explicit reason for rejecting it is a bad one,[41] turning as it does on an equation of 'act' with 'deed'. He points out that what we *do* in perception is *look*. On looking we see, but in seeing we are passive. We can choose where to look but not what to see.

100. Berkeley's real reason for rejecting the act-object account is to be found in the principle that the *esse* of what is perceived is *percipi*, i.e., to be sensed. The act-object metaphor implies that what is perceived could exist without being perceived, and hence implies, in traditional terms, a real distinction between perceiving and its object. Could there, however, be a perceiving that lacked an object? Is it a contingent fact that perceivings only come into being when there is an appropriate object to which it can be related? Does it even make sense to suppose a perceiving without a something perceived? Perhaps there could be a modification of the mind that had no 'object', but that *would* be a perceiving, *if* there were something appropriately related to it. One thinks: Why not? A seeming to see would be a seeing only if there was something appropriately related to it. Indeed, but is there not a sense in which even a *mere* seeming to see has an 'object'? And is not this sense of 'have an object' the basic sense? In *this* sense there could no more be a perceiving without an 'object,' i.e., *something per-*

ceived than there could be a believing without an 'object,' i.e., *something believed.* Surely, it is tempting to conclude, there is at most a distinction of reason between perceiving and what strictly speaking is perceived.

101. But what is perceived in this strict or minimal sense is, for example, a red triangle.[42] Hence in this case a red triangle is the 'object' of perception. But, then, there is only a distinction of reason between the perceiving of 'the' red triangle and 'the' red triangle perceived. The situation, however, is symmetrical. There is a red triangle? It is perceived.[43]

102. It surely does not distort the situation too much to say that for Berkeley a perceiving of a red triangle does not have the form

(perceiving) R (a red triangle)

but rather

(of a red triangle) perceiving,

i.e., to interpret him as holding that for a perceiving to be 'of a red triangle' is for it to be a perceiving of a certain sort.

103. Now a *conceiving* of an angel can occur without the actual existence of a certain angel of which it is the conceiving, or even of any angels at all. To be a conceiving of an angel as such is to be a conceiving of a certain kind, for example, the conceiving that is a constituent of a mental act of the

[an angel was dancing on the point of a pin one day]

kind.

104. The same is clearly true where the conceiving of an angel is the conceiving of a specific kind of angel, as in a thought of the kind,

[a rosy cheeked, blond, blue-eyed angel was dancing on the point of a pin one day].

No matter how specific we make the content of the conceiving, the conceiving can occur without the extra-conceptual existence of the object conceived. And, of course, no matter how specific the content of the conceiving of an angel, the conceiving never becomes an angel.

105. Now Berkeley clearly insists that that which is perceived is always of an absolutely specific character.[44] Suppose, now, two perceptions each of which is *of* something red$_{29}$ and triangular$_{30}$. They are perceptions 'of the same'. Does it follow that there is a 'same something' of which they are perceptions? *Only*, of course, in the sense that they belong to the same *kind*, i.e., are two perceptions each of which is *of* something red$_{29}$ and triangular$_{30}$.

106. But is there not another sense in which these two perceptions can be perceptions of the same *thing* (or, for that matter of different *things*)? Of course. If we construe *things* as patterns of actual and obtainable perceivings, two perceivings can be 'of exactly the same' (i.e., belong to the same *kind*) without being perceptions that are *of the same thing* in the sense of being among its constituents.

107. It is important, therefore, to see that Berkeley so uses the word 'particular' that to say of a perception that it is of a *particular* triangle is simply to say that its content is, as *we* would put it, completely *determinate*, i.e., to use the more traditional term, completely *specific*. Thus there can in Berkeley's sense be a perception of a particular triangle without there being what *we* would call a particular triangle, i.e., an individuated triangular item. What corresponds to the latter in Berkeley's ontology is, for example, a triangle on a blackboard—an appropriate pattern of actual and obtainable perceivings, some of which would, of course, *in the internal or classificatory sense* be perceivings of something determinately triangular. It is, of course, such patterns of perceivings that are *individuated*, ultimately by virtue of the individuation of the minds in which they occur.

108. In short there can be a perception of a particular triangle without there being a particular (i.e., individual) triangle of which the perception is a perception. The perception can, even in the internal sense, be said to be 'of an individual', but only if all implications pertaining to *individuation* have been removed from 'individual', leaving only the consideration that the perception is not of the abstraction triangularity$_{30}$, but of an *item* (a *something*) which is triangular$_{30}$.

109. The rationale of Berkeley's insistence that perceptions

are in the above sense particular (i.e., specific or determinate) can best be grasped by laying aside geometrical examples, and considering that strand of his theory of ideas which directly involves the assimilation of ideas to feelings of pain. A pain simply *is* a feeling of pain. (There was a pain? It was felt.) In the case of shape, we can distinguish between an *individual triangular object* (e.g., the triangle on the blackboard) and an *individual perception of a triangle.* As was noted above, an individual perception of a triangle need not be a perception of (i.e., a constituent of) an individual triangular object. On the other hand, *all there is to the individuality of a pain is the individuality of a feeling of pain.*[45] Thus we can mobilize the classical principle that all individuals are completely specific (most determinate) in character to argue,

All individual pains are determinate with respect to pain.

Individual pains are individual feelings of pain.

Therefore, individual feelings of pain are determinate with respect to pain, i.e., are feelings *of* determinate pain.

110.   If a case of color[46] is a perception of color as a pain is a feeling of pain, then, by parity of reasoning, a perception of color is always a perception of a determinate color.

111.   The assimilation of color to pain would amount, in terms of the distinctions drawn at the beginning of this section, to the equation of

α is an {a red item} perception

with

α is a red item,

an equation he would never have considered in the case of shape. Thus the *direct* use of the above pattern of argument in connection with perceptions of shape would have involved the puzzling premise

a (case of) shape is a perception of shape.

Sensing this, Berkeley relies on the identity in ontological status of the color and the shape in a perception of a shaped color to extend his conclusion to shape by analogy.

112. Of course, Berkeley *could* have recognized that a perception can be *of a red item* without being a red item, i.e., can be an {a red item} perception without being red, and argued from the premise that 'everything which exists is particular' that an individual perception cannot be *of a red item* unless it has some determinate form of the property of being *of a red item*. But then it would remain to be shown why being *of a red$_{29}$ item* is a determinate form of being *of a red item*.

113. As a matter of fact, however, it is built into the explanatory framework of sensations that the structure of determinates and determinables pertaining to the perceptually distinguishable features of physical objects is reflected in the predicates of sensation. Thus the *determinable* predicate 'red', which applies to physical objects, has as its counterpart the *determinable* sensation predicate 'of a red item'—in our notation '{a red item}'—just as the *determinate* physical object predicate 'red$_{29}$' has the *determinate* counterpart '{a red$_{29}$ item}'. And as a physical object cannot be red without being some determinate shade of red, e.g., red$_{29}$, so a sensation cannot be {a red item} without being, e.g., {a red$_{29}$ item}.[47]

114. Thus, even if Berkeley had not confused between

  α is an {a red item} perception

and

  α is a red item,

he could legitimately have argued that α cannot be an {a red item} perception without being *of* a determinately red item, thus an {a red$_{29}$ item} perception.

115. But the case of shape was crucial. Berkeley clearly would not wish to say that a perception of a triangle is a triangle. Obviously not in the metaphysically interesting sense in which the surfaces of material objects (the "unthinking things" of the "Materialist") might be triangular. Nor, of course, does he think that a perception of a triangle can be a triangle in the sense in which, on his own positive view, the triangle on the blackboard[48] is a triangle. And failing to realize that it could be an {a triangular item} perception without being a triangular item, he, like Descartes, opts for the alternative that it [is]

293

a triangular item, i.e., (equivalently) that it is an [a triangular item] perception. Like Descartes he assimilates the being-for-sense of a triangular item to the being-for-the-understanding of a triangular item.

> . . . It may perhaps be objected, that if extension and figure exist only in the mind it follows that the mind is extended and figured; since extension is a mode or attribute, which (to speak with the Schools) is predicated of the subject in which it exists. I answer, those qualities are in the mind only as they are perceived by it, that is, not by way of *mode* or *attribute*, but only by way of idea; and it no more follows that the soul or mind is extended because extension exists in it alone, than it does that it is red or blue, because these colors are on all hands acknowledged to exist in it, and no where else.[49]

116. Yet compared with Berkeley, Descartes was clear about the difference between being for sense and being for the understanding. Berkeley *blithely* puts all ideas, including sensations and images, in the understanding.[50] The inevitable result was to collapse the delicate unity of the being-for-the-understanding of *this red triangle* and the being-for-sense of a red triangle in an ostensible seeing of a red triangle, into the being-for-the-understanding of a determinately red and triangular item as such —without any of the signs of discomfort manifested by Descartes' appeal to naïve childhood beliefs, *from childhood*.

IX

117. Now if one is aware of the relevant distinctions, he need find no immediate discomfort in the idea that the *conceptual* aspect of an ostensible seeing *of a red triangle as such* might have a *determinable* content. Why might it not involve generic concepts of *red* and *triangular*, and have as its content *this red and triangular item* without having this content in a *determinate* form, for example, *this red$_{29}$ and triangular$_{30}$ item*? After all, it might be argued, the content of a non-perceptual thought can be simply *an angel dancing on the point of a pin* as contrasted with, for example, *a blue-eyed, etc., seraph*

294

waltzing thus-and-so-ly on the point of a pin made of brass, etc.

118. At this point a venerable ghost returns to haunt us. Must not an individual act of the understanding have a *determinate* character?—a vexing problem in classical philosophies of mind, as unavoidable as it was insoluble. Suppose there to be an act which is a thinking of a triangle, but not of a determinate sort of triangle. Would the act, exactly insofar as it is *of a triangle*, have a determinate character? Surely the character of an act that really exists must be determinate in all respects. Can being *of* something *generic*, thus being an [a triangular item . . .] be a *specific* feature of the total character of a mental act? If one thinks that the specific features of a mental act, α, must be, so to speak, 'qualities' that are quasi-perceptually discerned by the mind's eye, one will be puzzled. Finding no such specific features, one will be confronted by two alternatives: (a) Hold that acts of the understanding, while having a determinate character *in other respects*, need only, with respect to what they are *of*, have the character of *being of it*. From this point of view

α [is] a triangle

could be true without, for example,

α [is] a triangle$_{30}$

being true. Or, using intentional predicates instead of the intentional copula,

α is an [a triangle] act

could be true even though no attempt was made to construe '[a triangle]' as somehow a determinate predicate, nor to argue that

α is an [a triangle$_{30}$] act

must also be true, where '[a triangle$_{30}$]' is supposed to be a determinate predicate.[51] (b) Continue to insist, on general metaphysical grounds, that even with respect to what it is of, an act of the understanding must have a determinate character, and ostensibly *find* this character in the rich internal structure of minimal perceptual takings, and the imaginings that are their free-floating cousins.

295

119. Of these two alternatives, it is fair to say Descartes and, in general, the Platonic tradition adopts the former. Berkeley, on the other hand, clearly opts for the latter. It is important, however, to see that in rejecting abstract general ideas, Berkeley is essentially following in Aristotelian footsteps.

X

120. How, then, according to Berkeley, do we think of a triangle simply as such, if there is no such thing as a mental state that can be said to be *of a triangle as a triangle* without being *of some specific kind of triangle as of that specific kind*? The first step in the answer is the Aristotelian one that we apprehend the common (generic or specific) in a *phantasm*, i.e., a direct representation of an individual, the content of which is completely specific.[52] This approach, tidily carried out, requires a distinction between two kinds of mental states: (a) phantasms having determinate content; (b) acts of 'noticing', 'considering', and 'making use of' more of less generic features of that content.

121. According to the type of view we are considering, in order for the understanding to be aware of something *as* generically a triangle, it must begin with a representation of a *determinate* kind of triangle *as a triangle of that determinate kind*, e.g., *of a triangular$_{30}$ item as triangular$_{30}$*. It can then consider the triangular$_{30}$ item in its generic character as triangular. For the contents of phantasms *have* generic features, even though these features cannot occur other than as features of more specific contents.[53]

122. It is important to note that when Berkeley insists that all ideas are particular, he is *not* insisting that all ideas are 'particulars' in the contemporary sense of the term. He does, of course, think that ideas as modifications of mind are dependent individuals, individuated by the minds that have them, their place in the temporal order, and the sorts to which they belong. But the particularity he primarily has in mind concerns not the *individuation* of an idea but the absolute *determinateness* of its content, i.e., of the sort to which it belongs. Thus two

ideas that are of a red$_{29}$ triangle$_{30}$ are in the relevant sense particular, not by virtue of the individuation by which they are *two*, but by virtue of the fact that their content is determinate. They are both of exactly the same determinate sort by virtue of the fact that each is *of a red$_{29}$ triangle$_{30}$*.

123. Consider, now, two idea-occurrences, one of a red$_{29}$ triangle$_{30}$, the other of a red$_{29}$ triangle$_{15}$. They are, of course, not of the same determinate sort with respect to shape, but they are of the same generic sort, for each of them is *of* a triangle of *a* determinate sort. Either idea, then, can be the occasion on which one becomes aware of a triangle simply as a triangle. In the first case one begins, so to speak, by being aware of a triangle$_{30}$ as a triangle$_{30}$ and proceeds to 'notice' that generic feature of its content by virtue of which it is *of a triangle*. In the second case the point of departure is different (an awareness of a triangle$_{15}$ as a triangle$_{15}$), but here also the generic feature by virtue of which its content as a triangle-content is 'noticed'.

124. It is at this point that Berkeley makes the move that reveals the hollowness of his strategy. It is not, however, the silly move that is usually attributed to him, i.e., the view that a mental reference to items having a common character, determinable or determinate, consists in a certain 'use' of an item that actually has this character; for example, a determinately triangular item, say an equilateral triangle, which item is *somehow* 'mind dependent', to 'represent' all items that are, in some respect, of the same sort—thus, all equilateral triangles or all isosceles triangles or all triangles or even all shaped items. As has been repeatedly pointed out by Berkeley's critics, such an account would be obviously circular, presupposing an awareness of the item *as* an equilateral triangle, as an isosceles triangle, *as* a triangle, *as* having shape and hence, in the relevant sense, an awareness of common characters.

125. The crucial point is that for Berkeley an idea of an equilateral triangle is *not* simply a 'mind dependent' equilateral triangle—though, properly understood, it is that. It is an awareness of an equilateral triangle *as such*, a conflation of an equilateral triangle of which the *esse* is *being sensed* with a conceptual awareness of the form [this equilateral triangle].

Berkeley's problem is not that of constructing an awareness of sorts out of an awareness of 'mind dependent' entities having color and shape. Ideas are *ab initio* awareness of items *as determinately shaped and colored.* His problem was rather that of accounting for our awareness of *generic* sorts without acknowledging mental states that are merely of the generic as such.

126.　Thus Berkeley *begins* with the assumption that we can be aware of a triangle$_{30}$ not only *as a triangle$_{30}$* but *as (generically) a triangle.*[54] He then takes it for granted that this provides the key to understanding how we can think of *any item* (or *all items*) of the same sort, determinable or determinate, as the item that is the content of a given idea-occasion. It enables us to understand how, given an idea of a triangle$_{30}$, we can think of all triangles$_{30}$, of all isosceles triangles (supposing triangularity$_{30}$ to be a determinate form of isosceles triangularity), and, even, of all triangles. Berkeley put this, of course, in terms of thinking of all *ideas* of the same sort (as the given idea-occasion),[55] but it must be remembered that the content of an idea is not really distinct from the idea-occasion of which it is the content. Counting contents is counting kinds; counting idea-occasions is counting individuals belonging to a kind. Two idea-occasions can be the same (in kind) without being the same *idea-occasion.*

127.　In the example Berkeley offers to illustrate his theory of general ideas,[56] the structure of the argument is obscured. Using as an example of a particular idea, "a black line of an inch in length" drawn by a geometrician, presumably on a piece of paper, the *particularity* of the line, which consists in its *specific* character of being one inch in length (as contrasted, for example, with two inches in length), is not distinguished with the necessary care from its *individuality* as *this* black line, one inch in length, on *this* piece of paper. In his attempt to speak with the vulgar, Berkeley has blurred an essential distinction.

128.　Once he returns to the language of the learned, Berkeley makes his point correctly:

. . . Thus, when I demonstrate any propositions concerning triangles, it is to be supposed that I have in view the universal idea of a triangle; which ought not to be understood as if I could frame an idea of a triangle which was neither equilateral, nor scalenon, nor equicrural. But only that the particular triangle I consider whether of this or that sort it matters not, doth equally stand for and represent all rectilinear triangles whatsoever, and is, in that sense, universal.

XVI. *Objection.—Answer.* But here it will be demanded, *how we can know any proposition to be true of all particular triangles, except* we have first seen it *demonstrated of the abstract idea of a triangle* which equally agrees to all? For, because a property may be demonstrated to agree to some one particular triangle, it will not thence follow that it equally belongs to any other triangle, which in all respects is not the same with it. For example, having demonstrated that the three angles of an isosceles rectangular triangle are equal to two right ones, I cannot therefore conclude this affection agrees to all other triangles, which have neither a right angle, nor two equal sides. It seems therefore that to be certain this proposition is universally true, we must either make a particular demonstration for every particular triangle, which is impossible, or once for all demonstrate it of the *abstract idea of a triangle*, in which all the particulars do indifferently partake, and by which they are all equally represented. To which I make answer, that though the idea I have in view whilst I make the demonstration, be, for instance, that of an isosceles rectangular triangle, whose sides are of a determinate length, I may nevertheless be certain it extends to all other rectilinear triangles, of what sort or bigness soever.[57]

It is surely clear that in this passage this term 'particular' means *absolutely specific or determinate*, rather than *individual*, and that when he writes that "[the demonstration] extends to all other rectilinear triangles, of whatever sort or bigness soever," the reference to "all other rectilinear triangles" is *directly* to *all other determinate sorts of triangle*, and only derivatively to all *individual* triangles of these sorts.

129. The nagging question remains, however: How, on Berkeley's principles, can there be an act of the understanding that has as its content either

Any (all) idea(s) of a triangle is an (are) idea(s) of an item which has the area $= 1/2$ bh

or

Any (all) triangle(s) has (have) an area $= 1/2$ bh?

299

The point is a simple one. The 'grammatical' subject of such a propositional act is an act-element that corresponds to a *referring* expression of the form 'any ϕ' (or 'all ϕs') where 'ϕ' stands either for the generic character of being an occurrent idea of a triangle or the generic character of being a triangle-content. Is the feature by virtue of which this act-element has such a generic reference a determinate feature? The problem of the determinateness of acts of generic reference has simply been postponed.

130. It is at this point that one can appreciate Hume's attempt to replace ostensible mental acts that refer to all ideas of the same *generic* sort by associative connections between determinate *ideas* and generic *words*, so that the only acts of the *understanding* involved in the awareness of the generic would be 'particular' idea-occasions, that is, idea-occasions with determinate content. Unfortunately, as should be obvious, the problem of accounting for mental reference to all items that are *generically* of the same sort is but a special case of the more general problem of accounting for mental reference to all ϕs, no matter how determinate ϕ may be. To explore the confusions that made it possible for Berkeley and, for that matter, Hume to suppose that they had clarified *this* aspect of the activity of the understanding will be the concluding topic of this essay.

131. The sophisticated Aristotelians of the late scholastic period, with their keen sense of logical form,[58] were, of course, not unaware of this problem. As a result they were less strident than was Berkeley in what they had to say about those acts of the understanding that ostensibly have a merely generic character. They realized that even though, in their opinion, there might be good empiricist reasons for tying generic (not to mention analogical) intellectual references to features of the determinate contents of phantasm-occasions, this tie-in provides by itself no *explication* of the concept of general reference to all items of the same sort, whether generic or specific.

XI

132. A final sharpening of tools. If, as is reasonable, one takes it to be a *part* of the truth about generic or determinable

characters that they are exclusive disjunctions of specific or determinate characters,[59] it would follow that one could not be aware of something as having a generic character without being *implicitly* aware of it as having one or other, though not more than one, of the determinate characters that belong to the appropriate family. By 'implicitly aware' I mean, for present purposes, aware as one is aware of a person's being unmarried by virtue of being aware that he is a bachelor.

133. Implicit awareness, of course, should not be construed in quasi-perceptual terms. But to take, as Berkeley did, as one's paradigm for being aware of something *as of a certain character*, the state of seeming to see (or imagining) a triangular item as such, enables the fact that the *non-conceptual* aspect of the state must be of a determinate character to mobilize the above partial truth about generic characters in a way that enriches the confusions involved in the concept of an idea.

134. Thus the fact that a mind in which there occurs a conceptual act, α, with a generic content,

α is [this triangle]

is 'implicitly aware' of 'the' triangle *as either isosceles or scalene*, in that there is 'available' to that mind a further act that is [that isosceles or scalene triangle . . .],[60] is bred to the fact that a sensation or image, s, can't be an {a triangle} state without being an {isosceles triangle} state or an {a scalene triangle} state and, in the last analysis, an {a triangle$_1$} state or an {a triangle$_2$} state, and so on.[61] The result is the conviction that the awareness of a triangular item as such is always, at least in the first instance, an awareness of a *determinately* triangular item as such. For the fact that in its *sensory* aspect the seeming to see or imagining must be a sensation or image of a determinate triangle, that is, must be, for example, {a triangle$_{30}$}, leads, by a confusion of sensory of-ness with conceptual of-ness, to the conclusion that the seeming to see (or imagining) must be, at least in the first instance, an awareness of a triangle$_{30}$ *as a triangle$_{30}$*, which implies that in its *conceptual* aspect it is [this triangle$_{30}$].

135. As I see it, then, one element involved in the mass of confusions that is the Berkeleian theory of ideas is the confu-

sion between an awareness of a disjunction and a disjunction of awareness,[62] which leads to the notion that the awareness of a generically triangular item as generically triangular must be an awareness of a triangle of *one* of the disjunction of determinate sorts *as of that determinate sort*. The fact that an awareness of the generic is 'implicitly' an awareness of an exclusive disjunction of specifics, e.g., that the awareness of an item as generically triangular is 'implicitly' an awareness of an item *as either isosceles or scalene*, has been confused with the fact that a sensory state that has a generic sensory character, e.g., is of a triangular item, i.e., is {a triangular item}, must have one (and only one) of the specific characters falling under that genus, i.e., must be *either* {an isosceles triangle} or {a scalene triangle}.

XII

136. One final ingredient of the witches' brew, certainly not the least interesting one, remains to be isolated. Notice that the *predicates* that apply to sensory states are constructed from expressions that, though they *contain* predicates, are actually *referring* expressions. Thus, the expression 'a triangle', which occurs as a predicate in

This is a triangle

occurs as an indefinite referring expression in

A triangle is on the blackboard

and as a general referring expression in

A triangle is a relatively simple construction.

137. Now a sensation of a triangle owes its classification as an *of a triangle* sensation—an {a triangle} sensation—to the fact that it is, according to the explanatory framework of sensations, of a kind normally brought about by the presence of *a triangle*, and that the conceptual space of its intrinsic attributes is analogous to that of the attributes of *a triangle*. (Note the indefinite references!)

138. Furthermore, the conceptual aspect of a seeming to see, e.g., that by virtue of which it is an awareness *of a triangle as a triangle*, is its aspect as a [this triangle] awareness. It is a mental *reference* and though, correctly understood, it is a singular-demonstrative reference, it is not improper, provided one is careful, to characterize it informally as 'a reference to a triangle'. The indefinite article keeps the question 'reference to *which* triangle?' sufficiently at bay to make comfortable, even in this case, the material mode of speech use of the rubric 'reference to . . . ' to *classify* referential expressions and mental acts, rather than *to make references*.

139. The phrase 'a triangle' as it occurs in the description of a seeming to see is thus available as a verbal bridge to the idea that the mental state in question *contains* a general reference to triangles. The verbal bridge is indeed a strong one, since both the conceptual and the sensory aspects of the seeming to see (or imagining) are described by the use of the referring expression 'a triangle'.

XIII

140. With the addition of this final ingredient we can now understand how the confusing of the conceptual and the sensory aspects of a seeming to see generates the following properties of a Berkeleian 'idea.'

(1a) The idea is of a determinately triangular (e.g., $triangular_{30}$) item; it cannot be an {a triangular item} idea without being, e.g., an {a $triangular_{30}$ item} idea.

(1b) The idea is of a $triangular_{30}$ item *as such*; it is a [this $triangular_{30}$ item] idea.

(2a) The idea is of an item that is generically triangular by virtue of being of an item that is triangular in some specific way (e.g., $triangular_{30}$); the idea is an {a triangular item} idea because it is an {a $triangular_{30}$ item} idea.

303

(2b)   The idea is of an item that is generically triangular *as such* by virtue of being of an item that is specifically triangular$_{30}$ as such; the idea is a [this triangular item] idea by virtue of being a [this triangular$_{30}$ item] idea.

Here we can put our finger on a key symptom of the confusion. For while being {a triangular$_{30}$ item} is, indeed, a determinate form of being {a triangular item}, the same is not true at the conceptual level, i.e., using the corresponding bracketed expressions. The latter are, indeed, interestingly related, but nothing that is [a triangular$_{30}$ item] can also be [a triangular item]—any more than a linguistic inscription can be a token of both 'a triangular$_{30}$ item' and 'a triangular item'.

141.   Notice that the confusion involves treating being aware *of a triangular$_{30}$ item as a triangular$_{30}$ item* as a species of being aware *of a triangular item as a triangular item*. For once one sees that this is not the case, one would have to fall back on the thesis that a mind which is aware *of a triangular$_{30}$ item as triangular$_{30}$* is only 'implicitly' aware *of a triangular item as triangular*, i.e., the thesis that a thought about a triangular$_{30}$ item as triangular$_{30}$[63] is appropriately picked up by, for example, a thought about a triangular item as triangular.[64]

142.   It is worth pausing to notice that the distinctions we have been drawing throw light on the internal structure of the Berkeleian (and Aristotelian) theory of geometrical knowledge. Thus, to continue,

(3a)   The idea is of an item that is (generically triangular by virtue of being specifically triangular$_{30}$); it is an {a (triangular because triangular$_{30}$) item} idea.[65]

(3b)   The idea is of an idea that is (generically triangular by virtue of being specifically triangular$_{30}$) *as being generically triangular because specifically triangular$_{30}$*; it is a [this (triangular because triangular$_{30}$) item] idea.

At this stage, the confusion injects an awareness of logical connections into ideas. Since, as has been emphasized, Berkeley's confusions are simply a special case of confusions endemic to the

Aristotelian tradition, we have put our finger both on the source of the plausibility of theories of geometrical knowledge based on a concept of 'intuitive induction', and on the explanation of Berkeley's conviction that his account of geometrical knowledge was unproblematic.[66] Thus,

(4a) The idea is of an item that is (equilateral because equiangular); it is an {an (equilateral because equiangular) item} idea.

(4) The idea is of an item that is (equilateral because equiangular) *as (equilateral because equiangular)*; it is a [this (equilateral because equiangular) item] idea.

143. But we have not yet crossed the verbal bridge described at the beginning of this section. It takes us from (1b) above to

(1c) The idea is a general reference to triangular$_{30}$ items as such; it is an [a (any, all) triangular$_{30}$ item(s) is (are) . . .] idea.

and from (2b) to

(2c) The idea is a general reference to generically triangular items as such; it is an [a (any, all) triangular item(s) is (are) . . .] idea.

XIV

144. To the extent that Berkeley saw, as through a glass darkly, that an awareness of a triangular$_{30}$ item as a triangular$_{30}$ item cannot be identical with an awareness of a triangular$_{30}$ item as triangular, or of a triangular item as triangular, he can be said to construe the latter awarenesses as somehow 'implicit' in the former, to take them as additional *aspects* of one and the same idea, aspects that can be brought to the center of the stage by such 'unproblematic' acts of the understanding as 'noticing,' 'comparing' or 'considering'.

305

145. It is at this point that the most sympathetic reader will find it difficult to contain any longer the following objection: You have gone to great trouble to explain by a dialectical depth-analysis how Berkeley *might* have come to think that ideas themselves *contain* a general reference. But is it not a simple, unblinkable fact that according to Berkeley an idea becomes general *by being used to stand for all ideas of the same sort*? Does this not directly imply a distinction between the idea (which I grant to be an awareness of a ϕ item as ϕ) and the *reference* to a (any, all) ϕ item(s)? Surely it is gratuitous to attribute to Berkeley the view that an idea-occasion that is of a triangular$_{30}$ item as triangular$_{30}$ *contains* a general reference to triangular$_{30}$ items, let alone to triangular items. Surely his view (however confused he may be) is that such an idea-occasion is simply a necessary condition for the occurrence of an *additional* act of the understanding of the form

[an (any, all) item(s) of the same sort as *this* . . .]

where for an item to be of 'the' same sort as *this* is for it to be either of the same *specific* sort, e.g., a triangular$_{30}$ item, or of the same *generic* sort, e.g., a triangular item.

146. Berkeley's point, the objector might add, is simply that although the *referring act* is other than the *idea-occasion*, it is not *really distinct* from the latter, for it could not occur in its absence, as is shown by its demonstrative reference.

147. The force of this objection is weakened when we remember that Berkeley's account of how 'particular' ideas become 'general' is that positive account he offers to replace the rejected doctrine of *abstract* general ideas. Thus it is open to us to reply that Berkeley is thinking of 'particular' ideas, i.e., idea-occasions with *determinate* content (e.g., an idea of a triangle$_{30}$), as not only an awareness of *a triangle$_{30}$ as a triangle$_{30}$*, but as a general reference to *a triangle$_{30}$*. After all, his task, as he saw it, was to explain how we come to be able to think of all items of a *generic* sort. To Berkeley (and to Hume) it is the generic or determinable that poses the problem.

148. It should also be borne in mind that the post-scho-

lastic period was not *that* clear about the distinction between *universality* (the *common*) and *generality* (general reference) on which the above objection turns—nor, for that matter, between a *character* that is most determinate 'in all respects' and an *individual*.[67]

149. The point can be brought to a focus as follows: To the extent that Berkeley confusedly thinks of ideas as *containing* a general reference to any item of a determinate sort, then no distinct act of the understanding having the logical form of general reference would need to be introduced at this level. To the extent that Berkeley confusedly thinks of an idea of a triangle$_{30}$ as not only an awareness of a triangle$_{30}$ as a triangle$_{30}$, but also as an awareness of a triangle$_{30}$ as a triangle, he can think of acts of noticing, considering, and comparing, as *simply* noticings, considerings and comparings, i.e., as lacking content of the sort possessed by idea-occasions. They would be, so to speak, acts of peering into contents that they cannot have.

150. On the other hand, Berkeley does tell us that 'particular' idea-occasions become general ideas of *generically* characterized items *as such*, by virtue of an act of the understanding that *uses* the idea-occasion to represent all idea-occasions of the same generic sort. He clearly thinks of this use as including the noticing and the considering a generic feature of the content of the idea-occasion. Does it also include a *distinct* (though not, of course, *really* distinct) act of the understanding which has the logical form

Any (all) item(s) of the same generic sort as *this* . . . ?

or should we construe the understanding as simply 'disengaging' or 'highlighting' a reference that is 'implicit' in the idea itself? After all, if the idea contains a general reference to any item of a *determinate* sort, does it not enfold a general reference to any item of the relevant *generic* sort? The answer, of course, is a disappointing "yes and no." The most we can say is that, as in the case of the other elements in his confusions, the concept of a distinct act of general reference finds explicit recognition only when the context clearly demands it.

1. *The Philosophical Works of Descartes*, trans. E. S. Haldane and G. T. R. Ross, 2 vols. (New York: Dover, 1934), 2:52–53 (hereafter cited as HR).

2. Ibid., 1:159.

3. Ibid.

4. Ibid., 1:340.

5. Ibid., 1:340–41.

6. Ibid., 1:249–50.

7. One can imagine Berkeley reading Principle LXX (ibid., 1:249) according to which "we can find no intelligible resemblance between the color which we suppose to exist in objects and what we are conscious of in our senses. . . . It is easy to allow ourselves to fall into the error of holding that what we call color in objects is something entirely resembling the color we perceive, and then supposing that we have a clear perception of what we do not perceive at all," nodding his head and saying, "Indeed, only a sensation (perception, idea) can be like a sensation (perception, idea)."

8. At least as one pyramid resembles another—for the concept or resemblance can be extended to cover all sorts of 'analogies'.

9. *Principles of Philosophy*, Part II, Principle III (HR, 1:255).

10. Ibid., Part IV, Principle CXCI (HR, 1:291); *Meditations*, VI (HR, 1:193).

11. HR, 1:193.

12. A related point concerning the "material falsity" of "the idea of cold" is made in his *Reply to Objections IV* (HR, 2:106).

13. HR, 1:250.

14. If the point is pressed, i.e., must not α have a *determinate* character by virtue of which it represents what it does, a problem is posed that will be explored in connection with Berkeley's rejection of abstract general ideas.

15. Malebranche would be a case in point, but an examination of the nature and motivations of his doctrine that we see all things in God would require the space of another essay.

16. To be sure, we might want to add that the color is 'matter' and the shape is 'form,' but this distinction, important though it is, cuts across the categories with which we are concerned in this paper.

17. Yet one can envisage a position according to which the sensation of blue, *qua* sensation, has a character, not itself triangularity, nor the character of *intending* a triangle, by virtue of which *it*, rather than the state of the pineal gland, is the direct cause of the perception of a triangle. This would naturally develop into the view, adumbrated in paragraph 36 above, that there is an 'analogical' sense of 'triangular' in which the sensation itself might actually *be* triangular.

18. HR, 1:248.

19. If this position were represented by the slogan 'the *esse* of blue is *sentiri*', the latter would be a cousin of the slogan that 'the *esse* of abstractions is *concipi*', i.e., that abstractions as such have no formal being in extra-mentality.

20. See the passage quoted in paragraph 28 above.

21. In the sense of Definition II quoted in the opening paragraph of this essay.

22. The points made in this paragraph are spelled out in my essay, "Meditations Leibniziennes," *American Philosophical Quarterly* 2 (1965):105–18, (reprinted as chapter 6 in *Philosophical Perspectives*, [Springfield, Ill.: C. C. Thomas, 1968]).

23. The essay referred to in the previous note explores certain themes that are common to Leibnitz and Spinoza by constructing a fictitious Leibnoza.

24. In this essay I shall so use the expression 'proper sensibles' that shape as well as color is a 'sensible' proper to vision.

308

25. It is customary to use the term 'veridical,' a fact that reflects the insight, not always fully appreciated, that ostensible seeings do not have explicit propositional form. Since, however, as we shall see, ostensible seeings have propositional correlates, the necessary adjustments are unproblematic.

26. Even the notion that it 'has' sensible qualities, or even that it *is*, for example, red, was watered down to the notion that it somehow 'consists' of sensible qualities. That this does violence to the very category of *quality* and makes nonsense of *relations* is a familiar story.

27. Even if the example were '*this* cat', it could have limited referential success by virtue of the fact that a pure demonstrative on the surface, e.g., 'this' in 'this is a cat' is a transformation of 'this' + [criterion], where the criterion is contextually supplied.

28. I have argued in an unpublished paper, "Givenness and Explanatory Coherence," that the referential aspect of a perceptual taking is best construed as a reference to the sensory aspect of the taking. Thus, in terms of our contrived example, the reference of

This red triangle

would be to a sensing of a red triangle. Since the latter is, of course, *not* a red triangle, the reference, thus construed involves a *miscategorizing*, and can be characterized as a 'successful' reference to the sensing only in a dramatically extended sense of the 'limited success of a reference' explored in paragraph 82 above.

29. Where failure of reference is a possibility, we should gloss 'reference' as 'ostensible reference'.

30. The following remarks stress what I have called 'same level' inference patterns. The dimension of linguistic functioning that I have called 'language-entry transition' —thus, 'This red triangle' as a response to red and triangular objects in standard conditions—involves the validity of such inference patterns as

Jones candidly uttered "This red triangle is . . . ," so, *ceteris paribus*, there is a red triangle in front of him.

There is a red triangle in standard conditions in front of Jones' open sightful eyes, so, *ceteris paribus*, he has a propensity to say, "This red triangle is. . . ." .

31. That the cluster of inferences by virtue of which an expression refers to a red triangle as such (or a bachelor as such) are open-textured and variable, and need only have a family resemblance from context to context, is the truth contained in Quine's attack on the analytic-synthetic distinction. My central concern over the years in stressing *material* rule of inference has been *not* to deny the point Quine is making—indeed, to a behavioristically oriented anti-Platonist, the denial would be foolish—but rather to insist that inference patterns other than those formulated by logical truths *are essential to meaning and reference*. That these extra-logical inference patterns do not neatly divide into 'explicit' and 'implicit' definitions, and that they trail off into contingent generalizations, are theses that have emotional charge only for those who are still fighting the battle of the Museum.

32. In general to specify the 'content' of a conceptual episode is to classify it in terms of the inference patterns appropriate to the concepts involved.

33. This is as far as Smart's topic-neutral approach gets one.

34. To refer to something as 'the' cause is, of course, to isolate it from propitious circumstances, in this case, for example, the presence (or absence) of a certain mental 'set'.

35. These qualities and relations are to be construed in what are often called

'naïvely realistic' terms. Thus physical objects are literally colored in the aesthetically interesting sense of color—as contrasted with merely having causal powers with respect to color experiences—Locke's 'secondary qualities'.

36. The Cartesian would have been well advised either to think of the 'mind' as consisting of a 'sensorium' as well as a faculty of conceptual thinking, or to stick, at least initially, with the Aristotelian conception of a person as a substance having faculties ranging from 'physical' to 'intellectual', one of which would be the ability to sense.

37. Thus, for example, a state that is {a uniform case of red} cannot also be {a uniform case of blue}.

38. HR, 1:153.

39. One cannot help but remember, in this connection, Berkeley's confusion between the idea that a feeling of intense heat is a painful feeling, and the idea that it is a feeling of pain.

40. Although, like Berkeley, one makes a brave effort to speak with the vulgar.

41. *A New Theory of Vision and Other Select Philosophical Writings*, ed. by A. D. Lindsay, (London: J. M. Dent, 1938), pp. 226 ff.

42. For a less minimal sense in which a red triangle can be an object of perception for Berkeley, see below, paragraph 107.

43. See previous footnote.

44. Both with respect to perceptible qualities and, presumably, though the point is for the most part implicit, perceptible relations to other perceived items.

45. A twentieth-century Berkeleian might demur by arguing that it does make sense to say, "That is the same pain again," where this does not simply mean the same kind of pain. In this usage the pain would be an individual in the sense in which the triangle on the blackboard is an individual. But to attribute this idea to Berkeley himself would surely be an anachronism.

46. I use 'a case of color' instead of 'a color' because the latter normally refers to shades of color.

47. To use a simpler notation which establishes connection with the widespread (but contrived) usage in which one speaks of 'red sensations'—at the cost of obscuring the logical structure of sensation predicates—it cannot be {red} without being, e.g., {red$_{29}$}.

48. In a less interesting sense an 'unthinking thing'.

49. *A Treatise Concerning the Principles of Human Knowledge*, section XLIX, pp. 136–37 (hereafter cited as *Principles*).

50. See, for example, entries, 280, 282, 286, 579, 587, and 878 in the *Philosophical Commentaries* in *The Works of George Berkeley*, vol. 1, ed. A. A. Luce and T. E. Jessop (London: Thomas Nelson, 1964).

51. We shall shortly see that it does not make sense to suppose that α might be both an [a triangle] act and an [a triangle$_{30}$] act—a fact that is only more neatly disguised by the use of the intentional copula.

52. By speaking of the representation as 'direct', I mean that it does not have the form of a definite description, e.g., 'the tallest man in London'. It is a representation of a *this-such*, where, according to the Aristotelian, the *such* aspect is not an application of a general concept but the very source of general concepts. This aspect of the Aristotelian tradition is elaborated in chapter one of my *Science and Metaphysics*. It should be noted that Kant's concept of a perceptual intuition belongs directly in this tradition, though with distinctively Kantian variations. The concept of a perceptual taking as a believing *in* also belongs to this tradition. See also my essay "Kant's Transcendental Idealism," in the *Proceedings* of the 1974 Kant Congress held in Ottawa, Canada.

310

53. Compare the view of moderate realism, according to which individuals *in rerum natura* have generic features, though these features of individuals are not themselves *individuals*, and cannot occur save as features of individuals that are completely specific in character.

54. ". . . It must be acknowledged, that a man may consider a figure merely as triangular, without attending to the particular qualities of the angles or relations of the sides" (*Principles*, XVI, p. 104).

55. ". . . An idea, which considered in itself is particular, becomes general by being made to represent or stand for all other particular ideas of the *same sort*" (Introduction to the *Principles*, XII, p. 100).

56. Ibid.

57. Ibid., XV-XVI, pp. 103-4.

58. Which soon disappeared, not to be recovered until the Kantian revolution.

59. More accurately that G-ness has the form $(S_1$ *or* S_2 *or* . . . $S_n)$-ness, where '*or*' stands for exclusive disjunction, and 'G' and 'S_i' represent generic and specific predicates of the same family.

60. Or, to climb down the ladder of determinates [this triangle_1 or triangle_2 . . . or triangle_n or . . .].

61. Notice that in classifying the *conceptual* states the 'or' occurs *inside* the brackets, whereas in classifying the *non-conceptual* states it occurs *outside* the braces.

62. One only needs to take into account the fact that 'and' and 'or' are interchangeable in certain ordinary language contexts to understand the confusion involved in Locke's unhappy (but diagnostic) reference to ". . . the general idea of a triangle . . . [which] must be neither oblique nor rectangle, neither equilateral, equicrural, nor scalenon; but all and none of these at once" (*Essay*, IV, 7,9).

63. Strictly, a thought of the [*this* triangular_{30} item . . .] kind.

64. Thus, a thought of the [*that* triangular item is . . .] kind, where the [*that*] component picks up the reference of the [*this*].

65. Compare the physical object statement, "This is a (triangular because triangular_{30}) item" can be generated, by transformation, from "This item is triangular because it is triangular_{30}."

66. Of course, Berkeley denies the 'extra-mental' existence of geometrical objects, but his theory of how we know necessary truths about geometrical objects, whatever their ontological status, is clearly in the Aristotelian tradition.

67. Thus in the absence of a clear understanding of the category of individuated substance, there was a constant temptation to construe the idea of an individual as an idea of determinates, $D_1, D_2, D_3, \ldots D_n, \ldots$, where D_1 is, for example, *white*, and the idea is the idea of a white individual, by the sheer aggregation on more elements like *white*.

Chapter Eleven

BERKELEY'S THEORY OF THE IMMEDIATE
OBJECTS OF VISION

(For H. H. Price)

The fundamental negative thesis of Berkeley's theory of vision is that distance from the perceiver is not among the immediate objects of sight. The final form of his chief argument for it is found in his dialogue *Alciphron*.[1]

> *EUPHRANOR.* Look, Alciphron, do you not see the castle upon yonder hill?
> *ALCIPHRON.* I do.
> *E.* Is it not at a great distance from you?
> *A.* It is.
> *E.* Tell me, Alciphron, is not a distance a line turned endwise to the eye?
> *A.* Doubtless.
> *E.* And can a line, in that situation, project more than one single point on the bottom of the eye?
> *A.* It can not.
> *E.* Therefore the appearance of a long and of a short distance is of the same magnitude, or rather of no magnitude at all, being in all cases one single point.
> *A.* It seems so.
> *E.* Should it not follow from hence that distance is not immediately perceived by the eye?
> *A.* It should
> *E.* Must it not then be perceived by the mediation of some other thing?
> *A.* It must.
> *E.* To discover what this is, let us examine what alteration there

may be in the appearance of the same object, placed at different distances from the eye. Now, I find by experience that when an object is removed still farther and farther off in a direct line from the eye, its visible appearance still grows lesser and fainter; and this change of appearance, being proportional and universal, seems to me to be that by which we apprehend the various degrees of distance.

A. I have nothing to object to this.

(Alc., IV, 8: III, 150–51)

Earlier versions of this argument, both less complete and less persuasive, are set out in the *New Theory of Vision* and *Three Dialogues.*[2]

My objects in this brief study are: (1) to elucidate what Berkeley, in the passage quoted, professed to prove; (2) to determine whether or not he succeeded in proving it; and (3) to ascertain what light the considerations he presented in connection with it throw on the nature of vision itself. As is often the case with the work of a great philosopher, the better Berkeley's argument is understood historically, the greater is seen to be its permanent philosophical significance.

In commenting on a paper of Karl Britton's, in which all theories of sensation in terms of non-physical objects of seeing. hearing, and the rest were summarily dismissed, H. H. Price observed that in views such as Britton's "(visual) perception [was] being abolished altogether, and something else, something to do with judging and believing, [was] being substituted in its place."[3] Berkeley discerned a similar philosophical tendency in his own predecessors and contemporaries; and he ascribed it to "the snares of popular language," which betray us into saying things that are "strictly speaking neither true nor consistent" (*TVV*, 35: I, 263). "In the contrivance of vision," he wryly noted, ". . . Providence seemeth to have consulted the operation, rather than the theory, of man; to the former things are admirably fitted, but, by that very means, the latter is often perplexed" (*TVV*, 36: I, 263).

To remove these perplexities, Berkeley argues that it is necessary to distinguish three "lights" in which, for different purposes, vision may be considered:

313

1. the geometrical, treating of "the application of lines and angles for *praxis* or theory, in dioptric glasses and mirrours" (*TVV*, 37: I, 264);

2. the physical, treating of "the eye, nerve, coats, humours, refractions, bodily nature, and motion of light" (*TVV*, 37: I, 264); and

3. the philosophical, treating of the nature of vision itself.

He explains why as follows.

> To explain how the mind or soul simply sees is one thing, and belongs to philosophy. To consider particles moving in certain lines, rays of light as refracted or reflected, or crossing, or including angles, is quite another thing, and appertaineth to geometry. To account for the mechanism of the eye is a third thing, which appertaineth to anatomy and experiments. These two latter speculations are of use in practice, to assist the defects and remedy the distempers of sight. . . . But the former theory is that which makes us understand the true nature of vision, considered as a faculty of the soul. (*TVV*, 43: I, 266)

Seeing is not to be confounded with the physical conditions (treated in geometrical optics), or with the bodily mechanisms (treated in anatomy and physiology), that make it possible. What, then, is it?

Perhaps the most fundamental distinction Berkeley draws in developing his philosophical theory of the true nature of vision, considered as a faculty of the soul, is that between seeing and other forms of sensation on one side, and on the other intellect or understanding, the chief functions of which are judging and inferring. He made it explicit in the *Theory of Vision Vindicated*: "To perceive is one thing; to judge is another. So likewise, to be suggested is one thing, and to be inferred another. Things are suggested and perceived by sense. We make judgments and inferences by the understanding" (*TVV*, 42: I, 265). It follows that seeing something is not the same as making a perceptual judgment on the basis of seeing it. It is one thing to see a patch of red color, and another to judge either that a red patch is before you, or that you are seeing it. In addition, it is one thing for something to be seen (or perceived by sight), and another for it to be suggested by something seen.

Most philosophers today who, like F. I. Dretske, distinguish between seeing proper and perceptual judgment, hold that seeing proper is non-epistemic.[4] Berkeley does not: "The real objects of sight [he declares] we see, and what we see we know. And these true objects of sense and knowledge, to wit, our own ideas, are to be considered, compared, distinguished, in order to understand the true theory of vision" (*TVV*, 20: I, 258). There is a knowledge of objects of sense that is not analyzable as knowledge *that* they are such and such; for all knowledge *that* is a matter of judgment, and to see is one thing, to judge is another.

What are these "real" or "true" objects of sight, which must be "considered, compared, distinguished" in order to understand the true theory of vision? It is not in question that they are objects of the first sort Berkeley refers to in the *New Theory of Vision* when he maintains that

> in order to treat accurately and unconfusedly of vision, we must bear in mind that there are two sorts of objects apprehended by the eye, the one primarily and immediately, the other secondarily and by intervention of the former. Those of the first sort neither are, nor appear to be . . . at any distance off; they may indeed grow greater or smaller, more confused, or more clear, or more faint, but they do not, cannot approach or recede from us. Whenever we say an object is at a distance . . . we must always mean it of the latter sort, which . . . are not so truly perceived as suggested by the eye in like manner as thoughts by the ear. (*NTV*, 50: I, 189-90)

This passage provides us with a working hypothesis about the definitions of 'immediate' and 'mediate' object of vision implicit in Berkeley's analysis: namely, that an immediate object of vision may be defined as a seen object, the seeing of which is *not* a matter of its being suggested by something else that is seen; and that a mediate object of vision may be defined as a seen object, the seeing of which *is* a matter of its being suggested by something else that is seen. These definitions do not exclude the possibility that the same object may be, in different circumstances, both an immediate and a mediate object of vision.

To a normally sighted witness in broad daylight, the red color of human blood is something the seeing of which is not a matter of its being suggested by something else that is seen; but at dusk, when chromatic differences are hard to see, it may be suggested as being the color of the fluid seen to flow from a human wound.

A further working hypothesis is supported, although not conclusively verified, by Berkeley's distinction between perception and judgment: namely, that mediate objects of vision are, strictly speaking, objects of judgment. A mediate object of sight is one the seeing of which is a matter of its being suggested by something else that is seen. And *prima facie*, the suggestion made by the seen object is taken up, not by the visive faculty, but by the faculty of understanding. To take a suggestion is an act of judgment. This is confirmed by the way in which Berkeley sums up the conclusion of his first set of arguments in the *New Theory of Vision* about the seeing of distance.

> The judgment we make of the distance of an object, viewed with both eyes, is entirely the result of experience. If we had not constantly found certain sensations arising from the various disposition of the eyes, attended with various degrees of distance, we should never make those sudden judgments from them concerning the distance of objects; no more than we would pretend to judge of a man's thoughts by his pronouncing words we had never heard before. (*NTV*, 20: I, 175)

Here Berkeley unmistakably presents the taking of a suggestion prompted by a seen object, in conjunction with kinesthetic sensations in the muscles of the eyes, as a "sudden" act of judgment.

Berkeley's analogy between the various senses and different languages provides further confirmation of the hypothesis that he conceived mediate objects of vision as, strictly speaking, objects of judgment. Several commentators, above all Colin Murray Turbayne, have pointed out that this analogy, which is a cardinal tenet in the explicit immaterialism of the *Principles of Human Knowledge* and *Alciphron*, is also fundamental to the *New Theory of Vision.*[5] In *The Theory of Vision Vindicated*, Berkeley

316

described the conclusion of the *New Theory* in terms of it: namely, as being that "*Vision is the Language of the Author of Nature*" (*TVV*, 38: I, 264). He explained what he meant as follows:

> A great number of arbitrary signs, various and apposite, do constitute a language. If such arbitrary connexion be instituted by men, it is an artificial language; if by the Author of nature, it is a natural language. Infinitely various are the modifications of light and sound, whence they are each capable of supplying an endless variety of signs, and accordingly, have been each employed to form languages; the one by the arbitrary appointment of mankind, the other by that of God himself. A connexion established by the Author of nature, in the ordinary course of things, may surely be called natural; as that made by men will be named artificial. And yet this doth not hinder that the one may be as arbitrary as the other. (*TVV*, 40: I, 265)

Artificial languages such as Latin or English assign different meanings to different morphemes (visible) and phonemes (audible). A morpheme or phoneme of English suggests to a speaker of English whatever significance is arbitrarily assigned to it in English. In seeing or hearing it, he makes a sudden judgment as to that significance. Berkeley's position is that the various things that, by virtue of experience, the immediate objects of vision and hearing suggest to us are significances assigned to them, with equal arbitrariness, by the Author of nature. The sudden judgments by which we appreciate those significances are identical in kind with the sudden judgments by which we grasp the significances of words in the artificial language we speak. For, since it is not in question that the significances of words in artificial languages are grasped by acts of judgment, it follows that grasping what is suggested by an immediate object of vision or hearing must also be an act of judgment.

Provisionally assuming that our working hypotheses are true, that the definitions of 'immediate' and 'mediate' objects of vision we extracted from Berkeley's writings are in fact presupposed in them, and that he did in fact take mediate objects of vision to be,

317

strictly speaking, objects of judgment, does the argument from *Alciphron* with which we began succeed in establishing that distance from himself is not an immediate object of a perceiver's vision, but a mediate one?

That argument becomes easier to understand in the light of his views about what the immediate objects of vision are. His fullest pronouncement on the question is in the *New Theory of Vision*:

> All that is properly perceived by the visive faculty amounts to no more than colours, with their variations and different proportions of light and shade. . . . There are divers of [these objects] perceived at once, and more of some and less of others: But accurately to compute their magnitude and assign precise determinate proportions between things so variable and inconstant, if we suppose it possible to be done, must yet be a very trifling and insignificant labour. (*NTV*, 156: I, 234)

This passage is echoed in the *Theory of Vision Vindicated*:

> The proper, immediate object of vision is light, in all its modes and variations, various colours in kind, in degree, in quantity; some lively, others faint; more of some and less of others; various in their bounds and limits; various in their order and situation. (*TVV*, 44: I, 266)

Naturally interpreted, in these cardinal passages Berkeley is asserting that the whole of what a perceiver immediately sees at a given moment is a manifold ("divers of [these objects] perceived at once"), consisting of colored shapes ("colours" having "bounds and limits"), each having a definite size ("more of some and less of others") and position relative to the others ("various in their order and situation"), and each being more or less bright and more or less intense ("various . . . in degree, in quantity").

Although he lays down no exact conditions of identity through time, Berkeley in one place or another refers to immediate objects of vision (that is, colored shapes) as remaining the same while undergoing changes with respect to every immediately visible property: hue, shape, size, relative position, brightness, and intensity. This is not careless. That immediate objects of vision normally change rapidly and continuously is one of his chief reasons for denying that they are what geometry is about: "the perpetual *mutability* and fleetingness of these immediate objects of sight render them incapable of being managed after the manner of geometrical figures" (*NTV*, 156: I, 234; my emphasis). A continuant can be an object for geometry only inasmuch as its geometrical properties remain the same.[6]

What *kinds* of shape does Berkeley take the immediate objects of vision to be? Some of his pronouncements on this question, and his arguments for them, are perplexing:

> What we strictly see are not solids, nor yet plains variously coloured; they are only diversity of colours. And some of these suggest to the mind solids, and others plain figures, as they have been experienced to be connected with the one or with the other. . . . (*NTV*, 158: I, 235)

Both planeness or flatness (cf. *NTV*, 157: I, 234) and solidity are here implicitly declared to be mediate objects of vision. But how is this consistent with Berkeley's earlier statements that the immediate objects of vision have shape or "figure"? A shape or figure necessarily has two or more dimensions: that is, the points on its boundary are specifiable by reference to two or more coordinates. What is not so specifiable has no definite shape at all. Must not a visible shape then be geometrical? Furthermore, Berkeley himself describes the "visible moon," that is, my immediate object of vision when I mediately see the moon, as "a round, luminous plain of about thirty visible points in diameter,"[7] and again, as "a small, round, luminous flat" (*NTV*, 44: I, 187). Is this too a contradiction?

Both inconsistencies are only apparent. For Berkeley explains that the planeness or flatness that he denies the immediate objects of vision to have is geometrical; and he further explains that geometrical planeness or flatness is a property of certain objects in three-dimensional space. "The first elements of plain geometry," he observes, require the use of "the rule and compass" in constructing straight lines and circles; and proofs of the equality of angles and plane figures require "the placing of one plain or angle on another," all of which are operations in three-dimensional space. He even goes on to declare that "some idea of distance [i.e., depth] is necessary to form the idea of a geometrical plain, as will appear to whoever shall reflect on it," perhaps having in mind the definition of a plane as a two-dimensional surface of zero curvature (*NTV*, 155: I, 234). In short, his assertion that the immediate objects of vision "are of a nature intirely different" from geometrical planes as well as from geometrical solids implies no more than that they are neither planes nor solids in three dimensional space (cf. *NTV*, 158: I, 235). It is perfectly compatible with their being non-geometrically flat, in the sense of being two-dimensional figures that are not in three-dimensional space at all; and it is in that sense that he describes the visible moon as flat.

Hence it would be a serious mistake to portray Berkeley as holding that the immediate objects of vision are indeterminate with respect to geometrical planeness or solidity. He consistently holds that they are neither. Nor are they two-dimensional objects whose geometrical shape is indeterminate, neither their curvature nor their angle to the line of sight being determinate. They cannot be geometrically indeterminate in these ways, because they are not in three-dimensional space at all. Since, in Berkeley's view, visual space is two-dimensional and so non-geometrical, questions about its curvature or angle to the line of sight are absurd. Visual space has no spatial relation to the three-dimensional space of geometry. Hence, unlike two-dimensional geometrical figures, whose flatness or otherwise is contingent upon whether the surface on which they are inscribed is planar, Berkeley's immediate objects of vision are necessarily flat.[8]

I do not think that it has ever been questioned that, if there are immediate objects of vision in Berkeley's sense, then colored shapes, more or less bright, and more or less intense, are among them. If it is agreed that there are such objects, what is disputable in Berkeley's theory of them is that they are all two-dimensional. Why should not distance from the perceiver be such an object?

With these preliminaries in mind, let us return to the argument in *Alciphron* with which we began (IV, 8: III, 150). Notwithstanding its apparent simplicity, it draws upon presuppositions of seventeenth- and eighteenth-century visual theory that are by no means obvious, for which Berkeley's immediate sources were Locke and Molyneux. It is important not to forget that what is now most controversial in Berkeley's theory, his doctrine that distance is not immediately seen, was the received opinion among his more sophisticated contemporaries.

Indeed, the whole argument quoted from *Alciphron* no more than amplifies a statement by Molyneux in his *Dioptrika Nova* (London, 1692), which Nicholas Pastore has labeled "Molyneux's Premise."[9] In Molyneux's words, it is that "*distance* of itself, is not to be perceived; for 'tis a line (or a length) presented to our eye with its end toward us, which must therefore be only a *point*, and that is *invisible*" (*Dioptrika Nova*, prop. 32). This "premise" is really an argument: because distance presents only a point to our eye, and because a point is invisible, therefore distance of itself is not to be perceived. In the *New Theory of Vision* Berkeley adds nothing significant to it (cf. *NTV*, 2: I, 171). But in *Alciphron* he makes its character clearer. He begins by presenting Molyneux's physical premise separately:

(P_1) Distance, being a line turned endwise to the eye, cannot project more than one single point on the bottom of the eye. (cf. *Alc.* IV, 8: III, 150)

And he presents his premise about what is seen as a conclusion inferred from the physical premise:

(*C*) Therefore the appearance of a long and of a short distance is of the same magnitude, or rather of no magnitude at all, being in all cases one single point. (*Alc.* IV, 8: III, 150)

Now since (*C*) evidently does not follow logically from (P_1), Berkeley's argument, '(P_1), therefore (*C*)', is an enthymeme. Its suppressed premise, however, is easily restored. It would be something equivalent to:

321

(P_2) If two seen objects project images of equal magnitude on the bottom of the eye, then their appearances, that is, the immediate objects of vision by which they are seen, will be of equal magnitude.

(P_2) is a special form of what, following Köhler, has become known as the "constancy hypothesis," namely, that the spatial properties of objects (immediately) seen correspond to the spatial properties of the retinal images by means of which they are seen.

If Berkeley's theory of the relation of the mediate objects of vision to the immediate were an attempt to solve a problem in information theory, plausible arguments for (P_2), and for more general forms of the constancy hypothesis, could be found. Berkeley presented his immaterialism as an intelligible metaphysical account of the results of natural science, not as a denial of them; and it is a possible scientific position that all the information received by man's "visive faculty" is, in Berkeley's word, "intromitted" by the irradiation of the retina. If that should be so, and if Berkeley's problem was how a perceiver can proceed from information received to what that information suggests, then what he calls the immediate objects of vision, the information received by the visive faculty, will presumably correspond to the images upon the retina, since it is through them that that information is transmitted. Ascribing to Berkeley this information-theoretic version of the constancy hypothesis, Thrane has interpreted his argument as being that, since all information received by the visive faculty is intromitted by means of the retinal images, and since the retina is sensitive to nothing except the physical counterpart of a two-dimensional array of colors, and of their intensity and hue, the visive faculty itself can receive no more than a corresponding two-dimensional array.[10]

Interpreted in this information-theoretic way, Berkeley's argument is extremely persuasive. And I am inclined to think that he himself at least sometimes so understood it; for I find it difficult to explain, on any other hypothesis, why he regarded its soundness as obvious. Yet, on his own methodological principles, he ought not to have offered it.

He himself laid it down that the true nature of vision, considered as a faculty of the soul, can be understood only if it is viewed in a philosophical "light," as distinct from a geometrical or a physical one. Of course, when Berkeley wrote, "philosophical" did not mean anything distinct from "scientific": his point was simply that there is a direct philosophic-scientific procedure for investigating what the nature of vision is, as distinct from what are its physical conditions, or the bodily mechanisms that make it possible. We need not suppose that if, in investigating any particular problem about the true nature of vision, the direct "philosophical" method should fail, Berkeley would have denied that a "philosopher" might legitimately seek whatever indirect help optics, anatomy, and physiology may furnish. However, it may be remarked that, even in his late *Theory of Vision Vindicated*, the only use he explicitly acknowledges geometry or "anatomy and experiments" to have is practical: "to assist the defects and remedy the distempers of sight" (*TVV*, 43: I, 266).

It is a matter of geometry that distance from a perceiver can project only a point on his retina. And it is established by a combination of direct "philosophical" inquiry into what we see, and of "anatomy and experiments" (including what we now call physiology), that in general, we immediately see what we do by means of our retinal images. But that is not enough to establish Berkeley's tacit premise P_2, that the magnitude of every object that is immediately seen corresponds to the magnitude of some element in a retinal image by means of which it is so seen, so that nothing can be immediately seen unless some element of positive magnitude in a retinal image corresponds to it. Like the general proposition that we immediately see by virtue of having retinal images, P_2 plainly has a "philosophical" side, which Berkeley's own methodology obliged him to investigate "philosophically". Such an investigation would presumably begin by attempting directly to ascertain what the various kinds of immediate objects of vision are, and would go on to determine whether to each there corresponds some element in a retinal image. Whether or not distance from the perceiver is an immediate object of vision would therefore be at issue in the very first phase of a philosophical inquiry into P_2. On his own principles, Berkeley had no right to affirm P_2, or any form of the constancy hypothesis, until he had directly shown that distance from the perceiver is not immediately seen. The fundamental objection to his argument in *Alciphron* is that he needed its conclusion in order to establish its crucial tacit premise.

Can it be shown "philosophically," in Berkeley's sense, that distance from the perceiver is not immediately seen? Although, like most empiricists, Berkeley believed that "every one is himself the best judge of what he perceives, and what not" (*NTV*, 12: I, 173), he was not unaware that, should somebody be ignorant of certain facts about himself or his situation, he may honestly make a false judgment about what he sees. Thus, a man who is red color-blind may honestly judge that he immediately sees both the distinct colors red and green, because, owing to the usual presence of "cues" other than color, he has never found any difficulty in distinguishing red from green. Yet when he takes a color-blindness test, in which he is shown a card covered with red and green spots, the red ones forming a numeral surrounded by green ones, he will truthfully report that he sees a card wholly covered with green spots.

Here it is of the first importance both to keep in mind Berkeley's distinction between seeing and judging, and to distinguish between two kinds of judgment. Berkeley was chiefly concerned to distinguish (immediately) *seeing* something from judging that something is there on the basis of "cues" or suggestions supplied by what is immediately seen. But it is also necessary to distinguish *judging* that something is immediately seen from judging that something is there on the basis of such cues. Color-blindness tests are designed to distinguish the power to see immediately certain colors from the power to make correct judgments about what colors are there on the basis of other visual cues. And they do so by requiring the perceiver to make a judgment about what he immediately sees, while depriving him of all visual cues for making a judgment about what colors are there, except those colors themselves.

Unfortunately, it is very hard to contrive a situation in which a perceiver must make a judgment about whether or not he immediately sees a distance from himself, while depriving him

324

of all visual cues for judging whether such a distance is there, except that of distance itself. Empty three-dimensional space is invisible; virtually all objects in three-dimensional space furnish cues for judgments of distance: for example, their apparent movement in relation to one another when the perceiver moves his head, their changed appearance when viewed from different angles, the occlusion of part of one object by another, the relation of their apparent relative size to their known relative size, and their clarity or faintness.

Berkeley's confidence in the methodologically improper argument he advanced in the *New Theory* and *Alciphron* may partly explain why he contributed so little to the work of specifying visual situations in which perceivers may reliably judge whether or not they can immediately see distance. His immediate predecessors, Locke and Molyneux, defined the two problems that were to remain central to the discussion, until their solution by the work of Wheatstone, Bailey, and Helmholtz. Those problems are: (1) Can a three-dimensional object, some seen parts of which are at a greater distance than others, be visually indistinguishable from a two-dimensional object? and (2) Molyneux's problem, Can a blind person, who has learned by touch what a sphere and a cube are, on gaining his sight recognize a sphere and a cube when he sees them?

Let us consider each of these problems separately.

The first is implicit in the following remarks by Locke: "When we set before our eyes a round globe of any uniform colour, e.g., gold, alabaster, or jet, it is certain that the *idea* thereby imprinted in our mind is of a flat circle, variously shadowed, with several degrees of light and brightness coming to our eyes."[11] That Locke took the point of this example to be that a round globe of uniform color would be visually indistinguishable from a suitably shaded and placed circular disk, unless other cues led the perceiver to expect a globe to be there, is shown by his allusion to *trompe l'oeil* painting: "the *idea* we receive from [such a globe] is only a plane variously coloured, as is evident in painting."[12]

The puzzling character of Locke's example is shown by Condillac's tergiversation in his two discussions of it. In his

Essai sur l'origine des connaissances humaines (1746), according to Pastore, Condillac declared, against Locke, "For my part, when I look at a globe, I see something other than a flat circle."[13] Eight years later, however, in his *Traité des sensations* (1754), he retracted this, endorsed Locke's position, and explained his mistake on the Berkeleian ground that he had confounded a sudden judgment ultimately founded on the cooperation of sight and touch with a simple act of seeing.[14]

Condillac's vacillation confirms Locke's contention that under appropriate circumstances—when both are of the same color and uniformly illuminated, when their surroundings provide no cue as to depth, and when the perceiver sees both from the same position, the disk being at right angles to his line of vision—a globe and a disk are visually indistinguishable. Yet even if Locke were right about that case, it would not follow that distance cannot be immediately seen. The proposition that distance can be so seen does not entail that whenever a three-dimensional field is presented to sight, some distance is so seen. It does not entail, for example, that when the full moon is viewed with the naked eye, the viewer must immediately see the distance from himself between its visible centre and a point on its edge.

Another case, like Locke's except for one particular, is more enlightening. Consider an evenly lit, gray upright cube that can be viewed from only a single position, and that is fastened to a black background by a rod that it hides from view. Nine of its edges are plainly visible, as illustrated in figure one. Let us

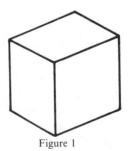

Figure 1

suppose this cube to be interchangeable with a flat hexagonal card at right angles to the line of sight, as far from the viewer as the nearest edge of the cube. This card is to have the same shape as that which the cube would project on a diaphanous screen in the same plane, as shown in figure two. Suppose now that a

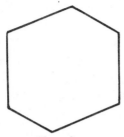

Figure 2

painter skilled at *trompe l'oeil* paints this flat card to resemble the cube, simulating the three "inner" edges. Would such a card, given that the painter captured the exact effect of the light on the inner edges, be visually indistinguishable from the cube?

It may be well at this point to remind ourselves of what our object is in asking such a question. Our interest is in what the perceiver immediately sees, not in what he judges is there. However, since it is difficult to judge what one immediately sees, as distinct from what one judges to be there, we have contrived a situation in which the perceiver has no non-visual cues, and in one case (the hexagonal card) no distance, but has some visual cues for seeing it; while in the other case (the cube) he has those same cues and distance as well. If he judges that the flat card is three-dimensional, or that the cube is two-dimensional, then it is a reasonable inference that, when he ordinarily judges that a cube is three-dimensional, he does so because of cues other than the immediate seeing of distance. If, however, he judges the dimensionality of the cube and the card correctly, it is a reasonable inference that he immediately sees the distance in depth between, say, the nearest upper corner and the farther upper corners of the cube. On what else could his judgment be founded?

It may be unnecessary to add that the phenomenon known as 'seeing as', which has attracted a good deal of attention from philosophers since the appearance of Wittgenstein's *Philosophical Investigations*, is here irrelevant. A suitably shaded and shaped hexagon may be seen as a cube, and a cube may (with rather more difficulty) be seen as its own projection on a diaphanous screen at right angles to the line of sight; but in all such cases, seeing one thing as something else goes with the capacity to see it also as it is. Seeing the vertical distance between two points on an upright two-dimensional card *as* a distance in depth between points on a horizontal surface of a solid is not *seeing* distance in depth. In many ways, it is more like imagining it.

It will not surprise you to be told that I have not carried out the test I have described, except as a *Gedankenexperiment*. However, my results in that *Gedankenexperiment*, and my reading of standard scientific works of reference on the subject (H. Davson, "Eye and Vision, Human" in *Encyclopaedia Britannica*, 15th ed., provides most of what is needed for our purposes), leave me in no doubt of what the result would be for normal binocular perceivers. They would have no difficulty in distinguishing the cube from the flat hexagon; and they would report that they *see* a distance in depth between, say, the two corners on the upper side of the righthand visible face of the cube, but only a vertical distance between the corresponding corners on the hexagon painted as a cube.

Assuming that these results would be obtained (and without carrying out the test, Berkeley would not have believed it), Berkeley's principles in the *New Theory of Vision* imply that there is a physical basis for them. And, of course, there is, although it was not uncovered until Charles Wheatstone's "Contributions to the Physiology of Vision" (*Phil. Transactions Roy. Soc.* 128 [1838]: 371–94).[16] According to Wheatstone, a cube is seen at a glance to be three-dimensional, and a flat perspective representation of a cube to be two-dimensional, because the images of the faces of the cube on the two retinas of the perceiver are not congruent and what is seen is determined by both, whereas the images of the flat perspective representations of the faces of a cube on the two retinas are congruent, so that binocularity makes no difference to what is seen. The case of a globe, however, is special. Although it is three-dimensional, it presents no faces the two retinal images of which would differ,

328

and so can be discriminated from a flat disk at right angles to the line of sight only by Berkeleian cues.[17] It should be obvious that most solid objects, like the cube, present distinguishable faces. Locke had the misfortune, or the perverse genius, to hit on a misleading exceptional case.

Let us now turn briefly to Molyneux's problem, and to a case reported by the anatomist William Cheselden, about which Berkeley should have been more wary than he was.

Molyneux posed his problem as follows:

> Suppose a man born blind, and now adult, and taught by his touch to distinguish between a cube and a sphere of the same metal, and nighly of the same bigness, so as to tell, when he felt the one and the other, which is the cube, which the sphere. Suppose then the cube and sphere placed on a table, and the blind man be made to see: *Quaere*, whether by his sight, before he touched them, he could now distinguish and tell, which is the globe, which the cube?[18]

Molyneux's own answer, which Locke endorsed, was: "Not. For, though he has obtained the experience of how a globe, how a cube affects his touch, yet he has not yet obtained the experience that what affects his touch so or so must affect his sight so or so."[19] Berkeley accepted Molyneux's "Not," but not his reason for it. In his *Philosophical Commentaries* he explained the newly sighted man's foreseen inability by the heterogeneity of visible and tangible distance, which he declared to be "demonstrated . . . from Molyneux's problem wch otherwise is falsely solvd by Locke & him."[20]

Berkeley gave his ground for rejecting Molyneux's reason for his solution as follows:

> . . . If a square surface perceived by touch be of the same sort with a square surface perceived by sight, it is certain that the blind man here mentioned might know a square surface as soon as he saw it: It is no more but introducing into his mind by a new inlet an idea he has been already well acquainted with. (*NTV*, 133: I, 225)

On this point Berkeley's criticism, although it contains a major error, is not unsound. Molyneux offered his reason, that experience of how a sphere or a cube feels is not experience of how it looks, as necessitating the prediction that a man who had only the former experience would not, on gaining his sight, recognize the latter. But Berkeley correctly pointed out that, if sufficiently acute, such a man *might* work out that the shape he sees for the first time is a cube or is a sphere, provided that the same shapes can be both touched and seen.[21] He also correctly pointed out that, on his own stronger premise that felt shapes and seen shapes are heterogeneous, such an inference would be an unfounded guess.

Nevertheless, in his criticism of Molyneux Berkeley made a serious error. Molyneux's formerly blind man has the task of judging whether he is seeing a sphere or a cube; and for that he must have "ideas," in the sense of concepts, of both *sphere* and *cube*. But the ideas of sphere and cube that he will exercise in judging, "This is (is not) a sphere," and "This is (is not) a cube," are not "ideas" in the Berkeleian sense of objects seen or felt. Berkeley has forgotten his own principle that to see is one thing, to judge is another. Except for his impugned contention that distance is not immediately seen, he has offered no persuasive reason for holding that the same concepts, *sphere* and *cube*, may not apply to objects both of touch and of sight. Nor has he shown that this would entail the absurd consequence that if somebody sees and feels the same object, it must be immediately obvious to him that it is the same object that he both sees and feels. All that would follow is that, with appropriate prior experience, he might be acute enough to work it out.

The upshot is simple. On the anti-Berkeleian view that distance can be immediately seen and that the same things can be both seen and touched, it is possible, nay likely, that a blind man who has gained his sight will not at once correctly identify by sight objects he can correctly identify by touch. On the other hand, it is also possible that, if he is very acute, he will do so. By contrast, on Berkeley's view, the latter possibility is excluded. Except by a lucky guess, such a man could not make correct visual identifications.

The obvious inference to draw from this is that the Molyneux problem affords a possible test for Berkeley's theory, but not for that of his adversaries. A well-authenticated case of a blind man recovering his sight and at once making correct identifications of seen shapes would overthrow Berkeley's theory. On the other hand, well-authenticated cases of inability to make such identifications would not confute his adversaries.

Hence, it is astonishing that Berkeley should cite Cheselden's case, which is of the latter kind, as "not a little confirm[ing]," by "fact and experiment, those points of [his] theory which seem the most remote from common apprehension" (*TVV*, 71: I, 276). The case was of a patient suffering from congenital cataracts, able to distinguish the colors black, white, and scarlet in a good light, but not to see the shape of anything. On this patient Cheselden carried out the operation of cutting an aperture through the iris of one of his eyes, a little above the pupil. As a result, according to Cheselden, he became able to see the full range of colors, but "the faint Ideas he had of [colours] before, were not sufficient for him to know them by afterwards." As for perception of shape, size, and distance:

> When he first saw, he was so far from making any Judgment about Distances, that he thought all Objects whatever touched his Eyes, (as he express'd it) as what he felt, did his Skin. . . . He knew not the Shape of any Thing, nor any one Thing from another, however different in Shape, or Magnitude; but upon being told what Things were, whose Form he before knew from feeling, he would carefully observe, that he might know them again; but having too many Objects to learn at once, he forgot many of them.[22]

Plainly, even taken at face value, as a case satisfying Molyneux's statement of his problem, Cheselden's report is as consistent with Locke's and Molyneux's theory, or with Leibniz's, as with Berkeley's. Hence it cannot corroborate Berkeley's against theirs.

It should also be remarked that Berkeley did not treat Cheselden's report with the caution its inexact and almost sensational formulation calls for. First of all, it gives no exact optical information about what the patient became able to see because of the operation. It defies belief that, even after his second eye had been operated on, his vision had become normal. Secondly, the report neglects to make clear which of the patient's reported judgments were serious. If at any time he seriously believed that whatever he saw touched his eyes, as what he felt did his skin, he must have been virtually half-witted. Hence it is hard to contest Samuel Bailey's verdict: "The narrative of Cheselden, which has been so celebrated, and thought to be conclusive, appears to me . . . exceedingly loose, meagre, and unsatisfactory."[23]

Although Berkeley's theory of vision was generally received as true for over a century, so much of it depends on the false proposition that distance cannot be immediately seen that it has long been discredited. Yet Armstrong has rightly judged the *New Theory of Vision* to be "a work of genius," the great importance of which is independent of Berkeley's immaterialism. However, even Armstrong finds its value to lie in its "ingenious and careful" deductions from premises that, plausible or not in themselves, are false.[24] Berkeley's work indeed has merit of that sort; but it also has merit of another sort, and greater.

In the last twenty-five years, both the representative theories of perception Berkeley combated, and the phenomenalist theories most of his followers embraced, have become as unfashionable as the fox-trot. They have been replaced by materialist causal theories, according to which situations in the physical world, both outside and inside the perceiver's body, cause his perceptions; the effects of those causes are nothing but states of the perceiver's central nervous system, which give rise to dispositions to behave in certain ways, including dispositions to utter sounds and inscriptions construable as linguistic signs. Such theories may do as philosophy of science; but they pay the high price of implicitly repudiating the existence of what they are ostensibly about, viz. perception itself. .

In his extreme old age, the great physiologist Sherrington gave philosophers inclined to adopt such theories a reminder, unforgettably vivid, if in minor respects philosophically inaccurate:

> The physical basis of mind encroaches more and more upon the study of mind, but there remain mental events which seem to lie beyond any physiology of the brain. . . . A pencil of light from the sun enters the eye and is focused there on the retina. It gives rise to a change, which in turn travels to the nerve layer at the top of the brain. The whole chain of these events, from the sun to the top of my brain, is physical. Each step is an electrical reaction.

But now there succeeds a change wholly unlike any which led up to it, and wholly inexplicable by us. A visual scene presents itself to the mind; I see the dome of the sky and the sun in it, and a hundred other visual things beside. . . . When this visual scene appears I ought, I suppose, to feel startled; but I am too accustomed to feel even surprised.[25]

Berkeley saw that a physical-physiological theory of what Sherrington was talking about, the act of seeing and its visual objects, was impossible; and he also saw that an adequate philosophical account of man must include a theory of the nature of that act and of its objects. Although the theory of them that he developed in his various writings on vision was unsatisfactory, he nevertheless divined the kind of thing such a theory would be. That is why I have tried to work out a Berkeleian critique of one of Berkeley's cardinal doctrines. What we need is not a non-Berkeleian theory of vision, but a true Berkeleian theory. Of course, the temptation will remain to evade the need for such a theory, by consigning what it is a theory of—vision itself—to oblivion.[26]

1. All references to Berkeley's writings are to A. A. Luce and T. E. Jessop, eds., *The Works of George Berkeley, Bishop of Cloyne*, 9 vols. (London: Thomas Nelson & Sons, 1948–57). In each case, following standard references by title, numbered book or dialogue (where appropriate), and numbered section (where appropriate), the numbers of the relevant volume and page in the Luce-Jessop edition are given. The following abbreviations of Berkeley's titles are used (conventional abbreviations being indicated by brackets):

Alc. = *Alciphron:* [*or, the Minute Philosopher*] (1st and 2d eds. London and Dublin, 1732; 3d ed. London, 1752)

NTV = [*An Essay towards*] *a New Theory of Vision* (1st ed., Dublin, 1709; 2d ed. Dublin, 1710; 3d and 4th eds., London and Dublin, 1732, annexed to 1st and 2d eds. of *Alciphron*)

PC = *Philosophical Commentaries* (manuscript in British Museum, Add. MS. 39305)

Princ. = [*A Treatise concerning*] *the Principles of Human Knowledge* (1st ed. Dublin, 1710; 2d ed. London, 1734, together with the 3d ed. of *Three Dialogues*)

TD = *Three Dialogues* [*between Hylas and Philonous*] (1st ed. London, 1713; 2d ed. London, 1725; 3d ed. London, 1734, together with the 2d ed. of *The Principles of Human Knowledge*)

TVV = *The Theory of Vision* [*or Visual Language shewing the immediate Presence and Providence of a Deity*] *Vindicated* [*and Explained*] (London, 1733)

2. *NTV*, 2:1,171; *TD*, I: II, 202. Gary Thrane's "Seeing: a Modern Assessment of Berkeley's Theory of Vision" (Ph.D. diss., University of Chicago, September 1973), a study to which, in writing this paper, I have owed more than to any other, characterizes the argument in *NTV* as 'physiological', that in *TD* as 'phenomenological', and that in *Alc.* as 'physical (physiological?)-phenomenological' (pp. 11–12).

3. H. H. Price, 'Seeming', *Aris. Soc. Supp.* 26 (1952): 217.

4. Cf. F. I. Dretske, *Seeing and Knowing* (London: Routledge, 1969), chap. 2.

5. Cf. Colin Murray Turbayne, "The Origin of Berkeley's Paradoxes," in W. E. Steinkraus, ed., *New Studies in Berkeley's Philosophy* (New York: Holt, Rinehart & Winston, 1966), pp. 31–42, esp. pp. 33–36, 39–41.

6. I pass over the argument for distinguishing visible from geometrical shape, which Berkeley derives from his doctrine that the size of a visible shape is a matter of how many *minima visibilia* it contains (*NTV*, 80–82: I, 204–5; *Princ.*, 123, 127–34: II, 97–98, 100–103). The fatal difficulties in Berkeley's views about *minima sensibilia* are exposed by D. M. Armstrong in *Berkeley's Theory of Vision* (Melbourne: Melbourne University Press, 1960), pp. 42–45.

7. "Berkeley actually says at one point that the moon looks to be about thirty points in diameter. But this is just bluff. In fact most lines and surfaces look continuous, and if they look continuous, then, on Berkeley's view, what is immediately perceived *is* continuous and so not made up of minima" (Armstrong, op. cit., p. 44).

8. My view of the two-dimensionality of Berkeley's immediate objects of vision is largely derived from Armstrong, op. cit., pp. 5–8, 13–14. I am also indebted to Thrane's "Seeing," but cannot accept his view that Berkeley's two-dimensional visual array consists of "infinitely various shapes and distances" ("Seeing," p. 77; and cf. pp. 29–33, 73–88).

9. See Nicholas Pastore, *Selective History of Theories of Visual Perception: 1650–1950* (New York: Oxford, 1971), pp. 68–70. Both the following quotation and reference are from this work.

10. Cf. Thrane, "Seeing," pp. 52–56, esp. p. 53. Thrane, however, takes the immediate object of vision in Berkeley's theory to be "the pattern of light projected on the retina" rather than the visual counterpart of that physical pattern. For another hint as to a possible information-theoretic interpretation of Berkeley, see K. M. Sayre, *Consciousness: A Philosophic Study of Minds and Machines* (New York: Random House, 1969), pp. 213–14, 219.

11. John Locke, *An Essay Concerning Human Understanding*, ed. J. W. Yolton, rev. ed. (London: Dent, 1965), Bk. II, chap. 9, sec. 8 (vol. i, 113).

12. Ibid., II, 9, 8 (vol. i, 114).

13. Pastore, op. cit., p. 193.

14. Ibid., pp. 101–2.

15. For Berkeley's use of such an 'occlusion screen' (Thrane so describes it because the image projected on the diaphanous screen, if painted on with opaque pigment, would be the smallest possible figure that would occlude the three-dimensional object projected) see *TVV*, 55–57: I, 270–71. Berkeley uses it only in discussing visible size, but his use of it is evidence that he takes the immediate objects of vision to be visually indistinguishable from two-dimensional shapes on such a screen.

16. I owe the reference to Pastore, who gives an excellent short account of Wheatstone's work: op. cit., pp. 13–16.

17. "A special condition is given by a uniformly illuminated sphere; this is three-dimensional, but the observer would have to use special cues to discriminate this from a flat disk lying in the frontal plane. Such a cue might be the different degree of convergence of the eyes required to fixate the centre from that required to fixate the

334

periphery, or the different degree of accommodation" (Davson, *Encyclopaedia Britannica*, 15th ed. [Chicago 1974], Macropedia, vol. 7, 115*a*).

18.   Locke, op. cit., II, 9, 8 (I, 114).

19.   Ibid.

20.   Berkeley, *PC*, B 49: I, 12.

21.   Leibniz agreed: "[Given] that the question is that of distinguishing alone, and that the blind man knows that the two figured bodies, which he should distinguish, are there, and that thus each of the appearances which he sees is that of the cube or that of the globe . . . it appears to me beyond doubt that the blind man who ceases to be such can distinguish them by the principles of reason [drawing upon his other empirical knowledge]. For I do not speak of that which he will do perhaps in fact and immediately, dazzled and confused by the novelty, or from some other cause little accustomed to draw inferences" (G. W. Leibniz, *Nouveaux essais sur l'entendement humain*, trans. Langley, 3d ed. [LaSalle, Ill.: Open Court, 1949], 139).

22.   Cheselden, *Phil. Transactions Roy. Soc.* 35 (1728): 448 (reprinted photographically in Pastore, op. cit., p. 414).

23.   Quoted in Pastore, op. cit., p. 207, from Samuel Bailey, *Review of Berkeley's Theory of Vision: Designed to Show the Unsoundness of That Celebrated Speculation* (London, 1842).

24.   Armstrong, op. cit., pp. vii, xi, 103.

25.   Charles Sherrington, "Introductory", in Peter Laslett, ed., *The Physical Basis of Mind* (Oxford: Blackwell, 1952), p. 3.

26.   To the audiences at Columbus who endured and criticized either the first or the second version of this paper, I owe much, and especially to the following, who caused me to remove particular errors from one or the other: Paul Eisenberg, Alan Hausman, Peter Machamer, Gareth Matthews, George Pappas, Nicholas Pastore, George Pitcher, and Robert Turnbull.

335

Chapter Twelve

JOSEPH PRIESTLEY ON SENSATION AND PERCEPTION

The *Examination of Dr. Reid's Inquiry into the Human Mind, on the Principles of Common Sense, Dr. Beattie's Essay on the Nature and Immutability of Truth, and Dr. Oswald's Appeal to Common Sense in Behalf of Religion*, first published in 1774, is one of the least known of Joseph Priestley's lesser works. Yet it was the spark to an explosion of publication that constitutes our only detailed statement of Priestley's position on metaphysics and psychology, and the nature of his criticism of Reid makes Priestley's book a pivot on which to hang a discussion of the major protagonists of late eighteenth-century British theories of sensation and perception—theories that were to lead, in the nineteenth century, to the opposition of nativists and empiricists.

As early as 1765, Priestley was to write of his intention to compile "*Illustrations of David Hartley's Doctrine of Association of Ideas, and farther Observations on the Human Mind.*"[1] Publication of such a study might well have been, as Priestley later suggests, his most original contribution to learning, but the several volumes of notes and hints kept for the work over a period of nearly thirty years were all destroyed in the Birmingham Riots of 1791.[2] Fortunately, earlier events had already prompted publication of some parts of what Priestley had intended to write on Hartley—and on his own psychological ideas. During the composition of Part III of his *Institutes of Natural and Revealed Religion*, published early in 1774, Priestley's attention was drawn to the writings of Oswald, Beattie, and Reid, which were then attracting favorable notice. Though he had earlier dismissed Reid and Beattie as unworthy of serious attention, careful reading of Oswald excited his "indignation and astonishment" and he reread Reid and Beattie. Of Oswald's *Appeal* he was to write, "I really do not remember that I ever read a work so large . . . that contained so little; I do not mean of truth, but of any thing"; and of Reid's *Inquiry* he declared " . . . I do not find in it a single observation that is *new*, and at the same time *just*."[3] Nonetheless, he proceeded to write a three hundred and seventy page *Examination* of these (and Beattie's) works, followed this with an edition of substantial parts of David Hartley's *Observations on Man* (as *Hartley's Theory of the Human Mind*) with three introductory Essays, published in 1775, and followed this with his *Disquisitions Relating to Matter and Spirit* of 1777 and his *Free Discussion of the Doctrines of Materialism and Philosophical Necessity* of 1778.

These four works: The *Examination, Hartley's Theory, Disquisitions*, and *Free Discussion* together comprise a criticism of Reid's "Common Sense" approach to the psychology of perception and a substitution of Priestley's own theory based on a combination of Hartley's associationism and his own spiritualized materialism. The four were, incidentally, written and published during the years of Priestley's most intensive and creative chemical researches. By 1777 the metaphysical psychology had so commanded his interest that he declared his intention, in the third volume of his *Experiments and Observations on* . . . *Air*, to devote himself, henceforth, to this different kind of speculation.[4] By 1779 he had decided that he could do both chemistry and metaphysics.[5] Events were perhaps to show that he was wrong, and it is open to suggestion that concentration on one or the other of these subjects might have been better for his reputation and for the world of learning. It should be noted, however, that his most substantial contribution to each subject was made during those hectic years between 1774 and 1778, when he worked on both together under the influence, so far as metaphysical psychology was concerned, of intense reaction against the early proponents of the philosophy of Common Sense.

Oswald, Beattie, and Reid, therefore, deserve our attention, if only out of gratitude to their effect on Priestley's production of what would most surely have otherwise been lost in the riotous fires lit by Birmingham's "men of common understanding." James Oswald, however, has been described (correctly) as a vulgarized Beattie; and James Beattie, though his work earned him an honorary L.L.D. from Oxford and a pension of 200£ a year from George III, has been described (again correctly) as a trivialized Reid. It is then on the work of Thomas Reid that we shall focus attention. This is the more reasonable as it was Reid who was the founder of the school of Scottish Common Sense philosophy, which once held some favor as an alternative to transcendental idealism (and is now enjoying an unaccountable revival), and it was from Reid that nativist psychology derived some part of its inspiration.

Reid, like Kant, was wakened from his "dogmatic slumbers" by the reading of David Hume's *Treatise on Human Nature*.[6] The philosophic nightmares accompanying Reid's slumbers were, however, based on the writings of George Berkeley, which he had studied between the ages of 12 and 16 as a student at Marischal College, Aberdeen, and from which, it appears he never entirely recovered.[7] Reid went from Aberdeen to a career as parish preacher (interrupted for a few years as librarian) before family influence gained him appointment in 1752 as professor of philosophy at King's College, Aberdeen, where he helped organize a discussion club at which the materials published in 1764 as his *Inquiry into the Human Mind* were first read. Publication of the *Inquiry* won him election to the chair in moral philosophy at Glasgow, in succession to Adam Smith, where he remained until his retirement from active teaching to prepare for the publication of his *Essays on the Intellectual Powers of Man* in 1785 and *Essays on the Active Powers of the Human Mind* in 1788. These last two works (and presumably the Glasgow lectures on which they were based) are more carefully argued and written than the *Inquiry*. They conceal, therefore, some of the obvious superficialities in Reid's understanding of previous philosophies and particularly avoid the blustering, patronizing quality that mars the *Inquiry*. The *Essays* also develop other parts of the doctrine of Common Sense at greater length. It should be noted, then, that it was the *Inquiry* that Priestley read and answered, whereas it was the *Essays* that earned the admiration of Dugald Stewart and, through Stewart, of Sir

William Hamilton. The fundamental nature of the sensation-perception arguments remain the same, however, from the *Inquiry* to the *Essays*, and the earlier version is the more revealing in its nominalistic nakedness. It is to the *Inquiry* that we shall most refer, though the *Essays* will occasionally provide amplification.[8]

Reid felt himself to be opposing a train of philosophizing that led inexorably to skepticism. For if one accepted, as he did, the Cartesian dichotomy of mind and body *and* adopted the concept that mind is conscious only of ideas, then, he felt, Locke necessarily follows Descartes and Berkeley, Locke, and Hume, Berkeley until we arrive finally and necessarily at the conclusion that the mind is aware only of "ideas and impressions, without any subject on which they may be impressed."[9] "Thus, the wisdom of philosophy ("a kind of metaphysical lunacy") is set in opposition to the *common sense* of mankind. . . . If this be wisdom, let me be deluded with the vulgar."[10] It was this flavor of vulgar anti-intellectualism permeating the *Inquiry* that partially explains Priestley's *Examination* of it "in a manner," as he later wrote, "that I do not entirely approve."[11] But there is more to Reid than rhetorical obscurantism, for he attempts to construct a new line of argument that does not lead to unacceptable consequences.

If the system, stemming from Descartes, that Reid calls "the ideal system" necessarily entails skepticism, then the *foundations* of that system must be reopened to examination, and it appears that its defect lies in the concept of idea. "No solid proof has ever been advanced of the existence of ideas," Reid declares, and our knowledge of the existence of external objects must be rationalized from another base.[12] That base, for Reid, lies in the duality of sensation and perception as distinct operations of the mind. Reid has been called (incorrectly, I believe) the first person to distinguish clearly between sensation and perception; certainly he does make an explicit point of separating the two in theory, though his practice sometimes confuses the issue—particularly as his implied definitions of these operations were not wholly acceptable even to followers of the philosophy of Common Sense.

Sensation, Reid holds, is a simple and original affection of the mind; it is purely passive, has no object distinct from itself, and as its essence consists simply in being felt, it cannot be either right or wrong; it just is.[13] Priestley, and others after him, objected that there were disordered sensory organs, malfunctioning nerves, or injured and delerious brains that produce false sensations, and Reid addresses such problems (to some extent) in the *Essays*. But, on the whole, he and other Common Sense philosophers ignored such criticisms with the observation that these were not considerations of the normally constituted faculties of the person of common understanding. They never quite understood how observations of pathological circumstances might lead to analysis of normal sensory processes any more than they understood how the observations of contemporary physicians on threshold intensities, durational variations, and differential frequency responses might need taking account of in the examination of sensations.[14] And, in the sense that Reid understood sensation, these criticisms and observations *are* essentially irrelevant, for physiology does not seriously enter the sensory considerations of Common Sense philosophy, which is basically introspective.

Indeed, the whole problem of the relationship between sensation and any process by which external objects impress on a sense organ is evaded in a Berkeleyan assumption that no relevant information is acquired by examination of an object-sensation relationship:

> . . . Neither the organ of smell, nor the medium, nor any motions we can conceive excited in the [pituitary] membrane . . . or in the nerve or animal spirits, do in the least resemble the sensation of smelling; nor could that sensation of itself ever have led us to think of nerves, animal spirits, and effluvia.[15]

It is, in fact, a major part of Reid's argument in the *Inquiry* that previous philosophers had supposed a likeness between sensation and the quality sensed, a likeness that did not and could not exist. Priestley, and at least one later quasi-follower of Reid, Thomas Brown, accuse Reid of taking cheap shots at his opponents with such an argument. Priestley writes:

. . . He appears to be misled—merely by philosophers happening to call ideas the *images* of external things; as if this was not known to be a figurative expression, denoting not that the actual shapes of things were delineated . . . upon the mind, but only that impressions of some kind or other were conveyed to the mind by means of the organs of sense and their corresponding nerves, and that between these impressions and the sensations . . . there is a real and necessary though at present an unknown connection.[16]

Now Reid does use this kind of criticism in demagogic declamations, as when he writes: "If a man run his head with violence against a pillar, I appeal to him, whether the pain he feels resembles the hardness of the stone. . . . "[17] On the other hand, Locke, for example, does suggest that our ideas of primary qualities differ from those of secondary ones by their "resemblance" to the qualities that produce them, and as late as 1826 it was still necessary for Johannes Müller to argue against the notion that perception reveals the nature of external objects by way of some representational similarity in sensation.[18] No doubt Reid makes a useful contribution to our understanding by his insistence that the sensations relate not to objects but to feelings. We do not smell a rose, but an odor, or hear a coach, but sounds, and so on. Nonetheless, the distinguishing of sensations from objects, without consideration of processes by which objects might produce them, leads to the problem of how sensations might then relate to perception of objects. This Reid answers with the doctrine of natural signs.

It is curious that Reid, who insists on an epistemology of observation and experiment, who declares that "no man ever more distinctly understood, or happily expressed, the nature and foundation of the philosophic art" than Bacon, should fall back upon an approach which so nearly resembles Plato's doctrine of reminiscences.[19] For sensations act as "natural signs" to suggest the "original perceptions" by which we become aware of the existence of objects and their qualities. The relationship between sensation and "original perception" is not a causal one but that of constant and simultaneous conjunction. By the nature of man's constitution as an original principle of human nature, prior to habit, experience, or education, certain sensations suggest to the mind the conception of qualities and create a belief in them.[20] In this doctrine of "original perception," Reid departs from Berkeley—for man thus attains a genuine knowledge of external objects, and that knowledge relates to the Lockeian "primary qualities" of body: hardness, extension, figure, movement. These generally involve signification by sensations of touch and sight, though some of the sensations of touch (e.g., heat) and sight (e.g., color) and all sensations of smell, hearing, and taste signify existence of an object, but are not originally its qualities. Knowledge of secondary qualities and their association with particular objects is obtained through "acquired perception," a gradually unfolding power of the mind.[21]

The distinction between original and acquired perceptions approaches the position that knowledge of physical objects is the result of inferences drawn from experience—which one would have thought Reid to be against. Priestley, indeed, claims that "this hypothesis of the gradual *unfolding* of the powers of the mind very much resembles the gradual acquisition of them, from the impressions to which we are exposed."[22] And it is at this point that Thomas Brown later introduces the doctrine of associationism into Common Sense philosophy. Perhaps Reid would not have objected, so long as one recognized that the nature of all sensation was simply as a set of signs by which innate faculties of mind simultaneously perceived the existence and primary qualities of body and subsequently identified secondary qualities with specific bodies previously acknowledged to exist. Acquired perceptions, like original ones, are not, that is, learned, though the nature of the former is "unfolded" whereas the latter are immediate. It is not entirely clear whether acquired perceptions are passive as original perceptions are, nor is Reid entirely consistent as to the invariable truth of perceptions. In the *Essays on Intellectual Powers*, he declares, "There is no fallacy in original perception, but only in that which is acquired by custom"; yet he also declares there that a perception conjoined by nature with a sensation can, in some instances, be fallacious though sensation cannot be.[23]

Reid declared that he held no theory of perception and one cannot but fervently agree, if by theory one means something more than a description of perceptional combinations. Indeed, the effect of Reid's substitution of scientific agnosticism for Humeian skepticism[24] is to put an end to analysis of the nature and cause of perception. In a mode strikingly similar to that adopted by his contemporaries in the physical sciences, Reid forestalls reduction of perceptional phenomena into more primitive elements. Just as the fluids of heat, electricity, and magnetism, or chemical compounds were formally defined by their operative qualities, essentially ending investigation as to the cause of those qualities other than the presence and variation in quantity of the fluids, so Reid defines a set of innate perceptive principles of the mind that thenceforth exist without cause other than the instinctive operation of mind.[25] Priestley, citing Newton's Occamist "Third Rule of Reasoning" in indignant rejection of this approach, claims that Reid identifies as many as twelve such "instinctive principles," "including awareness of extension, space, and motion, of human veracity, and of the validity of causal relationships."[26] If one was not inclined to accept as explanation of a phenomenon a formal cause recognizable to all persons of common sense, e.g., man perceives an object in space because he is endowed by the Creator with the faculty of perceiving objects in space, some answer other than, or in addition to, Reid's was required. For Priestley that other answer was to be found in David Hartley's *Observations on Man*.

David Hartley (1707–57) was educated for the clergy at Jesus College, Cambridge, but a reluctance to assent to the thirty-nine articles of the Church of England prompted him to become a physician instead. Whatever his initial qualifications for this curious response to religious scruple, he became a popular and successful physician with a care for the cure of his patients' souls as well as their bodies. The motivation in Hartley's publication in 1749 of his *Observations on Man, his Frame, his Duty, and his Expectations*, is, like that of Reid and of Priestley, primarily theological. As Hartley saw theology necessarily to involve consideration of determinism (what Priestley was later to call "philosophical necessity") and as he thought that determinism was entailed by the mode through which man perceived and thought, the first volume of his *Observations* in-

343

cludes a detailed study of the physiology of sensation and the formation and association of perceptions and ideas.[27]

Out of his background as a physician, Hartley distinguishes (fifteen years before Reid) between perceptions and sensations. Perceptions are ideas of the mind, whereas sensations are "those internal Feelings of the Mind" that arise from the impressions made by external objects upon the several parts of our bodies.[28] Verbally, the distinction is perhaps not as clear as we should like; for though he insists that he does not "comprehend *Sensations* under Ideas," he also describes ideas as "other internal Feelings" and then, using that phrase which Reid later attacks and Priestley excuses, says that "Ideas of Sensation" (his usual form for perception) are those ideas which "resemble Sensations."[29] Nonetheless, as a part of the process by which sensations arise in the mind is described in physiological detail, the distinction becomes operationally evident. For sensations are directly related to immediate physical transformations produced in the brain, and these, in turn, are a consequence of physical action by external objects on sense organs, transferred along (or through) the nerves. Exactly how effects on the material substance of the brain are manifest in the immaterial substance of the mind is not clear to Hartley (he suggests the action of some mediating infinitesmal elementary substance between brain and mind), but that this happens is clear from observations in physiology and anatomy where changes effected in the brain, nerves, or sensory organs invariably are followed by changes in ideas.[30]

Hartley initially bases his physiological speculation upon a suggestion from Query 12 in Newton's *Opticks*:

> Do not the Rays of Light, in falling upon the bottom of the Eye, excite Vibrations in the *Tunica Retina*? Which Vibrations, being propagated along the solid Fibres of the optic Nerves into the Brain, cause the Sense of seeing.[31]

The reasonableness of this "vibration theory" of sensation being confirmed by such observations as persistence of vision, after-images, and the character of the physical phenomena producing sounds, Hartley supposes that all external objects impress upon sense organs characteristic vibrations that are propagated through or along the nerves (as electricity is propagated along a hempen cord) and into the similar substance of the brain. ". . . Each Nerve and Region is originally fitted to receive . . . and sympathize with such vibrations as are likely to be impressed upon them in the various Incidents of Life. . . . "[32] The vibrations as received in the brain may differ from one another in their frequencies and intensities and in the region and direction by which their nerve-carriers enter the brain. Once in the brain, the vibrations propagate freely over the whole substance, diminishing in strength in proportion to the quantity of matter.[33] The vibrations are not translatory movement of substance but transfer of motion about positions of equilibrium and with respect to one another. It is this variation of particle-position, greater or lesser depending upon the intensity of the vibration, that is transformed somehow into simple sensation, initially always some form or combination of pain or pleasurable feeling.

For the way in which simple pleasure or pain sensation is to be related to perception of the object causing it, we must add Hartley's physiological version of the doctrine of association of ideas derived, in the first instance, he tells us, from Locke and a Reverend John Gay.[34] If sensory vibrations are frequently repeated, or are especially intense, they will "beget in the medullary substance" a disposition to diminutive vibrations (or vibratiuncles) that correspond to themselves.[35] This is the physiological analogue of the "Simple Ideas of Sensation" (i.e., perception), the "vestiges, types or images of themselves" left in the mind by frequently repeated sensations.[36] Now it is the nature of vibrations (as seen in the case of sounds in air) that they can coexist in the same medium without interfering with one another. Hence an infant will initially receive a chaos of sensations without any perception of cause. But as the sensory vibrations are "fixed" in vibratiuncles—perhaps through a process by which discontinuities are produced in the living substance of the brain—and particularly as such vibrations are frequently repeated, and certain sets occur simultaneously or in precisely contiguous instants of time, they acquire power to set up sympathetic vibrations in other vibratiuncles, so that vibrations

345

A, B, C, and so on, initially producing seperately miniature vibrations a,b,c, and so on; but being often and regularly associated, soon vibration A alone can excite miniature vibrations b, c, and so on.[37] Thus, by experience, simple ideas of sensation become clustered and coalesce into complex ideas, and sensation becomes identified through perception with the object that causes it. Eventually by reflection, muscular responses, and trial-and-error, specific sensations are associated with particular qualities of bodies. Perception of the existence of bodies, their differentiation from one another, and the abstraction of their qualities are, therefore, always the determined consequence of the particular experiences of individuals, though the process begins so early and is so continually being carried on that we lose the power to identify simple sensation and to separate it from the clusters of ideas that are perceptions.

Now Hartley's publication of the *Observations* was undoubtedly done in ignorance of Hume's work, the *Treatise on Human Nature* of 1739 having fallen, its author tells us, stillborn from the press, and the *Inquiry Concerning Human Nature* having appeared too recently to make any impact on a work in gestation for eighteen years. Reid's publication of his *Inquiry*, in direct response to Hume, was apparently done in ignorance of Hartley, whose work was scarcely known before Priestley issued *his* version of it in 1775.[38] Since Reid, in pursuing his "original principles of human nature" into the *Essays on the Intellectual Powers of Man*, dismisses Hartley's vibrations as merely conjecture, it is clear that he does not believe Hartley to be an adequate response to Hume.[39] Priestley knew the work of both Hartley and Hume before writing his response to Reid; and though we cannot agree with Priestley that, compared with Hartley, Hume "was not even a child,"[40] we can, I think, agree that Hartley's vibrations and associationism are as adequate (and as inadequate) a response to Hume as Reid's "original principles," and that Hartley affords a better base for a scientific psychology than either Hume or Reid—particularly in the form that Priestley was to develop his ideas.

Joseph Priestley was not a philosopher; his mind was not profound, nor did he develop his ideas into a single, systematic treatise. Priestley's mind was, however, quick and critical, and he had a talent for adapting essential points from a wide variety of systems to his own purposes. Contrary to traditional interpretations, these purposes were not, as a rule, deliberately revolutionary, for Priestley was fundamentally conservative. And it was precisely that conservatism which was offended by the arguments of Reid and his immediate followers. Priestley had been introduced to the writings of David Hartley as a part of his formal education into science and metaphysics while a student at the Protestant dissenting Academy at Daventry between 1752 and 1755.[41] He had, that is, assimilated Hartley's reductionist physiology and his Lockeian associationism into what was increasingly an old-fashioned view of man and nature that included the physical reductionism of Newton, Stephen Hales, and John Rowning; the utilitarianism and theological toleration of Richard Baxter, John Locke, and Philip Doddridge; and the notion of rational Christianity that had characterized half a century of dissenting theology before him. To accept the vain multiplication of separate faculties of the mind as explanation of phenomena amerable to a single, simple mechanism was intellectually offensive; to accept as proof of those faculties an appeal to the potentially intolerant and explicitly non-rational instincts of "common understanding" would be foolishness—as a glance at Dr. Oswald's *Appeal* was to suggest in 1774 and the Birmingham Church-and-King riots were to prove in 1791. Yet, as is typical of British conservatism, when Priestley set about to prove the validity of the old, he did so with new arguments, and in doing so, established a new pattern.

His new approach to physiological psychology cannot be obtained in a single, self-consistent, and systematic form from any one work by Priestley. It must be constructed from elements in his four major metaphysical books and from the seemingly inexhaustable flood of pamphlets that Priestley was subsequently obliged to write in defense of them. Many of Priestley's criticisms of Reid in the *Examination* have already been cited. To there we need add only that he constantly recurs to the argument of historical process. The child learns, in time, by "deliberation," by voluntarily attending to his observations, and by bringing his sense organs (through reaching, turning the head, and so on) into various relations to objects, that the affections of his senses relate to particular external objects.[42] Perception is, therefore, a matter of experience—and, like experience, may have limitations. The sure conviction of truth of some perception, therefore, may well be merely a prejudice; it is nothing on which one can base a proof. Elsewhere, in connection with scientific observations, Priestley was to write: "The force of prejudice . . . biases not only our judgments . . . but even the perceptions of our senses . . . that the plainest evidence of sense will not entirely change."[43]

His criticism of Common Sense philosophy does not cease with the *Examination*. Although the edition of *Hartley's Theory of the Human Mind* was explicitly undertaken to *divert* attention from Reid's "incoherent scheme," it is not a general summary of Hartley's theory.[44] The doctrine of vibrations is left out—for reasons we shall return to later—and selections were made from the remainder of the text, presumably to convey the nature of Hartley's arguments. But the selections were carefully made to address just those "original principles of the mind" cited by Reid and to show they all had alternative explanations. From the range of possible examples, the most critical is, perhaps, that which relates to perceptions of magnitude, distance, motion, figure, and position. All of these may be acquired through sensations of sight and have, therefore, physiological associations in the effects of intensity of light stimulus, variation of iris size, muscular efforts of focusing, eye and head movements, inclination of optical axes in binocular vision, size and motion of impression made on the retina, and position on the retina on which light rays fall. There are, in addition, association of ideas relating to magnitude and distance comparisons, distinctness of detail in impression, number and size of intervening objects, and variation of light and shadow. The use of glasses (spectacles or telescope?) may initially falsify associations and produce erroneous judgments until experience substitues new associations. Judgments made by sight concerning these qualities are to be acknowledged as true or false, according to their agreement with associated judgments made by touch.[45]

348

That other critical problem, the relation of experience to knowledge of causation, is not clearly dealt with in the edition of *Hartley*, since it there becomes entangled with theological doctrines of determinism and free will. Reid interprets Hartley and Priestley, in the *Essays*, as believing that constant conjunction in time is proof of causality, but he is certainly wrong—perhaps because he disagrees with both on determinism. It is no doubt that same disbelief in determinism which caused Reid to write in the *Inquiry* what appears to be a denial of causality:

> What we commonly call natural *causes*, might, with more propriety, be called natural *signs*, and what we call *effects*, the *things signified*. The causes have no proper efficiency or causality, as far as we know; and all we can certainly affirm, is, that nature hath established a constant conjunction between them and the things called their effects; and hath given to mankind a disposition to observe those connections, to confide in their continuance, and to make use of them. . . . [47]

It rather appears that Reid has chosen to deal with Hume's criticism of man's notion of causality by accepting it, on the surface, and then reasserting causality through a Berkeleyian redefinition.

Priestley, at least, would have none of this approach, and says so in his *Letters to a Philosophical Unbeliever* of 1780, addressed particularly to the writings of Hume. The plan of nature, from which the wisdom of God is inferred, requires intelligibility, and intelligibility requires a system of natural laws. It is the knowledge of the existence of natural law, obtained by way of our knowledge of God, that leads to belief in the causal connection of events in temporal conjunction—note the other way around.

> . . . Having found, in all such constant conjunctions . . . with respect to which we have been able to make any discovery at all, that the conjunction was really necessary, we conclude that the conjunction, if constant, is equally necessary, even when we are not able distinctly to perceive it. . . . When we say that two events, or appearances, are necessarily connected, all that we can mean is, that some more general law of nature must be violated before those events can be separated. [48]

349

For the remaining "primary quality" of matter to be perceived, that of hardness, we must return first to the edition of *Hartley* and the doctrine of vibrations. Priestley did not leave that doctrine out of the edition because he disbelieved in it. Indeed, "Dr. Hartley has produced sufficient evidence for it, or as much as the nature of the thing will admit."[49] It was, rather, that the doctrine of vibrations and the anatomical disquisitions made Hartley's theory seem difficult, and associationism could stand on its own without the vibrational hypothesis. Association of ideas, Priestley wrote, "wears the face of that simplicity in causes and variety in effects, which we discover in every other part of nature"—and he quotes Pope's *Essay on Man*:

> In human Works, tho' labored on with pain,
> A thousand movements scarce one purpose gain;
> In God's, one single can its end produce;
> Yet serves to second too some other use.[50]

Yet Priestley's introductory essays repeat, in brief, the major vibrational arguments and then go beyond them to query Hartley's supposititious immaterial substance, intermediary between mind and brain. In the major work that follows, his *Disquisitions Relating to Matter and Spirit* of 1777, Priestley develops that query into a thorough-going "materialism" in which he asserts that the powers of sensation and perception, as well as all other powers termed mental, are the result of the organization of matter in the brain. To the objection that sensation and thought bear no resemblance to any of the qualities of matter, he presents a twofold response: first, one can no more describe how *immaterial* substance can think than one can how material substance might do so; second, the received opinion relating to the qualities of matter is fundamentally incorrect.[51] Arguing out of a tradition that starts, for him at least, with the Cambridge Neoplatonists and Isaac Newton and continues through Stephen Hales and John Rowning to culminate in John Michell and the Abbé Roger Joseph Boscovich, and bolstering those arguments with personal observations garnered during more than ten years of interpreting experimental results, Priestley asserts that matter is not basically hard, inert, and extended but rather consists of geometrical points surrounded by concentric spheres of repulsive and attractive forces. Sensible bodies consist of complex structures of these points, and their apparent solidity is the repulsive action of *their* forces on those of any other body which attempts to penetrate their structures.

If this is materialism, it is curiously spiritualized, for matter is divested of all properties but the forces by which it acts upon other matter, and its motion and distribution in space. Priestley admitted to one critic, " . . . I have chosen to say that man is *wholly material*, rather than wholly spiritual, though both terms were in my option."[52] Mind and brain could, together, be called one thing or the other, but he was not prepared to admit any essential difference between them. Priestley has materialized the whole of man, but only by spiritualizing the whole of matter. One of the consequences of this hypothesis, as Priestley acknowledges in the *Free Discussion of the Doctrines of Materialism and Philosophical Necessity* of 1778, is that "matter is . . . resolved into nothing but the *divine* agency, exerted according to certain rules. . . . "[53] Another consequence, when the hypothesis is considered independently of its theological overtones, is that it becomes impossible for the mind directly to perceive, either through its sensations *or* through Reid's "innate perceptive principles," anything of the essential character of things as they are. What man senses is the complex action of varying forces, and all that he can possibly perceive is the consequence of elaborate rationalization of his experiences with sensation. One may note as well, though Priestley never says so, that it is possible to find in his statement that "matter is . . . resolved into nothing but the *divine* agency" an explanation of how this spiritualized matter might think. For if the forces that *are* matter represent the divine agency, they may be said to be an aspect of God's will—and, as matter is defined by force, matter *is* thought as well.

With this conclusion Priestley should have set a challenge to generations of philosopher-psychologists, but a disposition to concentrate on words rather than meanings diverted attention from either the radical theological idealism or the psychological challenge of his theories. Priestley had declared himself a materialist, materialism meant atheism, and atheism was alone

351

justification for ignoring the challenge until it could be forgotten. Not for nearly three-quarters of a century was there to be another physical-physiological empiricist theory of sensation and perception as completely articulated as Priestley's; not that is, until another physical scientist, Herman von Helmholtz, who was also a physiologist, joined the nativist-empiricist battle, and Helmholtz's theory was developed from a different metaphysical base.

1. At least that is the implication of his statement, in *An Appeal to the Public on the Subject of the Riots in Birmingham* (Birmingham, 1792), p. 38, that he had promised publication of this work "in the Preface to my *Essay on Education.*" My edition of the *Essay on a Course of Liberal Education,* which is the only title approaching that cited by Priestley, does not contain such a promise, but I do not possess the first edition of 1765. It is clear, at least, from his publications of the late 1760s that Priestley had already acquired his great admiration for the work of Hartley.

2. Priestley, *Appeal,* p. 38.

3. Priestley, *Institutes of Natural and Revealed Religion,* Part III, 2d ed. (Birmingham, 1782; first published in 1774), pp. 159, 160.

4. Priestley, *Experiments and Observations on . . . Air,* vol. 3 (London, 1777), p. vii.

5. Priestley, ibid., vol. 4 (London, 1779), pp. v-vi: ". . . The speculations . . . , which were of a metaphysical nature, did not happen to engage so much of my attention as I expected, and did not, at any time, much interfere with my philosophical [i.e., scientific] pursuits."

6. Paraphrased from Timothy Duggan's introduction to his edition of Thomas Reid, *An Inquiry into the Human Mind* (Chicago: University of Chicago Press, 1970), p. ix.

7. For a discussion of Reid's philosophical education at Marischal and particularly of the influence of his Berkeleyian teacher, George Turnbull, on Reid's lifelong respect for the meaningfulness of common speech forms, see G. E. Davie, "Hume and the Origins of the Common Sense School," *Revue internationale de philosophie* 6 (1952): 213–31.

8. I have used the Duggan edition of the *Inquiry* cited above and the reprint edition, Thomas Reid, *Essays on the Intellectual Powers of Man* (Cambridge, Mass.: MIT Press, 1969), with an introduction by Baruch A. Brody.

9. Reid, *Inquiry,* p. 14.

10. Ibid., pp. 76, 77.

11. Priestley, *Memoirs of Dr. Joseph Priestley* (London: H. R. Allenson, 1904), p. 51; note that this is a reprint of the *Memoirs* first published in 1806.

12. Reid, *Inquiry,* p. 19.

13. Ibid., p. 23.

14. See, for example, William Cullen, *Institutes of Medicine. Part I. Physiology,* 1st ed. (Edinburgh, 1772). Cullen was professor of medicine at Glasgow until shortly before Reid's arrival there and continued lcturing on medicine at neighboring Edinburgh during Reid's tenure at Glasgow.

15. Reid, *Inquiry,* p. 22.

16. Priestley, *Examination of Dr. Reid's Inquiry . . . ,* 2d ed. (London, 1775), p. 30.

17. Reid, *Inquiry,* p. 62.

18. See Edward Boring, *Sensation and Perception in the History of Experimental Psychology* (New York: Appleton, 1942), p. 17.

19. Reid, *Inquiry*, p. 66.

20. Ibid., pp. 66–67.

21. Ibid., extracted from chaps. 5–6; see especially pp. 69, 83–84, 108–9, 210–19.

22. Priestley, *Examination*, p. 40.

23. Reid, *Essays* (see note 8 above), pp. 302, 271.

24. For Reid's disavowal of a theory of perception, see S. A. Grave, *The Scottish Philosophy of Common Sense* (Oxford: Clarendon Press, 1960), p. 161. The reference of Reid's "scientific agnosticism" and what follows is a paraphrase of Boring, *Sensation and Perception*, p. 14.

25. For "materialist" theories of fluids and elements, see Robert E. Schofield, *Mechanism and Materialism* (Princeton, N.J.: Princeton University Press, 1970), passim.

26. Priestley, *Examination*, p. 9.

27. I have used the facsimile of the 1749 London edition of David Hartley, *Observations on Man, His Frame, His Duty, and His Expectations* (Hildesheim: George Olmes, 1967).

28. Hartley, *Observations*, p. ii (i.e., 2).

29. Ibid.

30. Ibid., pp. 34, 7.

31. Sir Isaac Newton, *Opticks: or, A Treatise of the Reflections, Refractions, Inflections & Colours of Light*, rpt. of 4th ed. of 1730 (New York: Dover Publications, 1952), p. 345; Queries 23 and 24, pp. 353–54, continue the same line of argument and make specific the analogy drawn to sound and hearing.

32. Hartley, *Observations*, p. 42.

33. Ibid., p. 24.

34. Locke is referred to only by inference, whereas the "Rev. Mr. Gay" is cited (ibid., p. v).

35. Ibid., p. 58.

36. Ibid., p. 56.

37. Ibid., pp. 36, 65.

38. It appears that Abraham Tucker, writing under the name Edward Search, in his *Light of Nature*, 7 vols. (London: 1768–77), was the only "Philosopher" to have taken public notice of Hartley's theories before Priestley made an issue of them.

39. Reid, *Essays*, pp. 86–98; he also refers, in passing, to Hartley or Priestley, pp. 134, 201, 591, and to Priestley (but not Hartley) without understanding in the *Essays on the Active Powers of the Human Mind*, rpt., with introduction by Baruch A. Brody (Cambridge, Mass.: MIT Press, 1969), p. 271.

40. Priestley, *Letters to a Philosophical Unbeliever*, Part I, 2d ed. (London, 1787), p. 126.

41. For Priestley's science at Daventry, see Robert E. Schofield, ed., *Scientific Autobiography of Joseph Priestley, 1733–1804* (Cambridge, Mass.: MIT Press, 1966), pp. 3–6; for his metaphysical studies, Schofield, *Mechanism and Materialism*, pp. 264–65.

42. Priestley, *Examination*, p. lvi.

43. Ibid., pp. 42–43; Priestley, *Experiments and Observations* (London, 1775), 2:30.

44. Priestley, *Examination*, p. xii.

45. Priestley, *Hartley's Theory of the Human Mind* (London, 1775), pp. 61–65.

46. Reid, *Essays*, p. 591.

47. Reid, *Inquiry*, p. 66.

48. Priestley, *Letters*, pp. 94–95.

49. Priestley, *Hartley's Theory*, preface, p. iii.

50. Ibid., p. xxiv.

51. Priestley, *Disquisitions relating to Matter and Spirit* (London, 1777), pp. 82, 7–16.

52. Priestley, *A Free Discussion of the Doctrines of Materialism and Philosophical Necessity* (London, 1778), p. 254.

53. Ibid., p. 250.

Nicholas Pastore

Chapter Thirteen

HELMHOLTZ ON THE PROJECTION
OR TRANSFER OF SENSATION

A general feature of Helmholtz's theory of sensory perception concerns the decomposability of a percept into two sorts of mental contents: sensation and psychical activities. Sensation, the direct correlate of stimulation of a sensory surface, constitutes the contribution of the body to the mind. On the other hand, psychical activities, though contingent on sensation, constitute the contribution of the mind itself. Such activities include judging, inferring, and the forming of associations. These and other psychical activities mediate the transition from sensation to perception, and without them a percept as we know it as normal adults would be nonexistent. That is to say, a hypothetical individual, one who is deprived of any psychical activity, would be reduced to a state of mere sensation. Psychical activity, in Helmholtz's view, is always involved in the formation of a percept even in the here and now of any particular percept that we may have when a sensory surface is stimulated. We are conscious, however, only of the finished product—the percept.[1] The theory represents a continuation of the classical tradition that had evolved, namely, that the mind is passive in respect to sensation but active in respect to perception.[2]

Helmholtz, consistent with the classical tradition, supposes that the mind or intellect, upon receiving the data of present and past sensations, has the special power of fashioning percepts.[3] The important problem with which Helmholtz must cope concerns the explanation of the origin of this power. Did it arise from "experience" and the association of ideas? Or did it re-side, at least latently, in an innate or intrinsic faculty of the mind to be subsequently elicited by "experience" and the association of ideas? A decisive determination of Helmholtz's attitude and answers to these questions is somewhat problematic. On the one hand, he espoused, as is well known, the empiristic theory in the explanation of percepts. His exposition of the theory can be interpreted as implying a positive answer to the first question and a negative answer to the second. Yet on the other hand, and perhaps not as well known, is his reliance on Kant for a significant underpinning of his theory. This implies a negative answer to the first question and a positive answer to the second.

Helmholtz's reliance on Kant is exhibited in his positing of innate properties or laws of the mind, especially in regard to an innate or a priori law of causality. The apriority of this law apparently is essential to his theory of (unconscious) inductive inference, which for him is a crucial factor in the formation of sensory perception. A percept, he says, represents the conclusion of the inference. Although the Kantian influence in respect to sensory perception is apparent in Sec. 26 of his famous work on physiological optics,[4] it is more conspicuous in his relatively brief and unknown work of 1855.[5] This latter work, which was a popular lecture on human vision delivered in Königsberg in honor of Kant, contains, as Helmholtz indicated, the essential features of his theory of perception.[6] This work will be an important source for this discussion.

The interpretation of his theory in general, and the evaluation of the Kantian influence in particular, is no simple matter, because he does not clearly distinguish the psychology of perception from the epistemology of perception. By the psychology of perception, I mean, at a minimum, a description of a current percept and a description of the antecedent alleged mental event, such as visual sensation or visual image, which would constitute the foundation for the development of that percept. Consider, for example, single vision. The current percept, when the eyes are properly directed to a single object, may be described thus: "I see one object." For Helmholtz its foundation consists of two sensations, one from each eye, that arrive in "consciousness" separately.[7] Epistemology, we may note, is irrelevant in the mere comprehension of the descriptions, and also in assessing the validity or adequacy of some proposed explanation that would account for the transition from sensation to the percept. And by the epistemology of perception, I mean that branch of philosophy that deals with the question concerning the nature of the external world and the inferences that one can make about this world on the basis of perception. To make this more specific, let us denote the external object by X, an object that by the mediation of a physical agent stimulates a sensory surface, say, the retina, and let us suppose that the stimulation gives rise to a perception. The following questions, presupposing perception, arise: How do we know X exists? Supposing the existence of X, how can we discover the nature of X, and also the nature of the mediating physical agent ("light")? Furthermore, what sort of limitation does the visual apparatus impose on us in the effort to attain true knowledge about X and the mediating physical agent? Such questions preoccupied Helmholtz even when he was concerned with the psychology of perception. Given this double interest, it is possible to assent to his epistemology of perception but to disagree with his psychology of perception. My particular interest lies in the psychology of perception.

A basic premise of Helmholtz can be interpreted from the standpoint of both the epistemology and psychology of perception. The premise:

> We never perceive the objects of the external world directly. On the contrary, we only perceive the effects of these objects on our nervous apparatuses, and it has always been like that from the first moment of our life.[2]

First, consider the epistemological bearing of this complex premise as Helmholtz might have envisaged it. The object X is at some distance from the body of the perceiver and produces an "effect" in the perceiver's body by the mediation of ether vibrations. Therefore, there can be no direct perception of X. The premise implies that X, indeed, is perceived but indirectly. This implication is noted by Helmholtz when he indicates that X is perceived by an inference.[9] That sometimes he speaks of the "knowledge" of X that is arrived at by inference, the inference presumably being mediated by a percept or idea, would serve to show that his interest is in epistemology. The second sentence of the premise, where Helmholtz indicates that the "effects" of X "on" the nervous apparatus are directly perceived, may be construed in a sense consistent with an epistemological interest. That is, by 'perceived effects' he meant perception rather than 'perceived nervous effects.'[10] On the other hand, Helmholtz's discussion of the premise also indicates a psychological interest, inasmuch as the direct mental result of the 'perceived effect' is regarded as sensation. In effect, Helmholtz is announcing his intention to concern himself with the explanation of the transition from sensation to perception. In passing, we may remark that in a consistent theoretical system, the psychological question should take precedence over the epistemological question. It would appear, however, that Helmholtz fails to note the logical priority of the psychological question.[11]

A major theme of my presentation arises from a rewording of the second sentence of the premise, namely, "We only perceive the sensations of these objects in our nervous apparatuses. . . ." For emphasis, sensations are *in* the nervous apparatuses. Such rewording is justified by Helmholtz's other versions of the premise[12] and by his reiterations that sensation is in the retina, in the optic nerve, in the brain, or that sensation is propagated from the retina to the brain along the optic nerve.[13] Helmholtz's usual starting point in the discussion of some percept is sensation in the retina, and this will be ours too. We may observe that Helmholtz has the special problem of getting the sensation out of the retina, as it were, and placing it in external space and in a particular region thereof. In any case, it is sensation so localized that is the basis of his discussion of the projection or transference of sensation into the so-called external field of vision. Of course, the alleged problem can be dismissed out of hand from the standpoint of the present day because it makes no sense at all to say that sensation (or retinal "image") can leave the nervous system to enter into external space. But rather than to berate Helmholtz from a contemporary standpoint, my

358

purpose is to examine the issue from Helmholtz's own standpoint and to indicate the problems to which it led in his theory, especially in regard to external reference.

External reference is a general feature of all visual percepts. When I open my eyes and look about me, the objects I see have a "thereness" in space. I see them as detached from my body and usually at some distance from it. When I look at my hand and then at some other object, say, a pencil on the desk, the pencil is evidently at some distance from my hand. Of course, I see other objects or surfaces in the space between my hand and the pencil. Upon closing one eye, I can see part of my nose and also that all other objects are at some distance away from it. When my finger touches an object, I still see this object as detached from my finger (i.e., not part of my body), though, to be sure, I do not see, and cannot see, any distance separating them. I can say all this with the absolute conviction that I have correctly described the way things look to me in reference to my body. I can also say, though perhaps not with the same degree of conviction, that all of you in this room see things as I do. External reference is also a trait of illusory percepts (X absent), such as the pressure phosphene. When the outer side of the right eyeball is pressed with a finger, a luminous circle appears on the side opposite in the general direction of, and near or at, the nasal bridge.

Helmholtz in various ways indicates his recognition of the problems in explaining external reference in general and the pressure phosphene in particular. Such problems arise from his assumption that sensation is in the retina and, therefore, does not have the trait of external reference. It would appear that his basic resolutions of the problems presuppose innate psychical activity that, as it were, creates the externalization of a percept or, in his language, produces the transference of sensation to the external field of vision. And it would also appear that for this reason he appealed to Kantian formulations. We shall begin with the pressure phosphene because Helmholtz devotes more attention to this than to the general problem of external reference.

359

I

In preparation for explaining the phosphene in his lecture of 1855, Helmholtz sets forth a number of significant statements. Having pointed out that light sensation is not vision, he states, "Light sensation becomes vision only insofar as we attain knowledge of the objects of the external world by means of it."[14] He insists that the "understanding of light sensation" is essential to vision and, in respect to sensory illusions in general, he avers that "we deceive ourselves in the understanding of sensation."[15] For emphasis, we observe that "knowledge" of objects and "understanding" of sensation are considered to be prerequisites for vision. Furthermore, he points out as a remarkable fact that "each light sensation occasions the idea of something luminous before us in the field of vision."[16] This statement, which already implies the recognition of the problem of external reference, is made more specific when he says that stimulation of a particular spot of the retina evokes the "idea" of a luminous body in a particular spot in space. Immediately continuing in his first reference to the pressure phosphene, he says:

> [We] always transfer the origin of any light sensation, which arises in [a particular] point of the retina, to the corresponding spot of the external field of vision. If you press the outer angle of the eye with your finger nail, a small light-image arises. Perhaps at first you will not even notice it because you would seek it where you exert pressure. Wide of the mark! It appears as a small luminous circle exactly on the opposite side of the field of vision near the bridge of the nose.[17]

The first sentence of this extract, concerning the transfer of sensation, is not justified in the text up to this point. The comment on the illusory light appearance seems to imply that it ought to be experienced at the place of pressure, and this is why the perceiver would look for it there. In any case, this implication becomes obvious in further discussion of the phosphene.[18]

Helmholtz's explanation of the phenomenon, which he apparently regards as clear, actually is vague and logically inadequate. Therefore, only a portion of his explanation will be chosen for discussion. Having intimated that inference and logical reasoning are involved, he writes: "In the experience of our entire life we have sought and found the origin of the light which strikes the most extreme part of the retina at the bridge of the nose, and our idea without hesitation also transfers the apparent light of the pressure to the same place."[19] Presumably the transference occurs by means of inference, which, of course, would have to be unconscious. This extract implies two distinct cases: (a) X is present, (b) X is absent. The second case need not detain us at all, since the transference could only occur on the condition that it has already occurred when X is present. In respect to the first case, let X represent an actual object at the bridge of the nose. Furthermore, let the effect of X on the extreme part of the retina be denoted by E and the seeing of an object at the nasal bridge by V. The proper interpretation of a 'lifetime of experience' presupposes the existence of V when E is given. This experience, in our view, represents acts of verification. That is, Helmholtz, in effect, is asserting that when V is given, the presence of X has been verified by movements of the body and the sensations arising therefrom—the sensations of the motions of the arm and hand in seeking and grasping X. Furthermore, such acts of verification would have taught us that the location of X corresponds to the location indicated by V. Additionally, the lifetime of experience implies that every act of verification has been successful, including the very first one.[20] Apparently Helmholtz assumed that on the first occasion of an E, V was its consequence.[21] In other words, he presupposed the transference of sensation from the retina to a particular spot of the external field of vision on this first occasion. Since this transference could not be the result of training or education of the senses, it would appear that he must have supposed that the transference is the result of a psychical act originating in an innate faculty of the mind.

I have alluded to the logical inadequacy of the omitted portion of Helmholtz's explanation of the phosphene. He asserted that the "image of the nasal bridge is projected on the outer side of the retina," but he failed to mention the necessity of the transference of the retinal image or sensation of the nasal bridge to the appropriate place in the external field of vision.[22] Apparently, he supposed its transference to have already occurred on the first occasion of the series of experiences of a life time. Quite possibly, Helmholtz, here too, must have supposed that innate psychical activity produced this transference.

Our interpretation concerning Helmholtz's presupposition of innate powers of the mind is corroborated, at least to some degree, in Helmholtz's appeal to Kant toward the end of the 1855 lecture. Before taking this up, we may reconsider the assumed fact that "each light sensation occasions the idea of something luminous before us in the field of vision" for still another relevant aspect. The occasioned idea, which is related to the problem of transference, exemplifies external reference. This idea, the origin of which has not yet been explained by Helmholtz, presumably goes along with the light sensation at its first occurrence. Therefore, this idea also can be regarded as originating in innate psychical activity. Consistent with this interpretation is the fact that Helmholtz often speaks of a connection between sensation and idea, thus implying that an idea is an existent term for participation in the connection.

II

In the Kant section at the end of the 1855 lecture, Helmholtz writes, "If a connection is to be formed between the idea of a body of certain figure and certain position, and our sensations of sense, then we first have to have the idea of such bodies."[23] Here he recognizes the logical problem that for a connection to be formed between two terms, both terms must be on hand for the formation of the connection. In the discussion that follows, the problem of the origin of the idea receives no explicit answer. Immediately subsequent to the quotation, Helmholtz, having stated the basic premise we have quoted in the above, frames a critical question and answers it.

Now, in which way have we for the first time passed over from the the world of sensations of our nerves to the world of reality? Obviously only through an inference; we have to suppose the presence of external objects as the *causes* of our nervous excitations, for there cannot be a cause without an effect.[24]

It would appear that his question concerns the psychology rather than the epistemology of perception since, after all, the sensations are presumed to be in the nerves and perception still must be accounted for. After a brief discussion of the causal law, he concludes: "The investigation of sensory perceptions finally leads us also to the knowledge already established by Kant: that the proposition, 'No effect without a cause,' is a law of our thinking given before all experience."[25] This law, Helmholtz holds, is "innate."[26]

Supposing that the "world of reality" refers to the trait of external reference of sensory perception, a question surely can be raised as to the way in which the a priori causal law, together with the location of light sensation in the retina, can lead to this "world." That is, how can the mind, given this law, pass over from sensation to perception? It seems to us that Helmholtz supposed that the mind is responsible for the transference and also creates the perception or, in his language, "idea." It would then follow that the inference involved would have to be in-nate. Of course, it is possible that Helmholtz has swerved from the psychology of perception to the epistemology of perception. Should this be the case, the basic problems arising from the assumed localization of sensation in the retina remain unre-solved.

However, that Helmholtz, in his appeal to Kant, was con-cerned with the psychology of perception receives confirmation in the similarity between him and Schopenhauer that had al-ready been noticed shortly after 1855.[27] Schopenhauer, begin-ning with a work on vision in 1816, believed that all sensations were subjective. Any sensation, he insisted, "only exists within the organism and under the skin." And in regard to visual sen-sation, the localization of this sensation was presumed to be the retina. In order to account for the objectification of sensa-tion, that is, its projection, he invoked a version of Kant's a priori law of causality. According to him, the "understanding," presumably a faculty of the mind, employed the a priori causal law to transform the subjective sensation into objective perception. That Schopenhauer is dealing with the psychology of perception is particularly evident when he considers the case of a hypothetical man who, in viewing a broad prospect, is suddenly deprived of his "understanding." From the standpoint of this man, all that would remain of the whole prospect is the "sensation of a very varied affection of his retina which, as it were, is the raw stuff from which his understanding previously created that perception."[28]

III

A certain tradition has developed in recent times, especially in American psychology, to the effect that Kantianism was rejected by the advocates of empiristic theory such as Helmholtz, and that it influenced nativists such as Hering. This tradition, however, is not firmly anchored in a textual analysis of the works of Helmholtz and others.[29] Surely, this tradition will have to be reexamined in detail. Perhaps it should be pointed out that, strictly from an empirical standpoint, Kantianism did not stand in necessary contradiction to empiristic theory. Toward the end of the nineteenth century, Kant himself had been claimed as an advocate of empiristic theory.[30] Schopenhauer, whose Kantianism is so strikingly evident, could, without too much difficulty, be considered as espousing basic features of empiristic theory when he undertook the explanation of the development of the perceptions of human infants.[31] It would appear that Helmholtz, despite his stout advocacy of empiristic theory, should have at least one foot firmly placed on Kantian ground.

Occasionally, however, Helmholtz suggests that human perceptions are to be explained exclusively in terms of associations of visual and tactile sensations. His theory can be, and has been, so interpreted.[32] But such an interpretation overlooks what Helmholtz asserts or implies about the role of unconscious inference in the projection of sensation and the full range of his comments on Kant. For the sake of argument, we may consider certain implications of his theory from the standpoint of associationism, to the exclusion of any Kantian influence. My point will be that the implications are such that Helmholtz would have had to postulate occult powers of the mind anyway in order to explain a visual percept and its feature of external reference. Let us suppose, the left eye being closed, that there is an X near or at the nasal bridge. Both X and the nasal bridge project images on the right-hand side of the right retina, and there give rise to light sensations. When the hand is raised to reach and to touch X, the hand likewise projects an image to a particular part of the retina, and the affected part also would give rise to light sensation. The retinal situation can be figuratively described as follows. The light sensation of the hand approaches the light sensations of nasal bridge and X along the surface of the retina. Since the retinal surface is bidimensional, all light sensations are similarly bidimensional.[33] That is, the solidity or third dimension of a percept is not a property of any light sensation. That any visual percept and its feature of externality could ever develop in terms of such assumptions is inconceivable. And this is still the case on the supposition that the tactile sensations derived from movements of the hand could be superadded to, or associated with, the retinal sensations.[34] The mind would forever be trapped in its subjective world of body-localized sensations.[35]

IV

The assumption that sensation is body-localized, of course, receives no confirmation at all in the here and now of perceiving. Thus, in my seeing you at some distance away, I am not aware, and I cannot make myself aware, of any sensation in my eye. Helmholtz, in his discussion of the phosphene, clearly recognizes the introspective nonverifiability of the light sensation and its supposed locus on the right-hand side of the retina by the subject who presses his eyeball.[36] In conceding its nonverifiability, Helmholtz's only recourse is to allege or imply its unconscious presence in seeing a luminous circle to the left. The question naturally arises as to what led Helmholtz to postulate the existence of a mental fact, namely, eye-localized sensation, which is not introspectively verified by anyone. We may first consider an answer from Helmholtz's own standpoint. This concerns the introspective nonverifiability of the mental activities responsible for the transformation of sensation into sensory perception. According to him, psychology relied on self-observation, that is, introspection, as the technique for gaining knowledge of the mind. But he points out that psychology is of no help in providing a description of the mental activities at the basis of perception because they are not accessible to "self observation."[37] This reflection, however, only repeats the question in another form. His decisive answer is that the existence of those activities is disclosed through, and proved by, the physiological investigation of the senses.

However, it may be remarked that physiological investigation as such can provide no information of any kind in regard to the nature, and even possible existence, of the mental activities (or sensation) that might ensue from the stimulation of a sensory surface.[38] In returning to his basic premise, all he would be entitled to say from a physiological standpoint, at most, is that objects of the external world produce effects in the nervous apparatus, and not that such effects are perceived. However, Helmholtz tacitly included sensation in the province of physiological investigation. And for the particular problem that concerns us, he also tacitly included the localization of sensation in the retina, or, more generally, in the nerves. In short, he assumed that sensation and nervous excitation were coterminous events.[39]

V

Up to this point I have probably succeeded in conveying the impression that Helmholtz always considered light sensation to be unconscious. This requires correction because he must have supposed consciousness of sensation in his extensive discussions of the Müller law of the specific energies of sense. Additional problems in the understanding of Helmholtz's theory arise from this consideration. In accordance with this law, which Helmholtz always considered to be a most significant discovery in the physiological investigation of the senses, any mode of stimulation of a particular sensory nerve produces a sensation that is specific to it. Any stimulation of the retina and optic nerve occasions nothing but light sensation. For instance, transection of the optic nerve of a patient requiring surgery for a tumor, as Helmholtz points out, gives rise not to pain but to the seeing of a flash of light.[40] Notwithstanding the limitations of introspection that he sets forth in other contexts, it is clear that he is relying, as he must, on the subject's report of his self-observation in setting forth the empirical basis of the Müller law.

Actually, the Müller law does not represent a victory for physiological investigation as such, since the physiologist obtained his knowledge of "sensation" from the introspecting subject of an experiment or surgical procedure. Indeed, it was such a subject that made it possible for the physiologist to obtain significant knowledge of nervous structure and nervous action.[41] Occasionally, Helmholtz indicates the role of the introspecting subject but without sufficient appreciation of its scope. When setting forth the range of facts at the basis of the Müller law, he fails to note the important fact that the subject does not localize a sensation in the retina or anywhere else in the nervous system.

VI

Controversy over the theoretical implications of the vision of animals, especially newborns, forms a significant chapter in the history of perceptual theory. This was also true in Helmholtz's period, and Helmholtz himself became the target of criticism. Critics, friends, and adversaries alike held that animal data embarrassed his general theory of the development of human sensory perception and called his attention to relevant data derived from either naturalistic observations or experiments.[42] Generally, Helmholtz's discussion of animal data and response to criticism were inadequate. In any case, since he does not have any explicit discussion of animals relevant to the themes of this presentation in his works, the implications of his theory for animal vision have to be inferred and hence must be somewhat speculative.

367

Helmholtz's basic premise does not appear in its immediate meaning to be restricted to the human species. Restating it in specific reference to the chimpanzee, it reads:

> The chimpanzee never perceives the objects of the external world directly. On the contrary, the chimpanzee only perceives the effects of these objects on its nervous apparatus, and it has always been like that from the first moment of the chimpanzee's life.[43]

The justification for the inclusion of the chimpanzee within the scope of the premise is as follows. The argument that X produces an effect in the nervous system of humans applies with equal force to the chimpanzee. That effect for both man and chimpanzee is located inside the body. And if we allow perception to the chimpanzee, it will perceive sensation in its retina. According to Helmholtz's theory, as developed by Helmholtz himself or as interpreted by others, two options are logically available for the explanation of the sensory perceptions of the chimpanzee. It could be argued that the Kantian a priori causal law operates in the "mind" of this animal. This, of course, would represent an interesting extension of Kantian principles.[44] On the other hand, it could be argued that the perceptions of this animal are wholly explicable in terms of the association of visual and tactile sensations. In that case, however, the chimpanzee would always be confined to a world of subjective sensation, provided that occult mental powers are not attributed to it. But even the postulation of such powers is foreclosed when "duck" replaces "chimpanzee" in the premise. The duck does not possess tactile or prehensile organs as does the chimpanzee. Therefore, the possibility of invoking those occult powers that might arise through tactile sensations in their association with visual sensations is excluded.[45]

Thus far, I have supposed that an animal has mental abilities, that it has light sensation, and that it perceives and sees. Helmholtz's explicit or implicit comments on animals sanction these statements and hence justify the relevancy of our discussion of animals in the understanding of his over-all theory of perception. He attributes "mental activity" to animals,[46] and also the ability to form "inductive inferences" similar to man.[47]

In his explanation of the results of Spalding's experiments on chicks, he notes, "Of course we have to consider that they have already previously pecked in the egg-shell, and perhaps have also seen when doing so. . . ."[48] Since he grants the possibility that the chick could have "seen" when in the egg, it appears probable that he would have maintained that the chick could *see* after hatching. He intimates that animals are subject to visual illusions—a bird, he says, pecks at the painting of a grape as though the real object were present. This comment, in its context, indicates that Helmholtz was of the opinion that the bird sees the painted grape as a three-dimensional object just as we would.[49]

In a presentation of the empirical data supporting the Müller law, Helmholtz notes:

> That the optic nerve and the retina, both capable of being stimulated by so delicate an agency as light, are tolerably insensitive to the roughest mechanical maltreatment, that is, have no sensation of pain, has seemed a remarkable paradox. The explanation, however, is simple, because the quality of all sensations of the optic nerve belongs to the group of light sensations.[50]

Before interpreting this passage, we may observe that the subject of the maltreatment is omitted. Man or animal? The context of the passage does not provide a decisive clue. Moreover, Helmholtz does not supply the citation for the observation. However, the observation most likely is based on the experimental work of the physiologist Magendie, who, incidentally, expressed great surprise at the results of his experiments. Animals—dogs, for instance—were the subjects of his experiments. He reports that a dog did not give any "appearance of pain" when he lacerated its retina and optic nerve. He was surprised because he had anticipated (as had other physiologists) signs of excruciating pain. Wishing to know whether this result was generalizable to humans, he undertook an experiment with an adult female patient who was to undergo surgery for double cataracts. However, he confined himself only to lightly touching the retina with the point of a needle several times. The patient, he reported, did not experience pain at all. Instead, in another result that as-

369

tonished him, "the woman, at the same instance in which I touched the nervous membrane, expressed her delight at seeing light again." Having obtained similar results with another patient, he concluded that the human retina gives rise only to light when stimulated, and in this respect "we do not differ from animals."[51]

Returning to the Helmholtz passage, the subject must be an animal. Also, his mode of expression is unusual: "The optic nerve and the retina . . . have no sensation of pain. . . . " Unusual because of the implication that sensation is a property of the animal's nervous system. Furthermore, he implies that animals localize light sensation in the nervous system, as the next sentence indicates. It seems probable that Helmholtz assumed for animals, as he had for man, the coextensivity of sensation and nervous excitation.

VII

Scientists interested in perception accept, explicitly or otherwise, a causal theory of perception, a theory that rests on the distinction of mental and physical facts. The scientist justifiably claims that certain physical happenings in the brain cause, give rise to, or are correlated with, mental facts.[52] As a corollary, the theory prescribes a mode of description that is alien to common sense. In ordinary life, when we see objects and describe them, we regard these objects as physical. However, we are actually referring to and describing mental facts. In the terminology of Gestalt psychology, the physical object of ordinary life is a phenomenal object, and the description pertains to the latter object.[53] In the definition of external reference, which I gave from my standpoint, "object," "pencil," "desk," "nose," and "hand" are, from the standpoint of the causal theory, phenomenal objects. Furthermore, the "distance," such as that between hand and object, is a phenomenal distance between phenomenal objects. "Colors" and "light," which in ordinary life are regarded as properties of physical objects or circumambient physical space, also are mental facts. Any visual illusion illustrates the necessity of the description imposed by the corollary.[54] Helmholtz accepted the causal theory of perception or some version of it. But he did not explicitly formulate the distinction of mental and physical facts. That he did recognize it is evident when he calls attention to the misuse of "light" as designating those ether-vibrations that excite the "sensation of light." "Properly speaking," he says, "the word should be used only . . . to denote the sensation that is produced by this means."[55] In other words, light belongs to the domain of mental facts and not to the domain of physical facts. However, he typically confused the two kinds of facts. The assumed location of sensation in the retina or optic nerve illustrates this confusion. A sensation, which is a mental fact, is considered as being coterminous with nervous excitation, which is a physical fact, in an anatomical structure, which is also a physical fact.[56]

1. The above represents an attempt to summarize key aspects of Helmholtz's theory drawn from his extensive writings on sensation and perception. However, a sufficient justification of the summary can be had in the appreciation of his "modification rule" and psychological explanation of simultaneous color contrast. The rule implies that an actual sensation is always present in a percept, though the perceiver is not aware of it. His explanation of color contrast presupposes the rule. See Nicholas Pastore, *Selective History of Theories of Visual Perception: 1650–1950* (New York: Oxford University Press, 1971), chap. 9, for definitions and discussion.

2. Ibid., pp. 35, 37, and passim.

3. Helmholtz's theory implies that acts of the mind do not have specific concomitants or counterparts in the nervous action in the brain (or elsewhere in the nervous system), and, perforce, unfold independently of physiological activity. The theory, in short, violates the psychophysical postulate (for William James's definition of the postulate and its discussion, ibid., pp. 224–25). As far as can be judged, the only place where Helmholtz attempts to accommodate his theory to physiology is in the final section of his work on physiological optics: "If one does not wish to reckon these processes of association and of the natural flow of ideas among the psychical activities, *but to attribute them to nervous substance*, I will not quarrel over names" (my emphasis): Hermann von Helmholtz, *Handbuch der Physiologischen Optik* (Leipzig: Voss, 1867), sec. 33, p. 804 (hereafter cited as *Optik*). That the issue was merely verbal is questionable, for if he had framed explanations in terms of "nervous substance," or better, in terms of innate and acquired brain mechanisms, he would have surrendered his particular emphasis on psychological factors. Incidentally, that Helmholtz, in the quoted passage, is concerned with psychological and physiological explanations is obscured in the standard English translation as reprinted by Dover, vol. 3, p. 541: "If anyone objects to including these processes of association and the natural flow of ideas among the psychic activities I will not quarrel over names" (*Treatise on Physiological Optics*, ed. J. P. S. Southall, translated from the 3d German edition, 3 vols. [New York: Optical Society of America, 1924]. (hereafter cited as *Optics*.) In the Dover reprint (New York, 1962) vols. 1 and 2 are combined in one volume. All citations to the translation will be from the Dover reprint).

An important source in my interpretation of the *Optik* is the French translation that appeared in the same year (*Optique Physiologique*, trans. E. Javal and N. Klein [Paris: Masson, 1867]). Incidentally, the translation carries the same pagination as the original. Of historical interest, to which I have alluded elsewhere (*Selective History*, p. 394), is the fact that Helmholtz guaranteed the authenticity of the translation in his preface to the *Optique*: " . . . Having re-read all the proofs, I believe I can guarantee its exactitude."

I wish to acknowledge the assistance of my colleague, Dr. Peter Dietrich, in the translation of Helmholtz's *Optik* and other works.

4. In this section of the *Optik*, Helmholtz, in effect, argues, against J. S. Mill, that an a priori law of causality must be involved in the determination of the major premise of an inference. Incidentally, I shall not attempt any detailed exposition of "unconscious inference" and its alleged role in the formation of sensory perception. Helmholtz is too vague on this subject. Also, in my view, "inference" constitutes a secondary issue necessitated in his theory by his basic presuppositions on the nature of sensation. One such presupposition, namely, that sensation is in, or a property of, the nervous system, is selected for examination here.

5. *Ueber das Sehen des Menschen* (Leipzig: Voss, 1855). My citations will be to this edition, although the lecture was reprinted in the first volume of Helmholtz's *Vorträge und Reden*, 2 vols., 5th ed. (Braunschweig: Viewig, 1903).

6. *Optik*, sec. 33, p. 819.

7. Nicholas Pastore, "Helmholtz's 'Popular Lectures on Vision'," *Journal of the History of the Behavioral Sciences* 9 (1973): 190–202, 198. Retrospectively, perhaps "mind" in this context is the more appropriate translation of "*Bewusstsein*" than "consciousness". Otherwise, Helmholtz essentially would be presupposing an 'unconscious consciousness'.

8. *Ueber das Sehen des Menschen*, p. 40. Although the premise represents a general statement, it will be restricted to vision. Incidentally, the appellation "basic premise" or "premise" is my own.

9. "But if consciousness (*Bewusstsein*) does not perceive directly at the place of the objects themselves, it can only arrive at its knowledge through an inference. For only through inferences can we know at all what we do not directly perceive" (ibid., p. 36).

10. The second sentence of the premise is being interpreted in a way favorable to Helmholtz. Nervous excitations are produced by X. These excitations give rise to the "effects" that are "perceived." In this interpretation no intermediate mental content such as inference is interposed between "excitations" and "effects". An unfavorable interpretation, on the other hand, is that the "excitations" themselves are perceived ("effects" equated with "excitations"), in which case some sort of interposed mental content becomes necessary. For discussion of *tertium quid* mental content in Helmholtz and other thinkers, see my "Reevaluation of Boring on Kantian Influence, Nineteenth Century Nativism, Gestalt Psychology, and Helmholtz," *Journal of the History of the Behavioral Sciences* 10 (1974): 375–90.

11. Suppose, on "seeing one object," the question is asked as to how one would know that there is a single X in space. To deal with this question, it would have to be explained how, given two sensations, one from each eye, the percept "seeing one object" could arise.

12. For instance, in the *Optik*, sec. 26, p. 430.

13. As will become evident in our quotations and discussion of Helmholtz. For additional quotations see my previously cited "Helmholtz's 'Popular Lectures' " and "Reevaluation of Boring."

A noteworthy passage from Helmholtz's *Die Thatsachen in der Wahrnehmung* merits quotation: "[The] objects present in space appear to us clothed in the qualities of our sensations. They appear to us red or green, cold or warm, they have smell or taste, etc., while these sensory qualities belong, after all, only to our nervous system and do not at all extend into outer space" (quoted after W. Köhler, "An Old Pseudo-problem," trans. E. Goldmeier, in *The Selected Papers of Wolfgang Köhler*, ed. M. Henle [New York: Liveright, 1971], p. 125 n; cf. *Selected Writings of Hermann von Helmholtz*, edited, with introduction, by Russell Kahl [Middletown, Conn.: Wesleyan University Press, 1971], p. 377). In effect, Helmholtz implies that sensory qualities truly "clothe" the nervous system, in which case he has the significant theoretical problem of explaining the appearance of a quality as an apparent attribute of an "object."

14. *Ueber das Sehen des Menschen*, p. 20.

15. Ibid., p. 20.

16. Ibid.

17. Ibid., p. 21. Incidentally, the problem under discussion is related to the problems of single vision and erect vision (ibid., pp. 29, 39).

18. Ibid., p. 22.

19. Ibid., p. 21. Helmholtz obviously personifies "idea" (*Vorstellung*). Personification of "idea" and similar entities, which was common in nineteenth-century discussions of vision, continues into the present. For instance, Harmon M. Chapman: "Sensation is clearly prior to perception in that it provides the raw materials on which perception operates" (*Sensations and Phenomenology* [Bloomington: Indiana University Press, 1966], p. 72).

20. The immediate above quotation in the text does not imply any exception. See note 21 below.

21. In the *Optik*, Helmholtz writes: "When we have felt excitation in those nerve mechanisms whose peripheral endings lie on the right hand side of both retinas, we have found in million-fold repeated experiences of our entire life that a luminous object lay before us on our left side. We had to raise the hand to the left in order to hide the light or to grasp the luminous object, or we had to move toward the left in order to come closer to it" (sec. 26, p. 448). This passage clearly implies his concern with acts of verification. Furthermore, consider the perceptual situation on the first trial of the apparently successful millionfold repetition of verificatory acts. If "luminous object" defines V, then V is present on this first trial and therefore is not the product of learning. If "luminous object" defines X (as I believe it does), then V, in this passage, is not specified. In other discussion that follows the quoted passage, the "seeing of a light to the left" can be taken as the definition of V (ibid., p. 449). Parenthetically, a failure of a verificatory act does not necessarily imply the absence of V; I may see a light to left but move my hand to the right.

22. *Ueber das Sehen des Menschen*, p. 21.

23. Ibid., p. 40. We may remark that "sensation" and "idea," in our notation, respectively correspond to E and V.

24. Ibid., p. 41.

25. Ibid.

26. Ibid. For other quotations from, and discussion of, Helmholtz's *Ueber das Sehen des Menschen*, see Pastore, "Reevaluation of Boring."

27. Apparently the similarity was such that Frauenstädt, a follower of Schopenhauer and editor of his works, could claim shortly after Helmholtz's *Ueber das Sehen des Menschen* that Helmholtz had plagiarized Schopenhauer's revision of Kant along with its application to perception; Helmholtz and his father discussed this accusation in the course of their correspondence in 1856 (Leo Koenigsberger, *Hermann von Helmholtz*, 3 vols. [Braunschweig: Viewig, 1902], 1:278, 285, 291, 293). The allegation of plagiarism is of interest here only because, serving as a measure of the degree of perceived similarity, it provides insight into the understanding of Helmholtz's theory.

Others who commented on the similarity (not necessarily restricted to Helmholtz's

Ueber das Sehen des Menschen) include: August Classen, *Ueber den Einfluss Kants auf die Theorie der Sinneswahrnehmung* (Leipzig: Grunow, 1886), pp. 114–15; Luigi Luciani, *Human Physiology*, trans. F. A. Welby, 5 vols. (London: Macmillan, 1911–21), 4:12; Wilhelm Wundt, *Elements de psychologie physiologique*, trans. E. Rouvrier, 2 vols. (Paris: Alcan, 1886), 2:195–96; Johann C. F. Zöllner, *Ueber die Natur der Cometen*, 3d ed. (Leipzig: Staackmann, 1883), pp. 140–43.

28. The above discussion of Schopenhauer is based principally on his *Ueber das Sehn und die Farben* (Leipzig: Hartknoch, 1816), chap. 1. See also A. Schopenhauer, *On the Fourfold Root of the Principle of Sufficient Reason and On the Will in Nature*, trans. K. Hillebrand, rev. ed. (London: Bell, 1903), secs. 21, 22; William James, *Principles of Psychology*, 2 vols. (New York: Holt, 1890), 2:33 n, 273–75.

29. Pastore, "Reevaluation of Boring."

30. Ibid.

31. Schopenhauer, *On the Fourfold Root*, pp. 84–87.

32. W. James, J. Sully, and W. Wundt placed Helmholtz in the tradition of English associationism (quoted and discussed in Pastore, *Selective History*, pp. 161, 227, 394).

33. This statement concerning bidimensionality reflects Helmholtz's acceptance of the constancy hypothesis—another significant assumption in his theory; this assumption was not restricted to vision with one eye (for quotations and discussion, see Pastore, *Selective History*, chap. 9; Pastore, "Helmholtz's 'Popular Lectures'," pp. 193–96).

34. For emphasis, "mental chemistry" (an occult power of the mind) is excluded in my above account of associationism. For justification of my point concerning inconceivability, see Pastore, *Selective History*, pp. 85, 140–42, 183–85, pp. 198–201, 215–16, 224. Parenthetically, it is also inconceivable that the "mind" could ever attain any knowledge of the external world and objects therein.

35. This represented a classical predicament. Condillac wrote in 1754: "How can sensation extend beyond the organ which feels and circumscribes it?" (Pastore, *Selective History*, p. 100).

36. *Optik*, sec. 26, p. 449.

37. *Selected Writings of Hermann von Helmholtz*, p. 142; *Ueber das Sehen des Menschen*, p. 34.

38. For emphasis, physiological investigation may be interpreted as a natural science in the sense that it is concerned with physical events—nervous structures and 'molecular action' in the nerves.

39. An assumption of Helmholtz recognized by James (*Principles of Psychology*, 2:33).

40. *Ueber das Sehen des Menschen*, p. 15.

41. That transection of the optic nerve gives rise to the sensation of a light flash could only have been ascertained from an introspecting subject. See also note 51 below.

42. See, for instance, the comments of Tyndall, Helmholtz's friend, in his famous 1874 Belfast address (John Tyndall, *Fragments of Science*, 5th ed. [New York: Appleton, 1883], p. 526). Tyndall called Helmholtz's attention to the relevancy of Spalding's experiments on animals; in response, Helmholtz revised his previous interpretation of animal data (Pastore, "Helmholtz's 'Popular Lectures'," pp. 201–2).

43. I discuss Berkeley's theory of vision from a similar standpoint in my paper, "In His Eye, or Rather in His Mind," in a work edited by E. Hilfstein and P. Czartoryski published in *Studia Copernicana* (XVI), under the auspices of the Polish Academy of Science: Institute of the History of Science, Education, and Technology (Ossolineum: in press).

44.   Schopenhauer took this step in his discussion of animal vision (Schopenhauer, *On the Fourfold Root*, p. 89).

45.   Suppose an object is close to the duck's head on one side and somewhat above its bill. The duck does not possess the means for "hiding" or "grasping" the object.

46.   Pastore, "Helmholtz's 'Popular Lectures'," p. 201.

47.   *Selected Writings of Hermann von Helmholtz*, p. 508. The "inferences" are not related to the possible origin of animal perception.

48.   Pastore, "Helmholtz's 'Popular Lectures'," p. 201.

49.   Helmholtz, "Optisches ueber Malerei," in *Vorträge und Reden*, 2:96 (see translation in H. Helmholtz, *Popular Scientific Lectures*, selected and introduced by M. Kline [New York: Dover, 1962], p. 251). Having recognized this visual illusion in birds, Helmholtz, to be consistent, would have had to regard the bird's three-dimensional percept either as involving "unconscious inferences" along with an a priori causal law or as the exclusive result of acquired associations. Consider his assumption of the constancy hypothesis (note 33 above). The only assignable reason at the basis of this assumption is the bidimensionality of the human retina. Since the avian retina is also bidimensional, his theory demands that the bird, in reference to sensation, should see everything bidimensionally.

50.   *Optics*, 2:11.

51.   François Magendie, "Suite des expériences sur les fonctions de la cinquième paire de nerfs," *Journal de physiologie expérimentale et pathologique* 4 (1824): 302–15; idem, "Sur l'insensibilité de la rétine de l'homme," *Journal de physiologie expérimentale et pathologique* 5 (1825): 37–41. Obviously the above observations and conclusions derived from human subjects had to depend on their introspections. According to the theoretical assumptions of the period, it was anticipated that the stimulation of the retina by a coarse agent, such as a needle, should give rise not only to pain but also to the most excruciating pain known to man. Introspection falsified these assumptions. It also led to the unexpected phenomenon of the seeing of light and color. Furthermore, the reports of the introspecting subject led to, or reinforced, a new conception of nervous action and structure: (a) that stimulation of different nerves by the same external agent gives rise to sensation that is specific to a particular nerve, (b) that stimulation of the retina by any external agent gives rise to light sensation, (c) that the retinal receptors do not include "pain" receptors.

In our view the experiments on animals do not necessarily weaken the importance we have given to the introspecting subject. When interested in ascertaining the generalizability of his results to humans (thus conceding the possibility of a difference between man and animal in respect to "function"), Magendie relied on the introspection of his human subjects. Of particular significance in this regard is the subject's "seeing of light"—a result not attributable to a dog based on the presence or absence of its motor reactions (as had been the case in Magendie's interpretation that the dog did not give the "appearance of pain" when its optic system was mechanically mistreated). Furthermore, Magendie's motivation in undertaking experiments with animals (which he did not fully explain) might have been undertaken in the knowledge of the antecedent observations on human subjects who underwent surgery for cataracts that had been reported by Sir Charles Bell in 1811 (Leonard Carmichael documents Bell's priority and quotes Bell in respect to the theoretical significance of cataract operations in "Sir Charles Bell: A Contribution to the History of Physiological Psychology," *Psychological Review* 33 [1926]: 188–217). Bell wrote: "In the operation of couching the cataract, the pain of piercing the retina with a needle is not so great as that which proceeds from a grain of sand under the eyelid. . . . [The] pain is occasioned by piercing the outward coat, not by the affection of the expanded nerve of vision. If the sensation of light were conveyed to us by the retina, the organ of vision, in consequence of that organ being as much more sensible than the surface of the body as the impression of light is more delicate than that pressure which gives us the sense of touch; what would be the feelings of a man subjected to an operation in which a needle were pushed through the nerve. Life could not bear so great a pain But there is an occurrence during this operation on the eye, which will direct us to the truth: when the needle pierces the eye, the patient has the sensation of a spark of fire before the eye" (*Idea of a New Anatomy of the Brain*: A Facsimile of the Privately Printed Edition of 1811, with a Bibliographical Introduction [London: Dawsons of Pall Mall, 1966], pp. 10-11).

52. Here we are concerned with the "mental effects" of only the final physical term of the causal chain of physical events.

53. For instance, see Köhler, "An Old Pseudoproblem."

54. For instance, to cite an illusion of personal interest: Two phosphorescent painted rods, one directly above the other, are viewed in a dark room. Contours joining their ends are seen so that a complete rectangular surface is perceived (the space between the contours appears luminous). When the distance between the rods is increased, the length of the contours also increases as though being stretched. As distance further increases, the contours gradually approach each other at their centers as though being pinched together. Clearly, the contours along with their stretching and convergence represent mental or phenomenal facts. Moreover, the "phosphorescent rods," the ends of which are joined by contours, also represent phenomenal facts. Köhler, of course, selected "visual illusions" for the purpose of emphasizing the necessity to distinguish between phenomenal and physical facts ("A Task for Philosophers," in *Selected Papers of Wolfgang Köhler*, pp. 91-95).

55. *Optics*, 2:4.

56. Helmholtz's confusion of phenomenal and physical facts, which dominates his theory of perception in general and his theory of projection in particular, has been recognized by many theorists. See Ewald Hering, *Outlines of a Theory of the Light Sense*, trans. L. M. Hurvich and D. Jameson (Cambridge, Mass.: Harvard University Press, 1964), pp. 4-6; James, *Principles of Psychology*, 2:33-34; Köhler, "A Task for Philosophers," p. 94.

Chapter Fourteen

SCIENCE AND ANTI-SCIENCE IN THE
PHILOSOPHY OF PERCEPTION

Even though at the end of the nineteenth century there was little concern for empirical science in the dominant idealist philosophy, the ensuing realist revival led to a good deal of cross-fertilization between philosophy and science (physiological and psychological). Indeed, in the work of some famous figures, such as W. James and G. F. Stout, it is by no means easy to say where philosophy leaves off and psychology begins; and Russell and Broad took the evidence from physics and physiology on the causation of perception very seriously as providing a crucial epistemological problem and, in turn, as providing an important field for the application of the sense-datum theory. Today idealism is rarely supported, but in the mainstream of contemporary philosophy (at least in Britain), with its preoccupation with conceptual analysis and its constant homage to Wittgenstein, the sciences are dismissed from the consideration of perception. Neurology and physiology are claimed to present no philosophical problems—only a temptation to fallacious causal theory; the philosophical psychology of, e.g., Stout is felt to be the kind of introspective concern with inner conscious processes from which philosophers have been emancipated; and modern experimental psychology has been condemned by Wittgenstein and his followers as vitiated by conceptual confusions.[1] There have been, of course, exceptions to this trend, particularly in the United States, but the breach between philosophy and science of perception has become so marked in Britain that it is worthwhile to examine the main reasons for it.

The sense-datum theory of Russell, Moore, Broad, and Price was the dominant philosophical approach in the first half of the twentieth century, so let us take as our first witness Price's book *Perception*.[2] In his first two pages he explains why science cannot answer the philosophical question of how our sense experiences justify our beliefs about the physical world. The physiological account of the causal processes in perception cannot help since it is based on the observational propositions into whose validity the philosopher is inquiring; indeed, if physiology is used to undermine ordinary observation, a gross fallacy is committed. Again, science only tells us the causes of perceiving, whereas the philosopher inquires into what perceiving itself is, a question "outside the sphere of science altogether."

I shall discuss Price's second point in its later development as the view that philosophy has a special task of conceptual analysis insulated from science. His first point was partly motivated by the skeptical implications of the representative theory, which I shall also consider later. But it primarily developed from the central epistemological aim of the sense-datum theory, viz., to provide foundations for empirical knowledge of the world on the basis of data that are (1) absolutely certain and (2) "given," i.e., not the result of inference or other mediating intellectual processes. This double requirement was often stated by saying that the data sought were objects of knowledge by acquaintance; and what were held to fill the bill were, for example, shaped patches of color, sounds, smells, and tactile sensations.

This drew philosophy away from concern with the findings of science partly because, as Price indicates, it was thought of as providing a foundation for the observation of the world on which science depended, and partly because the methods and principal suppositions involved in this kind of enquiry were diametrically opposed to those of science. To see this, consider how Price introduced sense-data:

> When I see a tomato there is much that I can doubt. I can doubt whether it is a tomato that I am seeing, and not a cleverly painted piece of wax. I can doubt whether there is any material thing there at all. Perhaps what I took for a tomato was really a reflection, perhaps I am even the victim of some hallucination. One thing how-

ever I cannot doubt; that there exists a red patch of a round and somewhat bulgy shape, standing out from a background of other colour-patches, and having a certain visual depth, and that this whole field of colour is directly present to my consciousness. (*Perception*, p. 3)

The assumption behind this is that what matters is what is contained in one individual's single act of perception, what one might call the solo snapshot approach. This is true to a strong philosophical tradition noticeable, for example, in Descartes. And the individualism is reminiscent also of a trend in Christianity; the mind faces the world in knowledge like the individual soul facing his God. By contrast science is cooperative and based on the repetition of observations and experiments that can be confirmed by anyone. Consider how one might settle the doubts that Price raises about the tomato. "It may be wax": then cut it and taste it; "it may be a reflection": then move around and try to touch it, and look for mirrors; "it may be a hallucination": then use the evidence of other persons as well as that of other senses or perhaps a photograph, and so on. The point here is that if one is really seeking what is with certainty the object of perception, why stick at one look when one can discover it through a simple series of tests using the evidence of the other senses, other persons, attempts to manipulate the object, and so on—i.e., in the main, public transactions?

The sense-datum theorist would reply to this that there is no certainty about the assumption that these various tests are all directed on the same object of knowledge. When we say that two persons see the same thing, they are actually acquainted with different sense-data that we suppose to belong to the same object; and similarly, my claim to see and touch the same thing is based on the different sense-data I obtain. Consequently the objection misses the point that the basic data of knowledge in all these cases are the sense-data.

This reply depends on prior acceptance of the view that our direct or actual acquaintance is not with objects but with sense-data, and why should we accept this? The sense-datum theorists could have brought in the scientific account of perceiving, equating the sense-data with the effects of sensory stimulation, but that would have been anathema to them. Hence they rely on the argument from illusion. If A and B see a dish from very different viewpoints, then A will see, or rather be acquainted with, a round shape and B will be acquainted with an elliptical one' hence they cannot both be acquainted with the same thing; viz, the dish, for the dish cannot *be* both round and elliptical. This argument only seemed plausible to so many eminent philosophers because of their assumption that immediacy or givenness guarantees truth. The elliptical shape with which B is immediately acquainted is "given," and so there must be an elliptical existent—as Price says, "in the sphere of the given what seems, is" (*Perception*, p. 10). As far as the deliverances of the different senses are concerned, he would have claimed that the data of touch and the data of sight are so different in phenomenal character that we could not strictly be seeing and touching one and the same object. The rock-bottom hard datum at any moment is what is given to one sense of one individual, and the relations of this to other data and to the object must be constructed by correlations that are liable to error. What is thus primary to the scientist (observation of things) is shown by the epistemologist to be derivative, and the field separate from science is opened up by the philosopher.

The central weakness in all this is the assumption that givenness or immediacy for consciousness guarantees certainty; both this and its development in the argument from illusion have come under such fire in recent years that all I need do here is point to how surprising it is that so little of the psychologists' controversy about nativism and empiricism or their experiments about the effects on perception of learning, set, cues, and so on, filtered through to the philosophers. Broad, it is true, does discuss the staircase figure and other alternating figures briefly and allows that past experience and present expectation affect the sense-data that we have, but Price does not consider them at all; and neither discusses object constancy,[3] in which the content of perception varies according to attitudes and even beliefs and differs from what a camera records. The point surely is that since sense-data are affected by subjective factors of a psychological or, for that matter, physiological nature, they cannot be objective data of knowledge on which to base the epistemological structure.

Although one must reject Pricean sense-data, nevertheless the concern with the data of consciousness was valuable and led to an emphasis on the phenomenology of perceiving that helped to wean philosophers away from point sensations, Lockeian simple ideas, or the postulated sensations of Helmholtz's constancy hypothesis. The sense-data were the products of careful inspection rather than of perceptual theory, although as in any observation this inspection was theory-guided; and so the search for the foundations of knowledge of objects led by Price's time to distinguishing as one datum the whole front surface of an object with visual depth rather than one color patch (perhaps Gestalt theory had an unrecognized influence here). Unfortunately theory prevented the further step of regarding ostensible objects as given, e.g., an ostensible tomato or a hand; the identification involved was thought to be an intellectual element akin to judgment and so not part of acquaintance or givenness, though it is unclear why it was supposed that we do not similarly identify colors and shapes. Also the inspection went too far in eventually attributing to the sense-datum full perspective quality and minute variations of light and shade and such—what the artist paints. Thus Price identifies Gibson's visual field with what sense-datum philosophers sought to isolate.[4] This then lays them fully open to Firth's criticism that the product of perceptual reduction cannot be regarded as a content in normal unreduced perception.[5] But if not carried to excess, this interest in the content of consciousness is a salutary corrective to that enthusiasm for behaviorist theories of perception which may lead philosophers to forget the sensuous character of looks and sounds and to produce a jejune travesty of our familiar perceptual experiences.

There is another way in which the sense-datum theorists' preoccupations still bear fruit. Even though Austin and other common-sense realists have shown that the arguments from illusion and hallucination do not prove the case for sense-data, one cannot so readily dismiss as unproblematical the experiences contained in these phenomena. If they are not sense-data, what is the second object (a bottle perhaps) seen in double vision, the blue color seen when looking at distant green hills in evening? What moves across the cinema screen? What was the seeming dagger that Macbeth saw? One bottle looking double, green hills looking blue, quickly successive stationary patterns, hallucinatory images confused with reality? Some of these hardly do justice to the experience, but more importantly they pose problems of explanation. How is it that the bottle looks double (even if that is a legitimate expression); that the hills look blue; and so on? What are the images and how are they produced? Or another point, how does the pain in the phantom limb occur? To answer these, anyone with that natural curiosity which Aristotle claimed to be the origin of philosophical inquiry would be driven to the physics and physiology of perceiving or to the psychological process therein—all things that many modern philosophers would like to exorcise from the philosophy of perception. And even if we have no bell and candle for the exorcism, there are plenty of books.

One line developed by Ryle is that inquiries into the physiology of perception have been misrepresented as explaining seeing and hearing. Such explanations would merely be in causal terms, and though partly satisfactory to the scientist (only partly, so that sense impressions have to be postulated), they do not deal with the questions "which are of interest in epistemology": these "are not causal questions . . . but questions . . . about the *crafts* or *arts* of finding out things by seeing or hearing—including questions about the nature of mistakes and failures in perception." Again, these "questions of technique" are not answerable by "answers to questions about causal conditioning."[6] We may also recall Price's summary rejection of inquiry into the causes of perceiving.

No one would, of course, claim that causal questions and explanations are the only ones in perception, but Ryle's alternative characterization of epistemological questions as questions of technique is strange and unconvincing. It suggests the sort of training in the technique of observation given in the armed forces, e.g., scan the whole field of view systematically rather than randomly. And questions about mistakes or failures might similarly be satisfied by a non-philosophical answer, e.g., because of carelessness, inexperience, preoccupation, or clever camouflage. Ryle's obsession with the chess analogy, already partly responsible for the divorce of language from the world in current theory of meaning, leads him to think of perceiving as a game and of the relevant questions as ones of how best to play it. Mistakes may be overcome by technique in that one learns to discount or distrust what one sees, but technique does not stop the green hills from looking blue in the evening or the moon from looking larger near the horizon; it does not alter strobo-scopic effects or prevent hallucinatory visions presenting similar sensuous characteristics to veridical perceiving; nor does it en-able one to understand what these are. Technique in chess alters the content of one's play; technique in perceiving has only a limited effect in altering the content of awareness.

The root trouble is that neither Ryle nor Price realizes that the causal data and explanations *pose* philosophical problems of a kind that have long been the stuff of epistemology because they make knowledge of the external world difficult to under-stand. Hence they cannot be put in a separate scientific casket and decently buried. The philosopher, with his traditional synop-tic task of considering *all* the facts, has to fit them into his pic-ture of perceiving, which thus has more than a scientific dimen-sion: he must provide a theory of perception that shows the mutually connected roles of physiological and experiential data in an integrated whole, in terms of which hallucinations, illu-sions, and other variations can be explained. Of course, philos-ophy cannot advance a developed scientific theory—the subject matter is insufficiently quantifiable and there is no scope for experiments to confirm or falsify predictions. But it can use other criteria to justify its theories such as consistency, com-prehensiveness (covering experiential as well as scientific facts), simplicity (in the sense of fewer ontological hostages to for-tune, no repeated coincidences or *deus ex machina*), and su-periority to all suggested alternatives.

A more radical attack comes from Wittgenstein. His view in the *Philosophical Investigations* is not that philosophers seek to explain different things from the scientist but that they should not seek to explain at all: "We may not advance any kind of theory . . . we must do away with all *explanation*, and description alone must take its place." Philosophical problems "are solved by looking into the workings of our language" (*PI*, p. 109). "Philosophy may in no way interfere with the actual use of our language: it can in the end only describe it. It leaves everything as it is" (*PI*, p. 124). "Philosophy simply puts everything before us, and neither explains nor deduces anything" (*PI*, p. 126). These statements are equally outrageous in their falsity, if a description of philosophical practice through the ages, or in their obscurantism, if a prescription for it; hence they themselves require explanation. It is intriguing that a leading pundit of the Vienna of Wittgenstein's youth claimed that science only describes and does not explain, so-called explanations being merely complete descriptions of events. But tempting as is the irony in supposing that Mach's account of science has been transferred to philosophy in order to show that the latter is not science, it would hardly do justice to the general tone of the *Philosophical Investigations*. It is more plausible to follow a conventional view[7] and regard Wittgenstein's statements as a manifestation of a therapeutic approach to philosophy. Philosophy is the treatment of a self-induced occupational disease of philosophers, the relief of the mental torment and confusion caused by straying beyond the limits of what can sensibly be said—an illness that few who try to wrestle with problems about the nature of man, mind, or society can escape. By the assemblage of reminders of the multifarious uses of language (*PI*, p. 127) the victim is brought to see his errors, confesses, and is purged.

But the test of therapy is pragmatic, and in the cure of a disease of irrationality, irrational methods from shock to counterbewitchment may work best. Hence instead of the aim of reason, system, and proof, one gets an unsystematic impressionistic approach, more that of the artist than of the scientist, with flashes of illumination and striking analogies. But when the cure works, what then? "Once the clarity is achieved they can go on to do other things," Fann puts it (*WCP*, p. 108). Philosophy leaves everything as it is because it is self-cancelling; all that is changed is the brain-washed philosopher.

Both this tame and restrictive conclusion and the disorderly method by which it is achieved put Wittgenstein firmly on the side of anti-science. Indeed, he saw himself as keeping science out of philosophy. But at what a price! If the therapy is all that philosophy should aim at, then there are no philosophical problems, only problem philosophers. But if there are problems facing the traditional philosophical task of understanding the nature of man and his mental and moral life, then even if the therapy is legitimate and successful it has only cancelled a false start, demolished faulty hypotheses. The problems still remain unsolved. If the metaphysician's stretching of language is nonsensical, then some other way must be found; merely to stick within everyday language games is to abandon the search for solutions. This is not to say that Wittgenstein has not exposed confusions one must beware of, e.g., treating sensations as objects or neglecting the social nature of language; and as his reminders tend to be of how we learn language as much as of how we use it, he has in spite of himself advanced theses that not everyone agrees with, e.g., "an 'inner process' stands in need of outward criteria." But what one must take a stand against is the claim that all philosophical problems are problems of language, due to its bewitchment of the intelligence (*PI*, p. 109).

It is worthwhile pausing a little longer on this because the *sub rosa* circulation of Wittgenstein's ideas long before their publication led to the development, particularly in Oxford, of the doctrine that the task of philosophy is the analysis of ordinary language, the clarification of ordinary usage or meanings, the plotting of the logical geography of our concepts. Though this is intended to dissolve away philosophical problems, there is emphasis also on ordinary language as a worthwhile subject of systematic philosophical study in its own right. Furthermore some tend to treat as the arbiter of the philosophically permissible what is ordinarily said rather than what, granted our present concepts, makes sense.[8]

The movement has had to face obvious criticisms. What counts as ordinary? Why, except perhaps as an occasional corrective by robust common sense, should one worry about what one's landlady would say, as she may well have an ill-informed, unreflecting view of the world? Or how is one to decide what is the correct use, the correct logical geography—does one take a vote, and of whom? These criticisms have led to some modification of aim and practice. The concern is said to be not with usage but with use, conceived of as a function that is language-neutral; it is better, therefore, to talk of concepts or meanings. Landladies are forsaken for the "minimum knowledge common to all educated men."[9] And though condemnation as linguistically odd is fatal and declarations of what one cannot say all-important, these are not to be settled by Gallup poll or to be refuted by contrary examples that may be jokes or mistakes. The logical geography of a concept is primarily a matter of its relation to others, "the various connections between the concepts which people handle in their ordinary life without any particular difficulty,"[10] i.e., it encompasses entailments, consistency, compatibility, and incompatibility in a complex system of relations. If misapplied you get absurdity that is conceptual rather than linguistic, a matter of intelligibility and understanding not of felicity of expression.

Philosophical problems have shown themselves remarkably resistant to dissolution by these methods. There are difficulties also in the notion of language-neutral uses and concepts. Cultures corresponding to the different Indo-European languages (let alone more outré ones) reveal all sorts of untranslatable concepts, e.g., "gravitas" or "gentleman." In the field of perception the color spectrum is notoriously divided up differently by different peoples, while the phrase "concept of mind" is itself scarcely translatable.[11] But though one may agree that, following the respectable Aristotelian tradition, it is useful and important to begin with the clarification of ordinary concepts in philosophy, the main difficulty is that the "begin-all of philosophy" in Austin's phrase has been elevated to the be-all and end-all.

This has led to the ignoring of psychology and science or, where they have been considered, to implausible attacks. For instance, it is claimed that since ordinarily one asks for an explanation only when something unusual happens, explanations of the normal do not make sense and so the scientist or philosopher must not seek them.[12] But science has thrived on attempts

386

to explain everyday things like the fall of an apple. Moreover one can explain *how* as well as *why*, and understanding how the normal happens, i.e. a general theory about it, is required for a full explanation of why the unusual did. Again it is said that it is a mistake to think that psychology can by factual inquiry say what perception is. For "perception is . . ." is a conceptual question to be settled by direct philosophical inquiry into what we mean when we say that we perceive something.[13] Presumably, then, we must refuse to listen to the physicist who tells us what matter, energy, light, or heat are. The point surely is that the ordinary understanding of a phenomenon, and so the ordinary concept, is normally very limited. Although adequate for everyday social life, it cannot cope with the discoveries of psychology and the natural sciences, or even with phenomena such as illusion and hallucination—cannot cope in that in order to make sense of these facts one has to extend the human mind, to advance beyond the trammels and conservatism of ordinary language and unenlightened common sense, by means of new or extended concepts, new ways of looking at things. One is of course told that Wittgenstein did not deny that ordinary language can be improved (though he apparently allowed only minor ways), only that *philosophy* must not interfere with it (*PI*, pp. 132, 124). But if not philosophers, who else? The scientist perhaps, but scientists are trained to deal with what is publicly observable and quantifiable, i.e., with only part of the data in mental phenomena. They have thus no special claim to marry the private experiential side to the physiological, and if they attempt it, they tend toward a form of representative theory that faces serious epistemological, i.e., philosophical, problems. So if there were not a discipline with the task of facing these larger issues, one would need to invent it. Fortunately there is one, viz, philosophy—indeed, modern philosophy started when Descartes wrestled with the skeptical implications of the knowledge of the causal processes in perception then recently discovered, knowledge displayed clearly, and sometimes with remarkable sophistication for its time, in *Principles*, part IV, or the *Dioptrics*.

Since the philosophical relevance of the science of perception has been so little recognised, I must now attempt to spell out more exactly the nature of the philosophical problems it poses and deal in more detail with some attempts to dismiss them.

The basic problem is that perceiving an object involves a causal chain: in sight, for example, object → light waves → the eyes → the optic nerve → the brain; as a result we get the experience of seeing the object. What matters primarily is not the detailed character of the stages but the fact that one has a process of several successive stages. For when one has such a chain of events, it is always theoretically possible that intervention at some intermediate stage can produce the same final stages as normally occur from the whole. Thus it might seem that object X is perceived when in fact the light is coming from object Y or even when there are no early causative stages at all; the perception will then be illusory or hallucinatory. The situation is analogous to a counter-espionage agent transmitting a bogus message on the radio of a captured spy in the spy's code. This theoretical possibility of intervention seems actualized in fact in several cases; e.g., direct electrical stimulation of the cortex can make people see colors or hear sounds,[14] and even pressure on the closed eye, as Descartes pointed out, can cause a visual color pattern; again, in phantom limbs irritation of the pain nerves can cause the same pain experience as if the non-existent toes were being crushed, and after-images or the colors "seen" on a rotated Benham disk seem due to non-veridical stimulation of the retina. Moreover it is difficult to see how one can explain dreams or eidetic imagery without supposing them to be the product of (or identical with) brain activity similar to that in normal perception of the experienced scenes; similarly, a whole range of psychological data implies modification to the later stages of the process.

If this is accepted as generally correct, it means that the final stages in the brain (activity in the sensory and association areas)[15] are a sufficient condition of the experience we call perceiving—i.e., in sense-datum language, both sensing and sense-data or sense-contents are "generated by" the brain—or that the experience is identical with brain activity caused by stimulation of the senses. But this poses the well-known "barrier of ideas" problem for epistemology, of how are we to know that the experience is due to (or identical with) brain activity that is caused by an external object of the corresponding kind, or even to an external object at all.

I take it, therefore, that the function of a causal theory of perception is, first, to show that the scientific facts pose this problem and, second, to try to answer it. But three main kinds of attempt have been made by recent writers on perception to dismiss this problem.

Ryle, in his *Dilemmas*, argues that perceiving is the instantaneous scoring of an investigational success and so cannot be the end stage of a physiological process.[16] Let us accept his positive account for the sake of argument, despite the difficulties that one can perceive without investigating and may perceive a thing unsuccessfully in the sense of getting the qualities wrong. The vital point is that his analysis of perception does not avoid the causal and epistemological problems, for the latter are concerned with *how* we perceive, how we attain the success or how we fail; this, as I have said, is not primarily a matter of technique. True, perceiving is not an end stage in a process in the sense of one more stage of the same kind as impulses in the nerves; it supervenes on the last of the physical stages, or is the last stage understood in a certain way. But it presupposes the series of physical activities, and so the latter cannot be excluded from the full understanding of it, particularly as the intervention problem transforms the whole question.

Whereas Ryle seeks to exclude the physiological processes, Pitcher and Armstrong attempt to bypass the epistemological problem by omitting the experience. Their formula, that perceiving is the acquisition of true beliefs about the object by means of the sense organs or causal processes, is only a half-truth at best. One can of course quarrel with the phrase "acquisition of true beliefs," and it certainly needs a lot of qualification as Pitcher shows; but let us accept it as a way of characterizing the investigational success of which Ryle speaks. The question then of how do we attain the success becomes now one of how does stimulating the sense organs and brain enable us to acquire these beliefs. Pitcher's answer is that these beliefs are dispositions to behave in certain ways and that they are brought about by conditioning; correct behavior and belief are rewarded by success in manipulating objects or in the practical affairs of life. "All behaviour is subject to conditioning, and so it is only to be expected that the dispositions to it, that according to our theory go to make up the way things look (sound, feel, and so on) to people, should also be subject to conditioning."[17]

This is very general and vague. Pitcher only gives details for a few special cases, viz, experiments where how things look varies with one's desires or emotional states (and this does not have to be explained by conditioning), or the experiments with distorting spectacles, where the evidence is unclear as to whether the appearance of things regressed to normal or simply that one's behavior adapted to the change as one adapts to using mirrors. It is unclear how conditioning works in normal perception or why, if it does, there is so much novelty in the content of perception. How could we observe new and unfamiliar things as well as we do, noting unexpected detail about them, if how they looked depended upon conditioning? The real trouble with Pitcher's answer is that it treats human beings as if they are simply machines. Pitcher claims it as a virtue of his theory that the mind/body problem does not arise on his "happy physicalistic world view" (A Theory of Perception, p.216; cf. p.61), but this is the objection to it. There is no mind/body problem for robots because they do not have conscious experiences; however, humans are different. Surely the overwhelming *fact* about perceiving is that it involves complex and characteristic presentational experiences varying in sensuous character according to the sense organ stimulated. Insofar as we acquire beliefs about the world, it is by means of these presentational experiences; the beliefs are understood in terms of them and our manipulations of objects are guided by them. Pitcher's answer to this objection is that it cannot make clear what is left out—the seeing (*qua* belief or success) is in and the object is, so what else is required? If the answer is "sense-data," then they have been shown to be the product of false hypotheses. The objection, he claims, is therefore an irrational and prejudiced expression of dissent (ibid., pp. 74–77).

Now since what Pitcher rejects is the overwhelmingly obvious distinguishing feature of perception, one is somewhat non-plussed. In the final analysis one has to appeal to everyone's experiences as a percipient, but the appeal may be supported by the following points:

1. Seeing, hearing, and touching differ not just in the sense organs involved but in something far more basic and all-pervading, viz, what we subjectively experience as the difference between these senses in their presentational manifold. A symptom of Pitcher's failure to deal with the data in perception is that his conditioned disposition account cannot do justice to the differences between the different senses: "belief," "dispositions," and "conditioning" are all neutral with respect to these dominating sensory differences because they result from, and do not constitute, the sensory presentation. A similar point can even be indicated within one sense. Look at the sky and the grass; the difference in color as experienced is what Pitcher leaves out—the distinction is more than that one is punished in a different way if one tries to walk on the sky.

2. When people listen to music, are they just acquiring beliefs; and if so, what beliefs?

3. Sense-data can be understood in two ways—as supposed private mental entities, or neutrally as shaped patches of color, sounds, tastes, and so on, discerned by attentive observation. We may allow Pitcher's dismissal of the first but not of the second. For even if one does not want to talk of sense-data, one must recognize, as he does not, that one can distinguish what has been called the phenomenological look of things—their "look (ph)" in Mundle's terminology.[18] Actually there is a range of looks under this heading, stretching from the minute detail perceived in close reductive observation, through the color, shape, and such revealed to moderately careful everyday perception to the glimpses obtained in a hasty or preoccupied glance. It is important to note this range. Pitcher's ac-

391

count would only be plausible if all perception was jumping to conclusions from hasty glimpses or casual glances. Many writers, on the other hand, have been too ready to concentrate on the other end and court the objection that since close reductive observation requires special effort, nothing revealed by it can be the content of normal perception. But a moment's pause should convince us that a good part of normal perception reveals distinctive sensuous characteristics that can fairly be called "looks" in a phenomenological sense. Thus green hills look blue in the evening, the bottle looks double to a man with double vision, the round dish when seen at an acute angle of sight looks elliptical, the red tie looks orange in modern street lighting, in this sense of "looks." By contrast we might also say that the dish looks round and the tie looks red, i.e., that discounting the misleading circumstances of perception which make them look different in the phenomenological sense, we judge or estimate them to be that. Pitcher's analysis of "looks" cannot deal satisfactorily with those cases where phenomenological look clashes with look as judged or estimated. He analyzes "this line looks straight to x" as "he causally receives the belief that it is straight," i.e., as is disposed to act in a complex set of ways with respect to it, ways appropriate to its being straight. But when we know the facts, we may believe the phenomenological look is faulty and so not be disposed to act appropriately to it. Even if the railway lines phenomenologically appear to meet in the distance, we do not try to stop the train lest it be derailed.

It might be replied that in such cases the disposition analyzing "looks" (as estimated) suppresses the disposition or tendency corresponding to "looks (ph)." But that would be to play on the ambiguity in "suppress." Experientially the "look (ph)" survives strongly, i.e., is at most only partially suppressed; but behaviorally the "looks (ph)" disposition is nonexistent, i.e., here "suppress" means "abolish or totally suppress." Even if the lidless round cookie tin over there "looks (ph)" elliptical, I have *no* behavioral inclination to seek an elliptical lid for it.[19]

A third kind of attempt to show that the scientific evidence poses no epistemological problem has been made by Quinton.[20] He argues that the evidence about causal processes is compatible with the direct realism of common sense and opposes the contrary view that science shows a space gap and a time gap between external objects and perception (as an act of mind that is the last stage of a causal process over time and space from the external object), so that the direct object of perception must be numerically different from the external object.

So far as the space gap is concerned, Quinton (following Reid) says that it is absurd to suppose that "mind can only operate where it is," i.e., in the brain. If mind is nonspatial, as interaction theory supposes, this may be so, though what then are the functions of brain and sense organs? But Quinton adds:

(a)   on an identity theory there is no justification for supposing that perceiving and its direct object must be spatially contiguous brain processes—objects too close to us cannot be seen at all;

(b)   the directness denied by a spatial gap is not the philosophically relevant directness, namely, lack of inference;

(c)   intervention in the causal process, e.g., direct stimulation of the brain, only causes a false belief and so does not mean that the object of awareness is in the person or the brain.

In answer to (a), I would say that although Russell talked of perception as perceiving (events in) our brain, that muddle must not be fathered on the identity theory (and muddle it is because we do not perceive our brains by use of our eyes when observing the external world). Any identity theory must suppose that perceiving, or rather perceptual consciousness, though it seems of act/object character to the percipient is really (i.e., from the point of view of the theoretician trying to encompass all the facts of perception) an "adverbial" activity in which perceiving and content, i.e., ostensible object, are one, as is more clearly the case in dreams and imagery;[21] and though this activity as a whole is identified with brain activity at the end of the causal chain, one does not separate out the content and identify it with a different brain activity, or suppose that perceiving is one brain process directed on another contiguous one. The identity theory does however imply that the content (even though it seems to the percipient to be way out in space) cannot be numerically identical with the external object, since it and the experience with which it is indissolubly linked are identical with brain activity (it is numerical non-identity, not spacegap, that matters). As to (b), admittedly the causal theories are operating with a different meaning of "direct" from non-inferred; for them "direct" means "without intervening processes such as activity in sense organs." But this is philosophically relevant, for if an awareness in perceiving is direct, i.e., of a mental content not perceived via sense organs and light rays, then the epistemological "barrier of ideas" immediately arises. As to (c), Quinton seems to be avoiding the intervention problem by a Pitcher-type move; but provided that one accepts (i) that normal perceiving involves a sensuous content, a sensory presentation, and (ii) that in the intervention situations, including imagery and dreams, a generally similar content or presentation is identical with, or generated by, brain activity without a corresponding external object, it is difficult not to suppose a similar relation between brain activity and content in normal perception, so that this content cannot be numerically identical with the external object.

So far as the time gap is concerned, Quinton argues that in the astronomical cases the time lag does not mean that I do not see the star directly (non-inferentially) but only that I have a false belief about it, viz, "that it has a certain temporal property, that of being contemporaneous with my act of seeing," and that this is no worse than mistaking its color. Other writers have just said bluntly that if I see the star as it was some years ago, I still see the star, i.e., seeing can reach back in time. All this misses the point. If light takes ten years to come from a star and I see the star now as it was ten years ago, then it may have exploded and disintegrated in the ten years so that I am seeing now what no longer exists now, just as much as if I now have a visual hallucination of a house knocked down ten years ago. This is worse than mistaking color, and cannot be the direct perception of an existing object, which is what perceiving is supposed on realist views to be. Also one needs to know how it happens, and the explanation involves separating the content of awareness (generated now by light arriving from the star) from the origin of causal processes in the star (dated ten years ago).

Granted, however, that there is a problem set by the causal processes in perception, particularly by the intervention situations, it needs to be met by an explanatory theory—a causal theory in the full sense as opposed to causal analyses of the concept of perceiving which have been given that name by Price, Grice, and Chisholm.[22] Traditionally, the theory that tried to do this was the representative theory, and its real or apparent fallacies have been a potent reason for anti-scientific attitudes among philosophers. I say "real or apparent" because the theory has been widely misunderstood, not least by its scientific advocates, and has often been so misstated as to seem ridiculous. For instance, it has been put forward as the view that we do not perceive external objects but only mental representations of them (ideas or sense-data), and this was attributed to Locke by Aaron. But clearly, the evidence for the theory consists of scientific data which presuppose that one can observe and theorize about external physical objects including sense organs and nerves; it would therefore be self-refuting for the theory to allege that we do not really perceive such things. Further, since the theory is usually put forward as an account of how we perceive external objects, it would be foolish for it to conclude that we do not perceive them. In fact, when Locke is talking carefully about "natural philosophy", as he puts it, in *Essay*, Book II, Chapter 8, he speaks of ideas as the *immediate* objects of perception and in several passages talks of our perceiving external objects, though of course he also talks about perceiving ideas. Again Russell, who should have known better, writes, "The observer, when he seems to himself to be observing a stone, is really . . . observing the effects of the stone upon himself."[23] But this is also a misstatement, for a bruise might be the effect of the stone—the relevant effects are of a special kind, mental representations, and are not observed with eyes as stones are. Similarly Helmholtz' view (as in the quotation given by Pastore, p. 357 above) is open to all these criticisms. So to do the best for the theory, as we should for any philosophical theory, we should reformulate it: we perceive external objects by means of an immediate or direct perception of representations (ideas, sense-data) caused by the object's action on our senses.

This kind of formulation has been criticized as suggesting that there are two species of a common genus of perceiving, but rather what is alleged is a relation of means to result. Perceiving external objects on the theory must be understood as discovering their existence and properties; one might even put it in the way that Ryle or Pitcher does—scoring investigational successes or acquiring beliefs about such objects. The immediate perception of representations is then the presentational part of perceiving; we make the discoveries by means of direct awareness of a sensuous presentation that represents them. What then does "represent" mean? Not "resemble," as Locke pointed out. So far as secondary qualities are concerned, there is no resemblance though there normally is a detailed correspondence, e.g., different textures of object surface correspond to, and by reflecting light at different wave frequencies cause, different color sense-data. So far as primary qualities are concerned, a resemblance is claimed, though it is often by analogue. This is difficult to reconcile with dualist views of mind; but certainly sense-data (in the phenomenological sense) do seem to have spatial extension, and the relations between the sides and angles in a rectangular sense-datum correspond closely to the measurable relation between sides and angles in, for example, the box lid that is causally related to the sense-data.

Even so the theory is open to grave objections. The first is the barrier of ideas. If our direct awareness is of mental representations, if sense-data in the phenomenological sense are really sense-data in the theoretical sense, i.e., private and mental, then how do we know that they represent external objects, or still more, that they resemble them in certain ways? Normally when we say a picture resembles, or is of, an object, we can establish this by observing both, but we cannot make the direct observation of objects that would establish this for representations. This objection is not only to the representative theory; it affects Pitcher's view (how do we know the beliefs are correct since testing them only gives more conditioned beliefs?). Here, as Lovejoy and Russell have shown,[24] there is a reasonable defence of the theory.

396

If we accept that our direct awareness is of mental data then the best explanation of the groupings and sequences of such data is that they are in fact representations, i.e., that by them we are discovering a real world. The main alternative, i.e., that there is no external physical cause, whether this is in Berkeley's or Hume's version or that of modern phenomenalism, is much less plausible; it is unable to explain the operation of unseen causes, and has to allow as quite inexplicable the observation of one object by several people simultaneously or the possibility of their communicating about it—things that the hypothesis of external physical causes of our data can deal with easily.

One must note here that this kind of justification is a theoretical one after the event. The ordinary percipient does not reason in this way or infer the existence of external objects from sense-data; he simply assumes that the data are external and public, and finds this assumption continually confirmed by manipulation and communication. The anti-scientific philosophers have, I think, made out a good case against the idea that we even unconsciously infer the existence of external objects from private sense-data. It is not just that we are not conscious of any such inference, but that such inferences would require a premise (I am directly aware of such-and-such private data) that the ordinary perceiver never attains and cannot be supposed ever to have had as a starting point. It is more difficult to grasp than the assumption that the data are in fact external, and needs a considerable argument to support it. A more recent variation of this objection comes from Wittgenstein's private-language argument. Whatever its faults, that argument does at least point to the social nature of language and to the way in which we learn and check the use of sensation words in public contexts. Consequently we could not even formulate the inference from sense-data to objects if we started with a world of purely private data recognized as such. It is important to realize what is involved here. Quinton wrongly uses this as an argument against the intelligibility of the whole representative theory (viz, that if it were correct, then our language would be based on the private data of immediate awareness—which is impossible—and material objects would be unintelligible [*The Nature of Things,* pp.174–75]). But

397

it is the theoretician trying to explain the causation of perception who says that when two people see a book they are directly aware of similar but numerically different private data that have a common public cause. The plain man has no reason to doubt that the two people are directly aware of one and the same public object, and so no call to infer it. So far as learning or using language is concerned, what are in fact similar private experiences with a common public cause function just as well as direct awareness of a public object, provided that they are assumed to be just that.

One must admit, though, that the representative or causal theory has been linked historically with the idea that percipients unconsciously infer the existence of external objects; it does not, I think, have to be. But whatever account one gives of the psychological processes in perceiving (e.g., operation of attention and selection, nature of recognition and identification, the role of learning and past experience, and so on), it has to be grafted onto the theory. This may force a restatement or reconsideration of what "immediate perception" means. The version I have suggested, for example, involves dropping the idea of a sensing or simple direct awareness of sense-data. The immediate perception must be regarded as a form of perceptual consciousness (i.e., a seeming awareness of objects, not just of sense-data) that is the product of a complex set of sensory and modificatory activities covering the psychological processes. Until this has been brought into the theory, it cannot cover all the facts of perception; but this is a weakness shared by the common-sense realism that many of its opponents support.

The other main objection to the representative theory is that it does not explain perceiving, it merely duplicates it. Thus if we take the analogies commonly suggested by modern versions of the theory, the immediate perceiving is likened to seeing a cinema or television picture or a map of the external world; and Russell, like Locke, tends to use "perceive" indiscriminately of sense-data or objects. But the analogy makes nonsense of the theory, for television and cinema pictures and maps are publicly observable things unlike ideas or sense-data, and one sees them in exactly the same way as one sees the external world, i.e., by the use of one's eyes and as the result of complex processes involving light rays and nerve impulses. The problem the theory seeks to solve is just reintroduced. Clearly, if the theory is to make any sense at all, the immediate perception must be quite different—it is direct or immediate in the special sense that it does not require intervention of sense organs and such. It must, as I have suggested, be regarded as a mode of consciousness that though seeming of an act/object nature to the percipient, is really of adverbial character in which awareness and content are one.

But I cannot hope here to develop a fully satisfactory causal theory; I have tried that elsewhere.[25] All I have sought to do in the final part of this paper is to show psychologists and other scientists that crude versions of the representative theory are open to serious philosophical objections, and to show anti-scientific philosophers both that the scientific evidence about perception poses a serious philosophical problem and that to accept this does not mean that one has to accept the more obviously fallacious type of causal theory. Once these points are recognized, the way should be open for closer cooperation between the two sides in an attempt to solve what is a common problem of importance to both disciplines.

1. "The confusion and barrenness of psychology is not to be explained by calling it a 'young science'. . . . For in psychology there are experimental methods *and conceptual confusion*" (L. Wittgenstein, *Philosophical Investigations* [Oxford: Blackwell, 1958], pt. II, p. xiv [cited hereafter as *PI*]). Cf. D. W. Hamlyn, *Psychology of Perception* (London: Routledge & Kegan Paul, 1957) (cited hereafter as *PP*).

2. H. H. Price, *Perception* (London: Methuen, 1932).

3. In their exposition of sense-datum theory. G. Pappas pointed out that Price refers to shape constancy, in P. A. Schilpp, ed., *The Philosophy of C. D. Broad* (New York: Tudor Publishing, 1959), p. 476.

4. In a review of Gibson's *Perception and the Visual World* in *Mind* 62 (1953): 407.

5. R. Firth, "Sense-data and the Percept Theory," *Mind* 58 (1949): 458-61, reprinted in R. J. Swartz, ed., *Perceiving, Sensing, and Knowing* (New York: Doubleday, 1965), pp. 233-38 (cited hereafter as *PSK*).

6. G. Ryle, "Sensations," in H. D. Lewis, ed., *Contemporary British Philosophy, Third Series* (London: Allen & Unwin, 1956), pp. 441-42; reprinted in Swartz, *PSK*, pp. 200-201.

7. K. T. Fann, *Wittgenstein's Conception of Philosophy* (Oxford: Blackwell, 1969), chap. 10 (cited hereafter as *WCP*). Wittgenstein himself compared solving (eliminating)

philosophical problems to "therapy" (*PI*, p. 133). Cf. "The philosopher's treatment of a question is like the treatment of an illness" (*PI*, p. 255).

8. Wittgenstein also is reported as saying, "What would my bed-maker say of this kind of abstract talk? . . . What the bed-maker says is all right but what [the metaphysicians] say is all wrong" (W. Mays, "Recollections of Wittgenstein," in K. T. Fann, ed., *Wittgenstein, The Man and His Philosophy: An Anthology* [New York: Dell, 1967]; quoted in Fann, *WCP*, p. 100).

9. Antony Flew, "Philosophy and Language", in Antony Flew, ed., *Essays in Conceptual Analysis* (London: Macmillan; New York: St. Martin's Press, 1966), p. 18.

10. P. F. Strawson in conversation with Popper and Warnock, in Bryan Magee, ed., *Modern British Philosophy* (London: Secker & Warburg, 1971), pp. 136–37. (Paladin edition, p. 171).

11. "Mind," "esprit," and "Geist" only partly overlap. The Italian title of Ryle's book is *Lo spirito come comportamento*. Flew attempts to deal with untranslatable foreign terms by saying "they provide concepts not available in the stock of our language group" (op.cit., p. 4), and so "broaden the mind" (p. 6). But apart from the fact that foreign concepts may *clash* with ours, a similar mind-broadening increase in stock can equally well be provided by the technical terms and technical extensions of English words which linguistic philosophers object to in traditional philosophy.

12. Hamlyn, *PP*, pp. 20 ff. Cf. H. P. Grice, "The Causal Theory of Perceptirn", *Proceedings of the Aristotelian Society*, Supp. vol. XXXV (1961), p. 144. (Reprinted in Rz J. Swartz, *PSK*, p. 464).

13. Hamlyn, *PP*, p. 6. Note the words he italicized in the following passage on that page: " . . . As a result of a factual investigation a person may *incidentally* come to understand something about what is meant by 'perception', but *only* in the ways in which he would come to do so, and perhaps more quickly, by a direct conceptual investigation, a direct inquiry into what we mean when we say that we or other people perceive something."

14. In these cases the stimulus is crude—artificial direct production of the same cerebral activity as occurs in normal perception is beyond us at present—and so the result is generally of colors, "stars," "wheels," or ringing or clicking sounds, rather than of objects. But stimulation of the temporal lobe can produce "flash back"—a seeing or hearing again of past scenes or events more vivid than normal memory. Cf. W. Penfield and L. Roberts, *Speech and Brain Mechanism* (Princeton, N.J.: Princeton University Press, 1959), pp. 36, 45–55.

15. More than the sensory areas are involved, because to perceive one must be conscious and reasonably attentive; a good deal of sensory information is filtered out before reaching consciousness, and this is presumably a cerebral process.

16. G. Ryle, *Dilemmas* (Cambridge: At the University Press, 1954), pp. 101 ff. I criticize his view in more detail in G. W. Wyburn, R. W. Pickford, and R. J. Hirst, *Human Senses and Perception* (London: Oliver & Boyd; Toronto: University of Toronto Press, 1964), pp. 290–91 (hereafter cited as *HSP*).

17. G. Pitcher, *A Theory of Perception* (Princeton, N.J.: Princezon Nniversity Press, 1971), p. 151. Cf. D. M. Armstrong, *Perception and the Physical World* (London: Routledge & Kegan Paul, 1961).

18. C. W. K. Mundle, *Perception: Facts and Theories* (London and New York: Oxford University Press, 1971), p. 17.

19. Cf. Pitcher's 'Last Cases' in his preliminary analysis (op. cit., p. 93), and the footnote and the puzzlement on p. 94. Unfortunately, this kind of case is not worked out behaviorally in his final analysis (p. 154).

20. A. Quinton, *The Nature of Things* (London and Boston: Routledge & Kegan Paul, 1973), pp. 195 ff.

400

21. The point of using the word 'adverbial' is to stress that perceptual consciousness is experiencing in a certain way; though having a content or intentional object, it does not presuppose an actual distinct object. I explain this in Wyburn et al., *HSP*, pp. 326 ff. It is essential at all times to distinguish how perceiving seems to the percipient from how it is characterized by the theorist in the light of other evidence.

22. Price, *Perception*, chap. 4. Grice, "The Causal Theory of Perception." R. M. Chisholm, *Perceiving: A Philosophical Study* (Ithaca, N.Y.: Cornell University Press; London: Oxford University Press, 1958).

23. B. Russell, *Enquiry into Meaning and Truth* (London: Allen & Unwin, 1940), p. 15. He attributes this to "physics" but apparently accepts it.

24. A. O. Lovejoy, *The Revolt against Dualism* (LaSalle, Ill.: Open Court, 1929), pp. 266 ff. B. Russell, *The Analysis of Matter* (London: Allen & Unwin, 1927), chap. 20.

25. In Wyburn et al., *HSP*, chaps. 14 and 15. Cf. also R. J. Hirst, *The Problems of Perception* (London: Allen & Unwin, 1959), chap. 10.

George S. Pappas

Chapter Fifteen

BROAD, SENSA, AND EXPLANATION

Sense-datum theories of perception are often associated with specific epistemological doctrines of a "foundationalist" sort. Sense-datum philosophers sometimes claimed, with others, that empirical knowledge rests on, or must rest on, a secure foundation of some kind; and, since most philosophers of this persuasion were, broadly speaking, empiricists, it was also felt that the foundation for empirical knowledge would have to be perceptual or, more generally, experiential. Sense-data, we know, were often introduced as those perceptual entities which were either themselves known non-inferentially and with certainty (as in Russell and Price), or as those entities about which observers often have non-inferential and certain perceptual knowledge. Since it was also held, on various grounds, that the foundations of empirical knowledge would have to consist either wholly or partially in non-inferential certain knowledge, perceptual knowledge of sense-data became that perceptual knowledge at the basis of all other empirical knowledge.

Given such a view of sense-data as those perceptual entities immediate and certain knowledge of which forms the basis for empirical knowledge, it was perhaps natural that philosophical theories of perception came to be reckoned as primarily concerned with elucidating the senses in which knowledge of the external world could be or is based on knowledge of sense-data. In fact, even those philosophical theories of perception that eschewed sense-data were taken as (and often still are taken as) theories of the ways in which sense experiences could serve to justify or help justify claims and beliefs about, e.g., the external world. As an illustration of this point, consider Quinton's claim:

The problem of perception is to give an account of the relationship of sense-experience to material objects. This relationship has traditionally been seen as logical, a matter of showing how beliefs about objects can be established or supported by what we know in immediate experience.[1]

"Lockean causal theories," Quinton tells us,

> assert that the connexion between experiences and objects is contingent and that knowledge of experience is good inductive evidence for beliefs, logically distinct from it about objects. The species of inference involved is transcendental hypothesis of the type to be found in scientific arguments for the existence of such unobservables as electrons or chromosomes.[2]

By contrast, "phenomenalism" is a theory of perception that holds that

> the connexion between experiences and objects is necessary, to speak of objects is to speak in an abbreviated way about certain pervasive kinds of regularity in experience. The species of inference is simple inductive extrapolation.[3]

Presumably, since "naïve realism" is usually taken as a theory that is opposed to both causal and phenomenalist theories, it, too, would be a theory of the manner in which sense experiences serve to justify beliefs about the physical world.[4]

Theories of the sort Quinton describes might better be called 'theories of perceptual knowledge'.[5] As such, each would, when suitably expanded, comprise an important ingredient in more general theories of empirical knowledge of various sorts. But typically philosophers have construed such theories as philosophical accounts of perception with the result, I believe, that much different theories with an equal claim to the label 'philosophical theories of perception' are obscured from view. Broad's theory of sensa, it seems to me, is not an account of the manner in which observers have non-inferential certain knowledge of perceptual particulars other than external physical objects. And neither is the theory of perception he develops from the theory of sensa a theory of perceptual knowledge.

A distinct though somewhat related view of philosophical theories of perception can be drawn from a remark of Ayer's. With regard to the causal theory, Ayer wrote:

> . . . Whatever may be said in defence of the causal theory, it cannot be regarded as furnishing an analysis of our perceptual judgments. It may provide an explanation of the facts which make them true, but it tells us neither what they mean nor how we are justified in accepting them.[6]

We have already noted that Quinton and others take the causal theory, and other theories of perception, as accounts of how certain empirical statements are justified. What Ayer adds here that is different is the claim that the causal theory, and, we may presume, other philosophical theories of perception as well, should tell us the *meaning* of perceptual judgments. On such a view, a philosophical theory of perception is an analysis of various perceptual judgments or statements. For example, the causal theory might be reckoned as essentially the claim that

> the elucidation of the notion of perceiving a material object will include some reference to the role of the material object perceived in the causal ancestry of the perception (or of the sense-impression or sense-datum involved in the perception).[7]

As Grice, the author of this remark makes clear, such a task amounts to elucidating or characterizing the ordinary notion of what it is to perceive a material object. And as with causal theories, so with other philosophical theories of perception: each would, on the present construal, be taken as an analysis of the meanings of certain sorts of perceptual statements; or, perhaps we could also say, each will purport to be an analysis of the ordinary concept of perception. Such analyses, presumably, will provide us with logically necessary and jointly sufficient truth conditions for the appropriate perceptual statements.[8]

Given such a view of theories of perception, presumably what would be involved with sensations as well would be analyzes. An account of sensations would amount to an analysis of the meaning of various sensation-statements. But, as we will see below,

Broad's theory of sensa, though a theory of some sensations, is not an analysis at all. And neither, I believe, is his causal theory of perception an analysis, or would-be analysis, of the meaning of perceptual judgments or statements.

There is a fourth, and final, preliminary point to be made. Proponents of sense-datum theories often deployed various arguments that were supposed to show that there are sense-data and that they, and perhaps they alone, are directly perceived. Descriptions of specific perceptual experiences, together with various other contingently true statements, in different arguments were held to logically imply that some particular with some sensible qualities was directly perceived, and that the particular in question was not itself an external physical object or a part of one. And such arguments, e.g., from perceptual relativity, from hallucinatory experiences, from the causal factors involved in perception, and from the time lag involved in perceptual processes, were typically held to be fully generalizable, so that the relevant descriptions of perceptual experiences, causal claims, and other appropriate truths would jointly imply that in each perceptual experience some particular that had at least one sensible quality and that was not itself an external physical object or a part of one was directly perceived. Such entities were variously denominated, sometimes being called 'sense impressions', sometimes 'sensa', but more commonly 'sense-data'.[9]

It seems at first glance that Broad utilizes these arguments in his attempt to justify his theory of sensa. He certainly does make use of, e.g., perceptual relativity arguments and arguments from hallucination, in connection with this theory. However, I believe that Broad's remarks in behalf of his theory of sensa are importantly different in structure from the usual deployment of the above-noted arguments. His idea is not that certain perceptual, causal, and other facts logically demand the result that some particular with some sensible qualities is directly perceived; rather, Broad's claim is that the best initial explanation of the relevant facts is that some appropriate particular with some sensible quality is directly perceived. The theory of sensa is introduced and subsequently defended on explanationist grounds.

405

For Broad, sensa are not introduced as perceptual entities about which observers have non-inferential certain perceptual knowledge. The problems motivating his introduction of sensa are phenomenological rather than epistemological. The theory of sensa is not an analysis of the meaning of sensation-statements, and Broad's theory of perception is not an analysis of the meaning of perceptual statements, or an account of perceptual knowledge. It is, instead, a theory of the nature of perception and of the nature of the external world.

I

Broad begins his protracted discussion of perception in *Scientific Thought* with a discussion of what he termed 'sensible appearances'.[10] He brings out what he means by this term by the use of examples, some of which are well-known and were hackneyed even then (1923). We need only consider one case, the familiar one of the round penny that, from a certain distance and perspective, is supposed to look elliptical. Broad supposes that the penny is round, that it is lying face up on a flat surface, and that from a certain position it looks, or appears, elliptical to some observer. Let us here ignore the oft-made criticism that under the stated conditions the penny will look round rather than elliptical. In this case, the term 'sensible appearance' designates a 'peculiar experience', namely, the experience of the penny's looking elliptical to the observer. (*ST*, p. 237)

The term 'look' (and kindred terms such as 'appears') in this context do not have what Chisholm[11] has called their 'hedging' use. That is, the term is not being used, as Broad intends it, to make a guarded statement, one that is more cautious than, say, "I see an elliptical penny." Nor does the term have an *epistemic*[12] use or sense: in claiming that the penny looks elliptical to the observer, Broad is not claiming that the observer believes, or is inclined to believe, that the penny is elliptical, or that he is visually experiencing something that is elliptical. As Broad claims,

406

Appearance is *not* merely mistaken *judgment* about physical objects. When I judge that a penny looks elliptical I am not mistakenly ascribing elliptical shape to what is in fact round. Sensible appearances *may* lead me to make a mistaken judgment about physical objects, but they *need* not, and, so far as we know, commonly do not. (*ST*, p. 236)

As Broad is using the term 'look', I think, the expression "the penny looks elliptical to the observer" functions to describe the perceptual experience the observer has. 'Looks', and kindred terms such as 'appears', are used by Broad in descriptive or phenomenological ways; "the penny looks elliptical to the observer," as Broad intends it here, functions to describe the phenomenological character of the perceptual experience.[13]

Broad's aim in considering sensible appearances is to uncover what they are or are best explained to be. In our penny case, this amounts to asking about the nature of the 'peculiar experience' of the penny's looking elliptical to the observer. Broad's answer to this question is that there are two different theories (or kinds of theories or, as he also says, analyses) of sensible appearances: the multiple relation theory, and the object theory (*ST*, p. 236). On the former sort of theory, sensible appearances are unanalyzable relations. In the penny case, as Broad construes this view, the relation would hold between the penny, ellipticality, and the observer's mind. Broad opts for an object theory, according to which the sensible appearance of the penny's looking elliptical is explained as the observer being directly aware of some object that *is* elliptical. Stating the object theory in a general way, Broad says,

Whenever I truly judge that x appears to me to have the sensible quality q, what happens is that I am directly aware of a certain object y, which (a) really does have the quality q, and (b) stands in some peculiarly intimate relation, yet to be determined, to x. (Ibid., p. 239)

Objects such as y, Broad calls 'sensa'.

Of course, simply giving such entities the name 'sensa' has no implications with respect to whether these entities have the sorts of characteristics philosophers usually attributed to sense-data, or sensa. What sort of things sensa are, at this stage of Broad's discussion, is left completely open. Accordingly, there actually are a number of distinct-object theories of sensible appearances, depending on whether one reckons the objects as phenomenal particulars, physical objects, parts of physical objects, parts of the surfaces of physical objects, and so on.

Broad, we know, takes sensa to be phenomenal particulars, each of which has at least one non-relational sensible quality. But why opt for an object theory in the first place? And why, given that one has so opted, should one construe the relevant objects as phenomenal individuals rather than, say, external physical objects or parts of them? Broad's answer to the first of these questions is that the object theory (= the theory of sensa, stated generally in the last quoted passage) can be used to explain the specific phenomenological character of sensible appearances. It is in answer to the second of these questions that Broad marshalls the familiar arguments from perceptual relativity and the like.

To help understand Broad's first answer, consider again the elliptical-looking penny case. Instead of saying that the penny looks elliptical, we could also say that the penny appears the way one would expect an elliptical penny to appear under normal circumstances. Or, one could say that the observer's visual experience is just like the visual experience one would expect to have if one were to see an elliptical penny. Each of these ways of describing the sensible appearances is adequate for some purposes. But in saying that the penny looks elliptical, we make some reference to the penny, and, presumably, we will want a way of describing sensible appearances in cases where there is nothing that appears to the observer. This problem confronts the first alternative description given above, too; descriptions of that form would not be adequate for purposes of describing hallucinations. Descriptions of the form 'such-and-such visual experience is just like such-and-such other visual experience' are capable of accommodating hallucinatory and other non-veridical perceptual experiences. However, such descriptions introduce problems of their own (specification of the meaning of 'just like') that it would be nice to avoid, if possible. To do this, let us say that, in the penny case, the observer is ostensibly presented with an elliptical penny.[14]

Use of such a terminology allows us to easily describe non-veridical perceptual experiences. Of the drunkard's visual hallucination, we can say that he is ostensibly presented with pink rats; and of the person who sees double when he holds his finger at the appropriate place in front of his nose, we could say that he is (visually) ostensibly presented with two fingers. In neither case is it implied that anything at all is actually perceptually presented to the observer; *a fortiori*, it is not implied by such descriptions that pink rats or two fingers are actually perceptually presented to the observer.

Notice that generally physical objects are ostensibly presented to observers. It is an elliptical penny that is ostensibly presented to the observer, and not an elliptical penny-like sensum or sense-datum. Philosophers who champion widely different theories of perception can agree that, for the most part, physical objects are ostensibly presented in perceptual experiences. Such philosophers will disagree with respect to what, if anything, is actually presented in perceptual experiences.

In Broad's penny case the phenomenological character of the visual experience is *objective*; i.e., an elliptical penny is ostensibly presented to the observer. Perceptual experiences typically are objective, as we noted above; physical objects are typically those entities that are ostensibly presented in perceptual experiences. It is this objective phenomenological character of sensible appearances, I think, that Broad claims needs to be explained if we are to understand the nature of sensible appearances. And, it is this objective phenomenological character that his own object theory, the theory of sensa, is invoked to explain.

Broad writes: "If, in fact, nothing elliptical is before my mind, it is very hard to understand why the penny should seem *elliptical* rather than any other shape" (Ibid., p. 240). Concerning the straight stick that, when half immersed in uncloudy water, looks bent, Broad says, ". . . It is very hard to understand how we could seem to ourselves to *see* the property of bentness exhibited in a concrete instance, if in fact *nothing* was present to our minds that possessed that property" (ibid., p. 241).

In these passages Broad is making the point that it is hard to

409

see how the objective phenomenological character of the perceptual experiences he discusses can be explained if the observer is not directly aware of something that has the relevant sensible quality. This is not to say that it is impossible, or even unlikely, that some alternative to an object theory might explain these same phenomenological facts; it is only the weaker claim that it is not initially clear how those explanations would be effective. In fact, Broad explicitly allows that there may well be alternative explanations of these facts. He tells us, "I do not now regard this argument as absolutely conclusive, because I am inclined to think that the Multiple Relation theory can explain these facts also" (ibid., p. 240). The argument Broad refers to here is that given in the two previously quoted passages.

The two passages in which Broad says he finds it hard to understand how alternatives to object theories can explain the phenomenological facts do not serve to make the additional claim that object theories *can* explain these facts. However, when those passages are read in the light of the passage quoted last to the effect that alternative theories "can explain these facts *also*," it is clear that Broad holds that object theories of the sort he proposes can explain the phenomenological facts.

Generalizing on the penny and stick cases, we could say that, phenomenologically construed, sensible appearances are objective in the sense that physical objects are ostensibly presented, perceptually, to observers. Philosophers of perception are, in general, interested in the nature of such sensible appearances, and Broad is no exception to this. By explaining sensible appearances as cases of direct awareness of objects with the apropriate sensible qualities, the objective phenomenological character is explained. And it is this latter fact that renders the object theory initially plausible; that is, it is this fact that renders Broad's theory of sensa initially plausible.

Broad actually has very little to say concerning the sense in which the phenomenological facts are explained by his theory. But we may note, first, that the observer must be directly aware of the sensible quality of the relevant object. For example, in the penny case again, the observer must be directly aware of the elliptical quality of the directly perceived object (sensum).

No explanation of the facts will be achieved if the observer is merely directly aware of an object that happens to be elliptical if, at the same time, he is not directly aware of its elliptical quality. Second, we should notice that Broad's technical term 'directly aware,' as well as the term he uses interchangeably with it, viz, 'sense,' are not to be taken in some epistemic way or sense. Being directly aware of an elliptical entity (sensum), or sensing such an entity when the penny looks elliptical, does not amount to gaining or having non-inferential certain perceptual knowledge of the elliptical entity. This point holds, I believe, whether the knowledge in question is reckoned as knowledge that the perceived entity is elliptical; or as some knowledge or other of some perceived entity that, as it happens, is elliptical; or as knowledge that the sensible quality of ellipticality is perceptually present.

Broad himself does not explicate the notion of direct awareness (or sensing). But, in support of the above claims, we may note, first, that in the relevant phenomenological sense of 'looks,' a penny may look elliptical to an observer who has not the slightest idea of what elliptical shape is. More generally, an object may appear in a determinate sensible way to some observer even though the observer lacks the concepts necessary to knowing how the object then appears. So for such observers, if 'directly aware' or 'sense' is epistemic in a way that demands knowledge that some perceived entity is elliptical, say, or knowledge that some elliptical quality is perceived, no explanation of sensible appearances will be achieved by Broad's object theory. Or at least, if such an explanation is achieved thereby, it will not be because any such knowledge is gained. For many observers it will not be thus gained, and in such cases the statements making up the explanations are false.[15]

Moreover, for purposes of the explanations Broad needs, of the objective phenomenological character of sensible appearances, no epistemic sense need be attributed to 'directly aware' or to 'sense' as used by Broad. What is essential to effect the relevant explanations is just that the observers be in some way perceptually aware of the relevant entity and its sensible quality. Having knowledge of the entity in question is superfluous, from the standpoint of explaining the phenomenological facts. It is also irrelevant, I would add, that the observer have any of the beliefs that would be required if 'directly aware' were used in some weaker epistemic way (see note 15 below).

Finally, we may note that in a comparatively late paper, where Broad is concerned in part to explain what he took his theory of sensa to amount to, some explanation of the meaning of the perceptual term used in connection with sensa is given. In this paper Broad uses the term 'prehending' rather than 'sensing' or 'being directly aware', and about his use of this term he says, "I have intended to use this phrase ('prehending a particular') as equivalent to one which was introduced many years ago by Earl Russell, viz., *being acquainted with* a particular'" ("SER," p. 43).

Now Russell's concept of acquaintance is surely epistemic; particulars with which one is acquainted are those one knows immediately and with certainty;[16] in addition, objects of acquaintance are given or presented without any intervening (perceived) object. But I believe Broad's use of 'prehends' is such that the epistemic component of the notion of acquaintance is dropped. To see this, consider Broad's claim that "an essential feature of any experience which Russell would describe as 'being acquainted with a certain particular' is that the latter presents itself to the observer as having a certain quality, e.g., as red, as hot, as squeaky, etc." (ibid.). Broad also says, "I use the expression 'S prehends x as red' as precisely equivalent to the phrase 'x sensibly presents itself to S as red'" (ibid.). And, lastly, to help dispel any idea that the notion of being presented *as* is epistemic, notice that Broad writes:

> Consider, again, the case of a cat or a dog, which has eyes very much like ours, but presumably lacks general concepts and therefore cannot literally know or judge that a certain predicate belongs to a certain subject. It may have, and very likely does have, experiences which would be described by saying that certain particulars sensibly present themselves to it as red or as hot or as squeaky. (Ibid.)

This last passage, I take it, makes clear that in Broad's view animals prehend particulars in just the way persons do and that,

412

as he sees it, animals do not thereby gain the appropriate knowledge or beliefs. 'Prehending a particular,' then, is not to be explicated in some epistemic way. And if we assume, as I do here, that Broad's later use of 'prehend' is equivalent to his earlier uses of 'directly aware' and 'sense' (see *Exam*, vol. II, pt. 1, p. 56), then the latter terms are not used epistemically either.[17]

Thus far we have seen that the problems motivating Broad's theory of sensa are phenomenological and, so to speak, metaphysical. The latter concern is reflected in Broad's interest in giving some account of the nature of sensible appearances; the former is reflected in his concern to explain the objective phenomenological character of sensible appearances.[18] The problems motivating the introduction of sensa, then, are not epistemological; and sensa are not introduced as those perceptual entities about which observers have non-inferential and certain perceptual knowledge. Sensa are introduced as those perceptual entities that are sensed, or that observers are directly aware of in some non-epistemic perceptual fashion.[19]

II

'Sensa', we have seen, is the name Broad gives to those entities the direct perception of which serves to explain certain facts about sensible appearances. But now what of our second question raised earlier: What sorts of entities are sensa? For Broad, sensa turn out to be phenomenal individuals each of which has at least one non-relational occurrent sensible quality. Why this result rather than some other?

To see how Broad argues regarding the nature of sensa, consider again the penny case. The penny's looking elliptical to the observer, Broad said, is to be explained as the observer's being directly aware of an object that is elliptical. The rest of Broad's case goes over (now) familiar ground. The above elliptical entity cannot be identical with the penny, since the former is elliptical and, *ex hypothesi*, the penny is round. Further, Broad holds that when one alters one's position relative to the penny so that the distance or angle of vision or both are changed, then the penny will look more or less elliptical than it did from the first position. In each case, given the theory of sensa,[20] the observer directly perceives some object that *is* elliptical in that degree to which the penny appears elliptical. None of these entities can be identified with the penny, again because they are, but the penny is not, elliptical.

Nor can we hold that any one of these elliptical entities is identical with the facing surface of the penny. This surface is assumed to be round, and each of the entities in question is elliptical. Moreover, Broad points out, there is variation in these entities; there is a different degree of ellipticality in what is directly experienced from one place from that experienced elsewhere. The facing surface of the penny, though, is assumed to remain unchanged, so none of the experienced elliptical entities is the facing surface of the penny.

One might hold, of course, that the round entity one is directly aware of when the penny is viewed from directly above is the top-facing surface of the penny. And one might hold that each of the entities sensed, both elliptical and round, is a part of the facing surface of the penny. Broad does not seriously consider either of these possibilities. But the former possibility is not plausible, especially if the size of the round entity sensed will vary as distances are varied directly above the penny. And the latter possibility is not plausible because, as Price put it, not all these entities could "fit" the facing surface of the penny.[21] Since it is also unreasonable to think that any of these sensed entities, whether elliptical or round, is identical to, or a part of, a non-facing surface of the penny, we reach the general result that none of these sensed entities is identical to the penny, a part of the penny, or a surface or part of a surface of the penny. And since, *ex hypothesi*, the penny is the only perceived external physical object, we reach the conclusion that none of the sensed entities is an external physical object.

The penny case is used by Broad as an example, and the points it serves to bring out and the conclusions reached concerning it are supposed to be applicable to other perceptual cases. Accordingly, the results reached with respect to the penny case are held to be generalizable across all other visual cases, and further generalizable across the other sense modalities.

414

Hence Broad reaches the fully general result that whenever someone has a perceptual experience, then some sensum is sensed, where the sensum is never an external physical object or any part of one.

It should be clear from the foregoing remarks, that Broad deploys familiar arguments from perceptual relativity and variation in the attempt to show that sensa are not external physical objects or parts of them. The structure of his over-all argument to this point, then, is as follows: (1) an initially plausible explanation of the fact that the phenomenological character of perceptual experiences is objective, is that certain entities, called 'sensa', are in each case directly perceived; and, (2) arguments from perceptual relativity (and from hallucination and from time-lag, not here discussed) show that sensa are not external physical objects or parts of them. This "explanationist" argument, though, differs sharply from some related arguments other philosophers used in support of sense-data.

To help show this, we can consider a late paper by Moore; the arguments he there uses, I think, are representative of many other sense-datum arguments.[22] Moore considers just cases of seeing, and in particular just cases of seeing opaque external physical objects under conditions in which the observer is not seeing double and his view is not partly obstructed by other objects. Moore asks "What *is* the puzzle in the case of opaque objects seen under these conditions?"[23] He then goes on to answer his own question thus:

> It arises from the fact, which everybody knows, that even where there is only one single part of an opaque object's surface which a man is seeing, and that part is large enough to entitle him to say correctly that he is seeing the object, yet the part of its surface in question may 'look' different to two different people who are both seeing that surface at the same time.[24]

Here, as Moore explains, he is using 'looks' in what we earlier called its 'phenomenological use'. The puzzle arises because "what is meant by saying that the same surface 'looks' different to two different people is that each is 'seeing', in a sense which I have called 'directly see', an entity which really *is* different from what the other is seeing."[25] For Moore, the puzzle is two-fold: (1) how is it that although each observer sees the same opaque object, they nonetheless directly see something differ-ent; and (2), how is it that the directly seen entity (for Moore a sense-datum) is related to the opaque external physical object in such a way that by directly seeing the sense-datum, the ob-server thereby sees the physical object? Moore struggled with this puzzle for much of his career but never, so far as I know, reached answers that satisfied him fully.

We will not stop to examine this puzzle; for our purposes, the main point was made in the last quotation. There Moore makes a claim about the *meaning* of 'looks', namely, the claim that what it *means* to say that such and such a surface looks a certain way, say ϕ, to an observer (where 'ϕ' stands for an ap-propriate non-relational occurrent sensible quality) is that the observer directly sees an entity that *is* ϕ. So, when 'looks' is used phenomenologically, Moore says, "it seems to me quite plain that the proposition that a physical surface looks bluish-white to me, entails that I am directly seeing an entity that *is* bluish-white."[26]

If we generalize on the claims Moore makes here, we get the following: (using our jargon) various physical objects are os-tensibly presented in perceptual experiences. We must, *logically* must, acknowledge that observers directly perceive entities that have the ostensibly presented sensible qualities. These directly perceived entities, called 'sensa-data', turn out on further argu-ment to be not external physical objects or parts of them. How such entities are related to external physical objects, and how the direct perception of them is related to our perception of ex-ternal physical objects, remain open questions.

The differences between Broad's arguments for the theory of sensa and the arguments for sense-data represented here by Moore's remarks should be clear. Broad holds that the theory of sensa provides a plausible explanation of the phenomenological facts, whereas Moore claims that the phenomenological facts logically require the view that specific entities are directly per-ceived.[27] Given the introduction of such directly perceived en-tities, each philosopher employs various well-known relativity arguments in the attempt to show that these entities are not external physical objects or their parts. Succinctly put, for Broad the theory of sensa provides a (putatively) plausible explanation of the phenomenological facts, whereas for Moore, the phenomenological facts together with certain other contingent truths, entails a theory of sense-data.[28]

III

It should be clear from the foregoing remarks that Broad's theory of sensa is not an analysis of sensible appearances in the sense of an elucidation of the meaning of 'sensible appearance statements'. Nor is his theory of perception an analysis of the meaning of perceptual statements.

The theory of sensa is not itself an account of perception. It is simply an account of the nature of sensible appearances in terms of the direct awareness of sensa. Broad's theory of perception, which he called the 'critical scientific theory', is a non-representative version of indirect realism. Very briefly and roughly, we may characterize this theory as follows: it includes a certain realist account of the nature of the external world, according to which there are perduring, publicly perceivable external physical objects that have some of the occurrent sensible qualities they are perceived to have (the so-called primary qualities) but that lack other occurrent sensible qualities that they are perceived to have (the so-called secondary qualities). The occurrent sensible quality of, e.g., color, on Broad's view, is had only by sensa. Roughly, then, though Broad adds many qualifications and modifications, which we will not take up here,[29] his account of the nature of the external world is essentially that developed classically by Locke and others.

Since Broad holds that no sensum is a part of, or identical to, an external physical object, and since he rejects phenomenalist views of the external world, Broad cannot hold that we directly perceive external physical objects by directly perceiving some sensa that are constituents of such objects. On the other hand, we know that the direct awareness of at least one sensum is an essential ingredient in every perception of a physical object. To see what Broad takes perceiving an external physical object to amount to, consider his claim that

> all words like "seeing," "hearing," etc. are ambiguous. They stand sometimes for acts of sensing, whose objects are of course sensa, and sometimes for acts of perceiving, whose objects are supposed to be bits of matter and their sensible qualities. This is especially clear about hearing. We talk of "hearing a noise" and of "hearing a bell." In the first case we mean that we are sensing an auditory sensum, with certain attributes of pitch, loudness, quality, etc. In the second case we mean that, in consequence of sensing such a sensum, we judge that a certain physical object exists and is present to our senses. Here the word "hearing" stands for an act of perceiving. (*ST*, p. 248)

What holds for hearing holds in general; perceiving turns out to be a special sort of judgment, what we might call 'perceptual judgment'.

As presented by Broad, the critical scientific theory is an account of the nature of perception. It includes essentially two components: (1) an account of the sensuous content of perception in terms of the direct awareness of sensa; and (2), an account of what it is to perceive physical objects. The latter is dependent on the former. For, although perceiving external physical objects is mainly a judgment, or an act of judgment, it is not merely that. It is a judgment occasioned by, and that has as its sensuous content, the direct awareness of a sensum or group of sensa.[30]

Much more needs to be said, of course, about this view of perception, especially since Broad claims that we are never (or nearly never) conscious of such acts of judgment, while at the same time he heavily qualifies the notion of a judgment in this context so that it amounts to nothing more than a vaguely felt "quasi-belief."[31] Instead of going into these matters, we will make two last observations.

It is likely that Broad's critical scientific theory of perception has important implications for the manner in which, and the extent to which, perceptual physical object statements are justified. But the critical scientific theory is not itself an account of the manner in which this justification is effected. It is true that, on this theory, acts of perceiving physical objects are acts of judgments of specific sorts, or acts of acquiring quasi-beliefs. But the critical scientific theory tells us neither whether, nor if so how, such judgments or beliefs are justified. Nor is it intended to provide such information.

We noted earlier that Broad allows that there may be alternative plausible explanations of the phenomenological facts of perception; in fact, he goes so far as to allow that there *are* such alternatives. Given such alternatives, it seems likely that there will be many different plausible theories of perception as well, distinct from the critical scientific theory he adopts. Broad's defense of his own theory is not that it alone succeeds in providing an analysis of perceptual physical object statements. Instead, his defense is that his account of perception and the external world provides the best over-all account of the phenomenological facts, the scientific facts about perceptual processes and the nature of the external world, and of the facts, or beliefs, of common sense.[32] Of course, whether Broad is right in his assessment of the critical scientific theory is another matter altogether.

1. A. Quinton, "The Problem of Perception," *Mind* 64, (1955); reprinted in, and quoted from, R. Swartz, ed., *Perceiving, Sensing, and Knowing* (New York: Doubleday, 1965), p. 497.

2. Ibid.

3. Ibid., pp. 497–98.

4. This is, in part, how Ayer construed theories of perception in *The Problem of Knowledge* (Baltimore: Pelican, 1956), chap. 3. For Ayer, too, the relevant theories are naïve realism, phenomenalism, and the causal theory. It should be noted that each of these is best taken as a species of theory; there will be many different variants within each species. Ayer also regarded philosophical theories of perception as "furnishing an analysis of our perceptual judgments," a point I take up below.

5. This is a term used by Pollock to designate a range of very similar theories. See his "Perceptual Knowledge," *Philosophical Review* 80 (July, 1971): p. 287 ff.

6. *The Problem of Knowledge*, p. 116.

7. H. P. Grice, "The Causal Theory of Perception", in Swartz, ed., *Perceiving, Sensing and Knowing*, pp. 438–39.

8. Construing philosophical "theories" of perception as analyzes of the meaning of perceptual statements, or of the concept of perception, is quite common. In addition to Grice, see D. Hamlyn, *The Psychology of Perception*, (London: Routledge & Kegan Paul, 1957), pp. 7 ff; and F. Sibley, "Analysing Seeing," in *Perception*, ed. F. Sibley, (London: Methuen, 1971). I have discussed Sibley's view in "Seeing$_e$ and Seeing$_n$," *Mind* 85 (April 1976).

9. For a thorough, detailed discussion of these arguments, see J. Cornman, *Materalism and Sensations* (New Haven: Yale University Press, 1971), pp. 193–227.

10. C. D. Broad, *Scientific Thought* (London: Routledge & Kegan Paul, 1923), pp. 234 ff. Much of his discussion there is reprinted under the title "The Theory of Sensa," in Swartz, op. cit., pp. 85–129. I shall use the following abbreviations for Broad's different writings:

ST = *Scientific Thought.*

"TS" = "Theory of Sensa," in Swartz, op. cit.

MPN = *Mind and Its Place in Nature* (London: Routledge & Kegal Paul, 1925).

"TES" = "Konrad Marc-Wagau's 'Theorie der Sinnesdaten', I and II," *Mind* 56 (1947).

"SER" = "Some Elementary Reflexions on Sense-Perception," *Philosophy* 27 (1952); reprinted partially in Swartz, op. cit. References are to this reprint.

Exam = *Examination of McTaggart's Philosophy*, vols. I and II, pts. 1 and 2 (Cambridge: At the University Press, 1933, 1938).

"Reply" = "A Reply to My Critics," in P. A. Schilpp, ed., *The Philosophy of C. D. Broad* (New York: Tudor Publishing, 1959).

11. R. Chisholm, *Theory of Knowledge*, (Englewood Cliffs, N.J.: Prentice-Hall, 1966), p. 31.

12. See ibid., p. 31, as well as R. Chisholm, *Perceiving* (Ithaca, N.Y.: Cornell University Press, 1957), pp. 43–44.

13. On such uses of 'looks' and appears-words, see Chisholm, *Theory of Knowledge*, pp. 31 ff, and his "Verification and Perception," *Revue Internationale de Philosophie*, No. 17–18, Fasc. 3–4 (1951), pp. 5–6; and C. W. K. Mundle, *Perception: Facts and Theories*, (New York: Oxford University Press, 1970), chap. 1.

14. I take this term from Cornman; see his "Materialism and Some Myths About Some Givens," *The Monist* 56 (April 1972); Cornman, in turn, gets the term from Firth, "Sense-Data and the Percept Theory," *Mind* 58 (1949) and 59 (1950). Firth's paper is reprinted in Swartz, op. cit., pp. 204–70. Compare Broad's terminology in "TES," pp. 3–6; and his different terminology in *MPN*, pp. 140 ff.

15. This point may not hold if 'directly aware', or 'sense', is explicated in some epistemic way that does not require knowledge of any sort. For example, '*S* is directly aware of an elliptical object x' might be construed to mean something such as '*S* has (gains) a non-inferentially justified perceptual belief that *x* is elliptical', or perhaps '*S*'s belief that he perceives something elliptical cannot be mistaken.' (For the latter concept of direct awareness, see N. Malcolm, *Knowledge and Certainty* [Englewood Cliffs: Prentice-Hall, 1963], p. 89). But I believe that neither of these notions of direct awareness is appropriate to those cases in which the relevant observers lack the appropriate concepts. In such cases, the observers will not have the necessary perceptual beliefs.

16. See B. Russell, *Problems of Philosophy*, (London: Oxford University Press, 1912), pp. 11, 19, 46. See, further, Cornman, *Materialism and Sensations*, pp. 222–23.

17. Notice that this claim might be true even if 'directly aware' is not wholly non-epistemic in the fashion discussed by Dretske. That is, the claim might not be true even if it is false that '*S* is directly aware of *x* at *t*' does not entail that *S* gains some belief at *t*. For Dretske's discussion, see his *Seeing and Knowing*, (New York: Humanities, 1969), chapter 1.

18. Compare W. Sellars: "Sense-datum theorists have . . . claimed that facts of the form *x looks red to X* are to be analysed in terms of sense-data. Some of them, without necessarily rejecting this claim, have argued that facts of this kind are, at the very least, to be *explained* in terms of sense-data. Thus, when Broad writes 'If, in fact, nothing

elliptical is before my mind, it is very hard to understand why the penny should seem *elliptical* rather than any other shape . . . .' he is appealing to sense-data as a means of *explaining* facts of this form" (*Science, Perception and Reality*, [New York: Humanities, 1963], p. 141).

19. This should not be construed to imply that being directly aware of a sensum is irrelevant to whether one has non-inferential knowledge of such entities. Still less should it be taken as the claim that, for Broad, we do not have non-inferential certain knowledge of sensa, or that, for Broad, empirical knowledge does not rest on a foundation made up of non-inferential certain knowledge of sensa.

20. By the term 'theory of sensa', here, all that is meant is the object theory discussed above. No implication that sensa are phenomenal individuals is to be carried by the expression.

21. See H. H. Price, *Perception* (London: Methuen, 1932), p. 35.

22. G. E. Moore, "Visual Sense-Data," in C. A. Mace, ed., *British Philosophy at Mid-Century*, (London: Allen & Unwin, 1957); reprinted in, and here quoted from, Swartz, op. cit., pp. 130–37.

23. Ibid., p. 133.

24. Ibid.

25. Ibid.

26. Ibid., p. 135.

27. I here assume, without argument, that Moore's term 'directly see' has pretty much the same meaning as Broad's term 'directly aware', or 'sense', or 'prehend', except, of course, that Moore's term is more restricted, having to do solely with vision. Support for this interpretation of Moore can be found in his *Some Main Problems of Philosophy*, (London: Allen & Unwin, 1953), p. 77 n. 1. I thus strongly disagree with the interpretation given by Malcolm, in *Knowledge and Certainty*, p. 89.

28. In this "explanationist" reconstruction of Broad's case for introducing sensa, I have concentrated on his discussion in *Scientific Thought*. In *MPN* Broad's argument is different. There he *assumes* that in all perceptual situations there is some perceived object (objective constituent), and he then goes on to consider what sort of entity this might be. He defends the sensum theory against some competitors on best explanationist grounds. That is, he argues that it is more reasonable to regard objective constituents of perceptual situations as phenomenal particulars than as anything else since so regarding them best accounts for all the relevant facts. His argument in "SER" parallels that given in *MPN* in important respects.

29. For some of them, see *The Mind and Its Place in Nature*, (London: Routledge & Kegan Paul, 1925), pp. 195–208. See also Broad's reply to Yolton in "Reply," pp. 808–12.

30. Compare Price's comment: "If anyone says 'I do not see sense-data, I see material objects' Prof. Broad will heartily agree with him. He has never maintained that we do see sense-data (or rather sensa). He has only maintained that we *sense* them, or as he sometimes says, intuitively apprehend them. Nor has he denied that we see material objects. What he has done is to propose an analysis of what this seeing of them consists in. It consists, he thinks, in holding a certain sort of belief, or quasi-belief, about some visual sensum which we sense, the belief that this sensum is related in a specially intimate way to such and such a material object (or sometimes, to a physical event, such as a lightning flash)!" (H. H. Price, "The Nature and Status of Sense-Data in Broad's Epistemology," in Schilpp, op. cit., pp. 473–74).

31. Cf. *MPN*, pp. 152–53 and pp. 208 ff.

32. *MPN*, p. 160 ff. Unfortunately, Broad does not really consider a fair sample of theories of perception. Neither does he consider a fair sample of accounts of the nature of sensible appearances.

Chapter Sixteen

THE PERCEIVING OF HIDDEN SURFACES

INTRODUCTION: THE ENVIRONMENT

The terrestrial environment consists of more or less permanent surfaces. A surface is the interface between a *substance* and the *medium*, that is, air. Natural surfaces are rough, not smooth like a mirror; and they are usually illuminated. They are generally opaque, not transparent; that is, they reflect light instead of transmitting it. Substances differ in their chemical inertness and the degree to which they resist dissolution or disintegration; hence their surfaces also differ in persistence. Some surfaces are relatively permanent, like the Pyramids; some are less persistent, and some are transitory, like clouds. In short, the layout of the environment is both *persistent* in some respects and *non-persistent* in others. These are facts of physics, but at a neglected level that might be called *ecological* physics.

The illuminated medium is filled with what I call *points of observation*. A point of observation need not be occupied by an observer for there to exist an *optic array* at that point. A point of observation may be fixed, but normally it is moving. At any fixed point of observation some of the existing surfaces of the environment will be *hidden* and the remainder *unhidden*. I mean that some will be *out of sight* and the rest *in sight*, that some will be *concealed* and the rest *revealed*. To use a term from geometry, some of the layout will be *projected* at that point and the remainder *unprojected*.

The above description of the environment is unusual. The accepted prototype is that of bodies in space, that is, detached objects in a three-dimensional void. This is the model of the world given us by Isaac Newton, in the tradition of Euclidean geometry and Cartesian coordinates. But it seems to me inappropriate for biology and psychology. We live in surroundings, not in space, and what we perceive is the environment around us, not bodies in air. What there is to be perceived, in fact, is a layout of surfaces *some of which are hidden*.

Exact terms for this fact of hiddenness are not found in the common language. There are words like *visible-invisible* and *seen-unseen*, but they are vague and slippery. These include the case of being hidden by darkness, and I do not. I mean *concealed, screened*, or *covered*, and I have defined a technical term, *optical occlusion*.[1] The projection or non-projection of opaque illuminated surfaces is a basic fact of ecological optics but not of physical or geometrical optics. The concept of projection being used is quite different from that found in projective geometry, where all planes are taken to be ideally transparent.

HIDDEN AND UNHIDDEN SURFACES

The perceiving of the *unhidden* surfaces of the environment is one problem; the perceiving of the *surfaces* of the environment in general is another problem entirely. The perceiving of *projected* surfaces is governed by the laws of what the ancients called "natural perspective." This discipline was founded by Euclid and Ptolemy. After the discovery of the retinal image, it was almost forgotten, and it was further obscured by the working out of the laws of "artificial perspective" for a picture-plane. In ancient optics there was said to be a "visual cone" for every object in the world, more exactly, a visual solid angle the size and shape of whose cross-section depended on the distance and the slant of the object. This rule can be brought up to date by saying that for every *projected* surface in the environment there is a visual solid angle, and that the solid angles are *nested within one another* up to the whole spherical angle of the ambient optic array.

All current theories of sensation-based perception try to explain the perception of projected surfaces; the only question is

423

how they can be seen at their true distances and their true slants, or how they could have size-constancy and shape-constancy. It seems to me that what needs to be explained, however, is the perception of the whole layout of surfaces including the hidden ones. We do not see a patchwork of forms, we see surfaces with *solidity* and *superposition*.

To summarize so far:

1. A surface is the interface between a substance and the medium. A surface goes out of existence when it has no substance.

2. An illuminated surface is projected at a fixed point of observation if it has a visual solid angle in the ambient optic array at that point. If not, it is unprojected, hidden, or out of sight.

3. For every fixed point of observation the layout of the environment is divided into hidden and unhidden surfaces. Reciprocally, for every existing surface the points of observation are divided into those at which it is hidden and those at which it is not.

TWO KINDS OF HIDDEN SURFACES IN THE NEAR ENVIRONMENT

Excluding consideration for now of the distant environment, there are two kinds of hidden surface. One is the *far side* of an object, and the other is the *ground* of an object. The far side of a topologically closed surface is continuous with the near side. The ground or background of such a solid is *not* continuous with it. This holds for the case of what I have called a "detached" object; in the case of an "attached" object, the surface will be continuous with the ground.

The environment does not consist of bodies in empty space, as Newton has been taken to imply, but it does, of course, contain movable objects like falling apples and rolling stones. Thus the ambient optic array does not consist of closed contour forms in an otherwise empty field, as psychologists imply who take the figure-ground phenomenon to be the basis of vision, but it does contain forms that correspond to the edges of moveable objects.

In summary:

424

4. An object hides both its far side and the ground behind it.

THE LAW OF REVERSIBLE OCCLUSION: THE INTERCHANGE OF THE HIDDEN AND THE UNHIDDEN

We live in what I have called a "cluttered" environment, not an "open" environment such as the desert or the sea where everything is projected to every point of observation. The terrestrial earth is a substratum, a subground as distinguished from a background, but it is always partly hidden by the *features* of the earth, by *objects*, and by the surfaces of *enclosures*. The sky, the upper hemisphere of our environment, is a non-surface, but even the sky is often hidden by trees and walls and ceilings.

I suggest that we *perceive* the surface of the earth despite the features, objects, and enclosures that hide it. In an extended sense of the term, but a proper one, we perceive the surfaces of the environment that are out of sight as well as those that are in sight. There are two reasons for this: first, that surfaces go out of sight and come into sight; and second, that they are separated by what I call occluding edges. Consider now the first reason.

The projected surfaces are continually *interchanging* with unprojected surfaces. The transitions between one and the other are observed. The concealed is revealed, and the revealed is concealed. This transition is perfectly reversible. It happens whenever there is a reversible motion of an object or a reversible locomotion of an observer.

This transition is not described by saying that an object "vanishes" or "disappears." Ordinary language is careless of the subtleties of visual perception. These verbs do not distinguish between the projective event of going out of sight and the substantial event of going out of existence. To "vanish" behind a corner is not to "vanish" into thin air, but the word does not separate the two different events.

The reasons for reversible occlusion are that points of observation are not fixed and that objects are displaced. Animals move about, and the layout shifts. A frozen optic array at a stationary point of observation is a limiting special case; typically

425

there is a changing array at a moving point of observation. The frozen optic array, like the frozen retinal image, is not the case with which to begin the study of vision. Any displacement of an observer in the environment can in theory be *cancelled* by an opposite displacement, and similarly any displacement of an object can be cancelled. Just as the movements are cancellable, so the corresponding optical transitions are opposable.

To summarize:

5. The hidden surface of an object turns into the unhidden surface and *vice versa* when the object rotates. A part of the ground is covered and another part is uncovered when the object is displaced.

6. The hidden parts of the layout come into sight and the unhidden parts go out of sight as the point of observation moves.

7. To the extent that reversible motion and locomotion occur, any persisting surface that goes out of sight will sooner or later come into sight. Every movement that makes a surface go out of sight has an opposite that makes it come into sight. This is the law of reversible occlusion. But a surface that goes out of *existence* at one time will not come into existence at another.

THE LOCI OF OCCLUSION, OCCLUDING EDGES, AND CONVEXITIES

The second reason why we perceive hidden surfaces is that we notice the "edges" that hide them. The term *edge* is not adequate to describe the place where occlusion occurs; it can be either a sharp edge or a curved convexity. This locus is neither an "objective" fact nor a "subjective" fact, for it depends on both the point of observation and on the surfaces observed. It seems to have escaped notice in both physics and psychology. But I suggest that a locus of occlusion is seen for what it is. It is *not* perceived as a line, or a margin, or a border, or a contour, or the mere junction of two flat surfaces at a dihedral angle. It is seen to be the place where one surface *covers* another. It is not just that there is "depth" at the edge but that a surface continues *behind* the edge. It is not just that the contour is "one-sided," as Rubin described it, but that something is hidden at that place. This is a fact, not a construction of the mind.

I am saying that to perceive the place where one surface hides another is to perceive the hidden surface. If we add to this the fact that the hidden is regularly being *converted* into the unhidden, that assertion no longer sounds like such a paradox. We perceive both the locus of occlusion and the change of occlusion, both the separation of the projected and the unprojected and the interchange between them.

8. Although surfaces shift between the projected and the unprojected state they are always separated by the loci of occlusion. Observers perceive these edges and convexities along with the continuation of the projected into the unprojected.

THE PERCEIVING OF VERY DISTANT SURFACES AND OBJECTS

It is now time to consider the distant environment. If the terrain is more or less uncluttered and the horizon is given in the optic array, a surface or an object can become unprojected if its visual solid angle becomes zero at the point of observation. We then say that an object has gone out of sight "in the distance," or that a part of the terrain is out of sight "at the horizon." It has reached a so-called vanishing point.

When a balloon in the sky becomes too far away to see, or when Mickey Mouse shrinks to a point in the animated cartoon, the structure of its visual solid angle has undergone *minification* (the opposition of magnification). The components of its structure, the nested solid angles, have all been diminished alike. This *diminution* is an optical transition of a quite different sort than the transition of optical *foreshortening* to an edge, or that of optical *deletion* to an edge. These are characteristics of the near environment, or what might be called the *habitat*.

To summarize:

9. The distant parts of an open terrain can become unprojected by the graded diminution of their visual solid an-

gles to zero, that is, at the horizon. The surface of a detached object can also become unprojected by the diminution of its visual solid angle to zero.

THE PERCEIVING OF A SURFACE GOING OUT OF EXISTENCE

Many surfaces of the environmental layout are persisting, but some are not; that is, some go out of existence, and some others come into existence. One kind of environmental change is the destruction of surfaces. When a solid goes into the gaseous state by sublimation, for instance, the surface ceases to exist. There are other ways in which a surface is destroyed: by evaporation, dissolution, combustion, disintegration, and decay. In all such cases there is a loss of the *topological integrity* of the surface.

These events, be it noted, are not reversible. The destruction of a surface is not the opposite process to the formation of that surface; they are not reciprocal. Occlusion can be nullified by reversing a movement, but destruction cannot.

A surface that goes out of existence is no longer projected to any point of observation, since it ceases to reflect light. A surface that goes out of sight continues to be projected to some points of observation, since it continues to reflect light.

The optical transitions corresponding to evaporation, dissolution, combustion, disintegration, and decay are not at all the same as those of optical deletion, foreshortening, and minification, corresponding to things going out of sight. I suspect that young children notice the difference between these two kinds of optical transition. The former *cannot be cancelled* and the latter can—how could they fail to notice this fact? If they do notice it, they will distinguish the going out of existence of a surface from the going out of sight.

The processes by which a surface comes into existence are condensation, freezing, crystallization, precipitation, aggregation, and biological growth. As already noted, these are not the opposites of the processes by which a surface goes out of existence. They are not reversible.

It should now be quite clear that what I call a *substance* in ecological physics is not what is called *matter* in physical physics. There is no law of the conservation of substance like the law of the conservation of matter.

Consider the tricks of the conjuror. They consist in large part of making it appear that something has gone out of existence when in fact it has only gone out of sight, and then that it has come into existence when in fact it has only come into sight. The optical information to specify the changing occlusion has been carefully suppressed by the magician, as in "palming" an object.

To summarize:

10. A surface may come to be unprojected everywhere because the interface between its substance and the medium is destroyed in one of several ways. A surface may come to be projected at some points of observation because an interface between substance and medium is formed. But these events are not reversible, and neither are the optical transitions that specify them.

IMPLICATIONS FOR THE THEORY OF MEMORY
AND IMAGINATION

It has always been assumed that perceiving depends on remembering in some sense of that term. Hence most psychologists would maintain that what I have called the perceiving of hidden surfaces is actually the remembering of those surfaces, albeit a kind of memory they call "immediate" or "primary" or "short-term." This seems to me conceptual confusion, and I prefer to assume that perceiving occurs over time, not at the "travelling present moment" of time.[2] How otherwise could anyone perceive the motion of an object?

In what he called the "tunnel experiment," Michotte displayed an object that went behind one edge of a screen and came from behind the other edge. He found that the object was *perceived* during the interval and that it was "almost seen" behind the

429

screen.[3] My interpretation of this result is that the object was seen to be a persisting surface, inasmuch as to perceive it being concealed is to see its continued existence, and to perceive it being revealed is to perceive its preexistence.

I suggest that all the different phenomena lumped together under the vague term *memory* should be separated into their components. We could then reserve the term *to recall* for the visualizing of surfaces and objects that have gone out of existence, like the house I once lived in that burned down. We could reserve the term *to imagine* for the visualizing of the surfaces of the house I hope to build, and for which there are plans. But the visualizing of the surfaces of the house I now live in, even when I am sitting in one room and temporarily facing the north wall, should be called *perceiving*. For the fact is that when I sit in one room, I can apprehend the other rooms behind the walls that hide them. It is not that I have X-ray vision, like Superman, but only that I perceive the layout of surfaces over time. It is not that the walls of my house are transparent but only that the hidden and the unhidden surfaces interchange at the edges of the doors.

Failing to conceive the difference between these kinds of visualizing in terms of surface existence can lead to all sorts of mystical nonsense. The distinction between a person who is out of sight and a person who is out of existence has been blurred in the history of human thought by the doctrine of spirits or ghosts. Perhaps there is a far place above the sky or below the earth where spirits exist, and perhaps they can make the journey back. But this is a case of imagining, not of perceiving or remembering.

Similarly, the belief in the possibility of seeing through opaque walls and at great distances, clairvoyance, is encouraged by our failure to develop a coherent theory of the perceiving of *reversibly* hidden surfaces.

11. The visualizing of briefly hidden existing surfaces should be distinguished from the recalling or imagining of surfaces that are nonexistent.

IMPLICATIONS FOR THE PROBLEM OF ORIENTATION

Animals and men are properly said to be oriented to their environment, or at least to their habitat in the total environment, but we have no adequate theory to explain this fact. We can all find our way about in the environmental maze, or learn a new maze. We are capable of "homing." What is the state of being oriented to all the places we might want to arrive at? Most of them are hidden places. It is surely not a chain of conditioned responses to stimuli. But neither is it the possession of an internal cognitive *map* of the habitat, for that implies a sort of internal perceiver who consults a map. Perhaps the theory of reversible occlusion provides an answer.

An alley in a maze, a room in a house, a street in, a town, and a valley in a countryside each constitutes what I have called a *vista*.[4] A vista is the set of projected surfaces within a semi-enclosure, with unprojected surfaces beyond. Vistas are serially *connected*. At the edge of the doorway, the next room opens up; at the corner of the street, the next street opens up; at the brow of the hill, the next valley opens up. To go from one place to another involves the opening up of the vista ahead and the closing in of the vista behind. There is usually a choice of vistas. To "know the way" from one place to another hidden place is to know which vistas to magnify at the openings, that is, which occluding edge hides the goal. One vista leads to another in a continuous set of reversible sequences.

Oriented locomotion within a semi-enclosure is not hard to explain—the observer has only to magnify the visual solid angle corresponding to his goal.[5] The difficulty is to explain orientation to the surfaces behind the walls, beyond the trees, or over the hill. My suggestion is that the oriented observer can *visualize* his possible goals behind the edges that hide them. This is implied by the fact that a man can *point to* a goal, for example, his home. A rabbit cannot, but nevertheless he "knows" where his rabbithole is.

This theory can be extended to objects as well as to places or enclosures. An object of value is often *caused* to be hidden, both by animals and men. It can be buried in the ground or put away in a drawer. If one has seen it going out of sight, one can visualize it, be oriented to it, go get it, and even point to it. One perceives where it is. A monkey can go directly to a canister that hides a lure if he has seen it being covered. A raven can choose a flowerpot that hides food if he has seen it going out of sight. Surely

431

this is a phenomenon of perception, not a delayed reaction to a "stimulus."

To summarize:

12. Within the habitat of an observer and to the extent that he has reversibly connected its surfaces, he is visually oriented to *all* the places and objects that interest him.

IMPLICATIONS FOR EPISTEMOLOGY

One of the problems in the theory of knowledge is to ask how we can all perceive the same environment and agree on what we perceive despite the fact that the visual sensations of each observer are unique and the perspective appearances of the world are thus different for different observers. We now have a new way of resolving this old puzzle. We can afford to reject the assumption that visual sensations and perspective appearances are the necessary basis of the perception of the environment.

It is true that there is a unique ambient array for each fixed point of observation in the medium. It is also true that a set of different observers must occupy different fixed points at the same time. But observers move, and the same observer occupies a series of points at successive times. This same path of locomotion may be traveled by different observers. To each path of locomotion there corresponds a unique *change* of the ambient array. If the set of observers move around, each observer will experience the same group of optical changes as any other observer.

Another way of putting this is to say that, although at any given time some points of observation in the medium are *occupied* and the remainder are *unoccupied*, the one set can go into the other.

One can summarize this by saying:

13. For every point of observation, there is a different optic array; but for moving points of observation, the same information is available to all observers as invariants over time. An environment can thus be perceived that is common to all observers.

It is also a fact, of course, although neglected, that the perceiving of the world usually entails the awareness of where one is in

432

the world, and of being in the world at that place. To the extent that an observer has moved from place to place in his habitat, from vista to vista, he can stand still in that place and *see where he is*, in other words, *where he is relative to where he might be.* This is entailed in the state of being oriented.

Furthermore, to the extent that an observer has moved from from place to place, he has perceived all the places of his habitat. This is true for any observer in that locale. If different observers have perceived the same places, there will be a *consensus* of their perceptions. And the more distant the travels have been, the larger will be the environment perceived.

Still further, an observer who can perceive the persisting layout from other points of observation than the one he occupies can perceive it from the position of another observer. He can "see things" from his point of view, as we say, or "take" his point of view. The common assertion, then, that "I can put myself in your position" has an exact meaning in ecological optics and is not a mere figure of speech. It means *I can perceive surfaces that are hidden at my point of view but that are revealed at yours.* It means *I can see one thing behind another.* And thus it implies, *we both see the same world.*

IMPLICATIONS FOR EGOCENTRISM

Psychologists sometimes talk about *egocentric perception.* An egocentric perceiver or person is taken to be one *who can see the world only from his own point of view.* It should now be clear that this way of speaking is quite mistaken. To be sure, an egocentric or introspective person can habitually pay attention to where he is, and to his own body, but this is what I call proprioception, not perception. This is an activity that *accompanies* perception of the environment but should never be confused with it.

The evidence from child psychology does *not* suggest that the earliest visual experiences are those of projected surfaces only, of the patchwork of pictorial perspectives. More likely the first percepts of the infant are based on what may be called "formless invariants."

433

THE HIDING OF ONESELF

The body of the observer is subject to the same laws of occlusion as any other body. To be hidden is to make one's body unprojected at points of observation likely to be occupied by other persons, or at a point actually occupied by another person. Among animals the prey hides from the predator. Sometimes the predator hides from the prey, in ambush. Among children, concealment is practiced in the game of "hide and seek." In fact, the law of reversible occlusion is learned very early by infants in the game of "peek-a-boo." The baby learns to see the occluding edge, either when the other person peeks at him around the corner or when he peeks at the other person.

The seeking of caves, burrows, or shelters among animals and men seems to derive from the need to hide one's body as well as the need for protection from wind, cold, rain, and sun. We seek "privacy" in our housing, and thus we put screens, curtains, or blinds on our glass houses.

Finally, the human habit of covering the body with clothing (or its modern opposite of displaying the body *without* clothing) can only be understood in terms of the social optics of hiding parts of the skin. I will not undertake an analysis of stripping and streaking in this paper, but only suggest that they fall within the neglected topic of the perceiving of the hidden relative to the unhidden.

This paper is a preliminary version of a chapter from a forthcoming book entitled *An Ecological Approach to Visual Perception* (in press, Houghton Mifflin).

1. J. J. Gibson et al., "The Change from Visible to Invisible: A Study in Optical Transitions," *Perception and Psychophysics* 5 (1969): 113–16.

2. J. J. Gibson, "The Problem of Temporal Order in Stimulation and Perception," *Journal of Psychology* 62 (1966): 141–49.

3. A. Michotte et al., "Les Complements amodaux des structures perspectives," *Studia Psychologica* (Louvain: Publications of the University of Louvain, 1964).

4. J. J. Gibson, *The Senses Considered as Perceptual Systems* (Boston: Houghton Mifflin, 1966).

5. J. J. Gibson, "Visually Controlled Locomotion and Visual Orientation in Animals," *British Journal of Psychology* 49 (1958): 182–94.

Chapter Seventeen

GIBSON AND THE CONDITIONS FOR PERCEPTION

J. J. Gibson's theory stands as a source for a certain causal view about perception. By sketching certain aspects of his theory and remarking upon particular points in it, I hope to provide a basis for an adequate theory of visual perception. The theory is a functional, causal theory, though I shall not be concerned here to explain the functional characteristics of it. Instead, based upon Gibson's approach, I shall propose a set of conditions for the truth of 'O sees I,' where O is an organism and I is what O sees. I shall confine my conditions and remarks to very low-level seeing, where O need not be conscious or aware of what he sees.

I

Gibson has argued that the traditional account of the causal facts of perception has been misguided, and that certain assumptions in psychology and philosophy have led us to misdescribe what the facts are.[1] Because of this misdescription of the causal facts, the theories that were developed to account for them were wrong (or wrong-headed) also. The traditional theory briefly can be schematized in the following stages: (1) Stimulus → (2) Reception → (3) Sense-impression → (4) (sometimes) plus Memory → (5) Perception. Elaborations of this schema have provided the basis for most theories of perception in both psychology and philosophy. I wish, following Gibson, to suggest that the model is inaccurate and does not capture what actually occurs in perception. If this inaccuracy claim is correct, then it is small wonder that no theory of perception thus far elaborated has been entirely successful.

In order to make plausible the above claim, I shall sketch some of the major aspects of Gibson's way of setting out the causal facts about perception. This sketch is useful for understanding exactly what a theory of perception must explain, and also for understanding the conditions that I shall set out later.

As is well known, there are objects existing in a world. Various of these objects emit light, and almost all reflect light.[2] Even those "things" in the world that do not reflect light are surrounded by light reflected from other objects that serve as a background to the thing in question. (The class of things I have in mind here are things like shadows, holes, and so on). Again, as is well known, the eye is the organ of reception for a perceiver and is activated by particular incoming light rays from the environment. Geometrically the eye is in a position to register all the light rays that are reflected to it. But these incoming light rays are not all the same—they vary from ray to ray in certain essential properties such as wave lengths and intensities. This fact is of crucial importance, and serves as the basis for Gibson's theory of ecological optics.[3]

Most objects in the environment reflect light rays of varying intensities and frequencies depending upon the substance and properties of the object (ambient light). The most obvious and most discussed property in this regard is the color of the object.[4] Another equally obvious, though not so often mentioned, property is the position of the facing surface of the object with respect to the light source (sun or artificial source). Other important properties are the spatial relations that the object has to other objects in its immediate environment and the locations of the various surfaces of the object with respect to one another and with respect to the light source.

Gibson has suggested that the primary structuring of the light that occurs is caused by the following kinds of properties of objects and relations between objects: borders that exist because objects have different faces inclined in different planes to the light source (differential facing); borders that exist because of the difference in substances of the adjoining surfaces in the environment (e.g., wood reflects differently from metal); and various environmental obstructions to the light source that result in shadow patterns or lack of reflectance. Likewise the environmental properties of transparency, refraction, and polarization of light also bring about differential intensities and wave lengths in reflected light. All of these factors and more need to be taken into account in specifying how light is reflected to the eye and in elaborating the various causes for the differing intensities and wave lengths of the light rays that reach the perceiver.

Gibson's main point can now be stated. All of the light that is reflected by a given object (or environment) is structured by that object (or environment). The way an object reflects light depends on its shape, its color, its location, surrounding environment, and so on. Thus the light that is reflected from an object is somewhat specific to that object. If the object's shape, location, and such were different, the pattern of reflected light coming from it would be different (keeping the light source constant). This is true of every object in the environment of a perceiver at a given time. Each object in the environment will reflect light differently from other objects that surround it. Similarly, the set of objects in a given environment at a particular time will reflect light in ways that are peculiar to those objects in their particular arrangements. Alternatively one could say that a particular pattern of reflected light specifies the object(s) from which it was reflected.

Succinctly stated, Gibson's theory (of ecological optics) holds that a particular environmental set-up structures the light rays reflected from it in causally specific ways. A set of reflected rays available to an observer at a given location has a structure that is (according to Gibson, uniquely) related to the objects and properties that caused that structure.[5] I shall call the properties of objects that are causally responsible for the particular structuring of the set of rays the visible or structural properties of those objects. Thus there will be determined for each set of rays picked up or extracted by a perceiver a set of properties of the object(s) that causally structured the ray. Gibson calls such structured sets of light rays ambient arrays.

Two such arrays of structured light are picked up by a normal perceiver at a given place and time, one by each eye. For any given point an observer is stationed at, there are two causally efficacious arrays. Additional properties of the objects and their interrelations are registered when an observer moves through an environment (or even when the eye moves or scans). When a perceiver moves, he picks up a sequence of arrays. Such sequences of arrays over time themselves have properties that are different from those present in any single array. Gibson says some of these properties remain invariant over sequences. For example, as I move about a table, a sequence of arrays reaches my eyes. The order of succession of these incoming arrays and the relations between them are determined by the properties of the object and by the facts concerning my movement. A table reflects light to my eyes in a way that depends upon the substance the table is made of, its color (pigmentation), its texture, and its shape. As I move about the table, structured light specific to each of these features is picked up at each point in my journey. In addition, properties of the sequence itself are picked up—the sequence provides information about, say, the shape and three-dimensional character of the table. This information is carried in the properties that belong to the sequence of arrays rather than to the properties belonging to the individual arrays. By moving about a table, I can pick up properties that will allow me to distinguish between a table and an arrangement of wires, which at one point I might have taken to be a table (e.g., a version of an Ames demonstration). Similar high level properties or invariants are specified by an object's movement through the environment (while the perceiver is stationary).

On Gibson's theory the effective variables or stimuli that are picked up or extracted by an observer and that give him information about the physical world cannot be present in a single (fixed) array.[6] Rather, these information variables are defined by differences and continuities that are picked up when two or more different arrays succeed each other in being available to an observer. Sequential differences in the structure of arrays are talked about as being transformations. Transformations of structure are due to movement in the environment of the structuring objects or to movement on the part of the observer. The latter may be gross exploratory activity involving the whole body or simply eye movement (even blinking). Gibson calls such higher-order, sequential variables *invariants*. Again, invariants are the information-carrying variables.

Gibson is not always clear about the fact that his theory requires pickup or extraction over time. He suggests, at one point, that stimulation (or as he later would say, information) consists of adjacencies and successivities.[7] Adjacencies, presumably, are invariants defined by differences present in a single array; and successivities are invariants defined by differences over time. In contrast to this claim, I would argue that Gibson must, and should, hold that perception is of change (or movement), and that change, of course, must be over time. The change depends upon non-change to specify it. The argument for this fact about perception is simple and can be stated from many bases. First, if in fact everything in a person's environment was completely static, i.e., there was no motion of either observer, observer's eyes, or the environment, then there would be no perception of that environment. The experiments, by Ditchburn and others, concerning stabilized retinal images and experiences with the Ganzfeld attest to this fact.[8] Unless there is movement or change resulting in differential sorts of stimulation available to the visual system (retina, et al.), then the world ceases to be perceived and all that is seen is a dull gray, diffused light. Second, considering the character of the receptors will again provide a basis for arguing the necessity of change. Receptors fire only to changes in stimulation. For example, a given point on the retina will fire only when it receives suitable stimulation that is different from what it was receiving in a prior moment.[9] The visual system responds to changes; constancy of stimulation over time to each point will prevent it from registering. Even in cases of exposure to brief stimulation, such as in tachistiscopic experiments, such change is essential. Change is present when from darkness the tachistiscopic image is suddenly illuminated, causing a different pattern of impingement upon the system than was present previously. Likewise, unless eye movement of some type (blinking or scanning) occurs, the image fades from view to be replaced by the static dull gray of the unseen.[10]

439

If I were to strictly follow Gibson's terminology, I would talk about information rather than causal properties. The structure of the light reflected from objects in an environment (the ambient array), specifically the properties or variables defined by the sequences of the structures over time, are said to contain the *visible information* in the environment. These patterns of reflected light carry information about the properties of the object(s) that caused the light to be reflected in the way it was. Such arrays contain *visible* information in that the information is contained in invariants that are effective on the visual system in a way that, for example, ultraviolet radiation from the environment is not. The arrays and sequences of arrays are said to contain information about the environment because of the specifying relation that exists between the object and the light reflected from it, viz, only that object (or objects of similar kinds) will reflect light in those arrays and will present an observer with those sequences.

The sequence of arrays over time define higher-order variables or invariants. These are the effective variables of stimulation that cause the organism's visual system to resonate. Thus the observer is said to extract or pick up those invariants. The invariants are structures remaining constant over time, defined by the changes in the sequence. These invariants specify the environment. The specificity of invariants to their sources in the environment is what is meant by Gibson when he speaks of the optical form changing but the substantial form remaining constant. The substantial form, or deep structure of the changing array, is the relevant relation between the visible or structural properties of the objects in an environment that are causally responsible for the invariants in the sequence of arrays that an observer picks up.[11]

The above discussion suggests that Gibson's talk of information is unproblematic, since it is deletable in favor of purely causal talk. Later I shall explain further how a harmless concept of information can be treated as a functional concept.

There is a problem with Gibson's claim that each ambient array is specific to the object or environment causing it. Gibson claims there is proof that each structured array picked up by an observer is unique to the pickup point.[12] This claim for absolute uniqueness, as far as I can see, has no justification. There is no reason why two different, though quite similar objects, or environments should not identically structure two arrays. This would be the case, e.g., in two rooms that were constructed to be identical. An observer in the one room would receive an array that is structurally identical to an observer at the same point in the other. In a room with a sphere in the center, illumined by a bulb immediately overhead in the center, many observation points would provide identical arrays.

I do not think this possibility of causal indeterminateness is overly worrisome. All that is needed for purposes of a theory of perception and knowledge is that an array or sequence of arrays is more or less specific to a kind of state of affairs (or to kinds of objects in kinds of contexts). Similarly a causal theory only needs the claim that a series of arrays is more or less specific to a given set of events that caused it. An array or finite series of arrays need not unambiguously pick out a particular object or even kind of object, though, most likely, the longer the series and the more complex the environment, the more specific the properties will be to a particular object or event and its environment. In nature the specificity is sufficient for the most part. Indeed, Gibson needs to allow for the possibility of such ambiguity or indeterminateness in order to account for illusions, where illusions are said to be the result of insufficiently specific information.

Briefly, then, in the environment of a perceiver there exists at a time and over time specific relationships between objects in the environment. All objects in the environment reflect and absorb light in various ways depending upon their natures (substance, properties, and so on) and their positions relative to the light source. An observer at a particular point picks up incoming rays from some of these objects. The properties and relations between these objects cause particular reflectance patterns that converge and register on the observer's eye. The temporal succession of reflectance patterns causes further properties that converge on both eyes, as either the observer or part of the environment changes position. Such sequences of arrays are

441

continuous transformations of the structure in the original array. Pickup of such successive transformations allows, e.g., for the perception of motion.

I hope that enough has been said to at least make intelligible and somewhat plausible the conception of the environment as reflecting structured patterns of light rays, i.e., the environment as filled with reverberating illumination. It is this patterned light that is picked up or extracted by a perceiver. Thus this patterned light makes vision possible.

The retina, of course, is not a mere receptor. It has a selective function and acts upon the available arrays.[13] This retinal pickup is just one stage in the functioning of the visual system. When the properties of the object that were present in the environment cause a reaction at the cortical level, the whole visual system has been put into action; the system is, to use Gibson's terminology, resonated. Before reaching this cortical stage, there have been many changes in the energy that began as reflected light.

Some of the reflectance patterns and sequential transformations from the environment are "processed" by the visual system ending in the cerebral cortex, where, according to the work of Hubel and Weisel,[14] certain patterns can be correlated with the firings of certain cells. The firing of certain cortical cells at a particular excitation level is the pickup stage of the observer (or the last stage of the pickup process). The state the observer is in when the cell fires in the appropriate way is caused by the visible properties that were present in the environment as specified by transformations of the ambient array. One can establish which properties caused which state (which neuronal firings) by correlating a given cell's maximal firings and inhibitions with the presence or absence of certain kinds of environmental (or distal) stimuli. Since I am concerned with only a rather tight causal connection, it is not worrisome that the types of energy, which can be functionally described as carrying the information (or within which the information is contained), are different at different stages in the process.

The final stage in the visual process is some complex state of the visual system, which when it is resonated (or activated) con-

stitutes the person's perception of his environment. This resonated state is the state of the person's being appeared to by
the environment, though at the level I am treating he need not be
conscious or aware of being in this state. The content of the
state he is in is causally determined by the properties of the objects that were the initial cause of the activation of the visual
system. It should be again emphasized that not all properties of
objects in the environment are effective and can find "realiza-
tions" in the visual system, so that the perceiver's state is a
function both of the environment and of the selectivity of the
receptors and various processing devices in the resonating
visual system. These latter, in turn, depend upon his genetic
heritage and his prior perceptual learning. At higher levels it is
likely that memory, needs, and such might also play some selective or emphatic function relative to this pickup state. I shall not
discuss such functions at length in this paper. A general conclusion from all this seems to be that in cases where the perceiver
is perceiving the environment his perceptual state or the content
of his perceptual state is causally determined by the properties
of the objects present to him in the environment that he is perceiving.[15] In the most general terms, Gibson's theory as I have
sketched it holds that a perceiver has the perceptual beliefs he
has because he is caused to have them by the world, and the way
that the world is determines the content of the perceiver's
state when he is seeing.

A recent dispute with Gyr and others caused Gibson to be
more explicit concerning the active nature of a perceiver.[16]
Perceiving is not the mere passive pickup of information, but is
an active extraction or sampling of information available in the
environment. The organism samples the information around
him by moving about in the environment and by purposefully following up information that is significant to him. This active aspect of perception and the linkage between behavior and perception is a central part of Gibson's theory. The organism picks
up a bit of information about his environment, and then acts in
an appropriate fashion toward the information he has picked up.
He may seek additional information if the content of information
contained in his state is not determinate enough to specify

the properties, objects, or events in his environment. He may flee, duck, or stick his head in the sand if the information specifies something harmful to him. In every case there is the possiblity of subsequent behavior that is appropriate to the information attained.

This idea of appropriate behavior is required by Gibson in order to account for perceptual learning. In many cases it is only through the organism's responses to the environmental causes of his information that he is able to modify or change his perceptual abilities. Often he learns, through action toward his environment, to discriminate new kinds of information. Under pressures from his environment, he comes to be able to pick up new kinds of information concerning that environment. The need for such a behavioral component also lies in its utility in providing an identification criterion for a given perceptual state.

Perception as I have so far described it requires that there are particular states of the visual system that have (relatively) unique causal ancestries in terms of the visible properties that gave rise to them. The significance of this is that, following Dennett, Fodor, Harman, and other functionalists, we can describe the state of such a perceiving organism in functional terms, which takes us beyond the low-level causal talk used above. For example, it is quite appropriate to talk of a given cell as being in an excited-by-an-edge state. The description of the state of the cell, and, further of the global visual state at this level is intentional with respect to a description of the object(s) causing that state. Such a state is said to have a description of the causing object or properties as its content, in that the state is about or specific to the cause. As will be seen, the rationale underlying the intentional description of the state is that the state is characterizable as a function of the effective stimulus and has an output that is appropriate, suitable, or specific to that stimulus.

The description of the neurological state in functional terms serves, thus, to specify the content of that state by reference to the causal antecedents in the environment. This device of content ascription seems to be an explication of Gibson's (and others') claim that the information from the environment is contained (literally) in the state of the perceiver, when he is perceiving. Further, there is, at this level of description, no mediating entity that must be interpreted or otherwise acted upon by the brain or mind. Perception, this functional sense, is directly of the world; though this is quite compatible with there being many parts to the causal sequence that brought the perceiver to this state.

It is worth reiterating at this point, that Gibson has defined perception as the pickup or extraction of available information from the environment. It was noted above that Gibson's concept of information is not very clear, though I suggested it could be explicated in purely causal terms. The above remarks concerning functional states and content ascription suggest that one can treat Gibsonian-style information as just a specific content ascription to a state of a system, e.g., to a human perceiver.

Gibson talks about his concept of information in two ways. In *The Senses Considered as Perceptual Systems*, he says that information means only specificity to something.[17] He says that in all cases a property of the stimulus is univocally related to a property of the object by virtue of physical laws. The information is said to be contained in the environment, in the effective stimulus or sequence of ambient arrays (what is actually in contact with the visual system), and in the perceiver (who picks up the information as carried to him). The idea of specificity I discussed when talking about a causally specifiable process leading to the existence of a particular functional state. The state is said to be specific to the object(s) that caused it; it is intentional with respect to that object(s), having a description of the object(s) as its content.

The distinction between a stimulus object and the effective stimulus should cause some worries in this context. Gibson's next characterization of information touches upon this point. Information is said to be structure. The information is contained in invariants under transformation in the optic array. Such invariants under transformation are said to contain information about the environment. These invariants of Gibson seem to correspond to what I have called an effective stimulus. They are high-order variables, which are the crucial variables in ex-

445

plaining which parts of the structure of the ambient arrays are actually effective upon the visual system. It is because these variables are the effective stimuli that they are preserved in the state of a perceiver. The state is said to have these effective variables as its content, since they are descriptive of the state as well as of the stimuli.

In the same way that information is always information about something, the functional state of a perceiver is always a state having a content. The way in which information is specific to the environment is the way in which the content of a perceiver's state is causally specific to the effective stimulus in the environment. Thus it seems possible to read Gibsonian information in completely causal or functional terms. The state of a perceiver can be described as a functional state, but it might also be described as a state of information pickup. The information picked up is the content of the state.

It will undoubtedly have been noticed that so far I have confined my attention and talk to cases where a perceiver is perceiving the physical world (and solely to cases of vision). Similar moves for the other modes of perception and for perception that depends on more than one mode are elaborated by Gibson, but I shall not discuss them at present (following good historical prejudice).[18] I do need to say something about perception in cases where one is hallucinating or otherwise not perceiving the environment. A general argument for including such cases under perception rests on the point made famous by the sense-datum philosophers, viz, many of these hallucinatory or otherwise odd cases are phenomenologically similar to cases of perceiving the environment. This similarity is a datum that needs accounting for, and seems to lend some plausibility to calling hallucinatory and like cases perceptual. Likewise, being untouched by some philosopher's distinction of many different senses of 'see', it seems perfectly sane and plausible to me to say things like "I saw last night what you saw in your hallucination today." Now one need not talk that way, but one can—and one can be understood when he does so speak. This too is a datum that needs accounting for. Finally, though I have hinted at this above, in hallucinations and similar cases men do speak often about what they see. None of these facts is conclusive in establishing that hallucinating is a kind of perceiving. But whatever we end up calling hallucinations and like cases, it is worth noting that hallucinations differ from perceptions of the environment in one crucial respect: they are not caused by the environment. Their "proximate" cause is internal to the perceiver. This then is a crucial fact in presenting a theory of perception that can account also for hallucinations and like cases.

II

In a larger study I would explicate in considerable detail the various components and the explanatory import of the functional talk that I introduced toward the end of the last section. I shall not do that here. Instead, I shall assume that such talk can be made plausible and coherent and, using it, shall attempt to set out necessary and sufficient conditions for seeing something. I take the conditions I offer to be compatible with, and derivative from, Gibson's theory. I shall first motivate and, then, state the conditions. Finally, I shall end this paper by discussing some of the implications that follow from this way of viewing visual perception.

I want to treat perception as a state of a perceiver. In order to understand perception, we have to understand the nature of this state. I suggested, but have not shown, that the state in question will be a functional state; thus, a state that has a content. If we can treat perception as a functional state, the content of the state should allow us to account for the facts concerning the intentionality of perception. To identify functional states, one has to refer to the causal conditions that brought about those states. Also one can repress any behavioral condition as long as it is shown that behavior could and sometimes does, in fact, result from that state.[19]

It is this set of facts that will allow me to set out the basic theory of perception. I must remind you again that the perception that is meant to be explained by the set of conditions that follow is of a very low level, e.g., it need not involve awareness or consciousness of what is being perceived. The attempt now is to make plausible the claim that perceptual states are a kind of functional state. They will be states in which subsequent behavior, R, is missing for the most part. Perception often occurs without appropriate behavior following. In addition, the fact that perception seems to be an afferent state suggests that the correct description of the perceptual state should be in terms of that state's specificity or relatively unique causal relation to the objects, events, or properties that cause that state to occur. As shown above, this is a major component of Gibson's theory.

To capture this specificity, one needs to isolate a description of an effective stimulus, I. The stimulus, I, under that description, is the cause of an organism's, O's, state. Roughly, I want to say that O is in the state of seeing I if, and only if, he has been caused to see I by I in the proper way and that way is sufficient to justify the ascription of a functional state to O, where the functional state has a description of I as its content. What makes the seeing state a visual state, as opposed to any other sort of functional state, is just that the ways in which I caused O to come to be in that state are peculiar to seeing. The effective stimulus, I, worked through O's visual system in appropriate ways.

Intuitively I have an idea of what is appropriate and what is not. If the effective stimulus should bump O's eye, it would not be appropriate; if it emits or reflects light rays and those light rays cause O to come to be in an appropriate state, then O is seeing. In terms of a paradigmatic functional schema, O's state would be appropriate to I if O's state was the cause of a behavior R and R was appropriate to I. If a frog was in the state of seeing the dragonfly, then his state would, if he were hungry, lead him to flick his tongue out to catch the fly so that he could eat it. For humans the case is obviously more complex. I shall assume it to be true that any information a human picks up concerning his environment is picked up so that he may better satisfy his needs, desires, and purposes. Much of what is picked up and stored in memory is such that it may not turn out to be useful for such satisfying purposes, but the point nonetheless remains: such things are picked up so that they may be useful (even if, in fact, they turn out not to be). A large part of the adaptiveness of the human organism derives from the fact that he picks up much that does not seem to be immediately relevant to fulfilling his needs, desires, or purposes. Perhaps it is plausible, and I shall assume it so, to count all information pickup as purposeful in this evolutionary or learning sense. When we talk about set phenomena and what is consciously picked up or searched for, the picture changes somewhat. But I shall not speak to this point in this paper.

The position now is that when O sees I he is in a state that is a pickup-of-information state. That state can be said to be an appropriate state since O's need or purpose is to pick up information about his environment or about himself. But what are the conditions that must be fulfilled for O's state to be appropriate to I. First, I must be the cause of it. Second, the state must be describable in such a way that it is (relatively) causally unique to I. This much is true of all functional states. The causal uniqueness claim is such that it establishes that I is linked with O's state in an appropriate way. Finally, O's state must be caused in the proper way by I and not just in some accidental fashion. In nonhelpful prose, I must be an appropriate visible or structural object, event, or property; O's state must be a visual state appropriate to I; and the causal connection between O and I must be described in the manner appropriate for seeing. The question is how to specify the seeing state in ways that capture the appropriate appropriateness.

The criteria for someone's seeing something can be stated in the form of two conditions. The first condition is disjoint and falls into three parts, any one of which must be fulfilled. "O sees I" is true if, and only if,

1. (A) O is in a physical state, S_1, at a time, t_2, that is (a) an effect of an external cause, I, where I is a set of objects, or events, or a set of properties of such sets, persisting over some previous time, in an environment E_1; and (b) the state, S_1, that O is in at t_2 is such that it is appropriate to I, at t_1, where 'appropriate' means that S_1 is relatively causally unique to I and its surrounding environment, E_1, and that, normally, if O were to act on the basis of S_1 (or

its output), he would behave in ways appropriate to S_1 and I; and (c) the structure of the light rays (ambient array) intervening between I and its surrounding environment and O's visual system is that which was casued by I and its surrounding environment and not by objects, events, or properties other than I, and I acted through the medium of light rays and through O's visual system in normal ways (i.e., resonated O's visual system).

(B) O is in a physical state, S_1, that is the effect of an internal cause (some internal disturbance or stimulation in O) and this internal cause brought about a state that could have been brought about if there had been an external cause, I, and O's visual system had been functioning normally, and O had been caused to be in that state, S_1, by I by satisfying (1A).

(C) P is in a physical state, S_1, that is an effect of a combination of the causal factors in (1A) and (1B).

2.   The physical state, S_1, which O is in by virtue of satisfying condition 1, is a functional state of O that has a description, I*, as its content, where 'I*' is a correct description of I that was the cause (or, in 1B and 1C cases, that could have been the cause) of S_1.

A not-too-straightforward example may be helpful at this point. It will be true that Jim sees the bottle of Chateau Lafite if, and only if, Jim is in a physical state at that time which is an effect of an external cause, the bottle of Chateau Lafite, and Jim's state is appropriate to the bottle of Lafite in that the state is relatively causally unique to bottles of Lafite. If Jim were to act on the basis of his seeing the bottle of Chateau Lafite, he would act appropriately, e.g., moan reverently and drool in joyous expectation. The structure of the light rays between Jim and the bottle of Lafite was caused by that bottle and the bottle structured the light rays that resonated in Jim's visual system. Finally, the state Jim is in is a functional state that has the bottle of Chateau Lafite as its content, for 'bottle of Chateau Lafite' is a correct descrip-

450

tion of a bottle of Chateau Lafite, and it was that bottle which caused him to be in that perceptual state.

In this example it should be noted that had Jim been affected by the bottle in other ways, e.g., by being hit by it, touching it, and so on, he usually would have come to be in a different state. Further, in order that he be in the state of seeing a bottle of Chateau Lafite, something about the bottle must have indicated that it was Chateau Lafite, e.g., the label must have been visible to him and been part of the cause of structuring of the light rays. (Or, it might have been that Jim has learned to discriminate the bottles used by Lafite from other Bordeaux bottles.) In any event, the cause, I, of Jim's state will be described differently in cases where he is seeing a bottle of wine, or just a bottle filled with something, than when he is seeing a bottle of Lafite. I shall return to ramifications of this claim later.

The effective stimulus, I, specified in condition 1(A) needs to be further explicated. As stated, it is a set of objects, events, or properties of such objects or events. It can be a unit set, containing just one object, and so forth. Specifying what I is, for a particular case of seeing, would involve us in describing the relevant parts of the environment, which caused the structuring of the ambient arrays and which were effective in causing O to see that part.

The temporal indices are included in 1(A) to allow for O's picking up information about I over time, and also to allow for O or I's movement. That is, as the condition stands, I can be a set of events persisting over time, which events are constituted by changes in the objects or relations between objects. The use of I as a single variable in the condition is meant to indicate that it is some invariant property of the environment to which O is responding, even if O is responding to its environment over time. The temporal indices also allow for the inclusion of the infamous case of seeing stars that have become extinct. The causal process between I and O takes time, so that O will always be in a state that was determined by I as it was some time previous to O's being in that state. Further, the environment that causes O to be in the state of seeing I need not be—in the last analysis—O's immediate environment. The environment that is causally crucial is the environment in which I is located, which is linked by some spatiotemporal causal chain to O. In this respect it can be remarked that condition 1(A) entails an existence claim about I. If (A) is true, then there is or was some I that caused O to be in the state he is in.

The state, S_1, that O is in is some complex physical state. I am not requiring, as some philosophers have, that S_1 be a brain state. It is most likely, as Gibson and others have noted, that a perceptual state involves much more than just the brain, including the states of the various peripheral mechanisms and, perhaps, even proprioceptive states. The point is that the state is only a physical state of the organism that is capable of being correctly described as required by conditions 1 and 2.

Condition 1(Ab) makes use of the troublesome concept of appropriateness. This was talked about above when discussing functional states and will not be allowed to trouble us at this point. It should be noted, though, that as theories of the workings of the perceptual system are elaborated in the works of physiological researchers, one will be able increasingly to avoid any reference to *overt* behavior on the part of the perceiving organism. The basic point is that the output of a state is appropriate to its input and to its own internal structure.[21]

Relative causal uniqueness is a feature of Gibson's theory that is preserved here. In cases where the content of O's state is such that it is not very unique, i.e., it is specific to more than one set of I's, it is still true that O is seeing his environment veridically. What is not true in such cases of indeterminate information pickup is that O will normally respond appropriately to the environment of which I is a part. Thus if O is in the state of seeing some brown object, he will not have enough information to base an appropriate response to that object under any other description than brown. If the object happens to be a bear, this could lead to dire consequences, but not because of faulty seeing.

Which aspects of the environment O sees, or picks up information about, depends upon the species of O (its evolutionary heritage) and upon the selective environmental, psychological, and social pressures that acted upon O during his lifetime. As O learns to discriminate more and more things, he is capable of seeing more and more. This is just the phenomenon of perceptual learning. A further complication should be noted: because of differing circumstances, specifically those dealing with the prior states of O (perceptually and otherwise), sometimes O picks up information about the environment that he did not or will not on other occasions. That is, even if O has the perceptual ability to discriminate or pick up information about a particular I, it does not follow that whenever I is present he will resonate to it or pick it up. The explication of this fact would be an explanation of set phenomena in perception. But I shall not say more at this point.

The clause (b), about the causal uniqueness of the relation between the state of O and the visible properties of I, is needed to rule out certain kinds of contents as not proper. Such causal uniqueness can be restated in functional terms, requiring that the state O is in has as its content a description of the visible or structural properties of I and/or other objects present in I's environment. This brings out one aspect of the relation between the causal conditions and the doxastic condition 2. Clause (b) also allows me to rule out O's being caused to have weird beliefs as a result of his picking up information about his environment. For example, clause (b) allows me to rule out as an example of seeing a case where O, seeing Stewball in the field grazing, is caused to be in a state where he has the belief that Stewball won the Preakness.[16] We should not, I think, want to call the belief that Stewball won the Preakness a perceptual belief in this case, since the property of Stewball's winning the Preakness is not one of the visible properties in O's environment. Thus O does not satisfy condition 1 (A) by being caused to have *that* belief.

Clause 1 (Ac) includes a reference to light rays (or, the ambient array) for three reasons: (i) it is by light rays that the causal connection is established; (ii) the clause as stated serves to rule out cases that would be left if it were not there, e.g., the case where a man is brought to see "stars" by being hit in the eye with a rock; and (iii) the inclusion of the light rays structured by sets of objects and their properties is necessary to account for cases where no light is reflected from an object itself, e.g., where there is a shadow or a hole. In such cases the hole can be identified by means of the differential intensities of the stimuli coming from the total environment. In the case where O sees a hole, there is no light reflected from the hole itself (it is not a reflecting surface). The location of the hole is specified by the light reflected from the surrounding landscape, i.e., the ground around the hold. Thus O sees the hole by means of picking up light rays from the landscape in which the hole was dug; O fulfills our condition.

Some philosophers might object to the inclusion of light rays in condition 1(A), clause (c), on the grounds that though light rays are involved, in fact, in everything we see in the external world, this is only a contingent fact. It is possible, someone like Fred Dretske might say,[22] that we could see something by other means (by a different causal mechanism). My reply to this is three-pronged: (i) I am quite unclear about whether or not it would be true that if someone was caused in a weird and bizarre manner to be in a state that we are caused to be in by light rays that I should want to claim he was seeing. A case, considered by Dretske, of a man who "sees" something behind an opaque wall is to the point, for it is not at all clear that it is fitting and proper or true to say that the man sees the object behind the wall. (ii) The contingent status of 1(Ac) is not worrisome because I see no reasons for the theories to be composed of necessary truths. This is brought out in my next rejoinder. (iii) Even if an example could be constructed where one was tempted by virtue of its similarities with a standard case (and there could be no other reason for being so tempted) to call it a case of seeing, the use of 'seeing' as applied to this new case would involve an extension of the present concept. In such cases, where our present concept undergoes extension or modification, it seems quite reasonable to expect that the truth conditions for sentences using that concept will undergo analogous extensions or modification. Such extension or modification would also be required if we, all of a moment, began to pick up the rays from ultraviolet or gamma sources. In such a case, if we were to call it a case of seeing, we would have to modify the light-ray-clause (c) in our condition. But this is just what should be expected, for it is in this respect that the new case differs from the standard. The possibility of finding reasons that would lead us to change our present concepts is, I take it, always open for every concept (arithmetic possibly excepted). Even under such circumstances, our perception conception would be little different; except for 1(Ac), the set of truth conditions would remain constant.

George Pitcher, in his book, *A Theory of Perception*, does make use of something like my light-ray-clause. He includes, "We use our eyes in the standard way."[23] This may seem more acceptable to some philosophers, but such a feeling would be illusory. The only meaning at all clear that one can attach to "the standard way" is that of receiving reflected light rays. (Pitcher admits as much.) Otherwise the phrase is merely vacuous and non-informative. If by means of light rays is the standard way, then why not say so and avoid obscurities and illusions of sense that attach to "standard way"? Such specification will also allow us to determine when a conceptual change has occured, and exactly what the change consists in, for we should have to modify in quite specific ways the manner of causal connections that are allowable in satisfying condition 1(A).

The 'normal ways' occuring in my clause 1(Ac) refers to the manner of processing that goes on when the stimulus affects the visual system. It is shorthand for a series of processes commencing in the retina, moving through the optic nerve, and ultimately into the cortex. All that needs to be noted about these processes is, in Gibson's words, that the information contained in the ambient array is likewise contained throughout the visual system. The information is carried through the system. The physical state referred to in 1 and the functional state referred to in 2 are both conceived as states of the whole system. I take no position on whether or not a given bit of information is contained in a specific part of the system at a specific time. Understanding the relevant states in such a global way actually obviates the need for the phrase 'normal ways,' since the focus is not on the processing (and the mechanism by which it occurs), but rather on the resultant state of the organism, i.e., on the state it is caused to be in.[24]

Consider the following troublesome case: There is a silvery

moon in the sky, shining upon a silvery tray. The moon's perceived properties are identical with the tray's perceived properties (e.g., both are the same apparent size, have the same texture so far as can be seen by O, and so on). Since the tray is illumined only by the moon's light, the moon is obviously involved in the causal process that causes O to see. Condition (c) and its requirement that I does the structuring rather than some other object(s) is meant to allow us to determine whether O sees the tray or the moon, despite the fact that both would look the same to him.[25]

The phrase 'visual system' occuring in 1(Ac) may seem worrisome due to the occurrence of 'visual.' I do not think that any vicious circularity results from its inclusion. The phenomenon of seeing can be identified independently, in many cases, of any knowledge of what is occurring in the visual system, e.g., by perceiver's reports. Given those cases in which seeing occurs and is identified independently of looking at the visual system, we can then physiologically begin to ascertain what the mechanism is that brings about this phenomenon. This is the method used in most physiological research. After some knowledge of what the system is and how it works, we develop independent grounds (anatomical in this case) for identifying the constituents of the system. These seem to be what are set down in texts describing the visual system. Thus it is possible for us to know what the visual system is and what its normal manner of functioning is like (more or less). This possibility of independent identification allows the use of the phrase 'visual system' in the conditions for 'O sees I' without its being question-begging or vicious.

Condition 1(A) explains the way in which the external world is related to O when he is seeing something in that world. There is no need to postulate sense-data, sensations, or the like in order to account for O's seeing. This is another crucial feature of Gibson's theory of perception.

In fulfilling condition 1(B), it is possible that there can be an external cause that brings about the internal cause of the hallucination. In the case of someone who sees "stars" by being hit in the eye with a rock, there is a sense in which being hit in

456

the eye with a rock is the cause of his seeing "stars." But there is another and more important sense for our purposes, in which the cause of his seeing what he does was the internal disturbance that resulted from the impact of the rock with his head.

Consider another strange case: O is caused by a bright light hitting his eyes to see "stars."[26] O believes, as he would in some normal hallucination cases, that he is seeing something that looks like stars. In this case O is satisfying condition 1(B), since the bright light set off an internal disturbance in O that caused him to see "stars." This case does not satisfy 1(A) because O's state is not brought about solely, without *abnormal* internal disturbances, by the light rays from the bright light hitting his eyes and by the normal functioning of the visual system. O is in a state brought about by the light rays from the bright light, and from their causing in him some internal effect that in turn caused O to be in a star-seeing-state.

This abnormal qualification requires understanding 1(A) in a certain way. The normality of the process is packed into a spelling out of what comprises the visual system. When these parts, and these alone, are causally responsible or constitutive of O's state, O is in a veridical state of seeing. (At higher levels of seeing, I shall of course allow certain memory states and other functional, neurological states to have a role in O's seeing, but this modification still necessitates O's total visual system being involved.) If some other, non-visual part of O's nervous system is brought into play and substitutes for one of the normal links in the chain causing vision, then we can say there is an internal disturbance.

This would seem to allow for the following problem: in some cases of ablation or brain damage, parts of the normal visual system are destroyed, and it is possible that other parts of the cortex can take over the functions of the destroyed parts. In such a case there would seem to be veridical seeing, though in an abnormal way, of the kind I just attempted to rule out. But to even conceive of this possibility of substitution depends upon knowing the normal parts and their functions in the visual system. Only with such knowledge can one justifiably claim that the other part took over the normal part's function. In such cases, which are obviously abnormal, the visual system for such

457

a person would be abnormal also. This abnormal person fulfills condition 1(A) in an abnormal way, but in a way that is functionally equivalent. My condition 1(A) can tolerate some abnormality. Such an abnormal person would fulfill 1(B) and not 1 (A) if in some way that was abnormal to *his* normal state he came to be in a particular seeing state.

The qualitative similarity between some hallucinations and some perceptions of the environment are easily explained upon condition 1(B). The state the perceiver is in, in both cases, is identical; it is only the causal routes by which they are arrived at that differ.

Condition 1(C) is necessary for explaining integrated hallucinations. Since 1(C) is just a causal composite of 1(A) and 1(B), it can raise no problems that are not raised by 1(A) and 1(B). No more need be said about it.

Generally, it is worth noting that in any particular case, whether O is seeing because he is fulfilling 1(A), (B), or (C) is a fact that we might ascertain from O's reports (where O reports he is hallucinating and so on) or from the context in which O is and which we have knowledge of (though O may not); for example, we know, though O does not, that he has just been given a dose of DMT. Normally, unless there is some information to the contrary, we assume that a perceiver is fulfilling the 1(A) condition. In cases where we do not assume O is fulfilling 1(A), there has generally been some tip-off that O is fulfilling the 1(B) or 1(C) alternatives. One such tip-off could come from O's report or from the context if we have acquired reason to think that the existence condition (entailed by 1(A)) is not being fulfilled.[27] O may be able to ascertain whether he, himself, is hallucinating from various "introspective" data. It has been suggested that if O moves (and from proprioceptive information knows he is moving), what he sees in a hallucination will move with him without change whereas an environmentally caused perception will undergo perspectival transformation.[28]

Condition 2, though stated as a content condition, could be stated as a belief or doxastic condition. Minimally I am assuming that whenever O is in such a state he has a dispositional belief appropriate to that state. The state that O is in will cause him, if certain appropriate conditions are present, to act as though a certain proposition were true. The proposition in question contains 'I*', in an essential way.

The descriptive content of S_1, viz, 'I*', is the functional content ascribed to O's state as specified in condition 1. In 1(A) cases, 'I*' is also descriptive of some object or properties available in O's environment. Say O has perceived a table during the time t_1 through t_3. One of the higher-order properties of the table (an effective stimulus) he will have been stimulated by, if he was moving about the table, was that the object was three-dimensional. This he would have picked up from the perspectival transformations of the various table-caused arrays. The content of the state is about a three-dimensional object. The content of O's state is that there is a three-dimensional object. The belief state O is in is that there is a three-dimensional object. This way of describing the content of O's state is compatible with, and explicated by, the earlier description given of function states and their rationale and conditions.

As noted above, the content of O's state, S_1, in veridical cases can be described as the information that O has picked up about his environment. Information is always information about a set of objects, events, or properties in the environment. Such information can be expressed in the form of a proposition, where the proposition describes the relevant causal properties, objects, or events that caused O to be in S_1. To specify content or information in this way may seem cumbersome, since one often sees more than is easily describable. The reason for the fact is easily grasped. The information in question is being presented pictorially. There is no reason to expect that a simple description will be able to express the simplicity (or other properties) or the pictorial content. For example, to describe the shape of a fleur-de-lis would take a rather complex sentence. A perceiver can be said to have picked up information about its shape even though neither he nor we are able to accurately express the complex sentence that describes what he is seeing.

For each resonated state of a perceiver there is a sentence or set of sentences that are true because of the properties, events, or objects that are causally responsible for his perceiving state.

459

If one takes the conjunction of all such sentences, the resulting sentence expresses the content of the perceiver's state at the time. The same information could be expressed, and often more accurately expressed, pictorially, e.g., by a drawing of the properties of the object and environment.

The description given of O's state is often one that *we* or some suitably knowledgeable third person could give in reporting about what O believes is true of I. It is not the case that O need have another belief about I, though he normally will; the only belief O need have about I is that I*, where 'I*' might be something like 'there is something large'!

That O is caused to have a belief by seeing I or the fact that O is in a state having a description of I as its content does not imply that O is conscious of I. For O to believe that there is a three-dimensional object, he need not know or consciously believe anything about three-dimensional objects. Beliefs of the type I am attributing to all perceivers are held by infant and, even, animal perceivers. Such beliefs are often quite low-level beliefs in that their content could be, e.g., the common information in the states of an infant, an Eskimo, and a Pasadena housewife, all seeing the same refrigerator.

I have not required that O have some true belief about an actually existing object, I. This would be an especially awkward requirement if O were fulfilling 1(B). Condition 2 is compatible with O's belief being true of I, though it is not necessitated by it. In 1(A) cases the beliefs will, in fact, be true.

It follows from Condition 2 that all seeing is doxastic, i.e., that it has positive belief content.[29] The seeming dispute concerning epistemic/non-epistemic perception can be resolved at this point. If one considers a state satisfying my conditions to be very low-level and thinks that purely causally defined states are not epistemic, then this would be the level of non-epistemic perception. Higher-level cognitive states would then be epistemic, especially those involving attention and (long-term) memory. I think the dispute is of little philosophical consequence.

There is one important ambiguity that must yet be remarked. Insofar as the sentence 'O sees I' is meant to convey the content of the state that O is in when seeing I, that far will it be true that 'seeing' makes an opaque context. When one uses 'O sees I' to express a truth claim about the content of O's state, one cannot freely substitute co-referential descriptions for I. 'O sees I,' with such speaker's intention, is true only under an intentional description where 'I' is the description of the causing environment and constitutes O's state. There is another sense of the sentence 'O sees I' that is common parlance. In this latter sense 'O sees I' is true under any co-referential description of I. There are normal limits to which kinds of descriptions would be accepted by ordinary speakers, but in logical terms any co-referential description would suffice to preserve truth. In such contexts 'O sees I' is treated transparently.

Literally, by condition 2, the content of O's state, I*, is intentional with respect to the causing object under a given description. Thus if O has picked up information about a pointed green edge, then all that is true of him is that he sees a pointed green edge. This claim, of course, is subject to the caveats noted above concerning whether or not the information is represented in visual or linguistic form. If, however, that pointed green edge happened to be the top leaf of a tall tree, one would ordinarily take it to be a warranted inference that O sees the leaf. In other, more exotic circumstances, such as looking for trees hiding behind billboards, one could take such seeing to warrant a claim that O sees a tree; or even, O sees the tree with the rotten heart. In the most strict non-transparent sense, all that O directly sees, or has picked up information about, is what is represented as the content of his state. There are epistemological problems concerning the validation of such claims; e.g., how can one determine whether O is in a seeing-a-green-edge state or in a seeing-a-leaf state? These are the problems that arise when one tries to provide conditions for justified functional state ascriptions.

The point at hand, though, is not how can we solve this particular methodological problem in particular cases, but when are we warranted in using 'see' transparently or opaquely to describe third persons. The third-person point of view is generally the appropriate one for the level of seeing that we wish to describe, for recall that O does not have to be conscious or aware of what he sees. Roughly, if the information O has picked up, viz, I*, is sufficiently relative to a given set of circumstances and to O's background knowledge and learning to justify a claim that a certain kind of object or event is present, then we are justified in claiming that O, besides strictly seeing I*, also sees that object or event which is warranted on the basis of his information.[30] If Baby Huey sees the green, pointed edge and under those circumstances that would not be sufficient for him to justify a claim that a leaf is there, we would not be justified in saying that Huey saw the leaf; just as, in such a case, we would not be justified in saying Huey saw the tree. Again, *ex hypothesi*, all that Huey directly saw was the green, pointed edge. When in fact Huey broadens his visual horizons, by perceptually learning to discriminate leaves from other green pointy things (like elves' hats), then we may attribute to him the state of seeing the leaf. In this last case, there would be no inference on either his or our part; in the former case there was inference on our part, though not on his. The terminology of "seeing as" is helpful at this point, but I shall not go into it here.[31]

Clearing up this ambiguity allows me to handle cases like that suggested by George Pitcher.[32] Pitcher proposes a hunter who is looking at a bush and grasses in which a pheasant is hidden. The pheasant is perfectly still, and some of her brown shows through the brownish surroundings. The hunter stares directly at that part of the bush where the pheasant's feathers show through. The puzzle is, does the hunter see the pheasant? On this account, insofar as the pheasant's feathers are the actual cause of the hunter's seeing state, and insofar as his state is feather specific, then the hunter does see the pheasant's feathers. Of course, the hunter need not be conscious or aware that he is seeing the pheasant's feathers. But, if the camouflage is good, and the pheasant's feathers convey to the hunter the same information that would be conveyed if, in fact, they were part of the bush, then *his* state would not be feather-specific. There still remains the fact that we could be justified in saying that he is seeing the pheasant's feathers (or relevant bits of it). In such circumstances, though, we would be unwise to hazard the claim that the hunter (non-transparently) sees the pheasant. It is precisely in those circumstances that many cognizant and conscious hunters miss pheasants; and unless he could, contrary to assumed fact, somehow distinguish the bit of pheasant feather from the surrounding bush, neither we nor he would be justified in claiming that there was a pheasant present.

Let me return to the start and end by having a last word concerning Gibson's theory of perception and its relation to alternative, constructive theories. There is nothing in the conditions for seeing as I have laid them down that requires one to distinguish between Gibson's theory and the constructivist, processing approach. I have borrowed in obvious ways, with hopefully not too liberal a hand, basic elements and grander inspiration from Gibson's work; but the theory I have sketched requires only a description of an I, structuring between I and the visual system, and finally a state that has I* as its content. There is nothing to stop a constructivist from using the theory I have here put forward. One can speak either with Gibson and say that some high level variable, I, specific to some aspect of the environment resonates O's visual system, which is O's being in S_1; or, speak from a processing theory, like Bruner's, which holds that a stimulus object, I, presents O with cues that are processed (categorized), resulting in O's being in a state S_1. Bruner's categorized stimulus cues, and Gibson's resonating visual system seem to be functionally equivalent. S_1 is the same for both theories, though each would define I differently. It seems then that this is a case where hypothesizing mechanisms for the internal functioning of the visual system is appropriate. It looks as though only when the two different mechanisms are hypothesized and tested will there be reasons to choose one theory over the other. Until that time both programs should be elaborated. In all probability further research will show that the visual system both picks up directly and processes. The two are not necessarily incompatible.

Telling the rest of the story of perception would take me into considering the mechanism of attention and its attendant consciousness, the role of memory, and the higher cognitive abilities.

Also, it would require a more detailed explication of functional states and their contents. But that story is too long to be told at present.

I thank George Pappas, who, during the seminars of 1971 and 1974 and at sporadic moments in between, has been a most harsh critic and source of considerable insight. James Bogen joined Pappas in the summer of 1971 in providing constant stimulation, and he later played midwife to various revisions when the paper was read and discussed at Pitzer College and the Claremont Graduate School. At that time helpful comments were provided by Morton Beckner and Ronald Rubin. I should like to thank Dean Owen, of the Ohio State University Psychology Department, for many valuable talks about perception, especially about Gibson's theory. I am grateful to those persons who spoke out at a colloquia at Ohio State (in 1971), and at Glasgow (in 1973) and to most of the graduate students in my perception seminars. Finally I owe a debt to the participants in the perception program that led to this volume. In particular, I wish to thank J. J. Gibson, who provided me with comments on the first half of this paper, and Romane Clark, who pointed out to me some bad things.

1. J. J. Gibson, *The Senses Considered as Perceptual Systems*, (Boston: Houghton Mifflin, 1966).

2. Gibson seems to hold that only reflected, or ambient, light can carry information. This neglects the information contained in emitted light. Astronomers, spectroscopy analysts, and other stargazers will be surprised to learn that on Gibson's theory they could not have picked up any information about the star they are looking at; e.g., its distance, magnitude, composition, and so on. I presume Gibson's slighting of emitting objects is primarily rhetorical, and is meant to overstate the case for the more neglected structural properties of ambient light; cf. Gibson, op. cit., p. 186.

3. Gibson demurred at this last sentence. I am not sure why.

4. Gibson seems to treat colors as properties of objects, though, at some points, he deletes 'color' and refers to the object's pigmented surface (op. cit., pp. 183, 211).

5. Gibson, op. cit., p. 189.

6. Gibson objects to the use of 'stimulus' in this sentence. But I shall use 'stimulus' to mean 'the effective variables in stimulation.' I do not think he would object to this.

7. J. J. Gibson, "The Problem of Temporal Order in Stimulation and Perception," *J. of Psychol* 62 (1966): 146.

8. Cf. R. W. Ditchburn and D. H. Fender, "The Stabilized Retinal Image," *Opt. Acta* 2 (1955): 133, and R. W. Ditchburn, "Eye-Movements in Relation to Retinal Action," *Opt. Acta* 1 (1955): 171 f.

9. Cf. the second paper by Ditchburn, mentioned in note 8 above. Also see Charles Butter, *Neuropsychology: The Study of Brain and Behavior* (Belmont, Calif.: Brooks/Cole, 1968), pp. 48-51.

10. Gibson remarked on the draft of this paper that this paragraph only speaks about *stimulation* involving change, and not about the *perception* of change with non-change. Therefore, he holds this data to be irrelevant to perception. I have left it in because it certainly is relevant for ascertaining what an organism picks up and, thus, to what it perceives.

11. J. J. Gibson, "A Note on the Concept of 'Formless Invariants' in Visual Perception," mimeo, dated, March 1972. To appear in *Leonardo*.

12. J. J. Gibson, *Senses*, p. 192.

13. Part of the selective function probably is due to feedback from higher cortical states and varies with the neurological state of the organism at immediately preceding times. Cf. K. Pribram's conception of "feed-forward" mechanisms.

14. D. H. Hubel and T. N. Wiesel, "Receptive Fields of Single Neurons in the Cat's Striate Cortex," *J. Physiol.* 148 (1959): 574 f., and D. H. Hubel and T. N. Wiesel, "Receptive Fields and Functional Architecture of Monkey Striate Cortex," *J. Physiol.* 195 (1968): esp. 238-42. A review article by D. H. Hubel of this work appeared in *Scientific American*, November 1963, under the title, "The Visual Cortex." A summary of Hubel and Wiesel's findings is provided in Butter, *Neuropsychology*, pp. 39-57.

15. I say 'determined' rather than 'completely determined' because at this point I wish to leave open many questions concerning the role that memory or prior knowledge might have upon perception. These questions should be addressed when one considers the role of attention and higher cognitive processes.

16. John W. Gyr, "Is a Direct Theory of Perception Adequate," *Psychol. Bull.* 77 (1922): 246-61; also see papers by Gyr, Gibson, and others in J. R. Royce and W. Rozeboom, eds., *The Psychology of Knowing*, (New York: Gordon & Breech, 1972).

17. J. J. Gibson, *Senses*, p. 187.

18. See ibid., chaps. 4-8.

19. Though the literature on functionalism seems to grow daily, there still does not exist a definitive and careful statement of the position. Thus in this paper I rely, as others have, upon certain intuitive-sounding phrases. But, in order to provide a little more content to those phrases, let me suggest the following characterization of a functional state: An organism, O, in environmental conditions E, is in a functional state, S_1, having a content ϕ at time t_2 if:

1. There is a stimulus, I_1, that has a description, 'ϕ,' true of it at t_2 or before (where the stimulus is a set of objects, events, or properties thereof, in an environment E_1, persisting over time);

2. I_1 causally affects O and is the cause of O's being in state S_1;

3. S_1 causes O to behave at t_3 in a way, R, that is appropriate to O's being in S_1 under conditions E and appropriate to I_1 under description ϕ, in conditions E_1;

4. The descriptions of I and R must either be justifiable by appealing to an accepted theory and its use or else be correct according to the established rules of language, etc., of the community to whom the ascription of the functional state is communicated;

5. There must exist, or be the real possibility of developing, criteria for identifying the state that are independent of the particular instances of I and R mentioned above.

It will be noted that since I claim behavior can be repressed, it follows that 3 above is not necessary. Though, as indicated, I hold that 3 must be true in some cases.

20. These particular examples of appropriate behavior are probably not the best, since it is unlikely that these would be mainfest without Jim's being aware that he was seeing a bottle of Lafite. Though this is most likely the case, it seems possible to imagine a wine drinker who is so conditioned that all this information is taken in and acts upon his effector system in a wholly unconscious manner.

21. This point can be elaborated by further considering functional systems in terms of the subsystems that serve as mechanisms for producing outputs of appropriate kinds. This way of ultimately eliminating a reference to overt behavior was suggested by Jerry Fodor in conversation.

22. Fred Dretske sets out such a case in his *Seeing and Knowing*, (Chicago: University of Chicago Press, 1970), pp. 50-51.

23. G. Pitcher, *A Theory of Perception*, (Princeton: Princeton University Press, 1971), pp. 70-89.

24. This point may help explain why Gibson is opposed to information-processing theories of perception, or why he thinks the processing details are interesting but, in the end, irrelevant in explaining perception.

25. This weird case was suggested by James Bogen.

26. This case was suggested in prototype by George Pappas. It was made bizarre by James Bogen.

27. Cf. Dretske, op. cit., p. 48–49.

28. Cf. J. J. Gibson, "On the Relation between Hallucination and Perception," *Leonardo* 3 (1970): 425–27.

29. Under one interpretation of Dretske's theory, all seeing would be epistemic since fulfillment of condition 2 would entail that O has some belief or set of beliefs. If Dretske wants merely to claim that no one single, specific belief is entailed in all cases of O's seeing, then seeing under my conditions, at this level, is non-epistemic. Dretske, also, does not require that the beliefs be true.

30. This problem was raised by Morton Beckner, when he commented on a very early version of this paper. The criterion was developed in some detail by Ronald Rubin.

31. A tentative account of "seeing as" occurs in my paper "Understanding Scientific Change," *Studies in the History and Philosophy of Science*, 5 (1975): 375–76.

32. Pitcher, *A Theory of Perception*, pp. 78 f.

Dean H. Owen

Chapter Eighteen

THE PSYCHOPHYSICS OF PRIOR EXPERIENCE

A survey of the history of perceptual theory, like that represented by this volume, reveals a great deal of effort expended on the problem of discovering the locus of perception. For vision, does perception occur in the crystalline humor, in the retina, in the cortex, or somewhere else in the organism? While the problem of anatomical localization has been taken over by sensory physiology, the attention of most perceptual theorists has shifted to hypotheses about what activities or processes must occur in those loci, wherever they turn out to be. In current information-processing nomenclature, for example, the loci become stages or levels of processing.

Accordingly, one of the major problems with which theorists have confronted themselves since the beginning of attempts to explain perception is how and at what locus prior experience comes to have an influence on subsequent perceiving. One observer may see something that another does not, or the one may see something in a way that the other does not. The difference in perception of the same object or event by two observers and the difference in perception of the same object or event by the same observer from one time to the next must be accounted for by an adequate theory of perception.

The problem of dealing with prior experience has led to a generally used distinction between the *physical* determinants of perception arising from differences and changes in the environment and the *organismic* determinants of perception arising from changes in the perceiver as a function of this past history of stimulation. The methodologies of psychophysics have been developed to account for variability in experience and/or behavior as a function of environmental variability, that is, the physical determinants.

For the purpose of theorizing about organismic determinants, a wide variety of mental processes have been proposed to intervene between proximal stimulation (the distribution of energy on a sentient surface) and the perceptual experience. Past experience, then, is supposed to have its influence on the process so that proximal stimulation is interpreted in different ways following different experiences. If two observers have the same kind of sensory system, it can be inferred that had their past histories of stimulation been exchanged, each would perceive as the other does. The influence of past experience on the process mediating between stimulation and perceptual experience becomes an explanation for perceptual learning. The difference between the state of an observer before and after his experience of the environment is a difference in the way in which stimulation is interpreted. The interpretation of stimulation by the observer is his contribution to perceiving. Names given the organismic determinants of perception have varied depending on the requirements of the theorist: unconscious inference (Helmholtz, 1925); accrual of context to sensory core (Titchener, 1910); schema (Bartlett, 1932); organization field forces in the brain (Köhler, 1947); stimulus generalization (Hull, 1943); acquired equivalence or distinctiveness of cues (Miller and Dollard, 1941); cue-weighting strategy (Brunswik, 1956); unconscious assumptions (Ittelson, 1960); categorization (Bruner, 1957; Liberman et al., 1967); stimulus-as-coded (Lawrence, 1963); efferent readiness (Festinger et al., 1967); and analysis by synthesis (Neisser, 1967). Terms like "stimulus" and "cue" are often used to designate entities considered to be inside the organism, so that both conceptualizations of the processes and *what* is processed are mental entities.

Theorists who believe that perceiving is direct rather than mediated propose that the distinction between past and present experience is a false dichotomy because perceiving is an event over time (J. J. Gibson, 1966a; Michotte, 1963). In other cases it is proposed that the perceiver learns to differentiate characteristics of stimulation not previously distinguished. Application of the new skills is described as abstraction of relevant information, filtering of irrelevant information (E. J. Gibson, 1969) and, in general, the education of attention (J. J. Gibson, 1966b).

The important question seems to be: What should constitute credible evidence that prior experience influences perceiving? After the criteria for acceptable evidence are worked out, the problem of what to call the influences should be considerably simplified.

There are four aspects of the problem to which the theorist/ researcher may devote his attention: (1) specification of the objects or events experienced by the observer at an earlier time, (2) specification of the objects or events experienced during later testing, (3) specification of the relation(s) between the previous and the subsequent objects or events, and (4) specification of change and nonchange in objects or events as events-over-time, which may encompass everything entailed by the other three aspects. The major experimental effort of perceptual research has been devoted to demonstrations that the interpretive process is active during perceiving through the use of illusions, reversible figures, and patterns providing constrained, ambiguous, or inadequate information. The major theoretical effort has been devoted to justifying the need for the mediating *psychological* processes and descriptions of their role in current perceiving. Much less attention has been given the specification of objects or events previously perceived and their relation to objects or events subsequently perceived.[1] This state of affairs persists in spite of the parsimony of defining the purported processes and describing their functioning in terms of the above four classes of *physically* specifiable information. Such an approach would require development of a psychophysics of prior experience, since current perceptual experience or behavior indexing current perceiving would be accounted for entirely in terms of physically specifiable variables.

The development of a psychophysics of prior experience has relevance for the study of several basic problems in perception. (a) Adaptation: how does an observer adjust to a change in stimulation so that the new point of central tendency becomes the neutral point to which differences and changes in stimulation are related? (b) Perceptual learning: how does an observer learn where to look, what invariants to look for, and what differences and transformations to look for? (c) Perceptual set or readiness: after learning to make the necessary distinctions, how can the perceptual system of an observer be prepared for the activities described in (b) before stimulation occurs? (d) Recognition memory: how is an observer able to distinguish "old" (previously experienced) patterns, objects, and events from "new" (not previously experienced) things? The activities of adaptation, perceptual learning and set, and recognition, as well as the explanatory concepts (unconscious inference, education of attention, or whatever) should be definable in terms of measurable manipulations of environmental variables.

Although no general experimental paradigm has been worked out, the need for a psychophysics of prior experience has been expressed by theorists representing a variety of viewpoints. Bartlett (1932) was aware of the problem and its potential resolution when he wrote the following:

> Perhaps an experimental study of the perceptual processes which precede any particular instance of recognising might be able to help us to understand why sometimes the specific mechanism is by comparison and judgment, sometimes by feeling, and sometimes, apparently by direct "knowing" of relations. . . . Experimenters have analyzed the final stage of recognising, and each has tended to claim a complete solution in terms of his particular analysis. In fact, nobody can understand recognition by confining his attention to what happens at the moment of recognition. (P. 192)

Much of the literature on prior experience has been concerned with the nativist-empiricist controversy. Unfortunately, due to the nature of the experiments conducted, most of the articles consist largely of exchanges of rhetoric (see, for example, Duncker, 1939; Zuckerman and Rock, 1957). Pratt (1950), seeing the need for an operational criterion, argued adamantly *against* empiricistic explanations of perceptual phenomena (and in favor of innate "organized properties of neural excitation set into operation by the action of external stimuli") when the result of an experiment could be accounted for by a psychophysical correlation:

> If the dependent variables . . . can be described as functions of the eternal stimuli, . . . the relationship thus formulated needs no further elaboration at the psychological level. (P. 88)

> An appeal to the past to explain the present is likely to be *ad hoc* or merely *faute de mieux* if the appeal is not based on experimental or statistical evidence. A general appeal to past experience . . . runs the risk of becoming a wastebasket into which are lightly tossed all difficulties met up with in accounting for the results of experiments. (P. 92)

As J. J. Gibson (1950) pointed out, however, the correspondence of perception to the information available in stimulation does not have to be a wholly innate and unchanging correspondence. Psychophysical correspondence can be refined with practice and effort. It is at least implicit in all of the above quotations that a particular kind of empiricistic explanation would be acceptable—if differences in objects or events previously experienced can be specified and shown to correlate with differences in a dependent variable when subsequent test stimulation is held constant.

Helson (1959) developed a quantitative model based upon just such a conception to account for changes in judgments as a function of adaptation. The experience of any given state of the environment is assumed to be relative to an adjustable internal standard or adaptation level. A judgment is assumed to be the log-weighted mean of (a) the focal stimulus to which attention is paid, (b) background stimuli presented simultaneously, and (c) residual stimuli. According to Helson, residual stimuli are

> determinants of behavior having their locus within the organism, such as effects of past experience and constitutional and organic factors which interact with present stimulation. . . . The concept of adaptation level is, in current parlance, an "intervening variable" but it differs from many intervening variables in being operationally defined in stimulus terms. (P. 567)

471

It is possible to study past stimulation as an experimental variable under laboratory conditions if advantage is taken of the fact that controlled stimulation at one time functions as "past experience" at a later time. (P. 592)

Helson's logic and paradigm are acceptable according to the criteria for a psychophysics of prior experience, but his theoretical account seems to fit the structuralist mold of combining sensations (current stimuli) and memory images (residual stimuli). This is apparently a misguided attempt to adhere to the principles of stimulus-response behaviorism. The determinants of responses must be stimuli even if the same word used to describe objects and events in the environment must also be used to describe states of the organism. Pratt (1950) made a more favorable interpretation and in addition demonstrated his own acceptance of a psychophysical criterion for empiricistic explanations of perceptual phenomena as well as for nativistic accounts:

By residual stimuli Helson means levels and frames of reference which are leftovers, as it were, from previous experiences. It is significant that he uses the expression residual stimuli. The independent variables in all psychological experiments, so Helson would seem to imply, should be some form of stimulus; and by stimulus he obviously means some factor which in the experimental design can be controlled, measured, or at worst deduced from the results by impeccable logic or some mathematical process of elimination. Only in this fashion can past experience be removed from the region of vague *ad hoc* supposition and treated as a truly independent experimental variable. (P. 104)

As Hochberg (1957) expressed it in assessing the Gestalt attack on the empiricist postion, ". . . It is extremely difficult to refute any general 'explanation' couched in terms of past experience. Consequently, we must *specify* the relationship between past and present stimuli and percepts, or we have 'explained' little more by invoking 'past experience' than by invoking 'human nature' " (p. 77).

J. J. Gibson (1974) has taken the position that perception is

472

not localized in the receptors *or* in the brain *or* in the muscles. It involves the *entire* system when a perceptual system is active. Perceiving does require a sentient organism with certain perceptual abilities, but it also requires an environment with perceivable characteristics. From this point of view, then, the distinction between physical and organismic determinants of perception is not a useful dichotomy. Gibson holds that perception must be defined in terms of the *reciprocal relation* between the perceiver and the perceived, and that the functioning of the perceptual systems can be understood by determining what variables and invariants constitute the information gained by perceiving. In keeping with his general theory, he (J. J. Gibson, 1959) proposed that,

> in the whole history of psychology it has never become clear just what "the effect of past experience" on perception or behavior is. . . . Learning itself has proved impossible to define. . . . A helpful procedure might be to forget all terms like memory, association, reinforcement, insight, or adjustment and to make an empirical survey and a classification of the known *effects of previous stimulation on the activity induced by subsequent stimulation.* (Pp. 488–89)

For J. J. Gibson, objects and events have successive order, as well as simultaneous order, and the information for both change and nonchange can be specific to either the continuity of or the relation between earlier and later experiences. This assertion can encompass phenomena as diverse as motion perception (considered as the pickup of information specifying a transformation over time) and recognition (considered as the ability to detect recurrence of an event after other events have intervened). According to his theory, it should be possible to relate changes in perceiving to information available during prior and subsequent experiences. If so, differences in information specific to objects and events experienced earlier should account for differences in perceiving by two observers when the information obtainable at a later time is identical for both. Adaptation, perceptual learning and set, and recognition all entail variables

473

and invariants of the environment to be adapted to, learned about, set for, and recognized. It follows that all these phenomena should be specifiable in psychophysical terms.

The purpose of the section that follows is to clarify by example how credible evidence for the influence of prior experience on the activity of perceiving can be generated from a general paradigm. The criteria for selecting the experiments were that in each case: (1) the patterns, objects, or events experienced by the organism prior to testing were physically specified and controlled; (2) the relation between prior experience and the test condition was controlled; (3) the pattern, object, or event presented during testing was physically specified and controlled; and (4) the test condition was exactly the same following all conditions of prior experience so that differences in performance could be unambiguously attributed to the effects of differences in earlier experiences and not confounded with differences in test conditions. Only a small number of studies met the selection criteria, but fortunately a wide variety of theories and perceptual phenomena are represented. Several of the studies use animal subjects because most conditions of controlled environments are too severe for the rearing of human infants. The sequence of presentation of the examples is roughly from lower- to higher-order perceptual phenomena, rather than according to any chronological or theoretical organization.

THERMAL ADAPTATION

The logic appropriate to a psychophysics of prior experience is not new. Locke (1690) observed that water "may produce the idea of cold by one hand, and of heat by the other. . . . " In 1846 Ernst Weber did an experiment with three containers of water at 20 degrees (C.), 30 degrees, and 40 degrees. One hand was placed in the 40-degree water and allowed to adapt at the same time the other hand was adapted to the 20-degree water. Then both hands were placed simultaneously in the 30-degree water, where it was demonstrated that the same physical temperature can feel cold to one hand and warm to the other (Geldard, 1972).

Although the phenomenon has been used for centuries as an obvious demonstration that perception is relative, it also serves as a simple example of how the information picked up by a sentient system can be accounted for by physical specification of prior and subsequent stimulation and the relation between the two. When only the test situation is considered, the demonstration can be interpreted as support for the notion that perception is' not in correspondence with the water temperature. If, however, the relevant physical variable is considered to be a *change* in temperature of the water, psychophysical correspondence can be demonstrated since the system is simultaneously sensitive to information that the water is cooler-than-before for the one hand and warmer-than-before for the other hand. The difference in experiences of the 30 degree water is specific to the difference in direction of change in temperature.

APPARENT MOTION

Wertheimer (1912) made use of the prior experience paradigm in his seminal experiments on the phi phenomenon, an illusion of motion observed when two light sources are successively illuminated and extinguished at appropriate brightness, spatial relation, and rate of alternation. He arranged two illuminated lines as shown in figure 1a so that the angle between line x and the baseline y could be varied. Lines x and y were flashed in succession with a brief interval between them. Under the condition of figure 1a, with no previous experience with the other

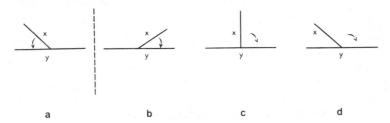

a   b   c   d

Fig. 1. The conditions used by Wertheimer to demonstrate the effect of objective set on apparent motion. Line x always preceded line y with a brief interval between. Conditions (a) and (d) are physically identical, but perceived differently when (b) and (c) precede (d). See text for complete explanation.

conditions, a single line will appear to move from x to the left half of y in the direction of the arrow. In the condition shown in figure 1b, however, the apparent motion will be in the opposite direction to the right half of y. Now, if the observer first experiences the condition of figure 1b, and the angle between line x and the baseline is progressively increased in 10-degree steps through the vertical (figure 1c) to the obtuse angle of figure 1d, the motion will *continue* to appear between x and the right half of y, whereas with no such preceding experience, the apparent motion was x to the left half of y (figure 1a). If the order of the conditions is reversed (d through c to b), then in condition b the apparent motion will be from x to the left half of y.

Koffka (1922), in the Gestalt tradition, explained the effect as produced by the observer's attitude, where the concept of attitude was a readiness to carry out a structural (organizational) process. He later described this process as fusion between the two separate excitations (Koffka, 1935). In terms of a psychophysics of an event-over-time, the difference in direction of apparent motion when the two instances of succeeding stimulation were the same is explained in terms of the change and direction of change in the angle of line x. According to his students (Luchins and Luchins, 1972), Wertheimer himself came to make a similar interpretation during a seminar in 1941:

> . . . Wertheimer pointed out that the direction of the movement was lawfully determined and not arbitrary. He referred to the operation of the factor of Einstellung and added that Einstellung was not subjectively but was objectively determined by the way line (x) was presented. The successive exposures were given in a certain rhythm . . . each exposure was seen as part of a structure, as part of a unitary series in which a line fell from left to right. He noted that the factor of Einstellung or objective set was one of the principles of organization. . . . (P. 311)

Again, if the physical variable is considered to be a change, psychophysical correspondence can be demonstrated since the difference in direction of apparent motion is specific to the difference in prior displacements of the line over time. As J. J. Gibson (1959) pointed out,

476

the neglected variables of succession are unquestionably stimuli for the sense organ. . . . Change of stimulus pattern is itself a kind of stimulus pattern. The change does not have to be continuous in time to be perceived as a change; the facts of stroboscopic movement prove that a discontinuous transformation may be the equivalent of a continuous transformation. (P. 489)

The psychophysical explanation is that displacement of a pattern over time and space is an adequate event for motion perception, and different orders of displacement result in the perception of different motions.

LONG-TERM EFFECTS OF EARLIER EXPERIENCE

Empiricists have long claimed that perception is acquired by the individual in the course of his development as a result of his dealings with the environment. Researchers have either assumed that the previous environments of two groups of human observers differed in specific ways, or they have directly controlled the environment in which an animal was reared. In both cases, tests are conducted to assess the perceptual effect of the earlier experience.

Allport and Pettigrew (1957) found that, under marginal conditions for obtaining the rotating trapezoid illusion, rural Zulus report the illusion only 14 percent of the time, as contrasted with urban Zulus who report it 64 percent of the time. It was argued that the environment of the urban Zulus was more likely to be of the carpentered, rectilinear variety filled with parallel horizontal and parallel vertical edges with their intersections at corners, whereas the environment of the rural Zulus consisted largely of rounded objects and openings. Since no difference obtained between urban and rural Zulus under more optimal conditions for producing the illusion, Allport and Pettigrew were cautious in interpreting their data. They were willing, however, to conclude that under marginal conditions object connotation or meaning based on closely relevant cultural experience helps to determine the nature of perceived movement. Others (Slack, 1959; Segall et. al., 1966) have been impressed by the positive result and view it as support for an empiricist theory of perception.

477

Working from the same general hypothesis, Annis and Frost (1973) tested the acuity of Euro-Canadian and Cree Indian subjects for lines of various orientations. The observers were told to turn the pointer of the response apparatus to match the orientation of a line grating. They were informed that the lines would always be in one of four possible orientations: horizontal, vertical, or left or right oblique. The Euro-Canadian subjects, reared in a carpentered environment, had better acuity for grating patterns in the horizontal and vertical orientations than in oblique orientations. In contrast, the Cree Indians from along the eastern shore of James Bay, Quebec, were reared in traditional tepee-like tents and lodges that present contours in virtually all orientations. Acuity scores for the Cree did not vary significantly with line orientation. The difference in adult visual acuity for orientation was correlated with the difference in frequency of various contour orientations in the early visual environments of the two groups of observers. For Annis and Frost, the most parsimonious explanation of the acuity difference is that orientation-specific neural line and edge detectors are tuned by the character of the early visual environment.

In order to make a direct test of just such a notion, Blakemore and Cooper (1970) reared kittens in a dark room from the age of two weeks to five months except for five hours each day spent in one of two special environments. A kitten was allowed binocular vision while standing on a clear glass platform inside a tall cylinder, the entire inner surface of which was covered with either horizontal or vertical black and white stripes. The kitten wore a wide black collar that restricted its visual field to a width of about 130 degrees, so that it could not see its own body.

When first tested at five months of age, the kittens showed no visually guided placing of their paws when brought up to a table top and no startle response when an object was thrust toward them. Within about ten hours of normal vision they showed startle responses and visually guided placing, and would jump with ease from a chair to the floor.

Other deficits seemed to be more permanent and specific to the horizontal and vertical environments. The kittens were virtually blind for contours perpendicular to the orientation they had experienced during rearing. They showed no startle response for an approaching plastic sheet covered with black stripes, nor would they place their paws with visual guiding on such a pattern, if the stripes were oriented opposite to those in the rearing environment. When two kittens, one having horizontal-stripe experience and the other vertical-stripe experience, were tested simultaneously with a long black or white rod, the difference was marked. If the rod were held vertically and shaken, the appropriate kitten would follow it, run to it, and play with it, whereas the second made no response. When the rod was held horizontally, the other kitten was attracted and the first completely ignored it.

Neurophysiological evidence convergent with the behavioral result was obtained by recording the activity of single cortical neurons when the kittens were seven and a half months old. While stimulating the eye with a thin bright line projected on a screen before the anaesthetized kitten, the orientation of the line was varied until the frequency of firing was maximized. Of 125 neurons studied in two kittens, one horizontally and the other vertically experienced, 124 had distinct orientation selectivity. The distributions of optimal orientation of the line were very abnormal. Not one neuron had its optimal orientation within 20 degrees of the inappropriate axis, and there were only 12 cells within 45 degrees of it.[2] In a second experiment, Blakemore and Mitchell (1973) varied from one to thirty-three the number of hours that a dark-reared kitten experienced the vertically striped environment on or about the twenty-eighth day of life. With a control kitten that had received no visual stimulation at all, they were unable to find any neuron that had more than the vaguest orientation preference. By contrast, virtually every cell of the kitten with only one hour of experience responded actively over a narrow range of orientations strongly biased toward the vertical.

From these studies Blakemore and his colleagues conclude that the visual cortex may adjust itself during maturation to the nature of its visual experience, perhaps adapting to match the probability of occurrences of features in the visual input. They further suggest that the environmental modification of cortical cells may be the physiological manifestations of learning and memory.

The effect of constrained early visual experience may ultimately be shown to have its effect by "setting" a labile system to be more sensitive to some sources of information than to others or by atrophy due to inactivity of a genetically determined system originally sensitive to a wider variety of patterns and objects (see, for example, Hubel and Wiesel, 1963). In either case, from the point of view of a psychophysics of past experience, it was demonstrated that differences in perceptually guided behaviors during the various visual tests were specific to the nature of the stimulation previously experienced. Stimulation during testing was the same for both groups of kittens, so that the differences in behavior, physiological activity, and presumably perception correspond to physically specifiable differences in environments previously experienced. The results can be compared with, and may provide an explanation for, findings from the experiments with adult human observers for which a direct interpretation cannot be made because previous experience was not under precise control.

INFANT HABITUATION

That the paradigm can be used to study the perceptual abilities of the newborn human infant is illustrated by an investigation of phenomena called "habituation" and "dishabituation." What is meant by these terms should become clear from the way in which the phenomena are studied. Friedman (1972) repeatedly presented one of two visual patterns to forty normal infants aged one to four days. The pattern was either a two-by-two (four squares) or a twelve-by-twelve (144 squares) black and white checkerboard. The pattern was presented repeatedly until a set criterion of habituation was reached, as measured by a decrement in the time the infant spent looking at the pattern. Each pattern was used both for the habituation trials and as a pattern to test for habituation with different groups of infants, so a particular combination will be used for clarification. One group of infants was habituated by repeated exposure to the two-by-two checkerboard, and a second group was habituated with the twelve-by-twelve checkerboard. When the set decrement in time spent looking was reached, infants in both groups received the *same* pattern, for example, the two-by-two checkerboard, in order to assess the effects of familiar and novel visual patterns on recovery of the habituated response. The results indicated that infants receiving the same pattern with which they had been familiarized on the habituation trials showed no increase in time spent looking. Infants receiving a novel pattern did show an increase in the visual response.

Use of the paradigm allows the decrement in looking time to be attributed to habituation rather than fatigue of the response system itself. Since visual fixation time recovered when the novel pattern was presented, the previous decrement must have been perceptually related rather than response related. Most important for the present argument, the paradigm makes credible the conclusion that newborn infants have the capacity to recognize a visual pattern as reflected by their ability to detect and respond to a change in the pattern presented. By physical control over the difference in patterns previously experienced and the relation between preceding and test patterns, the criteria set forth by Bartlett (1932) for the study of recognition memory are met. The experiment serves to demonstrate the utility of the psychophysical paradigm for the study of the ontogenetic development of perceptual memory.

SPEECH ADAPTATION

To demonstrate generalizability of the prior experience paradigm to the auditory system, two related psychophysical studies of the perception of synthetic speech are described.

Ladefoged and Broadbent (1957) divided the kinds of information conveyed by speech sounds into three classes: linguistic information, which enables the listener to identify the words; socio-linguistic information, which enables him to appreciate something about the background of the speaker (place of origin,

481

social status); and personal information, which aids in identification of the speaker. To investigate a listener's ability to detect the personal information conveyed by vowels and use that information to identify words, a speech synthesizer was used to generate six versions of the sentence "Please say what this word is." The sentence was chosen to provide a suitable context of personal information because the formant frequencies of the sounds vary over a wide range. (A formant is a region of high-energy concentration of frequency over time as revealed by a speech spectrogram. See figure 2 for examples.) The formants of a speech sound have properties specific to the shape of an individual's vocal tract and therefore convey idiosyncratic information about the speaker. The six versions were identical except for differences in the range over which the first and second formants varied. With the exception of one that did not sound like normal speech, the different versions sounded like the same sentence pronounced by people who had the same accent but differed in their personal characteristics.

A version of the sentence was presented before one of four test words of the form [b]–(vowel)–[t]. The first and second formant frequencies were varied for the middle of the vowel in each of the words. The listener was told that he would hear a series of words, each of which might be "bit," "bet," "bat," or "but." He was instructed to make a mark on an answer sheet by the alternative he had heard.

There was no doubt that identification of the test word was influenced by the properties of the context sentence that preceded it. For example, when one of the test words followed one version of the introductory sentence, it was identified as "bit" by 87 percent of the sixty listeners. When the *same* word followed a version of the sentence in which the first formant varied over a lower range, it was identified by 90 percent of the listeners as "bet." Auditory perceptual constancy, as indexed by identification of a vowel sound with fixed physical properties, was shown to depend on the *relations* between the frequencies of the vowel's formants and the frequencies of the formants of other vowels occurring in a preceding, physically controlled auditory context.

It might be argued that a given test word sounds phenomenally the same after each version of the context sentence but is interpreted differently. The following study of the effect of prior experience on the identification and discrimination of synthetic speech sounds is an attempt to clarify the issue.

Eimas and Corbit (1973) used synthetically produced phonemes (the smallest unit to which an acoustic event can be reduced and yet sound like speech) in an attempt to demonstrate the existence of "feature detectors" for linguistic information by selective adaptation to speech sounds. They hypothesized from physiological and psychological studies of vision (in the vein of the Blakemore et al., experiments cited earlier) that there are "detector mechanisms in the brain" that are uniquely sensitive to particular and relatively restricted patterns of stimulation. To test their hypothesis, they varied voice onset time that is sufficient for perceived distinctions between the voiced and voiceless stop consonants in the initial position of English phonemes. A stop consonant followed by a steady-state vowel is perceived as a phoneme. Very short lags are perceived as voiced stops, as in [ba], [da], and [ga]. Relatively long stops are perceived as voiceless stops, as in [pa], [ta], and [ka]. Voice onset time is controlled synthetically by varying the lag in onset of voicing, shown in the duration-by-frequency spectrograms of figure 2 as 10 and 100 milisecond lags. The spectograms for the first three formants are coded F-1, F-2, F-3 in figure 2 for the phonemes [ba] and [pa].

As voice onset time is varied in small steps, sounds in the series are identified as starting with either the voiced or the voiceless stop consonant. The conclusion drawn from these results is that speech perception is categorical, that is, at points along the relevant physical continuum, one or the other of two discrete sounds is heard. Adult speakers of at least ten other languages also show the categorical effects, and by use of a habituation paradigm similar to that described for the Friedman experiment cited earlier, it has been found that one-month-old human infants show the categorical effects as well. Although speech categorizing appears to be universal, suggesting to some theorists that it is a manifestation of the basic, specialized perceptual structures of the human brain, there is also evidence

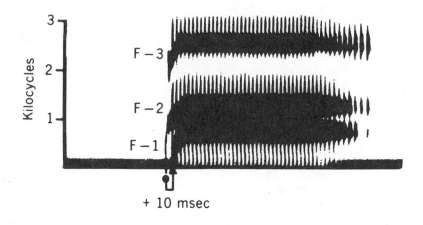

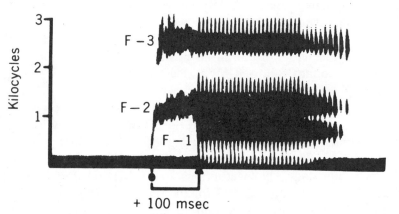

Fig. 2. Spectrograms of synthetic speech showing two values of voice onset time: a slight voicing lag represented by [ba] in the upper figure and a long voicing lag in the lower figure, represented by [pa]. The symbols F-1, F-2, and F-3 represent the first three formants, that is, the relatively intense bands of energy in the speech signal. (From P. D. Eimas and J. D. Corbit, "Selective Adaptation of Linguistic Feature Detectors," *Cognitive Psychology* 4 [1973]: 99–109. Copyright © 1973 by Academic Press; reprinted with permission.)

that prior experience has an influence in determining how speech sounds are heard. Some languages, for example, Thai, have a third long-voicing lead and an apporpriate perceptual category boundary. This fact led Eimas and Corbit to theorize that the "categorizers" might be differentially tuned to the acoustic consequences of speech production. From this theoretical assumption, they hypothesized that repeated presentation

484

of a particular duration of voice onset time to which a given "categorizer" is sensitive should fatigue the neural mechanism and reduce its sensitivity.

Two series of fourteen synthetic speech sounds were prepared by means of a synthesizer. The time between the onset of the first formant and the onset of the second and third formants was varied over a range of short voice onset times for a series starting with sounds readily identifiable as [ba] and ending with sounds readily identifiable as [pa]. The second series with slightly longer voice onset times ranged from [da] to [ta]. Ten identifications of each of the twenty-eight sounds were made after adaptation to [ba], [da], [pa], and [ta], which had voice onset times of –10, 0, +60, and +80 milliseconds respectively. Each adaptation sound was presented 150 times in a two-minute period at the beginning of each session and 75 times in a one-minute period before each identification test.

The phonetic boundary between the two categories of speech identification moved an average of eight milliseconds (in voice onset time) closer to the adapting sound indicating a greater number of identifications representing the unadapted mode of voicing at the new boundary than before adaptation. For the clearest case, shown in figure 3, (top), the event with a voice onset time of thirty-five milliseconds was identified by unadapted subjects as [da] 70 percent of the time and as [ta] 30 percent of the time. By contrast, the *same* voice onset time was identified as [da] 100 percent of the time after adaptation to the [ta] sound and as [ta] 100 percent of the time after adaptation to the [da] sound. The shifts in phonetic boundary occurred even when the adapting and identification test sounds were from different series. For example, adaptation to the sounds in the [da], [ta] series resulted in shifts of the category boundary when the identification test was made with sounds from the [ba], [pa] series.

The clearest example of cross-series adaptation is revealed in figure 3 (bottom) at forty milliseconds voice onset time. This event was identified by unadapted subjects as [da] 25 percent of the time and as [ta] 75 percent of the time. After adaptation to the sound [pa], however, the *same* sound was identified as [da]

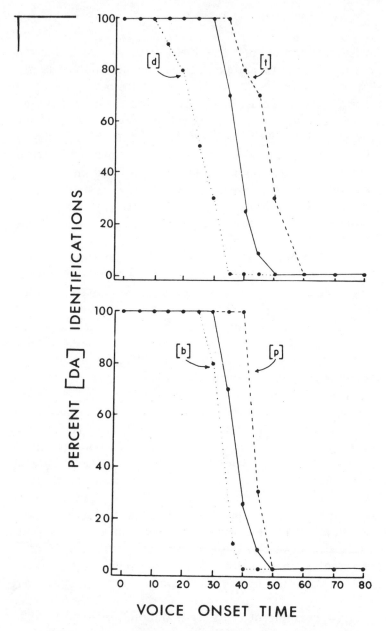

Fig. 3. Percentages of [da] identification responses obtained with and without adaptation. The solid lines indicate the unadapted identification functions, the dotted lines indicate functions after adaptation to short voice onset times ([da] or [ba]), and the dashed lines indicate functions after adaptation to long voice onset times ([ta] or [pa]). The phonetic symbols indicate the adapting sound. (From P. D. Eimas and J. D. Corbit, "Selective Adaptation of Linguistic Feature Detectors," *Cognitive Psychology* 4 [1973]: 99–109. Copyright © 1973 by Academic Press; reprinted with permission.)

100 percent of the time and as [ta] 100 percent of the time after adaptation to the sound [ba]. From the cross-series results, Eimas and Corbit argue that they must have adapted "categorizers" for complex information in the sound pattern, namely, voice onset time, rather than simply for information specific to a single sound. Recovery of the adaptation effect is not more than 50 percent complete by ninety seconds and they suggest that complete recovery may require thirty minutes or more.

When an identification task is used, however, the inferred perceptual categories are confounded with the response categories required of the perceiver. For this reason speech perception researchers have developed a discrimination task that does not require responses that are specific to the speech sounds. Three sounds are presented in a sequence, the first sound differing from the second whereas the third sound is the same as either the first or the second. The task of the listener is to determine whether the third matches the first or the second. The task is supposed to provide convergent evidence for the category theory since the discrimination accuracy is usually high when the two sounds are from opposite sides of a category boundary and near chance (50 percent) when the two sounds are from within the same category, even though the difference along the physical continuum is kept the same in both cases. If discrimination were not categorical, then accuracy would be equally good over the range of events including two identification categories and the boundary between them, in which case the accuracy function would be flat.[3]

Assuming the categorical nature of the speech perception process, Eimas and Corbit hypothesized that the shift in the identification boundary with adaptation should be paralleled by a shift in the peak of the discrimination accuracy function. They used the same adaptation procedure as in the identification experiments, except that the discrimination problem replaced the single identification test sound. The adapting sound had a long voice onset time and was perceived as [pa]. Eleven synthetic speech sounds from the [ba], [pa] series were used in pairs to make up the discrimination test problems. To obtain a function without adaptation, the discrimination problems were presented in random order.

As shown in figure 4, repeated exposure to the voiceless stop [pa] resulted in a shift in the discriminability peak that corresponded to the shift in the identification boundary. Sounds became more or less discriminable after adaptation depending on their proximity to the phoneme identification boundary. From these results Eimas and Corbit concluded that there are two linguistic feature detectors in the [ba], [pa] range of stimulation, each of which is sensitive to a restricted range of voice onset times and mediates perception of one of the two consonant voicing distinctions.

With regard to interpretation of the results in terms of the psychophysics of prior experience, it is important to note the lower graph in figure 3. At the point where voice onset time equals forty milliseconds, the *same* sound is identified on 100 percent of the trials as [pa] after adaptation to a sound with a short lag and is identified on 100 percent of the test trials as [ba] after adaptation to a sound with a long lag. Which of the two phonemes will be identified when this physical event occurs is dependent on the properties of the sounds previously experienced. This application of the psychophysical paradigm suggests that the perception of a given acoustic event can be influenced by preceding experience with speech sounds. The Ladefoged and Broadbent (1957) results also demonstrated that, at least for personal characteristics, the categorizing system can adjust as a function of a brief prior experience. Since their introductory sentence did not include exemplars of many of the vowels influenced, their effect, like that of Eimas and Corbit, is not specific to the sounds heard. The dynamic nature of the boundaries may further account for the ability to adapt to regional accents that were difficult to categorize correctly at first, but become easily understood as the perceiver adapts to the shifts in sounds with experience.

ADAPTATION TO VISUAL REARRANGEMENT

When the medium between the objects and events of the environment and the eyes is changed in some fashion, perception and concomitant behavior are usually in error. The perturbation of the medium may be as natural as the addition or removal of atmospheric haze or as unnatural as requiring the observer to wear goggles containing wedge prisms or colored filters. In

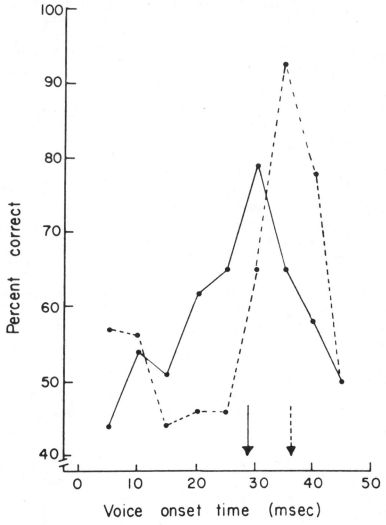

Fig. 4. The discrimination accuracy functions without adaptation (solid line) and after adaptation to [pa] (dashed line). The points are plotted midway between the two values of voice onset time being discriminated. The arrows indicate the locus of the phonetic boundaries found from identification functions with (dashed arrow) and without (solid arrow) adaptation to [pa]. (From P. D. Eimas and J. D. Corbit, "Selective Adaptation of Linguistic Feature Detectors," *Cognitive Psychology* 4 [1973]: 99–109. Copyright © 1973 by Academic Press; reprinted with permission.)

most cases the result is a gradual adjustment of the system to "normalize," "ignore," or "adapt to" the change, so that the environment is specified as before. Since the experiments relevant to the psychophysics of prior experience have been concerned with adaptation to the effects of wedge prisms, attention will be focused on that problem. Two perceptual effects result from wearing the prisms: (1) apparent displacement of all aspects of the environment away from the base of the prism and (2) apparent curvature of all lines and edges parallel to the prism's base. With experience, responses indicating the locus of points in space and the apparent curvature of lines become more accurate.

Two broad classes of theories have been developed to account for the adaptation phenomena. One class of theories proposes that the visual system adjusts to correspond to the changes necessary in the motor system in order to respond accurately. Festinger's theory of "efferent readiness" (see Festinger et al., 1967) is representative of the point of view that perception is somehow mediated by motor activity. The theory is an attempt to account for changes in conscious experience with adaptation as well as for perceptual-motor recoordination. Opposing theorists (Wallach et al., 1963; Rock, 1966) maintain that the information from perceiving alone can be adequate to allow, and perhaps to determine, changes in perception.

Wallach et al. (1963) had observers view their own legs through base-right prisms while standing. The observers initially perceived their feet displaced toward the left and their legs on a slant emerging from their torso at an angle. The slant at which the legs appeared was assumed to be in conflict with the vertical direction that the legs represent to a standing individual not wearing prisms. By about midway through the ten-minute viewing period, the observers reported that their legs now seemed straight. After the experience with prismatic displacement, two different tests of visual direction were used to converge upon modification of a single perceptual process by reducing the possibility that an adaptation effect would be connected with a particular response. Both tests were conducted in the dark to prevent the observer from seeing either his limbs or reference

490

points in the environment. One test required the observer to point only once at a glowing bulb filament. A second test determined apparent forward direction by requiring the observer to instruct the experimenter to move the bulb filament horizontally until the glowing point appeared to be straight ahead. The observers were tested with and without the prisms before and after viewing their legs. Comparison of before and after scores indicated both an adaptation *effect* as tested with the prisms and an adaptation *aftereffect* as tested without the prisms. The pointing test and the test of apparent forward direction measured about the same magnitude of adaptation, suggesting that a change in a common perceptual system had occurred.

According to Wallach et al., the observers were simultaneously exposed to two different conditions of stimulation: the "cues representing the visual direction and the cues on which the perception of the vertical direction is based" (p. 576), which normally give rise to the same perceptual property (verticality). By

> so altering one of [the "cues"] that it misrepresents the objective situation, a discrepancy is produced between the perceptual processes that result from the two conditions of stimulation and may lead to modification of one or both of these processes. . . . (P. 568)

> When [the observer] wears a prism, the slant with which his legs are now given will be in conflict with the vertical direction which his legs represent to a standing [observer]. (P. 569)

The explanation of the adaptation effects (and aftereffects) is that apparent visual direction is modified to correspond to the more dominant "cues for verticality." The latter were never specified by Wallach et al., but presumably are proprioceptive.

As a further test of their theory that adaptation resolves a perceptual discrepancy between two sources of information specifying the same property, Wallach et al. eliminated the verticality discrepancy by having the observer lie on his back with his head raised to permit him to see his legs through the prism.

491

It was assumed that the remaining "discrepancy between the displaced visual location of the legs and their location according to postural data . . . would be insufficient to cause an adaptation" (p. 577). Twelve of the twenty-three supine observers, in fact, never reported the displacement of their legs.

The notion that vision can dominate other sources of information is supported by a number of observations. Stratton (1897) wore an optic system that inverted the optic array, leaving the retinal image right side up rather than inverted as is normal. After wearing the apparatus for eight days, he reported that when "the scene was involuntarily taken as the standard of right directions, and my body was felt to be in an inharmonious position with reference to the rest. I seemed to be viewing the scene from an inverted body" (p. 469). In another experiment Stratton (1899) mounted two mirrors such that his body appeared horizontally in front of him at the height of his head. Free movements of body, head, and hands were possible. After wearing the apparatus for a total of twenty-four hours, he reported, "In walking I felt as though I were moving along above the shoulders of the figure below me, although this too was part of myself. . . . I had the feeling that I was mentally outside my own body" (p. 496). Stratton came to the conclusion that "if we were always to see our bodies a hundred yards away, we would probably also feel them there" (p. 498).

Visual dominance has also been observed in the study of adaptation to the curvature of lines and edges that results when wedge prisms are worn. In evaluating the hypothesis that adaptation toward decreased apparent curvature occurs in order to resolve a conflict between two experiences, J. J. Gibson (1933) discovered that "the kinaesthetic perception, in so far as it was consciously represented, did *not* conflict with the visual perception. When a visually curved edge such as a meter stick was felt, it was felt as *curved*. This was true as long as the hand was watched while running up and down the edge. If the eyes were closed or turned away, the edge of course felt straight, as in reality it was" (p. 5).

Festinger et al. (1967) verified Gibson's observation and proposed a theory to account for why vision dominates so that the hand is felt as moving in a curved path. According to their theory of "efferent readiness,"

> the conscious perception of the path of movement of a limb is not the organization of the informational input from the receptors in that limb, but is rather the organization of the efferent signals issued from the central nervous system to that limb. The arm would be felt to move in a curved path if the efferent signals issued through the motor pathways directed the arm to move in a curve." (P. 4)

Festinger et al. argued further that having to issue a new set of efferent responses that correspond to the actual straightness of an edge when the retinal input is curved would result in visual adaptation to curvature, since the way things look comes to correspond to the new "efferent readiness" that develops as movements are made and visual "reafference" provides information about the relative success of the movements.

Following the performance of various perceptual-motor tasks while wearing wedge prisms, Festinger et al. gave observers a version of a test of apparent curvature developed by J. J. Gibson (1933). The observer viewed two parallel rods and turned a knob to adjust the rods until they appeared straight. The deviation of apparently straight from actually straight was measured at the midpoints of the rods. With appropriate opportunity to learn a new "afferent-efferent association," observers adjusted the rods to be less curved than without such experiences.

It is an assumption of theories of "reafference" and "efferent readiness" that relevant motor movements are necessary to produce visual adaptation. It is of interest, therefore, to determine whether any adaptation will occur under conditions that allow an observer no relevant movements during either the initial experience or the test task. J. J. Gibson (1966b, 1968) has proposed that transformations and invariants in the optic array are information for both locomotion of the observer and motion of an object. Transformations can be generated by the changes in perspective that occur when an observer makes exploratory movements about an object. It might be hypothesized that the visual transformations, which Gibson proposed as adequate to specify observer and object motion, are also adequate information for adaptation to prism-induced distortion. Movements of the observer, according to this perceptual explanation, allow the visual transformations necessary to specify the true nature of objectively straight edges, rather than providing information for the adjustment of mediating mechanisms.

Allowing an observer to make exploratory movements in a prism adaptation experiment unfortunately confounds perceptual and perceptual-motor explanations of any adaptation effect. It is possible, however, to maintain a single observation point and use the transformations of the optic array as information about an object in motion. The observer becomes passive in order to optimize the pickup of object motion, a common strategy of predatory animals.

As a research strategy for the study of adaptation to distortion, use of a passive observer is particularly appropriate. As both J. J. Gibson (1933) and Festinger et al. (1967) pointed out, when prisms are mounted in spectacle frames, eye movements provide no information about the distorting effect of the prisms. Eye movements made in scanning the straight edge of an object must travel a curved path to move in correspondence with the curved image in the optic array behind the prism. Therefore, eye movements can provide no information about the distorting effect of the prism.

A recent experiment from the author's laboratory (Rea, 1974) was designed to determine whether adaptation to curvature is possible without movements related to the objects used during adaptation or during the test for adaptation. Head movements were constrained by having the observer look through artificial pupils with his head supported by a chin rest. In the frame behind each artificial pupil a 45-degree prism was mounted with the base to the left. The adapting experience consisted of viewing a skeleton cube constructed of white rods that either rotated at one revolution per minute (dynamic condition) or remained fixed in one position (static condition). Due to differential bending of light by the prisms, the centers of the vertical rods of the cube appeared bowed to the left.

The test for adaptation was similar to those used by J. J. Gibson (1933) and Festinger et al. (1967). After viewing the cube

494

for three minutes, and while still looking through the prisms, the observer verbally directed the experimenter to adjust a vertical rod until it appeared to be straight. The experimenter made the adjustments so that the observer could receive no feedback about the objective nature of the test rod from either performatory or exploratory movements. The measure of apparent curvature was the distance in millimeters of the midpoint of the objectively curved (but apparently straight) rod from its objectively straight position. Any adaptation to curvature over successive three-minute exposures to the cube would be indicated by reduction in the deviation of the apparently straight rod from its objectively straight position.

The results of the experiment are shown in figure 5. Each point on the graph is a mean of three adjustments for each of twenty observers. While the increase from the pre-adaptation test to the test after the first adaptation period was not anticipated, the effect of the two different types of experience was clear. No adaptation occurred after viewing the static cube, whereas the test rod was adjusted to be less curved after each succeeding exposure to the rotating cube.

The experiment demonstrated that adaptation to prism-induced curvature can take place without movements that might lead to a change in "efferent readiness." An observer who is free to move his head makes available transformations in the optic array by his movements. But when the transformations are made available to a fixed perceiver viewing a dynamic object, adaptation also occurs. When conditions are appropriate, changes in visual perception can take place based only on information provided by the visual system. The criteria for a psychophysics of prior experience were met, since the test situations were identical for the static and dynamic conditions, and the *difference* in magnitude of adaptation was specific to the *difference* in the two types of preceding experience.

THE ATTAINMENT OF PERCEPTUALLY BASED CONCEPTS

A distinction can be made between perceptually based concepts and concepts that require the development of an associa-

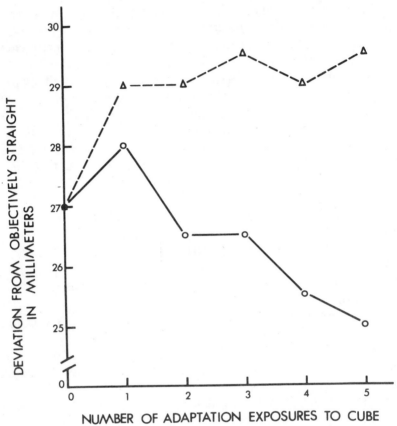

Fig. 5. Apparent curvature of the test rod expressed as deviation of the midpoint of the rod from objectively straight (zero on the ordinate scale). Zero on the abscissa represents the preadaptation test, while each unit represents the test after three additional minutes spent in observing the cube. (From M. S. Rea, "An Example of Visual Adaptation without Mediation" [M.A. thesis, Ohio State University, 1974].)

tion. The difference parallels the distinction between perceptual meaning and verbal meaning made by J. J. Gibson (1966b). Briefly, perceptual concepts require no other information than that which is available via perceiving, that is, taking note of similarities, invariants, differences, and changes in patterns, objects, or events. Associational concepts, on the other hand, are based upon arbitrary relations among things and typically require feedback or reinforcement for their attainment. According to this distinction, then, "E" and "e" are members of the

496

same class by virtue of association with each other and with the same acoustical sound, whereas "C" and "c" can be classified on the basis of common shape characteristics. To be classified separately, as must be done for upper- and lower-case distinctions, the size difference (also available perceptually) must be noted. The following series of studies illustrate the attainment of concepts on the basis of information specified by perception.

Jones (1970) developed a pattern reproduction task that allowed observers fifteen seconds to memorize a nine-column bar graph made up of O's. Then the observer was presented with a pattern exactly like the one memorized except that three columns were omitted. He was asked to draw in the missing columns to the same height as in the original pattern. One group of observers received twenty copies of the same (prototype) pattern with selection of the three omitted columns determined randomly for each trial. Another group received twenty variants of the prototype pattern produced by randomly adjusting each of the nine columns to heights of from +2 to –2 units from those of the prototype pattern.

To test for transfer of differential ability to abstract the "schema" underlying the variants, the last twenty patterns received by both groups were *identical*. These were twenty new variants of the prototype constructed according to the same rules. "Schema" learning could simplify the memorizing component of the task by allowing the observer to determine which columns conformed to the prototype, so that he could devote his attention to the columns that deviated from the "schema." These latter columns made each variant distinctive.

The group that memorized only variants showed no improvement over the forty patterns, reproducing on the average only one column correctly. The group that memorized the prototype was reproducing on the average about 2.75 columns correctly by the twentieth pattern. For the last twenty patterns (the same twenty variants received by the control group), the group trained with the prototype reproduced 1.5 columns correctly on the average, significantly better performance than the one column achieved by the group trained with variants.

The results suggested that the group trained with the prototype

497

had a "schema" available to aid them in performing the task. Members of the group receiving only variants were not able to abstract the "schema" and were therefore forced to deal with each pattern individually. The difference in performance of the two groups on the last twenty problems was specific to the difference in the nature of the patterns they had encountered during the first twenty problems.

It might be argued that the improvement in performance by the group trained with the prototype had nothing to do with memorizing the columns to be reproduced. Instead it might be proposed that the subject is guessing the height that a column had in the prototype pattern, which will be correct one-fifth of the time for an omitted column of a variant. By application of a variation of the same paradigm, Jones and Holley (1970) demonstrated that memorization of "deviations-from-schema" can in fact take place. Twelve-column patterns were constructed such that the first four column heights were determined randomly for each pattern and were *identical* in the patterns that two groups of subjects received. The possible column heights ranged from one to fifteen units so that the probability of guessing a column height correctly was 1/15. The sequence of the last eight column heights was always the same for one group, but varied for the other. Again, observers were allowed fifteen seconds to commit a pattern to memory and asked to reproduce the omitted columns, in this case a total of six, two randomly selected from among the first four columns and four from among the last eight.

Scoring was restricted to the two columns omitted from the first four columns in common for the two groups of observers. The group receiving patterns with the variable last eight columns averaged about 40 percent correct over the first twenty-five patterns, with a slight improvement over the last five patterns. In contrast, performance of the group receiving the constant sequence for the last eight columns improved monotonically from 50 percent to nearly 100 percent over the thirty patterns. The patterns were constructed to eliminate the possibility that a "schema" could be used for better-than-chance guessing of columns from the first four, since only the last eight columns remained unchanged. Therefore, superior performance must

498

have been due to use of a "schema" to simplify the memory requirements of the task, allowing attention to be devoted to the four columns that varied from pattern to pattern. This strategy was not possible for the group with the variable last eight columns, so that attention was divided among the entire twelve columns of each new and different pattern, with the resulting poorer performance on the first four columns.

In both of the above experiments (Jones, 1970; Jones and Holley, 1970), the paradigmatic criteria for the psychophysics of prior experience were met. In these examples whole patterns or parts of patterns remained invariant over a series of problems. Attending to, learning about, and memory for the invariants was possible and useful for correct performance on subsequent problems. There is no need, however, to invoke the notion that "schemata" are stored in memory in order to mediate later perceiving. Rather, by borrowing from the psychophysical approach to schema theory outlined by Evans (1967), schema and deviations from schema can be considered measurable characteristics of populations of patterns. The invariants and variations are made available to the observer, and his performance indicates whether he can attend to, learn about, and remember them. Evans labeled the development of these abilities "schematic concept formation" that leads to concepts that are defined by objects and events in the environment and are by no means arbitrary. As distinguished from arbitrarily associated "didactic concepts," schematic concepts are based only upon information derived from perceiving objects and events, without feedback concerning whether or not a response is correct (see Edmonds et al., 1966).

E. J. Gibson (1969) takes a similar position with her differentiation theory of perceptual learning. The need to reduce uncertainty by obtaining information from the environment is considered a strong motive in its own right. The discovery of invariant properties and distinctive features that are in correspondence with physical variables of objects and events is both the goal and the affirmation of perceptual learning. Support for the theory is exemplified by the classic transfer experiments conducted by Pick (1965). The experiments were designed to contrast distinctive feature theory with the hypothesis that "schema" are constructed through repeated experience and stored in memory for later comparison with sensory data. Kindergarten children were trained to discriminate "standard" patterns from specified transformations of them (see figure 6). The transformations involved one or two changes from straight to curved line, reversal, and rotation, as well as size and perspective changes.

TRANSFORMATIONS

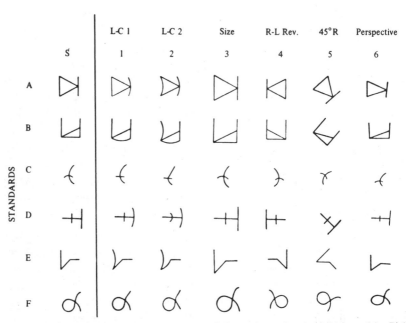

Fig. 6. The six standard patterns and six transformations of each of them used by Pick (1965). (From E. J. Gibson, *Principles of Perceptual Learning and Development* [New York: Appleton-Century-Crofts, 1969], p. 97. Copyright © 1969 by Meredith Corporation; reprinted with permission.)

By using different combinations of standards and transformations during training and a test for transfer of training, three conditions were developed to assess perceptual learning. Children in the control condition received three standards and three transformations all of which were different from those used in training. The control group, therefore, had no opportunity to apply what they had learned about particular patterns or about particular differences between patterns, and their performance was used as

500

a base line with which to compare the transfer performance of the other two groups. One of the experimental groups received the same standards during the test for transfer as they had received during training, but had to distinguish them from three new transformations of these standards. These children had the opportunity to learn about characteristics of the standard that could aid them during the test trials, but could not learn to detect the differences between the test transformations and the standards. The third condition was designed to reflect the extent to which distinctive feature learning had occurred during training. Children in this group received three new standards, but the same three types of transformations as during training. If these children could discover how the transformations differed from the standards during training, they had the opportunity to apply this skill in solving the problems used in the test for transfer of distinctive feature learning.

Three experiments were conducted with kindergarten and first-grade children. In the first experiment a child was presented with a set of fifteen cards containing two copies of each standard and three transformations of each standard and instructed to give to the experimenter any card with a pattern exactly the same as one of the three standards displayed on a stand before him. On the transfer test problems, the control group made a total of 101 errors, whereas the "schema" learning group made 69 and the "distinctive feature" group made only 39 errors.

To test the generality of the results, a second experiment was designed to test for improvement in tactual discrimination. The patterns were of raised lines on a smooth metal background. A blindfolded child was instructed to feel two forms, a standard and one of its transformations, with his dominant hand and to report whether the two forms were the same or different. On this task the control group made 48 total errors on the transfer test, whereas the "schema" group made 24 and the "distinctive feature" group made 25.

Under the assumption that "schema" learning was as useful as "distinctive feature" learning because the standard had to be remembered while the transformed pattern was being tactually explored, a third experiment allowed simultaneous comparison of the two patterns, one explored with each hand. In this test situation the control group made 32 errors, the "schema" group 31 errors, and the "distinctive feature" group only 9 errors.

Caldwell and Hall (1970) argued that due to the way Pick chose her combinations of standards and transformations for training and test of transfer, the children in the two experimental conditions were given different information regarding the experimenter's concepts of "same" and "different." For example, a child in the "schema" group, trained to reject line-to-curve and size transformations, had no way to know that the rotation transformations encountered during the transfer test were not acceptable as "same" to the experimenter. Children in the "distinctive feature" condition, on the other hand, could learn what transformations were not acceptable during training and apply the same concept to the test problems. In replicating Pick's first experiment with appropriate counterbalancing plus training to allow equal opportunity to learn the concepts, Caldwell and Hall found no difference in transfer between the two types of learning.

The Pick transfer paradigm produced a different result, however, when used by Aiken (1969) in an auditory discrimination task. Aiken's procedure closely paralleled the second experiment by Pick with successive tactual discrimination. He used standards of four easily discriminable frequencies, with three kinds of transformations of each: amplitude, duration, and direction (from the apparent left or right). The listener reported whether the standard and comparison (either the standard repeated or one of the transformations) sounds were "same" or "different" when separated by an interval of 1.5 seconds. His control group made 124 errors, the group receiving the same standards but new transformations made 73 errors, and the group receiving the same transformations of new standards made 95 errors.

Viewed in terms of Pick's original goal of distinguishing operationally between schema theory and what has become E. J. Gibson's (1969) differentiation theory, the series of studies reviewed above present a confusing picture. Perhaps, however, asking a slightly different and less theoretically loaded question will allow seemingly disparate results to be integrated within a common framework. There are at least three general kinds of

502

differences in patterns to which a perceiver can learn to attend. One of these is the class of differences between figure and ground that Attneave (see Olson and Attneave, 1970) has labeled *morphophoric* (patterning-bearing) variation. Although obviously an important and interesting area—learning to detect the protective coloration and patterning of an animal, for example— apparently no study of the problem using a transfer paradigm has been conducted. A second class following Attneave's lead, might be called *morphological* differences. Each pattern, object, or event has characteristics that make it unique; and if specified perceptually, a pattern can be matched or recognized on the basis of these properties. J. J. Gibson (1963) has called these invariant variables, because they are invariant under transformations for a particular object or event, but vary from one object to another. Discriminations and classifications are often, if not usually, made on the basis of morphological variables. A third category of physical differences is that which provides information about a change or transformation and might therefore be called *metamorphic*. These are differences which indicate that an object has been bent or rotated, a tune has been transposed, a face looks older or happier, and so forth.

This taxonomy is not just a scheme for classifying physical variables. It is, rather, a functional taxonomy taking into account the reciprocal roles of the environment and the organism. Differences are categorized according to their usefulness for a perceiver with the ability to detect them. It follows, then, that a given physical difference may fall in more than one category depending on the purpose it serves, that is, what the difference in the environment provides information about.

Several selected examples should suffice to illustrate the principle. The letters V and I can be distinguished morphologically by the difference in orientation of the line elements, allowing an observer to respond "different" to the pair in a discrimination task. Figure 7 shows that the difference between V and I can also serve a morphophoric function in distinguishing the letter M from the background. The red color of an apple can serve two functions simultaneously, to morphophorically isolate the apple from surrounding foliage and to convey metamorphic information about the ripening process. While the distinction between the patterns M and W would normally serve a metamorphic purpose indicating a 180-degree rotation of the same pattern, in the Roman alphabet they are morphologically distinct and must be identified differently. It was for the latter purpose that Pick used the various transformations of a standard pattern. She found that size and perspective transformations proved impossible for many children to distinguish from the standard long after other transformations had been distinguished. The difficulty undoubtedly arises because the invariants left unchanged by the transformations typically are information for shape constancy, whereas the transformations usually give information for the location of the pattern relative to the observer or indicate what has happened to the pattern (bending, for example). There must be a kind of unlearning and relearning taking place when children are required to consider two perspectives of a pattern as different. What Pick considered to be learning of "schema" can in the same functional framework be considered the learning about invariants for the purpose they usually serve, the distinguishing of the standards. Learning to recognize the standards aids the "schema" group in the test for transfer, but not the "distinctive feature" group who must learn to recognize a new set of standards.

To return from the digression, the conditions of the transfer studies need not be opposed as supporting one theory or another, but rather, can be considered as evidence that the individual solving the problems used one or the other or both of the kinds of information available in the only way(s) he was allowed. The demands on the individual vary widely from condition to condition and experiment to experiment, and it is reasonable to expect that sometimes one kind of information will be more useful, sometimes the other, and sometimes both will be equally useful. The value of the studies is in demonstrating the utility of a paradigm that will allow determination of the conditions under which each kind of information is useful. In this fashion a psychophysics of prior experience can be developed appropriate to the learning of perceptually based concepts.

Fig. 7. Use of the differences between the letters V and I to morphophorically specify the letter M.

PRIOR EXPERIENCE WITH DIRECTION OF LIGHTING

The study that follows serves as a transition between examples of successful use of the psychophysical paradigm and experiments for which nonperceptual explanations are plausible. In the experiment described, the criteria for the general paradigm were met, but the variables manipulated were not appropriate to the perceptual phenomenon for which the hypothesis was supposed to account.

505

The human perceptual phenomenon is illustrated by figure 8, which shows two copies of a photograph of a dented steel tank, one an inversion of the other. In the one case the tank appears to have dents in it, whereas the inverted copy appears to be a tank with bumps on it. Given a long history with sources of illumination from above, the distribution of light and shade on and around an object provides useful information for the perception of relative depth. Inversion of the light and shade distribution, then, results in an apparent reversal of depth when the photographs are turned upside down. Cast in terms of the nativist-empiricist controversy, is it the prior history of the species that is important? (Those individuals with perceptual systems sensitive at birth to depth information congruent with solar illumination of the terrestrial environment would be more likely to survive.) Or is the prior history of the individual important in learning to make use of the information?

Hess (1950) conducted what he purported to be a study of the illusion phenomenon to determine whether sensitivity to the depth information is innate or must be learned. Chicks were used in the experiment since it was known that the chick uses shading in making spatial discriminations and since the direction of lighting could be easily controlled from the time of hatching. A preliminary experiment demonstrated that chicks reared under natural lighting conditions would peck more often at a photograph of grain illuminated from above than at an inverted copy of the same photograph. The two copies of the photograph used to test the effects of prior experience are shown in figure 9.

When tested with the photographs shown in figure 9, chicks reared for seven weeks in cages illuminated from *above* pecked predominantly at the photograph on the left. Chicks reared with illumination from *beneath* the screen bottom of their cage (with the top and all sides covered with opaque cloth) and fed grain in clear glass dishes, pecked most often at the photograph on the right. A second experiment was conducted under the same conditions with some chicks tested immediately after hatching and some tested weekly up to seven weeks. The chicks tested soon after hatching pecked at one copy of the photograph equally often as at the other, but progressively pecked at the copy

506

Fig. 8. Examples of objects with attached shadows that can result in depth reversals when inverted. For (a) the dents in the tank look like bulges and the rivet heads look like dents. (From D. D. Wickens and D. R. Meyer, *Psychology*, rev. ed. [New York: Holt, Rinehart & Winston, 1961]. Copyright © 1961 by Holt, Rinehart & Winston; reprinted with permission.) For (b) the volcanic crater looks like a mesa. (From J. O. Whittaker, *Introduction to Psychology* [Philadelphia: Saunders, 1966]. Copyright © 1966 by W. B. Saunders; reprinted with permission.)

Fig. 9. Photographs used to test pecking responses of chicks after experiencing lighting from above or below. (From E. H. Hess, "Development of the Chick's Responses to Light and Shade Cues of Depth," *Journal of Comparative and Physiological Psychology* 43 [1950]: 112–22. Copyright © 1950 by the American Psychological Association; reprinted with permission.)

appropriate to their rearing illumination as they became older. Hess concluded that the direction of lighting in the first weeks of life determines the nature of a chick's responses to light and shade information for depth.

The problem arises in relating the conclusion to the human illusion and Hess's original hypothesis. Can it be inferred from their pecking behaviors that the chicks experienced an illusion so that grain illuminated from the direction opposite to that experienced previously appears to the chicks as depressions in a surface? An evaluation of the information available in shadows reveals that such an interpretation is inappropriate. There are two types of shadows: (1) shadows attached to an object itself by its interruption of light from a source, and (2) shadows cast by an object upon another surface when the object is located between the source and the surface. Dents and bumps have attached shadows that can reverse if the information about them is ambiguous. Kernels of grain have, in addition, cast shadows that provide unambiguous information about objects and their relations to a surface and a source of illumination. Consequently, objects with cast shadows do not show depth reversals.

Hershberger (1970) properly distinguished the two types of shadows and corrected the flaws in the Hess study by rearing chicks in cages illuminated from below and testing them with photographs that produce the reversal illusion for humans. The chicks were trained to discriminate between concave and convex dents by being rewarded for pecking at one but not the other. Light panels placed on either side illuminated the bump and dent used during discrimination training. As shown in the top half of figure 10, the two configurations had nearly identical attached shadows, but could be discriminated on the basis of binocular and motion parallax. When a chick began averaging four or more correct choices for each incorrect choice, it was tested with two photographs, both of either objective dents (one illuminated from below, one from above, as shown in the bottom half of figure 10) or both of objective bumps (one with the attached shadow on top, the other with it on the bottom).

Chicks trained to peck at the dent preferred the photographed dent with the attached shadow on top, whereas those trained to

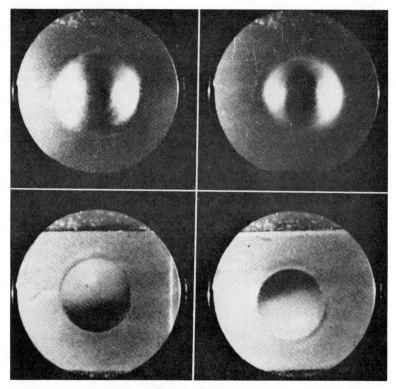

Fig. 10. Side-illuminated pictures of a bump and a dent used in discrimination training of chicks (top pair) and of a dent illuminated from below and above used to test for the reversal illusion (bottom pair). (From W. Hershberger, "Attached Shadow Orientation Perceived as Depth by Chickens Reared in an Environment Illuminated from Below," *Journal of Comparative and Physiological Psychology* 73 [1970]: 407–11. Copyright © 1970 by the American Psychological Association; reprinted with permission.)

peck at the bump chose the photographed bump with the attached shadow on the bottom. In other words, every chick responded as though there were an overhead source of illumination in the test cubicle, even though there never was. Hershberger concluded that "the perceptual parameter corresponding to 'overhead source of illumination' by which orientation of attached shadow is interpreted as depth is innate" (p. 410).

Since Hess made a reasonable application of the psychophysical paradigm, some other explanation than depth reversal must be appropriate. The difference in the chick's responses to

510

the two photographs was specific to the difference in direction of illumination experienced. A plausible candidate might be a superordinate configuration of kernel-plus-cast shadow, which differs in orientation for the two directions of lighting. In any case, additional manipulation and control of the information available during rearing and testing would be necessary to determine what was distinguished differently by the chicks with different prior experiences.

Evaluated in terms of the paradigm for a psychophysics of prior experience, the Hess and the Hershberger experiments demonstrate that choices of patterns, objects, or events for the prior experience and test conditions as well as the relation between the two conditions are extremely critical for interpretation of the data.

PERCEPTUAL VERSUS NONPERCEPTUAL EXPLANATIONS

All of the experiments described so far were selected to show the value of physical controls in ascribing an effect to the functioning of a perceptual system. Meeting the criteria of the prior-experience paradigm can lead to perceptual explanations of phenomena, however, only if perceptual effects are not confounded with effects due to the demands and constraints of the task that the perceiver must perform. The following experiment will illustrate the problem.

Helson (1959) proposed that the influence of past history on current perceiving can be understood by taking advantage of the fact that controlled stimulation at one time functions as "past experience" at a later time. In support of the notion, he cited an experiment by Nash (1950) in which two groups of raters categorized lifted weights on a nine-step scale ranging from very, very light through medium to very, very heavy. One group began with a set of five heavy weights and, after five judgments of each weight in random order, the heaviest was deleted and replaced by a weight fifty grams less than the lightest of the original five. The deletion procedure was continued until the final set of weights no longer overlapped with the

511

original set. A second group began with the lightest set, and the procedure was reversed by discarding the lightest weight and adding a heavier weight, ending with the heaviest set of five weights. The adaptation level, theoretically the equilibrium or neutral point against which the weights in a set were judged (effectively, the magnitude of weight to which the response "medium" would have been given), was estimated for each set and is shown in table 1. The influence of prior experience on adaptation level for the *same* set of weights embedded in either a descending or an ascending series is apparent. Experiencing

TABLE 1

EFFECTS OF PRECEDING STIMULATION UPON
JUDGMENTS OF WEIGHTS

Weights in Grams	Adaptation Level for Descending Series	Adaptation Level for Ascending Series
400-600	418	361
350-550	384	332
300-500	356	301
250-450	315	257
200-400	269	227
150-350	232	202
100-300	186	165

SOURCE: Data from Nash (1950) abstracted from table 2 of Helson (1959).

heavier sets of weights resulted in judging weights from succeeding sets as ligher relative to the high adaptation level that had developed. The opposite held for previous experience with lighter sets in that succeeding weights were judged heavier relative to a lower adaptation level. The net effect is that a given weight will be judged lighter following experience with heavy weights and heavier following experience with light weights than it would without a bias in prior experience.

Whereas Helson was willing to equate differences in judgments with differences in perception, there is no way to determine whether the change had simply been in the use of the scale. The rater was given a fixed scale of nine categories, and he may have been sliding the response scale to progressively encompass the new range of weights experienced in each succeeding set. Therefore, the neutral point on the scale will correspond to a higher physical value of weight for any set in the descending series than for the ascending series, and vice versa. It is possible that in this case the effect of prior experience may be an artifact of the categorical judgment task.

The reasonableness of a nonperceptual alternative explanation of the effect does not, however, preclude the possibility that the same weight did *feel* lighter after heavier weights had been experienced (that is, relative to a higher adaptation level in the descending series) or did not *feel* heavier in the ascending series (relative to a lower adaptation level). The logic of maintaining physical control over prior experience remains appropriate if an experimental effect is to be described as an adjustment of a perceptual system sensitive to relative magnitude. But implementation of that logic alone is not sufficient to isolate a phenomenon as perceptual. In addition, the task must be such that perceptual effects are not confounded with effects attributable to nonperceptual systems (decision, association, or response selection systems, for example).[4]

The problems of interpretation are compounded when psychophysical criteria are not met, and the psychological literature is replete with attempts to demonstrate the influence of prior experience without adequate physical control of patterns, objects, or events. As a consequence, alternative, nonperceptual explanations are possible and often compelling. A single example should suffice to illustrate the problem and to show, by contrast, the advantage of psychophysical criteria.

In an experiment designed to study perceptual set, Bruner and Minturn (1955) controlled the preceding experience of observers by requiring them to draw and verbally identify a series of block Roman capital letters *or* a series of two-digit Arabic numerals. As a test for the effect of set induced by having previously identified either letters or numbers, the observers were presented briefly with the pattern shown in figure 11. Relative to a control condition in which the preceding series consisted of letters mixed with numbers, having identified only letters resulted more frequently in reports of "B," whereas having identified only numbers resulted more frequently in reports of "13." Bruner and Minturn interpreted the results in terms of Gestalt organizational principles: they proposed that a centrally mediated categorizing process resulted in an observer's "noticing" the gaps between the two parts of the test figure when set to expect a number and "not noticing" the gaps when set to expect a letter. It was also suggested that the test figure was *seen* as categorized and as subsequently reported and drawn. In a later account, Bruner (1957) interpreted the result in terms of accessibility of the elements of the "memory trace system" to

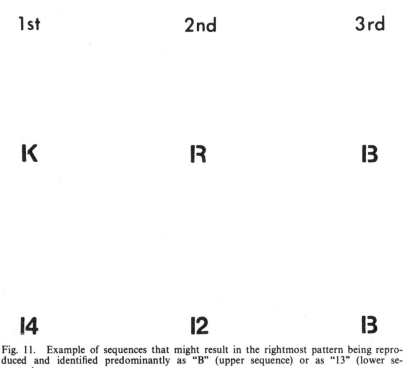

Fig. 11. Example of sequences that might result in the rightmost pattern being reproduced and identified predominantly as "B" (upper sequence) or as "13" (lower sequence).

stimulus input. Perceptual set is accounted for by assuming that when a "stimulus process" is equally similar to two memory traces, it will "make contact with" the trace having the higher probability of being matched by environmental events.

The problem with invoking the operation of organizational processes during perceiving is that an equally plausible nonperceptual explanation is possible. The pattern may have *looked* like neither of the figures reported, and, instead, the observer might have been set to select identification or reproduction *responses* from either a capital letter category or a two-digit number category. The point, then, is not to claim that the Bruner and Minturn explanation of their result was incorrect, but rather that there is no way to ascertain whether the perceptual system or some other system was affected by the preceding experiences. The outcome of their experiment is as ambiguous for the perceptual theorist as the information provided by the test pattern was for their observers.

The Bruner and Minturn example is made even more instructive in light of a clever visual search experiment. Jonides and Gleitman (1972) hypothesized that visual recognition can depend upon how a pattern is conceptually categorized (according to an association) rather than upon its physical characteristics. They proposed that for an effect to be credibly attributed to a conceptual process, all physical variables must be held constant. To this end, the same target pattern, the symbol 0, was presented under two different conceptual sets. To insure the appropriate set, all other target symbols were unambiguous members of either an uppercase letter category or a single-digit Arabic number category.

The observers were presented with a display of two, four, or six symbols. One group of observers was informed that they would receive displays of only letters, a second group was told that they would be presented only with displays of numbers. Before each trial the observer was told the *name* of the target symbol for which he was to search the display (for example, "A," "two," "zero"). For half the observers, the target symbols were the three uppercase letters A, Z, and O (specified as the vowel "ō"); for the other half, the target symbols were the three digits 2, 4, and 0 (physically identical to the O employed in the letter set, but now specified as "zero"). The display was flashed for 150 milliseconds, and half the observers in each group pressed a response key when the test symbol was present, the other half when it was absent. The time from presentation of the display to initiation of the key press was recorded to be interpreted as time taken to process the information necessary to solve each problem.

The results of the experiment are shown in figure 12 separately

515

for the conceptually unambiguous target symbols and the conceptually ambiguous target symbol (O). The important point is

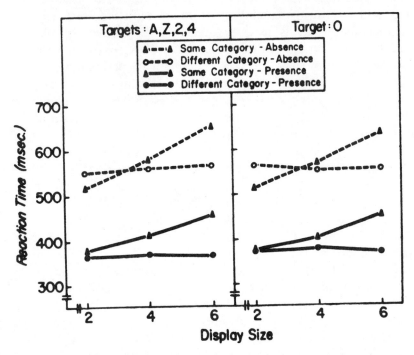

Fig. 12. Mean reaction time in milliseconds as a function of number of symbols displayed for unambiguous and ambiguous symbols when the symbol searched for and the symbol displayed are of the same and of different categories. (From J. Jonides and H. Gleitman, "A Conceptual Category Effect in Visual Search: O as Letter or as Digit," *Perception & Psychophysics* 12 [1972]: 457-60. Copyright © 1974 by the Psychonomic Society, Inc.; reprinted with permission.)

to note that the results are the same for both conditions. It did not matter that the symbol searched for could be either the letter "ō" *or* the digit "zero"; the observer treated it conceptually as it had been named by the experimenter. Consequently, Jonides and Gleitman concluded that the conceptual category effect implies a flexible processing repertory because the choice of processing strategy depended upon the situational context.

Again, the distinction between perceptual and verbal meaning is appropriate. According to J. J. Gibson (1966b) perceptual meaning is related to the environment by physical law, whereas verbal meaning is related to its referent by social convention.

Accordingly, two explanations of the Jonides and Gleitman results are possible. The observer may have used one of two strategies based upon perceptual learning. He may have been set (1) to test for the ways in which the constant pattern differs from the possible letters, or (2) to test for the ways it differs from the possible numbers.[5] On the other hand, he may have been set to conceptually categorize the pattern and code it either (1) by letter associate or (2) by number associate. If told to check for "zero" and letters appeared, he may have made a decision that it could not be in that category without searching the entire display (since his reaction time was as fast for six- and four-symbol displays as for two). If told to check for "zero" and digits were displayed, he may have changed his strategy (as indicated by the increase in reaction time with an increasing number of symbols displayed), perhaps making an item-by-item search of the display.

The perceptual and associational interpretations differ markedly, but in neither the Bruner and Minturn nor the Jonides and Gleitman experiments were there operations appropriate to distinguish them. It should therefore be instructive to contrast these two studies with the application of physical controls in all the experiments on perceptual concept attainment described earlier. In both uses of the prior-experience paradigm, there was manipulation of the set of patterns previously experienced, while the patterns used in the test situation were held constant for all conditions. The critical difference is in the nature of the control over the earlier experience, either physically specified in order to infer the isolation of a perceptual system effect or specified by association to assess the effect on a coding system.

It might be argued that perceptual concepts and associational concepts are merely two ways in which the perceiver can represent the variables of stimulation. This is the case made by Lawrence (1963) in assuming that the correlation between the response and stimulation is never direct but rather always mediated by an intervening event. The mediating event for Lawrence is a coding operation, and the code item that results then represents the stimulation. It is this "stimulus-as-coded" that is directly associated with, and elicits, the overt behavior being measured.

J. J. Gibson (1972), on the other hand, believes that environment perception is direct and not any kind of coding, whereas pictorially or verbally mediated perception is not direct. For a theory of direct perception, psychophysical criteria are essential. Therein lies the theoretical rub and sets the stage for some concluding remarks.

CONCLUSION

The purpose of the preceding sections was to clarify how credible evidence can be obtained from experiments in which prior experience is controlled in order to demonstrate its influence on subsequent perceiving. As should by now be apparent, the empirical findings generated by application of the paradigm do not fall into place in an all-encompassing, unified theory of perception. The objects, events, variables, and invariants chosen by a researcher, as well as the interpretation made of the results, will likely be repugnant to those working from other theories. This is reasonable if differences among theories ultimately reflect the nature of the objects, events, variables, and invariants that are acceptable to the different theorists thus leading them to different conclusions, rather than in the so-called facts that are "discovered" by application of the experimental method. The question is not which theory is correct about the contribution of the organism, but rather which changes in the environment are relevant to perception.

The approach recommended requires no paradigm shift like that described by Kuhn (1970). Rather, it is argued that an acceptable paradigm is already available and that exploitation of it can contribute considerably to a better understanding of perception. Although the argument is largely methodological, it is by no means atheoretical. Use of a psychophysical paradigm for assessing the influence of prior experience on perceiving by definition entails a psychophysical criterion for the study of perception, and that in itself is a theoretical statement. The suggested logic of experimental design and interpretation harks back to Watson's (1913) behavioristic criticism that the attention given by psychologists to conscious processes was not fruitful for an understanding of how and why an individual functions. There need be no concern for central processes, he argued, because "the individual is always examining objects . . . " (p. 174). His concern was for determining how a physically specified property of the environment was a factor in the individual's adjustment. Therefore, he wanted to know which properties are effective and which differences in properties must be maintained in order to afford bases for differential responses (see p. 171, Watson, 1913).

Due to the pervasive interest of early American psychology in the development of habits and associations, the study of perception was relegated to the problem of discrimination learning. The historical trend, well under way with Hull's (1943) work, has resulted in a proliferation of hypothetical mechanisms to mediate between "sensory input" and overt response. The functional problem of how sensitivity to environmental change allows adjustment to that change via appropriate response variability received much less attention. The variety of experimental topics described above, however, demonstrates that a great breadth of application is possible.

If psychophysical criteria are applied to assess the influence of prior experience, then distinctions like the following (from an argument against confounding effects of "meaningfulness" with effects of "suggestion") have no utility: "To assert that experiential factors operate, necessitates evidencing their spontaneous intervention in perceptual processes. No basis would otherwise be provided for drawing a line between effects of past experience and experimentally induced set" (Toch and Ittelson, 1956, pp. 203–4).

By applying a psychophysical criterion, perceptual set becomes possible *because of* an earlier experience. Perceptual set is that kind of readiness which is specific to, and defined by, a particular experimentally controlled prior experience. Rather than *intervening* in perceptual processes, previous experience has its impact by allowing the perceiver to discover new ways to make information available or to pick up information already available but not previously attended to. After such perceptual

519

learning has taken place, the subsequent pickup of certain information can be favored because the system can be readied for one of at least two possible sources of information. *What* an observer is set to perceive must be specific to a former perceptual experience.

To be complete, a theory of perception must account for an organism sensitive not only to the variables and invariants of objects and events but also to the variables and invariants that specify how the objects and events have and have not changed. Although this assertion may have the constructionist ring of producing percepts by adding information from the past to that currently being picked up, no such meaning is intended. Instead, following J. J. Gibson's (1966b) proposal, the influence of prior experience is a change in the sensitivity of the perceiver. When an observer becomes sensitive to new variables of change and to new invariants in spite of change, he can perceive something that he did not before.

The strategy of research and theory in perception should not, then, be a search for mechanisms. Rather, the study of perception must be conceived as an attempt to answer the question: What in the environment has to be varied over time to allow the perceiver to report seeing, or otherwise respond to, an object or an event in a certain way? The answers will aid in understanding the perception *of* motion, *of* looming, *of* speech sounds, *of* oldness and newness; discrimination *of* green fruit from ripe; adaptation *to* decreased illumination, *to* prismatically induced distortion, *to* a regional speech accent; readiness *for* a specific face, or attention *to* the tannin content of a wine. It follows that the functions served by perceiving need no longer be labeled as activities inferred to take place inside the perceiver. The constructing, judging, and coding processes can be discarded and replaced by the empirically assessed reciprocities of the perceiver and the perceived.

I would like to thank James J. Gibson and Alan B. McConkie for their discussions and comments on this paper. I have also appreciated and benefitted from the opportunity to share an interest in perception with Peter K. Machamer and George S. Pappas of the Ohio State University Philosophy Department.

1. It has been much more popular to assume past experience with one of two objects, or patterns that represent the objects. A pattern is then constructed so that it conveys either conflicting or approximately equal information about both patterns previously experienced. Reports are elicited to assess whether past experience influences interpretation of the pattern to yield one of the two "equipotential percepts" more often than the other.

2. Since the kittens in the Blakemore studies were free to move their eyes, head, and bodies, their pretest experience was with either vertical or horizontal lines in the environment, rather than on the retina. Unfortunately, environmental and retinal orientation were perfectly correlated during the physiological tests, so it could not be determined to which orientation the effect was specific. To test for the distinction, Horn and Hill (1969) found a cell in an adult cat's cortex sensitive to vertical line orientation, and then tilted the cat 45 degrees so that the line was at a 45-degree orientation on the retina. The cell continued to respond maximally to a vertical line in the environment, indicating that the system detecting line-at-an-orientation was adjusted by the gravity-sensitive vestibular system to maintain information specific to the environment rather than the retina. If the link between vestibular and visual systems is functional at birth, then Blakemore's kittens may have had cortical cells sensitive to all orientations on the retina, but only vertical or horizontal lines in the environment. The implication for a direct theory of perception should be clear.

3. Data proffered to demonstrate categorical perception should be interpreted with caution. Kopp and Livermore (1973) had observers learn to identify one tone by pressing a left-hand button and a second tone by pressing a right-hand button. Ability to discriminate was tested by presenting pairs of tones selected from the frequency continuum and asking for judgments of "same" or "different." "Different" judgements were correct more frequently near the boundary between the identification categories, but errors of reporting "different" when the two tones were the same increased as well. Signal detectability analysis indicated that discriminability was constant along the continuum, whereas observers reported "same" more often at the extremes and "different" more often near the boundary. It is possible that a similar nonperceptual bias may be operating in experiments with synthetic speech sounds. At present it is difficult to determine whether speech adaptation effects have the same explanation as adaptation to visual rearrangement or belong in the class discussed later as having nonperceptual explanations. Are the sounds discriminated as *heard* or as *identified*, or possibly both if, as Bruner (1957) and others have proposed, phenomenal experience follows categorization? The answer may depend on the development of more objective perceptual reports as occurred with adaptation to curvature.

4. Note that the binary reports appropriate for the three-bowl adaptation experiment discussed earlier are less susceptible of nonperceptual explanations, for example, "same" or "different," "warm" or "cool," or perhaps most suitable, "warmer-than-before" or "cooler-than-before."

5. The perceptual interpretation was suggested by Alan B. McConkie.

REFERENCES CITED

Aiken, E. G. Auditory discrimination learning: Prototype storage and distinctive features detection mechanisms. *Perception & Psychophysics* 6 (1969): 95–96.

Allport, G. W., and T. F. Pettigrew. Cultural influence on the perception of movement: The trapezoidal illusion among Zulus. *Journal of Abnormal and Social Psychology* 55 (1957): 104–13.

Annis, R. C., and B. Frost. Human visual ecology and orientation anisotropies in acuity. *Science* 182 (1973): 729–31.

Bartlett, F. C. *Remembering.* Cambridge: At the University Press, 1932.

Blakemore, C., and G. F. Cooper. Development of the brain depends on the visual environment. *Nature* 228 (1970): 477–78.

Blakemore, C., and D. E. Mitchell. Environmental modification of the visual cortex and the neural basis of learning and memory. *Nature* 241 (1973): 467–68.

Bruner, J. S. On perceptual readiness. *Psychological Review* 64 (1957): 123–52.

Bruner, J. S., and A. L. Minturn. Perceptual identification and perceptual organization. *Journal of General Psychology* 53 (1955): 21–28.

Brunswik, E. *Perception and the representative design of psychological experiments.* Berkeley: University of California Press, 1956.

Caldwell, E. C., and V. C. Hall. Distinctive-features versus prototype learning reexamined. *Journal of Experimental Psychology* 83 (1970): 7–12.

Duncker, K. The influence of past experience upon perceptual properties. *American Journal of Psychology* 52 (1939): 255–65.

Edmonds, E. M., M. R. Mueller, and S. H. Evans. Effects of knowledge of results on mixed schema discrimination. *Psychonomic Science* 6 (1966): 377–78.

Eimas, P. D., and J. D. Corbit. Selective adaptation of linguistic feature detectors. *Cognitive Psychology* 4 (1973): 99–109.

Evans, S. H. A brief statement of schema theory. *Psychonomic Science* 8 (1967): 87–88.

Festinger, L., C. A. Burnham, H. Ono, and D. Bamber. Efference and the conscious experience of perception. *Journal of Experimental Psychology Monographs* 74 (1967) (4. Whole No. 637).

Friedman, S. Habituation and recovery of visual response in the alert human newborn. *Journal of Experimental Child Psychology* 13 (1972): 339–49.

Geldard, F. A. *The human senses.* 2d ed. New York: Wiley, 1972.

Gibson, E. J. Principles of perceptual learning and development. New York: Appleton-Century-Crofts, 1969.

Gibson, J. J. Adaptation, after-effect and contrast in the perception of curved lines. *Journal of Experimental Psychology* 16 (1933): 1–31.

Gibson, J. J. *The perception of the visual world.* Boston: Houghton Mifflin, 1950.

Gibson, J. J. Perception as a function of stimulation. *In* S. Koche, ed., *Psychology: A study of a science,* vol. 1. New York: McGraw-Hill, 1959.

Gibson, J. J. The useful dimensions of sensitivity. *American Psychologist* 18 (1963): 1–15.

Gibson, J. J. The problem of temporal order in stimulation. *Journal of Psychology* 62 (1966): 141–49. (a).

Gibson, J. J. *The senses considered as perceptual systems.* Boston: Houghton Mifflin, 1966. (b).

Gibson, J. J. What gives rise to the perception of motion? *Psychological Review* 75 (1968): 335–46.

Gibson, J. J. A theory of direct visual perception. *In* J. R. Royce and W. W. Roseboom, eds. *The psychology of knowing.* New York: Gordon and Breach, 1972.

Gibson, J. J. A theory of direct perception. Colloquium at the Ohio State University, 23 May 1974.

Helson, H. Adaptation level theory. *In* S. Koch, ed. *Psychology: A study of a science.* New York: McGraw-Hill, 1959.

Helmholtz, H. *Physiological optics,* vol. 3. Ed. J. P. C. Southall. Optical Society of America, 1925.

Hershberger, W. Attached shadow orientation perceived as depth by chickens reared in an environment illuminated from below. *Journal of Comparative and Physiological Psychology* 73 (1970): 407–11.

Hess, E. H. Development of the chick's responses to light and shade cues of depth. *Journal of Comparative and Physiological Psychology* 43 (1950): 112–22.

Hochberg, J. E. Effects of the Gestalt revolution: The Cornell symposium on perception. *Psychological Review* 64 (1957): 73–84.

Horn, G., and R. M. Hill. Modifications of receptive fields of cells in the visual cortex occurring spontaneously and associated with bodily tilt. *Nature* 221 (1969): 186–88.

Hubel, D. H., and T. N. Wiesel. Receptive fields of cells in striate cortex of very young, visually inexperienced kittens. *Journal of Neurophysiology* 26 (1963): 994–1002.

Hull, C. L. *Principles in behavior.* New York: Appleton-Century-Crofts, 1943.

Ittelson, W. H. Visual space perception. New York: Springer, 1960.

Jones, E. Schema learning with low redundancy patterns. *Psychonomic Science* 21 (1970): 74–75.

Jones, E., and J. R. Holley. Schema utilization in pattern perception. *Psychonomic Science* 18 (1970): 197–98.

Jonides, J., and H. Gleitman. A conceptual category effect in visual search. *Perception & Psychophysics* 12 (1972): 457–60.

Koffka, K. Perception: An introduction to the Gestalt-theorie. *Psychological Bulletin* 19 (1922): 531–85.

Koffka, K. *Principles of Gestalt psychology.* New York: Harcourt, Brace & World, 1935.

Köhler, W. *Gestalt psychology.* New York: Liveright, 1947.

Kopp, J., and J. Livermore. Differential discriminability or response bias? A signal detection analysis of categorical perception. *Journal of Experimental Psychology* 101 (1973): 179–82.

Kuhn, T. S. *The structure of scientific revolution.* 2d ed. Chicago: University of Chicago Press, 1970.

Ladefoged, P., and D. E. Broadbent. Information conveyed by vowels. *Journal of the Acoustical Society of America* 29 (1957): 98–104.

Lawrence, D. H. The nature of a stimulus: Some relationships between learning and perception. *In* S. Koch, ed., *Psychology: A study of a science*, vol. 5. New York: McGraw-Hill, 1963.

Liberman, A. M., F. S. Cooper, D. P. Shankweiler, and M. Studdert-Kennedy, Perception of the speech code. *Psychological Review* 74 (1967): 431–61.

Locke, J. *Essay concerning human understanding.* Book 2, chap. 8, par. 21 (1690).

Luchins, A. S., and E. H. Luchins. *Wertheimer's seminars revisted: Problems in perception*, I. Psychology Department Reports, State University of New York at Albany, Albany, New York, 1972.

Michotte, A. *The perception of causality.* New York: Basic Books, 1963.

Miller, N. E., and J. Dollard. *Social learning and imitation.* New Haven, Conn.: Yale University Press, 1941.

Nash, M. C. A quantitative study of effects of past experience on adaptation-level. Ph.D. diss., Bryn Mawr College, 1950.

Neisser, U. *Cognitive psychology.* New York: Appleton-Century-Crofts, 1967.

Olson, R. K., and F. Attneave. What variables produce similarity grouping? *American Journal of Psychology* 83 (1970): 1–21.

Pick, A. D. Improvement of visual and tactual form discrimination. *Journal of Experimental Psychology* 69 (1965): 331–39.

Pratt, C. C. The role of past experience in visual perception. *Journal of Psychology* 30 (1950): 85–107.

Rea, M. S. An example of visual adaptation without mediation. M.A. thesis, Ohio State University, 1974.

Rock, I. *The nature of perceptual adaptation.* New York: Basic Books, 1966.

Segall, M. H., D. T. Campbell, M. J. Herskovits. *The influence of culture on visual perception.* Indianapolis: Bobbs-Merrill, 1966.

Slack, C. W. Critique on the interpretation of cultural differences in the perception of motion in the Ames trapezoidal window. *American Journal of Psychology* 72 (1959): 127–31.

Stratton, G. M. Vision without inversion of the retinal image. *Psychological Review* 4 (1897): 341–60, 463–81.

Stratton, G. M. The spatial harmony of touch and sight. *Mind* 8 (1899): 492–505.

Titchener, E. B. *A text-book of psychology.* New York: Macmillan, 1910.

Toch, H., and W. H. Ittelson. The role of past experience in apparent motion: A revaluation. *British Journal of Psychology* 47 (1956): 195–207.

Wallach, H., J. H. Kravitz, and J. Lindauer. A passive condition for rapid adaptation to displaced visual direction. *American Journal of Psychology* 76 (1963): 568–78.

Watson, J. B. Psychology as the behaviorist views it. *Psychological Review* 20 (1913): 158–77.

Wertheimer, M. Experimentelle Studien über das Sehen von Bewegung. *Zeitschrift für Psychologie* 61 (1912): 161–265.

Zuckerman, C. B., and R. Rock. A reappraisal of the roles of past experience and innate organizing processes in visual perception. *Psychological Bulletin* 54 (1957): 269–96.

Romane L. Clark

Chapter Nineteen

CONSIDERATIONS FOR A LOGIC FOR NAÏVE REALISM

This is an essay in direct, or naïve, realism. An earlier paper,[1] from which this abstracts, was quite directly predicated upon an interpretation of the direct realism set forth in some articles by Professor Gibson. But since that earlier interpretation evidently does not coincide with Gibson's intentions,[2] the present paper (although it, like the earlier one, has been stimulated by Gibson's provocative articles) is not a revision of that first paper. What follows is a generalization that abstracts from the Ohio State seminar discussion of, and with, Professor Gibson.

Direct, or naïve, realism is a theory of perception. The word 'theory' sounds pretentious, falsely suggesting as it does that there is here a structured body of assumptions and concepts. But it reminds us that theories of perception, like all theories, have certain obligations to fulfill. They need, of course, to explain certain common, and certain uncommon, facts of perceptual experience. But in doing so, they need to supply as well answers to questions common to all theories. We need to know what theoretical entities are invoked in explaining the facts of perceptual life; we need to know how to detect these entities and how to count their occurrences. Few theories of perception meet even these minimal theoretical requirements.

'Sense impression' and 'perception' are terms commonly invoked in the explanation of illusions, hallucinations, and the facts of perspective. They are theoretical terms. We need to know how to identify and count the alleged occurrences of each kind of entity posited by these terms. We need to know how the one kind of entity, sense impressions, is related to the other, perceptions.

I see a small, bouncy, red rubber ball in the corner. How many perceptual acts have occurred? How many sense impressions have I had, and how are these related to my perceptions? How much have I seen, and how much, seeing what I do, do I judge or infer? Theories of perception should provide at least schematic characterizations for answers to questions like these. An adequate theory of direct realism should.

There are also, of course, general problems for theories of perception that are special to them as theories of *perception*. What provides the sensuous character of perception, by contrast with colorless judgments? What determines what is seen and how perceptions, unlike judgments, are provoked by, and linked to, the surroundings on the occasions of their occurrences? How is perceiving how things are qualified like or different from perceiving things as kinds of things? How are perceiving, judging, and inferring to be distinguished on specific occasions of their occurrences? It is with the latter questions that I am mainly concerned here, although preparatory remarks concerning the earlier questions will be necessary to provide a frame for the discussion of these last.

Naïve or direct realism is a semantical, not causal, theory of perception. As a semantical account of perception, direct realism holds that the naïve view is the correct view. Perceptions are directly of things and happenings in our physical surroundings. 'Directly' here means that however complicated the causal path may be from environment to perception, what we experience are items of our physical environment and not surrogates, or images, or intermediaries of them. (What we see through eyes, glasses, telescopes, and microscopes are physical things, not optical images, though, of course, scientific lore makes it clear that we see what we do by means of images. By contrast, when I see you reflected "in" a mirror or a lake what I do see is your mirror or lake reflection and not you. Again, of course, common knowledge and scientific lore allow me thereby to locate you as well as your reflection in my scheme of things.) 'Surroundings', and 'environment' here mean the physical regions sensuously available to perception on the occasions of a perceptual occurrence. Obviously, the physical extent and location of the sensuously available physical surroundings wax and wane with occasions of perceptual occurrence; contracting from the visible stars to the brush of a cobweb on the back of one's neck.

Since on the present account we do not perceive or ex- • perience intermediate objects that represent, or from which we infer, what is in our surroundings, it follows that sense impressions, if they play a role in perception, do not do so as phenomenal objects. (Phenomenal objects may be understood as Rosenberg has characterized them.[3] They are those objects of direct, non-inferential sensory awareness every quality of which replicates something in sensation. Phenomenal objects, unlike physical things with their natures, parts, and backsides, are completely manifest in the momentary beholding.) Sense impressions, then, are not phenomenal objects. They are, rather, impressions of a sense quality. In the standard case they are impressions of something in one's surroundings. Sense impressions are mental occurrences that, diaphonous in their own occurrent properties, nonetheless are the basis of the sensuous character of perception. They are impressions, or awarenesses, of the sense qualities, the Aristotelian proper- and common-sensibles, of things. As mental occurrences, they themselves, of course, are not physical objects; and an impression of something red no more manifests the color by which one is impressed than need the word "red" itself be inscribed in the color it denotes. In one respect, in their direct relation to objects of awareness, sense impressions are quite analogous to so-called 'rigid designators' or 'logically proper names'. These designators or names, if such there be, are syntactically simple and, what is more to the point here, also semantically direct. They are direct in the literal sense that whatever the causal circumstances may be that link the name-user to the object designated, the use of the name for the agent for whom it is rigid or logically proper secures reference to the designated object in any circumstances without reference to, or knowledge of, other objects. Formally, such names have no further names as proper parts. Semantically, the truth-conditions of sentences employing such logically proper names do not require the computation of prior assignments of individuals to other singular terms to determine that of the given name. So, too, sense impressions are simple mental occurrences that are similarly direct. An impression of a proper sensible has no constituent internal complexity, and an impression is a direct awareness of that which is sensibly qualified. It requires no awareness of an intermediate object from which the impression is then gained or inferred. The fundamental fact is that sense impressions stand to the objects of which they are impressions in a manner semantically, though not causally or conventionally, like that in which the primitive, undefined descriptive constants of a formal language stand to the objects of a model on a given interpretation. It is the directness of sense impressions to their objects of awareness that provides the directness of perceptions which is required by the theory of direct realism. It is the character of sense impressions as impressions of sense qualities that provides the sensuous nature of perceptions required on all theories.

Sense impressions, then, are, on the present view, not phenomenal objects or sense data but direct impressions of the sensible qualities of things. Our perceptions of how things are link to items in our surroundings precisely because they incorporate sense impressions of what is "before us", i.e., of what is in one's sensuously available surroundings. Perceptions are not, then, judgments merely causally provoked by the occurrence of, or based upon inferences from, occurrent sense impressions. Rather perceptions, all perceptions, literally incorporate as constituents sense impressions or sequences of sense impressions. The directness of perceptions, via the directness of the constituent sense impressions of the perceptions, carries implications for the formal characterization of the ascription of perceptual states to psychical agents. It is neither necessary nor desirable to encumber our logic with syntactical reflections of substantive perceptual theses, doubling our quantifiers as do Hintikka and Thomason,[4] or semantically enriching our domains of interpretation to include phenomenal as well as physical things. Standard-model resources, we shall suggest, suffice. No more, at least, is required by a naive realism.

I assume that perceptions are a species of judgment; that

seeing or hearing, say, how or what a thing is, is a way of judging how or what it is. As a species of judgment, perceptions have, then, a certain formal complexity. Just as, in the simplest cases, a judgment is about something and is a judgment that the thing it is about is thus or so, so too a perception is a perception of something and a seeing that what is seen is thus or so. There is in perceptions as there is in judgments generally a referential and an ascriptive component. I assume also that sense impressions are literally cognitive constituents of perceptions. They function in two ways in perceptual judgments. They serve on the one hand by their very occurrence to secure the direct reference of the perception to a specific item in one's environment. And they serve on the other hand, being, as they are, specific impressions of the sense qualities of what one is aware, to provide an ascriptive characterization to what is seen. A specific sense impression is, as the impression of a specific quality of a thing, a natural predicate ascribing a certain sense quality to what is perceived in one's surroundings. Sense impressions are to perceptions as predicate expressions are to assertions and as concepts are to judgments. A sense impression of red is, in the natural order, what an occurrence of the word "red" is in the conventional order of our native language. Semantically, a sense impression of red occurring in a perception of one's surroundings fulfills the same function as does the predicate "red" in the context of an assertion, though the nature of the impression is not, as the material attributes of the linguistic expression are, conventionally prescribed. Although sense impressions are semantically predicates in the natural order of experience, there is an important difference between the role they play in perception and that fulfilled by conventional quality predicates in the conventional, linguistic order. For although sense impressions, like primitive predicates, have no internal complexity, they perform a function predicates do not conventionally perform in English. As impressions they are tokens of a type, occurrences of which carry (at least part of) the ascriptive force of an occurrent perceptual judgment. But unlike tokens of conventional predicates, they do more. They provide demonstrative reference as well. They do this, not by their internal nature as the specific impressions of the sense qualities they are, but rather by their sheer occurrence in the contexts in which they occur. They are, in this latter function, like linguistic demonstratives—by contrast with proper names. Just as the reference of demonstratives, unlike that of proper names, is essentially a function of the contexts of their production, so too the occasions of the occurrences of sense impressions—the contexts in which they occur—together with their occurrences fix the objects of reference to which the quality of which one has an impression is ascribed. Features of the occurrence of a token of a linguistic demonstrative, in the contexts in which it is produced, are necessary to determine its reference on those occasions of its production. Similarly, the context of the occurrence of a sense impression is necessary in seeing its reference on the occasions of its natural occurrence. Sense impressions, as occurrent mental happenings, thus perform twin semantical functions. They provide, by their sheer occurrence in the contexts in which they occur, demonstrative reference to one's environment. As tokens of the type they are, as the impressions of the qualities they are, they provide ascriptive, sensuous attribution to the object of perceptual reference. It is as though we expressed, as a matter of convention, the fact that this (before me) is red by writing the demonstrative "this" in red ink.[5]

Performing these twin functions, sense impressions are in standard perceptual contexts minimal or basic perceptions. They are basic in two senses. Each is the single ascription of a primitive, fully determinate sense quality or relation—one of the proper or common sensibles, to something demonstratively "before" one. We have no sense impressions of the richer ascriptives we deploy in more complex perceptions; perceptions, say, of the nature, or kind, or tendencies of what we see. When we see the red, round, bouncy rubber ball in the corner, we have an impression of the color and of the shape but not of the matter—*rubber*—or the kind—*ball*—of what we see in the corner. How these basic perceptions are related to the richer, more complex but more common perceptions of everyday life is a central question to which we shall return in a bit.

Basic perceptions are basic in a second sense as well. They

530

have no internal, logical complexity either in their mode of reference or in what is ascribed. They presuppose no other perceptions or impressions. Each is a single, qualitative ascription to a single object of reference demonstratively indicated. (The characterization gives, thereby, identity and count conditions for sense impressions. It gives in a limited sense an answer in principle to the question of how much is seen on a given perceptual occasion. There are as many basic perceptions on an occasion as we on that occasion can distinguish.)

I call such basic or minimal perceptions *demonstrative perceptions*. It seems clear to me that these occur not only as a theoretical requirement of the present characterization of direct or naïve realism, but that we all have, occasionally, perceptions of just this sort of which we are quite aware. (I catch perhaps a flicker of movement at the periphery of my visual field. I see that something, I know not what, has moved.) I have heard it argued, however, that there can be no problem of contrasting demonstrative perception with ordinary perception, nor of relating the former to the latter, for there is in fact no demonstrative perception at all. All perceptions, it may be claimed, are perceptions of objects as kinds of things. The form, then, of the simplest perceptual judgments will accordingly be that the, or this, K-thing is a Q. However, this cannot, I think, be true. The fact is that I can sensuously encounter my environment without this required level of understanding, and even know that I do so. This can happen for various reasons. It can happen because my understanding is itself too limited. I do not know what to make of what is before me. Or it can happen because my information is itself too limited. I did not perceive well enough, or closely enough, or long enough what passed before me. (A cobweb brushing my cheek in the dark? Or perhaps no object at all, a draft of wind?) But anyway, if there were no basic perceptions, what could be the truth conditions for those simple perceptual judgments of the form: this K is a Q? But surely the truth of this requires that the percipient sees that this is a K. If so, then either some perceptions are, after all, demonstrative, or else to see that this is a K is to see that this K^*-thing is a K. But then the same reasoning can be applied, *ad infinitum*. I

531

shall suppose, then, that there are indeed demonstrative perceptions. If so, the earlier question remains, how are basic, demonstrative perceptions related to "ordinary" perceptions of everyday life, as when I hear or feel, say, that the carburetor of my car needs adjusting. This is the central question to which we promised to return.

If sense impressions, with their twin semantical functions, are the most primitive form of perceptions, and if perceptions are a species of judgment, then, of course, infants and brutes are capable of, and indeed do manifest, primitive conceptual activity. This is, I think, a welcome consequence. For this is exactly how we think of animals and babies, at least outside the philosopher's (and psychologist's?) closet. Surely, they have, as we have, sense impressions. But they too discriminate among, choose, and play with items in their surroundings.

This makes clear the need to distinguish a sense impression of something in the sensory surroundings from sensations as mediating physiological disturbances along the sensory tracts. What concept is manifest on a given occasion will vary, for example, in the same physical circumstances, perhaps from observer to observer similarly placed. The sense impression is a function not only of the environmental placing of agent and object but of the context of sensory occurrence, the agent's knowledge, maturation, and current physiological state as well. I trace, suppose, with felt pen the closed outline on a Polaroid print of the image of a standing coin, snapped from the oblique. The shape I trace is an ellipse. My impression is, however, of a round-faced coin. I have seen a coin and that it is circular. I have seen, not inferred, this. No doubt this is something to be learned, an enrichment of the primitive concept of circular shape. Perhaps infants and beasts, placed as I am placed, do not have the same impression of shape as have I. But this is precisely to record the fact that the "meaning" of a sense impression will vary with physical circumstance, and will vary with perspective, and will vary as well with the state of the observer: what he knows, how alert or tired he is, and so on. On the present view, a sense impression is not a phenomenal object of introspective awareness. It is not an object at all. It is rather an

532

awareness of a quality discriminable by one of the senses of an object in the physical environment. The awareness is an ascription by the sentient agent of a sense quality to an object. But what quality is ascribed will not be a simple function of material position and stimulation alone. I see, perceptually judge, that the coin is round. The quality I ascribe need not and typically will not be the shape outlined on the Polaroid print.

If we think of sense impressions as ascriptions of qualities to things, as conventional predicates are used to characterize things, then there are in a quite literal sense natural homonyms just as there are linguistic homonyms. For just as two words may be identical in sound but differ in meaning, the occasions of their production making the intended ascriptions clear, so also two sense impressions may in their occurrent, material properties be the same while the occasions of their occurrences may make it quite clear that different sense qualities are ascribed to what is "before" one by each. This, of course, is crucial for our coming to distinguish the way things appear from the way they are. Conversely, sense impressions different in their occurrent, material properties may be ascriptions in relevant contexts of the same sense quality. Having seen the coin from the oblique, we corroborate our perceptual judgment by facing it head on. From the side, and from the front, we see that the coin is round.

It should perhaps, with the clash of foundational and coherence theories of evidence in the back of our minds, be stressed that there is no certainty, no primitive guarantee of truth, to these primitive judgments. The child, seeing what I do from where I am, is wrong if he takes in his primitive way the thing before him not to be circular. The coin is indeed round. Equally, beast, child, and I are subject to illusions and may, knowingly or not, suffer hallucinations. But whatever may be the right causal account of these aberrant phenomena, we need not postulate special non-material objects of perception to account for what we experience. Train tracks, trailing off into the distance, look positioned the way converging sticks before us look. We see train tracks, not phenomenal tracks. Their characteristic appearance is the basis for our judgment of the constancy of the length of the ties placed between them to the horizon. Impressions of tracks in a plane parallel to one's line of sight are similar to one's impressions of sticks before one in a plane perpendicular to the line of vision. Impressions of tracks, so positioned, are our awareness of the tracks, and that they are parallel. Equally, if drugged or distraught I suffer visions, that too is the way the world appears to one in my specific condition. It is a matter not of the perception of phenomenal things but of pathological perceptions of things. (I assume that we speak here of perceptions, a matter of sensory stimulation, and not of imaging or dreaming, which is another matter. Hallucinating, eyes and senses closed, without sensory input, is not a form of perception.)

So far, we have briefly sketched an account of sense impressions.[4] The characterization of these is crucial to the present version of direct or naïve realism. Direct realism is understood here as a semantical thesis of the nature of perception. It is one that is intentionalistic, and that eschews phenomenal entities. We have assumed that perceptions are a kind of sensuous judgment, and we have assumed that sense impressions are cognitive constituents of perceptions. In the simplest cases sense impressions constitute primitive perceptions. Sketching these things, we postponed discussion of the logical implications of our assumptions; and we postponed discussion of the way in which sense impressions may be related to the common, non-primitive perceptions of everyday adult human life. We turn now to say something of each of these matters, beginning with the latter and concluding the paper with some discussion of the logic of it all.

If I sensuously judge that what is before me is a small, bouncy, red rubber ball, I have not only sensuously judged that something before me is red but I have judged something about the nature, kind, and capacities of what is there. And how can I see all that? I do not have sense impressions of *ball*, as I do of *red*. My impressions are of something red, uniformly round, with depth. And I know something of the characteristic look, feel, and behavior of balls. Do I then infer, given what I see, the presence of a ball, or do I see its presence given that characteristic set of impressions? And does this apply not only to detecting what kind of thing it is, a ball, but also what its matter and nature may be, rubber and bouncy?

534

There is a familiar sequence of increasingly complex perceptual occurrences leading on from the perceptual identification of things as the kinds things may be. I catch a glint of metal through the leaves by the drive. Do I see, or infer, that the car is there? And is this like judging that my son is home since I see that the car is there? Where and how do we draw the line between what is seen, directly seen, and what is inferred or judged on the basis of what is directly seen?

There is in the empirical tradition a tidy, systematic, but undiscriminating way to deal with such questions. All such cases are simple cases of judging, on the basis of what we do see, i.e., on the impressions we do have, what is before us. I judge that the car is there, inferring it from what I see, the flash of metal through the trees. I judge that this is a ball, inferring the fact from the manifest characteristic qualities of depth and roundness of which I have impressions. This may seem implausible, requiring as it does ubiquitous, unconscious inferential occurrences for the range of ordinary perceptual transactions of everyday life. Implausible or not, however, this is not necessarily to forsake direct realism. For the premises upon which such inferences are projected need not be the records of awareness of phenomenal objects. The premises can quite as well be viewed as turning on those basic perceptions, the sense impressions, that make up the sequences of our samplings of our environment together with our knowledge of the constancy of certain objects. The premises are, then, simply those basic and direct perceptions of objects the existence of which direct realism has all along posited.

Moreover, the implausibility of the view can perhaps by mitigated if we view the inference not as conscious deductive calculation but as a matter of abductively accommodating the data of our basic perceptions in a familiar way. Abduction is nondeductive inference of the puzzle-solving variety.[7] Typically, it proceeds from a set of background assumptions and beliefs, together with the facts that need to be explained, to an explanation of those puzzling facts.

The form of the abduction runs thus: A, but also E (the puzzling data that need to be explained, so it must be that H. H, then, is the hypothesis concluded sufficient if true to explain

535

the puzzling E consistently with our set A of relevant background beliefs and assumptions. The *validity* of an abduction requires at least that certain minimal conditions be met: the hypothesis concluded, H, must itself be consistent with the conjunction of members of the set of background assumptions and belief, A; the assumptions and beliefs must not themselves entail the facts to be explained; and the assumptions together with the concluded hypothesis must imply what was to be explained. An abduction will be *sound* just when it is valid, A and H are true, and (the joker) when it is true that E because H as well.

Applied to perception, the view runs this way. Perceptual judgment, ordinary seeing what is the case, is really the outcome of a complex but not necessarily conscious and not necessarily protracted process. We come to our perceptual environment on any given occasion with a background of knowledge and belief already accumulated. We come in a given state of readiness or distraction, tired or alert. We are on that occasion and in that location and with that physiological system immersed in a bath of stimulation. Air pumps the tympanic membrane, physical pressures displace our surface, radiation stimulates the eye. This is, so far, in Quine's sense, scientific lore.[8] The conscious facts of the matter at this point are that we have a certain sensuous awareness of what is before us. We see, perhaps, the glint of light on metal through the trees. We have, given our own piece of lore and given the present sensory impressions, to explain these impressions on this occasion. Why these and not some others? A conclusion sufficient to explain the occurrent impressions consonant with my background beliefs is that it is the car I see through the trees. If my abduction is sound, I see the glint because the car is there. I report that I see the car because I judge that the flash of metal I detect is the car's. But I do not—on this account—see the car the way I see the glint of something there.

This difference between what it is I directly see and what I judge as an abduction from what I do directly see comes clear in the context of justification for my abduction. Here my perceptual claims are the basis for describing the case as one of abductive inference (even though there has been no prior, conscious transaction from impression to conclusion). I justify my abductive conclusion, if challenged after the fact, by remarking the impressions that occurred and by reasoning about their possible causes. I do so against the background of common facts of perspective, positioning, and the like. I do not, it may be noted, in this way justify my reports of direct sensuous impressions. The truth of perceptual claims on this simpler level is typically established, not by reasoning about causes and perspective, but by verifying the occurrence. In these simpler cases we do not typically argue causes but look again, or look more closely.

Thus viewed abductively, the account of perception, though positing multitudes of undetected acts of inference for the most common perceptual cases, is not, I think, completely implausible. Think, for instance, of listening to a speaker in a foreign tongue. Completely conversant and at home with the language, we transact the move from auditory impression to expressed thought without conscious inference or momentary calculation. Completely unconversant, our impression will only be of a chatter of sounds. But partially conversant with the language and learning, we consciously pause and search the verbal context for clues to disambiguate a homonym, say. Standard perceptual occurrences are, on the abductive account, rather like hearing assertions in a language with which one is conversant. Only occasionally does the context or environment require our consciously puzzling out what is before us; of what our impressions are impressions.

Of course, not every valid, perceptual abduction is sound. Many distinct physical circumstances may, against the background of known assumptions and beliefs, be sufficient to explain our impressions. Hence any given sufficient explanation may on such an occasion not be in fact the correct explanation. (It may after all be a neighbor's car in the drive, not ours; or perhaps no car at all but a camper.) The determination of selection principles for choosing among alternative, sufficient hypotheses is, of course, the interesting and deep issue for abductive theories, but one concerning which we have nothing useful to say.

The abductive account of the relation between our common-sense perceptual judgments and basic perceptions is, however,

537

not the only account. There is a bold alternative, implicit I thought in Professor Gibson's writings, that is a radical extension of direct realism, at least to the perception of the kinds and natures of the things sensorily available to us in our surroundings. I shall call it "radical direct realism." It is a striking alternative to the abductive account as a general characterization of ordinary, non-basic perception. Unlike the abductive account, it holds that perceptions of the kinds and natures of objects in one's material surroundings are very often direct, non-inferential, and without intermediary objects. Just as, say, I directly see that this is red and spherical, so too I see, and do not infer, that this is a ball and rubber. Since I have no simple sense impressions of *ball* and *rubber*, as I do of *red* and the shadowed, textured surface, and since my perception is, by hypothesis on this alternative, direct and non-inferential, it must then be that sequences of sense impressions function in these cases as do the single, minimal sense impressions in our primitive awarenesses of our physical surroundings. The characteristic look of a given kind of thing typically involves a range of sensible visual qualities of color, shape, texture, size, both from some one perspective and also from an altered, but continuous, array of these as one cocks his head or leans forward slightly. It is in ascribing, tacitly, such sequences of sense qualities in a suitably ordered way that we thereby classify an object, visually before us, as a certain kind of thing. The occurrent sequences of sets of positional sense impressions determine, and on this view, constitute our visual classification. We do not infer from the sense impressions, suitably ordered, what kind of thing we see before us. In having the sequence, we see what it is. This seeing is not a new mental occurrence separately performed. Rather, in seeing that this before me is uniformly round, with depth, I *thereby* perceive that this before me is a ball. The occurrence of the sequence of sense impressions is, it literally constitutes on this account, the ascription of a classificatory concept. Thus sequences of sense impressions themselves literally have meaning, just as do the individual member impressions of the sequence. What identification is made, what kind is seen on a given occasion, will be a function of the sequence of impressions in the context of its occurrence together with the knowledge and state of the observer. What we see is a function of what we know as well as of the sequences of impressions. And just as the impressions of a coin from many angles may each be perceptual ascriptions of its roundness, so too here there will typically be many distinct sequences of impressions that constitute the recognition of what is before one, a coin or a ball, say.

Although the occurrence of suitable sequences of impressions literally is the ascription of a classificatory concept, it is not possible, I suppose, relative to any given individual or any arbitrary concept, to specify exactly what impressions are presupposed for that individual's recognition of that kind of thing. Probably no set of qualitative impressions is necessary or sufficient for the correct application of a classificatory concept. Detecting the merest trace or hint may on occasion suffice, and the fullest qualitative characterization may on other occasions deceive. Nonetheless, things visually identifiable do have characteristic appearances. Some reasonable subset of such relevant qualitative features is, other things equal, a sound justification for the application of a given classificatory concept. Thus I defend my claim to have seen a lemon by asking you to look, and to note, the characteristic color and shape. (I do so though of course we know, you and I, that there are misshapen brown lemons also.)

It seems certainly true, as Professor Gibson has stressed, that visual categorizations, at least, of physical substances and kinds, are subject to certain conditions of continuity, reversibility, and "free access." Failure to conform to such conditions will lead a psychical agent to withhold or suspend otherwise plausible perceptual identifications or judgments. This is not to be thought of as a conscious act, but rather as the occurrent sequence of impressions not constituting an awareness of an enduring *physical* kind, and so also not an awareness of some given specific physical kind. Visually (and perhaps tactually, though not generally in the auditory and olfactory cases) a human psychical agent will actively sample his visual environment. Slight turns of the head or eyes will present continuously altered sequences of patterns of sense impressions. Eyes and head can be reversed, returning to their initial position with a concomitant retrieval of the initial sequences of sets of sense impressions, or rather of sequences congruent with the initial ones. Although the sequences of sets of sense impressions (unlike the member impressions of the sequences) can be randomly permuted, still preserving the perception of a kind of physical thing, no one set has, in general, special preeminence as the visual entry point to one's awareness of the object. There is free access to the sequence, still preserving the visual classification.

Whatever further principles and complexities underlie the activation and application of visual occurrences of classificatory concepts, and whatever principles and conditions may be disposed across the other sense modalities, there is a certain epistemological simplicity and attractiveness to this program. For one thing, without appeal to further entities, it relates individual, qualitative sense impressions to the range of ordinary perceptions in a direct and plausible way. Sense impressions are, after all, literal constituents of these more complex perceptions. They are members in the sets of impressions the sequences of occurrences of which are the activation of, and constitute the ascriptions of, a concept of a kind of thing. The account explains our feeling that ordinary but complex perceptions are somehow groups or clusters of what, upon reflection, are sensuous ascriptions of simpler kinds. Our perception of *how* the thing before us is, as distinct from our perception of *what* it is, does not presuppose other, prior or constituent, perceptions. But our perception of *what* a thing before us is, as distinct from merely how it is, does so. We could not see, for example, what kind of thing something before us was without seeing something of how it is. We detect and identify natural kinds by their sense qualities. If challenged, we justify classifying them as we do on just this basis.

Thus, on this account, ordinary perceptions of the kinds and dispositions of things around us are provoked by, and linked to, these things through the literal incorporation of sense impressions in these acts of perception. It is these constituent sense impressions that, by their own demonstrative references, provide the demonstrative force present in all acts of perception. Unlike the free range of non-sensuous judgment, all perception is tied to the sensuous context of its occurrence. It is the incorporation of sense impressions that ties the perceptual act to the occasion of its occurrence. It is the occurrent sense impressions that give perceptual judgments, even complex ones, the specific singular reference they have. We see that the chair, *that* chair, is by the door. It is the sequence of impressions in their ordered occurrences which is the seeing that *what* is *there* is a chair.

An ordinary occurrent perception is a function of these sequences of impressions in the same way that an occurrent act of judgment is a function of, and is constituted by, its constituent acts of reference and ascription that constitute the thought. Just as one does not first mentally refer, then ascribe, and then also judge, so too ordinary acts of perception are not something supervenient upon the sequences of impressions of which they are constituted. One does not first have impressions, then judge what is "before" him.

Visual judgment, then, as a form of perception, does not consist in first seeing and then judging. But if it does not, do we never see and then judge what is the case on the basis of what is seen? And if we sometimes do this, how are we to distinguish such cases from cases of directly seeing? By what principle do we draw a line between abductive and direct perceptual judgments? By what tokens are instances of each kind to be distinguished? Is seeing the glint of metal through the trees by the drive, given the occasion and the requisite knowledge and background lore I bring to the context of stimulation, to see that the family car is there, or to infer it? And if it is to see it, are there never cases of inferring what is so from what is seen? I catch the glint of metal and judge that my son, whom I know to have had the car, is at home. Do I, as I do report it, literally see that he is home? But if I do not, why should we not also then say that we judge, or infer, rather than see that the car is there when we catch the glint? Indeed, why should we not go the whole way the classical, abductive account, and maintain that even in the simpler case I judge, or infer, that this is a ball before me given the impression I have?

Neither the abductive account nor the radical direct realist's account is plausible across the entire range of *prima facie* perceptual occurrences. Taken alone, too much is inferred on the abductive account. Taken alone, too little is on the radical realists'.

There is an obvious and completely natural general principle, of course, that secures a gross division of perceptual cases into those in which things are judged and those in which things are directly seen. It is, it may be suggested, a necessary condition that one can only see that of which one has some sense impressions. Thus, catching the glint of metal, I see that the car is there. But catching no impression of my son, I infer, but do not see, his presence given the presence of the car. Things are not so simple, however, as Professor Firth has pointed out.[9] There are Descartes' "men themselves" to reckon with. Looking down from above, we review the passing parade, a sea of coats and hats below us. Do we see the men themselves? We have no sense impressions causally initiated by them as distinct from the garments they wear. And there are the negative perceptual cases to consider as well. I open Russell's refrigerator, scan the contents, and see that the butter is not there. Or must I say that I have inferred this, there being no butter there and no impressions of butter to tie my judgment to my perception?

I should like to leave instances of logically complex perceptions, perceptions the verbal expression of which would involve the use of logical constants, to one side. They require, I believe, special characterization. Hence, I should like to set to one side the cases of negative perceptions. But for the remaining logically simple and affirmative cases, there remains more plausibility to the general, gross principle of division than we have yet done justice. We can of course always safeguard the principle by swallowing the bitter pill; we may hold that indeed we see not the men themselves, having no impressions causally initiated by them, but only their garments. We infer the existence of those human clothes racks. Similarly, we might think, seeing the outline of a boat under canvas, we do not see the presence of the boat itself but infer it.

But this safeguard is a too rapid capitulation. In the first place, the radical direct realists' account was not a causal but a semantical account. And commonsensically, I surely do not infer the presence of the men or the boat in the way I infer the presence of a yolk given a glimpse of an unbroken egg. The fact is that it is the men themselves we believe ourselves to see in the one case. It is the boat we say we see in the other. And the fact is that we do have impressions of each after all. Looking down, we can say a good deal of the size and shape of the men. Looking on, we can report the size and outline of the boat, not just its covering. We have in fact impressions of garmented men, not garmented automata. These are displayed in sequences of impressions of their characteristic movements, their strides, the rhythm and fluidity of their gaits.

It is a usual characteristic of our perception of things whose presence we directly see, but do not infer, that we can look again or look more carefully. This is a symptom of the fact that usually some of the sensible qualities of what is before us can be described in ever finer and ever fuller detail on the occasion of the perception. I can describe with ever more precision and greater detail the canvas-shrouded boat because the boat's shape and size are presented to me in the perception. I cannot so further describe my son from what I see in catching the glint of metal by the drive.

So the principle of division for perceptual cases remains, I believe, a plausible principle. It divides those perceptual cases where it is possible, although not necessarily true, to claim a direct perception of an object from those cases where this is not possible. I do, after all, see the men, although I do not see their faces, because I see their characteristic human stances and movements, displayed in the manner clothed humans manifest these.

This has a further epistemological and logical import. I, as a scribe, recording the psychical events of my world, will want to distinguish not only those cases that by the principle above cannot be cases of direct perception, lacking as they do sense impressions initiated by the object of an agent's judgment, but also those cases that, though satisfying the principle, are not perceptions that the boat is there or that men are passing below. These are instances in which I correctly describe the agent as seeing the boat or men, but not seeing that what he sees is a boat,

543

or are men. The necessary condition for direct perceptual judgment has been satisfied, but still the judgment is not forthcoming. 'Perception', as used here, has been a quasi-technical term. Perceptions have been assumed to be judgmental. Thus the form of a perceptual judgment, like the form of judgments generally, is propositional. But the object of a perception is perceived directly, demonstratively, and how are we to express that? If John sees that something has moved, then John sees something; if John sees that the boat is under the tarpaulin, then John sees the boat. And if the boat under the tarpaulin is the *Courageous* then John sees the *Courageous*, perhaps unknown to John himself. If, then, all perception is propositional, how are we to express these cases of "direct-object" awareness? And how are we to express the truth that there is something John sees, namely the *Courageous*, but John does not see or know it to be such. This we need to do on a naïve realists' theory without appeal to special phenomenal objects, and without appeal to special syntactical resources, like the double quantifiers of Hintikka or Thomason,[10] or special semantical interpretations.

Current fashion construes the logic of the ascription of occurrent states of knowledge or belief to a psychical agent as a modal logic. If perception is a species of judgment, a kind of sensuous knowing or believing, then, if current fashion has things right, the logic of the ascription of occurrent perceptual acts to psychical agents is also a modal logic. I assume here that this is so, that the logic of perception is a modal logic. By contrast, direct-objection constructions, recording simply the seeing of things, are not propositional. They are not then perceptions. They are not thus directly represented in this logic, though certain propositional surrogates for them will appear.

To every indicative sentence, P, there are mundane, modal indicative sentences, of the form $M^{(ao)} P$, indexed to an agent, a, and an occasion, o. These can be used to assert that the agent on the given occasion knows $(K^{(ao)})P$ or judges $(J^{(ao)})P$ that P. (a and o in $M^{(ao)}$) stand for (free) individual variables whose occurrences will often for ease be suppressed in what follows. In general, unless the opposite is clear, mundane formulas with free variables will be considered to be (tacitly) universally quantified. (There are problems with the occurrences of these variables, not usually discussed in the relevant literature. Thus, given iteration, an instantiation of $M(^{a\jmath o})M(^{a\jmath o})P(a)$ might read, "Jones believes on the occasion of the wreck that Jones believes on the occasion of the wreck that Jones is bleeding" rather than saying of Jones on that occasion that he believed he believed on that occasion that he was bleeding. These questions concerning the representation of pronomial self-and-other reference, which have been brought to our attention by Castaneda,[11] will, like the variables of the modal operators, also be suppressed in what follows.)

Since perception is a species of judgment, our ascription of perceptual acts to psychical agents ascribes knowledge or belief to the agent in a suitably modified way; i.e., as sensuous. Perceptions are visual, or tactual, or olfactory, . . . , instances of knowledge or belief. We add, then, to the vocabulary and formation rules of a standard epistemic/doxastic modal logic the resources for expressing perception as a kind of modified epistemic/doxastic occurrence. $SM(^{a\jmath o})P$ says that the agent, on occasion, o, sensuously knows or believes that P. The application of the generic operator-modifier S ("sensuously") to M will in specific cases have as typical instantiations 'visually believes that' or 'tactually knows that'. Since I take the "success connotations" of our commonsense use of 'sees', 'hears', and the like to be logically gratuitous, we divide the common perceptual occurrences into cases of visual knowing, which carries the link to truth of the everyday 'sees', and visual believing, which is like, perhaps, our saying that the agent thinks he sees when we know the facts are other than he takes them.

We think of expressions of the form 'SMP' as formalizations of mundane sentences, true or false of the actual world. They are the reports of a scribe (perhaps ourselves) recording the perceptual mental happenings of certain psychical agents. Exploiting the current way with modalities, to each such mundane sentence we set a certain unique transcription that no longer contains the modal operators, M nor the operator-modifiers, S, and which is simply an expression of standard first-order logic supplemented with some specific predicates and constants and supplemented with some specific assumptions governing those predicates. Mundane logical truths are those that have transcriptions that are theorems in the resulting extended, first-order logic. (This restriction to first-order logic means we shall lose here the formal reflection of the way perceptions of kinds incorporate, and thereby entail, the existence of basic perceptions.) While the "world-theory" transcription of mundane modal sentences is by now a familiar device, the transcriptions, assumptions, and their resulting consequences below are not altogether the usual ones.

Our transcriptions require three special predicates that have the effect of relativizing what is perceived or believed to the agent to whom the mental occurrence is ascribed. T is a relational predicate used in relativizing truth to a world. TwP says that the proposition P is true in (the world) w. B is a relational predicate expressing the presence, or membership, of an individual in a world. Bwa says that the individual a belongs to (the world) w. Finally, the relational predicate H (for Hintikka, who created the fashion with doxastic modalities that is so much exploited in recent literature) expresses a relation of accessibility across worlds. Hww' says that (the world) w' is an alternative to (the world) w. In particular, H will be (tacitly or explicitly) indexed always, $H(^{e^{a}o})$ expressing '___ is an epistemic alternative relative to the individual a on occasion o of . . .'. $H(^{s-d_{a}})$ expresses '___ is a sensuous (i.e., visual, tactual, . . . ,) doxastic alternative relative to the individual a of . . . ' A visual alternative, relative to a on o, is, e.g., a world such that all truths of it are compatible with all a sees on occasion o.

The transcription of the mundane $M(^{a}o)P$ (or the mundane $SM(^{a}o)P$) is first relativized to the world of the scribe who records the physical event: we have $tw^s(M(^{a}o)P)$ (or $tw^s(SM(^{a}o)P)$.) w^s is an individual constant referring to the scribe's (i.e., in non-iterated cases, to our own, the actual,) world. The truth-in-a-world predicate is next confined to atomic sentential occurrences in accord with the following general stipulations:

For closed, unquantified, and unmodalized P, we have simply, as in standard alethic modal systems,

$$TwMP \text{ to } (w')(Hww' \rightarrow Tw'P),$$

where H will be indexed with an e or d according to whether M is 'knows' or 'judges' (i.e., according to whether M is an epistemic or *d*oxastic operator.)

Similarly,

$$Tw\,SMP \text{ to } (w')(H^s ww' \rightarrow Tw'P),$$

where H will be further indexed as above according to whether M is an epistemic or doxastic operator.

We wish, however, to generalize the characterization of perceptual ascriptions to occurrences of the mundane operators that command within their scope truth-functional operators, or quantifiers, or govern contexts with free-variable occurrences or occurrences of individual constants or parameters. We stipulate, thus,

for truth-functions:

$$Tw(P \,\#\, Q) \text{ to } (TwP) \,\#\, (TwQ),$$

for any binary truth-functional connective, #, and, for negation,

$$Tw\!-\!P \text{ to } -(TwP);$$

for quantifiers:

$$Tw(\exists x)(Px) \text{ to } (\exists x)(Bwx \;\&\; TwPx),$$

and

$$Tw(x)(Px) \text{ to } (x)(Bwx \rightarrow TwPx);$$

for the occurrence of an individual constant, a,

$$Tw(Pa) \text{ to } (Bwa \;\&\; TwPa),$$

(the generalization to multiple occurrences of individual constants is clear but untidy, and suppressed here);

and for the occurrence of a free individual variable, x, in the scope of an epistemic or doxastic operator, we set

547

$Tw M^a Fx$ to $(w)(H^a ww' \to (\exists y)((Bw'y)$ & $Tw(x{=}y)$
& $Tw'Fy))$,

(also suppressing for expository ease multiple occurrences of individual variables; mundane formulas with free individual variables, we recall, are assumed to be [tacitly] universally quantified).

The confinement of the truth-in-a-world operator, T, across
psychical modalities that govern contexts with free variables
reflects the radical subjectivity of the scribes' ascriptions to an
agent. An agent need not, of course, share a scribe's concepts or
references nor even have them in his mental repertoire. But
however that may be, in all worlds compatible with the agent's
beliefs there will exist something that is in fact identical with the
scribes' referent though the agent need not know this. We need
not even assume that the agent has a developed human intellect
or conceptual capacities of any special sophistication. The agent
may be an infant or a beast. We, as scribes, then say that there
is something, in some way the object of his reference, that is the
same as the referent of our thought, even though it may be compatible with all the agent judges that this is not so. The agent,
infant or beast, perhaps, may not even be cognizant of us, the
scribes who record his judgment and assert this identity of referent, his and ours.

This relativity of knowledge or judgments to the agents to
which they are ascribed requires as well a restricted concept
of identity. The rule of Interchange of Identities accordingly
reads thus:

Given $Tw(a{=}b)$ and $Tw P(a)$, one may interchange any occurrence of a for b in P provided also that both Bwa and Bwb.

We assume as an axiom the matching, relativized, reflexivity
of identity, i.e. $\vdash (w)(x)(Bwx \to Tw(x{=}x))$.

Depending upon various (Kripke-like) assumptions made concerning the relations, H, and depending upon various "pop-
ulation" assumptions posited for B, distinct theorems emerge.
We shall not develop systems of these here. Instead, we shall
merely note certain interesting formulas that appear or not, as
theorems of our extended, first-order logic. We contrast some of
these with results in the literature.

For one thing, on the present view, perception is a kind of judging, so it ought to be that what one sensuously believes (or knows), he believes (or knows). I.e., it ought to be that

$$\vdash SM^a P \rightarrow M^a P.$$

This is forthcoming on the assumption that

$$(w)(w')(Hww' \rightarrow H^s ww').$$

That is, where H^s is a relation among sensuous (epistemic or doxastic) alternatives, and where H is a general relation among (epistemic or doxastic) alternatives, we have the following,

$$(w)(w')(Hww' \rightarrow H^s ww') \rightarrow [(w)(H^s w^s w \rightarrow TwP) \rightarrow (w)(Hw^s w \rightarrow TwP)],$$

as a theorem of first-order logic. (Here w^s is a constant whose intended interpretation is the scribes' world, that in which the original, mundane modal proposition is asserted to be true.) The principle assumed is a reasonable one. It says that if w' is an alternative of w, compatible with all that a knows or believes, then it is thereby a visual alternative as well, compatible with all that a sensuously knows or believes.

On the assumption of the transitivity of H, we have immediately that what one sensuously knows (or believes,) he then knows (or believes) that he knows (or believes) it. I.e., that

$$\vdash SM^a P \rightarrow M^a M^a P.$$

The transitivity of H suffices to establish that

$$\vdash M^a P \rightarrow M^a M^a P,$$

and we have by the previous result that

$$\vdash SM^a P \rightarrow M^a P.$$

More interesting, and controversial, are those consequences of the system that apply to knowledge and belief quite generally, as much as to the species of these, sensuous knowledge and belief. Perhaps the most striking of the consequences, given current extant literature, is the asymmetry that emerges between the ways in which the principles of Existential Generalization and the Interchange of Identities of classical non-modal logics are reconstituted or modified to be valid in our modal contexts. Clearly, on our understanding of knowledge or belief, whether sensuous or not, the following are not valid argument forms as their transcriptions would corroborate:

$M^a Pb$, $b=c$, therefore $M^a Pc$;

$MaPb$, therefore $(\exists x)\ M^a Px$.

Commonsensically, they fail however for quite different reasons, and the reconstituted valid versions of each are formally quite distinct. What goes wrong with the first inference, turning on identity as it does, is that the agent may not know that b is c. He may even have no beliefs about c at all. Clearly what is required is to relativize the identity premise to the agent's body of belief. What is crucial for the conclusion validly to follow is not the truth of the identity of b and c but that the agent believes the identity to hold. The following, mundane, inference form should be valid:

$M^a Pb$, $M^a(b=c)\ \vdash\ M^a Pc$.

It is as its transcription makes evident.

Existential Generalization by contrast fails for quite different reasons. Accordingly, it is quite differently reconstituted. It is in fact the existence of the object of the agent's belief that is crucial here, not the agent's belief in its existence. Making no special, relativizing assumptions about the range of the quantifier, we have that if an agent believes something, and if the object of that belief exists, then there is indeed something of whom the agent has the given belief. This is to say that the following, mundane, inference form, bolstered by a premise of existence, should be valid:

$M^a Pb, (\exists x)(x=b) \vdash (\exists x) M^a Px.$

It is as its transcription makes evident. The resulting, transcribed formulas together are an instance of a valid argument form in standard, first-order logic.

This is, I think, quite as common sense suggests it ought to be. But it is not the received view. Hintikka, for instance, in fact assumes the invalidity of this argument form in his earlier defenses of his own principles governing quantification into modal contexts.[12] Given that he does so, it is interesting to contrast as well some of the other differences in the consequences of this system and received systems of epistemic logic like Hintikka's. The formula,

$(x) K^a Px \rightarrow (x) Px,$

for instance, is not provable in Hintikka's original systems of *Knowledge and Belief*, which created the general style of construing epistemic and doxastic concepts as modal concepts. Yet, surely if it is true of everything there is, that an agent knows it to be *P*, then it must follow that everything is *P*. What is known is after all true. It is a desirable consequence that this is a logical truth of our system of epistemic and perceptual judgment. Its proof requires only that the relations H^c or H^{sc} be assumed reflexive, to secure the link of what is known to what is true, and that we invoke the relativized identity conditions mentioned earlier to sanction a required interchange.

On the other hand, the formula

$(x)(y)((x=y) \rightarrow M(x=y))$

is not derivable on the present way of construing mundane modal formulas. And this is again, I think, as it ought to be. For, without special ways of construing the quantifiers, this appears to assert that things are identical only if they are known to be so. That surely is false. Yet as John Tienson has pointed out (in an important critique of Hintikka's restrictions on the values of variables in the scope of psychical operations)[13] Hintikka has stated that defending the validity of this (*prima facie* implausible) formula is tantamount to defending his way of restricting quantification into epistemic or doxastic contexts.

Tienson, in his critique, further constructs a variant system to those of Hintikka. He does so as a vehicle to evaluating Hintikka's claims, and to provide a counter-example to Hintikka's argument. We cannot pursue that discussion here (see note 11 and its citation.) But Tienson notes that his counter-system fails to deliver as valid the following formula, which, commonsensically, we suppose any adequate system should:

$$(\exists x)MPx \rightarrow M(\exists x)Fx$$

(expressed in the notation of this paper). This is, however, a theorem of our present logic for the psychical modalities. Our transcription principles take it into a theorem of first-order logic.

It might seem that if we do not restrict, as Hintikka suggests we should restrict, the values of variables and constants in the scope of psychical operators to individuals who are known to the agent to whom the mental act is ascribed, we then face an evident *reductio ad absurdum*. For it may be thought that failing to safeguard these ascriptions by requiring, say, that values of such variables "must be referred to by a constant b such that $(\exists x)K^a(x=b)$ holds,"[14] we make psychical agents inconsistent agents. And, generally of course, that need not be the case. For suppose an object, b perhaps, exists and is identical with c. And suppose our agent, a, believes that b is P but does not believe that Pc. Surely then, without further safeguards, our agent is (not merely unknowing but) inconsistent for there is then an object such that he both believes of it that it is P and yet does not believe this of that same object. I.e., will not the following be derivable:

$$[(M^aPb) \,\&\, -(M^aPc) \,\&\, (b=c) \,\&\, (\exists x)(x=b)] \rightarrow (\exists x)(M^aPx \,\&\, -M^aPx)?$$

This is not, however, derivable in our system. Our transcription principles, without further safeguards, forestall inferences from premises like the antecedent to the consequent. Intuitively, the common individual b, i.e., c, splits in the worlds of the agent's beliefs.

Particularly for perceptual contexts, it is sufficient but *not necessary*, and certainly *not desirable*, to require that the agent knows the object seen. For perception can occur demonstratively, without recognition, identification, or categorization. For infants, brutes, beasts, and all of us on occasion, it is too strong to require that an object of an agent's perception "must be referred to by a constant b such that $(\exists x)K^a(x=b)$ holds." The agent may perceive something, he knows not what. He may hear and speculate over the cause of a thump in the night. There is something he hears yet precisely there is no "constant b such that $(\exists x)K^a(x=b)$ holds" for him. One may, of course, do as Hintikka does. One may separate the case of perception from doxastic and epistemic ascriptions to agents. One may, with Hintikka, and Thomason, distinguish styles of quantifiers as they range over individuals either perceptually or physically identifiable to agents. And one may exploit these styles of quantifier to handle recalcitrant occurrences of minimal cognitive information. One may do this, but one need not. In particular, a realistic alternative which exploits classical modal resources is quite available as we have tried to make plausible.

We can say, combining sensuous and non-sensuous operators (not quantifiers), that Agent (thinks he) sees something, he knows not what. We write: $(\exists x)VB^a(\exists y)((x=y)$ & $-(\exists w)((w\neq y)$ & $K^a (\exists z)(z=w)))$. We can say Agent (indeed) sees someone, namely Jones, but does not know it is Jones. We write: $(\exists x)((x=j)$ & $VK^a(\exists y)((x=y)$ & $-K^a(x=j)))$, the modifier V in each case is intended to be interpreted as 'visually.' If as scribes we record merely the fact that Agent indeed knowingly sees (recognizes) Jones, we write: $(\exists x)((x=j)$ & $VK^a(x=j))$. As scribes we record the facts that John thinks what he hears outside is a dog, but Mary thinks it is a racoon, by writing: $(\exists x)(Ox$ & $AB^j(Dx)$ & $AB^m (Rx))$, where A is a modifier for acts of audition and O, D, and R have the obvious translations. Finally, there is Macbeth who, hallucinating, thinks he sees a dagger. If he is taken in, and believes literally that, that a physical dagger is there, we record the event thus: $VB^m (\exists x)(Dx)$ & $-(\exists x)(Dx)$, 'D' encapsulating

553

the concept of being a dagger at the required location. If, however, Macbeth knows that it is an hallucination he suffers, his vision (= impressions!) being at odds with reality, our ascriptive, naïve realism takes on its adverbial character. Macbeth sees not visionary daggers; rather, Macbeth suffers dagger-like visions (= impressions!) We record this latter event thus: $VC^m(\exists x)(Dx)$ & $-(\exists x)(Dx)$ & $K^m-(\exists x)(Dx)$. Here, D is as before. The new operator, C, modified by V ('visually') is the defined, weak modal operator of Hintikka's systems of *Knowledge and Belief*. We read: "It is compatible with all Macbeth's visual experiences that there be a dagger before him, only there is not and he knows it." So much then for some attempted contact with common speech.

So far, we have gathered a few theorems and non-theorems and attempted a few formal paraphrases of common statements of perceptual facts. The theorems and non-therorems pretty well match our intuitions about the relations between what we, as scribes, record of what others believe or see and what those others should be committed to. Most of the sample formulas at least in part depend upon applications of the Confinement Principle for free variables in modal contexts for their validity or lack of it. The principle is central. It specifies in an explicit way truth-conditions for mundane occurrences of quantification into psychical ascriptions to agents. It is a condition of the truth of such mundane ascriptions that in all circumstances compatible with what the agent knows (or believes sensuously or not,) there be a certain object. It is this object that we as scribes know to be the agent's referent for that object to which we refer when quantifying into that context expressing the agent's mental act. There is no requirement that the agent knows the object to be such. And there are no conditions on the agent's way of thinking of the object. No "vivid names" need be presupposed; indeed, no names or verbal items need occur at all. (We recall, for instance, the existence of our pre-verbal, sentient agents.) It is quite appropriate, then, that given the Confinement Principle governing "quantifying in" the following is not valid (despite its similarity to the reconstituted analogue of Existential Generalization).

554

$$((x)MPx \ \& \ (\exists x)(x{=}a)) \rightarrow MPa.$$

This of course ought not be valid. For although a exists, and although each thing is such that the agent knows (or believes, sensuously or not) that thing to be P, still the agent may not know (or believe, and so on) b to be P. He may not even know that one of the things there is, is b.

Our claim, finally, for a logic for naïve realism comes to this: perceptual knowledge and belief do not literally have a special logic. Special assumptions, of course, will govern the sensuous operators determining what is unique about these as vehicles for expressing sensuous judgments. But the logic of perception is but a species of the general logic of the ascription of psychical states, like judgments, to agents. And this general logic, although enriched with categorematic operators with which to express these ascriptions, contains and requires no special syntactical, syncategorematic, forms. It requires no special semantical resources. This general logic is but a species of modal logic. The logic of perception is but a species of this general logic. There is plenty that is interesting and subtle in the logic of perception. But there is nothing that forces us to reflect epistemological distinctions in our logical syntax and gadgetry. There is a certain wry amusement in finding phenomenal objects reincarnated in contemporary logical studies after their decent epistemological burial. But we are not forced to countenance them by sheer logical considerations, and epistemologically, naïve realism is a perfectly viable alternative. Besides, it is the way everyone sees things.

Thanks are due the Ohio State University Philosophy Department and its sponsor for their generous and thoughtful support of the seminars and conference that were the occasions for these papers. My gratitude goes to the National Endowment for the Humanities for a grant, time from which was devoted to this paper.

1. "Realism and the Active Mind" (25-page typescript). This was presented to the Ohio State University Philosophy Department Seminar in Perception, May 1974, and presented at the conference on perception, June 1974.

2. The seminar and conference discussions at Ohio State with Gibson made it clear that he would not accept the account of sense impressions given in that paper,

555

and does not think of sequences of them as constituting our concepts of kinds of material things. Gibson's papers are nonetheless quite pertinent. See, e.g., J. J. Gibson, "Constancy and Invariance in Perception," in *The Nature and Art of Motion*, ed. G. Kepes (New York, 1965), esp. pp. 67 ff.; or, J. J. Gibson, "A Theory of Direct Visual Perception," in *Psychology of Knowing*, ed. Royce and Rozeboom (New York, 1972), pp. 215–40.

3. This comes from Jay Rosenberg's "The 'Given' and How to Take It—Some Reflections on Phenomenal Ontology" (typescript), pp. 37 ff., but esp. p. 39.

4. See, for example, the articles and work of J. Hintikka on knowledge and belief and perception, especially the earlier work. See, e.g., his *Knowledge and Belief* (Ithaca, N.Y., 1962), and his papers "Individuals, Possible Worlds, and Epistemic Logic," *Nous* 1 (1967); "Existential Presuppositions and Uniqueness Presuppositions," in *Models for Modalities* (Dordrecht, 1969); and "On the Logic of Perception," in *Perception and Personal Identity*, ed. N. Care and K. Grimm (Cleveland, 1969). See also R. H. Thomason, "Perception and Individuation," in *Logic and Ontology*, ed. M. K. Munitz (New York, 1973), pp. 261–85.

5. We adopt here for our use a suggestion Professor Sellars develops for his own purposes in his "Naming and Saying," in *Science, Perception, and Reality*, esp. pp. 232–36.

6. I have attempted somewhat lengthier discussions of sense impressions elsewhere. One, concerned with their sensuous ascriptive natures, is titled "The Sensuous Content of Perception," and will appear in a volume of essays honoring Professor Wilfrid Sellars (H. N. Castaneda, ed.). The other is concerned with the role of sense impressions in securing the reference of perceptual judgments and is entitled "Sensuous Judgments," *Nous* 7 (1973): 45–56.

7. The introduction of the concept of abduction and its initial characterization are due, of course, to C. S. Peirce. Others, like N. R. Hanson, later applied the notion particularly to observation and perception. The account I have in mind in this brief sketch of abductive inference is that of my colleague Edwin Martin. See his "Perceptual Processing" (28-page typescript).

8. See, e.g., W. V. O. Quine, "The Scope and Language of Science," *British Journal for the Philosophy of Science* 8 (1957): 1–17.

9. R. Firth, "The Men Themselves: Or the Role of Causation in Our Concept of Seeing," in *Intentionality, Minds, and Perception*, ed. H. N. Castaneda (Detroit, 1967), pp. 357–82.

10. See n. 4 supra.

11. See H. N. Castaneda, " 'He': A Study in the Logic of Self-Consciousness," *Ratio* 8 (1966): 130–57; "On the Logic of Attributions of Self-Knowledge to Others," *Journal of Philosophy* 65 (1968): 439–56; "Indicators and Quasi-indicators," *American Philosophical Quarterly* 4 (1967): 85–100.

12. See J. Hintikka, esp. "Individuals, Possible Worlds, and Epistemic Logic" (note 4 supra).

13. See J. Tienson's "Hintikka's Argument for the 'Basic Restriction' " 10-page typescript), esp. p. 7.

14. Ibid.

Romane Clark is professor of philosophy at Indiana University.

Alan Donagan is professor of philosophy at the University of Chicago.

James Gibson is professor of psychology at Cornell University.

David Hahm is professor of classics at the Ohio State University.

Alan Hausman is associate professor of philosophy at the Ohio State University.

R. J. Hirst is professor and chairman of the Department of Logic at the University of Glasgow.

Ronald Laymon is associate professor of philosophy at the Ohio State University.

Edward Lee is professor of philosophy at the University of California, San Diego.

David Lindberg is professor of history of science at the University of Wisconsin.

Peter Machamer is professor of history and philosophy of science at the University of Pittsburgh.

Gareth Matthews is professor of philosophy at the University of Massachusetts, Amherst.

Dean Owen is associate professor of psychology at the Ohio State University.

George Pappas is associate professor of philosophy at the Ohio State University.

Nicholas Pastore is professor of philosophy, Brooklyn College and the Graduate School and University Center, City University of New York.

A I. Sabra is professor of history of science, Harvard University.

Robert Schofield is professor of history of science, Case Western Reserve University.

Wilfrid Sellars is University Professor of Philosophy, University of Pittsburgh.

Robert Turnbull is professor and chairman, Department of Philosophy, Ohio University.

Heinrich von Staden is associate professor of classics and philosophy, Yale University.

INDEX OF NAMES